"Nolo's home page is worth bookmarking."
—WALL STREET JOURNAL

LEGAL INFORMATION
ONLINE ANYTIME

24 hours a day

www.nolo.com

AT THE NOLO.COM SELF-HELP LAW CENTER ON THE WEB, YOU'LL FIND

- Nolo's comprehensive Legal Encyclopedia, with links to other online resources
- SharkTalk: Everybody's Legal Dictionary
- Auntie Nolo—if you've got questions, Auntie's got answers
- Update information on Nolo books and software
- The Law Store—over 250 self-help legal products including:

  Downloadable Software, Books, Form Kits and E-Guides
- Discounts and other good deals, plus our hilarious Shark Talk game
- Our ever-popular lawyer jokes
- NoloBriefs.com, our monthly email newsletter

Quality LAW BOOKS & SOFTWARE FOR NON-LAWYERS

Nolo.com legal books and software are consistently first-rate because:

- A dozen in-house Nolo legal editors, working with highly skilled authors, ensure that our products are accurate, up-to-date and easy to use.
- We know our books get better when we listen to what our customers tell us. (Yes, we really do want to hear from you—please fill out and return the card at the back of this book.)
- We are maniacal about updating every book and software program to keep up with changes in the law.
- Our commitment to a more democratic legal system informs all of our work.

OUR "NO-HASSLE" GUARANTEE

Return anything you buy directly from Nolo for any reason and we'll cheerfully refund your purchase price. No ifs, ands or buts.

An Important Message to Our Readers

This product provides information and general advice about the law. But laws and procedures change frequently, and they can be interpreted differently by different people. For specific advice geared to your specific situation, consult an expert. No book, software or other published material is a substitute for personalized advice from a knowledgeable lawyer licensed to practice law in your state.

U.S.

★★★★★★★★★★★★★★★★★★★★★★★★

IMMIGRATION

★★★★★★★★★★★★★★★★★★★★★★★★

MADE EASY

By Immigration Attorneys Laurence A. Canter & Martha S. Siegel

**Seventh Edition updated by Professor Richard A. Boswell,
University of California, Hastings College of the Law**

Keeping Up-to-Date

To keep its books up-to-date, Nolo issues new printings and new editions periodically. New printings reflect minor legal changes and technical corrections. New editions contain major legal changes, major text additions or major reorganizations. To find out if a later printing or edition of any Nolo book is available, call Nolo at 510-549-1976 or check our website at www.nolo.com.

To stay current, follow the "Update" service at our website at www.nolo.com. In another effort to help you use Nolo's latest materials, we offer a 35% discount off the purchase of the new edition of your Nolo book when you turn in the cover of an earlier edition. (See the "Special Upgrade Offer" in the back of the book.) This book was last revised in: February 2000.

SEVENTH EDITION	FEBRUARY 2000
Editor	SPENCER A. SHERMAN
Illustrations	LINDA ALLISON
Book Design	TERRI HEARSH
Cover Design	TONI IHARA
Index	PATRICIA DEMINNA
Production	SARAH HINMAN
Proofreading	SHERYL ROSE
	ROBERT WELLS
Printing	BERTELSMANN INDUSTRIES SERVICES

International Standard Serial Number (ISSN) 1055-9647

ISBN 0-87337-404-5

Quantity sales: For information on bulk purchases or corporate premium sales, please contact the Special Sales department. For academic sales or textbook adoptions, ask for Academic Sales, 800-955-4775. Nolo.com, 950 Parker St., Berkeley, CA, 94710.

To Our Parents,

With Love and Gratitude

Table of Contents

CHAPTER

1

How to Use This Book

U.S. Immigration Made Easy was developed to give you the kind of help you need to be successful with the United States Immigration Service. Whether your aim is to live, work, invest, retire or study in the U.S., this book should assist you in reaching your goal and doing it legally. We will tell you about the different kinds of visas available and the qualifications you need to get each one. Then we will show you, step by step, how to prepare the paperwork for the visa you want. We will tell you how long it takes to get each visa and how to avoid common pitfalls. You will find out whether or not you have a realistic chance of immigrating to the U.S. We have also included some brief material on U.S. taxes for those with business interests or people who simply want to know the tax consequences of life in the U.S.

A. Basic Strategy for Immigration

Not everyone can immigrate to the U.S., but you can improve your chances by knowing the inside information on immigration. That's exactly what you'll find in this book. If you don't qualify to immigrate right now, we will examine the possibilities for your qualifying in the future. It isn't hopeless. There are things you can do. We're going to remove the mystery and tell you what those things are. The key to winning at U.S. immigration is information, the information you'll find in these pages.

U.S. immigration laws may not be what the immigrant expects. Often these laws were written as much to keep immigrants out as they were to provide orderly procedures for letting them in. Immigration policies are not always logical or sensible. Many people from other nations who wish to live in the U.S. and could make wonderful contributions to the country are the very people kept from getting green cards or visas. More and more, U.S. immigration law is a controversial issue among Americans. Everyone agrees there must be some limits. No one agrees on how these limits should work.

There is, however, a positive side to the ongoing debate. As U.S. opinions and priorities change, so do the country's policies toward immigrants. Every time the law changes it means new opportunities for people who never had a

chance before. As an example, the amnesty program from the Immigration Reform and Control Act of 1986 gave millions of undocumented aliens, most of whom had given up hope, the opportunity to get green cards. The Immigration Act of 1990 is an even farther-reaching reform of the system, the biggest in four decades.

One of the greatest changes brought about by the Immigration Act of 1990 is the major refocusing of U.S. immigration goals. Overall, the law has always favored immigrants who were family members of other recent U.S. immigrants. Now, some of the emphasis is being shifted away from family relationships and toward job skills, education levels and other business-related qualifications. Therefore, the Immigration Act of 1990 makes the biggest difference to those getting green cards and visas through employment with U.S. companies or institutions.

Since 1990, there have been several procedural changes in the ways certain types of visas are processed. Also, the government has increased its emphasis on deportation, now called removal, particularly of criminal aliens. In the future, you can expect even more changes. A number of proposals have been introduced into Congress to restrict the numbers of legal immigrants, though to date none have passed or become law. However, the passage of the Illegal Immigration Reform and Immigrant Responsibility Act (IIRIRA) of 1996 and the Antiterrorism and Effective Death Penalty Act (AEDPA) of 1996 have brought many new changes to the immigration code, most of them restrictive. The information in this book is the very latest available but it isn't written in stone. If you don't like the law the way it is, don't give up! Sooner or later, it will probably change.

Is it smart, then, just to wait until things get better? We don't think so. There's a lot you can do right now if you have all the facts. You'd be surprised at how few people do. We have written this book after spending many years working as immigration lawyers. A good deal of what appears here is in response to questions clients have asked us again and again. One lesson we learned over time is that often people fail at immigration because they just don't know enough about it. Information given out at U.S. consulates, embassies and the offices of the Immigration and Naturalization Service (INS) isn't always complete. Most immigration officials lack the time to share all their knowledge with you. It is unlikely that they will be willing to sit down with you, examine your case and spend an hour or more helping you think of ways to qualify for a visa, as attorneys do when clients come to their office. In this book, you will find much more information than any consulate or INS office has the time to offer.

For the immigrant, an even greater danger than having too little information is having information that is wrong. Common sources of confusion are well-meaning friends and relatives as well as general rumormongers, all of whom are only too happy to share their ignorance with you. Of all the false information in circulation, the stories from those who claim to have gotten green cards or visas by ignoring the rules or using special influence are by far the most creative. Enjoy them for their entertainment value, but don't harm yourself by believing them.

In this book we have made the rules and procedures of immigration as clear and understandable as possible, but we have not stopped with the laws themselves. In immigration, knowing the rules and regulations isn't enough. You must also know how things really work. Here we tell you both the law as it is written and the way things actually happen in real life. They are not always the same. Learning about such inconsistencies is a good way to make them become less frustrating or at least less frightening. Once you find these things out, you'll improve your chances of being an immigration success.

One of the biggest problems we face with our clients is that they rarely arrive in our office without having already heard plenty about immigration. Most of what they've heard comes from friends or relatives. When we tell clients something different from what they've heard before, they don't know what to think or whom to believe. We assure you that the contents of this book are accurate to the best of our knowledge and written with the benefit of many years of experience as practicing immigration attorneys. If what we tell you is not the same as what you've heard from others, we ask you to try it our way. We can't guarantee you will get the green card or visa you want. No one can do that. But we are confident that following the procedures in this book is your best chance for success at immigration.

1. Can You Cheat the System?

We've already mentioned briefly the stories in circulation about how some people have found shortcuts through the system, legal or illegal. We've been asked about cheating the system an endless number of times. Some people put it more politely than others, but the idea is always the same. Let's get it straight right now. If you know someone who

insists he or she walked into a consulate and got a green card immediately just for the asking, or successfully bribed a U.S. immigration official, most likely that person has an overactive imagination. The hard fact is that shortcutting the American immigration system is close to impossible.

Moreover, while bribing public officials is generally tolerated in some countries, it is not in the U.S. We do not make this statement as any kind of moral judgment on other nations. We point it out simply as a cultural reality because, unfortunately, it has the effect of making immigrants from certain countries where bribery is a common practice believe the same tactic will work in the U.S. It won't. Any U.S. government employee found guilty of selling visas will be severely punished. While there have been reports of corruption within INS, these occurrences are rare. The bottom line is immigration officials don't take bribes.

Another plan popular among those determined to bypass the system is asking for help from U.S. congressional representatives or senators. The offices of these officials are besieged with such requests. While a U.S. politician will always treat you courteously and may write a letter to INS asking for a status report on your case, one thing he or she will not do is fight with INS to get you a green card or visa. No matter how strong your political influence might be, no government official can get immigration benefits for someone who is not truly qualified, nor will he or she try to do so. It is a point of pride among Americans that even congressional representatives and senators are not above the law.

2. Can You Work the System?

Yes, you can work the system by knowing exactly how it operates. In our experience with thousands of immigrants from nearly every country in the world, we have seen that most people view their chances for successful immigration as either completely certain or totally impossible. One group believes that by filling out a few simple forms they will quickly and automatically be granted the right to do exactly as they please. They get angry and insulted when they find out the U.S. government isn't going to cooperate as quickly or as easily as they thought. The other group is made up of those who think the situation is hopeless. Usually they've based their conclusions on discussions with misinformed friends and relatives. The doomsayers and the optimists have one thing in common: They are both wrong.

Contrary to popular belief, immigration is much like any other area of the law. To prepare an immigration case, you must gather evidence, make arguments and complete paperwork. The finished product is then considered by an INS or consular officer. The officer looks at the case and makes a decision based on his or her knowledge of the law and evaluation of the evidence. While some cases are obviously stronger than others, nobody's case is either a guaranteed success or a certain failure. Each one is different. There are many variables in preparing a case and we'll tell you how to work the system for the best results. Meanwhile, keep in mind that there is no black or white in immigration. Each case is some shade of gray, and that means there is always hope.

3. Choosing a Category

Let's give away one of the biggest secrets of being successful at U.S. immigration right at the beginning. It's picking the visa category that's best for you. The cornerstone of the U.S. immigration system is a rigid group of visa categories. Each category carries with it a very specific list of requirements. Your job in trying to get any type of immigration benefit is, very simply, to prove that you fit into one of the categories. Much of this book is devoted to describing the categories and explaining how you can prove to the U.S. government that you do in fact fit into one of them. Once you know the requirements, you will be miles ahead of most applicants who file for immigration benefits.

There are no exceptions to the rule that you must meet the qualifications of some immigration category. If you cannot do so, you cannot get a green card or visa. You may find as you read on that you already fit into one or more qualifying category. If not, you have the option of trying to change your situation so you do. It is you and not the categories that will have to change. Keep in mind, however, that it is often perfectly possible to arrange your life or your business so you become qualified for a category, even if you are not right now.

As we said earlier, the Immigration Act of 1990 was written with the intent to give more consideration to the personal merit of the applicant. Although close family members of American citizens and green card holders are still favored, now there is also a much greater emphasis on education and career skills. Thanks to the new law, potential economic contributions to the U.S. are also a factor. If someone of financial means wants a green card, he or she can get one by investing in a business that creates jobs for U.S. workers. All of this is reflected in the visa categories now available.

Even though the new law has to some extent introduced more practical considerations into the immigration process, the overall system still is not completely fair or logical in giving immigration benefits only to the most worthy. Many people become angry when they realize this. They cannot understand why decent, hardworking, financially stable people are sometimes unwanted by the U.S. government. As unreasonable as it may seem, the fact is that INS has its rules and those rules are not very flexible. Once again, to put it simply, *if you do not fit within a category, you will not get a green card or visa.* Make it your business to know the categories. Do what you must to fit in. Then you will be a certain success at immigration.

4. The Visa System

The visa system can be divided into two major classes. The first is the permanent class, officially called permanent residence. Those who become permanent residents of the U.S. are given cards called Alien Registration Receipt Cards. These are more popularly known as green cards. They give you the right to live and work permanently in the U.S. Because the term *green card* is familiar to so many, we will use it here most of the time instead of the technically proper name.

There are many ways to get a green card, but once you get one, all green cards are exactly alike. Each one carries the same privileges: namely, the right to work and live in the U.S. permanently. Green cards are available mostly to those who have immediate family members in the U.S. or job skills in demand by a U.S. employer. Also, a large number of green cards are given to educated professionals, investors and refugees, or on a lottery basis to those with very few qualifications other than luck.

The second broad class of visas is temporary. People wanting to enter the U.S. on a temporary basis receive what are known as nonimmigrant visas. Unlike green cards, nonimmigrant visas come in a variety of types with different privileges attached to each. Generally, they are issued for specific purposes, such as vacation, study or employment.

Besides the fact that green cards are permanent while nonimmigrant visas are temporary, the most significant difference between the two is that the number of green cards issued each year is limited by a quota, while the number of nonimmigrant visas issued in most categories is unrestricted. Green cards in certain categories can be obtained very quickly. In other categories, even if you have the strongest qualifications possible for a green card, it can still take months or years to get one because of the quotas, and there is no way to speed up the wait. Nonimmigrant visas, however, can usually be obtained very quickly, sometimes on the same day you apply.

5. Timing

How long it takes to get a green card or visa is often affected by quotas. Most categories of green cards and a few non-immigrant visa categories are affected by them. Sometimes quotas move quickly and are not a problem. At other times, quotas can mean long waits.

Quotas can slow down the process of getting green cards and visas, but they are not the only source of immigration delays. U.S. consulates and immigration offices, which are typically understaffed, often get behind on paperwork. Human error, yours or theirs, can also cause processing to drag on. Sometimes files become lost in the system and that means taking time to straighten out the confusion. It is impossible to say exactly how long any one case will take because there are so many factors that influence its progress.

In this book, we give our best estimates of how long it takes to get an approval in each green card and visa category. As you go through the application process, use our estimates as guidelines. Check up if something seems overdue, but don't be disappointed if you must wait. To be successful at immigration as well as maintain your sanity, you must be realistic. Accept that the immigration process can take anywhere from several months to several years. Patience and persistence are important in being successful at immigration.

B. How to Use *U.S. Immigration Made Easy*

Now that you know a little bit about the U.S. immigration system, you are ready to learn how to use this book effectively. There are six steps you must follow:

1. Learn the types of visas available.
2. Choose the one right for your needs.
3. Decide if you have the proper qualifications for the visa you want.
4. If you do not qualify for the visa you want, think about what changes you can make to become qualified.
5. If you still cannot qualify for your first choice, consider what other visas are available and see if you can qualify for one of them.
6. Apply for the visa you choose, using the directions in this book.

Everyone should read this chapter and the following:

Chapter 2	Chapter 4	Chapter 26
Chapter 3	Chapter 14	

These chapters give you a basic knowledge of immigration. Until you have read these chapters through, you will not be able to understand the rest of the book.

Next, you should read the top portion and first section only of each of the following chapters:

Chapter 5	Chapter 10	Chapter 16	Chapter 21
Chapter 6	Chapter 11	Chapter 17	Chapter 22
Chapter 7	Chapter 12	Chapter 18	Chapter 23
Chapter 8	Chapter 13	Chapter 19	Chapter 24
Chapter 9	Chapter 15	Chapter 20	Chapter 25

Each of these chapters discusses a different green card or visa. The beginning of each chapter describes the privileges and limitations of the green card or visa category covered in that chapter. It also tells you how long it takes and who qualifies for the visa so you can find out if you are eligible to get the particular visa described. We strongly recommend that you read the first section in all the chapters listed, even if you think you aren't particularly interested in some of the green cards or visas discussed. It should take only a short time to do this. The introductory material is brief and reading it all is the only way you can discover the full range of options available to you. You may be unexpectedly pleased to learn that there are many ways of obtaining a green card or visa, and many ways of getting them that will give you all or at least some of the benefits you want.

After reading the introductory material of the recommended chapters, you will probably find that not all the green cards or visas described in this book interest you. When you select the one you want and for which you are qualified, you need not read about the others unless you want to. Each chapter devoted to applying for a particular green card or visa is complete within itself. You may notice that certain pieces of information are repeated over and over in each chapter. This has been done so you will not have to flip back and forth between pages to get all the information you need.

As you learn about the qualifications necessary for each green card or visa, you may find you do not meet all the requirements for the one of your choice. If that is the case, keep in mind the possibility of changing conditions in your life so you can fulfill the qualifications of the green card or visa you want. Making an investment in or opening a U.S. business is one step you can take to improve your immigration chances. Increasing your education or finding a job with a U.S. employer are some of the things you can do to qualify yourself for certain types of immigration benefits.

When we mention these options to our clients some can't wait to do whatever is necessary to help themselves. Others complain and repeat over and over "it's hopeless, it's hopeless." What they mean by hopeless is that they are unwilling to do what it takes. There is no question that making the necessary changes to qualify for a green card or visa when you are not already qualified is sometimes hard. It may require a major effort or even a sacrifice on your part. Is it worth the trouble? That is a personal decision only you can make. We believe it is. If you agree, you will be happy to know there is often a way to become qualified for U.S. immigration benefits if you want to badly enough.

C. Preliminary Strategies for Green Card or Visa Selection

As we've just explained, in this book we describe all of the methods of getting green cards and the most common types of nonimmigrant visas in detail. There is a separate chapter devoted to each green card or visa category. As you learn about the qualifications necessary for each green card and visa, you may find you do not meet all the requirements of your first choice. If that is the case, we have already suggested you should consider the possibility of changing conditions in your life so you can get the green card or visa you want.

Another strategy is to be sure you pick the right green card or visa category in the first place. You would be surprised how many people lose out just because they apply in the wrong category. They may choose one type of non-immigrant visa when another would better fit the situation. They may try to get a green card and fail because they are not qualified, without considering that some nonimmigrant visa, which they *can* get, will serve their purposes just as well. As you read the profile of each green card or visa category, see if you don't find several possibilities that meet your needs. As you read the "Who Qualifies" sections, if you don't qualify in one category, check another and you may have better luck. Consider your qualifications, needs and resources to see how you can fit into the green card or visa system. Weigh the pros and cons of each possibility as you would in making any other decision. Then pick the category that is your best choice.

Below are some examples of how certain groups might approach green card and visa selection. Perhaps you fall into one of these groups. If not, we strongly urge you to read about them anyway. Here you will get your first taste of the kinds of options available in the U.S. immigration system. You will learn a lot about certain categories that you didn't know before. Most important, you will start becoming prepared to analyze your own situation and do a good job of selecting the visa or green card category that makes the most sense for you.

1. Visitors

You can act as a tourist and transact temporary business for a foreign employer on a visitor's visa, but you cannot accept work. When someone enters the U.S. with a visitor's visa, he or she is usually given permission to stay for six months. There is a lot of confusion about the six months rule. Some people think the law allows foreign visitors to remain in the U.S. up to a maximum of only six months in any 12-month period. That is not true. Technically, you may leave the U.S.

at the end of six months, return the next day and be read-mitted for another six months. Alternatively, when one six-month period is up, you can apply for an extension of stay without even leaving. If the extension is approved, you will usually get to remain for another six months.

Some people, believing that they have found a loophole in the system, try to live permanently in the U.S. by taking short trips out of the country every six months and then returning again. Unfortunately, this tactic doesn't work for long. A condition of being admitted to the U.S. as a visitor is that you truly plan to leave at a specific point in time. You must also keep a home abroad to which you can return. The genuineness of your intent to leave the U.S. is measured by your acts. If an INS officer sees from the stamps in your passport or hears from your answers to questions at a border checkpoint that you are spending most of your time in the U.S., he or she will conclude that you are an unauthorized resident. Then you will be stopped from entering the country. You may get away with living in the U.S. on a visitor's visa for as much as a year or two without being discovered, but sooner or later you will be turned away.

On the bright side, if you can be content with dividing your time between the U.S. and some other country, you can continue that life-style indefinitely with a visitor's visa. As a visitor, you can engage in many activities. We've already mentioned that you may travel around as a tourist. You may also transact business for a foreign employer, or purchase real estate and make other investments. Finally, you may remain for at least six months, and it is all perfectly legal.

2. Retirees

Residents of many nations find the U.S. a desirable place to retire. This is especially true of Canadians and Europeans who want to trade their colder homelands for the warm climates of America's southern states. Unfortunately, there is no category specifically designed for those who simply want to retire in the U.S. The only way to get a green card as a retiree is by qualifying as a relative of a U.S. citizen or green card holder, a special immigrant or through one of the lottery programs now available.

If you don't have the necessary U.S. relative or don't win a green card lottery, the alternative is to get a green card through employment. To do so, you must find a job in the U.S. (See Chapter 8.) Even if you have saved enough money to support your retirement and may not need or want to work, you will still have to find a job for green card purposes. Under such circumstances, you must decide if moving to the U.S. permanently is important enough to make you postpone retirement plans by a few years. On the positive side, once you get a green card, it is yours forever. Although you must actually begin working in the U.S. in the job for which you were issued the green card, you will not lose your card if you retire only a year or so later.

After thinking it over, many retirees decide they don't need or even want green cards to meet their desired goals. Retirees are allowed to spend a long time each year in the U.S. as visitors. Holders of B-2 visitors' visas, or any Canadian visitor without a visa, can be admitted for a period of up to six months. The only restriction on your activities during this time is that you may not work. If you wish to buy and live in a winter residence, you may do so. In fact, many Canadians prefer this arrangement because it allows them to spend the winter months in the U.S. without losing government health benefits at home.

3. Families

The greatest number of green cards, by far, have historically gone to people with sponsoring relatives already in the U.S. Under current law, you may get a green card if you have a husband, wife, parent, child (who is over 21 years old), brother or sister who is a U.S. citizen. U.S. citizen stepparents and stepchildren, adopted children, half-brothers and half-sisters also count as sponsoring relatives. In addition, you may get a green card if you have a husband, wife or parent who is not a U.S. citizen but who holds a green card.

It is important to understand that your American relative must invite you to come to the U.S. and be willing to cooperate in the immigration process, including acting as your financial sponsor. It is also important to consider that some of the family categories, especially brothers and sisters of U.S. citizens, have very long waits under the green card quota. In some cases, these waits may be for many years. If you fall into a family category where there is a long wait, you may want to look at the possibilities in employment categories, or even the lottery, because those methods can take less time. Remember that just because you qualify for a green card in a family category doesn't mean you are barred from applying through some other method, if that is what you prefer.

4. Employees and Owners of Small Businesses

Small U.S. businesses frequently want to hire foreign workers. Even more often, small business owners want U.S. immigration benefits for themselves. A small business can sponsor a worker for a green card, but a small business owner normally cannot use his or her business to sponsor himself or herself. Therefore, the small business owner may have to choose between working for someone else who can act as a green card sponsor or being satisfied with one of the nonimmigrant visas.

Nonimmigrant categories available to employees of smaller companies are the B-1, E-1, E-2, H-1B, H-2B, and L-1 visas. E-1 and E-2 visas are especially useful for providing immigration benefits to owners as well as their employees. Although we list L-1 visas, called intracompany transfers, as a possibility for smaller businesses, they are usually difficult to get for companies having only a very few employees. L-1 is, however, another category where owners stand a good chance.

With any kind of work-related visa, the smaller company must be prepared to show the U.S. government that it is financially stable and able to pay foreign workers' reasonable wages. This is most likely to be an issue with companies having fewer than 100 employees.

5. Employees and Owners of Large Businesses

It is very common for large U.S. businesses to hire foreign workers. In fact there is probably no large business in existence that does not do so. The U.S. immigration system offers large businesses several different options for bringing foreign workers to the U.S. Green cards or nonimmigrant visas can be used. If a company wishes to hire the foreign worker on a permanent basis, the worker should have a green card. The biggest consideration for the company in picking the best category is time. If the worker has the equivalent of an advanced university degree, or at least a bachelor's degree and some experience, it may take several months to a year to get a green card. When the worker has no college degree and little experience, the wait will be a minimum of several years, up to ten years or more.

A large U.S. business can quickly bring in foreign workers on a temporary basis for periods ranging from several days to several years by getting them nonimmigrant visas. Frequently they can then go on to apply for green cards while they are working in the U.S. Many nonimmigrant visa categories may be used, depending on the particular circumstances and the formal legal structure of the business. B-1, E-1, E-2, H-1B, H-2B, L-1, O, P and R visas all serve the employment needs of U.S. businesses.

In many cases, these same visas are available to the large business owner. Although none of them are strictly available for the self-employed, many legal entities, such as corporations, are treated as separate from the individual who owns the company. Generally, only owners of larger businesses can be sponsored for green cards and visas as employees of their own companies.

6. Investors

The Immigration Act of 1990 created a special green card category for substantial business investors. In the past, investors had to be satisfied with E-2 nonimmigrant visas. Even these were available only to citizens of a selected 40 countries having investor treaties with the U.S. Since 1990, anyone who invests $1,000,000 ($500,000 in an economically depressed region) in a new U.S. business that hires at least ten full-time American employees can get a green card. Obviously, this category is not for everyone. If you are among the fortunate few who can meet the qualifications, take a close look at Chapter 10. If you are not so fortunate, consider the nonimmigrant investor visa described in Chapter 21. You'll find the money requirements in this category much more reasonable. Furthermore, nonimmigrant investor visas last many years.

7. Registered Nurses

If the U.S. government has a special interest in those who practice a certain occupation, there will be special rules or categories just for them. Nursing is an example of such an occupation. Nurses who qualify for special green cards do not have to go through the normal quota waits. The details of qualifying for a special green card as a registered nurse are discussed in Chapter 8.

8. Employees of the Entertainment and Sports Industries

Entertainment and sports employees are very interested in green cards. If you wonder why, think about how many popular Broadway musicals have British casts and crews, or how many non-U.S.-born players participate in tennis tournaments while living in the U.S. There are some special rules controlling green cards for those who are well known in the entertainment and sports industries.

Nonimmigrant visa category O is available for better-known individual athletes and entertainers and their support personnel. P visas are given to performers who are part of a well-known or unique troupe or entourage. These visas can be obtained quickly, sometimes within a matter of days, and last for the period of time needed to complete a season or tour. Less well-known entertainers and athletes get H-2B visas. H-2B visas can be issued for only one year at a time and take several months or more to get.

Other business-oriented nonimmigrant visas may offer some solutions to problems of those in the entertainment or sports industries that the O and P visas do not. Depending on the legal structure of the businesses involved, L-1, E-1 and E-2 visas are worth exploring.

D. Sponsorship

By now, you have probably noticed that you often need the cooperation of another person such as an employer or relative in order to get green cards and some nonimmigrant visas. Just exactly how much can another person do to help you with immigration? A question often asked is "Can I get a green card by finding a sponsor?" The answer is "yes and no." The word *sponsor* does not appear anywhere in the U.S. immigration laws. When relatives or employers participate in an immigration application, they are really acting as sponsors. However, they are called not sponsors, but *petitioners*. You will learn later the details of the role of the petitioner in each green card and visa application.

Years ago, a willing U.S. citizen could bring any foreigner into the U.S. simply by vouching for his or her character and guaranteeing financial support. Under present law, this type of sponsorship is no longer possible.

E. Inadmissibility

A darker side to the immigration outlook of some people comes in the form of a problem called *inadmissibility* (formerly called excludability). Inadmissibility is a condition that keeps certain otherwise qualified individuals from getting green cards. Generally, it affects those who have committed crimes or fraud, are mentally ill or have a communicable disease. Inadmissibility is also a factor in cases of former U.S. citizens who either deserted the U.S. Army or evaded the military draft. We say more about inadmissibility in Chapter 25. Right now, we want you to know that many conditions of inadmissibility can be overcome.

F. U.S. Citizenship

The ultimate achievement in most people's immigration outlook is U.S. citizenship. Becoming a U.S. citizen is considered by many immigrants the realization of a life-long dream. It is the highest form of immigration benefit a foreign national can get.

There is considerable confusion about how green cards compare to U.S. citizenship. Many people believe the only difference is that U.S. citizens can vote, while those who have green cards cannot. Of equal importance, however, is the fact that even if you live outside the U.S. indefinitely or commit a crime, you can keep your U.S. citizenship once you get it. Under the same circumstances, you might lose a green card.

In all but a very few special cases, no one can apply directly for U.S. citizenship. You must first get a green card and live in the U.S. as a permanent resident for a certain length of time. Only then can you become a U.S. citizen. Even if you have held a green card for the required length of time, becoming a U.S. citizen is not automatic. You must first go through an application process called *naturalization.*

Occasionally, a person born or raised in another nation is already a U.S. citizen but doesn't know it. This happens most often when a foreign national has an American parent or grandparent who was taken from the U.S. at an early age. Usually, the parent or grandparent is also unaware of a claim to U.S. citizenship. This is especially true where the U.S. citizen is a grandparent who passes U.S. citizenship to a parent, who in turn passes it to the foreign national. The skipping of a generation adds to the confusion.

U.S. citizenship is not an easy thing to lose. If there is anyone in your direct line of ancestry who you think might ever have been a U.S. citizen, you should explore that possibility. More than one person has come to our office frustrated over the difficulties of getting a green card, only to learn he or she is actually an American citizen already!

G. Should You Use a Lawyer?

We've talked to countless foreign nationals about whether or not they need a lawyer in the immigration process. What we've learned is that most people believe they can handle their own immigration work without professional help. In the great majority of cases we agree, and hope this book will get you the results you want without spending money on legal fees. However, each immigration case is different. Some cases are more complex than others. Sometimes human error or plain bad luck make things go wrong. Most administrative problems can be smoothed out with patience and the information you will find in these pages, but it is also smart to know when you need professional assistance. If things get really tough, it is often foolish as well as dangerous to go it alone. If you have read this book care-fully, given it your best try and things are going badly, the most useful advice we can give you is to hire a competent immigration attorney. There are times when nothing can substitute for expert help.

If you do feel a need for help, we can't emphasize too strongly that you should check thoroughly the credentials of the person you hire. How many years has the attorney been practicing immigration law? How many immigration cases has he or she handled? Does the attorney practice in many areas of law, or is the practice devoted exclusively to immigration work? Take the trouble to get some answers to these questions before choosing the person in whose hands you will place your future in America.

It is our sincere belief that most people will find all the help they need right here. If you are successful in reaching your immigration goals, it means that we have succeeded, too. Over the years, we have had the great pleasure of seeing thousands who have been able to begin new careers and new lives in the U.S. We hope you will soon be joining them. ■

CHAPTER 2

Basic Immigration Terms

Knowing the terms defined below is essential to understanding the other chapters of this book. These terms are the foundation of immigration procedure and you should become familiar with them from the beginning.

Green card. The well-known term *green card* is actually a popular name for an Alien Registration Receipt Card. We use the term green card throughout this book because it is familiar to most people. At one time, the card was actually green in color. It was changed to pink, but it is still called a green card the world over.

This plastic photo identification card is given to individuals who successfully become legal permanent residents of the U.S. It serves as a U.S. entry document in place of a visa, enabling permanent residents to return to the U.S. after temporary absences. The key characteristic of a green card is its permanence. Unless you abandon your U.S. residence or commit certain types of crimes, your green card can never be taken away. Possession of a green card also allows you to work in the U.S. legally. You can apply for a green card while you are in the U.S. or while you are elsewhere, but you can actually receive the green card only inside American borders. If you apply for your green card outside the U.S., you will first be issued an immigrant visa. Only after you use the immigrant visa to enter the U.S. can you get a green card.

Those who hold green cards for a certain length of time may eventually become U.S. citizens. Green cards have an expiration date of ten years from issuance. This does not mean that the permanent resident status itself expires, only that a new, updated green card must be applied for every ten years.

Alien Registration Receipt Card. An Alien Registration Receipt Card (ARC) is the official name used in immigration law for a green card.

Permanent resident. A permanent resident is a non-U.S. citizen who has been given permission to live permanently in the U.S. If you acquire permanent residence, you will be issued a green card to prove it. The terms permanent resident and green card holder refer to exactly the same thing. You cannot be a permanent resident without a green card and you cannot have a green card without being a permanent resident. Both words in the phrase permanent resident are important. As a permanent resident, you may travel as much as you like, but your place of residence must be the U.S. and you must keep that residence on a permanent basis. If you leave the U.S. and stay away for more than a year, you risk losing your green card.

Nonimmigrant. Nonimmigrants are those who come to the U.S. temporarily for some particular purpose but do not remain permanently. The main difference between a permanent resident who holds a green card and a nonimmigrant is that all nonimmigrants must have the intention of being in the U.S. only on a temporary basis. There are many types of nonimmigrants. Students, temporary workers and visitors are some of the most common.

Accompanying relative. In most cases, a person who is eligible to receive some type of visa or green card can also obtain green cards or similar visas for immediate members of his or her family. These family members are called accompanying relatives, and may include only your spouse and unmarried children under the age of 21 who will be traveling with you.

Visa. A visa is a stamp placed in your passport by a U.S. consulate outside of the U.S. All visas serve as U.S. entry documents. Visas can be designated as either immigrant or nonimmigrant. Immigrant visas are issued to those who will live in the U.S. permanently and get green cards. Everyone else gets nonimmigrant visas. Except for a few types of visa renewals, visas cannot be issued inside American borders, and so you must be outside the U.S. to get a visa.

Immigrant visa. If you are approved for a green card at a U.S. consulate or U.S. embassy, you will not receive your green card until after you enter the U.S. In order to enter the U.S., you must have a visa. Therefore, when you are granted the right to a green card, you are issued an immigrant visa. An immigrant visa enables you to enter the U.S., take up permanent residence and receive a permanent green card.

Nonimmigrant visa. Nonimmigrants enter the U.S. by obtaining nonimmigrant visas. Each nonimmigrant visa comes with a different set of privileges, such as the right to work or study. In addition to a descriptive name, each type of nonimmigrant visa is identified by a letter of the alphabet and a number. Student visas, for example, are F-1 and investors are E-2. Nonimmigrant visas also vary according to how long they enable you to stay in the U.S. For example, on an investor visa, you can remain for many years, but on a visitor's visa, you can stay only six months at a time.

Status. Status is the name for the group of privileges you are given when you receive immigration benefits, either as a permanent resident or a nonimmigrant. Nonimmigrant statuses have exactly the same names and privileges as the corresponding nonimmigrant visas. A green card holder has the status of permanent resident. Visas and green cards are things you can see. A status is not.

While you must be given a status with each visa, the reverse is not true. If you want nonimmigrant privileges, you can get a nonimmigrant status by applying in the U.S. and you can keep that status for as long as you remain on American soil. You will not, however, get a visa at the same time because visas can be issued only outside the U.S. The theory is that since a visa is an entry document, persons already in America do not need them. This is important for nonimmigrants, because they can travel in and out of the U.S. on visas, but not with a status. Those with permanent resident status do not have the same problem, of course, because they have green cards.

If you have nonimmigrant status, but not a corresponding visa, you will lose it as soon as you leave the U.S. You can regain your privileges only by getting a proper nonimmigrant visa before returning.

Special U.S. entry documents for refugees. Political refugees are granted refugee status when they apply for American protection while still outside the U.S. Applications for refugee status must be filed at one of the few INS offices located overseas. On approval, the refugee receives a special U.S. entry document, but no visa. This document is good for only one entry. After spending one year in the U.S., refugees can apply for green cards. Although refugees have the privilege of living and working anywhere in the U.S., they must apply to INS for a special refugee travel document if they want to leave the county and return again before getting a green card.

Asylum status. Those seeking political asylum status are in a different situation from refugees. Those applying for refugee status are outside the U.S., while potential political asylees must have already gotten to America. They apply for asylee status at INS service centers in the U.S., just as others do who are seeking statuses.

Parole. The term parole has a special meaning in immigration law. Under certain circumstances, a person may be allowed to enter the U.S. for humanitarian purposes, even when he or she does not meet the technical visa requirements. Those who are allowed to come to the U.S. without a visa in this manner are granted parole, and are known as parolees. Advanced parole may be granted to a person who is already in the U.S. but needs to leave temporarily, and return without a visa. This is most common when someone has a green card application in process and must leave the U.S. for an emergency or on business. Occasionally, an individual who is in the U.S. illegally may be granted advanced parole to enable him or her to leave the U.S. temporarily and return without getting a visa.

I-94 card. The I-94 card is a small green or white card given to all nonimmigrants when they enter the U.S. The I-94 card serves as evidence that a nonimmigrant has entered the country legally. Before the I-94 card is handed out, it is stamped with a date indicating how long the non-immigrant may stay for that particular trip. It is this date and not the expiration date of the visa that controls how long a nonimmigrant can remain in the U.S. A new I-94 card with a new date is issued each time the nonimmigrant legally enters the U.S. Canadian visitors are not normally issued I-94 cards.

Visa Waiver Program. Nationals from certain countries may come to the U.S. without a visa as tourists for 90 days. They can do so under what is known as the Visa Waiver Program. Persons coming to the U.S. on this program receive green-colored I-94 cards. They are not permitted to extend their stay or change their statuses. The Visa Waiver Program is covered in more detail in Chapter 15.

Quota. There are several ways to qualify for a green card. Certain categories of qualified green card applicants are allowed into the U.S. in unlimited numbers. Certain other categories are restricted by a quota. Approximately 400,000 green cards can be issued each year under the quota, with no more than 25,000 going to applicants from any one country. (With the exception of Hong Kong, dependent areas have a limit of only 5,000.) If there are more green card applicants than there are green cards allocated under the quota each year, a backlog is created and applicants must wait their turns. It is because of the quota that it can often take years to get a green card.

Immediate relative. If you are an immediate relative of a U.S. citizen, you are eligible to receive a green card. The number of immediate relatives who may receive green cards is not limited by a quota. The list of those who are considered immediate relatives is as follows:

- Spouses of U.S. citizens. This also includes widows and widowers who apply for green cards within two years of the U.S. citizen spouse's death.
- Unmarried people under the age of 21 who have at least one U.S. citizen parent.
- Parents of U.S. citizens, if the U.S. citizen child is over the age of 21.

Preference Categories. Certain groups of people who fall into categories known as *preferences* are given first chance at the green cards available under the annual quota. The preferences are broken into two broad groups: family preferences and employment preferences. The number of green cards available each year to the family preferences is around 480,000 and the number available in the employment preferences is 140,000. The categories are:

- **Family first preference.** Unmarried children (including divorced), any age, of U.S. citizens.
- **Family second preference.** 2A: Spouses of green card holders and unmarried children under 21 years, of green card holders; and 2B: unmarried sons and daughters (over 21 years) of green card holders.
- **Family third preference.** Married children, any age, of U.S. citizens.
- **Family fourth preference.** Brothers and sisters of U.S. citizens where the U.S. citizen is at least 21 years old.
- **Employment first preference.** Priority workers, including persons of extraordinary ability, outstanding professors and researchers, and multinational executives and managers.
- **Employment second preference.** Persons with advanced degrees and persons of exceptional ability, coming to the U.S. to accept jobs with U.S. employers for which U.S. workers are in short supply or where it would serve the national interest.
- **Employment third preference.** Skilled and unskilled workers coming to the U.S. to accept jobs with U.S. employers for which U.S. workers are in short supply.
- **Employment fourth preference.** Religious workers and various miscellaneous categories of workers and other individuals.
- **Employment fifth preference.** Individual investors willing to invest $1,000,000 in a U.S. business (or $500,000 in economically depressed areas).

Preference relatives. Preference relative is a general term for a foreign relative of a U.S. citizen or green card holder as defined in the preference categories listed above. Preference relatives and immediate relatives are the only foreign family members of U.S. citizens or green card holders who are eligible for green cards on the basis of their family relationships.

Qualifying relative. Qualifying relative is a general term for either an immediate relative or a preference relative. A qualifying relative is any green card applicant who has a U.S. citizen or green card holder family member legally close enough to qualify the applicant for a green card.

Labor Certification. If you are not a qualifying relative, you may be able to get a green card through a job offer from a U.S. employer. However, in many cases, the job offer alone is not enough to make you eligible for a green card. First you must prove that there are no qualified U.S. workers available and willing to take the job. The U.S.

agency to whom you must prove this is the U.S. Department of Labor and the procedure for proving it is called *Labor Certification*. People who fall under the employment second and third preferences usually need Labor Certifications in order to get green cards.

Attestation. Attestations are sworn statements that employers must make to the U.S. Department of Labor before being able to bring foreign workers to the U.S. Attestations may include statements that the employer is trying to hire more Americans, or it may simply be a statement that foreign workers will be paid the same as U.S. workers. Attestations are required only for certain types of employment-based visas.

Employee. Employee is a term used to describe a foreign person seeking U.S. immigration privileges through a job offer from a U.S. company. Both a green card in the preference categories and several nonimmigrant visas can be obtained if you have such a job offer.

Employer. An employer, for immigration purposes, is a U.S. company or individual who has made a firm job offer to a foreign person and is acting with that person in an attempt to acquire a preference category green card or nonimmigrant visa.

Diversity Program (the lottery). An annual green card lottery program is held for persons born in certain countries. Every year, the Department of State determines which countries have sent the fewest number of immigrants to the U.S., relative to the size of the country's population. Green cards are then given to a certain number of persons from those countries. People who receive the lottery green cards are selected at random from everyone who registers for that year's lottery. The object of this program is to insure that the immigrants who come to the U.S. are from diverse backgrounds. That is why it is called the Diversity Program.

Special immigrant. Laws are occasionally passed directing that green cards be given to special groups of people. There is an annual quota of 10,000 green cards that can be given to special immigrants. Common categories of special immigrants are workers for recognized religions, former U.S. government workers and foreign doctors who have been practicing medicine in the U.S. for many years.

Priority date. If you are applying for a green card in a preference category, your application is controlled by a quota. Since only a limited number of green cards is issued each year, you must wait your turn behind the others who have filed before you. The date on which you first make a formal filing for a green card is called the priority date. Your priority date marks your place in the waiting line. Each month the U.S. Department of State, in accordance with the quota, makes green cards available to all those who applied on or before a certain priority date. You can get a green card only when your date comes up.

Petition. A petition is a formal request that you be legally recognized as qualified for a green card or some types of nonimmigrant visas. Paper proof that you do indeed qualify is always submitted with the petition.

Petitioner. The petitioner is a U.S. person or business who makes the formal request that you be legally recognized as qualified for a green card or nonimmigrant visa. The petitioner must be your U.S. citizen relative, green card holder relative or U.S. employer. No one else may act as your petitioner. Almost all green card categories and some types of nonimmigrant visa categories require you to have a petitioner.

Sponsor. The word sponsor does not appear anywhere in the U.S. immigration laws. When people refer to a sponsor for immigration purposes, they usually mean a petitioner. A sponsor can be a U.S. citizen, U.S. permanent resident or U.S. employer who undertakes to bring an immigrant legally into the U.S. Close U.S. relatives or U.S. employers who need your services in their businesses are the only ones with the legal ability to act as sponsors. When they do so, they are called petitioners. Years ago, any willing U.S. citizen could bring any foreigner into the U.S. simply by vouching for his or her character and guaranteeing his or her financial support. Under the present U.S. immigration laws, this type of financial sponsorship is no longer possible.

Beneficiary. If your relative or employer is filing a petition on your behalf, you are a beneficiary. A beneficiary is a potential visa or green card applicant attempting to obtain some type of visa or green card in a category requiring a petitioner. Almost all green cards as well as certain types of nonimmigrant visas require petitioners, and whenever there is a petitioner there is also a beneficiary. A beneficiary is so called because he or she benefits from the petition by becoming qualified to make an application for a green card or visa.

Application. An application is a formal request for a green card or visa. In the case of most green cards and many nonimmigrant visas, an application cannot be made until you obtain proof that you are qualified. This is done with a petition. In some cases, a petition is not required and only an application is required to get immigration privileges.

Applicant. When you make a formal request for a green card or nonimmigrant visa, you are an applicant. In cases where the green card or visa requires the filing of a petition, usually you may not become an applicant until your petitioner has successfully completed a petition on your behalf. You may be called either an applicant or a beneficiary, depending on where you are in the overall immigration process.

Refugee and political asylee. Refugees and political asylees are persons who have been allowed to live in the U.S. indefinitely to protect them from persecution in their home countries. Refugees get their status before coming to the U.S. Political asylees apply for their status after they arrive in the U.S. in some other capacity. Both may eventually get green cards.

Temporary Protected Status (TPS). The Immigration Act of 1990 created a temporary status for persons already in the U.S. who came from certain countries experiencing conditions of war or natural disasters. Temporary Protected Status (TPS) allows someone to live and work in the U.S. for a specific time period, but it does not lead to a green card. At present, TPS is available to persons from Bosnia-Herzegovina, Guinea-Bissau, Honduras, Kosovo, Montserrat, Nicaragua, Somalia and Sudan.

Immigration and Naturalization Service. The Immigration and Naturalization Service (INS) is the U.S. government agency having primary responsibility for most matters taking place on U.S. soil concerning foreigners who enter the country. Petitions for visas and green cards, as well as U.S. filed applications for green cards and statuses are all submitted to offices of INS. INS is a branch agency of the U.S. Department of Justice.

Border Patrol. The Border Patrol is a sister agency of INS. Its primary function is to investigate information received on undocumented aliens. Most people recognize the Border Patrol as the agency responsible for rounding up undocumented aliens and taking them into custody.

U.S. embassies. U.S. embassies are agencies that represent the U.S. government in other countries. The U.S. has embassies located in many countries around the world. Most U.S. embassies accept and process green card and visa applications.

U.S. consulates. U.S. consulates are simply branch offices of U.S. embassies. They, too, are located all over the world. The U.S. government frequently operates both consulates and embassies in a single foreign country. Many consulates accept and process green card and visa applications.

Department of State. U.S. embassies and consulates are operated by the branch of the U.S. government called the Department of State (DOS). Generally, it is the DOS that determines who is entitled to a visa or green card when the application is filed outside the U.S. at U.S. embassies or consulates, but it is INS under the Department of Justice that regulates immigration processing inside the U.S.

National Visa Center. The National Visa Center (NVC), located in Portsmouth, New Hampshire, is run by a private company under contract with the DOS for the purpose of carrying out certain immigration functions. The NVC receives all approved green card petitions and green card lottery registrations directly from INS or the DOS. It is the NVC that initiates the final green card application process by sending forms and instructions to the applicant and forwarding the file to the appropriate U.S. consulate abroad.

Department of Labor. The Department of Labor (DOL) is a U.S. government agency involved with many types of visas that are job-related. It is the DOL that receives applications for Labor Certifications and decides whether or not there is a shortage of American citizens available to fill a particular position in a U.S. company.

Inadmissible. Potential immigrants who are disqualified from obtaining visas or green cards because they are judged by the U.S. government to be in some way undesirable are called *inadmissible* (formerly "excludable"). In general, most of these people are considered excludable because they have criminal records, have certain health problems, commit certain criminal acts, are thought to be subversive or are unable to support themselves financially. In many cases, there are legal ways to overcome inadmissibility.

Removal. Removal (formerly "deportation") is a legal proceeding carried on before a special immigration judge to decide whether or not an immigrant will be allowed to enter or remain in the country. While, generally speaking, a person cannot be expelled without first going through a removal hearing, someone arriving at the border or a port of entry can be forced to leave without a hearing or ever seeing a judge. If an immigrant is found removable, he or she can then be forced to leave the U.S. Those who are deported are barred from returning to the U.S. for at least five years unless a special waiver is granted by INS.

Naturalization. When a foreign person takes legal action to become a U.S. citizen, the process is called naturalization. Almost everyone who goes through naturalization must first have held a green card for several years before becoming eligible for U.S. citizenship. A naturalized U.S. citizen has virtually the same rights as a native-born American citizen. ■

Government Immigration Agencies: How They Work

You should become familiar with the various U.S. government agency offices that process immigration applications, and learn about the special problems in dealing with each of them. As you go on to the detailed explanations of how to get your green card or nonimmigrant visa, you will be told exactly where to file the paperwork for each. In this chapter, we will give you a general idea of what to expect when you do file.

Getting your green card or nonimmigrant visa may require you to deal with one, two or even three different U.S. government agencies. They are:

- The U.S. Department of State (DOS), through U.S. embassies and U.S. consulates located around the world
- The U.S. Immigration and Naturalization Service (INS), and
- The U.S. Department of Labor (DOL).

A. Department of State, U.S. Embassies and U.S. Consulates

U.S. visas are issued only *outside* the U.S. embassies or consulates issue visas. Embassies and consulates are part of the U.S. Department of State. Virtually every U.S. embassy and many U.S. consulates located in major cities worldwide have visa sections. However, not every consulate issues every type of visa. When you are ready to apply, you will have to locate the consulate nearest you that is authorized to issue the visa you want. Visa sections are subdivided into immigrant and nonimmigrant departments. Some consulates handle only one type or the other. A complete list of all U.S. consulates and embassies that issue visas is in Appendix I. If you find that a particular embassy or consulate with which you are familiar is missing from the list, that is because it is not authorized to perform immigration processing.

When you apply for a green card at a U.S. embassy or consulate, you must usually do so in the country where you live. Embassies and consulates located in nations other than your home country will normally refuse to accept your case. Occasionally, a consulate in a country other than your

present homeland may be persuaded to process your application, but those are exceptions and require advance approval. Furthermore, to get the right to apply in some other country, you must show a compelling reason why you are unable to apply at home. Usually, you will be allowed to apply for a green card outside your home country only if the U.S. has no diplomatic relationship with the government of your homeland.

Unlike green cards, you may apply for nonimmigrant visas at certain U.S. embassies or consulates authorized to issue the type of visa you seek, and which accept nonimmigrant visa applications from third country nationals, that is, nationals of neither the U.S. nor the country where the consulate is located. You must be physically present within its geographic jurisdiction.

Furthermore, if you have been present in the U.S. unlawfully, in general you cannot apply as a third country national. Even if you overstayed your status in the U.S. by just one day, your visa will be automatically cancelled, and you must return to your home country and apply for the visa from that consulate. There is an exception. If you were admitted to the U.S. for the duration of your status (indicated by a "D/S" on your I-94 form) and you remained in

the U.S. beyond that time, you may still be able to apply as a third country national. The State Department's current regulations seem to imply that you will be barred from third country national processing only if INS or an immigration judge has determined that you were unlawfully present. Because of the ambiguity, you may find that your success in applying as a third country national will depend on your country, the consulate and the relative seriousness of your offense.

If at all possible, it is thus usually best to apply in your country of residence because your case will receive greatest consideration there. A few countries may even decide to waive the requirement that you be physically present to apply. For example, the U.S. embassy in London insists that all applications (for U.K. nationals) be submitted by mail; your presence there is necessary only in cases requiring a personal interview.

Virtually all applications for green cards, as well as those for certain nonimmigrant visas, require a first step called the *petition*. Most petitions are filed at INS offices (see Section B, below) in the U.S. and not at embassies or consulates. However, if the petitioner is a U.S. citizen living abroad, the petition may be filed at the U.S. embassy or consulate in his or her country of residence.

In addition to operating the green card and visa sections of U.S. embassies and consulates, DOS is also responsible for running the green card lottery which takes place each year. You can participate in a green card lottery by mailing a registration form to DOS at a special address, during an annual registration period. (See Chapter 9.)

NATIONAL VISA CENTER

The National Visa Center, or NVC, is run by a private company under contract to DOS for the purpose of initiating final green card applications. After the INS approves a green card petition, NVC sends the first sets of forms and instructions to applicants and forwards their files to the appropriate U.S. consulates abroad. NVC also is responsible for processing green card lottery applications and selecting the winners.

B. Immigration and Naturalization Service

Most Immigration and Naturalization Service (INS) offices are located inside the U.S. INS is part of the U.S. Department of Justice. Various types of petitions and applications are filed with INS.

There are about 60 INS local offices placed all over the U.S., and several located within U.S. territories. INS local offices are classified as district or suboffices. Suboffices are primarily intake offices. They receive petitions and applications, but send the paperwork elsewhere for much of the actual processing. While interviews and some limited visa functions do take place at suboffices, the district offices perform more of the work on site. For this reason, you can often get faster results at a district office. A complete list of all INS district offices and suboffices with their addresses and phone numbers is in Appendix II.

Filing procedures vary somewhat from one INS office to another. Most permit paperwork to be filed either by mail or in person, but some allow only one method or the other. If the type of visa for which you are applying requires an interview, most offices will conduct the interview after the papers are processed. A few, such as the INS office in Honolulu, will interview at the time of filing, completing all procedures in just one day. It is a good idea either to call or visit your nearest INS local office to find out about procedures at that particular location. If you try to call, be prepared for the fact that many INS local offices are poorly staffed and the telephones are always busy.

Most people who apply for green cards or visas want them as soon as possible. While nothing can be done to shorten waits due to quotas, district offices and suboffices of INS do have the power to speed up the paperwork on cases not involving quotas or where the priority date has already come up. This special attention is reserved for those who can show a genuine and pressing need for quick action. Simple convenience of the applicant is not a good enough reason and, even when the need is truly urgent, requests for faster processing may be turned down. Still, such requests are given consideration and are often granted. Again, different offices have different policies. Call or visit your local INS office if you wish to ask whether expedited processing is available in your locale.

Four special INS offices, known as regional service centers, have full responsibility for certain types of cases. Virtually all applications that do not automatically require interviews must be submitted by mail directly to a regional service center. It is anticipated that in the future, all immigration petitions and applications may initially be filed at the service centers. A complete list of the regional service centers is in Appendix II.

Dealing with the regional service centers may be frustrating because public telephone access is limited and the possibility of a face-to-face discussion with an immigration examiner is almost nonexistent. This makes it difficult to get information on pending cases. The regional service centers have an automated phone inquiry system whereby punching in the file number provides limited information. Of course, to use this system, you must first have the file number. Regional centers also respond to fax inquiries concerning pending applications, if they have been filed and are awaiting a decision beyond the estimated processing time stated on your receipt notice.

C. Department of Labor

If your visa or green card application is based on a job with a U.S. employer, certain parts of the paperwork may have to be filed with and ruled on by the U.S. Department of Labor (DOL). Applications filed with INS or a consulate for most green cards based on the employment-related preferences must be accompanied by an approved Labor Certification. The exceptions are first preference employment sponsored green cards and Schedule A occupations, which do not require Labor Certifications. These are described in detail in Chapter 8. Other applications for green cards through employment, and for H-2 nonimmigrant visas, must be accompanied by an approved Labor Certification. If you read Chapter 2, *Basic Immigration Terms*, you will remember that a Labor Certification is an official recognition by DOL that no Americans are available and willing to take the U.S. job that has been offered to you. Procedures for getting Labor Certifications are handled by DOL. In certain types of cases, a Labor Certification must be obtained before a petition can be filed with INS.

In carrying out its duties to process Labor Certifications, DOL makes use of the services of the labor departments operated by each U.S. state. State employment offices act as agents of the federal government in performing certain parts of the Labor Certification procedure. It is at a state employment office where an application for Labor Certification is first filed. In some states, this is done at the local state employment office nearest the U.S. employer's place of business. In others, the state is divided geographically into regions and the application goes to the nearest regional office. Still other states have only a central filing, usually with a state job service office in the capital city. To find out where your Labor Certification should be filed, contact the office of the state labor department, division of employment, training and administration nearest your prospective employer.

Labor Certification applications can sometimes take as long as two years or more to complete. As with INS offices, waiting periods due to quotas cannot be speeded up, but delays due to paperwork backlogs can sometimes be overcome in an emergency. If you are applying for a nonimmigrant visa where quotas are not involved, and the need to get your visa quickly is truly urgent, or if your priority date for a green card has come up so that the quota is no longer a factor, you or your U.S. employer can explain the problem to the state labor department office and it may be willing to handle the case right away. Like INS, however, DOL grants requests for expedited processing only in the most unusual and compelling circumstances. ■

Green Cards: An Overview

People all over the world have heard of green cards. The term green card is not an official name. It is a common term for what is properly known as an Alien Registration Receipt Card. Years ago, these cards were green in color. Then, for a while they were red, white and blue. Today they are pink.

A lot of people mistakenly believe that green cards are nothing more than work permits. While a green card does give you the right to work legally in the U.S. where and when you wish, that is just one of its features. Identifying the holder as a permanent resident of the U.S. is its main function.

When you have a green card, you are required to make the U.S. your permanent home. If you don't, you risk losing your card. This does not mean your ability to travel in and out of the U.S. is limited. Freedom to travel as you choose is an important benefit of a green card. However, no matter how much you travel, your permanent residence must be in the U.S. or your card will be revoked.

All green cards issued since 1989 carry expiration dates of ten years from the date of issue. This does not mean that the residency itself expires in ten years, just that the card must be replaced. The requirement to renew green cards every ten years applies only to cards with expiration dates.

A. Categories of Green Card Applicants

INS has created nine categories of green card applicants.

1. Immediate Relatives

Most green card categories are subject to some type of quota. There is, however, no quota limit on the number of green cards that can be issued to immigrants who are immediate relatives of U.S. citizens. Immediate relatives are defined as:

- spouses of U.S. citizens, including recent widows and widowers
- unmarried people under the age of 21 who have at least one U.S. citizen parent
- parents of U.S. citizens, if the U.S. citizen child is over the age of 21

- stepchildren and stepparents, if the marriage creating the stepparent/stepchild relationship took place before the child's 18th birthday, or
- parents and children related through adoption, if the adoption took place before the child reached the age of 16—all immigration rules governing natural parents and children apply to adoptive relatives but there are some additional procedures (see Chapter 6).

Immediate relatives (other than adopted relatives) are discussed in Chapter 5.

2. Preferences

Those who receive green cards under the quota fall into one of several classifications called preferences. Although there are a number of preference categories, they actually cover only two general types of people: certain family members of U.S. citizens or permanent residents, and those with job skills wanted by U.S. employers.

a. Group I: Family Preference Green Cards

- **Family first preference.** Unmarried people, any age, who have at least one U.S. citizen parent.
- **Family second preference.** 2A: Spouses of green card holders and unmarried children under 21 and 2B: unmarried sons and daughters (who are over 21) of green card holders.
- **Family third preference.** Married people, any age, who have at least one U.S. citizen parent.
- **Family fourth preference.** Sisters and brothers of U.S. citizens who are over 21 years old.

b. Group II: Employment Preference Based Green Cards

- **Employment first preference.** Priority workers, including the following three groups:
  - persons of extraordinary ability in the arts, sciences, education, business or athletics
  - outstanding professors and researchers, and
  - managers and executives of multinational companies.
- **Employment second preference.** Professionals with advanced degrees or exceptional ability.

- **Employment third preference.** Professionals and skilled or unskilled workers.
- **Employment fourth preference.** Religious workers and various miscellaneous categories of workers and other individuals.
- **Employment fifth preference.** Individual investors willing to invest $1,000,000 in a U.S. business (or $500,000 in economically depressed areas).

Preference green cards are discussed in Chapters 5 and 8.

3.   Ethnic Diversity: Green Card Lotteries

A certain number of green cards are given to people from countries that in recent years have sent the fewest immigrants to the U.S. The purpose of this program is to insure a varied ethnic mix among those who immigrate to America. Therefore, green cards in this category are said to be based on ethnic diversity. The method used for distributing these green cards is a random selection by computer, so the program is popularly known as the *green card lottery*. The future of these lotteries is uncertain. If you are interested, do not procrastinate—the opportunities may disappear. Green card lotteries are discussed in Chapter 9.

4.   Investors

Ten thousand green cards are now available each year to people who make large business investments in the U.S. The investment must be in a new business that will hire at least ten full-time American workers. A minimum investment of $500,000 is required if the business is located in a rural or economically depressed area of the U.S. Otherwise, the minimum is $1 million. Green cards through investment are discussed in Chapter 10.

5.   Special Immigrants

Occasionally, laws are passed making green cards available to people in special situations. Groups singled out for these green cards are not included in the preference system and are referred to as special immigrants. The current special immigrant categories are:

- religious workers for legitimate religious organizations
- foreign medical graduates who have been in the U.S. since 1978
- former employees of the Panama Canal Zone
- foreign workers who were formerly longtime employees of the U.S. government
- retired officers or employees of certain international organizations who have lived in the U.S. for a certain time, their spouses and unmarried children
- foreign workers who have been employees of the U.S. consulate in Hong Kong for at least three years, and
- foreign children who have been declared dependent in juvenile courts in the U.S.

All special immigrant categories are discussed in Chapter 11.

6.   Refugees and Political Asylees

Every year, many people seek political asylum in America or try to get green cards as refugees. The two are often thought of as the same category, but there are some technical differences. A refugee receives permission to come to the U.S. in refugee status *before* actually arriving. Political asylum is granted only *after* someone has physically entered the U.S., either as a nonimmigrant or an undocumented alien.

The qualifications for refugee status and political asylum are similar. You must fear political or religious persecution in your home country. If you are only fleeing poverty, you do not qualify in either category. Both refugees and political asylees can get green cards. See Chapter 12 for details.

7.   Temporary Protected Status

The INS may decide to give citizens of certain countries temporary safe haven in the U.S. when conditions in their homeland become dangerous. This is called Temporary Protected Status (TPS). TPS is similar to political asylum except that it is always temporary, and will never turn into a green card. See Chapter 12 for more details.

8.   Amnesty

Congress added an amnesty for Nicaraguan and Cuban nationals in a 1997 bill called the Nicaraguan Adjustment and Central American Relief Act (NACARA). Some provisions, discussed in Chapter 13, also benefit Salvadorans, Guatemalans, and Eastern Europeans.

The Immigration Reform and Control Act of 1986 (IRCA) gave amnesty to aliens who had been living in the U.S. illegally since January 1, 1982 by making green cards available to them. The deadline for filing temporary residency applications as amnesty candidates was May 4, 1988, however, under certain circumstances late applications may still be accepted. If you believe you may be eligible for amnesty, check with an immigration attorney to see if you can still apply. Do not check first with an INS office because you risk being placed in deportation proceedings. Chapter 13 contains the details.

9.   Special Agricultural Workers (SAWs)

The Immigration Reform and Control Act of 1986 also contained an amnesty green card opportunity for agricultural laborers who worked in the fields for at least 90 days between

May 1, 1985 and May 1, 1986. Like other amnesty applicants, special agricultural workers (SAWs) got green cards in two steps. First, a temporary residency was granted and then, depending on a variety of factors, permanent green cards were issued one or two years later. The filing deadline for these temporary residency applications was November 30, 1988. However, late applications may be accepted under certain circumstances. Once again, check with an immigration attorney if you think you are eligible in this category. Chapter 13 contains additional details.

10. Long-Term Residents and Other Special Cases

The law also allows certain people who have lived illegally in the U.S. for more than ten years to obtain permanent legal residence. They must show that their spouse or children—who must be U.S. citizens—would face "extraordinary and exceptionally unusual hardship" if the undocumented alien were forced to leave the country.

Anyone who believes that they meet this requirement should consult with a lawyer before going to the immigration service to make an application. If they are clearly not within this category, they might be causing their own deportation by making themselves known to the authorities.

Individual members of Congress have, on occasion, intervened for humanitarian reasons in extraordinary cases, helping an individual obtain permanent residence even if the law would not allow it.

B. Quotas

There are no limits on the number of green cards that can be issued to immediate relatives of U.S. citizens. For those who qualify in any other category, there are annual quotas. Both family and employment based preference green cards are affected by quotas.

Green cards allocated annually to employment based categories, including investors and special immigrants, number 140,000 worldwide. Approximately 480,000 green cards worldwide can be issued each year in the family categories.

Only 7% of all worldwide preference totals added together can be given to persons born in any one country. There are, therefore, two separate quotas: one for each country and one that is worldwide. This produces an odd result because when you multiply the number of countries in the world by seven (the percentage allowed to each country) you get a much larger total than 100. What this means from a practical standpoint is that the 7% allotment to each country is an allowable maximum, not a guaranteed number. Applicants from a single country that has not used up

its 7% green card allotment can still be prevented from getting green cards if the worldwide quota has been exhausted. Right now, there are in fact waiting periods in most preference categories caused by the limits of the worldwide quota.

In addition to the fixed worldwide totals, 55,000 extra green cards are given each year through the ethnic diversity or lottery category. Qualifying countries and the number of green cards available to each are determined each year according to a formula. Chapter 9 gives the details of the lottery program.

C. How to Keep a Green Card Once You Get It

When you successfully complete an application for permanent residence at a U.S. consulate abroad, you do not get a green card immediately. First you are issued an immigrant visa. You must then use the immigrant visa within six months to enter the U.S. and claim your green card. If you do not act in time, the immigrant visa will expire and your right to a green card will be lost. If you are already in the U.S. when you apply for a green card you will not get an immigrant visa, and so will not have to deal with this deadline.

Once you receive a green card, there are only two conditions required to keep it for life. First, you must not become removable or inadmissible. The most common way of doing so is to be convicted of a serious crime.

The second requirement to keep your green card is that you not abandon the U.S. as your permanent residence. Residence, for immigration purposes, is a question of your intent when you depart the country. When you leave, if you do not plan to make your home somewhere else, then legally you are still a U.S. resident. Problems come up, however, because INS will try to judge what is in your mind by the way you act.

As a general rule, if you have a green card and leave the U.S. for more than one year, you may have a difficult time reentering the U.S. That is because INS feels an absence of longer than one year indicates a possible abandonment of U.S. residence. Anyone who is not a U.S. citizen must have either a visa or a visa substitute to enter the U.S. A green card serves as a visa substitute, but only if you have been away for less than one year. If you are gone longer, you may not be able to use your green card to get back in. Even if you do return before one year is up, that may not be enough, and it is best to come back within six months since by doing so you will not be subject to a full-scale inspection, unless you have been convicted of a crime or done other serious acts. It is a common misconception that to keep your green card all you need to do is enter the U.S. at least once a year. The fact is that if you ever leave with the intention of making some other country your permanent home, you give up your U.S. residency when you go. Once again, INS will look for signals that your real place of residence is not the U.S.

On the other hand, remaining outside the U.S. for more than one year does not mean you have automatically given up your green card. If your absence was intended from the start to be only temporary, you may still keep your permanent resident status. Staying away for more than one year does mean, however, that you may no longer use your green card as a U.S. entry document. Under these circumstances, you must either apply at a U.S. consulate for a special immigrant visa as a returning resident or you must get what is known as a *reentry permit.*

Reentry permits are for people who hold green cards and know in advance that they must be outside the U.S. for more than one year. Under such circumstances, INS can allow you to stay away for up to two years. You should apply for this privilege *before* leaving. If the application is approved, a reentry permit will be issued. The permit will help you prove that your absence from the U.S. is not an abandonment of residence. It also serves as an entry document when you are ready to return. Reentry permits cannot be renewed and can be applied for only inside the U.S. Therefore, if you want to stay away for more than two years, you must return briefly and apply for another reentry permit. You can apply for reentry permits by filling out INS Form I-131 and sending it to your nearest local INS office.

If you stay outside the U.S. for more than one year and do not get a reentry permit before leaving, then in order to come back again, you must apply at a U.S. consulate abroad for a special immigrant visa as a returning resident. To get this visa you will have to convince the consular officer that your absence from the U.S. has been temporary and you never planned to abandon your U.S. residence. You will have to show evidence that you were kept away longer than one year due to unforeseen circumstances. Such evidence might be a letter from a doctor showing that you or a family member had a medical problem. If you do not have a very good reason for failing to return within one year, there is a strong chance you will lose your green card.

THE COMMUTER EXCEPTION

Green card holders who commute to work in the U.S. from Canada or Mexico on a daily or seasonal basis may keep their cards even while actually living outside the country. INS will grant you commuter status if, when you get a green card, you advise them of your intention to live in Canada or Mexico. If you live in the U.S. with a green card but later move to the other side of the border, you will be given commuter status when you notify INS of your new address.

D. Green Cards and U.S. Citizenship

Green card holders can, after a certain time, apply for U.S. citizenship. Except in rare cases, no one can become a U.S. citizen without first receiving a green card. It is frequently said that green cards give all the benefits of U.S. citizenship except the rights to vote and hold public office. The differences between the two are actually greater. The most important distinction is that if you commit a crime or physically leave your U.S. residence for a year or more, you can lose your green card. U.S. citizenship cannot be taken away, unless you acquired it fraudulently or voluntarily give it up.

E. Green Cards and U.S. Taxes

Once you get a green card, you automatically become a U.S. tax resident. U.S. tax residents must declare their entire incomes to the U.S. government, even if part or all of that income has been earned from investments or business activities carried on outside American borders. This does not necessarily mean that the U.S. government will tax all of your worldwide income. International treaties often regulate whether or not you must pay U.S. taxes on income earned elsewhere. However, green card holders do have to at least report all income they have earned worldwide.

You may believe that the number of days you spend in the U.S. each year has some effect on whether or not you are a U.S. tax resident. This is true for people who have nonimmigrant visas. It is not true for green card holders. If you have a green card, your worldwide income must be reported to the U.S. government, even if you remain outside the U.S. for an entire year.

As a green card holder, you must file U.S. tax return Form 1040 each year by April 15th. Failure to follow U.S. tax laws may be considered a crime. If you are found guilty of a tax crime, your green card can be revoked and you may be deported. To find out exactly how to follow U.S. tax laws, consult an accountant, a tax attorney or the nearest office of the U.S. Internal Revenue Service. ■

Getting a Green Card Through Relatives

Privileges

- You may live anywhere in the U.S. and stay as long as you want.

- You may work at any job, for any company, anywhere in the U.S., or you may choose not to work at all.

- You may travel in and out of the U.S. whenever you wish.

- You may apply to become an American citizen after you have held your green card for a certain length of time.

- In some types of cases, if you qualify for a green card through relatives, then your spouse and unmarried children under the age of 21 may also get green cards automatically as accompanying relatives.

Limitations

- Your place of actual residence must be in the U.S. You cannot use a green card just for work and travel purposes. (The only exception to this is commuters, discussed in Chapter 4C.)

- You must pay U.S. taxes on your worldwide income because you are regarded as a U.S. resident.

- You cannot remain outside the U.S. for more than one year at a time without special permission or you risk losing your green card. (It is recommended that you return within six months.)

- If you commit certain crimes or participate in politically subversive activities, your green card can be taken away and you can be deported.

A. How to Qualify

Qualifying for a green card through relatives has some limitations.

1. Quota Restrictions

The preference relative categories are limited by quotas. The immediate relative category is not.

The forecasts for the preference relative categories quotas as of January 1998 are:

- **Family first preference.** Waiting periods of two years for natives of all countries except the Philippines and Mexico. Filipinos can expect quota waiting periods of at least 12 years. Mexicans can expect to wait about seven years.
- **Family second preference.** Waiting periods of four years can be expected for natives of all countries for family-based 2A (spouses and children of permanent residents) and six years for family-based 2B (unmarried sons and daughters over 21 years old).
- **Family third preference.** Waiting periods of at least three years can be expected for natives of all countries except Mexico, where the wait is about nine years and the Philippines, where the waiting periods are at least 11 years.

- **Family fourth preference.** Natives of all countries may expect waiting periods of at least ten years. Filipinos will have to wait at least 19 years.

Petitions are normally approved within two months. Green card applications take several months to a year after the quota becomes current.

2. Who Qualifies for a Green Card Through a Relative?

You qualify for a green card if you have a close family member who is a U.S. citizen or green card holder. You may qualify for a green card through relatives if you fall into one of the following categories:

- immediate relative of a U.S. citizen
- preference relative of a U.S. citizen or green card holder, or
- accompanying relative of someone in a preference category.

a. Immediate Relatives

These people qualify as immediate relatives:

- Spouses of U.S. citizens. This includes widows and widowers of U.S. citizens if they were married to the

DISCARD

U.S. citizen for at least two years and are applying for a green card within two years of the U.S. citizen's death.
- Unmarried people under the age of 21 who have at least one U.S. citizen parent.
- Parents of U.S. citizens, if the U.S. citizen child is over the age of 21.

Immediate relatives may immigrate to the U.S. in unlimited numbers. They are not controlled by a quota.

Stepparents and stepchildren qualify as immediate relatives if the marriage creating the parent/child relationship took place before the child's 18th birthday. Parents and children related through adoption also qualify as immediate relatives, if the adoption took place before the child reached the age of 16. In addition, the adopted child must have lived with the adoptive parent or parents for at least two years prior to filing the petition for a green card.

b.   Preference Relatives

In Chapter 4, *Green Cards: An Overview*, we listed a number of preference categories under which you can qualify for a green card. Four of them require family relationships with Americans. Here is a review of the qualifications needed for the four preferences based on relatives:

- **Family first preference.** Unmarried people, any age, who have at least one U.S. citizen parent.
- **Family second preference.** 2A: Spouses and children under 21 years old, of green card holders; and 2B: Unmarried sons and daughters of green card holders who are at least 21 years old.
- **Family third preference.** Married people, any age, who have at least one U.S. citizen parent.
- **Family fourth preference.** Sisters and brothers of U.S. citizens, where the U.S. citizen is at least 21 years old.

c.   Accompanying Relatives

If you get a green card as a preference relative and you are married or have unmarried children below the age of 21, your spouse and children can automatically get green cards as accompanying relatives simply by proving their family relationship to you. If, however, you qualify as an immediate relative, they *cannot*. This difference may create some real problems in cases involving parents with adult children or stepparents and stepchildren who wish to immigrate as a family. Below are a few examples to illustrate the practical effect of these laws. This is probably one of the most difficult areas in immigration to understand. It may take several readings before you grasp it completely. If you don't have adult children or stepchildren involved in your immigration plans, skip these examples, save yourself the trouble and read on.

EXAMPLE 1: Suppose your child is over age 21 and is a U.S. citizen. You are applying for a green card as an immediate relative with your U.S.-citizen child acting as petitioner. If you are married to someone other than your U.S.-citizen child's other parent, your spouse can't get a green card automatically as an accompanying relative because *accompanying relatives are included only with preference relatives, not immediate relatives.* Any children you may have, even if they are minors, cannot be accompanying relatives either, for the same reason.

If your U.S.-citizen child is the offspring of your spouse as well, your child may file petitions for each parent at the same time, but the two filings will be completely separate. The marriage between you and your spouse will not be relevant when INS considers your cases. Likewise, your U.S-citizen child may also sponsor his or her brothers and sisters under the family fourth preference, but again, the fact that you qualify for a green card will not help your children. There is a long wait under the quota for family fourth preference applicants, while there is no wait at all for immediate relatives. In this manner, members of the same family can be forced to immigrate on different time schedules.

EXAMPLE 2: Again, suppose you are the parent of a U.S.-citizen child who is over age 21. You are applying for a green card as an immediate relative with your U.S. citizen child acting as petitioner. You are married, but your spouse is not the other parent of your U.S.-citizen child. Clearly, you have a problem. Your spouse can't get a green card automatically as an accompanying relative because *accompanying relatives are included only with preference relatives, not immediate relatives.* Neither can your spouse be sponsored separately by your U.S.-citizen child because your spouse is not the child's parent.

If your present marriage took place before your U.S. son or daughter reached the age of 18, your problem is solved, because your spouse is, according to immigration law, a stepparent. Likewise, if your spouse adopted your child before the child's 16th birthday, your spouse qualifies as an adopting parent. Stepparent and adopting parents can qualify as the immediate relatives of a U.S. citizen and your child can petition for a stepparent or adopting parent just as if he or she were a natural parent.

What if your marriage took place after the petitioning child's 18th birthday? Now your spouse is not considered a stepparent for immigration purposes and so you will have to wait until you get your own green card before anything can be done for your spouse. Once you get your own green card, you will be able to act as petitioner for your spouse, who will then qualify under the family second preference as the relative of a green card holder. Unfortunately, this category is currently subject to a quota wait of several years, so your spouse will have to wait even longer before getting a green card.

The same sort of problem also comes up when the U.S.-citizen petitioner is the stepparent. The U.S. stepparent may easily petition for the alien husband or wife, but if the alien spouse has children by a previous marriage and those children were over the age of 18 when the present marriage took place, they will have no one to petition for them until their natural parent gets a green card and they qualify under the family second preference.

EXAMPLE 3: Suppose you are unmarried and under age 21. Your parent is a U.S. citizen and you are applying for a green card with your parent acting as petitioner. You are in the unique situation of being able to choose between classifications. You qualify either as an immediate relative or in the family first preference category. It would seem logical for you to choose the immediate relative category because preference relatives are limited by quota while immediate relatives are not.

Let us further suppose that you have a child of your own. It now seems logical to place yourself in the preference rather than the immediate relative category because then your child could automatically get a green card as an accompanying relative. On the other hand, preference relatives, limited by quotas, usually wait longer for green cards than immediate relatives. At present, the family first preference has waiting lists of from 18 months to two years for most countries, and waiting periods of seven and more than 12 years, respectively, for people born in Mexico and the Philippines. The first preference waiting period has moved abruptly back and forth in recent months, so you are well advised to consult the visa bulletin closely before making a choice between a preference category and immediate relative status.

d. Marriage to a U.S. Citizen

Almost everyone knows that there are immigration advantages to marrying a U.S. citizen. It is also no secret that many who are not fortunate enough to have U.S. citizen relatives try to acquire one through a marriage of convenience.

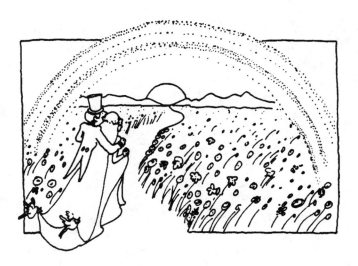

By law, green cards are not available to anyone who marries only for immigration purposes. Such marriages, even though they may be legal in every other way, are regarded by immigration officials as shams. Of course, it is very difficult for INS officers to tell which marriages are shams and which are not. However, INS and the Department of State assert that more than half of all the marriage applications they process are based on shams. It is not surprising, then, that INS is especially careful about investigating marriage cases.

It is a criminal offense to file a green card application based on a sham marriage. If you attempt to qualify for a green card in this way, you will risk a long jail sentence as well as deportation. In addition, you will almost certainly be permanently barred from getting a green card. The U.S. citizen also risks going to jail as well.

i. Conditions on Green Cards Through Marriage

Because INS is so suspicious of foreign nationals who marry U.S. citizens, there are some special restrictions on immigration benefits available to them. If you apply for a green card through marriage and INS believes the marriage is valid, and you are otherwise eligible, you will get a green card. However, if you have been married for less than two years when your application is approved, the card will be issued only conditionally. These conditional green cards last for two years. When that time is up, you must apply to INS to have the condition removed and your green card made permanent. If you are still married, you and your U.S. spouse should file an application together. Then, if INS continues to believe your marriage was not just for immigration purposes, you will receive a permanent green card.

If, however, you are divorced or your U.S. spouse simply refuses to cooperate, you must file for removal of the condition yourself. Under these circumstances you can still keep your green card if you can show one of the following three things:

- you are now divorced, but you originally entered into the marriage in good faith, or, in other words, your marriage was not a sham
- your eventual deportation will cause you extreme hardship, greater than that suffered by most people who are deported, or
- you were abused by your U.S.-citizen or green card-holder spouse.

If you have been married for close to two years, but for some reason have not yet applied for a green card, it makes sense to wait until your second wedding anniversary before applying. Likewise, if you are approaching the two-year mark and have a green card marriage interview scheduled shortly before your anniversary, you may want to consider postponing the interview until afterward. A green card approved after two years of marriage is permanent, with no condition attached.

Even when you stay married for two years or more and get your permanent green card, if you divorce at a later time, your immigration benefits are still restricted. Although you can keep the green card, should you eventually wish to remarry and your next husband or wife needs a green card, the INS will assume that your first marriage was one of convenience, unless and until you prove through convincing documentation that it was not. If you can make such a showing, you may sponsor your new spouse within five years of the first marriage. Otherwise you have to wait until the five years has passed.

ii. Shaky Marriages Heading for Divorce

What happens if you got married in good faith, are still married, but the marriage is failing—perhaps divorce proceedings are now being considered or have already begun? The courts have long held that the present strength of a marriage is not a factor in judging eligibility for a green card. All that matters is the intent of the parties at the time of the marriage, and whether or not you are still legally married now. Therefore, even if a divorce is in progress, if the marriage was legitimate from the beginning, and your American spouse is willing to file a petition, you can still get a green card. Just be absolutely certain that the divorce decree does not become final until the green card is issued. Remember, though, if you have been married for less than two years, your green card will be issued only conditionally, subject to the rules discussed above. It is important that your divorce lawyer have a thorough understanding of these rules.

You must be completely open with INS about the current state of your marriage. During your green card interview, you should mention that a divorce is in progress, even if you are not asked about it. Otherwise, the fact that this situation does not appear on the record may cause your honesty to be questioned later. This is especially true if you are receiving your green card only conditionally and will eventually be facing the removal of the condition alone.

iii. Battered Spouses and Children

If you are the battered or abused spouse or child of a U.S. citizen and he or she refuses to petition on your behalf, then you can petition for yourself. You are required to be physically inside the U.S. to take advantage of this opportunity.

You must also establish with credible evidence all of the following:

- that you were either battered or subjected to extreme cruelty
- that you resided with the spouse or parent inside the U.S.
- that your deportation would cause extreme hardship to yourself or your children, and
- if you're a spouse, that the marriage was entered into in good faith—that is, not just to get a green card.

iv. Marriage During Deportation

If you marry a U.S. citizen or green card holder while you are in the middle of deportation proceedings, you may still apply for a green card. However, an even stricter standard will be applied when your motives for marriage are examined. You will be required to produce clear and convincing evidence that your marriage is not a sham and you can expect a very detailed marriage interview. You would be well advised to hire an immigration attorney in such a situation.

v. Widows and Widowers

Special rules apply to foreign nationals who wish to get green cards as widows or widowers of U.S. citizens. They may do so, but only if they were married for at least two years before the American spouse's death occurred. Then, the surviving foreign national may file his or her own petition. This petition must be filed no more than two years after the death of the U.S. citizen. If the surviving foreign national remarries, then he or she loses the right to apply for a green card as a widow or widower. However, even if the widow or widower remarries after that, your green card will not be taken away for that reason.

These rules apply only to the surviving spouses of U.S. citizens. Husbands and wives of green card holders may get green cards themselves only if the petitioner remains alive until the card is actually issued. Even if a petition is filed and approved while the green card holder is alive, the spouse still cannot receive a green card if the husband or wife dies before the card is issued, unless there are extra-ordinarily sympathetic circumstances which could convince an INS officer to grant the green card even though the petitioner died.

3. Inadmissibility

If you have ever been arrested for a crime, were unlawfully in the U.S. for more than six months, lied on an immigration application, lied to an immigration officer or suffered certain physical or mental illnesses, among other circumstances, you may be excludable from receiving a green card unless you can qualify for what is known as a *Waiver of Inadmissibility*. See Chapter 25, *Inadmissibility*, to find out exactly who is in-admissible and how these obstacles can be overcome.

B. Getting a Green Card Through a Relative

Getting a green card through a relative is a two-step pro-cess. Certain parts of this process are technically the respon-sibility of your sponsoring relative. Other parts are meant to be done by you. As we give you step-by-step instructions for getting a green card, we will discuss each task according to who has the legal responsibility for carrying it out. How-ever, even if the law presumes your relative is performing a particular task, there is nothing to stop you from helping your relative with the paperwork and in fact we recommend that you do so. For example, you can fill out forms in-tended to be completed by your relative and simply ask him or her to check them over and sign them. With the help of this book, you will know how to do all that is required and it is completely legal as well as in your best interest to assist whenever possible. The less your U.S. relative must do, the more he or she will be willing to act as your petitioner.

1. Step One: The Petition

The petition is filed in most cases by your sponsoring rela-tive. In the case of widows or abused spouses, however, the petition, called a self-petition, is filed by you. Unless the pe-titioner is living outside the U.S., all petitions are submitted to INS local offices or regional service centers in the U.S. The object of the petition is to establish that you are what you say you are: namely, the qualifying relative of a qualify-

ing sponsor. If you are a preference relative and therefore subject to a quota, the date on which you file the petition is called your priority date. The priority date is important be-cause it marks the legally recognized moment when your waiting period for a green card starts. If all goes well, your petition will eventually be approved, but be aware that an approved petition does not by itself give you any right to be present, enter or work in the U.S. It is only a prerequisite to Step Two, submitting the application for a green card. Your petition must be approved before you are eligible for Step Two.

2. Step Two: The Application

The application is filed by you and your accompanying relatives, if any. The application is your formal request for a green card. Step Two may be carried out in the U.S. at an INS office or in your home country at a U.S. consulate there. If you file Step Two papers in the U.S. on the basis of a marriage to a U.S. citizen, you will usually submit them at the same time and in the same place as those for Step One. For this reason it is often called a one-step process. When Step Two is dispatched at a U.S. consulate abroad, or in the U.S. but at a separate time from Step One, you must wait to file the application until the Step One petition is first ap-proved.

The majority of relative Step Two applications are filed at consulates. Those filed in the U.S. are mainly marriage cases. If you are in the U.S. legally on a nonimmigrant visa and you are an immediate relative or a preference relative with a current priority date (you filed a petition earlier and your wait under the quota is over or you have not filed a petition, but the preference category under which you will file is up to date and there is no wait), you apply for your green card either inside or outside the U.S., whichever you prefer. If you are in the U.S. illegally, or entered legally but without a visa under the Visa Waiver Program (unless you are the immediate relative of a U.S. citizen), you may be barred from a U.S. filing.

If you have an approved petition (Step One) but your priority date is not yet current, you must wait until it is current to file your Step Two application. The consulate will advise you by mail when your priority date finally comes up. If you want to check quota progress from time to time, you may do so by calling the U.S. State Department in Washington, D.C., at 202-663-1541 for the latest quota information.

THE PENALTY PROVISION, GRANDFATHER CLAUSE AND OVERSTAY BARS

The rules concerning getting a green card in the U.S. are somewhat complicated. In general, if you entered the U.S. properly and maintained your nonimmigrant status, you can probably get your green card without leaving the U.S. Most people who marry U.S. citizens can get a green card in the U.S. even if they have fallen out of status or worked without authorization, as long as they did not enter without being properly inspected, such as a crewman or stowaway.

Other people may be barred from getting a green card in the U.S., even though they have an approved petition saying a visa number is available. For example, you cannot apply for adjustment of status (green card within the U.S.) as a second preference alien until your priority date is current. Many family members of petitioners thus are out of status for a long time waiting for a visa number. Once your priority date is current, you can apply for adjustment of status by paying the filing fee of $130 for the I-485, if your relative is in status and otherwise eligible for adjustment.

If, however, your relative is currently out of status, has worked without authorization or entered without inspection, he is eligible to apply for an adjustment only if he is grandfathered in under the old provision which allowed an adjustment of an otherwise ineligible applicant upon paying a $1,000 penalty. This law expired in the fall of 1997. Presently, the only people who can still use the penalty provision are those that had a visa petition or labor certification on file by January 14, 1998.

An additional problem is the bar to adjustment for people who were unlawfully present for six or twelve months after April 1, 1997, who subsequently left the U.S. and who now seek admission through adjustment of status or through consular processing. Such people would be subject to a three-year waiting period; the period is ten years if they were unlawfully present for one year after April 1, 1997. A waiver is available for the spouse, son or daughter of a U.S. citizen or permanent resident, if it would cause that spouse or child "extreme hardship." (See Chapter 25, *Inadmissibility*, for more details.)

3. Paperwork

There are two types of paperwork you must submit to get a green card through a relative. The first consists of official government forms completed by you or your relative. The second is personal documents such as birth and marriage certificates. We will tell you exactly what forms and documents you need.

It is vital that forms are properly filled out and all necessary documents are supplied. You or your U.S. relative may resent the intrusion into your privacy and the sizable effort it takes to prepare immigration applications, but you should realize the process is an impersonal matter to immigration officials. Your getting a green card is more important to you than it is to the U.S. government. This is not a pleasant thing to accept, but you are better off having a real understanding of your position. People from all over the world want green cards. There is no shortage of applicants. Take the time and trouble to prepare your papers properly. In the end it will pay off with a successful application.

The documents you or your U.S. relative supply to INS do not have to be originals. Photocopies of all documents are acceptable as long as you have the original in your possession and are willing to produce the originals at the request of INS. Documents submitted to U.S. consulates, on the other hand, must be either originals or official government-certified copies. Government-certified copies and notarized copies are not the same thing. Documents that have only been notarized are not acceptable. They must carry a government seal. In addition to any original or government-certified copies of documents submitted to a consulate, you should submit plain photocopies of each document as well. After the consulate compares the copies with the originals, it will return the originals.

Documents will be accepted if they are in either English, or, with papers filed at most U.S. consulates abroad, the language of the country where the documents are being filed. An exception exists for papers filed at the U.S. consulates in Japan, where all documents must be translated into English. If the documents are not in an acceptable language as just explained, they must be accompanied by a full, word for word, written English translation. Any capable person may act as translator. It is not necessary to hire a professional. At the end of each translation, the following statement must appear:

> *I hereby certify that I translated this document from (language) to English. This translation is accurate and complete. I further certify that I am fully competent to translate from (language) to English.*

The translator should sign this statement but it does not have to be witnessed or notarized.

Later in this chapter we describe in detail the forms and documents needed to get your green card through a relative. A summary checklist of forms and documents appears at the end of the chapter.

C. Who's Who in Getting Your Green Card

Getting a green card will be easier if you familiarize yourself with the technical names used for each participant in the process. During Step One, the petition, you are known as the *beneficiary* and your sponsoring relative is called the *petitioner*. In Step Two, the application, you are referred to as *applicant*, but your relative remains the petitioner. If you are applying in a preference category, and bringing your spouse and children with you as accompanying relatives, they are known as applicants as well.

D. Step One: The Petition

This section includes the information you need to submit the petition.

1. General Procedures

Your sponsoring relative submits the petition (I-130), consisting of forms and documents, to the INS regional service center that has been designated for your sponsoring relative's place of residence. If both Steps One and Two will be carried out in the U.S. and the person being petitioned for has a current priority date or is an immediate relative not subject to quota, the petition will be filed, together with Step Two paperwork, at the INS local office nearest your place of residence. (See Appendix II for a complete list.) Otherwise you must have your sponsoring relative file Step One papers at the regional service center, and then when a number is available you may submit Step Two papers to the local INS office. If your sponsoring relative lives abroad and the INS has an office in the country where he or she lives, the Step One papers must be filed there. Foreign cities that currently have an INS office are: Vienna, Austria; Frankfurt, Germany; Athens, Greece; Hong Kong; New Delhi, India; Rome, Italy; Nairobi, Kenya; Seoul, Korea; Ciudad Juarez, Mexico City, Monterrey, Guadalajara, and Tijuana, Mexico; Manila, the Philippines; Panama City, Panama; Singapore; Bangkok, Thailand; and London, the United Kingdom. In all other countries, Step One papers should be filed with the U.S. consulate in the country where your sponsoring relative resides abroad.

When your relative files by mail and defects or omissions such as unsigned forms or missing payment are found, all petition papers, forms and documents will be returned. The returned package will contain either a handwritten note or a form known as an I-797 telling your relative what corrections, additional pieces of information, or additional documents are expected. If the papers are properly filed but missing some evidence INS needs to approve the case, INS will keep the papers but issue a request for evidence (RFE). Your relative should make the corrections or supply the extra data and mail the whole package back to INS.

When Step Two, the application, will be executed at a U.S. consulate abroad, or if it will be filed in the U.S. but at a separate time from the petition, file the petition at the INS regional service center or U.S. consulate office nearest your U.S. relative petitioner's place of residence. (A complete list of U.S. consulates abroad, together with their addresses and telephone numbers, is in Appendix I. Appendix II contains a complete list of all INS regional service centers.)

If the petition is to be filed at an INS regional service center, it must be sent by mail. Certified mail, return receipt requested, is recommended so you will have proof that the petition arrived. You should also enclose a self-addressed, stamped envelope and request that INS send back a receipt for the fees paid.

No matter where or how you file, the filing fee for each petition is currently $110. Checks, money orders and cash are accepted. When filing by mail, it is not advisable to send cash. If you file in person, you will be given a written receipt for the filing fee. Keep it in a safe place, together with a complete copy of everything submitted. Then you can confirm on what date your petition was filed, and the number on the receipt will help locate your papers should they get lost or delayed in processing. When filing by mail, again, we recommend sending the papers by certified mail, return receipt requested, and keeping a complete copy of everything submitted for your records. Also, remember that your priority date for quota purposes is established on the day your petition is filed, so it is important to have proof of exactly when this took place.

Once your petition is approved, a Notice of Action Form I-797 will be sent to your relative, indicating the approval. If you plan to execute Step Two at a U.S. consulate abroad, INS will forward the file to the National Visa Center (NVC), located in Portsmouth, New Hampshire. NVC will then send a packet of forms and instructions to you so that you may proceed with Step Two.

2. Petition Forms

Copies of all forms can be found in Appendix III.

Form I-130

The basic form for Step One, the petition, is immigration Form I-130. It is used for all relative cases. Section B of the form asks only about your petitioning relative. Section C asks about you. Section D is relevant only if the petitioner has petitioned for other relatives before. If a particular question does not apply, it should be answered "None" or "N/A." Do not leave any spaces blank or INS will return the form.

If you are petitioning for yourself as a battered spouse, you will sign the form instead of your U.S. spouse. Use Form I-360 in that situation.

It is absolutely essential to answer each question truthfully, even if it means disclosing that you are in the U.S. illegally. Failure to reveal requested information may result in your being permanently barred from the U.S.

Box at the Top of the Form. Do not fill in this boldfaced box.

Section A. These questions are self-explanatory.

Section B. These questions are self-explanatory.

Section C, Questions 1–20. These questions are self-explanatory.

Section C, Question 21. If you are planning to process Step Two, the application, at a U.S. consulate, check the first box in Question 21 and fill in the location of the consulate in your sponsor's country of residence where you wish to have your petition sent. The U.S. consulate in your sponsor's country of residence is the only one legally required to accept your application. If there is an overwhelming need to file elsewhere, you can contact a consulate in some other country and ask if it will agree to process your application. That consulate is under no obligation to grant your request and is very likely to turn you down, but there is no harm in asking. Unless you have received permission in advance, don't write down the name of any consulate other than the one in your sponsor's country of residence. Your file will eventually end up at the consulate you indicate in Question 21 and it will be held at that location. If that consulate has not already agreed to process your case, it will automatically send the file to the U.S. consulate in your sponsor's country of residence. This brings about unnecessary delays and increases the chances of your paperwork being lost.

If you are eligible to process Step Two in the U.S. and wish to do so, check the second box of Question 21 and put down the location of the INS local office nearest your home in the U.S. Also, name a consulate where you wish your petition sent in the event that INS decides you really aren't qualified for U.S. filing.

Section D. These questions are self-explanatory.

Perforated Card. Do not forget to complete the perforated card attached to the bottom of the last page of the form. INS uses this as an office index card on your case, so it is crucial in preventing the loss of your file.

Form I-360

Remember, use this form only if you are petitioning for yourself as a battered spouse.

Part 1. Skip this section.

Part 2. Check the second box. Cross out the words "Widow(er) of a U.S. citizen who died within the past 2 years" and write "Battered spouse."

Part 3. Fill in information about yourself.

Part 4. Fill in information about yourself.

Part 5. Skip this section.

Part 6. Skip this section.

Part 7. At the very top, cross out the words "a Widow or Widower" and write "yourself." In Section A, cross out the words "or wife who died" if you are a battered wife. Cross out the words "husband or" and "who died" if you are a battered husband. The questions for Sections A and B are self-explanatory.

Part 8. This section is self-explanatory.

Part 9. This section is self-explanatory.

Part 10. Skip this section.

Form G-325A

In most types of relative cases, the G-325A Biographic Data Form is a part of Step Two, not Step One. If, however, your petition is based on marriage to a U.S. citizen and it is being filed separately from the application, Form G-325A must be filled out in Step One as well. In marriage cases, G-325A forms must be completed for both you and your U.S. spouse. This is the only type of case where full biographic data is requested on someone who is already a U.S. citizen. Form G-325A is meant to gather personal background information. The questions are self-explanatory.

3. Petition Documents

All relative petitions must be filed with evidence that the petitioner is a U.S. citizen or green card holder. If the petitioner is a U.S. citizen by birth, a birth certificate is the best proof. Only birth certificates issued by a U.S. state government are acceptable. Hospital birth certificates cannot be used. When the petitioner is a U.S. citizen born outside U.S. territory, a certificate of citizenship, naturalization certificate, U.S. consular record of birth abroad, or unexpired U.S. passport will serve as proof. If the petitioner is a U.S. citizen but does not have any of these documents, read Chapter 27 to learn how to obtain them.

If the petitioner is not an American citizen but is a permanent resident, this can be proven by showing the petitioner's green card, unexpired reentry permit or passport with an unexpired stamp indicating admission to the U.S. as a permanent resident. (The unexpired stamp in a foreign passport is used only in the few cases where the petitioner has just been approved for a green card but is still waiting to receive the card itself.) The card typically arrives by mail several months later. When green card holders act as petitioners, INS will not check its own records to establish the existence of the green card. Your petitioning relative is responsible for supplying this evidence.

The above described documents proving the eligibility of the petitioner to act as a sponsor must be part of every Step One submission. The next documents we will describe are not the same in all cases but differ according to which of your relatives will act as your petitioner. Don't forget, however, that in addition to the documents for specific relatives, there must be proof in every case that the petitioner is a U.S. citizen or green card holder.

a. Your Sponsoring Relative Is Your Spouse

When the basis of the petition is marriage to a U.S. citizen or green card holder, you must establish that you are lawfully married to the petitioner. Do this by showing a valid civil marriage certificate. Church certificates are generally unacceptable. (There are a few exceptions, depending on the laws of your particular country. Canadians, for example, may use church marriage certificates if the marriage took place in Quebec Province, but not elsewhere. If a civil certificate is available, however, you should always use it.) You may have married in a country where marriages are not customarily recorded. Tribal areas of Africa are an example. In such situations, call the nearest consulate or embassy of your home country for help with getting acceptable proof of marriage.

If either you or your spouse has been married before, you must prove that all prior marriages were legally terminated. This requires presenting either a divorce decree or death certificate ending every prior marriage. Where a death certificate is needed, it must be an official document issued by a government. Certificates from funeral homes are not acceptable. Divorce papers must be official court or government documents. If the death or divorce occurred in one of those few countries where such records are not kept, call the nearest consulate or embassy of your home country for help with getting acceptable proof of death or divorce.

It is also necessary to present one photograph each of you and your spouse. The photos should meet certain exact specifications. Instructions for having these photos made are in Appendix III on Form M-378.

b. Your Sponsoring Relative Is Your Child

Usually, you may verify a parent/child relationship simply by presenting the child's birth certificate. Many countries, including Canada and England, issue both short and long form birth certificates. Where both are available, the long form is needed because it contains the names of the parents while the short form does not.

c.   Your Sponsoring Relative Is Your Stepchild

U.S. stepchildren may petition for the green cards of stepparents where the marriage creating the family relationship took place before the child's 18th birthday. However, for a stepchild to act as petitioner for a stepparent, the marriage that created the stepchild/stepparent relationship must still exist. If the marriage ends, according to immigration laws, the stepchild/stepparent relationship also ends. Accordingly, you must prove you are currently married to the stepchild's natural parent. Do this by showing your present marriage certificate as well as divorce decrees or death certificates indicating that all prior marriages of you and your current spouse were legally terminated. Where a death certificate is needed, it must be an official document issued by the government. Certificates from funeral homes are not acceptable. It is also necessary to present your stepchild's long form birth certificate to show the names of his or her natural parents.

d.   Your Sponsoring Relative Is Your Illegitimate Child

U.S. illegitimate children may petition for the green cards of their parents. If you are the mother, legitimacy is irrelevant for immigration purposes. The documents needed are exactly the same as those for a petition by a legitimate child. If you are the father, however, something more is required. You must present documents proving two additional elements—paternity and either legitimation or the existence of a genuine parent/child relationship.

i.   Documents Proving Paternity

Paternity can be documented by presenting your child's birth certificate with your name on it, although it is common to find that the father's name is not registered on the birth certificate of an illegitimate child. If you want to prove paternity to INS, you should go to the government office that issued your illegitimate child's original birth certificate and try to get it amended to include your name.

When your name does not appear on your child's birth certificate and amending is not possible, INS may require a blood test to establish paternity. If INS deems this necessary, it will tell you so after you have begun Step One, and give you instructions on how to proceed. INS may allow you to substitute for the blood test a sworn affidavit from the child's mother identifying you as the father. INS has the discretion to demand whatever proof it wants.

ii.   Documents Proving Legitimation

Legitimation is a legal procedure where a father of an illegitimate child acknowledges before a court or government body that he is the parent of the child. Laws establishing legitimation procedures exist in many countries. Illegitimate children may petition for the green cards of their fathers if they were legitimated before their 18th birthday.

In matters of legitimation, INS recognizes the procedures and documents called for by the law of the country where the child was born. Some nations have abolished the legal difference between legitimate and illegitimate children. In Jamaica, for example, a father need only sign an acknowledgment of paternity and the legal distinction of illegitimacy is erased. In any country where legitimation laws are in effect, provided the law was enacted before the child's 18th birthday, INS will ask for the same legitimation documents required by the law in the child's home country.

iii. Documents Proving a Genuine Parent/Child Relationship

If the child was not legally legitimated prior to his or her 18th birthday, there is an alternative. Fathers may then choose to prove that before the child's 21st (not 18th) birthday and while the child was unmarried, a real father/child relationship existed, involving personal contact and financial support. Evidence of this might include documents showing that you and the child resided in the same house. Also valuable are affidavits from people who know your family, stating that you have acted as a father, or copies of the child's school records with your name registered as a parent. Proof that you contributed money to the child's support is considered particularly strong evidence of a paternal relationship. U.S. income tax returns declaring the child as a dependent, canceled checks or other common financial records can be used to show this.

e.   You Are a Battered or Abused Spouse or Child

If you will be petitioning for yourself as a battered or abused spouse or child, you must supply credible evidence of having been battered or subjected to extreme cruelty. Police reports or arrest records reflecting the abuse would be the strongest evidence. Medical reports if you sought treatment for the abuse would also be helpful. If no complaints were filed with the police and you never sought medical attention, you will probably then have to obtain affidavits from other knowledgeable people. Statements from any shelters you stayed in or friends or neighbors who were aware of the situation would all be useful. Your own statements without any substantiating evidence will probably not be sufficient.

f. Your Sponsoring Relative Is Your Adopted Child

Adopted children petitioning for adoptive parents must submit all the same documents as do natural children who petition for their parents. There are, however, some additional requirements that have been established in cases where adopted children are the petitioners or beneficiaries. See Chapter 6, *Getting a Green Card Through an Adoption*, for a full explanation.

g. Your Sponsoring Relative Is Your Parent

Usually, you can show that you are the child of a U.S. citizen or green card holder simply by submitting your long form birth certificate with your parents' names listed. When the petitioner is your father, you must also submit your parents' marriage certificate. It is, therefore, easier to choose your mother over your father as a petitioner if you have a choice, because you will then need one less document.

h. Your Sponsoring Relative Is Your Parent and You Are an Illegitimate Child

U.S. parents may petition for their illegitimate children. If your parents were not married at your birth, you will be treated as illegitimate. In that case, you must present the same documents required of a parent whose petitioner is an illegitimate child. See Section d, above, to see what documents you need.

i. Your Sponsoring Relative Is Your Parent and You Are a Stepchild

If you are a stepchild, your U.S. stepparent may petition for you when the marriage creating the family relationship took place before your 18th birthday. If the marriage has ended, the stepchild/stepparent relationship ceases to exist in the eyes of INS. If you are a stepchild, you must present all the same documents required of a parent utilizing a stepchild as petitioner. Therefore, you must prove that your parent and stepparent are currently married. Do this by showing their marriage certificate as well as divorce decrees or death certificates indicating that all prior marriages of each were legally terminated. You also must present your long form birth certificate to show the names of your natural parents.

j. Your Sponsoring Relative Is Your Parent and You Are an Adopted Child

Parents petitioning for adopted children must submit all the same documents as do parents who petition for their natural children. There are, however, some additional requirements that have been established in cases where adopted children are the petitioners or beneficiaries. See Chapter 6, *Getting a Green Card Through an Adoption*, for a full explanation.

k. Your Sponsoring Relative Is Your Brother or Sister (Includes Half-Brothers and Half-Sisters)

To petition for your green card, your brother or sister must be at least 21 years of age. You must also demonstrate that you and the petitioner have at least one common parent. Therefore, you should submit both of your birth certificates, which will have your parents' names listed. If the only common parent is your father, it is necessary to document that your father was married to your mother at the time of your birth, and to your sibling's mother at the time of his or her birth. This means verifying the existence of both marriages. You may accomplish this by producing all the same documents called for in the case of a U.S. spouse petition. See Section a, above.

l. Name Tracing Documents

A married woman participating in an immigration matter, whether as petitioner, beneficiary or accompanying relative applicant, should submit all marriage and divorce certificates so INS can follow the chain of all her name changes up to the present. It is routinely necessary to show that a woman whose name appears on a birth certificate is the same woman listed on an immigration form or marriage certificate, even though the names are different. This is equally true of a man who has ever used more than one name.

4. Petition Interviews

Personal interviews on the petition are held only in cases where the existence of the family relationship between you and the petitioner is in doubt. Most of the time, the facts are clear from the documents presented, so petition interviews are rarely held, except in cases where the petition is based on marriage.

MARRIAGE INTERVIEWS

Petition interviews are sometimes held in marriage cases, especially if the marriage recently took place or if there are great age or cultural differences between the spouses. Interviews are always held when the application is being filed in the U.S. but are usually not held on the petition if the application is being filed at a U.S. consulate. For this reason, there may be occasions when it would be best to use consular filing for the application even if you are eligible to apply for your green card inside the U.S.

Marriage interview procedures vary with the individual personality of the examining officer, and you should be prepared to adjust to that officer's interviewing style. You and your U.S. spouse may be brought into the interviewing room separately. Each of you may then be questioned about your life together, how you met, what sorts of things you do as a couple, daily routines, common friends, favorite places to go, what the inside of your home looks like, and so on. These questions are intended to reveal whether or not you and your U.S. spouse actually live together. You may refuse to answer some or all questions, but doing so could result in the petition being denied.

Many couples wonder if they will be asked about the more intimate details of their relationship. INS policy states that the interviewers should not ask embarrassingly personal questions, but sometimes INS officials believe it is necessary to ask intimate questions in an attempt to uncover a fraudulent case. Most INS offices now videotape all interviews, so the likelihood of abuse has been diminished. The best advice we can offer is be prepared for anything and cooperate as much as possible. If you become uncomfortable during the interview, try to think of it as simply the price of getting a green card.

5. Petition Appeals

When the family relationship between you and your U.S. relative has been poorly documented, or if your marriage to a U.S. citizen looks suspicious, the petition will probably be denied. Your sponsoring relative will then receive written notice of INS's unfavorable decision, a written statement of the reasons for the negative outcome and an explanation of how to make a formal appeal.

The best way to handle an appeal is to try avoiding it altogether. Filing an appeal means making an argument to INS that its judgment was wrong. If you think you can eliminate the reason why your petition failed by improving your paperwork, it makes sense to forget about the appeals process and simply file a new petition, being careful to see that it is better prepared than the first.

If the petition was denied because the petitioner left out necessary documents that have since been located, the new documents should be sent, together with a written request that the case be reopened, to the same INS office that issued the denial. This is technically called a *Motion to Reopen*. There is a $110 fee for filing this motion. Appeals often take a long time. A Motion to Reopen can be concluded faster than an appeal.

If your sponsoring relative does choose to appeal, he or she must do so within 30 days of the date on the Notice of Denial. The appeal should be filed at the same INS office with which your relative has been dealing. There is a $110 filing fee. INS will then forward the papers for consideration to the Board of Immigration Appeals in Washington, D.C. The appeals decision, which can take many months, will be sent to your relative by mail. The vast majority of appeals fail.

When an appeal to INS has been denied, the next step is an appeal through the U.S. judicial system. Your relative may not file an action in court without first going through the appeals process available from INS. If the case has reached this stage and you are living illegally in the U.S., we strongly recommend seeking representation from a qualified immigration attorney, as you are now in danger of being deported.

E. Step Two: The Application (Consular Filing)

Anyone with an approved petition and a current priority date can apply for a green card at a U.S. consulate in his or her home country or last country of residence. You must be physically present in order to apply there. Even if you have been or are now working and living illegally in the U.S., you can still get a green card from a U.S. consulate if you otherwise qualify. (First read Chapter 25, *Inadmissibility*, to make sure you are not subject to the three- and ten-year overstay bars or other new laws punishing individuals who were out of status and then departed and/or reentered the U.S.)

Citizens of countries not having formal diplomatic relations with the U.S. are faced with the problem of where to apply for immigrant visas. At present, the U.S. maintains no diplomatic relations with, and therefore makes no visa services available in, Afghanistan, Iran, Iraq, Lebanon, Libya and Somalia.

Persons from these countries who are physically present in the U.S. may have Step Two papers processed at the U.S. consulate in Ciudad Juárez, Mexico. For those who are not physically in the U.S., immigrant visas should be processed as follows:

Country of Citizenship or Residence	Apply for Visas in
Afghanistan	Karachi
Iran	Abu Dhabi, Ankara, Vienna or Naples
Iraq	Amman or Casablanca
Lebanon	Abu Dhabi, Damascus or Nicosia
Libya	Tunis or Valletta
Somalia	Nairobi, Dar es Salaam or Djibouti

1. Benefits and Drawbacks of Consular Filing

Anyone with an approved petition and a current priority date can apply for a green card at the appropriate consulate. That is not the case with U.S. applications since you must be physically inside the U.S. to apply there. If you are a preference relative and in the U.S. illegally, you must pay a substantial penalty, currently $1,000, to file in the U.S. In most cases, unless you had a visa petition or labor certification on file by January 14, 1998, you are not eligible to apply for your green card in the U.S. (See Chapter 25.) If you are not eligible to apply by paying the penalty, you can elect to file at a consulate, but under these circumstances, you may run into other difficulties due to the three- and ten-year waiting periods imposed on individuals who have violated their status. Be sure to understand these issues, discussed in Chapter 25, before proceeding.

A further plus to consular filing is that consulate offices may work more quickly to issue green cards than do some INS offices. Your waiting time for the paperwork to be finished may be months shorter at a U.S. consulate abroad than at U.S. INS offices. Remember, however, that the difference in waiting time between INS and consulate

offices applies only to processing paperwork. Quotas move at the same rate of speed no matter where your application is filed.

One drawback to consular filing is the travel expense and inconvenience you will experience in returning to your home country if you are already in the U.S. Another problem is that should your consular application fail, you will have fewer ways to appeal than a U.S. filing would offer.

2. Application General Procedures: Consular Filing

The law states that only a U.S. consulate or embassy where your sponsoring relative resides is required to accept your green card application. This is true for all individuals except persons from countries without U.S. embassies, discussed before Section 1, above. (A complete list of U.S. consulates that process visa applications, with addresses and phone numbers, is in Appendix I.) You can ask a consulate located elsewhere (that is *not* where your sponsoring relative resides) to accept your application, but it has the option to say no, and in fact most consulates turn down such requests unless you show extremely compelling reasons. If you do wish to ask for this privilege, you should contact the consulate of your choice before filing the Step One petition. That is because Form I-130 in Step One asks where you will file your application and you must be prepared with an answer to this question.

You may not file an application for a green card at a consulate until after your petition has been approved. At that time, the INS office where your petition was originally submitted will forward your file to the National Visa Center (NVC) in Portsmouth, New Hampshire. NVC will then forward your file to the U.S. consulate you have named on Form I-130 in Step One. At the same time, a Notice of Approval from Step One will be sent directly to your relative. NVC will send instructions and application forms to you within a month or two after petition approval. You will return all paperwork, however, directly to the consulate. If, after waiting a reasonable time, you have not heard from NVC, you should phone them and look into the matter.

NVC will send you Packet 3, containing forms and instructions. Complete and send Forms OF-230 I and OF-169 to the consulate as soon as possible. This will allow the consulate to begin a required security check into your background. Failure to return these forms promptly can significantly delay your green card.

The application for your green card is made in person, by appointment. Once your quota number is current and the consulate is ready for your final processing, it will then send another group of papers known as Packet 4. Packet 4 includes an interview appointment letter, instructions for obtaining your medical examination and still more forms to be completed. Other than Form OF-230 I, which should be mailed in as soon as you receive it, and Form OF-169, which you will send in when you are ready for your interview, do not mail your paperwork to the consulate. Instead, bring the rest of your forms and all documents with you at the time of your appointment. The fee for filing an application is $200 per person.

3.   Application Forms: Consular Filing

When you file at a U.S. Consulate abroad, the consulate officials will provide you with certain optional forms designated by an "OF" preceeding a number. Instructions for completing optional forms and what to do with them once they are filled out will come with the forms. We do not include copies of these forms in Appendix III. Copies of all non "OF" forms can be found in Appendix III.

Form I-864

There are two distinct requirements associated with this form: one is that all family-based immigrants (and employment-based immigrants where the applicant's relatives submitted the visa petition or own at least 5% of the petitioning company) must have it filed by the petitioner in order to apply for permanent residence; the second is that it satisfies or helps satisfy the requirement that an immigrant show she is not likely to become a public charge.

The requirements for this affidavit of support are very different from those of its predecessor, Form I-134. For example, the new form is legally enforceable by the government for most public benefits utilized by the sponsored immigrant. It is also enforceable by the immigrant-family member against the sponsor for support. It also requires that the sponsor show that she has at least 125% of income for a similar family size, according to the federal poverty level.

All family-based immigrants who file adjustment of status or immigrant visa applications on or after December 19, 1997 are required to have the new I-864 filed by the person who is sponsoring their immigrant petition. However, another person (a joint sponsor) may add her income to the sponsor's if the joint sponsor:

• is willing to be jointly liable
• is a legal permanent resident or citizen
• is over 18 years old, and
• resides in the U.S.,

as long as she meets the 125% income requirement for her own household.

The joint sponsor files a separate affidavit of support. Other household members may join their income to help reach the 125% level, but only if they have been living with the sponsor for six months and they agree to be jointly

liable by filing form I-864. Personal assets of the sponsor or the immigrant, such as property, bank account deposits, and personal property such as automobiles, may also be used to supplement the sponsor's income, if the primary sponsor's actual income does not add up to 125% of the federal income poverty guidelines. To use assets, however, the assets will have to add up to five times the difference between the 125% poverty income guidelines level for an equivalent family and the sponsors' actual income.

The sponsors must also notify the INS within 30 days of the sponsor's change of address, using form I-865. Failure to do so is punishable by fines of $250-$2,000, or $2,000-$5,000 if the sponsor fails to notify with knowledge that the sponsored alien received a public benefit. The requirements and paperwork burden of the new affidavit are complicated and substantial; most of the requirements are spelled out on the forms. If you have questions about meeting the eligibility requirements or the scope of your legal responsibility—which may be ten or more years for sponsors, or until the immigrant permanently leaves the country, dies or naturalizes—you may want to consult an immigration attorney.

4.   Application Documents: Consular Filing

The most important document in your application is the Notice of Action showing approval of your petition. It is sent directly from NVC in the U.S. to the consulate you named on Form I-130 in Step One. This is the only document you will not have to submit yourself. Do not mail in your other documents. Instead, bring them to your interview.

You must resubmit to the consulate virtually all of the documents first filed in Step One. Only the proof of U.S. citizenship or the green card of your petitioning relative need not be resubmitted. If not included in Step One, you must have your long form birth certificate and birth certificates of any unmarried minor children who are not immigrating with you. Copies of these documents will not be forwarded by INS to the consulate for you. Remember that Step One original documents should have been returned to you once they were checked by INS, so you should have them available to bring to the consulate.

It is also necessary to have in your possession a valid passport from your home country. The expiration date on the passport must leave enough time for the passport to remain valid at least six months beyond the date of your final application interview.

Unlike applications made in the U.S., you personally must collect police clearance certificates from each country you have lived in for one year or more since your 16th birthday. Additionally, you must have a police certificate from your home country and your country of residence at the time of visa application, if you lived there for at least six months since the age of 16 and from every country in which you lived for at least one year. You do not need to obtain police certificates from the U.S. Additionally, a consular officer can request that you obtain a police certificate from any country—regardless of how long you lived there—if he or she believes you have a criminal record there. Like all other documents, you should be prepared to present the necessary police clearance certificates at your interview. If you go to your interview without the required certificates, you will be refused a green card and told to return after you get them.

OBTAINING POLICE CERTIFICATES

You should contact the local police department in your home country for instructions on how to get police certificates. To obtain police certificates from nations other than your home country, it is best to contact the nearest consulate representing that country for instructions. Some nations refuse to supply police certificates, or their certificates are not considered reliable, and so you will not be required to obtain them from those locations. At this writing, police certificates are not required from the following countries:

Afghanistan	Haiti	Saudi Arabia
Albania	Honduras	Sierra Leone
Angola	India	Somalia
Bangladesh	Indonesia	Sri Lanka
Brunei	Iran	Sudan
Bulgaria	Iraq	Syria
Cambodia	Jordan	Tanzania
Chad	Laos	Thailand
Colombia	Liberia	Turkey
Costa Rica	Libya	United Arab
Cuba	Malaysia	Emirates
Dominican Republic	Mexico	United Kingdom
El Salvador	Mongolia	United States
Equatorial Guinea	Mozambique	Venezuela
Ghana	Nepal	Vietnam
Guatemala	Pakistan	

For applicants who once lived in Japan but do not reside there at the time their green card applications are filed, the Department of State recognizes that police certificates are available from Japan only as far back as five years from the date of the green card application.

Other countries, including the Netherlands, North Korea, South Africa and South Korea, will send certificates directly to U.S. consulates but not to you personally. Before they send the certificates out, however, you must request that it be done. Usually this requires filing some type of request form together with a set of your fingerprints.

You and each accompanying relative must bring to the interview three photographs taken in compliance with the instruction sheet found in Appendix III. Additional photo instructions are provided in Packet 4. Often Packet 4 will also contain a list of local photographers who take this type of picture.

A few consulates require you to submit fingerprints, though most do not. Consulates wanting fingerprints will send you blank fingerprint cards with instructions.

5. Application Interviews: Consular Filing

Consulates hold interviews on all green card applications. A written notice of your interview appointment is included when you receive Packet 4. Immediately before the interview you and your accompanying relatives will be required to have medical examinations. Some consulates conduct the medical exams up to several days before the interview. Others, including London, schedule the medical exam and the interview on the same day. You will be told where to go and what to do in your appointment letter.

The medical examinations are conducted by private doctors and you are required to pay the doctor a fee. The fees vary from as little as $50 to more than $150 per exam, depending on the country. The amount of the medical exam fee will be stated in your appointment letter. The exam itself involves the taking of a medical history, blood test and chest X ray. You will also need to present documentation that you have received vaccination against vaccine-preventable diseases, unless the INS' regulations state that vaccination is inappropriate for you or you are granted a waiver based on your moral or religious beliefs. The physician who performs your medical exam should have and fill out the form for this. Pregnant women who do not want to be X-rayed may so advise the consulate and their appointments will be postponed until after the pregnancy. The requirement to have an X ray taken cannot be waived.

The main purpose of the medical exam is to verify that you are not medically excludable. The primary medical exclusions are tuberculosis and HIV (AIDS). Medical exclusions usually can be overcome with treatment. See Chapter 25, *Inadmissibility,* for more details. If you need a medical waiver, you will be given complete instructions by the consulate at the time of your interview.

After the medical exam, you and your accompanying relatives will report to the consulate for the interview. At that time, you must pay two more fees: $170 per person when your papers are submitted, and an additional $30 per person at the end of the interview when your applications are approved. Some consulates accept payment only by certified check, money order or traveler's check. Others accept cash. You will be told the proper method of payment in Packet 4.

Bring with you to the interview the completed forms, photographs, your passports and all of the required documents discussed here. The interview process involves verification of your application's accuracy and an inspection of your documents. If all is in order, you will be asked to return later in the day when you will be issued an immigrant visa. You are not yet a permanent resident.

The immigrant visa allows you to enter the U.S. for six months. You acquire the full status of green card holder at the moment of making entry into the U.S. with your immigrant visa. At that time, your passport is stamped and you are immediately authorized to work. If you are bringing any accompanying relatives, they must enter at either the same time or after you do in order to become permanent residents. Permanent green cards for you and your accompanying relatives are then ordered. They will come to you by mail several months later.

MARRIAGE INTERVIEW

Some consulates, including the consulate in Ciudad Juárez, Mexico, often request the American spouse to appear at the interview in cases based on a marriage. Even though INS may have already conducted a marriage interview during Step One, these consulates feel they have the right to conduct another. The legal basis for this position is not clear and such consulates are in the minority, but you should be prepared for the possibility of a marriage interview at a consulate. When your U.S. spouse's appearance is specifically requested, but he or she is unable to attend, you should communicate this fact to the consulate in advance. If the consulate continues to insist that your American spouse must travel abroad to attend your interview, it may be wise to hire an immigration lawyer to deal with the consulate. Interviews of this kind must be handled with special care. Otherwise, the consulate could send the entire file back to INS in the U.S. with a request for a formal investigation of your marriage. This could delay the issuance of a green card by months or even years, and during that time, you might be forced to remain outside the U.S.

6. Applications Appeals: Consular Filing

When a consulate denies a green card application, there is no formal appeal available, although you are free to reapply as often as you like. When your green card is refused, you will be told the reasons why. The most common reason for denial is failure to supply all the required documents. Sometimes presenting more evidence on an unclear fact can bring about a better result. If the denial was caused by a lack of evidence, this will be explained in a written notice sent to you by mail.

Another common reason for denial of a green card is that the consular officer believes you are inadmissible. If you are found to be inadmissible, you will be given an opportunity to apply for a Waiver of Inadmissibility, if one is available. See Chapter 25 for directions on how to apply.

When all these possibilities are exhausted, if the consulate still refuses you a green card, your opportunities for further appeals are severely limited. Historically, the courts have held that there is no right to judicial review and there is no formal appeal procedure through any U.S. government agency. The State Department in Washington, D.C., does offer an informal review procedure through the mail. This agency will look at the factual elements of your case and decide whether or not the consulate made a correct decision. Even if the State Department rules in your favor, its decision is only advisory and the consulate is free to ignore the State Department, letting its own decision stand. At present, there does appear to be a trend developing where courts in the U.S. are more frequently accepting jurisdiction over consular decisions, so a court appeal may be a possibility to consider. The jurisdiction of U.S. courts to review consular decisions is, however, still an unsettled legal issue.

Your denial may be based on a question of law rather than fact. The State Department offers the same informal review for legal questions with the difference that any decision it makes is binding on the consulate. Appeals of this kind are very technical and should be handled by a competent immigration attorney. Even with representation by an attorney, most such appeals fail.

Overall, the best way to handle an application that has been turned down is simply to wait a while, reapply on a different basis, and hope for better luck next time. The fact that you have been turned down once does not preclude you from trying again.

F. Step Two: The Application (U.S. Filing)

If you are physically present in the U.S., you may apply for a green card without leaving the country, on the following conditions:

- you are simultaneously filing Step One paperwork for or have already received an approved petition, and
- a green card is currently available to you under the quota because your waiting period is up or because you are an immediate relative and therefore not subject to a quota.

Unless you can meet these terms, you may not file an application for a green card in the U.S.

1. Benefits and Drawbacks of U.S. Filing

The obvious benefit to applying for a green card in the U.S. is that if you are already in the country, you avoid the expense and inconvenience of overseas travel. Moreover, it is a rule of immigration law that once you file Step Two, you must remain wherever you have filed. If you depart the U.S. after filing and do not request permission to reenter the U.S., you will abandon your application and have to start all over again. When you file in the U.S., should problems arise in your case, you will at least be able to wait for a decision in America, a circumstance most green card applicants prefer. In most cases, you will also be able to renew your application in deportation proceedings, in case your application is denied by INS.

Another important benefit of U.S. filing is that you may receive permission to work while you wait for the results of your case. To obtain this benefit, you must make a separate application, in person, at the local INS office where your Step Two application has been filed. Most INS offices allow you to apply for work authorization a week or more after filing your green card application. If you do not need to work right away, you should probably still get your work authorization as soon as possible since many states require you to have it to apply for other benefits such as social security cards and driver licenses.

If your application for a green card is turned down, you have greater rights of appeal inside the U.S. than you do at a U.S. consulate. INS offices have different procedures from consular offices because they are controlled by different branches of the U.S. government.

There is a paperwork benefit to applying in the U.S. You will not have to obtain required police certificates and submit them yourself to INS. Instead, you will submit a fingerprint chart and INS will order all necessary police certificates directly.

There are some disadvantages to applying in the U.S. It may take longer to get results. Processing times at INS offices average six to twelve months, but at some offices may even be longer, even on cases not affected by quotas or those where quotas are current. While your case is pending at an INS office, you may not leave the U.S. without getting special permission. If you do leave without INS's permission, even for a genuine emergency, this will be regarded as a withdrawal of your application and you will have to start Step Two all over again when you return.

PROCEDURES FOR ADVANCED WORK AUTHORIZATION

If you want to work before your application for a green card is approved, you must file a separate application for employment authorization. This can be done by completing Form I-765 and filing it with the same local INS office where you filed the Step Two papers. Together with Form I-765, you must submit a copy of your filing receipts and photos, and pay a filing fee of $100. It is very important to keep the fee receipt INS gives you so you can prove that the I-765 was filed. Normally you will want to file the application for employment authorization at the same time as your application papers.

Some INS offices may approve your employment authorization and issue a work authorization card on the spot. Others, however, will give you an appointment to return, and you will receive your work authorization card at that time. INS is soon expected to change the procedure for issuing work authorization cards, requiring that they be mailed from a central facility, much like green cards. The purpose of this change is to make the cards more difficult to counterfeit. The new procedures are a response to public complaints that certain INS personnel have been "selling" work ID cards.

Legally, INS does not have to make a decision on your employment authorization application for up to 90 days. If for some reason you are not given a decision within 90 days, you will, at your request, be granted an interim employment authorization which will last 240 days. To receive an interim card, you must return in person to the INS local office where you filed your I-765 and show your fee receipt. Then your interim work authorization card will be issued.

If 240 days pass and you still have not received a final decision on the I-765, you must stop working. Interim work authorization cards cannot be renewed. However, if you reach this point, you have the option to file a new I-765 application and, if you do not get a decision on the new application within 90 days, you will then be entitled to another interim work authorization card.

2. Application General Procedures: U.S. Filing

When filing in the U.S., it is best to submit the application and the petition at the same time. The vast majority of U.S. filings are done this way. Concurrent filing of Steps One and Two require coordination with your sponsoring relative who, you will remember, has full legal responsibility for Step One. If the petition is filed separately, you must wait to submit the application until after the petition has been approved.

The application, consisting of both forms and documents, is submitted either by mail or in person to the local INS office nearest the place you are living. (Appendix I contains a list of all INS offices with telephone numbers and addresses.)

For U.S. filings, the basic form used in Step Two, the application, is INS Form I-485, Application for Permanent Residence. Form I-485 is filed to adjust your status in the U.S. "Adjusting status" is a technical term used only in U.S. filings. It simply means that you are presently in the U.S. as a nonimmigrant and are in the process of "adjusting" your current status (nonimmigrant) to the status of a permanent resident.

The filing fee for each application is $220 for applicants age 14 and over, and $160 for applicants under age 14. A separate application must be filed for you and each accompanying relative. In addition, if you are in the U.S. illegally, or entered without being inspected, you may also be subject to a $1,000 penalty fee. Checks and money orders are accepted. It is not advisable to send cash through the mail but cash is satisfactory if you file in person. Cash is accepted only in the exact amount. INS offices will not make change. We recommend filing your papers in person if at all possible, as you will be given a written receipt from INS and your papers are likely to be processed right away. Even if you submit the petition and application together, each has a separate filing fee which must be paid. If you choose to mail in your application, you should do so by certified mail, return receipt requested. In either case, keep a complete copy of everything you send in.

Once your application has been filed, you should not leave the U.S. before your application has been approved without first requesting advance permission to come back. Any unauthorized absence will be viewed as a termination of your application for a green card. If you want to leave the U.S. for any legitimate business or personal reason, you should go in person to the INS office processing your application, bringing three passport-type photographs and ask for an advance parole, by filing Form I-131 and paying a $95 filing fee. You may also file form I-131 with your application if you already know you want to travel. If approved, you will be allowed to leave the U.S. and return again with no break in the processing of your application.

Generally, after filing your application, you will not hear anything from INS for several months. Then you should receive a notice of your interview appointment. The interview notice will also contain instructions for getting the required medical exam, and will tell you if any further documentation is needed.

Applications cannot be approved without an interview. Your petitioning relative is usually required to attend the interview with you. If your application was filed together with a petition, both the petition and application will usually be acted upon together and a single interview will cover both Steps One and Two.

If everything is in order, your application will be approved at the conclusion of the interview. Your passport will be stamped to show that you have been admitted to the U.S. as a permanent resident, and your permanent green card will be ordered. The green card will come to you in the mail about two months after the interview.

3. Application Forms: U.S. Filing

Copies of all forms can be found in Appendix III.

Form I-485

While most of the form is self-explanatory, a few items typically raise concerns. If a particular question does not apply to you, answer it with "None" or "N/A." The questions on this form requiring explanation are as follows:

Part 1. This asks for general information about when and where you were born, your present address and immigration status. It also asks for an "A" number. Normally, you will not have an "A" number unless you previously applied for a green card or have been in deportation proceedings.

Part 2. Mark Box A if you are the principal applicant. Box B is marked if your spouse or parent is the principal applicant. Box C is for people who entered the U.S. on K-1 or K-2 fiancé(e) or children of fiancé(e) visas. Do not mark any other box.

Part 3. The questions in Sections A through C are self-explanatory. The nonimmigrant visa number is the number that appears on the very top of the visa stamp. It is not the same as your visa classification. The questions in Section C are meant to identify people who are inadmissible. With the exception of certain memberships in the Communist party or similar organizations, you will not be deemed inadmissible simply because you joined an organization. However, if your answer to any of the other questions is "yes," you may be inadmissible. Chapter 25 is intended to help you remove such obstacles. Don't lie on your answers because you will probably be found out, especially if you have engaged in criminal activity. Many grounds of inadmissibility can be legally overcome, but once a lie is detected, you will lose the legal right to correct the problem. In addition, a false answer is grounds for denying your application in itself and may result in your being permanently barred from getting a green card.

Form I-485A

This form is required only if you are subject to the $1,000 penalty fee for residing here illegally and are eligible to file because you had a visa petition or labor certification on file before January 14, 1998. The form is self-explanatory, and is intended only to determine if you are subject to the penalty.

Form G-325A

G-325A Biographic Data Forms must be filled out for you and each accompanying relative. You need not file a G-325A for any child under the age of 14 or any adult over the age of 79. If the basis of your immigration case is marriage to a U.S. citizen, a G-325A must be completed for both you and your U.S. spouse. This is the only type of case where full biographic data is requested on someone who is already a U.S. citizen. Please note that if yours is a marriage case and you are filing Step Two in the U.S., but at a separate time from Step One, you must include the G-325A forms in Step One as well as Step Two. Form G-325A is meant to gather personal background information. The questions are self-explanatory.

Form I-864

There are two distinct requirements associated with this form: one is that all family-based immigrants (and employment-based immigrants where the applicant's relatives submitted the visa petition or own at least 5% of the petitioning company) must have it filed by the petitioner in order to apply for permanent residence; the second is that it satisfies or helps satisfy the requirement that an immigrant show she is not likely to become a public charge.

The requirements for this affidavit of support are very different from those of its predecessor, Form I-134. For example, the new form is legally enforceable by the government for most public benefits utilized by the sponsored immigrant. It is also enforceable by the immigrant-family member against the sponsor for support. It also requires that the sponsor show that she has at least 125% of income for a similar family size, according to the federal poverty level.

All family-based immigrants who file adjustment of status or immigrant visa applications on or after December 19, 1997 are required to have the new I-864 filed by the person who is sponsoring their immigrant petition. However, an-other person (a joint sponsor) may add her income to the sponsor's if the joint sponsor:

- is willing to be jointly liable
- is a legal permanent resident or citizen
- is over 18 years old, and
- resides in the U.S.,

as long as she meets the 125% income requirement for her own household.

The joint sponsor files a separate affidavit of support. Other household members may join their income to help reach the 125% level, but only if they have been living with the sponsor for six months and they agree to be jointly liable by filing form I-864. Personal assets of the sponsor or the immigrant, such as property, bank account deposits, and personal property such as automobiles, may also be used to supplement the sponsor's income, if the primary sponsor's actual income does not add up to 125% of the federal income poverty guidelines. To use assets, however, the assets will have to add up to five times the difference between the 125% poverty income guidelines level for an equivalent family and the sponsors' actual income.

The sponsors must also notify the INS within 30 days of the sponsor's change of address, using form I-865. Failure to do so is punishable by fines of $250-$2,000, or $2,000-$5,000 if the sponsor fails to notify with knowledge that the sponsored alien received a public benefit. The requirements and paperwork burden of the new affidavit are complicated and substantial; most of the requirements are spelled out on the forms. If you have questions about meeting the eligibility or the scope of your legal responsibility—which may be ten or more years for sponsors, or until the immigrant permanently leaves the country, dies or naturalizes—you may want to consult an immigration attorney.

Form I-765

Block above Question 1. Mark the first box, "Permission to accept employment."

Questions 1–8. These questions are self-explanatory.

Question 9. This asks for your Social Security number, including all numbers you have ever used. If you have never used a Social Security number, answer "None." If you have a nonworking Social Security number, write down the number followed by the words "nonworking, for tax purposes only." If you have ever used a false number, give that number, followed by the words: "Not my valid number." However, be aware that if you have used false documents for employment or other purposes, you may be inadmissible. (See Chapter 25.)

Question 10. You will not usually have an Alien Registration Number unless you previously applied for a green card, were in deportation proceedings or have had certain types of immigration applications denied. All Alien Registration Numbers begin with the letter "A." If you have no "A" number but you entered the U.S. with a valid visa, or without a visa under the Visa Waiver Program, you should have an I-94 card. In this case, answer Question 10 by putting down the admission number from the I-94 card.

If you are from Mexico, you may have entered the U.S. with a border crossing card, in which case you should put down the number on the entry document you received at the border, if any. Otherwise simply put down the number of the border crossing card itself, followed with "BCC." If you are Canadian and you entered the U.S. as a visitor, you will not usually have any of the documents described here, in which case you should put down "None."

Questions 11–15. These questions are self-explanatory.

Question 16. Answer this question "(C)(9)."

4. Application Documents: U.S. Filing

An application filed in the U.S. for the spouse of a U.S. citizen is usually submitted at the same time as the petition. In the relatively few cases when the petition is filed earlier, for a family member of a permanent resident, you must submit the Notice of Action showing petition approval with the application.

In all cases, you must demonstrate the ability to support yourself and any accompanying relatives once you get a green card by having your family member-sponsor submit an I-864, Affidavit of Support, on your behalf (see Section 3 above).

You and each of your accompanying relatives are required to submit two photographs. These photos should meet the specifications on the photo instruction sheet found in Appendix III.

You must also submit a Medical Examination Report for each applicant, including proof of vaccinations. This is done on INS Form I-693, which must be taken to an INS authorized physician or medical clinic. The INS local office will provide you with this form and a list of approved physicians in your area. After completion of the medical exam, and upon obtaining the test results, the doctor will give you the results in a sealed envelope. *Do not open the envelope.*

Each applicant must submit an I-94 card if one was issued. Failure to do so may result in a conclusion that you entered the U.S illegally and are inadmissible or subject to the $1,000 penalty described earlier. This is the small white or green card you received on entering the U.S. If you are a Canadian citizen and entered the U.S. as a tourist, you will not need to present the I-94 card. If you are from Mexico and entered the U.S. with a border crossing card instead of a visa, you must submit your original border crossing card, which will be canceled.

The only other paperwork required is a fingerprint card. Beginning March 30, 1998, INS regulations changed so that all fingerprinting now takes place at an INS-run fingerprinting center. You will be notified where and when to appear after submitting your application forms. You will be required to pay INS $25 (often when you file your application papers) to cover the fingerprinting costs.

5. Application Interviews: U.S. Filing

Whenever a green card application is based on a marital relationship, a personal interview is required. Interviews can be waived on other types of cases, at the discretion of the local INS office. As already noted, in a U.S. filing the petition and application are usually submitted together. Likewise, in a U.S. filing, the petition and application interviews are normally held at the same time. Even though they are technically regarded as two separate interviews, the practical result is that the Step One and Step Two interviews are one and the same.

The part of the interview pertaining to the application is usually a simple matter. The INS officer will go over your application to make sure that everything is correct. He or she will also ask questions to ascertain whether or not you are inadmissible. (See Chapter 25, *Inadmissibility.*) Fingerprints will then be taken and you will be asked to sign your application under oath. Accompanying relatives, all of whom must attend the interview with you, will go through the same procedure.

The interview, including both the petition and application portions, normally takes about 30 minutes. If all goes well your case should be approved on the spot, although recently the INS has been postponing the final decision on many cases because they have not yet received the FBI clearance. You may be expected to wait for the results if this is the case. Most INS offices will place a temporary stamp in your passport showing that you have become a permanent U.S. resident. With this stamp you acquire all the rights of a green card holder, including the right to work and freedom to travel in and out of the U.S. as long as your passport remains valid. The stamp is not your green card. You will receive your permanent green card by mail several months later.

If your fingerprints have not been cleared yet, your application will be approved only provisionally pending clearance. In those cases, no stamp will be placed in your passport at the interview. Instead, you will receive a written notice of approval within a month or two. That notice serves as your proof of U.S. residency until you receive your green card, which takes yet another two to three months. If you need to travel outside the U.S. before your green card arrives, however, you must go back to the INS office with your passport and the written notice of approval. A temporary stamp will then be placed in your passport, enabling you to return after your trip. Never leave the U.S. without either your green card or a temporary stamp in your passport.

6.   Application Appeals: U.S. Filing

If your application is denied, you will receive a written decision by mail explaining the reasons for the denial. There is no way of making a formal appeal to INS when your application to adjust status is turned down. If the problem is too little evidence, you may be able to overcome this obstacle by adding more documents and resubmitting the entire application to the same INS office you have been dealing with, together with a written request that the case be reopened. The written request does not have to be in any special form. This is technically called a Motion to Reopen. There is a $110 fee to file this motion. Alternatively, you may wait until INS begins deportation proceedings, in which case you may refile your application with the immigration judge.

If your application is denied because you are ruled inadmissible, you will be given the opportunity to apply for what is known as a Waiver of Inadmissibility, provided a waiver is available for your situation. See Chapter 25 for directions on how to apply.

Although there is no appeal to INS for the denial of a green card application as there is for the denial of a petition, you have the right to file an appeal in a U.S. district court. This requires employing an attorney at considerable expense. Such appeals are usually unsuccessful.

G.   Removing Conditional Residence in Marriage Cases

As we've already mentioned, green cards based on marriage to a U.S. citizen are issued only conditionally when the marriage is less than two years old at the time the green card application is approved. This is true of cards issued both to spouses and stepchildren of U.S. citizens.

After holding your conditional green card for two years, if you are still married, you and your U.S. spouse should file a joint petition to remove the condition. The condition should be removed not only from your green card but from those of any children who came with you. If you are divorced, or your spouse refuses to join in the petition, you must file for a waiver of the requirement.

1.   Filing a Joint Petition With Your Spouse

You may file the joint petition even if you are separated or a divorce is in progress, as long as you remain legally married and your U.S.-citizen spouse agrees to sign. You may also file the petition on your own if your U.S.-citizen spouse died no more than two years ago. You cannot file the petition once the two-year conditional period has expired. If you fail to meet this deadline, you should be prepared to show an extremely good reason why you could not file on time.

The petition to remove the conditional status of your green card is made by filling out Form I-751. A copy of this form is in Appendix III. The form is self-explanatory. Where stepchildren are involved, one form may be used for the entire family. It must be signed by both you and your U.S. spouse, unless, of course, you are filing on your own because your spouse has died.

Together with your form, you must also supply documents to show that your marriage was not entered into only for immigration purposes. You must do this by proving that you and your spouse have been living together. This is best accomplished by submitting papers showing that you and your spouse held joint bank accounts, had automobiles and insurance policies in both names and rented or purchased your home in both names. Sworn affidavits from people who know both you and your U.S. spouse, stating that they observed you living together during a particular period are also helpful. If you wish, you may bring witnesses to the interview who can testify to observing that you and your U.S. spouse live together.

Forms and documents should be mailed together with a $125 filing fee to the INS regional service center nearest your home. A list of the INS regional service centers with their addresses is in Appendix II. Within a few weeks after mailing your petition to the regional service center, you will receive a written receipt by return mail. Provided you filed this petition before your two-year conditional residency period expired, you may continue to travel in and out of the U.S. at will for a period of one year by showing your conditional green card, and this receipt. Within that six-month period you should either get a decision approving your petition, or be asked to come to the INS local office for an interview. The interview is at INS's discretion and does not necessarily indicate a problem. If your interview is successful, you will usually be approved at that time. After approval, your permanent green card will be sent to you by mail.

2.   Getting a Waiver of the Requirement to File a Joint Petition

If you are unable to file a joint petition with your U.S. spouse to remove the condition on your residency, either because of divorce or because he or she refuses to co-operate, you must then file for a waiver of the requirement to file the joint petition. This waiver will be granted in only three circumstances:

- you entered into a good faith marriage but the marriage is legally terminated
- your deportation will result in an extreme hardship, one greater than that normally experienced by someone who is deported, and the marriage was originally entered into in good faith, or
- you were a battered or subjected to extreme cruelty by your U.S. spouse and the marriage was originally entered into in good faith.

Like the joint petition, an application for a waiver must be filed before your two-year conditional residency expires.

Waiver applications, like joint petitions, are filed on Form I-751. Where stepchildren are involved, one form may be used for the entire family.

Together with your form you must also supply documents showing that your marriage was not entered into only for immigration purposes. Proving that a marriage lasting less than two years was not a sham can be very difficult. First, you are not likely to have the cooperation of your ex-spouse, who in fact may even testify against you. In this situation, any other proof you can present to show that you married for love and not to get a green card can help.

This is best accomplished by submitting records that you and your spouse held joint bank accounts, had automobiles and insurance policies in both names, and rented or purchased your home in both names. Sworn affidavits from people who know both you and your U.S. spouse, stating that they observed you living together during a par-

ticular period of time are also helpful. If you had children together, this too is good evidence that your marriage was not a sham. If you are divorced, you should also provide a copy of your divorce decree.

Proving extreme hardship is more difficult. Situations that might qualify include serious illness, other close family members living in the U.S., financial loss such as vested pension benefits or lost career opportunities, and serious political or economic problems in your home country. You should submit a detailed, written statement in your own words explaining the circumstances of your marriage, what you gave up to come to the U.S, and what you will lose by returning to your home country. The statement should be supported by written documentation.

If the basis of your waiver is that you were abused by your U.S. spouse, you must supply evidence such as police reports, medical reports, photographs or affidavits from witnesses. If you are in divorce proceedings, court records including pleadings and depositions may be used. Your own personal written statement explaining the details of the abuse should also be submitted.

Your forms and documents must be mailed, together with an $80 filing fee, to the INS regional service center nearest your home. A list of the INS regional service centers with their addresses is in Appendix II. Within a few weeks, you will receive a written receipt by return mail. Provided you filed this application before your two-year conditional residency period expired, you may continue to travel in and out of the U.S. at will for a period of one year by presenting your conditional green card and this receipt.

Many applications for waivers will require a personal interview before being approved. If an interview is required in your case, you will be notified by mail. The interview will be held at the INS local office nearest your home. Due to the complexity of this type of application and the severe consequences of its failure, it is strongly recommended that you consider hiring an experienced immigration lawyer to assist you.

FORMS AND DOCUMENTS CHECKLIST

STEP ONE: PETITION

Forms

☐ Form I-130 (needed in all family cases except those involving widows and widowers or battered spouses).

☐ Form I-360 (needed for widows and widowers or battered spouses only).

☐ Form G-325A (needed only in marriage cases; one form is required for each spouse).

Documents

☐ Petitioner's proof of U.S. citizenship or green card status.

☐ Foreign national's long-form birth certificate.

☐ Relative's long-form birth certificate.

☐ If either the petitioner or beneficiary have ever been married, copies of all marriage certificates.

☐ If either the petitioner or beneficiary have ever been married, copies of all divorce and death certificates showing termination of all previous marriages.

☐ If you are applying as a battered spouse, evidence of physical abuse, such as police reports, medical reports or affidavits from people familiar with the situation.

☐ If you are a father petitioning for a child, certificate showing marriage to child's mother.

☐ If your are a father petitioning for an illegitimate child, documents proving both paternity and either legitimation or a genuine parent/child relationship.

☐ If the petition is for an adopted child:

    ☐ adoption decree, or child's new birth certificate showing you are the parent

    ☐ evidence you and the child have lived together for at least two years, and

    ☐ evidence you have had legal custody of the child for at least two years.

☐ If the petition is for a brother or sister, a copy of the parents' marriage certificate.

☐ In marriage cases, one photograph of each spouse.

STEP TWO: APPLICATION

Forms

☐ OF forms (available from U.S. consulate abroad for consular filing only).

☐ Form I-485 (U.S. filing only).

☐ Form I-485A (U.S. filing only).

☐ Form G-325A (U.S. filing only).

☐ Form I-864 (Consular and U.S. filing).

☐ Form I-765, if advanced permission to work is desired (U.S. filing only).

Documents

☐ Notice of approval of the petition.

☐ All documents originally filed with the petition, except the petitioner's proof of U.S. citizenship or green card.

☐ Passports for the applicant and each accompanying relative, valid for at least six months beyond the date of the final interview (Consular filing only).

☐ I-94 card for the applicant and each accompanying relative (U.S. filing only).

☐ Police certificates from every country in which the applicant and each accompanying relative has lived for at least six months since age 16 (Consular filing only).

☐ Military records for the applicant and each accompanying relative (Consular filing only).

☐ Three photographs of the applicant and each accompanying relative.

☐ Form I-864, Affidavit of Support, for the applicant and each accompanying relative.

☐ Fingerprints for the applicant and each accompanying relative between the ages of 14 and 75 (U.S. filing only).

☐ Medical exam report for the applicant and each accompanying relative.

Getting a Green Card Through an Adoption

Privileges

- The adopted child may live anywhere in the U.S. and stay as long as he or she wants.

- The adopted child may work at any job, for any company, anywhere in the U.S., or may choose not to work at all.

- The adopted child may travel in and out of the U.S. whenever he or she wishes.

- The adopted child may apply to become an American citizen after holding his or her green card for at least five years.

Limitations

- The adopted child's place of actual residence must be in the U.S. He or she cannot use a green card just for work or travel purposes.

- The adopted child will *never* be able to confer U.S. immigration benefits on his or her natural parents.

- The adopted child cannot remain outside the U.S. for more than one year at a time without special permission, or the child will risk losing his or her green card. We recommend that he or she return before being gone for six months.

- If the adopted child commits a crime or participates in politically subversive or other proscribed activities, his or her green card can be taken away and removal proceedings begun.

A. How to Qualify

Qualifying for a green card through an adoption has some limitations.

1. Quota Restrictions

The preference relative categories are limited by quotas. Orphan and immediate relative categories are not.

The forecasts for the preference relative category quotas are:

- **Family first preference.** Two and a half year waiting periods for natives of all countries except the Philippines and Mexico. Filipinos can expect quota waiting periods of at least eleven years. Mexicans can expect to wait from four to five years.
- **Family second preference.** Waiting periods of four years can be expected for natives of all countries for spouses and minor children; unmarried adult children (over 21) can expect to wait six years or more.
- **Family third preference.** Waiting periods of at least three years can be expected for natives of all countries except Mexico, where the wait is about nine years, and the Philippines, where the wait is at least 11 years.

Petition approval usually takes from one to six months. After petition approval and once a green card becomes available under the quota, it will take an additional one to six months for visa application approval.

2. Who Qualifies for a Green Card Through Adoption?

In Chapter 5, *Getting a Green Card Through Relatives*, we explained that children can get green cards through their American parents, and likewise, parents may get green cards through U.S. children. Both possibilities are available to adopted children and parents if certain requirements are met. The most significant requirement is that the adoption must have taken place before the child's 16th birthday. Often our adult clients ask us if having themselves legally adopted by a U.S. citizen is an effective way of becoming eligible for a green card. Clearly, if you are more than 16 years of age, the answer is "no."

Apart from immigration considerations, there are many adult U.S. citizens who genuinely want to adopt foreign children. This chapter contains the special instructions they need to get green cards for such children. Included are children already adopted, as well as those who will be adopted in the future.

When an adopted child has a parent who is a U.S. citizen or green card holder, the child may get a green card on the basis of the family relationship with that parent. It is not required that both adopting parents be U.S. citizens or green card holders. Only one parent need act as petitioner for the child's green card.

In Chapter 5, *Getting a Green Card Through Relatives*, we explained that there are several categories of relatives eligible for green cards. Foreign children who are adopted by U.S. citizen parents are considered immediate relatives of U.S. citizens. No quota applies to this category and so immediate relatives may immigrate to the U.S. in unlimited numbers. Adopted children of green card holders are in the preference relative category. This category is subject to quotas.

Immigration law divides adopted children into two classes—orphans and non-orphans.

Both classes are eligible for green cards, but the requirements for those categorized as orphans are dramatically different from those who are non-orphans. Sometimes a child may qualify as either an orphan or a non-orphan. In such cases the parent may choose the more favorable category.

a. Orphans

A child may obtain a green card as an orphan only if he or she is being adopted by a U.S. citizen. In the case of orphans, it is not sufficient that the adopting parents hold green cards. A child is an orphan if both natural parents are either deceased or have permanently and legally abandoned the child. In the case of an illegitimate birth, if the law of the native country confers equal benefits to illegitimate children as it does to legitimate, *both* parents must relinquish their rights. In addition, to be classified as an orphan, the child must be living outside the U.S. and, if not already adopted by the U.S. parents, must either be in the parent's custody or in the custody of an agent acting on their behalf in accordance with local law. Finally, the child must be under 16 years of age when the petition is filed.

Orphans may have green card petitions filed on their behalf either before or after the legal adoption by U.S. parents is completed. It is not essential that the adopting U.S. parents have met the orphan. In fact, it is not necessary that a particular child be identified before paperwork begins. There is a special procedure for those parents who know they will be adopting a child from a certain country but have not yet selected the particular child. To take advantage of this procedure, it is necessary that the adopting parents have satisfied any pre-adoption requirements existing in the laws of the U.S. state where they live, including a home study by the state government or an approved agency. If the adopting parent is single, he or she must be at least 25 years of age in order to act as petitioner in an orphan green card application. There are no age restrictions if the petitioner is married.

b. Non-Orphans

A non-orphan is any person already adopted, whose adoption was finalized prior to his or her 16th birthday. It does not matter how old the child is when the petition is filed. In addition to being legally adopted, the child must have been in the legal custody of and physically residing with the adopting parents for at least two years before applying for a green card.

For a non-orphan to get a green card, it is also necessary that the adopting parents meet certain requirements. They must be investigated by a U.S. state public or government-licensed private adoption agency. Such an investigation is usually part of standard adoption procedure in most U.S. states and so this qualification may have already been met prior to the adoption. If, however, the adoption takes place outside the U.S., or an investigation is not compulsory in the particular American state where the adoption occurs, this study must now be satisfactorily completed. The age of the petitioning parent is irrelevant in filing a non-orphan petition, even if the parent is unmarried.

3. Orphan or Non-Orphan: Benefits and Drawbacks

It is not unusual for a child to meet all the requirements of both the orphan and non-orphan categories. The U.S. parents can then choose which category will result in a simpler application. For example, the major benefits to an orphan filing are that the two-year cohabitation and legal custody requirements of the non-orphan category need not be met, and the petition can be filed before the adoption is completed. On the other hand, if a child is already adopted and physically residing in the U.S., the current age of the child is not important in a non-orphan filing. In an orphan filing, the child must be under the age of 16. Remember that only U.S citizens may petition for the green cards of orphans, whereas non-orphans may have either U.S. citizens or green card holders as their petitioners.

Parents who are planning to adopt a foreign-born child but have not yet located or identified a specific child, may nonetheless proceed with applying for a green card through advance processing in the orphan category. The parents are investigated in advance and the orphan petition pre-approved. Then, when the child is identified, the final processing goes much faster.

4. Inadmissibility

Like all green card applicants, children are subject to the grounds of inadmissibility. If they have been arrested for certain crimes or suffered certain physical or mental illness, they may be inadmissible from receiving a green card unless they are able to qualify for what is known as a Waiver of Inadmissibility. For example, medical grounds of inadmissibility for conditions such as tuberculosis are not uncommon in orphan cases from certain parts of the world. See Chapter 25 to find out exactly who is inadmissible and how these obstacles can be overcome.

B. Getting a Green Card for a Non-Orphan

If a child adopted by a U.S. citizen parent or green card holder falls into the category of non-orphan, the procedures for obtaining a green card are exactly the same as those described in Chapter 5 for blood-related children of parents who are U.S. citizens or green card holders. Read all of Chapter 5, following the instructions for immediate relatives. Note that for an adopted child, either a consular or U.S. filing is possible, depending on the physical location of the child when the application is submitted.

C. Getting a Green Card for an Orphan

Getting a green card for an orphan is a two-step process. Step One is called the petition. Step Two is called the application. The application is a formal request for a green card.

1. Step One: The Petition

The petition is filed by the U.S.-citizen adopting parent. All petitions are submitted to INS offices in the U.S. The object of the petition is to establish that the parent is a U.S. citizen and is qualified to adopt a foreign child, and that the child is legally available for adoption. If all goes well, the petition will eventually be approved, but be aware that an approved petition does not, by itself, give the child the right to come in to the U.S. It is only a prerequisite to Step Two, submitting the application. The petition must be approved before the child is eligible for Step Two.

Sometimes prospective U.S. parents looking for a foreign child to adopt wish to begin paperwork before they have actually identified the specific child. Although it is necessary, eventually, to go through all of the Step One procedures for a child already identified, prospective adopting parents may begin some of the paperwork before having identified the child by filing a preliminary application with an INS office. Once it is approved, and the parent has actually identified the child to be adopted, the rest of Step One may be completed. Since INS has by that time already finished its mandatory investigation of the prospective parents, the remainder of the petition procedures can usually be approved immediately.

2. Step Two: The Application

The application is technically filed by the child, although normally an adult, either the adopting parents, private attorneys or foreign adoption officials, will actually do all of the paperwork on the child's behalf. Step Two must be carried out in the child's home country at a U.S. consulate there. Step Two may not begin until the Step One petition is first approved.

3. Paperwork

There are two types of paperwork you must submit to get a green card for an adopted child. The first consists of official government forms completed by you. The second is personal documents such as birth, adoption and marriage certificates. We will tell you exactly what forms and documents you need.

It is vital that forms are properly filled out and all necessary documents are supplied. You may resent the intrusion into your privacy and the sizable effort it takes to prepare immigration applications, but you should realize the process is an impersonal matter to immigration officials. Your getting a green card for an adopted child is more important to you than it is to the U.S. government. This is not a pleasant thing to accept, but you are better off having a real understanding of your position. People from all over the world want green cards. There is no shortage of applicants. Take the time and trouble to prepare your papers properly. In the end it will pay off with a successful application.

The documents you supply to INS do not have to be originals. Photocopies of all documents are acceptable as long as you have the original in your possession and are willing to produce the originals at the request of INS. Documents submitted to U.S. consulates, on the other hand, must be either originals or official government certified copies. Government certified copies and notarized copies are not the same thing. Documents which have only been notarized are not acceptable. They must carry a government seal. In addition to any original or government certified copies of documents submitted to a consulate, you should submit plain photocopies of each document as well. After the consulate compares the copies with the originals, it will return the originals.

Documents will be accepted if they are in either English, or, with papers filed at U.S. consulates abroad, the language of the country where the documents are being filed. An exception exists for papers filed at the U.S. consulates in Japan, where all documents must be translated into English. If the documents are not in an acceptable language as just explained, they must be accompanied by a full, word for word, written English translation. Any capable person may act as translator. It is not necessary to hire a professional. At the end of each translation, the following statement must appear:

I hereby certify that I translated this document from (language) to English. This translation is accurate and complete. I further certify that I am fully competent to translate from (language) to English.

The translator should sign this statement but it does not have to be witnessed or notarized.

Later in this chapter we describe in detail the forms and documents needed to get a green card through an adoption. A summary checklist of forms and documents appears at the end of the chapter.

D. Who's Who in Getting an Adopted Child's Green Card

Getting a green card will be easier if you familiarize yourself with the technical names used for each participant in the process. For an orphan, during Step One, the petition, the adopting petitioning parent is known as the *petitioner* and the orphan is called the *beneficiary*. In Step Two, the application, the orphan is referred to as the *applicant* but the petitioning parent remains petitioner. For non-orphans, see Chapter 5.

E. Step One: The Petition

This section includes the information you need to submit the petition.

1. General Procedures When the Child Has Been Identified

A U.S.-citizen adopting parent submits the petition, consisting of forms and documents, to the INS local office nearest the place where he or she lives. Appendix II contains a complete list of all U.S. immigration offices with their current telephone numbers and addresses.

INS offices differ in their procedures. Some want the paperwork sent in by mail while others require that the file be delivered in person. A call or visit to the office will tell parents how and where to file Step One papers. If possible, it is preferable to file in person to insure that the arrival of

the petition is recorded. When the papers are brought in in person, they will be checked and any defects or omissions pointed out. If necessary, they will immediately be retrieved, the defects corrected or information supplied and the papers resubmitted. When filing is done by mail and defects or omissions are found, all petition papers, forms and documents, will be returned. The returned package will contain either a handwritten note or a form known as an I-797 (Request for Evidence), describing what corrections or additional pieces of information and documents are expected. The petitioner should make the corrections or supply the extra data and mail the whole package back to INS.

The filing fee for each petition is currently $155. Checks, money orders and cash are accepted. When filing by mail, it is not advisable to send cash. If the petitioner files in person, he or she will be given a written receipt for the filing fee. It should be kept in a safe place, together with a complete copy of everything submitted. Then the date the petition was filed can be confirmed and the number on the receipt will help locate the papers should they get lost or delayed in processing. When filing by mail, we recommend sending the papers by certified mail, return receipt requested and, again, keeping a complete copy as a record.

The length of time it takes to obtain an approved petition varies from one INS office to another, but in all cases will take a minimum of 90 days. That is because once the adopting parent files the petition, the INS office will contact the FBI to obtain police clearance for both parents, and this process takes 90 days.

Once the orphan petition is approved, a Notice of Action Form I-797, indicating approval, will be sent to the adopting parent. INS will also notify the consulate having jurisdiction over the child's residence, sending it a complete copy of the file.

2. General Procedures When the Child Has Not Been Identified

If a U.S. citizen knows he or she will be adopting a foreign child but has not yet identified the particular child, he or she may still begin processing the paperwork. A preliminary application consisting of forms and documents is sent to the INS regional service center having jurisdiction over the parent's residence. There is a $155 filing fee for this preliminary application, which has the effect of asking INS to begin the investigation of the parents at once. The purpose of the preliminary application is to save processing time once the child to be adopted has been identified. Approval will take a minimum of 90 days. Again, the 90-day minimum is due to the time it takes INS to receive FBI clearance on the prospective parents. Once INS completes its investigation, a Notice of Action form is sent to the petitioning adopting parent.

When the child finally has been identified, the parent may then proceed with Step One, the petition, as already outlined, but the $155 filing fee is not required. Since the INS investigation has already been completed, Step One can usually be approved in a day or two.

3. Petition Forms

Copies of both forms can be found in Appendix III. The fee for Form I-600 is $405 and for Form I-600A the fee is also $405.

Form I-600

(INS has been considering eliminating this form, and combining all orphan/adoption petitions on a new I-130 relative petition form. It is not known if or when the new form will come into use and be available.)

Questions 1–24. These questions are self-explanatory. Remember that all questions are being answered by the petitioner, and therefore "You" on this form refers to the adopting parents. Only one adopting parent needs to answer the questions, but if the petitioning adopting parent is married, both parents will have to sign the form.

Question 25. The petitioner must designate a U.S. consulate outside the U.S. to process the orphan's visa. Normally this should be at a U.S. embassy or consulate in the country where the child is living. A complete list of all U.S. consulates that process visa applications, together with their addresses and phone numbers, is in Appendix I.

Form I-600A (Used for Advanced Processing Only)

This form is completely self-explanatory.

4. Petition Documents When the Child Has Been Identified

Only U.S. citizens may petition for orphans. Therefore, it is necessary for the petitioner to provide proof of U.S. citizenship. If the petitioner is a U.S. citizen by birth, a birth certificate is the best proof. Only birth certificates issued by a U.S. state government are acceptable. Hospital birth certificates cannot be used. A certificate of citizenship, naturalization certificate, U.S. consular record of birth abroad or an unexpired U.S. passport will serve as proof of U.S. citizenship if the petitioner was born in another country. If the petitioner is a U.S. citizen but does not have any of these documents, read Chapter 27 to learn how to obtain one of them.

The petitioning U.S. parent must also submit evidence that the child is under age 16, that the natural parents are deceased or have legally abandoned the child, and that the adopting parents either have already obtained legal custody of the child in his or her home country, or the child is in the legal custody of an approved agency acting on their behalf. This will require presenting the orphan's birth certificate and either the natural parents' death certificates or the legal papers terminating their parental rights. If a birth certificate is unavailable, other evidence of the child's age must be submitted, such as a letter or affidavit from a doctor or anyone who knows when the child was born. Also required is a court or government order or acknowledgment concerning the legal custody of the child.

The marital status of the petitioner is relevant because if the petitioner is married, the fitness of both adopting parents will be evaluated. Therefore, if the petitioner is married, it is necessary to prove this by showing a valid civil marriage certificate. Church certificates are generally unacceptable. (There are a few exceptions, depending on the laws of the particular country where the marriage took place. Canadians, for example, may use church marriage certificates if the marriage took place in Quebec Province, but not elsewhere. If a civil certificate is available, however, it should always be used.)

The petitioners may have married in a country where marriages are not customarily recorded. Tribal areas of Africa are an example. In such a situation they should call the nearest consulate or embassy of their native country for help with getting acceptable proof of marriage.

If either parental spouse has been married before, it must be proven that all prior marriages were legally terminated. This requires presenting either a divorce decree or death certificate ending every prior marriage. Where a death certificate is needed, it must be an official document issued by the government. Certificates from funeral homes are not acceptable. Divorce papers must be official court or government documents. If the death or divorce occurred in one of those few countries where such records are not kept, call the nearest consulate or embassy of that country for help with getting acceptable proof of death or divorce.

It is necessary to present a home study done either by the U.S. state government agency handling adoptions in the particular state where the petitioner lives or any private agency licensed in that state to do home studies. Some U.S. states have additional pre-adoption requirements, such as that the parents must have met the child prior to adoption. If that is the case in the petitioner's state, he or she must present a letter or certificate from the agency regulating adoptions in the home state, verifying that the petitioner has satisfied all pre-adoption requirements under state law. Home studies must include statements that there is no history of abuse or violence within the household. All Step One orphan petition documents must be resubmitted to the consulate later during Step Two.

5. Petition Documents When the Child Has Not Been Identified

If the orphan has not yet been identified, but the prospective parents wish to apply for advanced processing to speed up immigration once the child is chosen, the documentation needed to accompany the advanced processing Form I-600A is identical to that required for a standard orphan petition as already described above, with only the following exceptions. It will not be necessary at the time of completing the Step One procedure to include the child's birth certificate or other proof of the child's age, nor will it be necessary to provide evidence that the natural parents are dead or have legally abandoned the child. Also, the petition may be filed without the home study in order to get things moving right away. The home study may be submitted up to one year later, but INS cannot approve the petition before receiving the home study.

Once the advanced processing is approved and the child has been identified, the petitioner must then submit the remainder of Step One forms and documents together with the Notice of Action from the advanced processing. It is also not necessary to submit the $155 fee with the Form I-600 since it was already paid at the time of advanced processing. This action must be taken within 18 months after approval of the advanced processing application.

6. Petition Interviews

Personal interviews on orphan petitions are held only in cases where there is a question about the likelihood that a legal adoption will actually take place. Most of the time, the facts are clear from the documents presented, so petition interviews are rarely necessary.

7. Petition Appeals

When the status of the child as an orphan has been poorly documented, the petition will probably be denied. The petitioning parent will then receive a Notice of Action advising of INS's unfavorable decision, a written statement of the reasons for the negative outcome and an explanation of how to make a formal appeal.

The best way to handle an appeal is to try avoiding it altogether. Filing an appeal means making an argument to INS that its reasoning was wrong. This is not something INS likes to hear. If the reason why the petition failed can be eliminated by improving the paperwork, it makes sense to disregard the appeals process and simply file a new petition, being careful to see that it is better prepared than the first.

If the petition was denied because the petitioner left out necessary documents that have since been located, the new documents should be sent, together with a written request that the case be reopened to the same INS office that issued the denial. This is technically called a *Motion to Reopen*, for which there is a $110 filing fee. Appeals often take a long time. A Motion to Reopen can be concluded faster than an appeal.

If the petitioning adopting parent does choose to appeal, it must be done within 30 days of the date on the Notice of Denial. The appeal should be filed at the same INS office that issued the decision. INS will then forward the papers for consideration by the Board of Immigration Appeals in Washington, D.C. As orphan cases frequently involve questions of foreign law, it may take many months before the petitioner will get back a decision by mail. In immigration matters generally, fewer than 5% of all appeals are successful.

When an appeal to INS has been denied, the next step is an appeal through the U.S. judicial system. The adopting parent may not file an action in court without first going through the appeals process available from INS. If the case has reached this stage we strongly recommend seeking representation from a qualified immigration attorney. The case obviously has problems and there may be ways to expedite getting the child to the U.S.

F. Step Two: The Application for Orphans

This section includes the information you need to submit the application.

1. Application General Procedures

The law states that only a U.S. consulate or embassy in the child's home country is required to accept his or her green card application. This is true for all except persons from countries without U.S. embassies, discussed below. A complete list of U.S. consulates that process visa applications, with addresses and phone numbers may be found in Appendix I. You can ask a consulate located elsewhere to accept your adopted child's application, but it has the option to say "no," and they do, in fact, turn down most such requests. If you do wish to ask for this privilege, you should approach the consulate of your choice before filing the Step One petition. That is because Form I-600 in Step One asks where you will file your application and you must be prepared with an answer to this question.

You may not file an application for a green card at a consulate until after your petition has been approved. At that time, the INS office where your petition was originally submitted will forward your file to National Visa Center in Portsmouth, New Hampshire (NVC). NVC will then forward your file to the U.S. consulate you have named on Form I-600 in Step One. NVC will send instructions and application forms to you within a month or two after petition approval. You will return all paperwork, however, directly to the consulate. If, after waiting a reasonable time, you have not heard from NVC, you should call and look into the matter.

NVC will send you Packet 3, containing forms and instructions. Complete and send Forms OF-230 I and OF-169 to the consulate as soon as possible. Failure to return these forms promptly can significantly delay your adopted child's green card.

The application for your adopted child's green card is made in person by appointment. Once the consulate is ready for his or her final processing, it will then send another group of papers known as Packet 4. Packet 4 includes an interview appointment letter, instructions for obtaining a medical examination, and still more forms to be completed. Other than Form OF-230 I, which should be mailed in as soon as you receive it, and Form OF-169, which you will send in when you are ready for your interview, do not mail your paperwork to the consulate. Instead, whoever will be taking the child through the consulate should bring the rest of the forms and all documents with them at the time of the appointment. Young children, under age 14, will normally be exempted from having a personal interview. The fee for filing an application is $200 per person.

CHILDREN FROM COUNTRIES WITHOUT U.S. EMBASSIES

Citizens of countries not having formal diplomatic relations with the U.S. are faced with the problem of where to apply for immigrant visas. At present, the U.S. maintains no diplomatic relations with, and therefore makes no visa services available in, Afghanistan, Bosnia, Iran, Iraq, Lebanon, Libya and Somalia. If you are adopting a child who is living in one of those countries, how his immigrant visa will be processed depends on whether he resides in his home country or a third country.

Persons from these countries who are still residing in their home countries will apply at a designated foreign consulate. Persons who are outside of their home country in a third country which conducts visa processing, will do visa processing in that country as if they were residents of the third country.

2. Application Forms

When you file at a U.S. consulate abroad, the consulate officials will provide you with certain optional forms, designated by an "OF" preceeding a number. Instructions for completing optional forms and what to do with them once they are filled out will come with the forms. We do not include copies of these forms in Appendix III. Copies of all non "OF" forms are in Appendix III.

Form I-864

It will be necessary for you to convince INS that once the child gets a green card, she will be supported. To show this, you must submit a completed Form 1-864, affidavit of support.

There are two distinct requirements associated with this form: one is that all family-based immigrants (and employment-based immigrants where the applicant's relatives submitted the visa petition or own at least 5% of the petitioning company) must have it filed by the petitioner in order to apply for permanent residence; the second is that it satisfies or helps satisfy the requirement that an immigrant show she is not likely to become a public charge.

The requirements for this affidavit of support are very different from those of its predecessor, Form I-134. For example, the new form is legally enforceable by the government for most public benefits utilized by the sponsored immigrant. It is also enforceable by the immigrant-family member against the sponsor for support. It also requires that the sponsor show that she has at least 125% of income for a similar family size, according to the federal poverty level.

All family-based immigrants who file adjustment of status or immigrant visa applications on or after December 19, 1997 are required to have the new I-864 filed by the person who is sponsoring their immigrant petition. However, another person (a joint sponsor) may add her income to the sponsor's if the joint sponsor:

- is willing to be jointly liable
- is a legal permanent resident or citizen
- is over 18 years old, and
- resides in the U.S.,

as long as she meets the 125% income requirement for her own household.

The joint sponsor files a separate affidavit of support. Other household members may join their income to help reach the 125% level, but only if they have been living with the sponsor for six months and they agree to be jointly liable by filing form I-864. Personal assets of the sponsor or the immigrant, such as property, bank account deposits, and personal property such as automobiles, may also be used to supplement the sponsor's income, if the primary sponsor's actual income does not add up to 125% of the federal income poverty guidelines. To use assets, however, the assets will have to add up to five times the difference between the 125% poverty income guidelines level for an equivalent family and the sponsors' actual income.

The sponsors must also notify the INS within 30 days of the sponsor's change of address, using form I-865. Failure to do so is punishable by fines of $250-$2,000, or $2,000-$5,000 if the sponsor fails to notify with knowledge that the sponsored alien received a public benefit. The requirements and paperwork burden of the new affidavit are complicated and substantial; most of the requirements are spelled out on the forms. If you have questions about meeting the eligibility or the scope of your legal responsibility—which may be ten or more years for sponsors, or until the immigrant permanently leaves the country, dies or naturalizes—you may want to consult an immigration attorney.

3. Application Documents

Except for the proof that the petitioning adopting parents are U.S. citizens, all of the documents first filed in Step One should be resubmitted to the consulate. Copies of these documents will not be forwarded by INS to the consulate. Remember that Step One original documents should have been returned to the petitioning parent once they were checked by INS, so they should be available to the child to bring to the consulate.

It is also necessary that the child have in his possession a valid passport from his or her home country. The expiration date on the passport must be such that it will remain valid for at least six months beyond the date of the final application interview.

Since a child must be under age 16 to qualify as an orphan, it is not necessary to collect police certificates, as is required in all other types of green card applications.

The child must bring to the interview three photographs taken in compliance with the instruction sheet found in Appendix III. Additional photo instructions are provided in Packet 3. Often Packet 3 will also contain a list of local photographers who take this type of picture.

The only other paperwork required is a fingerprint card. Beginning March 30, 1998, INS regulations changed so that all fingerprinting now takes place at an INS-run fingerprinting center. You will be notified where and when to appear after submitting your application forms. You will be required to pay INS $25 (often when you file your application papers) to cover the fingerprinting costs.

4. Application Interviews

Consulates hold interviews on all green card applications, although a formal interview is frequently waived for children under the age of 14. A written notice of the interview appointment is included with Packet 4. Immediately prior to the interview, the orphan, regardless of age, will be required to have a medical examination. Some consulates conduct the medical exams the day before the interview. Others, including London, schedule the medical exam and the interview on the same day. The child will be told where to go and what to do in the appointment letter.

The medical examinations are conducted by private doctors and a fee must be paid. The fees vary from as little as $20 to more than $100 per exam, depending on the country. The amount of the fee will be stated in the appointment letter. The exam itself involves the taking of a medical history, blood test and chest X ray and vaccinations or verification of vaccinations, if applicable. The requirement to have an X ray taken cannot be waived, though for a very young child, some of the blood tests may not be required.

The primary purpose of the medical exam is to verify that your adopted child is not medically inadmissible. The primary medical grounds of inadmissibility are tuberculosis and HIV (AIDS). Medical grounds of inadmissibility usually can be overcome with treatment. See Chapter 25, *Inadmissibility*, for more details. If a medical waiver is needed, you will be given complete instructions by the consulate at the time of your child's interview or final processing.

After the medical exam, the child will report to the consulate for the interview. At that time, two more fees must be paid: $170 when the papers are submitted, and an additional $30 at the end of the interview when the application is approved. Some consulates accept payment only by certified check, money order or traveler's check. Others accept cash. The proper method of payment will be explained in Packet 4.

The completed forms, photographs, the child's passport and all of the required documents discussed here should be brought to the interview. The interview process involves verification of the application's accuracy and an inspection of the documents. If all is in order, the child will be asked to return later in the day, when he or she will be issued an immigrant visa. The child is not yet a permanent resident. The immigrant visa allows the orphan to travel to and request entry to the U.S. as a resident. He or she will acquire the full status of green card holder at the moment of being inspected and admitted into the U.S. with the immigrant visa. At that time, the orphan's passport is stamped with an indication of permanent residence. A green card will then be ordered for the child. It will come in the mail several months later.

It is important to note that the orphan's immigration status will not be affected if the legal adoption never takes place. The child may keep the green card anyway. It is certainly possible that circumstances might arise which would stop an adoption from being finalized. However, it is illegal for a U.S. citizen to file an orphan petition simply to help the child but with no genuine intent to complete the adoption. Although the child will be allowed to keep the green card, the U.S. petitioner will risk criminal prosecution for filing a fraudulent petition.

5. Application Appeals

When a consulate denies a green card application, there is no formal appeal available, although the child is free to reapply. When a green card is refused, the consulate will explain why. The most common ground for denial is failure to present all required documents. Sometimes presenting more evidence on an unclear fact can bring a better result. If a lack of evidence is the problem, the child or his custodian will be so advised in writing.

Another common reason for denial of a green card is that the consular officer believes the child is inadmissible. If ruled inadmissible, the child will be given an opportunity to apply for a waiver of inadmissibility. See Chapter 25 for directions on how to apply.

FORMS AND DOCUMENTS CHECKLIST

ORPHANS

STEP ONE: PETITION

Forms

☐ Form I-600.

☐ Form I-600A (advanced processing only).

Documents

☐ Fingerprints (2 sets) for petitioner and spouse, if any.

☐ Child's long-form birth certificate or other proof of age.

☐ Proof that the child may be adopted:

    ☐ natural parents' death certificate

    ☐ proof that the child has been abandoned, or

    ☐ legal papers terminating parental rights.

☐ Proof that the child is in the legal custody of either the adopting parents or an approved agency acting on their behalf.

☐ Petitioning parent's birth certificate, or other proof of U.S. citizenship.

☐ If petitioner is married, marriage certificate.

☐ If either or both petitioners have ever been married, copies of all divorce and death certificates showing termination of each previous marriage.

☐ Documents showing completion of adoption agency home investigation.

☐ Documents showing the adopting parents have satisfied any pre-adoption requirements of the state where they live.

STEP TWO: APPLICATION

Forms

☐ OF forms (available at U.S. consulate only).

☐ Form I-864.

Documents

☐ Notice showing approval of orphan petition.

☐ All documents originally filed with the orphan petition, except the petitioning parent's proof of U.S. citizenship and fingerprint cards.

☐ Passport from the orphan's home country, valid for at least six months beyond the date of the final interview.

☐ Three photographs of the orphan.

NON-ORPHANS

See checklists for relatives in Chapter 5.

Getting a Green Card Through Your Fiancé(e): K-1 Visas

Privileges

- You and your minor unmarried children may come to the U.S. if you will be marrying a U.S. citizen.

- You may apply for permission to work immediately upon arriving in the U.S.

- If your U.S.-citizen fiancé(e) is unable to travel to your home country to marry you, the K-1 visa may be the only solution.

- Your minor, unmarried children under age 21 may come with you as accompanying relatives.

Limitations

- You must marry your U.S.-citizen petitioner within 90 days after you enter the U.S.

- You must still apply for a green card after you get married.

- It can take longer to get a K-1 visa than a green card through marriage.

- A K-1 visa lasts only 90 days. It cannot be extended beyond that period under any circumstances.

- If you fail to get married within the 90-day period, you may be forced to leave the U.S.

A. How to Qualify

There are no quota restrictions for K-1 visas. Petition approval normally takes from one to four months. After the petition has been approved, it will take an additional one to four months for the issuance of the visa.

1. Who Qualifies for a K-1 Visa?

If you intend to marry a U.S. citizen, your fiancé(e) may bring you to America for that purpose with a K-1 visa. Although it is a nonimmigrant visa, we have included it with the chapters on green cards because after you get married, it can easily be converted into a green card. In fact, a K-1 visa has no real value other than as a preliminary step to getting permanent residence. That is why most couples do not apply for K-1 visas. Instead, they simply marry and apply directly for green cards. A K-1 visa is most useful when there is some reason why the marriage cannot take place in either the U.S. or the foreign national's home country.

To get a K-1 visa, both members of the couple must be legally able to marry. That is to say, both must be single and of legal age. If either party is already married, a K-1 visa cannot be granted until a divorce takes place.

Not only must the couple actually intend to marry, but, with limited exception, they must have met and seen each other in person within the past two years. Under the right circumstances this requirement may be waived for people who practice religions in which marriages are customarily arranged by families and premarital meetings are prohibited. Generally, to be released from the requirement of having met your fiancé(e), you must show that both parties will be following all the customs of marriage and weddings that are part of the religion.

It is also possible to get a waiver of the personal meeting requirement if such a meeting would cause an extreme hardship to either member of the couple. Only the most extreme situations involving medical problems are likely to be regarded as a good enough reason for the waiver to be granted. Economic problems alone are not usually acceptable.

In summary, there are four conditions to getting a K-1 visa:

- the petitioner must be a U.S. citizen
- both members of the couple must be legally able to marry
- the foreign national must have a genuine intention to marry the petitioner after arriving in the U.S., and
- the couple must have met and seen each other within the past two years, unless they practice a religion that forbids couples to meet before marriage, or if their meeting would cause an exceptional hardship.

Accompanying Children

When you get a K-1 visa, any of your unmarried children under the age of 21 can be issued K-2 visas. This will enable them to accompany you to the U.S. They, too, will be able to apply for green cards once you get married. They will qualify as stepchildren of a U.S. citizen. (See Chapter 5, *Getting a Green Card Through Relatives.*)

2. Applying for a Green Card After Marriage

Once you marry, if the 90-day validity period of the K-1 visa has not yet expired, you may file for a green card without leaving the U.S. Simply follow the directions in Chapter 5, *Getting a Green Card Through Relatives*, starting with Step Two. Because you have already gotten a K-1 visa, you are excused from Step One. You will, however, be subject to the two-year conditional residency placed on green cards obtained through marriage to an American. This, too, is covered in Chapter 5. Read it carefully before applying for a fiancé(e) visa.

B. Getting a Green Card for a Fiancé(e)

Getting a K-1 visa is a two-step process. Step One is called the petition. Step Two is called the application. The application is your formal request for a K-1 visa.

1. Step One: The Petition

The petition is filed by your U.S.-citizen fiancé(e). All K-1 visa petitions are submitted to INS regional service centers in the U.S. The object of the petition is to prove three things:

- you have a bona fide intention of marrying a U.S. citizen within 90 days after you arrive in the U.S.
- both parties are legally able to marry, and
- you have physically met each other within the past two years—this requirement can be waived if you both practice a religion that forbids a couple to meet before marriage, or if it would be an extreme hardship for you to meet first.

An approved petition does not by itself give you any immigration benefits. It is only a prerequisite to Step Two, submitting your application. The petition must be approved before you are eligible for Step Two.

2. Step Two: The Application

Step Two must be carried out at a U.S. consulate in your country of residence. You must wait to file the application until the Step One petition is first approved. You may not, under any circumstances, complete Step Two while you are in the U.S. as you can with other nonimmigrant visas, since the whole objective of the K-1 visa is to allow your entry into the U.S. for the purpose of marrying. If you are already in the U.S., getting a K-1 visa is unnecessary. Instead, you should get married and then apply for a green card as outlined in Chapter 5.

3. Paperwork

There are two types of paperwork you must submit to get a fiancé(e) visa. The first consists of official government forms completed by you or your fiancé(e). The second is personal documents such as birth and marriage certificates. We will tell you exactly what forms and documents you need.

It is vital that the forms are properly filled out and all necessary documents are supplied. You or your fiancé(e) may resent the intrusion into your privacy and sizable effort it takes to prepare immigration applications but you should realize the process is an impersonal matter to immigration officials. Your getting a visa is more important to you than it is to the U.S. government. This is not a pleasant thing to accept, but you are better off having a real understanding of your position. People from all over the world want visas. There is no shortage of applicants. Take the time and trouble to prepare your papers properly. In the end it will pay off with a successful application.

The documents you or your fiancé(e) supply to INS do not have to be originals. Photocopies of all documents are acceptable as long as you have the original in your possession and are willing to produce the originals at the request of INS. Documents submitted to U.S. consulates, on the other hand, must be either originals or official government certified copies. Government certified copies and notarized copies are not the same thing. Documents which have only been notarized are not acceptable. They must carry a government seal. In addition to any original or government certified copies of documents submitted to a consulate, you should submit plain photocopies of each document as well. After the consulate compares the copies with the originals, it will return the originals.

Documents will be accepted if they are in either English, or, with papers filed at U.S. consulates abroad, the language of the country where the documents are being filed. An exception exists for papers filed at the U.S. consulates in Japan, where all documents must be translated into English. If the documents are not in an acceptable language as just explained, they must be accompanied by a full, word for word, written English translation. Any capable person may act as translator. It is not necessary to hire a professional. At the end of each translation, the following statement must appear:

I hereby certify that I translated this document from (language) to English. This translation is accurate and complete. I further certify that I am fully competent to translate from (language) to English.

The translator should sign this statement, but it does not have to be witnessed or notarized.

Later in this chapter we describe in detail the forms and documents needed to get your fiancé(e) visa. A summary checklist of forms and documents appears at the end of the chapter.

C. Who's Who in Getting Your K-1 Visa

Getting a K-1 visa will be easier if you familiarize yourself with the technical names used for each participant in the process. During Step One, the petition, you are known as the *beneficiary* and your U.S. fiancé(e) is known as the *petitioner*. In Step Two, the application, you are referred to as *applicant* but your U.S.-citizen fiancé(e) is still known as the *petitioner*. Your accompanying children will be known as *applicants* as well.

D. Step One: The Petition

This section includes the information you need to submit the petition.

1. General Procedures

The fiancé(e) petition, consisting of forms and documents, is filed by mail at the INS regional service center nearest the home of your U.S.-citizen fiancé(e). INS regional service centers are not the same as local offices. There are many INS local offices but only four INS regional service centers spread across the country. Appendix II contains complete lists of all U.S. immigration offices and regional service centers, with their addresses and telephone numbers.

As mentioned earlier, petitions filed at regional service centers are submitted by mail. The filing fee for the petition is $95. Checks or money orders are accepted. It is not advisable to send cash. We recommend sending your papers by certified mail, return receipt requested, and making a copy of everything sent in to keep with your records. Within a week or two after mailing your petition, your fiancé(e) should get back written confirmation that the papers are being processed, together with a receipt for the fees. This notice will also give your immigration file number and tell approximately when you should expect to have a decision.

If INS wants further information before acting on your case, petition papers, forms and documents may be returned to your fiancé(e), together with another form known as an I-797. The I-797 tells your fiancé(e) what additional pieces of information or documents are expected. Your fiancé(e) should supply the extra data and mail the whole package back to the INS regional service center.

Once your petition is approved, a Notice of Action Form I-797 will be sent to your fiancé(e), indicating the approval, and the file will be forwarded to the appropriate U.S. consulate abroad. The consulate will then contact you directly with instructions on how to complete the visa processing.

2. Petition Forms

Copies of all forms can be found in Appendix III.

Form I-129F

Section A, Questions 1–13. These questions, which pertain to your U.S.-citizen petitioner, are all self-explanatory.

Section B, Questions 1–8. These questions, which pertain to the K-1 visa applicant, are all self-explanatory.

Section B, Question 9. Alien Registration Numbers, which all begin with the letter "A," are given only to people who have applied for green cards, have applied for political asylum or have been placed in deportation proceedings. If you have an "A" number, put that number down and explain how you got it, such as "number issued from previous green card petition filed by my brother." If you do not have an "A" number, write down "None."

Section B, Questions 10–19. These questions are self-explanatory.

Section B, Question 20. Your fiancé(e) must designate a U.S. consulate outside of the U.S. where you will apply for your K-1 visa. A complete list of all U.S. embassies and consulates that issue visas, together with their addresses and phone numbers, is in Appendix I. Normally this should be in your home country. Other consulates can also be designated if necessary, but they are often reluctant to take K-1 cases from persons who are not residents or nationals of the country where the consulate is located. It is better not to press the issue if you can avoid it.

Section C. This applies only to petitioners who are in the U.S. armed forces overseas. This section is self-explanatory. If it does not apply to you put down "N/A."

G-325A

Both you and your U.S. fiancé(e) must complete this form, which is meant to gather personal background information. The questions are all self-explanatory.

3. Petition Documents

You must provide several documents with the petition.

a. Proof That the Petitioner Is a U.S. Citizen

The first document that must be filed with the petition is evidence that the petitioner is a U.S. citizen. If the petitioner is a U.S. citizen by birth, a birth certificate is the best proof. Only birth certificates issued by U.S. state governments are acceptable. Hospital birth certificates cannot be used. When the petitioner is a U.S. citizen born outside U.S. territory, a certificate of citizenship, naturalization certificate, U.S. consular record of birth abroad or unexpired U.S. passport will serve as proof. If the petitioner is a U.S. citizen but does not have one of these documents, read Chapter 27 to learn how to obtain one of them. A fiancé(e) petition cannot be filed without this proof.

b. Proof That You and Your Fiancé(e) Can Legally Marry

You and your fiancé(e) will have to prove you are both over the legal age of consent (usually 18) in the U.S. state where you plan to marry. Birth certificates for each of you will serve to prove this. If either of you has been married before, you must also prove that all prior marriages were legally terminated. This requires presenting a divorce decree or death certificate for every prior marriage. Divorce papers must be official court or government documents. Likewise, when a death certificate is needed, it must be an official document issued by the government. Certificates from funeral homes are not acceptable. If either of you comes from a country where divorces and deaths are not officially recorded, you should contact the nearest embassy or consulate representing that country to find out what other types of proof are available.

c. Proof of Intent to Marry

If a wedding is planned, which is strongly recommended in K-1 visa cases, your fiancé(e) should provide evidence that a wedding will take place, such as copies of wedding announcements, catering contracts, etc. A letter or affidavit from your pastor or justice of the peace stating that he has been contacted about performing your marriage ceremony is helpful. The petitioner should also prepare and submit a statement explaining how you met each other, why he or she cannot travel to your home country to marry you there and describing your wedding plans. This statement does not have to be in any special form, but simply in the petitioner's own words.

d. Proof That You Have Met Each Other

Your fiancé(e) must prove that you and he or she have met each other in person and have seen each other within the past two years. This is best shown by submitting photographs of the two of you together and letters you have written to each other indicating that there has been a meeting.

e. If You Haven't Met Each Other

Under recent changes in the law, it is virtually impossible to get an approval of a K-1 petition without a personal meeting unless both you and your fiancé(e) practice a religion that prohibits spouses from meeting each other before the wedding. If that is your situation, you must present evidence of your membership in such a religion. This is usually done with two documents: a letter from an official in your religious organization verifying that you and your fiancé(e) are members, and a detailed statement from a clergyperson explaining the religious laws concerning marriage.

If you are asking for a waiver of the requirement of having met, and your request is based upon a showing of exceptional hardship, you must submit a written statement explaining in detail why you cannot meet. If there is a medical reason why your U.S.-citizen fiancé(e) can't travel to meet you, include a letter from a medical doctor explaining the condition.

f. Identification Photographs

It is necessary to submit one photograph each of you and your U.S.-citizen fiancé(e). This is in addition to photographs that may have been provided showing you had previously met each other. These identification photographs must meet certain exact specifications. Instructions for having these photos made can be found in Appendix III.

4. Petition Interviews

Sometimes INS will request a personal interview with the petitioner prior to approving a fiancé(e) petition. The purpose of the interview is to ascertain if a marriage will really take place after you arrive in the U.S. and to confirm that you have previously met each other. All interviews are held at INS local offices. The regional service center will forward the file to the INS local office nearest the petitioner's place of residence for the purpose of the interview. The appropriate INS local office will send the petitioner a notice of when and where to appear for the interview, and instructions to bring additional documentation, if any is required.

5. Petition Appeals

Usually a fiancé(e) petition is turned down either because you and your fiancé(e) haven't met each other or your fiancé(e) hasn't convinced INS that you really intend to marry upon your arrival in the U.S. When the petition is denied, your fiancé(e) will then get a written statement of the reasons for the negative outcome and an explanation of how to appeal.

The best way to handle an appeal is to try avoiding it altogether. Filing an appeal means making an argument to INS that its reasoning was wrong. This is not something INS likes to hear. If you think you can eliminate the reason why your petition failed by improving your paperwork, it makes sense to disregard the appeals process and simply file a new petition, being careful to see that it is better prepared than the first.

If the petition was denied because your U.S.-citizen fiancé(e) left out necessary documents that have since been located, the new documents should be sent together with a written request that the case be reopened to the same INS office that issued the denial. This is technically called a Motion to Reopen, for which there is a $110 filing fee. Appeals often take a long time. A Motion to Reopen can be concluded faster than an appeal.

The fastest solution is for your U.S.-citizen fiancé(e) to travel to your country, marry you there, and then proceed to apply for a green card as an immediate relative of a U.S. citizen, as discussed in Chapter 5.

If your fiancé(e) does choose to appeal, it must be done within 30 days of the date on the Notice of Denial. The appeal should be filed at the same INS office which issued the denial. There is a $110 filing fee. INS will then forward the papers for consideration by the Administrative Appeals Unit of the central INS office in Washington, D.C. In six to eighteen months or more, your fiancé(e) will get back a decision by mail. Less than five percent of all appeals are successful.

When an appeal to INS has been denied, the next step is to make an appeal through the U.S. judicial system. Your fiancé(e) may not file an action in court without first going through the appeals process available from INS. If the case has reached this stage, we strongly recommend seeking representation from a qualified immigration attorney.

E. Step Two: The Application

This section includes the information you need to submit the application.

1. Who Is Eligible?

Anyone with an approved K-1 petition can apply for a K-1 visa at a U.S. consulate in his or her home country. You must be physically present in order to apply there. Even if you have at one time lived and worked illegally in the U.S., you can still get a K-1 visa from a U.S. consulate if you otherwise qualify. Remember, unlike most other visas, a K-1 visa cannot be obtained in the U.S.

2. General Procedures

The law states that any consulate will accept nonimmigrant cases, regardless of the residence of the applicant. A complete list of all U.S. consulates that process visa applications, together with their addresses and phone numbers, may be found in Appendix I. However, in the case of K-1 visas, the attitude of the consulates is usually different. Because K-1 visas are so closely related to green cards, all but the consulate in your home country are usually reluctant to accept your application. You can ask a consulate located elsewhere to accept your application, but it has the option to say "no" and will probably do so. Therefore, you should attempt to process your K-1 application in some other country only if it is absolutely essential. If you wish to ask for this privilege, you should approach the consulate of your choice before filing the Step One petition. This is because Form I-129F in Step One asks where you will file your application, and your fiancé(e) must be prepared with an answer to this question.

You may not file an application for a fiancé(e) visa at a consulate before your petition has been approved. The INS service center where your petition was originally submitted will then forward a complete copy of your file to the U.S. consulate you have designated on Form I-129F in Step One.

At the same time a Notice of Action from Step One will be sent directly to your U.S. fiancé(e). It typically takes a month or longer for the approved petition and file to arrive at the consulate. The consulate will in turn contact you directly by mail, sending the necessary forms and detailed instructions for your application. If, after waiting a reasonable time, you have not heard from the consulate, you should call and look into the matter. Files do get lost, so check up.

Once the consulate has received your file from INS, you will receive a letter containing the needed forms and instructions, including the requirements for obtaining a medical exam. One item it will contain is Biographical Information Form OF-179. Complete and return Form OF-179 to the consulate as soon as possible. This will initiate a security check. Failure to return Form OF-179 promptly can significantly delay your K-1 visa.

The application for your fiancé(e) visa is made in person, by appointment. When the consulate is ready for your final processing, it will send you an appointment letter and still more forms to be completed. Other than Form OF-179, do not mail your paperwork to the consulate. Instead, bring it with you at the time of your appointment. In most countries, there is no filing fee for the K-1 visa application.

3. Application Forms

When you file at a U.S. consulate abroad, the consulate officials will provide you with certain optional forms, designated by an "OF" preceeding a number. Instructions for completing optional forms and what to do with them once they are filled out will come with the forms. We do not include copies of these forms in Appendix III. Copies of non "OF" forms are in Appendix III.

Form I-864

K visa applicants will need to submit the new affidavit of support, Form I-864, with their green card application in the U.S. They will probably be allowed to use the less burdensome and older I-134 for the K visa, since the K visa is a nonimmigrant visa. But the newer and more complicated I-864 affidavit will eventually be required. So it makes sense to submit the I-864 in support of the K visa if it can easily and clearly be satisfied, since by doing so you will not have to duplicate your efforts. Due to the legal enforceability of the new affidavit, the U.S. citizen sponsor may in some cases wish to use the old I-134 initially, and then use the I-864 during the U.S. application.

There are two distinct requirements associated with this form: one is that all family-based immigrants (and employment-based immigrants where the applicant's relatives

submitted the visa petition or own at least 5% of the petitioning company) must have it filed by the petitioner in order to apply for permanent residence; the second is that it satisfies or helps satisfy the requirement that an immigrant show she is not likely to become a public charge.

The requirements for this affidavit of support are very different from those of its predecessor, Form I-134. For example, the new form is legally enforceable by the government for most public benefits utilized by the sponsored immigrant. It is also enforceable by the immigrant-family member against the sponsor for support. It also requires that the sponsor show that she has at least 125% of income for a similar family size, according to the federal poverty level.

All family-based immigrants who file adjustment of status or immigrant visa applications on or after December 19, 1997 are required to have the new I-864 filed by the person who is sponsoring their immigrant petition. However, another person (a joint sponsor) may add her income to the sponsor's if the joint sponsor:

  • is willing to be jointly liable
  • is a legal permanent resident or citizen
  • is over 18 years old, and
  • resides in the U.S.,

as long as she meets the 125% income requirement for her own household.

The joint sponsor files a separate affidavit of support. Other household members may join their income to help reach the 125% level, but only if they have been living with the sponsor for six months and they agree to be jointly liable by filing form I-864. Personal assets of the sponsor or the immigrant, such as property, bank account deposits, and personal property such as automobiles, may also be used to supplement the sponsor's income, if the primary sponsor's actual income does not add up to 125% of the federal income poverty guidelines. To use assets, however, the assets will have to add up to five times the difference between the 125% poverty income guidelines level for an equivalent family and the sponsors' actual income.

The sponsors must also notify the INS within 30 days of the sponsor's change of address, using form I-865. Failure to do so is punishable by fines of $250-$2,000, or $2,000-$5,000 if the sponsor fails to notify with knowledge that the sponsored alien received a public benefit. The requirements and paperwork burden of the new affidavit are complicated and substantial; most of the requirements are spelled out on the forms. If you have questions about meeting the eligibility or the scope of your legal responsibility—which may be ten or more years for sponsors, or until the immigrant permanently leaves the country, dies or naturalizes—you may want to consult an immigration attorney.

4. Documents

The most important document in your application is the Notice of Action indicating approval of your fiancé(e) visa petition. It is sent directly from the INS office in the U.S. to the consulate you designated on Form I-129F in Step One. This is the only document you will not have to submit yourself. Do not mail in your other documents, unless specifically requested to do so. Bring them with you to your interview.

You must resubmit to the consulate all of the documents first filed in Step One. Copies of these documents will not be forwarded by INS to the consulate for you. Remember that Step One original documents should have been returned to you once they were checked by INS, so you should have them available to bring to the consulate.

It is also necessary that you have in your possession a valid passport from your home country. The expiration date on the passport must be such that it will remain valid for at least six months beyond the date of your final application interview.

Police clearance certificates are required from each country you have lived in for one year or more since your 16th birthday. Additionally, you must have a police certificate from your home country or country of last residence, if you lived there for at least six months since the age of 16. You do not need to obtain police certificates from the U.S. Like all other documents, you should be prepared to present the necessary police clearance certificates at your interview. If you go to your interview without the required certificates, you will be refused a visa and told to return after you get them.

OBTAINING POLICE CERTIFICATES

You should contact the local police department in your home country for instructions on how to get police certificates. To obtain police certificates from nations other than your home country, it is best to contact the nearest consulate representing that country for instructions. Some nations refuse to supply police certificates, or their certificates are not considered reliable, and so you will not be required to obtain them from those locations. At this writing, police certificates are not required from the following countries:

Afghanistan	Haiti	Saudi Arabia
Albania	Honduras	Sierra Leone
Angola	India	Somalia
Bangladesh	Indonesia	Sri Lanka
Brunei	Iran	Sudan
Bulgaria	Iraq	Syria
Cambodia	Jordan	Tanzania
Chad	Laos	Thailand
Colombia	Liberia	Turkey
Costa Rica	Libya	United Arab
Cuba	Malaysia	Emirates
Dominican Republic	Mexico	United Kingdom
El Salvador	Mongolia	United States
Equatorial Guinea	Mozambique	Venezuela
Ghana	Nepal	Vietnam
Guatemala	Pakistan	

For applicants who once lived in Japan but do not reside there at the time their visa applications are filed, the Department of State recognizes that police certificates are available from Japan only as far back as five years from the date of the application.

Other countries, including: the Netherlands, North Korea, South Africa and South Korea, will send certificates directly to U.S. consulates but not to you personally. Before they send the certificates out, however, you must request that it be done. Usually this requires filing some type of request form together with a set of your fingerprints.

You and each accompanying child must bring to the interview three photographs taken in compliance with the instruction sheet found in Appendix III. Additional photo instructions are provided in your appointment letter, which may also contain a list of local photographers who take this type of picture.

A few consulates require you to submit fingerprints, though most do not. Consulates wanting fingerprints will send you blank fingerprint cards with instructions.

5. Application Interviews

Consulates hold interviews on all fiancé(e) visa applications. You will receive written notice of your interview with your appointment letter. Immediately prior to the interview, you and your accompanying children will be required to have medical examinations. Some consulates conduct the medical exams the day before the interview. Others, including London, schedule the medical exam and the interview on the same day. You will be told where to go and what to do in your appointment letter.

The medical examinations are conducted by private doctors and you are required to pay the doctor a fee. The fees vary from as little as $50 to more than $150 per exam, depending on the country. The amount of the medical exam fee will be stated in your appointment letter. The exam itself involves the taking of a medical history, blood test and chest X ray and verification or administering of vaccinations, if applicable. Pregnant women who do not want to be X-rayed may so advise the consulate and their appointments will be postponed until after the pregnancy. The requirement to have an X ray taken cannot be waived.

The main purpose of the medical exam is to verify that you are not medically inadmissible. The primary medical grounds of inadmissibility are tuberculosis and HIV (AIDS). Medical grounds of inadmissibility usually can be overcome with treatment. See Chapter 25, *Inadmissibility*, for more details. If you need a medical waiver, you will be given complete instructions by the consulate at the time of your interview.

After the medical exam, you and your accompanying children will report to the consulate for the interview. Bring with you to the interview the completed forms, photographs, your passports and all of the required documents discussed in this chapter. The interview process involves verification of your application's accuracy and an inspection of your documents. If all is in order, you will be asked to return later in the day when you will be issued a visa. Normally, you must use the visa to enter the U.S. within four months, though the consulate can extend this period if necessary. Upon entering the U.S. with that visa, your passport is stamped and you will be given an I-94 card showing that you are authorized to work. You will be authorized to remain in the U.S. for only 90 days. If you are bringing accompanying children, they must enter the U.S. at either the same time or after you do.

6. Application Appeals

When a consulate denies a fiancé(e) visa application, there is no formal appeal available, although you are free to reapply as often as you like. When your visa is refused, you will be told the reasons. The most common reason for denial is failure to supply all the required documents. Sometimes presenting more evidence on an unclear fact can bring about a better result. If the denial was caused by a lack of evidence, this will be explained in a written notice sent to you by mail.

Another common reason for denial of a visa is that the consular officer believes you are inadmissible. If you are found to be inadmissible, you will be given an opportunity to apply for a Waiver of Inadmissibility, if one is available. See Chapter 25 for directions on how to apply.

When all these possibilities are exhausted, if the consulate still refuses you a visa, your opportunities for further appeals are severely limited. Historically, the courts have held that there is no right to judicial review and there is no formal appeal procedure through any U.S. government agency. The State Department in Washington, D.C. does offer an informal review procedure through the mail. This agency will look at the factual elements of your case and decide whether or not the consulate made a correct decision. Even if the State Department rules in your favor, the decision is only advisory and the consulate is free to ignore the State Department, letting its own decision stand. At present, there does appear to be a trend developing where courts in the U.S. are more frequently accepting jurisdiction over consular decisions, so a court appeal may be a possibility to consider. The jurisdiction of U.S. courts to review consular decisions, is, however, still an unsettled legal issue.

Your denial may be based on a question of law rather than fact. The State Department offers the same informal review for legal questions with the difference that any decision it makes is binding on the consulate. Appeals of this kind are very technical and should be handled by a competent immigration attorney. Even with representation by an attorney, most such appeals fail.

EMPLOYMENT AUTHORIZATION

If you want to work before you get married and apply for your green card, you must file a separate application for employment authorization. This can be done by completing Form I-765 and filing it with the INS local office together with your Step Two application. Together with Form I-765 you must submit your I-94 card. The filing fee is $100. Applications for employment authorization may be filed in person or they may be filed together with your green card application.

Some INS offices may approve your employment authorization and issue a work authorization card on the spot, or you may be given an appointment to return within a few weeks, and you will receive your work authorization card at that time.

The INS is not required to make a decision on your employment authorization application for up to 90 days. If for some reason you are not given a decision within 90 days, you will, at your request, be granted an interim employment authorization which will last 240 days. To receive an interim card, you must return in person to the INS local office where you filed your I-765 and show your fee receipt. Then your interim work authorization card will be issued.

If 240 days pass and you still have not received a final decision on the I-765, you must stop working. Interim work authorization cards cannot be renewed. However, if you reach this point, you have the option to file a new I-765 application and, if you do not get a decision on the new application within 90 days, you will then be entitled to another interim work authorization card.

Instructions for completing Form I-765

Block above Question 1. Mark the first box, "Permission to accept employment."

Questions 1–8. These questions are self-explanatory.

Question 9. This asks for your Social Security number, including all numbers you have ever used. If you have never used a Social Security number, answer "None." If you have a nonworking Social Security number, write down the number followed by the words "nonworking, for tax purposes only." If you have ever used a false number, give that number, followed by the words: "Not my valid number." (Before submitting information about any use of false documents or false information, be sure to read Chapter 25.)

Question 10. You will not usually have an Alien Registration Number unless you previously applied for a green card, were in deportation proceedings, or have had certain types of immigration applications denied. All Alien Registration Numbers begin with the letter "A." If you have no "A" number but you entered the U.S. with a valid visa, you should have an I-94 card. In this case, answer Question 10 by putting down the admission number from the I-94 card.

Questions 11–15. These questions are self-explanatory.

Question 16. Answer this question "(A)(6)."

FORMS AND DOCUMENTS CHECKLIST

STEP ONE: PETITION

Forms

☐ Form I-129F.

☐ Form G-325A (one form is required for each party).

Documents

☐ One identification photograph each of the petitioner and the beneficiary.

☐ Documents proving the petitioner is a U.S. citizen.

☐ Documents proving that both parties are legally free to marry, including:

    ☐ copies of all divorce and death certificates, if either party was previously married, and

    ☐ if either party is under the age of legal consent in the U.S. state where the marriage will take place, appropriate written consent from a parent or guardian.

☐ Documents showing that the foreign national has a real intent to marry the petitioner, including:

    ☐ copies of wedding announcements

    ☐ letter or affidavit from a pastor or justice of the peace stating that he or she has been contacted about performing the marriage ceremony, and

    ☐ detailed letter from the petitioner explaining how the couple met, why the petitioner cannot travel to the beneficiary's home country and marry there and what plans have been made for the wedding ceremony.

☐ Documents proving that the couple has physically met within the past two years.

☐ If the couple has not met and their religion does not allow meeting before marriage:

    ☐ letter from an authority in the religious organization verifying that both parties are members of that religion

    ☐ detailed statement by a clergyperson explaining the religious laws concerning marriage, and

    ☐ detailed letter from the petitioner explaining how the couple will comply with all customs of the religion concerning marriage and weddings.

☐ If the couple has not personally met but to do so would cause extreme hardship:

    ☐ letter explaining the extreme hardship preventing the petitioner from traveling to meet the beneficiary, and

    ☐ if the hardship is medical, a letter from a licensed physician explaining the condition.

STEP TWO: APPLICATION

Forms

☐ OF forms (available from U.S. consulate abroad only for consular filing).

☐ Form I-864.

☐ Form I-765 (for work authorization only).

Documents

☐ Notice showing approval of the fiancé(e) visa petition.

☐ All documents originally filed with the petition.

☐ Long-form birth certificate for the applicant and each accompanying child.

☐ Passports for the applicant and each accompanying child, valid for at least six months beyond the date of the final interview.

☐ Police certificates from every country in which the applicant and each accompanying child has lived for at least six months since age 16.

☐ Three photographs each of the applicant and each accompanying child.

☐ Form I-864, Affidavit of Support, for the applicant and each accompanying child.

Getting a Green Card Through Employment

Privileges

- You may live anywhere in the U.S. and stay as long as you want.

- You may work at any job, for any company, anywhere in the U.S., or you may choose not to work at all.

- You may travel in and out of the U.S. whenever you wish.

- You may apply to become an American citizen after you have held your green card for a certain length of time.

- In some types of cases, if you qualify for a green card through relatives, then your spouse and unmarried children under the age of 21 may also get green cards automatically as accompanying relatives.

Limitations

- Your place of actual residence must be in the U.S. You cannot use a green card just for work and travel purposes. (The only exception to this is Alien Commuters, discussed in Chapter 4.)

- You must pay U.S. taxes on your worldwide income because you are regarded as a U.S. resident.

- You cannot remain outside the U.S. for more than one year at a time without special permission, or you risk losing your green card. (It is highly recommended that you return to the U.S. before you have been gone six months.)

- If you commit certain crimes, participate in politically subversive activities or engage in other prohibited activities, your green card can be taken away and you can be deported.

A. How to Qualify

Qualifying for a green card through employment has some limitations.

1. Quota Restrictions

There are currently no waiting periods other than the normal time that it takes to process visa applications. In general, waiting periods tend to be longer for people from China, India, Mexico and the Philippines. At this time, these countries are not experiencing backlogs, except for non-skilled workers.

The Department of State has a recorded message with information regarding quotas at 202-663-1541.

In addition to waiting for the visa number to become available ("quota"), applying for permanent residency under certain preference categories also requires certification that the alien worker is not taking a position that a U.S. worker could fill. This process is called labor certification. After a Labor Certification is issued, it will take one to three months for visa petition approval. Once the petition is approved and

the quota becomes current, it will take an additional four to eight months for green card application approval.

2. Who Qualifies for a Green Card Through Employment?

In order to qualify for a green card through employment:
- you must have a job offer from a U.S. employer
- you must have the correct background in terms of education and work experience for the job you have been offered, and
- there must be no qualified American willing or able to take the job—this rule does not apply to categories of green cards where Labor Certification is not required.

a. Job Offer From a U.S. Employer

You need a specific job offer from a U.S. employer to get a green card through employment. There are two main exceptions to this rule. The first is for those who can qualify as people of extraordinary ability. This is a small subgroup of the green card through employment category called *priority workers.* The second exception is for persons qualifying as having exceptional ability under the employment based second preference. This other exception usually applies when it is deemed in the national interest to do so. Both categories are described later in this chapter.

Labor Certification is one of the steps often necessary for getting a green card through employment. Labor Certification is a procedure required by the Labor Department to prove that there are no qualified Americans available to take a job being offered to a foreign national green card applicant. In all cases requiring Labor Certification, the employer acts as the petitioner in obtaining the green card. Many people are surprised to learn that they need a job offer *before* filing a green card application. The idea behind it is that you are getting a green card only because your services are essential to an American employer. Put another way, the U.S. government is issuing a green card not for your benefit, but to help an American company or institution.

In reality, it may be hard for you to find such an employer, for he or she must not only offer you a job, but also be willing to take part in the procedure of getting you a green card. The paperwork can include producing company financial records and tax returns for review by INS. Many employers are afraid to do this. Your prospective employer should also have the patience to wait because, although you need a job offer to apply, unless you already have a nonimmigrant work visa, you cannot legally start on the job until your green card application is approved. This can take anywhere from several months to several years, depending on your qualifications and nationality.

When a potential employer badly needs your skills, he or she will usually cooperate with the various requirements. Others may be reluctant. If you want to get a green card but do not have a U.S.-citizen relative or the luck to win a green card lottery, finding a willing employer is essential.

The employer who offers you a job may be a company, institution, organization or individual. If you yourself have a U.S. business, normally you cannot act as the petitioning employer for your own green card. The only situation in which you may be able to hire yourself is where the business is a corporation employing many others as well.

An agent who books your talents for a variety of jobs, as is common in the entertainment industry, may also be the source of your job offer. For an agent to act as petitioner, you must receive your salary directly from the agent.

WHAT TO TELL AN EMPLOYER

When you are trying to find a U.S. job, it may help if you can assure the employer that he or she is taking limited legal risks by participating in your green card application. As the petitioner for a green card, the employer assumes absolutely no financial responsibility for you during the application process or after you enter the U.S. except that it guarantees to pay you the market wage for the position during the time you are actually employed. The employer also has the right to withdraw the petition for any reason and at any time. Once you receive a green card and begin working, your employer is free to fire you at will.

Prospective employers will be asked to supply business financial records to INS. Many are afraid to do this. You can reassure them by explaining that INS checks these records for the purpose of proving the business has enough money to pay your salary.

b. Correct Background

You must have the correct background in terms of experience, training and education for the job you have been offered. For example, if you are a qualified nuclear scientist, but are asked to take employment managing a U.S. bakery, you cannot use that job offer to get a green card because you have no background in bakery management. It is irrelevant that your native intelligence and general knowledge of business may make you quite capable of handling the bakery job. Likewise, reliability, honesty or willingness to work hard, characteristics difficult to find and much in demand by real-world employers, are not an INS consideration. A match between your background and the job is the only thing that counts.

c. No Qualified Americans

Labor Certification may or may not be a requirement for you. It depends on your background and the kind of job you have been offered in the U.S. Later, we will explain which types of applications need Labor Certifications and which do not. Where a Labor Certification is required, there must be no qualified Americans available and willing to take the job you have been offered in the region where the job is offered.

Usually, to fulfill the requirement of no qualified Americans, there must be no American workers who meet the *minimum* qualifications. In the case of college professors or persons of exceptional ability in the arts and sciences, however, the standard is less difficult to meet. In these subcategories it is necessary to show that you are *more* qualified than any suitable American workers, but you do not have to be the only one available. This difference may seem small, but it really does make getting Labor Certifications much easier for college and university faculty.

Even in the majority of categories, where the requirement is that there be no minimally qualified American workers to fill the job, the standard may not always be hard to meet. It all depends on the occupation involved and where the job is located. Overall, it is not nearly as difficult to fulfill this requirement as people imagine. More jobs than you would think do go begging for want of either qualified or willing U.S. applicants. Jobs that typically make successful foundations for green card applications are those requiring workers with a college education, special knowledge or skills. Unskilled jobs that have odd working hours, or other undesirable factors are also good possibilities for green card applicants.

B. Employment Categories

Whether or not you need a Labor Certification to get a green card through employment depends on the work category in which you apply. Green cards through employment are divided into five preference categories. The first one has no Labor Certification requirements. The rest do. All employment preference categories are subject to quotas. The quotas for the first two employment preferences move more quickly than the third. In certain categories, you require a specific job offer from a U.S. employer. In others you do not. All in all, you can see that the amount of difficulty involved in getting a green card through employment depends on the category into which you fall. The five employment preference categories are:

- **Employment first preference.** Priority workers.
- **Employment second preference.** Workers with advanced degrees or exceptional ability.
- **Employment third preference.** Skilled or unskilled workers without advanced degrees.
- **Employment fourth preference.** Religious workers and various miscellaneous categories of workers and other individuals.
- **Employment fifth preference.** Individual investors willing to invest $1,000,000 in a U.S. business (or $500,000 in economically depressed areas).

1. Employment First Preference

Priority workers are divided into three subcategories: persons of extraordinary ability, outstanding university professors or researchers and executives or managers of multinational companies. No Labor Certification is required for any of these subcategories. To apply for a green card as a priority worker under two of the three subcategories, you first need a job offer from a U.S. employer, but if you are a person of extraordinary ability, you do not even require that.

a. Persons of Extraordinary Ability

You qualify for a green card as a priority worker if you have extraordinary ability in the sciences, arts, education, business or athletics. Your achievements must have been publicly recognized and resulted in a period of sustained national or international acclaim. A further condition of this subcategory is that your entry into the U.S. will substantially benefit America in the future. You do not need a specific job offer as long you will continue working in your field of expertise once you arrive in the U.S.

b. Outstanding Professors and Researchers

You qualify for a green card as a priority worker under the outstanding professors and researchers subcategory if you have an international reputation for being outstanding in a particular academic field. You need three years minimum of either teaching or research experience in that field. You must also be entering the U.S. to accept a specific tenured or tenure-track teaching or research position at a university. Alternatively, you may accept a job conducting research in industry or with a research organization. The U.S. company or institution employing you should have a history of making significant achievements in research and must employ at least three other full-time research workers.

c. Multinational Executives and Managers

You qualify for a green card as a priority worker under the multinational executives and managers subcategory if you have been employed as an executive or manager by a qualified company outside the U.S. for at least one out of the past three years, and you are now going to take a similar position with an American branch, affiliate or subsidiary of the same company. The U.S. company must have been in business for at least one year. The qualifications needed are similar to those for L-1 intracompany transfer visas, discussed in Chapter 20.

For U.S. and foreign companies to act as petitioners in this subcategory, they should fit one of the following three descriptions:

- they must be different branches of the same company
- one company must be a majority-controlled subsidiary of the other, or

- the foreign and U.S. companies must be affiliated in a way such that both companies are under the control of the same person, persons, company or group of companies.

Since the positions held by the green card applicant both in and out of the U.S. are required to be executive or managerial in nature, the exact meaning of these terms is important. A manager is defined as a person who has all four of the following characteristics:

- he or she manages the organization or a department of the organization
- he or she supervises and controls the work of other supervisory, professional or managerial employees, or manages an essential function of the organization
- he or she has the authority to hire and fire those persons supervised, or if none are supervised, works at a senior level within the organization, and
- he or she has the authority to make decisions concerning the day-to-day operations of the portion of the organization over which he or she has authority.

A supervisor below the level of middle management is often called a first-line supervisor. First-line supervisors are not normally considered managers for green card qualifying purposes unless the employees they supervise are professionals. The word "professional" here means a worker holding a university degree.

An executive is defined as a person who has all four of the following characteristics:

- he or she directs the management of the organization or a major part of the organization
- he or she sets the goals and policies of the organization or a part of the organization
- he or she has extensive decision-making authority, and
- he or she receives only general supervision or direction from higher level executives, a board of directors, or the stockholders of the organization.

2. Employment Second Preference

The employment second preference category of green cards through employment is for professionals holding advanced university degrees, and for persons of exceptional ability in the sciences, arts or business. To qualify in this category, you must be coming to the U.S. specifically to work in your field of expertise. With limited exceptions, you must have a definite job offer from a U.S. employer. Labor Certifications are normally required for this category. (For exceptions, see Section c, below.) This is another preference category that is divided into subcategories.

a. Advanced Degree Professionals

The plain term "professional" has long been defined by INS to mean a person in an occupation that requires, at a minimum, a baccalaureate degree or its equivalent from a college or university. Therefore, to qualify as an advanced degree professional takes something more. Specifically, you must hold a graduate level degree, or a professional degree requiring postgraduate education, such as is standard in law or medicine. Many who qualify for H-1 visas in professions like nursing and engineering do not qualify for green cards in this subcategory unless they have completed postgraduate degrees.

There is a substitute for having an advanced degree. If you have a bachelor's degree plus five years of progressively responsible professional work experience, you also qualify in this category.

ACADEMIC CREDENTIAL EVALUATIONS

Not every country in the world operates on the same academic degree and grade level system found in the U.S. If you were educated in some other country, INS, as part of judging your eligibility, will usually ask for an academic credential evaluation from an approved consulting service to determine the American equivalent of your educational level.

Evaluations from accredited credential evaluation services are not binding on INS, but they are very persuasive. When the results are favorable, they strengthen your case. If, however, the evaluation shows that your credentials do not equal those required for advanced degree professionals, you will not qualify in this subcategory.

A list of these services can be found at http://www.naces.org/members.htm.

We recommend getting a credential evaluation in every case where non-U.S. education is a factor. In addition, we advise getting the evaluation before INS asks for it. When the evaluation is favorable, you can automatically include it with your petition. This strengthens your case and saves time if INS decides to request it later. If your evaluation is unfavorable, submit the results only if INS insists you do. You may also wish to consider applying in a different category because your application in this one is likely to fail.

b. Persons of Exceptional Ability

The priority worker category described in Section 1a, above, covers the subcategory of persons of "extraordinary ability" in the sciences, arts, education, business or athletics. Do not confuse this with the exceptional ability subcategory of the employment second preference, which includes only those in the sciences, arts and business. Something less than the international acclaim required for extraordinary workers is enough for the exceptional ability subcategory. Proven sustained national acclaim in your field will meet the required standard. You must, however, still be considered significantly more accomplished than the average person in that profession, and you must also show that your presence in the U.S. will substantially benefit the economic, cultural or educational interests of the country.

c. Waiver of the Labor Certificate Requirement

If your presence will benefit the U.S. in the future, you may be exempted from having a job offer or Labor Certification. By "benefit," INS means that your coming to the U.S. will have a favorable impact on the economic, employment, educational, housing, cultural or other important aspect of the country. The impact must be *national* in scope, it must be *substantial* and it must derive from your talent or skills.

3. Employment Third Preference

This is the third broad category of green cards through employment. Like most of employment second preference, Labor Certifications are required for the entire category. No national interest waiver is available for the third preference. Employment third preference is also divided into sub-categories—professional workers, skilled workers and unskilled workers.

You may wonder what difference it makes whether you are classified as a professional worker, skilled worker or unskilled worker, since all three categories require Labor Certifications and draw green cards from the same 40,000 quota allocation. The answer is that of those 40,000 green cards available each year, only 5,000 are for unskilled workers. Accordingly, those classified as unskilled will have to wait much longer for green cards than workers in the other subcategories. That wait is currently at least seven and a half years.

a. Professional Workers (No Advanced Degree)

Immigration law is always vague about the definition of the term "professional," stating only that the meaning includes such occupations as architects, lawyers, physicians, engineers and teachers. Other occupations that have routinely been

approved as professional include accountants, computer systems analysts, physical therapists, chemists, pharmacists, medical technologists, hotel managers (large hotels only), fashion designers, certain upper-level business managers and commercial airline pilots of 747s or other large aircraft. The professional workers subcategory of employment third preference is for members of professions who hold only bachelor's degrees and have less than five years of work experience. As long as you have the necessary degree, proving eligibility in this category is simple.

b. Skilled Workers

Workers engaged in occupations that normally do not require college degrees, but do need at least two years of training or experience, qualify in the subcategory of skilled workers. How much experience or training may be necessary for a specific job is not always clear. Your local state labor department office can tell you the exact number of years of education and experience they consider a minimum for the particular job you have been offered. Or you can look it up in the Department of Labor's publication "Dictionary of Occupational Titles," available at a library or the local Government Printing Office bookstore.

c. Unskilled Workers

Any job not falling into one of the subcategories we've already described goes into the subcategory of unskilled workers. Generally, this includes occupations requiring less than two years training or experience. Whatever require-ments the job does have must be met by your own qualifi-cations or you will not be able to apply successfully for a green card in this subcategory. For example, if a job requires a one-year vocational training program, you must have completed such a program before you can begin applying for a green card on the basis of that job.

4. Employment Fourth Preference

This is the fourth category of employment based workers. It encompasses religious workers, which includes ministers and religious professionals. The fourth preference also includes various miscellaneous categories of workers. (See Chapter 11.)

5. Employment Fifth Preference

This employment category is for investors willing to invest a minimum of $500,000 to $1,000,000 in a U.S. business. The minimum amount depends on the location of the enterprise. (See Chapter 10.)

6. Schedule A Labor Certification

In addition to the specific categories that do not require Labor Certification, there are other alternatives to meeting the condition that there be no qualified Americans available to take the job. One alternative is called a Schedule A Labor Certification. It allows some people to get green cards through employment without first testing the market for the availability of American workers.

Schedule A is not a separate green card category, like the ones we just described above. Schedule A is a special list of occupations that would fall into categories normally requiring Labor Certification except that shortages of such workers are already a recognized fact.

The Schedule A list is not permanent. It changes as U.S. labor needs change. Below are the occupations presently on the Schedule A list.

a. Certain Medical Occupations

Physical therapists. You must be qualified for a license in the state where you intend to practice, but you need not be licensed already.

Professional nurses. This includes only registered nurses. Licensed practical nurses do not qualify. You must have graduated from either a U.S. or Canadian nursing school, or passed the Commission on Graduates of Foreign Nursing Schools examination. Alternatively, you qualify for Schedule A if you are licensed by the U.S. state in which you intend to practice. Although you still need to fill out the labor certification form, instead of filing it with the Department of Labor, you file it directly with the INS service center for your area.

b. People With Exceptional Ability in Arts or Sciences

It is difficult to qualify in this category. First, you must prove you are recognized in at least two different countries. The likely candidates under this category are internationally famous scientists, writers or fine artists such as painters and sculptors, and people of a high level of recognition and accomplishment in the performing arts and business.

If you try to avoid Labor Certification by using this category, your employer must submit extensive proof that you are recognized in at least two different countries. The employer can do this successfully if you have written evidence available to prove your recognition. Such evidence might include certificates for important awards you have won, copies of widely distributed books or articles you have written or newspaper articles about you and your work.

7. Schedule B: Low Level Jobs

INS has predetermined that in a number of unskilled occupations, there are generally no worker shortages. These are called Schedule B occupations. Usually Labor Certifications will be denied for any job listed on Schedule B. An employer is allowed to file a Labor Certification application for a Schedule B worker if he or she wishes, but he or she must overcome INS' presumption that there are adequate workers for these occupations. Here is the current Schedule B occupation list:

- Assemblers
- Attendants (amusement and recreation service)
- Attendants (automobile service station)
- Attendants (parking lot)
- Attendants (service workers such as personal service)
- Bartenders
- Bookkeepers II
- Caretakers
- Cashiers
- Charworkers and cleaners
- Chauffeurs and taxicab drivers
- Cleaners (hotel and motel)
- Clerk typists
- Clerks and checkers (grocery)
- Clerks (general)
- Clerks (hotel)
- Cooks (short order)
- Counter and fountain workers
- Dining room attendants
- Electric truck operators
- Elevator operators
- Floorworkers
- Groundskeepers
- Guards
- Helpers (any industry)

- Household domestic service workers, or housekeepers, unless you have at least one year of prior paid experience
- Janitors
- Keypunch operators
- Kitchen workers
- Laborers
- Loopers and toppers
- Material handlers
- Nurses aides and orderlies
- Packers, markers and bottlers
- Porters
- Receptionists
- Sailors and deck hands
- Sales clerks (general)
- Sewing machine operators and handstitchers
- Stock room and warehouse workers
- Streetcar and bus conductors
- Telephone operators
- Truck drivers and tractor drivers
- Typists (lesser skilled only)
- Ushers
- Yard workers

8. Accompanying Relatives

If you are married or have children below the age of 21 and you acquire a green card through employment, your spouse and children can automatically get green cards as accompanying relatives simply by providing proof of their family relationship to you.

9. Inadmissibility

If you have ever been arrested for committing a crime, lied on an immigration application, lied to an immigration officer or been afflicted with certain physical or mental defects, you may be inadmissible from receiving a green card unless you can qualify for what is known as a *Waiver of Inadmissibility*. See Chapter 25, *Inadmissibility*, to identify and find out how you may be able to overcome these problems.

C. Steps to Obtaining a Green Card

Once you have a suitable job offer, if one is required, getting a green card through employment is a three-step process for categories requiring Labor Certification, and a two-step process for categories that do not. Often, applicants expect their employers to handle the entire procedure for them and, indeed, many large companies have experienced workers who will do this for highly desirable employees. Even smaller companies may be prepared to do

whatever is necessary, including paying an immigration attorney's fees, to attract a key staff member. However, it is often the employee who is most interested in having the green card issued, and to U.S. employers, the red tape of hiring a foreign employee can be an unfamiliar nuisance.

1. Step One: Labor Certification

Labor Certification is filed by your U.S. employer. Employment first preference priority workers and those with occupations appearing on Schedule A do not have to go through the full Step One procedures. They may move directly to Step Two, though during Step Two they do have to present the Step One forms and documents to show that they qualify as either priority workers or for Schedule A.

The object of Labor Certification is to satisfy the U.S. government that there are no qualified American workers available and willing to take the specific job that has been offered to you. This must be proven to the U.S. Department of Labor (DOL), not INS. Therefore, your employer will file Labor Certification papers with DOL.

Since you are applying for a green card under a preference category, you are subject to a quota. The date on which your employer files the Labor Certification is called your priority date. The priority date is important because it marks the legally recognized moment when your waiting period for a green card starts to elapse. (Where formal Labor Certification is not required, your priority date is the date your application is filed at the INS).

If all goes well, the Labor Certification will eventually be approved, but be aware that an approved Labor Certification does not, by itself, give you any right to live or work in the U.S. It is only a prerequisite to Steps Two and Three, submitting the petition and application for a green card. Where Labor Certification is required, it must be approved before you are eligible for Steps Two and Three.

2. Step Two: The Petition

The petition is also filed by your U.S. employer. All petitions are submitted to INS regional service centers in the U.S. With the successful completion of Step One, your employer has proven that no qualified Americans are available for the job. The object of the petition is to prove that you do, in fact, qualify. In the case of priority workers, you must also prove as part of Step Two that you qualify in one of that category's three subgroups. In addition, it must be shown that your future employer truly needs someone with your skills and has the financial ability to pay your salary. Like the Labor Certification, an approved petition does not by itself give you any immigration privileges. It is only a prerequisite to Step Three, submitting your application. The petition must be approved before you are eligible for Step Three.

STEPS FOR SCHEDULE A

Step One procedures for Schedule A cases differ in many respects from those for standard Labor Certification. The principal difference is that it is not necessary to prove there are no U.S. workers available for the job. Instead, your employer will prove that you do in fact qualify for one of the groups on Schedule A. Another difference is that the Step One procedures in Schedule A cases are carried out simultaneously with, instead of before, those of Step Two, the petition. The differences in Schedule A procedures are explained where necessary throughout this chapter.

3. Step Three: The Green Card Application

The green card application is filed by you and your accompanying relatives, if any. This application is your formal request for a green card. Step Three may be carried out in the U.S. at an INS Service Center or in your home country at a U.S. consulate there. In either case, you may not file Step Three papers until both Steps One and Two have been approved.

The majority of work-related green card applications are filed at INS Service Centers inside the U.S., since usually the worker is already in the country. If you are in the U.S. legally on a nonimmigrant visa, and you have a current priority date, you may qualify to apply for your green card either inside or outside the U.S., whichever you prefer. If you are in the U.S. out of status or you entered legally without a visa under the Visa Waiver Program, you may be barred from filing your green card application inside the U.S., unless you had a visa petition or labor certification filed before January 14, 1998, in which case you must pay a penalty fee, which is currently $1,000. The penalty fee is in addition to the regular filing fee for such applications. Children under the age of 16 and immediate relatives of U.S. citizens are not subject to paying this penalty. If you are subject to these penalties and want to avoid them, you may instead elect to apply for your green card at a U.S. consulate abroad, but if you were in the U.S. out of legal status before leaving, you should be sure you are not inadmissible or subject to the three- or ten-year waiting periods before proceeding. (See Chapter 25.)

If you have an approved petition but your priority date is not yet current, you must wait until it is current to file your green card application. The consulate will advise you by mail when your priority date finally comes up, but if you want to check progress from time to time, you may do so by calling the U.S. State Department in Washington, D.C. at 202-663-1541 for the latest quota information.

4. Paperwork

There are two types of paperwork you must submit to get a green card through employment. The first consists of official government forms completed by you or your U.S. employer. The second consists of personal and business documents such as birth and marriage certificates, school transcripts and diplomas, and company financial statements and tax returns. We will tell you exactly what forms and documents you need. It is vital that forms are properly filled out and all necessary documents are supplied. The documents you or your U.S. employer supply to INS do not have to be originals. Photocopies of all documents are acceptable as long as you have the original in your possession and are willing to produce the originals at the request of INS. Documents submitted to U.S. consulates, on the other hand, must be either originals or official government certified copies. Government certified copies and notarized copies are not the same thing. Documents which have only been notarized are not acceptable. They must carry a government seal. In addition to any original or government certified copies of documents submitted to a consulate, you should submit plain photocopies of each document as well. After the consulate compares the copies with the originals, it will return the originals.

Documents will be accepted if they are in either English, or, with papers filed at U.S. consulates abroad, the language of the country where the documents are being filed. An exception exists for papers filed at the U.S. consulates in Japan, where all documents must be translated into English. If the documents are not in an acceptable language as just explained, they must be accompanied by a full, word for word, written English translation. Any capable person may act as translator. It is not necessary to hire a professional. At the end of each translation, the following statement must appear:

I hereby certify that I translated this document from (language) to English. This translation is accurate and complete. I further certify that I am fully competent to translate from (language) to English.

The translator should sign this statement but it does not have to be witnessed or notarized.

Later in this chapter we describe in detail the forms and documents needed to get your green card through employment. A summary checklist of forms and documents appears at the end of this chapter.

D. Who's Who in Getting Your Green Card

Getting a green card will be easier if you familiarize yourself with the technical names used for each participant in the process. During Steps One and Two, the Labor Certification and the petition, you are known either as the *beneficiary* or the *employee* and your prospective U.S. employer is known either as the *petitioner* or the *employer*. The petitioner may be either a business or an individual, but usually it is a business. In Step Three, the application, you are referred to as *applicant*, but your U.S. employer remains the *petitioner* or *employer*. If you are bringing your spouse and children with you as accompanying relatives, they are known as *applicants* as well.

E. Step One: Labor Certification

➡️ If you are in a green card through employment category that does not require Labor Certification, or practice an occupation listed in Schedule A, skip ahead to Section F.

1. General Procedures

Labor Certifications, consisting of forms and documents, are filed in the U.S. at the appropriate state labor department office in the state of the employer's place of business. We emphasize that this is an office of the state government, not the U.S. DOL. State labor department offices assist the DOL in the Labor Certification process by monitoring employers' efforts to locate American workers. However, a regional office of the U.S. DOL, where the file is forwarded after the state office finishes its work, makes the final decision on your employer's Labor Certification.

States differ as to the exact place and procedure for filing Labor Certifications. Most states have centralized filing at the labor department headquarters in the state capital. A call to the state labor department office in the state capital will tell you where and how to file Step One papers. Different states give different names to these offices, including labor department, job service, department of economic security, and employment commission. Correct names, addresses and telephone numbers of each state headquarters are listed in Appendix II.

There is no filing fee for a Labor Certification. If possible, it is better for the employer to file in person so you can be sure that the arrival of the papers is recorded. When the papers are presented in person, a dated written receipt should be requested. The receipt should be kept in a safe place, together with a complete copy of everything submitted. Then your employer can confirm on what date your Labor Certification was filed and help to locate the papers should

they get lost or delayed in processing. When filing by mail, we recommend sending the papers by certified mail, return receipt requested, and again keeping a complete copy for your records. Also, remember that your priority date for quota purposes is established on the day the Labor Certification is filed, so it is important to have proof of exactly when this took place.

Because there is no uniformity in operating procedures among the various state labor departments, the length of time it takes to get a Labor Certification approved varies from one state to another. A delay of as much as a year and a half to two years is not unusual in some places, even for the strongest cases. However, the time it takes for Labor Certification approval usually runs concurrently with the wait caused by the third preference quota. You will remember that you cannot begin Step Three of the green card process until your priority date is current. Since you must wait for your priority date to come up under the quota anyway, the processing time for a Labor Certification usually doesn't add anything to the total time it takes to get a green card. Because the second preference quota is often current, it is advantageous to qualify under that preference if possible. The Labor Certification may be completed long before your number under the quota is current. For this reason, even if DOL could process and approve your Labor Certification more quickly, you still would not get your green card any faster. However, if you are in a nonimmigrant status which may expire before the labor certification is approved, then you need to be concerned about the time it takes to process your application. See Chapter 25 on inadmissibility and penalties for being out of status.

2. Advertising Procedures

The Labor Certification process starts with the U.S. employer trying to recruit American workers for the position that has been offered to a foreign national. It is crucial to the success of the green card application for the employer to fail at this attempt. To demonstrate that American workers are in fact unavailable, the job must usually be publicly advertised. The employer must then wait to see if any qualified U.S. candidates come forward. DOL has established a specific procedure for this advertising.

The procedure begins when the employer files Form ETA-750 with the state labor department. Once this form is submitted, the state labor department will send back a letter to the employer acknowledging receipt of the form and assigning an identification number known as a job-order number to the case. The letter will also give instructions on how to advertise.

It is mandatory that the employer carry out the advertising procedures exactly as required. There are specific guidelines on how and where the advertisements must be placed. Three separate types of advertisements are necessary. First, the state labor department will enter a description of the position, identified by the job-order number, in its state-wide computer bank. For 30 days, anyone throughout the state who contacts the state labor department will have an opportunity to apply for the job.

Second, the petitioning employer must prepare a written advertisement for the classified section of a newspaper or professional journal. The ad must state the job title, salary and working hours of the position as well as describe the duties and qualifications. It is important that the job descriptions in the ad match the one that appears in the ETA-750 form. The employer can only reject an American job applicant for lacking qualifications which are listed on both the ad and the form.

The advertisement should not give the name or address of the employer's company. Instead, it must contain the address of the state labor department and the job-order number. Prospective U.S. job candidates will be asked to contact the state labor department office and make reference to this number. By having all job candidates contact them directly, the state labor department is able to monitor the results of the ad placed by the employer.

Normally, the employer should place the advertisement in the classified section of a standard newspaper circulated in the city where the employer's place of business is located. If the city has only one daily newspaper, the ad should be placed there. If there are two or more daily newspapers in the area, as is common in larger cities, the employer may choose whichever one he or she prefers. The same ad must be run for three consecutive days.

Sometimes the letter from the state labor department will suggest that the employer advertise in a professional journal, trade journal or national publication, instead of a local newspaper. The employer is not required to follow this suggestion, but unless there is a good business reason for not doing so, it is generally best to comply. When the ad is placed in a national newspaper or journal, it need appear only once instead of three times.

The third type of advertising required for Labor Certification is an official job notice posted at the employer's place of business. The notice must contain the identical language used in the newspaper or journal advertisement, but instead of giving the job-order number, prospective candidates should be asked to contact a specific person in the company. The notice must be posted for at least ten business days on an employee bulletin board or other suitable location on the company premises.

If the job being offered is one represented by a labor union or collective bargaining group, that union or group must also be sent a notice that a Labor Certification application has been filed. This gives the union an opportunity to refer union members for the job.

REDUCTION IN RECRUITMENT OR "RIR"

The DOL has begun to process cases on an expedited "reduction in recruitment" basis if the employer and the position meet certain criteria. The employer must have conducted *recruitment* for the position for the *six months* preceding the filing of the application. The DOL prefers to see at least one newspaper advertisement per month for the position during that period, although it may accept less. Other types of recruitment evidence should be submitted, as long as they are normal to the industry. There must be a documented *labor shortage* for the position in the region where the employer resides, and the employer must be offering the prevailing market wage for the position. The employer may not require experience or education for the position, which are not within the normal parameters as defined in the DOL's *Dictionary of Occupational Titles*. Although these are the principal requirements, there are myriad procedural requirements involved, and because it is a relatively new process, the standards and requirements are changing. You should probably retain or at least consult an experienced immigration attorney if you wish to be successful in an RIR labor certification.

It is also speculated that the RIR procedures may actually become the preferred way to do labor certifications, so that the non-RIR cases would take longer and longer, and receive less attention and processing priority from DOL. This is another reason you should check in with a knowledgeable expert if you are interested in a labor certification.

3. Handling Job Applications

If anyone applies for the job by responding to the advertisement or state labor department listing, the state labor department will collect resumes from the candidates and forward them to the employer. The employer must then review the resumes and be prepared to state in writing why each candidate does not meet the minimum qualifications for the job as described in the advertisement and on Form ETA-750. The same must be done with candidates who respond directly to the employer from the posting of the in-house notice. Even if a single requested qualification is missing from the resume, that is enough reason for the employer to reject an American job candidate in favor of you, if he wishes to do so. However, when some acceptable resumes do turn up, the employer must interview those people. After the interview, if the employer is unsatisfied and still wishes to employ you, he should again put in writing why the U.S. job candidates were not suitable. Once an interview has been held, the employer is no longer limited to rejecting candidates only because they do not meet the job description as stated in the ad or the ETA-750 form. Poor work habits, lack of job stability, questionable character and similar business considerations, if legitimate, are also satisfactory reasons. In addition, it sometimes comes out in an interview that the prospective worker's qualifications are not in fact what they appeared to be on the resume, or that the worker is not willing to relocate or is not otherwise willing to accept the job. This provides still another reason to turn down the U.S. candidate.

With the exception of college and university teachers, DOL does not consider the fact that you may be more qualified than any other candidate to be a valid reason for rejecting an American worker. Being the most qualified is not enough. You must be the only one who is minimally qualified. The employer cannot be forced to hire an American who happens to apply for the job as a result of the required advertising, but if a qualified American does turn up and your prospective employer cannot find a solid business reason to reject him or her, the Labor Certification application filed on your behalf will fail.

If no minimally qualified American job candidates present themselves, the Labor Certification will be approved. Then the stamped certification will be sent to your U.S. employer. Only the employer receives communications from DOL, because technically it is the company that is seeking Labor Certification in order to fill a staff need.

4. Labor Certification Forms

A copy of this form can be found in Appendix III.

Form ETA-750

Forms ETA-750 A and B are the only forms used in Step One, Labor Certification. They must be submitted in duplicate. Each of the two sets of forms must have an original signature, although the forms themselves may be photocopies.

All questions on the ETA-750 should be answered truthfully, as is the case on all government forms. Revealing that you are in the U.S. illegally will not affect the outcome of the Labor Certification, but giving false information on a government form is a criminal offense and could lead to your deportation from the U.S. There is some risk that if the ETA-750 form discloses that you are presently in the U.S. illegally, DOL will notify INS. Policies vary around the country. Even if DOL does notify INS, it may take months before deportation proceedings are initiated. Unfortunately, if you are in the U.S. illegally, it is a risk that you will have to take if you ever wish to get a legal green card.

Form ETA-750 is divided into Parts A and B. In Part A, the U.S. employer is asked to give a very detailed description of the job. Part B requires a great deal of information about your (the employee's) qualifications and experience. We already know that the employer thinks you are qualified for the job. Otherwise, he or she would not be filing a Labor Certification on your behalf. If, in Part B, it is indicated that you have fewer qualifications than your prospective employer has asked for in the job description as written in Part A, that means the company has not accurately written down its expectations for a job candidate to fill this position. Therefore, the job requirements should be reduced and the job description in Part A changed before it is filed with the state labor department. There should be no qualifications listed in Part A that you, as the potential employee, cannot meet, or you will not qualify for the position.

One of the questions asked in Part A is the number of years of work experience the job requires. Eventually you must prove that you have at least that much experience. When you count up how many years of relevant experience you have to offer, you cannot include experience gained from working for your petitioning employer in exactly the same job that is described in the ETA 750. It is a fact that many people seeking green cards through employment have already begun to work illegally for their petitioning employers before they receive green cards. Others take U.S. jobs legally on temporary work visas and then begin green card processing using the same employer as petitioner. If some or all of the required experience comes from years of working for the petitioning employer in exactly the same job used for the Labor Certification, or if considered to be a training position for that job, absent unusual circumstances, neither DOL nor INS will give you credit for these credentials.

Therefore, you must be prepared to prove that you met the minimum experience and education requirements as stated in Part A of the ETA-750 before you started working for the petitioner in the particular position described on the ETA-750, even if you have been employed in that job for some time. If, however, you have spent time working for your petitioning employer in a different job than the one described on the ETA 750, you may count that time toward your "related experience" requirement.

Suppose you had no experience when hired, but have now become very important to your employer. In fact, if your employer had to hire an inexperienced worker to replace you and then train that person, the business might fall apart. Your employer didn't need an experienced person when he first hired you, but now he must have an experienced person performing your job. His business needs have changed. Under these circumstances, you can include your experience with the petitioning employer in your job requirements. To do so, your employer must convince DOL there would be a substantial disruption of the business if he had to train a new person without experience. The term "substantial disruption" is not well defined and its practical meaning is open to debate. For this reason, it is best to avoid relying on experience that you gained through your work for the petitioning employer unless it is absolutely necessary in your case.

You will remember that the purpose of Step One is to convince DOL that there are no qualified Americans available for the job in question. Although Part B of Form ETA-750 does ask for your work and education background, DOL does not normally evaluate your job qualifications during this step. Nonetheless, DOL will sometimes send the ETA-750 forms back to your employer and ask for such proof. This is not a proper request for DOL to make. Still, when their demands are not too difficult to meet, giving them what they ask for is the easiest and quickest way to keep your case moving.

Although your job qualifications need not be verified in Step One, don't lose sight of the fact that this will eventually have to be done in Step Two. In Step Two, it must be proven to INS that you meet every requirement stated by the employer in Part A of Form ETA-750. A Labor Certification will be approved if no qualified American job candidates come forward, but that alone doesn't guarantee you a green card. If you can't meet the job qualifications either, the approved Labor Certification will turn out to be wasted effort. We also reemphasize that you must not only meet the job qualifications, you must also be able to prove you meet them. The discussion of documents under Step Two will explain how to do this.

Now we will look at Form ETA-750 question by question.

Part A, Questions 1–11. These questions are self-explanatory.

Part A, Question 12. DOL is concerned that a petitioning employer may offer a very low salary in order to discourage Americans from applying for the job. To insure this tactic won't work, DOL has salary guidelines that must be followed. The salary offer listed in Part A, Question 12 can be no more than 5% below the average salary paid to workers in the same type of job in the same geographical area where the employer's company is located. DOL calls this average salary range the *prevailing wage.* To find out the prevailing wage for your job, the state labor department makes a wage survey of similar jobs in the area, or relies on wage data and surveys to do so. You can find out what the state labor department believes the prevailing wage is by filing a "prevailing wage request" with the local unit in charge of determining prevailing wages. In many states, a publication is available listing by city or county the industry average wages for most occupations. Before submitting the ETA-750 form, the employer should make efforts to determine the prevailing wage, either by consulting the above-mentioned publication or by asking the state labor department. The employer may want to list the lowest wage possible, although he is required by law to pay the higher of either the prevailing market wage or the actual wage paid to workers who occupy the same position. Keep in mind, however, that the Labor Certification procedure tests the market only for people meeting the minimum requirements for the job and the prevailing wage is also for the minimum requirements. There is nothing wrong with paying a higher salary to someone whose qualifications are more than the minimum.

When an ETA-750 contains a salary offer that is too low and the Labor Certification is questioned ("assessed") for that reason alone, your employer has the option of raising the salary and resubmitting an amendment to the form with the higher salary listed. Then all advertising procedures will have to be repeated, adding more time and expense to the case. You will, however, be allowed to keep your original priority date. It is easier to find out in advance the amount of the prevailing wage. Then, if the petitioning employer is not willing to offer that much, at least everyone will be saved the effort of submitting a Labor Certification application that is guaranteed to fail. (Wage surveys are not required for Schedule A applicants.)

Part A, Question 13. Part A, Question 13, asks the employer to describe the job being offered. This question should be answered in as much detail as possible. Daily duties, typical projects, supervisory responsibilities, the kinds and uses of any machinery or equipment, foreign language skills needed and so forth should all be thoroughly explained. If there are special job conditions, such as the requirement to live on the work premises or unusual physical demands, these too must be described. The employer should not fail to put down any reasonably necessary skill or activity the job requires, as long as it is a normal requirement for the occupation. The ability to reject U.S. workers will depend completely on how well the American job candidates match up to the job description in Part A, Question 13. The more detailed the job description, the more possible reasons for rejecting American candidates.

While the employer should do his best to describe the position and its demands fully, he should not invent requirements that don't exist or seem ridiculous, simply to discourage American job applicants. For example, suppose the job opening is for a bakery manager but in the job description the employer states that all applicants must have a background in nuclear science. This sort of unreasonable demand makes it clear to the state labor department reviewer that the job description is not legitimate, but deliberately made up to keep American workers from applying. When the job description lacks real-world credibility, the ETA-750 will be sent back and the employer will be asked to justify the more unusual requirements. If the state labor department reviewer cannot be convinced that the job description reflects the employer's true needs, the Labor Certification will be denied.

The employer should also guard against asking for such a variety of requirements that the job seems more appropriate for two separate workers instead of one. For example, if the job is that of bakery manager and the job description requires the applicant not only to manage the shop but to do the baking as well, the reviewer might say the business really needs two people, a baker and a store manager. Once again, this will result in the Labor Certification being denied. This approach will work only if the employer can convincingly explain that the business will be unable to function unless a single individual is hired to perform these combined duties. On the other hand, if the bakery manager is required to know accounting so he can handle the books, baking techniques so he can supervise the bakers, retailing so he can effectively promote the bake shop and sales techniques so he can deal with customers, all of these tasks can be classified as management activities. Therefore, this job description is reasonable.

Part A, Question 14. Question 14, Part A asks for the minimum experience and education the job requires. The answer to this question should describe the demands of the job, not the personal qualifications of the green card applicant. For example, you personally may have a bachelor's degree representing four years of music education or several years of work experience as an artist, but if the position you have been offered is for a live-in housekeeper, music education or experience in art usually has nothing to do with being a housekeeper and therefore should not be mentioned in the answer to this question. Remember, in Part A

it is the job offer that is being described, not your own background and qualifications.

As with salary levels, DOL also has specific guidelines on what the minimum number of years of experience and education should be for a certain kind of job. If your employer references the DOL's *Dictionary of Occupational Titles*, he or she will be able to determine the exact number of years of education and experience considered a normal minimum for the particular job you have been offered. The number of years listed for each job in the *Dictionary of Occupational Titles* controls what you may put down in the answer to Part A, Question 14. You and your employer need not concern yourselves with the *Dictionary of Occupational Titles* unless you want to verify for yourselves that DOL does have a particular number in mind as an acceptable answer to this question, and that if you exceed that number your application will be in jeopardy.

The number of years of experience and education listed in the *Dictionary of Occupational Titles* for each job is the total allowable years of experience and education combined. (If you wish to learn more about the *Dictionary of Occupational Titles*, it can be found in most U.S. public libraries or ordered from the U.S. Government Printing Office. U.S. company personnel staff or others reading this book who work with Labor Certifications on a regular basis may find it useful to familiarize themselves with the *Dictionary of Occupational Titles* and its *Specific Vocational Preparation* (SVP) classifications which dictate the number of years of background presumed necessary for each job.) The employer may divide the years up between the two in any way he sees fit, as long as he does not exceed the overall total. For example, if the *Dictionary of Occupational Titles* says there should be a minimum of two years of background for the job you have been offered, your employer has a choice of requiring two years of education, two years of experience or one of each. He may even divide it by months, requiring, say, six months of training or education and 18 months of experience.

Suppose the employer truly believes he needs a person with more total years of education and experience than the *Dictionary of Occupational Titles* indicates? Then a letter from the employer should be submitted with the ETA-750 forms giving the reason why he feels additional years of background are justified. DOL will normally respect the employer's judgment if reasonable. In Part A, Question 14, if the employer puts down a higher total number of years than the *Dictionary of Occupational Titles* allows, the requirement must be supported with an explanatory letter, or the Labor Certification will be denied. This letter does not have to be in any special form. A simple explanation in your employer's own words will do. If you receive notice that such requirement is considered restrictive, it is advised that you contact an immigration attorney or other expert to advise you, due to the complexity of these issues. (Schedule A applicants are not subject to the limitation on experience set in the *Dictionary of Occupational Titles*. Therefore, an employer of a Schedule A applicant may answer this question in any manner he wishes without being concerned that the chances for the green card application's success will be harmed.) If possible, the employer should submit as supporting documentation evidence that other employers with similar positions also require the additional years of education or experience.

When a certain number of years appears in the box marked "experience," it is understood that this means experience in the same occupation as the job being offered. If the experience is in a different but relevant field, or in the same field but at a lower level, it should go in the box marked "related occupations."

Once again, if, in Part A, Question 14, the employer asks for a background of specific education or experience, make sure you yourself can meet these requirements. In Step Two, the petition, your employer will be asked to prove that you can fulfill the job criteria established in Part A of the ETA-750. If you cannot do so, you will not get a green card.

Part A, Question 15. This question asks the employer to state any essential requirements for the job over and above years of formal education or work experience. Any special knowledge or skills detailed in Part A, Question 13, such as foreign language ability, familiarity with certain types of machinery or special physical capabilities (strength to do heavy lifting, for example) should be repeated here. When you reach Step Two, you will have to prove in some way that you can perform the skills listed in Part A, Question 15, but you will not have to show an exact number of years of education or on-the-job experience as you will for the qualifications listed in Part A, Question 14.

Part A, Question 21. Part A, Question 21 asks your employer to describe past attempts to hire U.S. workers for the position being offered to you. At this stage, it is not essential that such efforts have already been made. If the U.S. employer has not yet tried to hire a worker for the job, he should write the following statement in Part A, Question 21:

"Advertisements and job posting to begin upon receipt of job-order number."

If, however, your employer has already made some attempt to hire a U.S. worker, the nature of these efforts (newspaper ads, use of employment agencies, etc.) and the results should be described here. Of course, we assume any prior efforts to fill the job have failed, or the employer would not be trying to hire you.

Remember, if your employer has already conducted six months of recruitment efforts that are similar to those required for the Labor Certification process, he or she may be able to get an expedited "reduction in recruitment" application approved.

If you are applying under Schedule A, this question should be answered as follows:

"Occupation is listed under Schedule A Group (number). No recruitment is required."

Part B, Questions 1–14. These questions are self-explanatory.

Part B, Question 15. You are asked to list any job experience you have had in your lifetime which is relevant to the job presently being offered. All your work activities for the past three years, relevant or not, must also be listed. Give full information on both these subjects. Don't explain one but not the other. Make sure your employer does not leave any gaps in accounting for your time during the past three years. If you were unemployed for any period, write this down. If an extra sheet of paper is needed to cover all your experience, note in this question that an extra sheet is attached.

5.   Labor Certification Documents

Most of the documents your petitioning employer will submit to DOL with the Labor Certification application are the written results of the mandatory advertising procedure which are not submitted with the forms but rather after completion of recruitment efforts. Be sure to read all communications from the state labor department, taking special note of the deadlines for filing various documents. Once the job-order number is received from the state labor department, the job will remain open in the state labor department computer banks for only 30 days. Then the job order will be closed out. All documents are due in the state labor department office no more than 45 days from this closeout date.

The submission of all the documents described below normally completes the Labor Certification procedure. Once your employer has submitted them, the forms and documents are eventually sent from the state labor department office to the regional certifying office of the DOL, where a decision on the Labor Certification is made. If no qualified Americans applied for the job and the paperwork has been carefully prepared, the Labor Certification should be approved on the first try. Sometimes, papers are returned to the employer with a request for additional information or instructions to remedy a defect in the advertising. After mistakes and deficiencies have been corrected, the papers should be returned to DOL. When papers are sent back for additions or corrections, the employer is given a limited time, usually 45 days, to respond. If deadlines for returning corrected papers are not met, the entire advertising procedure will have to be repeated and you will lose your priority date. When your employer has finally gotten the paperwork the way DOL wants it, he or she will eventually receive a written notice from DOL either granting or denying the Labor Certification.

a. Written Statement of Why Other Candidates Were Unacceptable

A key document is the employer's written statement explaining why each American who applied for the job is unqualified. By far the most acceptable reason for turning down a U.S. applicant is failure to meet the requirements as stated on Form ETA-750, Part A, and in the newspaper or journal advertisement. Other reasons are also considered adequate, as long as they reflect valid business concerns. If no U.S. applicants responded to the various advertisements, the employer should supply a written statement to that effect.

b. Publication Pages Containing the Advertisement

The pages from the publications where the advertisements appeared must be torn out and submitted. If the ad ran in a newspaper for three days, three pages must be presented, one for each day, even if the exact same ad was published on all three days. Photocopies of the ads are not acceptable. Your employer must obtain a copy of the publication each

time the ad appeared and tear out the entire page, showing each date the ad appeared.

c. Job Notice

A copy of the job notice that was posted inside the employer's place of business and sent to the appropriate labor union is still another document that must be turned in. A statement from the employer giving the dates when the job notice was posted, and the results should accompany the copy of the notice itself.

d. Special Documents for Special Cases

There are certain types of jobs for which DOL expects some special documents. These documents are required in addition to the standard advertising documents already described. (Except in the case of Schedule A applications, where the special documents are submitted in place of, rather than in addition to, the standard documents for Step One. See Section F4d, below, for Schedule A documents.) Unlike the advertising documents, credentials for special cases should be submitted together with the ETA-750.

i. Documents for Restrictive Job Requirements

Any job requirements that exceed the normal minimum requirements in terms of education or experience, or that combine two or more different occupations into one, are considered to be restrictive. The employer must then convince DOL that it is a "business necessity" to have these particular requirements because the business would be substantially disrupted if the person taking the position did not meet these requirements. The best document for this purpose is a detailed letter from the employer explaining the need for the restrictive requirements, why the business is dependent on those requirements and how the business would be affected if someone not meeting those requirements were hired. Again, if you receive a notice that your requirements are unduly restrictive, you would be well advised to consult an immigration attorney who specializes in this subject in order to have the best chance of approval.

ii. Documents for Live-in Domestics

One occupation needing special documents for Labor Certification approval is that of a live-in domestic. The term "live-in domestic" covers workers engaged in performing routine domestic chores such as cooking and cleaning, as well as individuals who care for children while living in the home of the employer.

If you have been offered a job as a live-in, you must produce documents proving that you already have at least one full year of paid domestic experience. Up to nine months of this experience may come from working for the petitioning employer, but at least three months must come from another employer. Strangely, however, if you have been working in the U.S. as a live-in domestic for someone other than the present petitioner, all of that experience can be counted toward your one-year total, even if you were working illegally at the time. To meet the one-year experience requirement, you need not have worked as a live-in for one consecutive year. The work periods may be at various times as long as they all add up to at least 12 months. To document your 12 months of live-in job experience, you will need letters signed by your previous employers stating that you have worked for them as a live-in and for how long. If possible, the letters should be notarized.

To get a green card as a live-in domestic, DOL must be convinced that live-in services are a business necessity of your petitioning employer. Therefore, the employer must provide DOL with a signed statement explaining why his or her household cannot function without a live-in. To pass the DOL test, the household must usually contain small children or invalids, and the able-bodied adults must be subject to erratic work schedules where they may be called away at any time, leaving the dependents unattended. A family where there are small children and both parents are physicians is a good example of a household that would qualify. The fact that your prospective employer simply prefers to have live-in help is not sufficient. DOL must believe there is an actual need and that no alternative arrangement will meet that need. Finally, be aware that the waiting period for third preference unskilled workers is long. If you have fallen out of status or are subject to any of the many bars to admissibility or adjustment of status, you may be wasting your time by applying for a labor certification. Read Chapter 25 carefully before starting to be sure you qualify for permanent residence.

iii. Documents Proving a Foreign Language Requirement

According to DOL, foreign language capability is not a valid requirement for most jobs, except perhaps the occupations of foreign language teacher or translator. By foreign language capability we mean the ability to speak English plus one other language. Some Labor Certification job descriptions contain unnecessary foreign language requirements because petitioning employers know it is a good way to decrease the chances that qualified Americans will apply for the job.

If your employer wants a foreign language capability in his job description, he must prove his need is real by preparing and submitting a signed statement explaining the business reasons for the foreign language requirement. The statement does not have to be in any particular form but it should answer obvious questions the language requirement might raise. What is it about the employer's business that makes knowledge of a foreign language necessary? Why does this particular position require knowledge of a foreign language if someone else in the company already speaks that language? Why couldn't the company simply hire a translator as a separate employee or use a translator on a part-time basis when the need arises? The statement prepared by the petitioning employer should provide good answers to questions like these. The employer must show that the need for the employee to speak a foreign language is very great and that no alternative arrangement will be an adequate substitute.

A good example of how to approach this problem can be seen in the case of an employer who owns a restaurant and is trying to justify a foreign language requirement for a waiter. Here, the employer can explain in his statement that a large percentage of the restaurant's customers speak the particular foreign language in question and expect to be addressed in that language when they come in to eat. If the restaurant's clientele demands it, it is reasonable that all employees of this restaurant who have contact with the public be able to speak the language of the customers.

DOL doesn't like foreign language requirements because it is well aware that most people who apply for green cards can speak a language other than English. DOL regards this as a poor excuse to keep an American worker from taking a job. Therefore, it is usually best not to include a language requirement, especially if the Labor Certification is likely to be approved anyway. If, however, the occupation being certified is relatively unskilled, as is the case with the job of a waiter, a language requirement supported by strong documents showing a real business need (and prior business transactions) may mean the difference between success and failure of the Labor Certification.

iv. Documents for Physicians

If you are a physician, your U.S. employer must show documents to DOL proving that you have passed Parts I and II of the National Board of Medical Examiners examination, commonly known in immigration circles as the visa qualifying examination or VQE. The VQE test is administered by the Educational Commission for Foreign Medical Graduates and all foreign physicians are required to pass. All foreign graduates of approved medical schools in the U.S. or Canada are exempt from taking the exam, even if they are not presently licensed in the U.S. However, in the case of most foreign physicians, successfully passing a standardized exam such as FLEX (used for licensing by many U.S. states), or other state licensing exams, is not sufficient. Passing the VQE is also necessary.

VQE INFORMATION

You can obtain information on taking the VQE exam by contacting:

Educational Commission for Foreign Medical Graduates
3624 Market Street
Philadelphia, PA 19104-2685
Telephone: 215-386-5900
Fax: 215-387-9963
Website: http://www.ecfmg.org
The exam is given twice a year, in July and January. The application deadline is 13 weeks prior to each exam date. Most graduate residency programs in the U.S. also require foreign medical graduates to have passed this exam for acceptance in the program.

v. Documents for College and University Teachers

To meet normal standards for Labor Certification approval, it must be shown that are no available American workers who meet the minimum requirements for the job that has been offered to the green card applicant. In other words, being the most qualified candidate isn't enough. You must be the only qualified candidate. For college and university teachers the test is different. Here, you can get Labor Certification if you are the most qualified applicant. This is the only occupation where a Labor Certification can be approved even though there are suitable American workers available in the field.

The employer may also be exempted from the standard Labor Certification advertising procedures, provided a competitive recruitment process was used for selecting the foreign worker, and it was done within 18 months of filing the Labor Certification application. Even if new advertising is required, instead of having to show why each of the other applicants is unqualified, the employer will simply prepare a written statement explaining why you are the best of the choices available. This statement does not have to be in any particular form, but must simply state why you are superior to any of the other candidates. An additional helpful document in this job category, if available, is a copy of the minutes of faculty search committee meetings or board of directors meetings, where discussions were held on the merits of the various job candidates. Those minutes should, of course, reflect the reasons why you are considered to be the best choice.

Because of the different standard, Labor Certifications for college and university teachers are easier to obtain than for members of any other occupation.

6. Labor Certification Appeals

If DOL thinks the Labor Certification application is unsatisfactory, it will issue a form called Notice of Findings. This notice will state that DOL intends to deny the application and will give the reasons why DOL has reached this decision. Labor Certification applications cannot actually be denied without first giving the employer an opportunity to present new evidence or answer the criticisms contained in the notice. The employer will be given 35 days to respond. If the employer does not answer, when the deadline passes the Notice of Findings automatically becomes a denial of the Labor Certification. Labor Certifications are frequently approved in spite of the issuance of a Notice of Findings. If a Notice of Findings is issued in your case, do not give up.

If the petitioning employer fails to respond in time to the Notice of Findings, he or she loses all other rights of appeal as well. Under these circumstances, if the employer still wishes to pursue a Labor Certification on your behalf, the only alternative is to wait at least six months and then file again, starting the procedure from the beginning.

If the employer does respond on time but the case is denied anyway, the employee will receive a written decision and an explanation of what further rights of appeal are available. The employer will then have 35 days to file what is known as a Notice of Appeal. This is filed with DOL and represents still another effort to make DOL change its mind about your case. At this stage, the decision will be made by three panel members from a national appeals board known as the Board of Alien Labor Certification Appeals (BALCA), which sits in Washington, D.C. If the employer loses the appeal to BALCA, he or she can take the case to U.S. district court for review.

A full explanation of the appeals process itself is beyond the scope of this book. Most appeals are unsuccessful. If the case has reached this point and your employer wishes to pursue an appeal, it is highly advisable to employ an immigration attorney. However, sometimes it is faster and cheaper to start over and try to avoid making the same mistakes twice. If you prefer simply to file a new Labor Certification application and start over, you must wait six months from the date of the denial before filing again, but appeals are likely to take much longer than that.

F. Step Two: The Petition

Once your employer has obtained an approved Labor Certification on your behalf, or if you are not required to have a Labor Certification because you are in the priority worker category or practice a Schedule A occupation, it is time to file the petition.

1. General Procedures

Your employer mails the petition, consisting of forms and documents, to the INS regional service center in the U.S. having jurisdiction over your employer's place of business. INS regional service centers are not the same as INS local offices. There are four INS regional service centers spread across the U.S.

When your employer files at a regional service center, within a week or so after mailing the petition, he or she should receive a written confirmation that the papers are being processed, together with a receipt for the fees. This notice will also give your immigration case file number and tell approximately when to expect a decision. If INS wants further information before acting on your case, it will send you a request for evidence ("RFE") form I-797. The I-797 tells your employer what corrections, additional pieces of information or additional documents are expected. Your employer should make the corrections or supply the extra data and mail them back to the INS regional service center with the request form on top.

The filing fee for each petition is currently $75. Checks or money orders are accepted. Regional service centers will not accept cash. When filing by mail, we recommend sending the papers by certified mail, return receipt requested, and keeping a complete copy of everything sent for your records. Appendix II contains complete lists of all INS regional service centers with their addresses, telephone and fax numbers.

The filing procedure is the same for all green card through employment petitions, but your employer must indicate which employment preference and subcategory is being requested. If you are turned down for one category, the petition will not automatically be considered for a lower category. However, your employer may always submit a new petition under a different employment preference or subcategory. For example, if you have a job offer that might fall under the skilled worker subcategory of the employment third preference, but you are not sure, consider filing two petitions, one as a skilled worker and another as an unskilled worker. This will save some time if the petition under the higher level subcategory is turned down.

It generally takes one to three months to get a decision on the petition. Once your petition is approved, a Notice of Action, Form I-797, will be sent to your employer, indicating the approval. If you plan to execute Step Three at a U.S. consulate abroad, INS will forward the file to the National Visa Center (NVC) located in Portsmouth, New Hampshire. NVC will then send a packet of forms and instructions to you so that you may proceed with Step Three, described later in this chapter.

2. Procedures for Schedule A and Priority Workers

If you qualify as a priority worker or Schedule A applicant, your employer must prove to INS that you do in fact qualify as a priority worker or for Schedule A. To do this, Step One forms and documents must be filed together with the Step Two forms and documents. The employer should not, however, follow the cumbersome Step One procedures. Only the paperwork is required. All papers are filed at the INS regional service center having jurisdiction over your employer's place of business. Although your employer must still fill out the same Step One form, the ETA-750, there will be an entirely different set of documents. A description of these documents is in Section 4d, below. When completing Form ETA-750, your employer may disregard any of the directions concerning how to meet and deal with certain standards set by DOL for the minimum number of years of job experience and the minimum salary. Instead, the employer may set his or her own standards, provided any minimum requirements for the priority worker or Schedule A categories are not listed. This is explained in more detail in the instructions on how to fill out Form ETA-750.

3. Petition Forms

Copies of all forms can be found in Appendix III.

Form I-140

The basic form for Step Two, the petition, is Form I-140. It is used for all green card through employment petitions. The form has one section asking for information about your petitioning employer and another section asking for information about you. If a particular question does not apply, it should be answered "None" or "N/A."

It is absolutely essential to answer each question truthfully, even if it means disclosing that you are in the U.S. illegally. Failure to reveal requested information may result in your being permanently barred from the U.S. (See Chapter 25.)

Part 1. Part 1 asks for basic information about the employer and is self-explanatory.

Part 2. Part 2 asks you to check the box indicating the classification you are seeking. Categories A, B and C are priority worker categories. Category D is for the employment based second preference. Category E is for skilled or professional workers applying under the employment third preference. Category F is for a classification that no longer exists. Category G is for unskilled workers applying under the employment third preference.

Part 3. Part 3 asks questions about you. Your current immigration status must be disclosed, even if you are in the U.S. illegally. "A" numbers are usually issued only to people who previously held green cards or have made previous green card applications. If any of the boxes do not apply to you, answer "N/A."

In listing your address, put down the address where you really live, even if it means revealing that you are in the U.S. without status. DOL and INS offices during Steps One and Two and INS offices or consulates during Step Three will send correspondence to the address you put down in Part 3, so be sure it is correct.

Part 4. Part 4 asks at which consulate you intend to apply for your green card and also requests your last foreign address, if you are currently living in the U.S. In listing a consulate, keep in mind that U.S. consulates in your last country of residence are the only ones legally required to accept your application. If there is an overwhelming need to file elsewhere, you can approach a consulate in some other country and ask if it will process your application there. It is

under no obligation to grant your request and is likely to turn you down, but there is no harm in asking. Unless you have gotten permission in advance, your employer should not write down the name of any consulate other than the one in your last country of residence.

If you are eligible to process Step Three in the U.S. and you wish to do so, we suggest writing in, under Part 4 at the bottom of the first page, the following, "Adjustment of Status Intended."

Part 5. Part 5 asks for additional information about the employer, including type of business, date established, gross and net annual income and number of employees. It also asks for a nontechnical description of the job, which should match the description put on Part A of the Form ETA-750 Labor Certification application.

In priority worker petitions for persons of extraordinary ability, no offer of employment is required. If that is the case, under type of petitioner the box "Self" should be marked. The remaining questions about the employer may be answered "N/A."

Parts 6. Part 6 asks for basic information about your proposed employment and is self-explanatory.

Parts 7–9. These parts request information on accompanying family members, and require signatures. They are self-explanatory.

Form ETA-750

If you are applying under Schedule A, you must still fill out this form and submit it in duplicate as part of Step Two. See Section E4, above.

4. Petition Documents

Documents filed with the petition are intended to prove three things:

- you have an approved Labor Certification, are a priority worker or qualify under Schedule A
- you are qualified for the job that you have been offered, and
- your petitioning employer has sufficient income to pay you the wage stated on the Labor Certification or petition.

a. Approved Labor Certification

The first and most important document your employer must submit with the petition forms is the approved Labor Certification. This is actually the ETA-750, Part A, which has been returned to your employer with a red and blue approval stamp. The original, approved form must be submitted. A copy is not acceptable. If you are applying as a priority worker or under Schedule A, instead of with an approved Labor Certification, the documents you will need are listed in Section 4d, below.

b.   Documents Proving Your Job Qualifications

Documents to prove your own qualifications for the job also go with the petition. There must be evidence that you have the minimum education and experience called for in the job description on Form ETA-750. If special requirements were written in Part A, Question 15 of the form, there must be proof that you have those skills as well.

Diplomas and transcripts from schools you attended must be shown to verify your education. INS insists on both a diploma and a transcript from each school where you graduated. If you attended a school but did not graduate, the transcript is required. If you were educated outside of the U.S., INS may request a credential evaluation from an approved evaluation service as explained in Section B2, above. Remember that an unfavorable evaluation should not be sent in unless requested. A bad evaluation should also give you reason to consider applying under a lesser preference or subcategory.

Evidence of your job experience should include letters or notarized affidavits from previous employers. These do not have to be in any special form but simply in your former employer's own words. The letters or affidavits should clearly indicate what your position was with the company, your specific job duties and the length of time you were employed. If letters from previous employers are unavailable, you may be able to prove your work experience with your personal tax returns or by affidavits from former co-workers. Proof of special knowledge or skills can be supplied through notarized affidavits, either from you or someone else who can swear you have the special ability (such as skill to use a particular machine or speak a foreign language) required. These, too, need not be in any special form.

c.   Salary Level Documents

Your employer must also supply documents to prove the business can afford to pay you. Many petitions filed by smaller businesses are turned down because the employer cannot show sufficient income to pay the required salary. To prove the ability to pay, your employer should present the company's U.S. tax returns for the past two years or, if tax returns are unavailable, bank statements showing capital in the company and balance sheets plus profit and loss statements. If your employer cannot produce tax returns, he should be prepared to explain why not. Usually the only excuse INS will accept is that the company is too new to have filed them.

Publicly held companies do not have to produce tax returns. For them, the annual reports of the corporation for the past two years are the accepted documents for proving ability to pay wages. As a general rule, the larger the company, the less evidence INS demands of its ability to pay additional salaries. When a company is nationally known, INS may require no proof at all.

d.   Special Documents for Priority Workers and Schedule A Occupations

For priority workers and Schedule A occupations, all Step One forms and documents are submitted directly to INS at the same time as the forms and documents for Step Two, the petition. The documents required depend upon the priority worker subcategory or Schedule A group under which you are applying.

i.   Persons of Extraordinary Ability

This category is reserved for only the most accomplished persons in the arts, sciences, education, business or athletics. Extensive documentation must include either evidence that you have received a major, internationally recognized award or achievement, or, alternatively, at least three of the following types of proof:

- Documentation of the receipt of several lesser nationally or internationally recognized prizes or awards for excellence. (If the award is major, as described above, only one is necessary.)
- Documentation of membership in associations which require outstanding achievements of their members.
- Published material about you in professional or major trade publications or other major media outlets relating to your work.
- Evidence of your participation as a judge of the work of others in your field.
- Evidence of your original scientific, scholarly, artistic, athletic or business-related contributions of major significance.
- Evidence of your authorship of scholarly articles in professional or major trade publications or other major media outlets.
- Evidence of the display of your work at artistic exhibitions.
- Evidence that you have performed in a leading or critical role for distinguished organizations.
- Evidence that you have commanded a high salary (at least $100,000 per year).

- Evidence that you have achieved commercial successes in the performing arts as shown by box office receipts or sales of records, cassettes, compact disks or videos.

ii. Outstanding Professors and Researchers

You must produce evidence that you have at least three years of teaching or research experience. This is best shown by letters from former employers. If you are coming to the U.S. as a university professor, the position must be a tenured or tenure-track position. A letter from the employing university should clearly state this. If the employer is a private industry, it must submit evidence that it has a history of significant achievements in research and employs at least three other full-time research workers.

Additional documentation must include at least two of the following:

- Evidence that you have received major prizes or awards for outstanding achievement in your academic field.
- Evidence of your membership in associations in your academic field which require outstanding achievements for membership.
- Published material in professional publications written by others about your work. Mere citations to your work in bibliographies are not sufficient.
- Evidence of your participation as the judge of the work of others.
- Evidence of your original scientific or scholarly research contributions to the academic field.
- Evidence of your authorship of scholarly books or articles in scholarly journals having international circulation.

iii. Multinational Executives and Managers

An applicant claiming priority worker status as a multinational executive or manager must document his eligibility in exactly the same way as he would do for Step One, the petition, of an L-1 visa application. Due to the length of that material, we will not repeat the full description of the documents here. Instead, we refer you to Chapter 19. Follow the instructions just as they are written there. We have, however, included a complete review of all the necessary forms and documents for this subcategory of priority workers in the summary checklist of forms and documents contained at the end of this chapter.

There are three categories of L-1 visa holders: managers, executives and those with specialized knowledge. The only L-1 visa holders who qualify as priority workers are managers and executives. *If you qualify for an L-1 visa only under the specialized knowledge category, you must go through standard Labor Certification procedures to get a green card through employment, unless you qualify as an executive or manager.*

iv. Physical Therapists

To qualify as a physical therapist, you must either be licensed in the U.S. state where you will work or be qualified to take the state licensing exam. If you are already licensed in some U.S. state, a copy of your license should be submitted. If you are not licensed, a letter from the state physical therapy licensing agency in the state where you will work must be submitted, stating that you meet all of the qualifications of that state to take the licensing exam.

v. Registered Nurses

To receive a green card as a registered nurse, you must submit a copy of your full and unrestricted nursing license issued by the U.S. state where you plan to work. A license from any other U.S. state is not sufficient. If you are not yet licensed, you must provide evidence that you have passed the Commission on Graduates of Foreign Nursing Schools (CGFNS) exam. You can get information on how to take this exam from:

CGFNS
3600 Market Street, Suite 400
Philadelphia, PA 19104
Telephone: 215-349-8767

vi. Persons of Exceptional Ability in the Sciences or Arts

To successfully document your qualifications as a person of exceptional ability in the arts or sciences, the law requires your employer to provide evidence from at least three of the following categories of documents:

- Evidence that you have an academic degree relating to your area of exceptional ability.
- Evidence that you have had at least ten years of full-time experience in the field.
- A license to practice your profession.
- Evidence that you have at some time commanded a high salary (at least $75,000 per year).
- Evidence of your membership in professional associations.
- Evidence of recognition for achievements and significant contributions to your industry or field.

If you are applying for a waiver of the job offer requirement and Labor Certification, you must also submit as a document Form ETA-750, Part B only, and a written statement explaining why an exemption from the job requirement is in the U.S. national interest.

vii. Religious Occupations

Evidence is needed to show that you are recognized by your religion as qualified for the particular occupation in which you engage. To prove this, you should present your official certificates or licenses, if any. You should also obtain a letter from the governing body of your religion certifying the nature of your occupation and how long you have worked in that capacity. You must have been engaged in your occupation for at least two years before you begin the paperwork for a green card.

INS INVESTIGATION OF QUALIFICATIONS

Sometimes in Step Two, INS will go beyond the documents your employer submits and attempt to verify, through an investigation of its own, that you've had the work experience you claimed to have in Part B of the ETA-750 form. This is particularly true with live-in housekeepers and specialty chefs such as Chinese cooks. If such an investigation is undertaken, you and your employer won't be told about it, but it could cause long delays in your case. When you find it is taking an unusually long time to get an approval on the petition, an investigation in progress could be the reason. Waits in excess of a year are typical under these circumstances.

If INS, through its own investigation, comes up with evidence showing you are not really qualified for the job, it must notify your employer of its intent to deny the petition and advise him of the nature of the evidence on which it is basing the denial. Your employer will then have ten days to argue against these findings.

---

5. Petition Interviews

Before approving a petition, INS occasionally requests an interview with the petitioning employer. This is fairly unusual. If the employer is a new company or an individual rather than a company (as is normally the case with employers of live-in housekeepers), an interview may be held concerning the employer's ability to pay wages. Interviews can best be avoided by providing good documentation from the beginning on both your job qualifications and the employer's ability to pay your salary.

6. Petition Appeals

When your job qualifications or the ability of your employer to pay your salary have been poorly documented, the petition will probably be denied. Your employer will then receive written notice of INS's unfavorable decision, a written statement of the reasons for the negative outcome and an explanation of how to make a formal appeal.

The best way to handle an appeal is to try avoiding it altogether. Filing an appeal means making an argument to INS that its reasoning was wrong. If your employer thinks he can eliminate the reason why the petition failed by improving the paperwork, it makes sense to disregard the appeals process and simply file a new petition, being careful to see that it is better prepared than the first.

If the petition was denied because your U.S. employer left out necessary documents that have since been located, the new documents should be sent, together with a written request that the case be reopened, to the same INS office that issued the denial. This is technically called a *Motion to Reopen*. There is a $110 fee for filing this motion. Appeals often take a long time. A Motion to Reopen can be concluded faster than an appeal.

If your U.S. employer does choose to file an appeal, it must be done within 30 days of the date on the Notice of Denial. The appeal should be filed at the same INS service center with which your employer has been dealing. There is a $110 filing fee. INS will then forward the papers for consideration to the Administrative Appeals Unit of the central INS office in Washington, D.C. In six months or more, your employer will get back a decision by mail. Few appeals are successful.

When an appeal to INS has been denied, the next step is to make an appeal through the U.S. judicial system. Your employer may not file an action in court without first going through the appeals process available from INS. If your case has reached this stage and you are living illegally in the U.S., we strongly recommend seeking representation from a qualified immigration attorney, as you are now in danger of being deported.

G. Step Three: The Application (Consular Filing)

Anyone with an approved petition and a current priority date can apply for a green card at a U.S. consulate in his or her home country or last country of residence. You must be physically present in order to apply there. Even if you have been or are now working and living illegally in the U.S., you can still get a green card from a U.S. consulate if you otherwise qualify.

CITIZENS OF COUNTRIES WITHOUT U.S. EMBASSIES

Citizens of countries not having formal diplomatic relations with the U.S. are faced with the problem of where to apply for immigrant visas. At present, the U.S. maintains no diplomatic relations with, and therefore makes no visa services available in, Afghanistan, Bosnia, Iran, Iraq, Lebanon, Libya and Somalia.

Persons from these countries who are still residing in their home countries will apply at a designated foreign consulate. Persons who are outside of their home country in a third country which conducts visa processing will do visa processing in that country as if they were residents of the third country.

1. Benefits and Drawbacks of Consular Filing

Anyone with an approved petition and a current priority date can apply for a green card at the appropriate consulate. (Be sure that none of the bars to immigrant visas or grounds of inadmissibility apply to you before departing the U.S. to do consular processing. (See Chapter 25 on inadmissibility.) That is not the case with U.S. applications since you must be physically inside the U.S. to apply there. If you entered the U.S. legally and have fallen out of status, you may be ineligible to file in the U.S. unless you had a certain visa petition or labor certification on file by January 14, 1998. If you elect to file at a consulate, be sure to understand the bars to admission discussed in Chapter 25 before proceeding.

A further plus to consular filing is that some consulate offices may work more quickly to issue immigrant visas than do some INS offices. Your waiting time for the paperwork to be finished may be months shorter at a U.S. consulate abroad than at U.S. INS offices. Please remember, however, that the difference in waiting time between INS and consulate offices applies only to processing paperwork. Quotas move at the same rate of speed no matter where your application is filed.

One of two drawbacks to consular filing is the travel expense and inconvenience you will experience in returning to your home country if you are already in the U.S. The other problem is that should your consular application fail, not only will you be outside the U.S. but you will also have fewer ways to appeal than a U.S. filing would offer.

2. Application Forms: Consular Filing

When you file at a U.S. consulate abroad, the consulate officials will provide you with certain optional forms, designated by an "OF" preceeding a number. Instructions for completing optional forms and what to do with them once they are filled out will come with the forms. We do not include copies of these forms in Appendix III. Copies of all non "OF" forms are in Appendix III.

Form I-134

It is necessary to convince the consulate that once you receive a green card you are not likely to go on public welfare. Since you have a job offer, that proves you have a way to support yourself and an I-134 need not be filed for you, unless a relative owns 5% or more of the business which is petitioning for you. (In that case, you would need to file Form I-864. A copy is in Appendix III and instructions for completing it are in Chapter 7.) You should still, however, fill out Form I-134, the Affidavit of Support, for any accompanying relatives. Because the consulate knows you will have an income, you must sign the I-134 forms and take financial responsibility for each of them.

If you are in the subcategory of priority workers that does not require you to have a specific job offer in order to get a green card, you have already submitted the documents in Step Two, showing your intent to continue working. These documents are also a sufficient substitute for Form I-134.

Form I-134, the Affidavit of Support, is your guarantee that you will take care of your accompanying relatives. In signing the Affidavit of Support, you are not actually promising to support your accompanying relatives. What you do promise is to reimburse the U.S. government for the sum total of any government support payments they might receive should they go on welfare. The Affidavit of Support binds you to this obligation for three years. Your responsibility to the government then comes to an end.

3. Application Documents: Consular Filing

The most important document in your application is the Notice of Action showing approval of your petition. It is sent directly from the INS office in the U.S. to the consulate you named on Form I-130 in Step Two. This is the only document you will not have to submit yourself. Do not mail in your other documents. Instead, bring them to your interview.

You must resubmit to the consulate all the documents first filed in Step Two. Additionally, you must have your long form birth certificate and birth certificates of any unmarried minor children who are not immigrating with you.

It is also necessary to have in your possession a valid passport from your home country. The expiration date on the passport must leave enough time for the passport to remain valid at least six months beyond the date of your final application interview.

Unlike applications made in the U.S., you personally must collect police clearance certificates from each country you have lived in for one year or more since your 16th birthday. Additionally, you must have a police certificate from your home country or country of last residence, if you lived there for at least six months since the age of 16. You do not need to obtain police certificates from the U.S. Like all other documents, you should be prepared to present the necessary police clearance certificates at your interview. If you go to your interview without the required certificates, you will be refused a green card and told to return after you get them.

OBTAINING POLICE CERTIFICATES

You should contact the local police department in your home country for instructions on how to get police certificates. To obtain police certificates from nations other than your home country, it is best to contact the nearest consulate representing that country for instructions. Some nations refuse to supply police certificates, or their certificates are not considered reliable, and so you will not be required to obtain them from those locations. At this writing, police certificates are not required from the following countries:

Afghanistan	Haiti	Saudi Arabia
Albania	Honduras	Sierra Leone
Angola	India	Somalia
Bangladesh	Indonesia	Sri Lanka
Brunei	Iran	Sudan
Bulgaria	Iraq	Syria
Cambodia	Jordan	Tanzania
Chad	Laos	Thailand
Colombia	Liberia	Turkey
Costa Rica	Libya	United Arab
Cuba	Malaysia	Emirates
Dominican Republic	Mexico	United Kingdom
El Salvador	Mongolia	United States
Equatorial Guinea	Mozambique	Venezuela
Ghana	Nepal	Vietnam
Guatemala	Pakistan	

For applicants who once lived in Japan but do not reside there at the time their green card applications are filed, the Department of State recognizes that police certificates are available from Japan only as far back as five years from the date of the green card application.

Other countries, including the Netherlands, North Korea, South Africa and South Korea, will send certificates directly to U.S. consulates but not to you personally. Before they send the certificates out, however, you must request that it be done. Usually this requires filing some type of request form, together with a set of your fingerprints.

You and each accompanying relative must bring to the interview three photographs taken in compliance with the instruction sheet found in Appendix III. Additional photo instructions are provided in Packet 4. Often Packet 4 will also contain a list of local photographers who take this type of picture.

A few consulates require you to submit fingerprints, though most do not. Consulates wanting fingerprints will send you blank fingerprint cards with instructions.

4. Application Interviews: Consular Filing

Consulates hold interviews on all green card applications. A written notice of your interview appointment is included when you receive Packet 4. Immediately before the interview, you and your accompanying relatives will be required to have medical examinations. Some consulates conduct the medical exams up to several days before the interview. Others, including London, schedule the medical exam and the interview on the same day. You will be told where to go and what to do in your appointment letter.

The medical examinations are conducted by private doctors and you are required to pay the doctor a fee. The fees vary from as little as $50 to more than $100 per exam, depending on the country. The amount of the medical exam fee will be stated in your appointment letter. The exam itself involves the taking of a medical history, blood test and chest X ray, and vaccinations, if required. Pregnant women who do not want to be X-rayed may so advise the consulate and their appointments will be postponed until after the pregnancy. The requirement to have an X ray taken cannot be waived. The vaccination requirement may be waived for religious, moral or medical reasons.

The main purpose of the medical exam is to verify that you are not medically inadmissible. The primary medical grounds of inadmissibility are tuberculosis and HIV (AIDS). Some medical grounds of inadmissibility usually can be overcome with treatment or by applying for a waiver. See Chapter 25, *Inadmissibility,* for more details. If you need a medical waiver, you will be given complete instructions by the consulate at the time of your interview.

After the medical exam, you and your accompanying relatives will report to the consulate for the interview. At that time, you must pay two more fees: $170 per person when your papers are submitted, and an additional $30 per person at the end of the interview when your applications are approved. Some consulates accept payment only by certified check, money order or traveler's check. Others accept cash. You will be told the proper method of payment in Packet 4.

Bring with you to the interview the completed forms, photographs, your passports and all of the required documents discussed here. The interview process involves verification of your application's accuracy and an inspection of your documents. If all is in order, you will be asked to return later in the day when you will be issued an immigrant visa. You are not yet a permanent resident.

The immigrant visa allows you to request entry to the U.S. You acquire the full status of green card holder at the moment of being inspected and admitted into the U.S. with your immigrant visa. At that time, your passport is stamped and you are immediately authorized to work. If you are bringing any accompanying relatives, they must enter at either the same time or after you do in order to become permanent residents. Permanent green cards for you and your accompanying relatives are then ordered. They will come to you by mail several months later.

5. Application Appeals: Consular Filing

When a consulate denies a green card application, there is no formal appeal available, although you are free to reapply as often as you like. When your green card is refused, you will be told the reasons why. The most common reason for denial is failure to supply all the required documents. Sometimes presenting more evidence on an unclear fact can bring about a better result. If the denial was caused by a lack of evidence, this will be explained in a written notice sent to you by mail.

Another common reason for denial of a green card is that the consular officer believes you are inadmissible. If you are found to be inadmissible, you will be given an opportunity to apply for a Waiver of Inadmissibility, if one is available. See Chapter 25 for directions on how to apply.

When all these possibilities are exhausted, if the consulate still refuses you a green card, your opportunities for further appeals are severely limited. Historically, the courts have held that there is no right to judicial review and there is no formal appeal procedure through any U.S. government agency. The State Department in Washington, D.C. does offer an informal review procedure through the mail. This agency will look at the factual elements of your case and decide whether or not the consulate made a correct decision. Even if the State Department rules in your favor, the decision is only advisory and the consulate is free to ignore the State Department, letting its own decision stand. At present, there does appear to be a trend developing where courts in the U.S. are more frequently accepting jurisdiction over consular decisions, so a court appeal may be a possibility to consider. The jurisdiction of U.S. courts to review consular decisions, is however, still an unsettled legal issue.

Your denial may be based on a question of law rather than fact. The State Department offers the same informal review for legal questions with the difference that any decision it makes is binding on the consulate. Appeals of this kind are very technical and should be handled by a competent immigration attorney. Even with representation by an attorney, most such appeals fail.

Overall, the best way to handle an application that has been turned down is simply to wait awhile, reapply on a different basis, and hope for better luck next time. The fact that you have been turned down once does not stop you from applying again.

H. Step Three: The Application (U.S. Filing)

If you are physically present and presently in legal status in the U.S., you may apply for a green card without leaving the country on the following conditions:
- you have an approved Labor Certification or are exempt from Labor Certification
- you have already received an approved petition
- a green card number is currently available to you because your waiting period under the quota is up, and
- you are admissible and none of the bars to adjustment apply to you.

Unless you can meet these terms, you may not be eligible to file an application (Step Three) for a green card in the U.S.

1. Benefits and Drawbacks of U.S. Filing

The obvious benefit to applying for a green card in the U.S. is that if you are already in the country, you avoid the expense and inconvenience of overseas travel. Moreover, it is a rule of immigration that once you file Step Three, you must remain wherever you have filed. When you file in the U.S., should problems arise in your case, you will at least be able to wait for a decision in America, a circumstance most green card applicants prefer.

Another important benefit of U.S. filing is that you may receive permission to work while you wait for the results of your case. To obtain this benefit, you must make a separate application, in person, at the INS local office where your Step Three application has been filed. Most INS offices will give you a separate appointment, several weeks later, to come in and have a work permit issued. If you do not need to work right away, but can wait until after getting your green card, you do not need to file this separate application.

If your application for a green card is turned down, you have greater rights of appeal inside the U.S. than you do at a U.S. consulate. INS offices have different procedures from consular offices because they are controlled by a different branch of the U.S. government.

There are some disadvantages to applying in the U.S. It may take much longer to get results. Processing times at several INS offices approach as long as one year, even on cases where quotas are current. While your case is pending at an INS office, you may not leave the U.S. without getting special permission. If you do leave without INS's permission, even for a genuine emergency, this will be regarded as withdrawal of your application and you will have to start your application over again when you return.

PROCEDURES FOR ADVANCED WORK AUTHORIZATION

If you want to work before your application for a green card is approved, you must file a separate application for employment authorization. This can be done by completing Form I-765 and filing it with the same service center where you filed the Step Three papers. Together with Form I-765, you must submit your I-94 card and pay a filing fee of $100. It is very important to keep the fee receipt INS gives you so you can prove that the I-765 was filed. Normally, you will want to file the application for employment authorization at the same time as your Step Two application papers.

Legally, INS does not have to make a decision on your employment authorization application for up to 90 days. If for some reason you are not given a decision within 90 days, you will, at your request, be granted an interim employment authorization which will last 240 days. To receive an interim card, file a request for interim work authorization at the INS service center.

If 240 days pass and you still have not received a final decision on the I-765, you must stop working. Interim work authorization cards cannot be renewed. However, if you reach this point, you have the option to file a new I-765 application and, if you do not get a decision on the new application within 90 days, you will then be entitled to another interim work authorization card.

2. Application General Procedures: U.S. Filing

You may not begin Step Three until you have an approved Labor Certification, if one is required, and an approved visa petition. The application, consisting of both forms and documents, is submitted by mail to the INS service center nearest the place you are living. Appendix II contains a complete list of all INS service centers and their addresses. All applications are filed only by mail to the regional service centers.

For U.S. filings, the basic form used in Step Three, the application, is INS Form I-485, application for Permanent Residence. Form I-485 is filed to adjust your status in the U.S. "Adjusting status" is a technical term used only in U.S. filings. It simply means that you are presently in the U.S. and are in the process of acquiring a green card.

The filing fee for each application is $220 for applicants age 14 and over, and $160 for applicants under age 14. A separate application must be filed for you and each accompanying relative. In addition, if you are in the U.S. illegally, you may still be able to apply for your green card by paying a $1,000 penalty, but only if your visa petition or labor certificate was filed by January 14, 1998. Checks and money orders are accepted. It is not advisable to send cash through the mail. You should send your papers by certified mail, return receipt requested. Keep a complete copy of everything you send in.

Once your application has been filed, you should not leave the U.S. for any reason before you have applied for and received advance permission to reenter the U.S. (advance parole). Any absence without this permission will be viewed as a termination of your application for a green card. If you want to leave the U.S., you should file Form I-131 at the service center together with three passport-type photographs and a short explanation for why you want to leave—you will need a bona fide personal or business reason. There is a $95 filing fee. If approved, you will be allowed to leave the U.S. and return again with no break in the processing of your application. However, if you were out of status for six or more months after April 1, 1997, you should not depart the U.S. even on the basis of an advance parole, as this may subject you to the three- or ten-year bars to permanent residence.

Generally, after filing your application, you will receive a receipt which estimates the processing time for your application. You should receive a notice of your approval in two–three months, unless INS requires additional evidence or information, in which case they will send you a Request for Evidence (I-797) requesting further documentation or information.

INS has the discretion to waive a personal interview in applications for green cards through employment, and in practice they do so unless there is a problem or issue in your case. Policies differ among the INS service centers. If an interview is not required, you will receive an approval letter in the mail, usually about four to eight months after the application is filed. If an interview is required and if everything is in order, your application will be approved at the conclusion of the interview. (The interview, if required, would be held at a local INS office near you.) Your passport will be stamped to show that you have been admitted to the U.S. as a permanent resident, and your permanent green card will be ordered. The green card will come to you in the mail about two months after the interview or after receiving notice of approval if no interview was required. If the interview is not required, your approval notice will instruct you where to go to a local INS office for your green card or "ADIT" processing.

3. Application Forms: U.S. Filing

Copies of all forms can be found in Appendix III.

Form I-485

While most of the form is self-explanatory, a few items typically raise concerns. If a particular question does not apply to you, answer it with "None" or "N/A." Some questions on this form require explanation.

Part 1. Part 1 asks for general information about when and where you were born, your present address and your immigration status. It also asks for an "A" number. Normally, you will not have an "A" number unless you previously applied for a green card or have been in deportation proceedings.

Part 2. In Part 2, you will mark Box A if you are the principal applicant. Box B is marked if your spouse or parent is the principal applicant.

Part 3. The questions in Sections A through C are self-explanatory. The nonimmigrant visa number is the number that appears on the very top of the visa stamp. It is not the same as your visa classification. The questions in Section C are meant to identify people who are inadmissible. With the exception of certain memberships in the Communist Party or similar organizations, you will not be deemed inadmissible simply because your joined an organization. However, if your answer to any of the other questions is "yes," you may be inadmissible. See Chapter 25, which is intended to help you remove such obstacles. Don't lie on your answers because you will probably be found out, especially if you have engaged in criminal activity. Many inadmissible conditions can be legally overcome, but once a lie is detected, you will probably lose the legal right to correct the problem. In addition, a false answer is grounds to deny your application and may result in your being permanently barred from getting a green card.

Form I-485A

This form is required only if you are eligible to use and subject to a $1,000 penalty for being in the U.S. illegally. The form is self-explanatory and is intended only to determine if you are subject to the penalty.

Form G-325A

G-325A biographic data forms must be filled out for you and each accompanying relative. You need not file a G-325A for any child under the age of 14 or any adult over the age of 79. The G-325A form is meant to gather personal background information. The questions are self-explanatory.

Form I-134

It is necessary to convince INS that once you receive a green card, you are not likely to go on public welfare. Since you have a job offer, this proves you have a way to support yourself, and an I-134 need not be filed for you, unless, as mentioned above, a relative is a 5% or more owner of the petitioning business. You should still, however, fill out Form I-134, the Affidavit of Support, for any accompanying relative. Because INS knows you will have an income, you must sign the I-134 forms and take financial responsibility for each of them.

Form I-134, the Affidavit of Support, is your guarantee that you will take care of your accompanying relatives. In signing the Affidavit of Support, you are promising to support your accompanying relatives and to reimburse the U.S. government for the sum total of any government support payments they might receive should they go on certain kinds of public assistance. The Affidavit of Support purportedly binds you to this obligation for ten or more years or until they become citizens. Only then does your responsibility to the government end.

Form I-765

Block above Question 1. Mark the first box, "Permission to accept employment."

Questions 1–8. These questions are self-explanatory.

Question 9. This asks for your Social Security number, including all numbers you have ever used. If you have never used a Social Security number, answer "None." If you have a nonworking Social Security number, write down the number followed by the words "nonworking, for tax purposes only." If you have ever used a false number, give that number, followed by the words: "Not my valid number." Be sure to read Chapter 25, however, before filing an application with such information.

Question 10. You will not usually have an Alien Registration Number unless you previously applied for a green card, were in deportation proceedings, or have had certain types of immigration applications denied. All Alien Registration Numbers begin with the letter "A." If you have no "A" number but you entered the U.S. with a valid visa or without a visa under the Visa Waiver Program, you should have an I-94 card. In this case, answer Question 10 by putting down the admission number from the I-94 card.

If you are from Mexico, you may have entered the U.S. with a border crossing card, in which case you should put down the number on the entry document you received at the border, if any. Otherwise simply put down the number of the border crossing card itself, followed with "BCC." If you are Canadian and you entered the U.S. as a visitor, you will not usually have any of the documents described here, in which case you should put down "None."

Questions 11–15. These questions are self-explanatory.

Question 16. Answer this question "(C)(9)."

4. Application Documents: U.S. Filing

You must submit the Notice of Action showing petition approval with the application. As a person applying for a green card through employment, you must show that the original job offer on which the Labor Certification was based is still open to you. Prove this by submitting a current letter from your employer stating again his intent to hire you. This letter will also serve as proof of your ability to support yourself and any accompanying relatives once you get a green card. If you are in a category that does not require a specific job offer, submit your Step Two documents proving your intent to work.

You and each of your accompanying relatives are required to submit two photographs. These photos should meet the specifications on the photo instruction sheet found in Appendix III. Additionally, you must submit your birth certificate or other record of birth, if married a marriage certificate and your spouse's birth certificate, and birth certificates for all your children under age 21, even if not immigrating with you.

You must also submit a Medical Examination Report for each applicant. This is done on INS Form I-693, which must be taken to an INS authorized physician or medical clinic. The INS local office will provide you with the form as well as a list of approved physicians in your area. After completion of the medical exam, and upon obtaining the test results, the doctor will give you the results in a sealed envelope. Do not open the envelope.

Each applicant must submit an I-94 card if one was issued. Failure to do so may result in a conclusion that you entered or remained in the U.S. illegally and either are not eligible to adjust your status or are subject to the $1,000 penalty described earlier. This is the small white or green card you received on entering the U.S.

The only other paperwork required is a fingerprint card. Beginning March 30, 1998, INS regulations changed so that all fingerprinting now takes place at an INS-run fingerprinting center. You will be notified where and when to appear after submitting your application forms. You will be required to pay INS $25 (often when you file your application papers) to cover the fingerprinting costs.

5. Application Interviews: U.S. Filing

As previously explained, personal interviews are usually waived in green card through employment applications. If an interview is not waived, you and your accompanying relatives will be asked to come in to the INS local office for final processing. The INS officer will go over your application to make sure that everything is correct. He will also ask questions to convince himself that you are not inadmissible. (See Chapter 25, *Inadmissibility*.) Try to find out the reason for the interview prior to appearing at the INS. If you have an issue or problem, you should probably consult an attorney in order to resolve the issue before the interview. A single fingerprint will then be taken and you will be asked to sign your application under oath. Accompanying relatives, all of whom must attend the interview with you, will go through the same procedure.

The interview normally takes about 30 minutes. If all goes well, your case should be approved on the spot. You will not be expected to wait for the results. Most INS offices will place a temporary stamp in your passport (as long as it is still valid) showing that you have become a U.S. permanent resident. With this stamp, you acquire all the rights of a green card holder including the right to work and freedom to travel in and out of the U.S. The stamp is not your green card. You will receive your permanent green card by mail several months later. If your fingerprints have not been cleared yet, your application will be approved only provisionally pending clearance. In those cases, no stamp will be placed in your passport at the interview. Instead, you will receive a written notice of approval within a month or two. That notice serves as your proof of U.S. residency until you receive your green card, which takes yet another two or three months. If you need to travel outside the U.S. before

your green card arrives, however, you must go back to the INS office with your passport and the written notice of approval, and a temporary stamp will be placed in your passport, enabling you to return after your trip. Never leave the U.S. without either your green card or a temporary stamp in your passport.

6. Application Appeals: U.S. Filing

If your application is denied, you will receive a written decision by mail explaining the reasons for the denial. There is no way of making a formal appeal to INS when your application is turned down. If the problem is too little evidence, you may be able to overcome this obstacle by adding more documents and resubmitting the entire application to the same INS office you have been dealing with, together with a written request that the case be reopened. The written request does not have to be in any special form. This is technically called a *Motion to Reopen*. There is a $110 fee to file this motion. Alternatively, you may wait until INS begins deportation proceedings, in which case you may refile your application with the immigration judge.

If your application is denied because you are ruled inadmissible, you will be given the opportunity to apply for what is known as a *Waiver of Inadmissibility*, provided a waiver is available for your ground of inadmissibility. See Chapter 25 for directions on how to apply.

Although there is no appeal to INS for the denial of a green card application as there is for the denial of a petition, you have the right to file an appeal in a U.S. district court. This requires employing an immigration attorney at considerable expense. Such appeals are usually unsuccessful.

FORMS AND DOCUMENTS CHECKLIST

STEP ONE: LABOR CERTIFICATION

Forms

☐ ETA-750 A & B.

Documents

☐ Statement from the employer justifying any unusual or restrictive job requirements.

☐ Tear sheets from all advertisements.

☐ Posted job notice with signed statement by the employer of the dates posted and the results.

☐ Statements from the employer of advertising results saying why each U.S. job candidate was turned down.

Additional Documents for Special Cases

LIVE-IN DOMESTICS

☐ Evidence that the domestic has at least one full year of paid domestic experience.

☐ Statement of the employer explaining the need for a live-in.

PHYSICIANS

☐ Evidence that the physician has passed Parts I and II of the National Board of Medical Examiners exam.

COLLEGE AND UNIVERSITY TEACHERS

☐ Statement of a university official explaining you are the best job candidate.

☐ Minutes of faculty search committee meetings.

☐ Evidence of previous advertising and the results.

STEP TWO: PETITION

Forms

☐ Form I-140.

☐ Form ETA-750.

Documents

☐ Approved Labor Certification or evidence of qualifying as a priority worker of extraordinary ability, Schedule A, the pilot pre-certification program, or as a second preference worker of exceptional ability.

☐ All forms and documents listed under Step One.

☐ Diplomas and transcripts from colleges or universities.

☐ Professional certificates.

☐ Documents proving previous job experience.

☐ Documents proving special skills.

☐ Tax returns of the employer's company for the past two years, if available.

☐ Financial statements, including profit and loss statements and balance sheets of the employer's company for the past two years, if available.

PRIORITY WORKERS

Persons of Extraordinary Ability

☐ Evidence you have received a major, internationally recognized award, or at least three of the following:

☐ Evidence you have received several lesser nationally or internationally recognized prizes or awards for excellence.

☐ Documentation of membership in associations which require outstanding achievements of their members.

☐ Published material about you in professional or major trade publications or other major media relating to your work.

☐ Evidence of your participation as a judge of the work of others.

☐ Evidence of your original scientific, scholarly, artistic, athletic or business-related contributions of major significance.

☐ Evidence of your authorship of scholarly articles in professional or major trade publications.

☐ Evidence of the display of your work at artistic exhibitions.

☐ Evidence you have performed in leading or critical roles for distinguished organizations.

☐ Evidence you have commanded a high salary (at least $100,000 per year).

☐ Evidence you have achieved commercial successes in the performing arts.

☐ Copy of the U.S. employment contract, or a written statement explaining how you will continue your extraordinary work in the U.S.

FORMS AND DOCUMENTS CHECKLIST

Outstanding Professors and Researchers

☐ Letters from former employers verifying that you have at least three years of teaching or research experience.

☐ If it is a university position, a letter or contract from the university stating that the U.S. position is either a tenured or tenure-track position.

☐ If the employer is in a private industry, evidence that it has a history of significant achievements in research and employs at least three other full-time research workers.

☐ At least two of the following:

    ☐ Evidence that you have received major prizes or awards for outstanding achievement in your academic field.

    ☐ Evidence of your membership in associations in your academic field which require outstanding achievements for membership.

    ☐ Published material in professional publications written by others about your work. Mere citations to your work in bibliographies are not sufficient.

    ☐ Evidence of your participation as the judge of the work of others.

    ☐ Evidence of your original scientific or scholarly research contributions to the academic field.

    ☐ Evidence of your authorship of scholarly books or articles in scholarly journals having international circulation.

Multi-National Managers and Executives

☐ Notice of approval of an L-1 visa petition, if any.

☐ Documents proving employment with the parent company for one of the past three years outside of the U.S. as an executive or manager.

☐ Articles of incorporation or other legal charter or business license of the foreign business.

☐ Articles of incorporation or other legal charter or business license of the U.S. business.

☐ Legal business registration certificate of the foreign business.

☐ Legal business registration certificate of the U.S. business.

☐ Tax returns of the foreign business for the past two years, if available.

☐ Tax returns of the U.S. business for the past two years, if available.

☐ If the company is publicly held, annual shareholder reports of both the U.S. and foreign companies.

☐ Accountant's financial statements, including profit and loss statements and balance sheets of both the U.S. and foreign company for the past two years.

☐ Payroll records of the foreign company for the past two years, if available.

☐ Promotional literature describing the nature of the employer's business, both U.S. and foreign.

☐ Copy of the business lease or deed for the premises of the U.S. business.

☐ If either company is publicly held, statements from the secretary of the corporation attesting to how the companies are related.

☐ For private companies, copies of all outstanding stock certificates.

☐ For private companies, a notarized affidavit from the corporations' secretaries verifying the names of the officers and directors.

☐ For private companies, copies of the minutes of shareholder meetings appointing the officers and directors.

☐ If a joint venture, copy of the joint venture agreement.

Persons of Exceptional Ability in the Sciences, Arts or Business

☐ At least three of the following:

    ☐ Evidence that you have an academic degree relating to your area of exceptional ability.

    ☐ Evidence that you have had at least ten years of full-time experience in the field.

    ☐ A license to practice your profession.

    ☐ Evidence that you have commanded a high salary (at least $75,000 per year).

    ☐ Evidence of your membership in professional associations.

    ☐ Evidence of recognition for achievements and significant contribution to your industry or field.

☐ If you are applying for a waiver of the job offer requirement and Labor Certification:

    ☐ Form ETA-750, Part B only, and

    ☐ written statement, support letters and other documentation explaining why an exemption from the job requirement is in the U.S. national interest.

FORMS AND DOCUMENT CHECKLIST

GROUP I: MEDICAL OCCUPATIONS

Physical Therapists

☐ Copy of the U.S. state physical therapist license, or

☐ Letter from the state physical therapy licensing agency stating that you meet all the qualifications to sit for the state exam.

Registered Nurses

☐ Copy of a full and unrestricted state nursing license, or

☐ Evidence of having passed the commission on Graduates of Foreign Nursing Schools exam.

GROUP II: EXCEPTIONAL ABILITY IN THE ARTS OR SCIENCES

☐ At least two of the following:

  ☐ Documents proving that you have won internationally recognized prizes or awards.

  ☐ Documents showing membership in selective international associations.

  ☐ Articles about your work appearing in professional publications.

  ☐ Documents proving that you have acted as a judge in international competitions.

  ☐ Documents describing your original scientific or academic research.

  ☐ Copies of scientific or academic articles by you that have been published in international journals.

  ☐ Documents proving that your work has been exhibited in at least two different countries.

STEP THREE: APPLICATION

Forms

☐ OF forms (available from U.S. consulate abroad for consular filing only).

☐ Form I-485 (U.S. filing only).

☐ Form I-485A (U.S. filing only).

☐ Form G-325A (U.S. filing only).

☐ Form I-765 (U.S. filing only).

☐ Form I-134 (Consular and U.S. filings).

☐ Form I-864 (If a relative owns 5% or more of the business).

Documents

☐ Notice of approval of the visa petition.

☐ Long-form birth certificate for you and each accompanying relative.

☐ Passport for you and each accompanying relative, valid for at least six months beyond the date of the final interview.

☐ I-94 card for you and each accompanying relative (U.S. filing only).

☐ Police certificates from every country in which you and each accompanying relative has lived for at least six months since age 16 (Consular filing only).

☐ Military records for you and each accompanying relative (Consular filing only).

☐ Fingerprints for you and each accompanying relative between the ages of 14 and 75 (U.S. filing only).

☐ Three photographs each of you and each accompanying relative.

☐ Letter from the petitioning employer verifying the job is still open.

☐ Medical exam report for you and each accompanying relative.

Getting a Green Card Through the Lottery

Privileges

- You may live anywhere in the U.S. and stay as long as you want.

- You may work at any job, for any company, anywhere in the U.S.

- You may travel in or out of the U.S. whenever you wish.

- You may apply to become an American citizen after you have held your green card for at least five years.

- If you qualify for a green card through the lottery, your spouse and unmarried children under the age of 21 may also get green cards automatically as accompanying relatives.

Limitations

- Your place of actual residence must be in the U.S. You cannot use a green card just for work and travel purposes. (The only exception to this rule is for Alien Commuters, discussed in Chapter 4.)

- You must pay U.S. taxes on your worldwide income because you are regarded as a U.S. resident.

- You cannot remain outside the U.S. for more than one year at a time without special permission or you risk losing your green card. (It is recommended that you return from your trip abroad before you have been gone six months.)

- If you commit a crime or participate in politically subversive activities or other proscribed activities, your green card can be taken away and you can be deported.

A. How to Qualify

Qualifying for a green card through the lottery has some limitations.

1. Quota Restrictions

There are 55,000 green cards per year given out under the lottery program. They are distributed by dividing up the world into regions and allocating varying percentages of the total green cards to each region. Additionally, each qualifying country within any region is limited to no more than 3,850 lottery green cards per year.

2. Who Qualifies for a Green Card Through the Lottery?

The Immigration Act of 1990 created a new green card category to benefit persons from countries that in recent years have sent the fewest numbers of immigrants to the U.S. In general, you can qualify for a green card through the lottery simply by being a native of one of these countries. Because the method used to select those who receive green cards through the lottery is that of random drawing, the program is popularly known as the *green card lottery*.

Different qualifying countries are selected each year, based on which ones, and which areas of the world, sent the fewest numbers of immigrants to the U.S. during the previous five years, in proportion to the size of their populations. U.S. job offers are not a requirement. The only other qualification is that the applicant have either a high school diploma or a minimum of two years experience in a job that normally requires at least two years of training or experience.

There is a new application period every year, usually occurring in late winter or early spring. Registrations submitted one year are not held over to the next, so if you are not selected one year you need to reapply the next year to be considered. Currently, the only countries not qualified for the lottery are:

Canada

China (mainland and Taiwan, except Hong Kong)

Colombia

Dominican Republic

El Salvador

Haiti

India

Jamaica

Mexico

Philippines

Poland

South Korea

United Kingdom (except Northern Ireland) and its dependent territories

Vietnam

3. Inadmissibility

As in all green card applications, if you have been arrested for committing certain crimes or afflicted with certain physical or mental defects, you may be inadmissible from receiving a green card through the lottery.

B. Getting a Green Card Through the Lottery

Getting a green card through the lottery is a two-step process.

1. Step One: Registration

The object of registration is simply to place your name among those who may be selected through the lottery drawing system to receive green cards. Acceptance of your registration does not mean you are eligible for a green card. It means only that you appear to come from a qualifying country.

2. Step Two: The Application

The application is filed by you and your accompanying relatives, if any. The application is your formal request for a green card. Step Two may be carried out at an INS office in the U.S. or in your home country at a U.S. consulate there. Step Two may not be filed until the National Visa Center has notified you that your registration was selected for green card processing.

The vast majority of lottery green card applications will be filed at consulates. Because many winners do not already reside in the U.S., and because consulates may process cases faster than INS offices in the U.S., it may be safer to have a lottery green card application processed there. If the green card cannot be issued by the end of the lottery (fiscal) year

(September 30), your application becomes invalid. If you are in the U.S. legally on a nonimmigrant visa with a current priority date, you apply for your green card either inside or outside the U.S., whichever you prefer.

If you are in the U.S. illegally or entered legally without a visa under the Visa Waiver Program, refer to Chapter 25 to see if you may still file your green card application inside the U.S. However, you should know that having a diversity petition on file before the "penalty grandfather date" of January 14, 1998 will not permit you to do a U.S. filing, since the grandfather petition does not apply to petitions filed with the Department of State. Be sure you are not subject to any grounds of inadmissibility or the bars (three- or ten-year waiting periods) to getting a green card, which result from being in the U.S. out of status and then departing the U.S. (See Chapter 25.)

3. Paperwork

There are two types of paperwork you must submit to get a green card through the lottery. The first consists of official government forms. The second is personal documents such as birth and marriage certificates. We will tell you exactly what forms and documents you need.

It is vital that forms are properly filled out and all necessary documents are supplied. You may resent the intrusion into your privacy and sizable effort it takes to prepare immigration applications but you should realize the process is an impersonal matter to immigration officials. Your getting a green card is more important to you than it is to the U.S. government. This is not a pleasant thing to accept, but you are better off having a real understanding of your position. People from all over the world want green cards. There is no shortage of applicants. Take the time and trouble to prepare your papers properly. In the end it will pay off with a successful application.

The documents you supply to INS do not have to be originals. Photocopies of all documents are acceptable as long as you have the originals in your possession and are willing to produce the originals at the request of INS. Documents submitted to U.S. consulates, on the other hand, must be either originals or official government certified copies. Government certified copies and notarized copies are not the same thing. Documents which have only been notarized are not acceptable. They must carry a government seal. In addition to any original or government certified copies of documents submitted to a consulate, you should submit plain photocopies of each document as well. After the consulate compares the copies with the originals, it will return the originals.

Documents will be accepted if they are in either English, or, with papers filed at U.S. consulates abroad, the language of the country where the documents are being filed. An exception exists for papers filed at the U.S. consulates in Japan, where all documents must be translated into English. If the documents are not in an acceptable language as just explained, they must be accompanied by a full, word for word, written English translation. Any capable person may act as translator. It is not necessary to hire a professional. At the end of each translation, the following statement must appear:

I hereby certify that I translated this document from (language) to English. This translation is accurate and complete. I further certify that I am fully competent to translate from (language) to English.

The translator should sign this statement but it does not have to be witnessed or notarized.

Later in this chapter we describe in detail the forms and documents needed to get your green card through the lottery. A summary checklist of forms and documents appears at the end of this chapter.

C. Step One: Registration

The present registration rules require you to type or print on a plain sheet of paper the following information, first for yourself, and then for your spouse and any unmarried children under age 21:

Full name
Place: City/Town, District/County/Province, Country
EXAMPLE: Munich, Bavaria, Germany. The name of the country should be the name currently used for the place where the applicant was born (Slovenia, rather than Yugoslavia; Kazakhstan rather than Soviet Union, for example).
Current mailing address
Last city and country of residence outside the U.S.

Place the sheet of paper in a business-sized envelope, on which you must type the special registration mailing address, which for the DV program is:

DV-2001 Program
National Visa Center
Portsmouth, NH 00--- (see below for appropriate code)
Asia: 00210
South America/Central America/Caribbean: 00211
Europe: 00212
Africa: 00213
Oceania: 00214
North America: 00215

While there is no special way to register, you *must* include all of the information noted above or the entry will be disqualified. You should use a plain sheet of paper and type or clearly print the information in English. It is best to provide the information in the order noted above. The entry must be submitted by air or regular mail to the address matching the region of the applicant's country of birth. Entries sent by express or priority mail, fax, hand messenger or any means requiring receipts or special handling will not be processed. The envelope must be between 6 and 10 inches (15 to 25 cm) long and 3-1/2 and 4-1/2 inches (9 to 11 cm) wide. Postcards are not acceptable, nor are envelopes inside express or oversized mail packets. In the upper left-hand corner of the envelope the applicant must show his/her country of birth, followed by the name and full return address. The applicant must provide both the country of birth as well as the country of the address, even if both are the same. Failure to provide this information will disqualify the entry.

Mail only one registration per person. Do not mail separate registrations for children unless they qualify on their own and are willing to immigrate without you. Although children automatically qualify to immigrate with their parents, if selected, the opposite is not true. If a child is selected, the parents will not get green cards unless they are selected separately.

D. Step Two: The Application (Consular Filing)

Anyone whose registration was selected for green card processing can apply for a green card at a U.S. consulate in his or her home country. If you have been or are now working and living illegally in the U.S. or you entered the U.S. improperly read Chapter 25, regarding grounds of inadmissibility and bars to getting a green card, before you depart the U.S. or apply for a visa or green card.

1. Benefits and Drawbacks of Consular Filing

Your waiting time for the paperwork to be finished may be shorter at a U.S. consulate abroad than at an INS office. This is a particularly important consideration with lottery green card cases because if your immigrant visa isn't issued before the end of the fiscal year for which you were selected, your registration becomes void and you lose your chance for the card. The deadline is the end of the fiscal year *for*, and not *in*, the year you were picked. The government fiscal years begin on October 1 and end on September 30. This means that if you were selected in the 2000 registration period (which was October 4, 1999, to November 3, 1999), your deadline for receiving a green card was September 30, 2000. Successful registrants would have been notified between April and July of 2000. Remember—this is the deadline for receiving your green card, not filing the application. You must, therefore, file much earlier to be sure the processing is completed in time. You can apply for a visa or green card based on your successful lottery DV-2000 registration from October 1999 through September 2000. (The registration period for the DV-99 program ran from February 3, 1997, to March 5, 1997; applicants who were selected must apply for permanent residence by September 30, 1999. However, if a DV-99 applicant was out of status, entered without inspection, worked without authorization or otherwise needed the penalty provision to adjust status, the green card application must have been filed by midnight of November 25, 1997.)

Another reason why speed is important is that it has been the practice of the National Visa Center to notify twice as many people as there are green cards available. This is done because NVC assumes some of these people either will not qualify or will change their minds about immigrating. If NVC's assumption is wrong and everyone selected does mail in applications, the green cards will be given on a first come, first served basis. It is therefore possible that even though you win the lottery, if that year's green card allotment is used up before your own interview is scheduled, you will not get a green card. Once again, the speedier consular filing offers some protection against this happening.

One drawback to consular filing is the travel expense and inconvenience you will experience in returning to your home country if you are already in the U.S. And, if you are living in the U.S. illegally you may be subject to the three- or ten-year waiting periods if you have been out of status over six or ten months, and then depart the U.S. Be sure to read Chapter 25 before making your decision on whether to consular process or apply in the U.S. Another problem is that should your consular application fail, you will have fewer ways to appeal than a U.S. filing would offer and if problems arise in your case, you will usually have to remain outside the U.S. until they are resolved.

NATIVITY IS THE KEY TO LOTTERY

To enter the lottery, an applicant must be able to claim what the law describes as "nativity" in an eligible country, and will be required to meet either the education or training requirement of the Diversity program. "Nativity" in most cases is determined by the applicant's place of birth. However, if a person was born in an ineligible country but his/her spouse was born in an eligible country, that person can claim the spouse's country of birth rather than his/her own. Also, if a person was born in an ineligible country, but neither of his/her parents was born there or resided there at the time of the birth, such a person may be able to claim nativity in one of the parents' country of birth.

To enter the lottery, an applicant must also have a high school education or its equivalent—defined in the U.S. as successful completion of a 12-year course of elementary and secondary education—or two years of work experience within the past five years in an occupation requiring at least two years of training or experience to perform. If a person does not meet these requirements, he/she will not be able to qualify and should not submit an entry to the Diversity program.

2. Application General Procedures: Consular Filing

The law states that only a U.S. consulate or embassy in your home country is required to accept your lottery green card application. A complete list of all U.S. consulates that process visa applications, with addresses and phone numbers, is in Appendix I. You can ask a consulate located elsewhere to accept your application, but it has the option to say "no," and in fact will turn down most such requests.

If you are selected, you will receive a letter from the National Visa Center in Portsmouth, New Hampshire. You may not file an application for a green card at a consulate until after you have been notified by NVC.

Your notification will include Packet 3, containing forms and instructions. Biographical Information Form OF-230 I will be included and should be completed and returned together with photocopies of all required documents. Do not send your original documents. You will need them later at your interview. Failure to return this form and the documents promptly can jeopardize your ability to get a green card.

The application for your green card is made in person by appointment. When the consulate is ready for your final processing, it will send you another group of papers known as Packet 4. Packet 4 includes an interview appointment letter, instructions for obtaining your medical examination, and still more forms to be completed. Other than Form OF-230 I, which should be mailed in as soon as you receive it, and Form OF-169, which you will send in when you are ready for your interview, do not mail your paperwork to the consulate. Instead, bring the rest of your forms and all documents with you at the time of your appointment. The fee for filing an application is $260 per person and there is a $75 surcharge for diversity visa applicants and a visa issuance fee of $65.

3. Application Forms: Consular Filing

When you file at a U.S. consulate abroad, the consulate officials will provide you with certain optional forms, designated by an "OF" preceeding a number. Instructions for completing optional forms and what to do with them once they are filled out will come with the forms. We do not include copies of these forms in Appendix III. Copies of all non "OF" forms are in Appendix III.

Form I-134

It is necessary to convince the consulate that once you receive a green card you are not likely to go on public welfare. A job is not required, but if you do not have a written offer of employment in the U.S., you must show that you are independently wealthy, or someone is filing an Affidavit of Support on your behalf. Form I-134, the Affidavit of Support, guarantees that someone is willing to take financial responsibility for you. INS offices insist that the person signing the Form I-134 be both your close relative and a U.S. resident. Consulates, however, are generally not as fussy about who it is that promises to guarantee your support. Consulates may allow more distant relatives or even friends to sign these forms and the signer's country of residence may not be a factor.

If you can show that you are financially independent or have a job offer in the U.S., an I-134 need not be filed for you. You should still, however, fill out Form I-134 for any accompanying relatives. Because INS knows you will have an income, in this case, you will be the one to sign the Form I-134, taking financial responsibility for each of them.

When you request a family member or friend to sign an Affidavit of Support on your behalf, he or she will doubtless wish to know the legal extent of the financial obligation. In signing the Affidavit of Support, the signer does not promise to support you. What he or she does promise to do is reimburse the U.S. government for the sum total of any government support payments you might receive should you go on welfare. The Affidavit of Support binds the person signing it to this obligation for three years. After that, his or her responsibility to both you and the U.S. government comes to an end.

4. Application Documents: Consular Filing

All green card applicants must supply birth records, marriage records, if married, birth certificates of all children under age 21, even those not immigrating with you, photographs, police clearances and evidence of financial support. Copies of these documents are first mailed to the NVC, but bring the originals with you to your interview.

In all cases, you must demonstrate the ability to support yourself once you get a green card. A source of support must be shown for your accompanying relatives as well. You have three alternatives. You can submit as a document a written job offer from a U.S. employer. As an alternative you can submit your own personal current financial documents showing you have sufficient savings and investment income to support yourself. The third possibility is to have a U.S. friend or relative sign Form I-134, Affidavit of Support, on your behalf. If this form is filed, then no further documentation is required. Each of your accompanying relatives must also submit proof of a job offer, evidence of independent financial assets or an I-134 signed on his or her behalf. When you have a job offer or sufficient financial means, you can sign Affidavits of Support for your accompanying relatives.

It is also necessary that you have in your possession a valid passport from your home country. The expiration date on the passport must leave enough time for the passport to remain valid at least six months beyond the date of your final application interview.

Unlike applications made in the U.S., you personally must collect police clearance certificates from each country you have lived in for one year or more since your 16th birthday. Additionally, you must have a police certificate from your home country or country of last residence, if you lived there for at least six months since the age of 16. You do not need to obtain police certificates from the U.S. even if you have lived there. Like all other documents, you should be prepared to present the necessary police clearance certificates at your interview. If you go to your interview without the required certificates, you will be refused a green card and told to return after you get them.

OBTAINING POLICE CERTIFICATES

You should contact the local police department in your home country for instructions on how to get police certificates. To obtain police certificates from nations other than your home country, it is best to contact the nearest consulate representing that country for instructions. Some nations refuse to supply police certificates, or their certificates are not considered reliable, and so you will not be required to obtain them from those locations. At this writing, police certificates are not required from the following countries:

Afghanistan	Haiti	Saudi Arabia
Albania	Honduras	Sierra Leone
Angola	India	Somalia
Bangladesh	Indonesia	Sri Lanka
Brunei	Iran	Sudan
Bulgaria	Iraq	Syria
Cambodia	Jordan	Tanzania
Chad	Laos	Thailand
Colombia	Liberia	Turkey
Costa Rica	Libya	United Arab
Cuba	Malaysia	Emirates
Dominican Republic	Mexico	United Kingdom
El Salvador	Mongolia	United States
Equatorial Guinea	Mozambique	Venezuela
Ghana	Nepal	Vietnam
Guatemala	Pakistan	

For applicants who once lived in Japan but do not reside there at the time their green card applications are filed, the Department of State recognizes that police certificates are available from Japan only as far back as five years from the date of the green card application.

Other countries, including the Netherlands, North Korea, South Africa and South Korea, will send certificates directly to U.S. consulates but not to you personally. Before they send the certificates out, however, you must request that it be done. Usually this requires filing some type of request form together with a set of your fingerprints.

You and each accompanying relative must bring to the interview three photographs taken in compliance with the instruction sheet found in Appendix III. Additional photo instructions are provided in Packet 4. Often Packet 4 will also contain a list of local photographers who take this type of picture.

A few consulates require you to submit fingerprints, though most do not. Consulates wanting fingerprints will send you blank fingerprint cards with instructions.

The lottery green card program requires applicants to have either a high school diploma or the equivalent, or job skills needing at least two years of experience or training to learn. Appropriate evidence would be either a copy of your high school diploma or proof of job skill training, such as a vocational school certificate, and proof of at least two years of skilled employment verified by letters from past employers. A specific job offer in the U.S. is not required.

5. Application Interviews: Consular Filing

Consulates hold interviews on all green card applications. A written notice of your interview appointment is included when you receive Packet 4. Immediately before the interview, you and your accompanying relatives will be required to have medical examinations. Some consulates conduct the medical exams the day before the interview. Others schedule the medical exam and the interview on the same day. You will be told where to go and what to do in your appointment letter.

The medical examinations are conducted by private doctors and you are required to pay the doctor a fee. The fees vary from as little as $50 to more than $150 per exam, depending on the country. The amount of the medical exam fee will be stated in your appointment letter. The exam itself involves the taking of a medical history, blood test, chest X ray, and vaccinations if applicable and/or recommended for you. Pregnant women who do not want to be X-rayed may so advise the consulate and their appointments will be postponed until after the pregnancy. The requirement to have an X ray taken cannot be waived.

The main purpose of the medical exam is to verify that you are not medically inadmissible. The primary medical grounds of inadmissibility are tuberculosis and HIV (AIDS). Medical grounds of inadmissibility usually can be overcome with treatment. See Chapter 25, *Inadmissibility*, for more details. If you need a medical waiver, you will be given complete instructions by the consulate at the time of your interview.

After the medical exam, you and your accompanying relatives will report to the consulate for the interview. At that time, you must pay two more fees: $170 per person when your papers are submitted, and an additional $30 per person at the end of the interview when your applications are approved. Some consulates accept payment only by certified check, money order or travelers check. Others accept cash. You will be told the proper method of payment in Packet 4.

Bring with you to the interview the completed forms, photographs, your passports and all of the required documents discussed here. The interview process involves verification of your application's accuracy and an inspection of your documents. If all is in order, you will be asked to return later in the day when you will be issued an immigrant visa. You are not yet a permanent resident.

The immigrant visa allows you to request entry to the U.S. You acquire the full status of green card holder at the moment of making entry (being inspected and admitted) into the U.S. with your immigrant visa. At that time, your passport is stamped and you are immediately authorized to work. If you are bringing any accompanying relatives, they must enter at either the same time or after you do in order to become permanent residents. Permanent green cards for you and your accompanying relatives are then ordered. They will come to you by mail several months later.

6. Application Appeals: Consular Filing

When a consulate denies a green card application, there is no formal appeal available, although you are free to reapply as often as you like. When your green card is refused, the reasons will be explained. The most common reason for denial is failure to supply all the required documents. Sometimes, presenting more evidence on an unclear fact can bring about a better result. If the denial was caused by a lack of evidence, this will be explained in a written notice sent to you by mail.

Another common reason for denial of a green card is that the consular officer believes you are inadmissible. If you are found to be inadmissible, you will be given an opportunity to apply for a Waiver of Inadmissibility if one is available. See Chapter 25 for directions on how to apply.

When all these possibilities are exhausted, if the consulate still refuses you a green card, your opportunities for further appeals are severely limited. Historically, the courts have held that there is no right to judicial review and there is no formal appeal procedure through any U.S. govern-

ment agency. The State Department in Washington, D.C. does offer an informal review procedure through the mail. This agency will look at the factual elements of your case and decide whether or not the consulate made a correct decision. Even if the State Department rules in your favor, the decision is only advisory and the consulate is free to ignore the State Department, letting its own decision stand. At present, there does appear to be a trend developing where courts in the U.S. are more frequently accepting jurisdiction over consular decisions, so a court appeal may be a possibility to consider. The jurisdiction of U.S. courts to review consular decisions, however, is still an unsettled legal issue.

Your denial may be based on a question of law rather than fact. The State Department offers the same informal review for legal questions with the difference that any decision it makes is binding on the consulate. Appeals of this kind are very technical and should be handled by a competent immigration attorney. Even with representation by an attorney, most such appeals fail.

E. Step Two: The Application (U.S. Filing)

If you are physically present in the U.S., you may apply for a green card without leaving the country on the following conditions:

- you have been notified by NVC that your registration has been selected for a green card
- your lottery registration number is available under the quota, and

• you are not subject to any grounds of inadmissibility or bars to adjustment of status (see Chapter 25).

Unless you can meet these terms, you may not file an application (Step Two) for a green card in the U.S.

1. Benefits and Drawbacks of U.S. Filing

The obvious benefit to applying for a green card in the U.S. is that if you are already in the country, you avoid the expense and inconvenience of overseas travel. Moreover, it is a rule of immigration that once you file Step Two, you must remain wherever you have filed. When you file in the U.S., should problems arise in your case, you will at least be able to wait for a decision in America, a circumstance most green card applicants prefer.

Another important benefit of U.S. filing is that you may receive permission to work while you wait for the results of your case. To obtain this benefit, you must make a separate application, in person, at the INS local office where your Step Two application has been filed. Most INS offices will give you a separate appointment, several weeks later, to come in and have a work permit issued. If you do not need to work right away, but can wait until after getting your green card, you do not need to file this separate application. However, you may need to get benefits such as a social security card and a drivers' license so you may want to apply for it even if you do not intend to work.

If your application for a green card is turned down, you have greater rights of appeal inside the U.S. than you do at a U.S. consulate. INS offices have different procedures from consular offices because they are controlled by a different branch of the U.S. government.

There are some disadvantages to applying in the U.S. It usually takes much longer to get results. Processing times at INS offices average eight to twelve months. We already discussed in Section D1, above, why speed is particularly important in lottery cases. Because lottery green cards must be issued by a specific date, INS delays could cause you to lose an opportunity.

While your case is pending at an INS office, you may not leave the U.S. without getting special permission. If you do leave without INS's permission, even for a genuine emergency, this will be regarded as a withdrawal of your application and you will have to start your application all over again when you return.

PROCEDURES FOR ADVANCED WORK AUTHORIZATION

If you want to work before your application for a green card is approved, you must file a separate application for employment authorization. This can be done by completing Form I-765 and filing it at the time you file your green card application or later at the same INS local office where you filed the application. Together with Form I-765, you must submit your I-94 card and pay a filing fee of $100. It is very important to keep the fee receipt INS gives you so you can prove that the I-765 was filed. Normally, you will want to file the application for employment authorization at the same time as your Step Two application papers.

Some INS offices may approve your employment authorization and issue a work authorization card on the spot. Usually, however, you will be given an appointment to return within a few weeks and you will receive your work authorization card at that time. INS is soon expected to change the procedure for issuing work authorization cards, requiring that they be mailed from a central facility, much like green cards. The purpose of this change is to make the cards more difficult to counterfeit. The new procedures are a response to public complaints that certain INS personnel have been "selling" work ID cards.

Legally, INS does not have to make a decision on your employment authorization application for up to 90 days. If for some reason you are not given a decision within 90 days, you will, at your request, be granted an interim employment authorization which will last 240 days. To receive an interim card, you must return in person to the INS local office where you filed your I-765 and show your fee receipt. Then your interim work authorization card will be issued.

If 240 days pass and you still have not received a final decision on the I-765, you must stop working. Interim work authorization cards cannot be renewed. However, if you reach this point, you have the option to file a new I-765 application and, if you do not get a decision on the new application within 90 days, you will then be entitled to another interim work authorization card.

2. Application General Procedures: U.S. Filing

The application, consisting of both forms and documents, is submitted either by mail or in person to the INS local office nearest the place you are living. Appendix II contains a complete list of all local U.S. immigration offices with their telephone numbers and addresses. The procedure is now undergoing a change. It is expected that eventually all applications will be filed only by mail to the regional service centers.

For U.S. filings, the basic form used in Step Two, the application, is INS Form I-485, application for Permanent Residence. Form I-485 is filed to adjust your status in the U.S. "Adjusting status" is a technical term used only in U.S. filings. It simply means that you are presently in the U.S. as a nonimmigrant and are in the process of acquiring a green card.

The filing fee for each application is $220 for applicants age 14 and over, and $160 for applicants under age 14. A separate application must be filed for you and each accompanying relative. In addition, if you are in the U.S. illegally, you may be subject to grounds of inadmissibility or bars to getting your green card in the U.S. See Chapter 25 before departing the U.S. or filing any forms with INS. Checks and money orders are accepted. It is not advisable to send cash through the mail but cash is satisfactory if you file in person. Cash is accepted only in the exact amount. INS offices will not make change. We recommend filing your papers in person if at all possible, as you will be given a written receipt from INS and your papers are likely to be processed right away. If you choose to mail in your application, you should do so by certified mail, return receipt requested. In either case, keep a complete copy of everything you send in.

Once your application has been filed, you should not leave the U.S. for any reason before your application has been approved. Any absence will be viewed as a termination of your application for a green card. If you want to leave the U.S. you should request advance parole by filing Form I-131 together with three passport-style photos and pay a $95 filing fee. You should include a short letter describing the purpose of your trip—which may be for any bona fide business or personal reason. Be sure you are not inadmissible and that you have not been out of status for 180 days or more after April 1, 1997 (before filing your adjustment application) or you may be prevented from getting your green card. (See Chapter 25.) If approved, you will be allowed to leave the U.S. and return again with no break in the processing of your application.

Generally, after filing your application, you will not hear anything from INS for several months. Then you should receive a notice of your interview appointment. The interview notice will also contain instructions for getting the required medical exam, and will tell you if any further documentation is needed.

3. Application Forms: U.S. Filing

Copies of all forms can be found in Appendix III.

Form I-485

While most of the form is self-explanatory, a few items typically raise concerns. If a particular question does not apply to you, answer it with "None" or "N/A." The questions on this form requiring explanation are as follows:

Part 1. Part 1 asks for general information about when and where you were born, your present address and immigration status. It also asks for an "A" number. Normally, you will not have an "A" number unless you previously applied for a green card or have been in deportation proceedings.

Part 2. You will mark Box A if you are the principal applicant. Also mark Box H, "other," and write in "Diversity Lottery Winner." Leave the other boxes blank.

Part 3. The questions in Sections A through C are self-explanatory. The nonimmigrant visa number is the number that appears on the very top of the visa stamp. It is not the same as your visa classification. The questions in Section C are meant to identify people who are inadmissible. With the exception of certain memberships in the Communist Party or similar organizations, you will not be deemed inadmissible simply because you joined an organization. However, if your answer to any of the other questions is "yes," you may be inadmissible. See Chapter 26, which is intended to help you remove such obstacles. Don't lie on your answers because you will probably be found out, especially if you have engaged in criminal activity. Many grounds of inadmissibility conditions can be legally overcome, but once a lie is detected, you will lose the legal right to correct the problem. In addition, a false answer is grounds to deny your application and may result in your being permanently barred from getting a green card.

Form I-485A

This form is required only if you are subject to a $1,000 penalty for being in the U.S. illegally. You are only eligible to apply under this provision if you had a labor certification or visa petition on file by January 14, 1998. (See Chapter 25.) The form is self-explanatory, and is intended only to determine if you are subject to the penalty.

Form G-325A

G-325A biographic data forms must be filled out for you and each accompanying relative. You need not file a G-325A for any child under the age of 14 or any adult over the age of 79. The G-325A form is meant to gather personal background information. The questions are self-explanatory.

Form I-134

It is necessary to convince INS that once you receive a green card you are not likely to go on public welfare. A job is not required, but if you do not have a written offer of employment in the U.S., you must show that you are independently wealthy or that someone is filing an Affidavit of Support on your behalf. Form I-134, the Affidavit of Support, guarantees that someone is willing to take financial responsibility for you. INS offices insist that the person signing the Form I-134 be both your close relative and a U.S. resident.

If you can show that you are financially independent or have a job offer in the U.S., an I-134 need not be filed for you. You should still, however, fill out Form I-134 for any accompanying relatives. Because INS knows you will have an income, in this case, you will be the one to sign the Form I-134, taking financial responsibility for each of them.

When you request a family member or friend to sign an Affidavit of Support on your behalf, he or she will doubtless wish to know the legal extent of the financial obligation. In signing the Affidavit of Support, the signer does not promise to support you. What he or she does promise to do is reimburse the U.S. government for the sum total of any government support payments you might receive should you go on welfare. The Affidavit of Support purportedly binds the person signing it to this obligation for three years. After that, his or her responsibility to both you and the U.S. government comes to an end.

Form I-765

Block above Question 1. Mark the first box, "Permission to accept employment."

Questions 1–8. These questions are self-explanatory.

Question 9. This asks for your Social Security number, including all numbers you have ever used. If you have never used a Social Security number, answer "None." If you have a nonworking Social Security number, write down the number followed by the words "nonworking, for tax purposes only." If you have ever used a false number, give that number, followed by the words: "Not my valid number." (Also read Chapter 25 before filing any applications with INS.)

Question 10. You will not usually have an Alien Registration Number unless you previously applied for a green card, were in deportation proceedings, or have had certain types of immigration applications denied. All Alien Registration Numbers begin with the letter "A." If you have no "A" number but you entered the U.S. with a valid visa or without a visa under the Visa Waiver Program, you should have an I-94 card. In this case, answer Question 10 by putting down the admission number from the I-94 card.

If you are from Mexico, you may have entered the U.S. with a border crossing card, in which case you should put down the number on the entry document you received at the border, if any. Otherwise simply put down the number of the border crossing card itself, followed with "BCC." If you are Canadian and you entered the U.S. as a visitor, you will not usually have any of the documents described here, in which case you should put down "None."

Questions 11–15. These questions are self-explanatory.

Question 16. Answer this question "(C)(9)."

4.   Application Documents: U.S. Filing

In all cases, you must demonstrate the ability to support yourself once you get a green card. A source of support must be shown for your accompanying relatives as well. You have three alternatives. You can submit as a document a written job offer from a U.S. employer. You can also submit your own personal current financial documents showing you have sufficient savings and investment income to support yourself. The third possibility is to have a U.S. friend or relative sign an I-134 Affidavit of Support on your behalf. If this form is filed, then no further documentation is required. Each of your accompanying relatives must also submit proof of a job offer, evidence of independent financial assets or an I-134 signed on his or her behalf. When you have a job offer or sufficient financial means, you can sign Affidavits of Support for your accompanying relatives.

You must also submit a medical examination report for each applicant. This is done on INS Form I-693, which must be taken to an INS authorized physician or medical clinic. The INS local office will provide you with the form as well as a list of approved physicians in your area. After completion of the medical exam, and upon obtaining the test results, the doctor will give you the results in a sealed envelope. Do not open the envelope.

You and each of your accompanying relatives are required to submit two photographs. These photos should meet the specifications on the photo instruction sheet found in Appendix III. Additionally, you must submit your birth certificate or other record of birth. If you are married, submit a marriage certificate, your spouse's birth certificate, and birth certificates for all your children, even those not immigrating with you.

Each applicant must submit an I-94 card if one was issued. Failure to do so may result in a conclusion that you entered or remained in the U.S. illegally and either are not eligible or are subject to the $1,000 penalty described earlier. This is the small white or green card you received on entering the U.S.

The lottery green card program requires applicants to have either a high school diploma or the equivalent, or job skills needing at least two years of experience or training to learn. Appropriate evidence would be either a copy of your high school diploma or proof of job skill training, such as a vocational school certificate, and proof of at least two years of skilled employment verified by letters from past employers.

The only other paperwork required is a fingerprint card. Beginning March 30, 1998, INS regulations changed so that all fingerprinting now takes place at an INS-run fingerprinting center. You will be notified where and when to appear after submitting your application forms. You will be required to pay INS $25 (often when you file your application papers) to cover the fingerprinting costs.

5. Application Interviews: U.S. Filing

All lottery green card applications require personal interviews. These are scheduled by appointment. You will receive written notice of the interview time a few weeks in advance. The interview is usually a simple matter. The INS officer will go over your application to make sure that everything is correct. He will also ask questions to convince himself that you are not inadmissible. (See Chapter 25, *Inadmissibility.*) A single fingerprint will then be taken and you will be asked to sign your application under oath. Accompanying relatives, all of whom must attend the interview with you, will go through the same procedure.

The interview normally takes about 30 minutes. If all goes well, your case should be approved on the spot. You will not be expected to wait for the results.

Most INS offices will place a temporary stamp in your passport showing that you have become a permanent U.S. resident. With this stamp you acquire all the rights of a green card holder including the right to work and freedom to travel in and out of the U.S. The stamp is not your green card. You will receive your permanent green card by mail several months later.

If your fingerprints have not been cleared yet, your application will be approved only provisionally, pending clearance. In those cases, no stamp will be placed in your passport at the interview. Instead, you will receive a written Notice of Approval within a month or two. That notice serves as your proof of U.S. residency until you receive your green card, which takes yet another two or three months.

If you need to travel outside the U.S. before you receive your green card, you must go back to the INS office with your passport and the written Notice of Approval, and a temporary stamp will be placed in your passport to enable you to return to the U.S. after your trip. Never leave the U.S. without either your green card or a temporary stamp in your passport.

6. Application Appeals: U.S. Filing

If your application is denied, you will receive a written decision by mail explaining the reasons for the denial. There is no way of making a formal appeal to INS when your application is turned down. If the problem is too little evidence, you may be able to overcome this obstacle by adding more documents and resubmitting the entire application to the same INS office you have been dealing with, together with a written request that the case be reopened. The written request does not have to be in any special form. This is technically called a *Motion to Reopen.* There is a $110 fee to file this motion. Alternatively, you may wait until INS begins deportation proceedings, in which case you may refile your application with the immigration judge.

If your application is denied because you are ruled inadmissible, you will be given the opportunity to apply for what is known as a *Waiver of Inadmissibility.* See Chapter 25 for directions on how to apply.

Although there is no appeal to INS for the denial of a green card application, you have the right to file an appeal in a U.S. district court. This requires employing an immigration attorney at considerable expense. Such appeals are usually unsuccessful.

FORMS AND DOCUMENTS CHECKLIST

STEP ONE: REGISTRATION

Forms

☐ Registration application. There is no official form. Simply write the following information on a plain sheet of paper:

- Name
- Date and place of birth
- Full mailing address
- U.S. consulate where you wish to have your case processed if you are selected, and
- Names, dates, and places of birth of your spouse (if any) and all children under age 21 who will immigrate with you.

  (Data required on registrations may change each year. Call 900-884-8840 for the latest information.)

Photographs

Attach with tape a recent 1.5 inches (37 mm) square photo, with applicant's name printed on back.

Signature

Be sure to sign the form or you will not be considered for the lottery.

Documents

None.

STEP TWO: APPLICATION

Forms

☐ OF forms (available from U.S. consulate abroad for consular filing only).

☐ Form I-485 (U.S. filing only).

☐ Form I-485A (U.S. filing only).

☐ Form G-325A (U.S. filing only).

☐ Form I-134 (U.S. and consular filings).

☐ Form I-765, if advanced permission to work is desired (U.S. filing only).

Documents

☐ Evidence of registration selection.

☐ Long-form birth certificate for you and each accompanying relative.

☐ Passports for you and each accompanying relative, valid for at least six months beyond the date of the final interview.

☐ Police certificates from every country in which you and each accompanying relative have lived for at least one year since age 16 (Consular filing only).

☐ Military records for you and each accompanying relative (Consular filing only).

☐ Fingerprints for you and each accompanying relative between the ages of 14 and 75 (U.S. filing only).

☐ Three photographs each of you and each accompanying relative.

☐ Proof of education or work background:

  ☐ Copy of high school diploma, or

  ☐ Letters from past employers verifying skills and experience.

☐ I-94 card for you and each accompanying relative (U.S. filing only).

☐ Marriage certificate if you are married and bringing your spouse.

☐ If either you or spouse have been previously married, copies of divorce and death certificates showing termination of all previous marriages.

☐ Medical exam report for you and each accompanying relative.

Getting a Green Card Through Investment

Privileges

- You may live anywhere in the U.S. and stay as long as you want.

- When you first receive your green card through investment, you may work in your own company. After a certain length of time, you may work anywhere you wish or not work at all.

- You may travel in or out of the U.S. whenever you wish.

- You may apply to become an American citizen after you have held your green card for at least five years.

- If you qualify for a green card through investment, your spouse and unmarried children under the age of 21 may get green cards automatically as accompanying relatives.

Limitations

- You must maintain a large business investment in the U.S. for at least three years.

- Your place of actual residence must be in the U.S. You cannot use a green card only for work and travel purposes. (The only exception to this rule is for Alien Commuters, discussed in Chapter 4.)

- You must pay U.S. taxes on your worldwide income because you are regarded as a U.S. resident.

- You cannot remain outside the U.S. for more than one year at a time without special permission, or you risk losing your green card. (It is recommended that you return from any trips abroad before you have been gone for six (6) months.)

- If you commit a crime or participate in politically subversive activities or commit other proscribed activities, your green card can be taken away and you can be removed from the U.S. (deported).

A. How to Qualify

Qualifying for a green card through investment has some limitations.

1. Quota Restrictions

Green cards for investors are limited to 10,000 per year, with 3,000 of those reserved for persons investing in rural areas or areas of high unemployment. Only principal applicants are counted in the quota. Accompanying relatives are not. Therefore, in reality, many more than 10,000 per year can be admitted with green cards through investment.

At present, green cards are available to all qualified applicants. It appears unlikely that waiting periods will develop in the near future. Petition approval normally takes from two to six months. After petition approval, application approval should take an additional one to six months.

2. Who Qualifies for a Green Card Through Investment?

Green cards through investment are available to anyone who invests a minimum of $1 million in creating a new U.S. business or expanding one that already exists. The business must employ at least ten full-time American workers. The investor, his or her spouse and their children may not be counted among the ten employees.

The required dollar amount of the investment may be reduced to $500,000 if the business is located in a rural area or in an urban area with an unemployment rate certified by the state government to be at least 150% greater than the national average. Rural areas are defined as any location not part of an official metropolitan statistical area or not within the outer boundaries of any city having a population of 20,000 or more. State governments will identify the parts of the particular state that are high in unemployment, and will notify INS of which locations qualify. Even if you know that the area of your intended investment has extremely high unemployment, it will not qualify for the lesser dollar amount unless the state government has specifically designated it as a high unemployment area for green card through investment purposes. Several states, including Texas, California, New York, Florida and Washington, have made such designations.

INS also has the authority to require a greater amount of investment than $1 million. This may occur when the investor chooses to locate the business in an area of low unemployment. At present, INS has adopted the policy of not raising dollar investment requirements on this basis.

The entire investment does not have to be made in cash. Cash equivalents such as certificates of deposits, loans and notes can count in the total. So can the value of equipment, or inventory. Borrowed funds may be used as long as the investor is personally liable in the event of a default, and the loan is not secured by assets of the business being purchased. This means that mortgages on the business assets disqualify the amount borrowed from being calculated into the total investment figure.

A number of investors may join together in creating or expanding a U.S. business and each may qualify for a green card through the single company. However, the individual investment of each person must still be for the minimum qualifying amount, and each investor must be separately responsible for the creation of ten new jobs. For example, if five individuals each invest $1 million in a new business that will employ at least 50 American workers, all five investors qualify for green cards.

Although it is expected that the investment will be well underway when the green card application is made, the law does require the investment to be in a completely new commercial enterprise. There is an exception to this rule. The investor can purchase an existing business if he or she increases either its net worth or the number of employees by at least 40%. The rules requiring a $1 million investment and ten employees still apply, however. Therefore, the existing business must be large enough so that a 40% increase will amount to the fixed required dollar and employment minimums in the category.

If the existing business purchased is in financial trouble, an investment designed to save that business will qualify the investor for a green card in this category. Purchasing a troubled business releases the investor from having to increase the net worth or the number of employees. It does not, however, excuse the $1 million minimum investment requirement. To qualify as a troubled business, the company must have been in operation for at least two years, and have had an annual loss during those two years equal to at least 20% of the company's net worth. An investor buying a troubled business is prohibited from laying off any employees.

A green card for an investor is first issued only conditionally. The conditional green card is granted for two years. When the two years are over, the investor will have to file a request with INS to remove the condition.

In deciding if the condition should be removed, INS will investigate whether or not the proposed investment has actually been made, if ten full-time American workers have been hired, whether or not the business is still operating and if the business is still owned by the investor who got the green card. When any of the required factors cannot be established to the satisfaction of INS or the petition for removal of the condition is not filed within the final 90 days of the two-year conditional period, the investor will lose his or her green card and be subject to removal from the U.S. (deportation). If, on the other hand, INS is satisfied that the investment still meets all requirements, the condition will be removed and a permanent green card issued.

3. Accompanying Relatives

If you are married or have children below the age of 21 and you acquire a green card through investment, your spouse and children can automatically get green cards as accompanying relatives simply by providing proof of their family relationship to you. Their green cards will also be issued conditionally and will become permanent when yours does.

4. Inadmissibility

If you have ever been arrested for a crime, lied on an immigration application, lied to an immigration officer or suffered certain physical or mental illness or are otherwise inadmissible, you may be inadmissible from receiving a green card unless you can qualify for what is known as a *Waiver of Inadmissibility*. See Chapter 25 to find out exactly who is inadmissible and how you can overcome these problems.

B. Getting a Green Card Through Investment

Getting a green card through investment is a two-step process. There is no sponsoring relative or employer involved in this type of green card. Therefore, the completion of both steps will be carried out by you alone.

1. Step One: The Petition

You file the petition on your own behalf. All petitions are submitted to INS regional service centers in the U.S. You should file in the office closest to where the business in which you are investing is located. The object of the petition is to prove that you either have made or are in the process of making a qualifying business investment in the U.S. An approved petition does not by itself give you any immigration privileges. It is only a prerequisite to Step Two, submitting your application. The petition must be approved before you are eligible for Step Two.

2. Step Two: The Application

The application is filed by you and your accompanying relatives, if any. The application is your formal request for a green card. Step Two may be carried out in the U.S. at an INS office or in your home country at a U.S. consulate there. In either case, you may not file Step Two papers until Step One has been approved.

The majority of green card applications are filed at INS offices inside the U.S., since usually the applicant is already in the country. If you are in the U.S. legally on a nonimmigrant visa with a current priority date, you can probably apply for your green card either inside or outside the U.S., whichever you prefer. If you are in the U.S. illegally or entered legally without a visa under the Visa Waiver Program, whether you may still file your green card application inside the U.S. depends on whether you had a visa petition or labor certification application on file by January 14, 1998. If you did, you may be able to get your green card in the U.S. by paying the $1,000 penalty fee. This is in addition to the regular filing fee for such applications. If you are subject to these penalties and want to avoid them, you may instead elect to apply for your green card at a U.S. consulate abroad, but in that case, you must be sure that you are not subject to any grounds of inadmissibility or bars to adjustment of status, before you leave. See Chapter 25.

3. Paperwork

There are two types of paperwork you must submit to get a green card through investment. The first consists of official government forms. The second is personal and business documents such as birth and marriage certificates, financial records and legal papers showing your business investment. We will tell you exactly what forms and documents you need.

It is vital that forms are properly filled out and all necessary documents are supplied. You may resent the intrusion into your privacy and sizable effort it takes to prepare immigration applications, but you should realize the process is an impersonal matter to immigration officials. Your getting a green card is more important to you than it is to the U.S. government. This is not a pleasant thing to accept, but you are better off having a real understanding of your position. People from all over the world want green cards. There is no shortage of applicants. Take the time and trouble to prepare your papers properly. In the end it will pay off with a successful application.

The documents you supply to INS do not have to be originals. Photocopies of all documents are acceptable as long as you have the originals in your possession and are willing to produce the originals at the request of INS. Documents submitted to U.S. consulates, on the other hand, must be either originals or official government certified copies. Government certified copies and notarized copies are not the same thing. Documents which have only been notarized are not acceptable. They must carry a government seal. In addition to any original or government certified copies of documents submitted to a consulate, you should submit plain photocopies of each document as well. After the consulate compares the copies with the originals, it will return the originals.

Documents will be accepted if they are in either English, or, with papers filed at U.S. consulates abroad, the language of the country where the documents are being filed. An exception exists for papers filed at the U.S. consulates in Japan, where all documents must be translated into English. If the documents are not in an acceptable language as just explained, they must be accompanied by a full, word for word, written English translation. Any capable person may act as translator. It is not necessary to hire a professional. At the end of each translation, the following statement must appear:

> *I hereby certify that I translated this document from (language) to English. This translation is accurate and complete. I further certify that I am fully competent to translate from (language) to English.*

The translator should sign this statement but it does not have to be witnessed or notarized.

Later in this chapter we describe in detail the forms and documents needed to get your green card through investment. A summary checklist of forms and documents appears at the end of this chapter.

C. Who's Who in Getting Your Green Card

Getting a green card will be easier if you familiarize yourself with the technical names used for each participant in the process. During Step One, the petition, you are the *petitioner*. In Step Two, the application, you are referred to as *applicant*. If you are bringing your spouse and children with you as accompanying relatives, they are known as *applicants* as well.

D. Step One: The Petition

This section includes the information you need to submit the petition.

1. General Procedures

The Step One petition is mailed to the INS regional service center in the U.S. having jurisdiction over your place of business. INS regional service centers are not the same as INS local offices. There are four INS regional service centers spread across the U.S.

Within a week or so after mailing the petition, you should receive a written confirmation that the papers are being processed, together with a receipt for the fees. This notice will also give your immigration case file number and tell approximately when to expect a decision. If INS wants further information before acting on your case, all petition papers, forms and documents will be returned to you, together with another form known as an I-797. The I-797 "Request for Evidence" tells you what corrections, additional pieces of information or additional documents are expected. You should make the corrections or supply the extra data and mail the whole package back to the INS regional service center.

The filing fee for each petition is currently $155. Checks or money orders are accepted. Regional service centers will not accept cash. When filing by mail, we recommend sending the papers by certified mail, return receipt requested, and keeping a complete copy of everything sent for your records. Appendix II contains a list of all INS regional service centers with their addresses, telephone and fax numbers.

It generally takes one to three months to get a decision on the petition. Once your petition is approved, a Notice of Action Form I-797 will be sent to you, indicating the approval. If you plan to execute Step Two at a U.S. consulate abroad, INS will forward the file to the National Visa Center (NVC) located in Portsmouth, New Hampshire. NVC will then send a packet of forms and instructions to you so that you may proceed with Step Two, described later in this chapter.

2. Petition Forms

A copy of this form may be found in Appendix III.

Form I-526

This form, called Immigrant Petition by Alien Entrepreneur, is the only Step One form you need to complete.

Part 1. Part 1 asks questions about you. Your current immigration status must be disclosed, even if you are in the U.S. illegally. "A" numbers are usually issued only to people who previously held green cards or have made previous green card applications. If any of the boxes do not apply to you, answer "N/A."

In listing your address, you will have to put down the address where you really live, even if it means revealing an illegal U.S. residence. If you are in the U.S. illegally, however, you may be ineligible to receive a change of status (from nonimmigrant to permanent resident) or even to get an immigrant visa. Again, be sure to understand if any grounds of inadmissibility or bars to permanent residence apply to you before you depart the U.S. or file your application. See Chapter 25.

Part 2. Part 2 asks you to check off the box indicating the classification you are seeking. Note that there are two "b" boxes. This is due to a misprint in the form. The first box "b" applies only if you are investing in an area of high employment for which the law requires more than a $1 million investment. To date, INS has decided not to utilize this provision, so the first box "b" will be checked only when INS policy changes. Check the second box "b."

Part 3. Part 3 asks basic questions about your business investment in the U.S. and is self-explanatory.

Part 4. Part 4 asks for financial information about your business investment. This should be self-explanatory.

Part 5. Part 5 asks questions about the jobs your investment will create. Remember that you must create at least ten new jobs to qualify, but you have up to two years to actually create them.

Part 6. Part 6 asks at which consulate you intend to apply for your green card, and also requests your last foreign address, if you are currently living in the U.S. In listing a consulate, keep in mind that U.S. consulates in your home country or last country of residence are the only ones legally required to accept your application. If there is an overwhelming need to file elsewhere, you can approach a consulate in some other country and ask if it will agree to process you application there. The consulate is under no obligation to grant your request and is very likely to turn you down, but there is no harm in asking.

Parts 7 and 8. These parts are merely for signatures and are self-explanatory.

3. Petition Documents

You must prove that you either have made or are actively in the process of making a qualifying business investment in the U.S. Generally, the amount invested must be at least $1 million. If your investment is in a targeted area of high unemployment or in a rural area, you should submit evidence of this. You must also show that the business will employ at least ten full-time American workers (which includes U.S. citizens, permanent residents and asylees/refugees) not including you or your immediate family. Finally, you must show that the investment was made *after* November 29, 1990.

Documents to prove your eligibility should include:

- bank wire-transfer memos showing the amount of money sent to the U.S. from abroad
- contracts and bills of sale for purchase of capital goods and inventory showing the amount spent
- leases, deeds or contracts for purchase of business premises
- construction contracts and blueprints for building business premises
- comprehensive business plans with cash flow projections for the next three years
- U.S. employment tax returns showing the number of employees on the qualifying company's payroll, and
- accountant's financial statements for the business, including balance sheets.

If you are in the process of starting up the business, you may be unable to produce all of the items listed above. In that case, at a minimum you will have to present evidence that you have sufficient funds to invest, such as bank statements or lines of credit sufficient to purchase the business, and a written contract legally committing you to make the investment. You must also include a detailed written explanation of the nature of the business containing statements of how much will be invested, where the funds for investment will come from, how the fund will be used, and a list of the specific job openings you expect to have over the first two years of the business, including job title, job description, salary, and when these jobs will become available. Finally, you should submit a comprehensive business plan supporting all of these documents.

In addition to the above, you should submit as many documents as possible to show that your investment is being made in a real, ongoing business that requires daily supervision. Passive investments such as land speculation do not qualify you for a green card in this category. Evidence of an active business should include:

- articles of incorporation or other business charter of the qualifying company
- bank statements from the qualifying company
- credit agreements with suppliers
- letters of credit issued
- leases or deeds for business premises and warehouse space
- income and payroll tax returns filed, if any, and
- promotional literature or advertising.

If the qualifying business is not incorporated, instead of copies of stock certificates you will need to present legal papers proving the existence and ownership of the company, such as partnership agreements, business registration certificates or business licenses, together with a notarized affidavit from an official of the company certifying who owns the business and in what percentages.

4. Petition Interviews

Personal interviews on the petition are very rare. There may be an interview only if the legitimacy of the paperwork in your case is questionable. If an interview is held, it will be at the INS local office nearest the place where your investment is located. You will be asked to explain all documents and to convince the INS officer that you intend to carry out your plans of investment and hiring American workers. INS permits you to be represented by an immigration attorney if you wish.

5. Petition Appeals

When the investment has been poorly documented, or if you have not been able to convince INS that you will be employing at least ten full time American workers, the petition will probably be denied. You will then receive written notice of INS's unfavorable decision, a written statement of the reasons for the negative outcome and an explanation of how to make a formal appeal.

The best way to handle an appeal is to try avoiding it altogether. Filing an appeal means making an argument to INS that its reasoning was wrong. If you think you can eliminate the reason why your petition failed by improving your paperwork, it makes sense to forget about the appeals process and simply file a new petition, being careful to see that it is better prepared than the first.

If the petition was denied because you left out necessary documents that have since been located, the new documents should be sent together with a written request that the case be reopened to the same INS office that issued the denial. This is technically called a *Motion to Reopen*. There is a $110 fee for filing this motion. Appeals often take a long time. A Motion to Reopen can be concluded faster than an appeal.

If you do choose to appeal, it must be done within 30 days of the date on the Notice of Denial. The appeal should be filed at the same INS office with which you have been dealing. There is a $110 filing fee. INS will then forward the papers for consideration by the Board of Immigration Appeals in Washington, D.C. The appeals decision, which can take many months, will be sent to you by mail. The vast majority of appeals fail.

When an appeal to INS has been denied, the next step is an appeal through the U.S. judicial system. You may not file an action in court without first going through the appeals process available from INS. If the case has reached this stage and you are living illegally in the U.S., we strongly recommend seeking representation from a qualified immigration attorney, as you are now in danger of being removed (deported).

E. Step Two: The Application (Consular Filing)

Anyone with an approved petition can apply for a green card at a U.S. consulate in his or her home country or last country of residence. You must be physically present in order to apply there. Even if you have been or are now living illegally in the U.S., you may still get a green card from a U.S. consulate if you otherwise qualify. (See Chapter 25 to be sure this is the case.)

CITIZENS OF COUNTRIES WITHOUT U.S. EMBASSIES

Citizens of countries not having formal diplomatic relations with the U.S. are faced with the problem of where to apply for immigrant visas. At present, the U.S. maintains no diplomatic relations with, and therefore makes no visa services available in, Afghanistan, Bosnia, Iran, Iraq, Lebanon, Libya and Somalia.

Persons from these countries who are physically present in the U.S. may have Step Two papers processed at the U.S. consulate in Ciudad Juárez, Mexico.

Persons from these countries who are still residing in their home countries will apply at a designated foreign consulate. Persons who are outside of their home country in a third country which conducts visa processing, will do visa processing in that country as if they were residents of the third country.

---

1. Benefits and Drawbacks of Consular Filing

Anyone with an approved petition can apply for a green card at the appropriate consulate. (Again, see Chapter 25 to make sure you are not inadmissible.) That is not the case with U.S. applications since you must be physically inside the U.S. to apply there. If you are a preference relative and in the U.S. illegally, you may be able to apply in the U.S. if you had a visa petition or labor certification on file by April 14, 1998, by paying the $1,000 penalty. Instead of paying the penalty, you can elect to file at a consulate, but under these circumstances, if you instead elect to file at a consulate, be sure that the "overstay" bars (relating to individuals who were out of status for over six months after April 1, 1997) and other bars on grounds of inadmissibility do not apply to you. (Se Chapter 25.)

A further plus to consular filing is that consulate offices may work more quickly to issue green cards than do some INS offices. Your waiting time for the paperwork to be finished may be months shorter at a U.S. consulate abroad than at U.S. INS offices.

One drawback to consular filing is the travel expense and inconvenience you will experience in returning to your home country if you are already in the U.S. Another problem is that should your consular application fail, you will have fewer ways to appeal than a U.S. filing would offer.

2. Application General Procedures: Consular Filing

The law states that only a U.S. consulate or embassy in your home country is required to accept your green card application. This is true for all except persons from countries without U.S. embassies. A complete list of U.S. consulates that process visa applications, with addresses and phone numbers is in Appendix I. You can ask a consulate located elsewhere to accept your application, but it has the option to say no, and in fact consulates turn down most such requests. If you do wish to ask for this privilege, you should approach the consulate of your choice before filing the Step One petition. That is because Form I-526 in Step One asks where you will file your application and you must be prepared with an answer to this question.

You may not file an application for a green card at a consulate until after your petition has been approved. At that time, the INS office where your petition was originally submitted will forward your file to the National Visa Center (NVC) in Portsmouth, New Hampshire. NVC will then forward your file to the U.S. consulate you have named on Form I-526 in Step One. At the same time, a Notice of Approval from Step One will be sent directly to you. NVC will send instructions and application forms to you within a month or two after petition approval. You will return all paperwork, however, directly to the consulate. If, after waiting a reasonable time, you have not heard from NVC, you should call and look into the matter.

NVC will send you Packet 3, containing forms and instructions. Complete and send Forms OF-230 I and OF-169 to the consulate as soon as possible. This will allow the consulate to begin a required security check into your background. Failure to return these forms promptly can significantly delay your green card.

The application for your green card is made in person by appointment. Once the consulate is ready for your final processing, it will then send another group of papers known as Packet 4. Packet 4 includes an interview appointment letter, instructions for obtaining your medical examination and still more forms to be completed. Other than Form

OF-230 I, which should be mailed in as soon as you receive it, and Form OF-169, which you will send in when you are ready for your interview, do not mail your paperwork to the consulate. Instead, bring the rest of your forms and all documents with you at the time of your appointment. The fee for filing an application is $200 per person.

3.   Application Forms: Consular Filing

When you file at a U.S. consulate abroad, the consulate officials will provide you with certain optional forms, designated by an "OF" preceeding a number. Instructions for completing optional forms and what to do with them once they are filled out will come with the forms. We do not include copies of these forms in Appendix III. Copies of all non "OF" forms are in Appendix III.

Form I-134

It is necessary to convince the consulate that once you receive a green card you are not likely to go on public welfare. Since your application is based on a large business investment, that alone should be sufficient proof that you have a way to support yourself and an I-134 need not be filed for you. You should still, however, fill out Form-134, the Affidavit of Support, for any accompanying relatives. Because the consulate knows you will have an income, you must sign the I-134 Forms and take financial responsibility for each of them.

Form I-134 is your guarantee that you will take care of your accompanying relatives. In signing the Affidavit of Support, you are not actually promising to support your accompanying relatives. What you do promise is to reimburse the U.S. government for the sum total of any government support payments they might receive should they go on welfare. The Affidavit of Support supposedly binds you to this obligation for three years. Your responsibility to the government then comes to an end.

4.   Application Documents: Consular Filing

The most important document in your application is the Notice of Action showing approval of your petition. It is sent directly from the INS office in the U.S. to the consulate you named on Form I-526 in Step One. This is the only document you will not have to submit yourself. Do not mail in your other documents. Instead, bring them to your interview.

You must resubmit to the consulate all the documents first filed in Step One. If not included in Step One, you must have your long form birth certificate and birth certificates of any unmarried minor children who are not immigrating with you. Copies of these documents will not be forwarded by INS to the consulate for you.

It is also necessary to have in your possession a valid passport from your home country. The expiration date on the passport must leave enough time for the passport to remain valid at least six months beyond the date of your final application interview.

Unlike applications made in the U.S., you personally must collect police clearance certificates from each country you have lived in for one year or more since your 16th birthday. Additionally, you must have a police certificate from your home country or country of last residence, if you lived there for at least six months since the age of 16. You do not need to obtain police certificates from the U.S. Like all other documents, you should be prepared to present the necessary police clearance certificates at your interview. If you go to your interview without the required certificates, you will be refused a green card and told to return after you get them.

OBTAINING POLICE CERTIFICATES

You should contact the local police department in your home country for instructions on how to get police certificates. To obtain police certificates from nations other than your home country, it is best to contact the nearest consulate representing that country for instructions. Some nations refuse to supply police certificates, or their certificates are not considered reliable, and so you will not be required to obtain them from those locations. At this writing, police certificates are not required from the following countries:

Afghanistan	Haiti	Saudi Arabia
Albania	Honduras	Sierra Leone
Angola	India	Somalia
Bangladesh	Indonesia	Sri Lanka
Brunei	Iran	Sudan
Bulgaria	Iraq	Syria
Cambodia	Jordan	Tanzania
Chad	Laos	Thailand
Colombia	Liberia	Turkey
Costa Rica	Libya	United Arab
Cuba	Malaysia	Emirates
Dominican Republic	Mexico	United Kingdom
El Salvador	Mongolia	United States
Equatorial Guinea	Mozambique	Venezuela
Ghana	Nepal	Vietnam
Guatemala	Pakistan	

For applicants who once lived in Japan but do not reside there at the time their green card applications are filed, the Department of State recognizes that police certificates are available from Japan only as far back as five years from the date of the green card application.

Other countries, including the Netherlands, North Korea, South Africa and South Korea will send certificates directly to U.S. consulates but not to you personally. Before they send the certificates out, however, you must request that it be done. Usually this requires filing some type of request form together with a set of your fingerprints.

You and each accompanying relative must bring to the interview three photographs taken in compliance with the instruction sheet found in Appendix III. Additional photo instructions are provided in Packet 4. Often Packet 4 will also contain a list of local photographers who take this type of picture.

A few consulates require you to submit fingerprints, though most do not. Consulates wanting fingerprints will send you blank fingerprint cards with instructions.

5. Application Interviews: Consular Filing

Consulates hold interviews on all green card applications. A written notice of your interview appointment is included when you receive Packet 4. Immediately before the interview, you and your accompanying relatives will be required to have medical examinations. Some consulates conduct the medical exams up to several days before the interview. Others, including London, schedule the medical exam and the interview on the same day. You will be told where to go and what to do in your appointment letter.

The medical examinations are conducted by private doctors and you are required to pay the doctor a fee. The fees vary from as little as $50 to more than $150 per exam, depending on the country. The amount of the medical exam fee will be stated in your appointment letter. The exam itself involves the taking of a medical history, blood test and chest X ray, and verification or administering of vaccinations, if applicable. Pregnant women who do not want to be X-rayed may so advise the consulate and their appointments will be postponed until after the pregnancy. The requirement to have an X ray taken cannot be waived.

The main purpose of the medical exam is to verify that you are not medically inadmissible. The primary medical grounds of inadmissibility are tuberculosis and HIV (AIDS). Medical grounds of inadmissibility usually can be overcome with treatment. See Chapter 25, *Inadmissibility*, for more details. If you need a medical waiver, you will be given complete instructions by the consulate at the time of your interview.

After the medical exam, you and your accompanying relatives will report to the consulate for the interview. At that time, you must pay two more fees: $170 per person when your papers are submitted, and an additional $30 per person at the end of the interview when your applications are approved. Some consulates accept payment only by certified check, money order or travelers check. Others accept cash. You will be told the proper method of payment in Packet 4.

Bring with you to the interview the completed forms, photographs, your passports and all of the required documents discussed here. The interview process involves verification of your application's accuracy and an inspection of your documents. If all is in order, you will be asked to return later in the day when you will be issued an immigrant visa. You are not yet a permanent resident.

The immigrant visa allows you to request entry to the U.S. You acquire the full status of green card holder at the moment of being inspected and admitted into the U.S. with your immigrant visa. At that time, your passport is stamped and you are immediately authorized to work. If you are bringing any accompanying relatives, they must enter at either the same time or after you do in order to become permanent residents. Permanent green cards for you and your accompanying relatives are then ordered. They will come to you by mail several months later.

6. Application Appeals: Consular Filing

When a consulate denies a green card application, there is no formal appeal available, although you are free to reapply as often as you like. When your green card is refused, you will be told the reasons why. The most common reason for denial is failure to supply all the required documents. Sometimes presenting more evidence on an unclear fact can bring about a better result. If the denial was caused by a lack of evidence, this will be explained in a written notice sent to you by mail.

Another common reason for denial of a green card is that the consular officer believes you are inadmissible. If you are found to be inadmissible, you will be given an opportunity to apply for a Waiver of Inadmissibility, if one is available. See Chapter 25 for directions on how to apply.

When all these possibilities are exhausted, if the consulate still refuses you a green card, your opportunities for further appeals are severely limited. Historically, the courts have held that there is no right to judicial review and there is no formal appeal procedure through any U.S. government agency. The State Department in Washington, D.C. does offer an informal review procedure through the mail. This agency will look at the factual elements of your case and decide whether or not the consulate made a correct decision. Even if the State Department rules in your favor, the decision is only advisory and the consulate is free to ignore the State Department, letting its own decision stand. At present, there does appear to be a trend developing where courts in the U.S. are more frequently accepting jurisdiction over consular decisions, so a court appeal may be a possibility to consider. The jurisdiction of U.S. courts to review consular decisions, is however, still an unsettled legal issue.

Your denial may be based on a question of law rather than fact. The State Department offers the same informal review for legal questions with the difference that any decision it makes is binding on the consulate. Appeals of this kind are very technical and should be handled by a competent immigration attorney. Even with representation by an attorney, most such appeals fail.

You may ask the consular office for a written notice of denial or an explanation to see if there is any way to fix the problem, such as providing additional documentation. Depending on the reason for the denial you may be able to apply again.

You may also simply wait awhile, reapply on a different basis, and hope for better luck next time. The fact that you have been turned down once does not stop you from trying again.

F. Step Two: The Application (U.S. Filing)

If you are physically present in the U.S., you may apply for a green card without leaving the country on the following conditions:

- you have already received an approved petition
- a green card is currently available to you because your waiting period under the quota is up, and
- you are in status and/or otherwise eligible to adjust status (see Chapter 25).

Unless you can meet these terms, you may not file an application for a green card in the U.S.

1. Benefits and Drawbacks of U.S. Filing

The obvious benefit to applying for a green card in the U.S. is that if you are already in the country, you avoid the expense and inconvenience of overseas travel. Moreover, it is a rule of immigration that once you file Step Two, you must remain wherever you have filed. When you file in the U.S., should problems arise in your case, you will at least be able to wait for a decision in America, a circumstance most green card applicants prefer.

Another important benefit of U.S. filing is that you may receive permission to work while you wait for the results of your case. To obtain this benefit, you should submit form I-765 to the service center along with your visa petition (form I-526). If you do not need to work right away, but can wait until after getting your green card, you do not need to file this separate application.

Be aware that if you work under your green card application work permit ("open market EAD") for a different employer than an authorized "H-1B" or "L" visa employer, you will be considered out of status should your green card application be denied. For this reason, it is better to continue working for your L or H employer until after your green card is approved. If you are working for such an employer, you should also request advance parole before departing the U.S., otherwise your green card application will be considered abandoned.

If your application for a green card is turned down, you have greater rights of appeal inside the U.S. than you do at a U.S. consulate. INS offices have different procedures from consular offices because they are controlled by a different branch of the U.S. government.

There are some disadvantages to applying in the U.S. It may take longer to get results. Processing times at INS offices can approach as long as one year. While your case is pending at an INS office, you may not leave the U.S. without getting special permission (advance parole). If you do leave without INS's permission, even for a genuine emergency, this will be regarded as withdrawal of your application and you will have to start your application over again when you return.

PROCEDURES FOR ADVANCED WORK AUTHORIZATION

If you want to work before your application for a green card is approved, you should file an application for employment authorization. This can be done by completing Form I-765 and filing it with the same INS service center where you file the Step Two papers. Together with Form I-765, you must submit your I-94 card and pay a filing fee of $100. It is very important to keep the fee receipt INS gives you so you can prove that the I-765 was filed. Normally you will want to file the application for employment authorization at the same time as your Step Two application papers.

Legally, INS does not have to make a decision on your employment authorization application for up to 90 days. If for some reason you are not given a decision within 90 days, you will, at your request, be granted an interim employment authorization which will last 240 days.

If 240 days pass and you still have not received a final decision on the I-765, you must stop working. Interim work authorization cards cannot be renewed. However, if you reach this point, you have the option to file a new I-765 application and, if you do not get a decision on the new application within 90 days, you will then be entitled to another interim work authorization card.

2. Application General Procedures: U.S. Filing

You may not begin Step Two until you have an approved Step One petition. The application, consisting of both forms and documents, is submitted by mail to the INS service center with responsibility over the place you are living. Appendix II contains a complete list of all INS service centers with their telephone numbers and addresses.

For U.S. filings, the basic form used in Step Two, the application, is INS Form I-485, Application for Permanent Residence. Form I-485 is filed to adjust your status in the U.S. "Adjusting status" is a technical term used only in U.S. filings. It simply means that you are presently in the U.S. as a nonimmigrant and are in the process of acquiring a green card.

The filing fee for each application is $130 for applicants age 14 and over, and $105 for applicants under age 14. A separate application must be filed for you and each accompanying relative. If you are in the U.S. illegally, or entered improperly, your ability to stay in the U.S. and get your green card may depend on whether you had a visa petition or labor certification on file by January 14, 1998. See Chapter 25 to be sure you qualify. Checks and money orders are accepted. It is not advisable to send cash through the mail, but cash is satisfactory if you file in person. Cash is accepted only in the exact amount. INS offices will not make change. We recommend filing your papers in person if at all possible, as you will be given a written receipt from INS and your papers are likely to be processed right away. If you choose to mail in your application, you should do so by certified mail, return receipt requested. In either case, keep a complete copy of everything you send in.

Once your application has been filed, you should not leave the U.S. for any reason before your application has been approved, or until you apply for and receive advance parole (advance permission to reenter the U.S.). Any other absence will be viewed as a termination of your application for a green card. If you must leave the U.S. you should apply for advance parole (form I-131) by mail to the appropriate service center, sending three passport-type photographs and proof of the reason (any legitimate personal or business reason). There is a $95 filing fee. If approved, you will be allowed to leave the U.S. and return again with no break in the processing of your application.

Generally, after filing your application, you will not hear anything from INS for several months. Then you should receive a notice of your interview appointment. The interview notice will also contain instructions for getting the required medical exam, and will tell you if any further documentation is needed.

If everything is in order, your application will be approved at the conclusion of the interview. Your passport will be stamped to show that you have been admitted to the U.S. as a permanent resident, and your permanent green card will be ordered. The green card will come to you in the mail about two months after the interview.

3. Application Forms: U.S. Filing

Copies of all forms can be found in Appendix III.

Form I-485

While most of the form is self-explanatory, a few items typically raise concerns. If a particular question does not apply to you, answer it with "None" or "N/A." The questions on this form requiring explanation are as follows:

Part 1. Part 1 asks for general information about when and where you were born, your present address and immigration status. It also asks for an "A" number. Normally, you will not have an "A" number unless you previously applied for a green card or have been in deportation proceedings.

Part 2. In Part 2, you will mark Box A if you are the principal applicant. Box B is marked if your spouse or parent is the principal applicant.

Part 3. The questions in Sections A through C are self-explanatory. The nonimmigrant visa number is the number that appears on the very top of the visa stamp. It is not the same as your visa classification. The questions in Section C are meant to identify people who are inadmissible. With the exception of certain memberships in the Communist Party or similar organizations, you will not be deemed inadmissible simply because you joined an organization. However, if your answer to any of the other questions is "yes," you may be inadmissible. See Chapter 25, which is intended to help you remove such obstacles. Don't lie on your answers because you will probably be found out, especially if you have engaged in criminal activity. Many grounds of inadmissibility can be legally overcome, but once a lie is detected, you will lose the legal right to correct the problem. In addition, a false answer is grounds to deny your application and may result in your being permanently barred from getting a green card.

Form I-485A

This form is required only if you are subject to the $1,000 penalty for entering, working in or living in the U.S. illegally. The form is self-explanatory, and is intended only to determine if you are subject to the penalty. (See Chapter 26 for an explanation of when it is required.)

Form G-325A

G-325A biographic data forms must be filled out for you and each accompanying relative. You need not file a G-325A for any child under the age of 14 or any adult over the age of 79. The G-325A form is meant to gather personal background information. The questions are self-explanatory.

Form I-134

It is necessary to convince INS that once you receive a green card you are not likely to go on public welfare. Since you have made a large business investment already, which proves you have a way to support yourself, an I-134 need not be filed for you. You should still, however, fill out Form I-134, the Affidavit of Support, for any accompanying relative. Because INS knows you will have an income, you must sign the I-134 forms and take financial responsibility for each of them.

Form I-134 is your guarantee that you will take care of your accompanying relatives. In signing the Affidavit of Support, you are not actually promising to support your accompanying relatives. What you do promise is to reimburse the U.S. government for the sum total of any government support payments they might receive should they go on welfare. The Affidavit of Support supposedly binds you to this obligation for three years. Your responsibility to the government then comes to an end.

Form I-765

Block above Question 1. Mark the first box, "Permission to accept employment."

Questions 1–8. These questions are self-explanatory.

Question 9. This asks for your Social Security number, including all numbers you have ever used. If you have never used a Social Security number, answer "None." If you have a nonworking Social Security number, write down the number followed by the words "nonworking, for tax purposes only." If you have ever used a false number, give that number, followed by the words: "Not my valid number." Before submitting the form, read Chapter 25 as it relates to grounds of inadmissibility for document fraud, to be sure you are not barred from getting a green card.

Question 10. You will not usually have an Alien Registration Number unless you previously applied for a green card, were in deportation proceedings or have had certain types of immigration applications denied. All Alien Registration Numbers begin with the letter "A." If you have no "A" number, but you entered the U.S. with a valid visa or without a visa under the Visa Waiver Program, you should have an I-94 card. In this case, answer Question 10 by putting down the admission number from the I-94 card.

If you are from Mexico, you may have entered the U.S. with a border crossing card, in which case you should put down the number on the entry document you received at the border, if any. Otherwise simply put down the number of the border crossing card itself, followed with "BCC." If you are Canadian and you entered the U.S. as a visitor, you will not usually have any of the documents described here, in which case you should put down "None."

Questions 11–15. These questions are self-explanatory.
Question 16. Answer this question "(C)(9)."

4. Application Documents: U.S. Filing

You must submit the Notice of Action showing petition
approval with the application. You and each of your accompanying relatives are required to submit two photographs.
These photos should meet the specifications on the photo
instruction sheet found in Appendix III. Additionally, you
must submit your birth certificate or other record of birth,
if married a marriage certificate and your spouse's birth
certificate, and birth certificates for all your children under
age 21, even if not immigrating with you.

You must also submit a Medical Examination Report for
each applicant. This is done on INS Form I-693, which
must be taken to an INS authorized physician or medical
clinic. The INS local office will provide you with the form
as well as a list of approved physicians in your area. After
completion of the medical exam, and upon obtaining the
test results, the doctor will give you the results in a sealed
envelope. Do not open the envelope.

Each applicant must submit an I-94 card if one was
issued. Failure to do so may result in a conclusion that you
entered or remained in the U.S. illegally and are not able to
get your green card in the U.S. unless you qualify under the
penalty provision (see Chapter 25). The I-94 is the small
white or green card you received on entering the U.S.

The only other paperwork required is a fingerprint card.
Beginning March 30, 1998, INS regulations changed so that
all fingerprinting now takes place at an INS-run fingerprinting center. You will be notified where and when to
appear after submitting your application forms. You will be
required to pay INS $25 (often when you file your applica-
tion papers) to cover the fingerprinting costs.

5. Application Interviews: U.S. Filing

As previously explained, personal interviews may be waived
in green card-through-investment applications. If an interview is not waived, you and your accompanying relatives
will be asked to come in to the INS local office for final
processing. The INS officer will go over your application to
make sure that everything is correct. He will also ask
questions to convince himself that you are not inadmissible.
(See Chapter 25, *Inadmissibility.*) A single fingerprint will
then be taken and you will be asked to sign your application
under oath. Accompanying relatives, all of whom must
attend the interview with you, will go through the same
procedure.

The interview normally takes about 30 minutes. If all
goes well, your case should be approved on the spot. You
will not be expected to wait for the results. Most INS offices
will place a temporary stamp in your passport showing that
you have become a U.S. permanent resident. With this
stamp, you acquire all the rights of a green card holder
including the right to work and freedom to travel in and
out of the U.S. The stamp is not your green card. You will
receive your permanent green card by mail several months
later. If your fingerprints have not been cleared yet, your
application will be approved only provisionally pending
clearance. In those cases, no stamp will be placed in your
passport at the interview. Instead, you will receive a written
notice of approval within a month or two. That notice serves
as your proof of U.S. residency until you receive your green
card, which takes yet another two or three months. If you
need to travel outside the U.S. before your green card
arrives, however, you must go back to the INS office with
your passport and the written notice of approval, and a
temporary stamp will be placed in your passport, enabling
you to return after your trip. Never leave the U.S. without
either your green card or a temporary stamp in your passport.

6. Application Appeals: U.S. Filing

If your application is denied, you will receive a written decision by mail explaining the reasons for the denial. There is
no way of making a formal appeal to INS when your application is turned down. If the problem is too little evidence,
you may be able to overcome this obstacle by adding more
documents and resubmitting the entire application to the
same INS office you have been dealing with, together with a
written request that the case be reopened. The written
request does not have to be in any special form. This is
technically called a *Motion to Reopen.* There is a $110 fee to
file this motion. Alternatively, you may wait until INS
begins deportation proceedings, in which case you may
refile your application with the immigration judge.

If your application is denied because you are found
inadmissible, you will be given the opportunity to apply for
what is known as a *Waiver of Inadmissibility,* provided a
waiver is available for your ground of inadmissibility. See
Chapter 25 for directions on how to apply.

Although there is no appeal to INS for the denial of a
green card application, you have the right to file an appeal
in a U.S. district court. This requires employing an
immigration attorney at considerable expense. Such appeals
are usually unsuccessful.

REMOVING CONDITIONAL RESIDENCE

As we've already stated, green cards through investment are first issued conditionally for two years. After the two years are up, in order to make the green cards permanent, you must then go through a procedure for removing the conditional residence. To remove the conditional basis of the green card, file form I-829 90 days prior to the second anniversary of your admission to the U.S. The spouse and children of the entrepreneur should be included on the form. In addition to the $345 filing fee, the petition to remove conditions should be accompanied by the following documentation:

- evidence that you actually established the commercial enterprise (such as federal income tax returns)
- evidence that you actively invested the required capital (such as financial statements)
- evidence that you have substantially met and maintained the capital investment requirement (such as bank statements, invoices, receipts, contracts, etc.)
- evidence that the enterprise has generated employment for (or will soon do so) ten U.S. workers, such as payroll records, tax documents, forms I-9. (If the investment was in a "troubled business," submit evidence that the pre-investment level of employees was maintained during the two-year conditional residence period.)

Failure to submit the I-829 and documentation prior to the 90-day window period will, under INS regulations, result in termination of the conditional resident status and INS may start deportation proceedings against the conditional resident and family members. If you miss the deadline you can still file the removal petition for "good cause and extenuating circumstances" up to the time INS commences deportation proceedings. After the matter comes under the jurisdiction of the immigration court, the judge may only terminate proceedings and restore permanent resident status with the INS' cooperation. Because of this, it is very important to make a timely filing of the I-829.

INS may waive the interview (in connection with the I-829 filing), if the accompanying documentation makes it clear you have fulfilled the requirements for the green card.

If INS requires an interview, it will be held at a local INS office near where the commercial enterprise is located. If you fail to appear for the interview, the INS regulations specify that INS should put the petitioner-entrepreneur under deportation proceedings and terminate the conditional status as of the two-year anniversary of the conditional status grant. If that happens, the entrepreneur can still write the INS director and request that the interview be rescheduled or waived. If it is rescheduled or waived, the CPR status is restored. Otherwise, the petition has to be considered in deportation court as discussed above. You can clearly save yourself a lot of time and trouble by filing the petition on time and appearing for the interview or timely requesting a waiver or rescheduling of the interview.

The primary purpose of the request to remove conditional status is to show all of the following:

- that you did actually make the investment
- that you did actually hire at least ten full-time American workers
- that the business in which you invested is still operating, and
- that you still own the business.

In addition to a request form, you are required to submit documents proving these facts.

On approval of your request to remove the conditional residence, your green card will become permanent. If you fail to file the request, or you are unable to prove that you still meet all the requirements for a green card through investment, your green card will be canceled. Your accompanying relatives will also lose their green cards. You and your family members will then have to leave the U.S. or be subject to deportation.

FORMS AND DOCUMENTS CHECKLIST

STEP ONE: PETITION

Forms

- [ ] Form I-526.

Documents

- [ ] Copies of all outstanding stock certificates, if the business is a corporation.
- [ ] Notarized affidavit from the secretary of the corporation, or, if the business is not a corporation, from the official record keeper of the business, stating the names of each owner and percentages of the company owned.
- [ ] Articles of incorporation or other legal charter or business license of the company.
- [ ] Letter from the state government certifying that the business is located in a rural or high unemployment area, if applicable.
- [ ] Tax returns of the company for the past two years, if available.
- [ ] Accountant's financial statements, including profit and loss statements and balance sheets of the company for the past two years, if available.
- [ ] Payroll records of the company for the past two years, if available.
- [ ] Promotional literature describing the nature of the business.
- [ ] Letters from banks or bank statements indicating the average account balance of the business.
- [ ] Evidence of deposits of funds in the business's bank account, and proof of sources of funds.
- [ ] Contracts for purchase and bills of sale for the purchase of capital goods and inventory.
- [ ] Lease agreements for the business premises, contracts to purchase or deeds for business real estate or construction contracts and blueprints for building the business premises.
- [ ] Comprehensive business plan with cash flow projections for the next three years.
- [ ] Detailed written statement describing the business, where the investment is coming from, how the investment will be used, and an itemization of full-time positions that will be filled with American workers, including duties, salaries, and when each job will become available.

STEP TWO: APPLICATION

Forms

- [ ] OF forms (available at U.S. consulate abroad for consular filing only).
- [ ] Form I-485 (U.S. filing only).
- [ ] Form I-485A (U.S. filing only).
- [ ] Form G-325A (U.S. filing only).
- [ ] Form I-134 (U.S. and consular filings).
- [ ] Form I-765, if advanced work authorization is needed (U.S. filing only).

Documents

- [ ] Notice showing approval of your petition.
- [ ] I-94 card for you and each accompanying relative (U.S. filing only).
- [ ] Three passport-type photographs of you and each accompanying relative.
- [ ] Long-form birth certificates for you and each accompanying relative.
- [ ] Marriage certificate if you are married and bringing your spouse.
- [ ] If either you or your spouse has ever been married previously, copies of divorce and death certificates showing termination of all previous marriages.
- [ ] Passports for you and each accompanying relative, valid for at least six months beyond the date of the final interview.
- [ ] Police certificates from every country in which you and each accompanying relative has lived for at least one year since age 16 (Consular filing only).
- [ ] Military records for you and each accompanying relative (Consular filing only).
- [ ] Fingerprints for you and each accompanying relative between the ages of 14 and 75 (U.S. filing only).
- [ ] Medical exam report for you and each accompanying relative.

STEP THREE: REMOVING THE CONDITIONS ON RESIDENCE

Forms

- [ ] Form I-829.

Documents

- [ ] Federal Income Tax Return.
- [ ] Financial Statements (profit & loss, balance sheet).
- [ ] Bank statements, invoices.
- [ ] Receipts, contracts.
- [ ] Payroll records, other tax documents, forms I-9.

Getting a Green Card As a Special Immigrant

Privileges

- You may live anywhere in the U.S. and stay as long as you want.

- You may work at any job for any company, anywhere in the U.S. or you may choose not to work at all.

- You may travel in and out of the U.S. whenever you wish.

- You may apply to become an American citizen after you have held your green card for a certain length of time.

- If you qualify as a special immigrant, your spouse and unmarried children under the age of 21 may get green cards as accompanying relatives.

Limitations

- Your place of actual residence must be in the U.S. You cannot use a green card just for work and travel purposes. (The only exception is for Alien Commuters, discussed in Chapter 4.)

- You must pay U.S. taxes on your worldwide income because you are regarded as a U.S. resident.

- You cannot remain outside the U.S. for more than one year at a time without special permission or you risk losing your green card. (It is recommended that you limit your trips abroad to under six months.)

- If you commit a crime or participate in politically subversive or other proscribed activities, your green card can be taken away and you can be deported.

A. How to Qualify

Qualifying for a green card as a special immigrant has some limitations.

1. Quota Restrictions

A total of 10,000 green cards are available each year for all special immigrant categories taken together. No more than 5,000 of that total can go to non-clergy religious workers.

At present, green cards are available on a current basis for all special immigrants except for non-clergy religious workers born in all countries, who may experience waits of up to seven months. Petitions are normally approved within one to four months. Green card applications take one to six months after the quota becomes current.

2. Who Qualifies for a Green Card as a Special Immigrant?

Occasionally, laws are passed making green cards available to people in special situations. These special groups are not included in the preference system. They fall under a differ-ent category called special immigrants. Special immigrant green cards are available to the following people:

- workers for recognized religious organizations
- foreign medical graduates who have been in the U.S. a long time
- former employees of the Panama Canal Zone
- foreign workers who were formerly longtime employees of the U.S. government
- retired officers or employees of certain international organizations who have lived in the U.S. for a certain time, their spouses and unmarried children
- foreign workers who have been employees of the U.S. consulate in Hong Kong for at least three years, and
- foreign nationals who have been declared dependent on juvenile courts in the U.S.

a. Religious Workers

There are two subcategories of religious workers: clergy and other religious workers. Clergy is defined as persons autho-rized by a recognized religious denomination to conduct religious activities. This includes not only ministers, priests and rabbis, but also Buddhist monks, commissioned officers of the Salvation Army, practitioners and nurses of the Christian Science Church and ordained deacons. Usually, to be considered a member of the clergy, you must have formal recognition from the religion in question such as a license, certificate of ordination or other qualification to conduct religious worship.

The subcategory of other religious workers covers those who are authorized to perform normal religious duties but are not considered part of the clergy. This includes anyone performing a traditional religious function, such as liturgical workers, religious instructors, religious counselors, cantors, catechists, workers in religious hospitals or religious health care facilities, missionaries, religious translators or religious broadcasters. It does not cover workers involved in purely nonreligious functions such as janitors, maintenance workers, clerical staff or fundraisers.

To qualify for a green card in either of the two religious subcategories, you must have been a member for at least the past two years of a recognized religion that has a bona fide nonprofit organization in the U.S. During those two years, you must have been employed by that same religious group. Your sole purpose in coming to the U.S. must be to work as a minister of that religion, or, at the request of the organization, to work in some other capacity related to the religion's activities in the U.S.

This provision of the law has been the subject of some controversy and there have been efforts in Congress to eliminate it as a way of getting permanent residency. Currently applications for special immigrant religious workers must be submitted before October 1, 2000.

b. Foreign Medical Graduates

If you are a graduate of a foreign medical school who came to the U.S. before January 10, 1978 on either an H or J visa, you qualify as a special immigrant when you can meet all of the following conditions:

- you were permanently licensed to practice medicine in some U.S. state on January 9, 1978
- you were physically in the U.S. and practicing medicine on January 9, 1978
- you have lived continuously in the U.S. and practiced medicine since January 9, 1978, and
- if you came to the U.S. on a J-1 visa and were subject to the two-year home residency requirement, you got a waiver of the home residency requirement, or you have a "no objection letter" from your home government (see Chapter 23).

c. Former Employees of the Panama Canal Zone

You can qualify for a green card as a special immigrant if you were a resident of the Panama Canal Zone on or before April 1, 1979, and you were employed for at least one year either by the Panama Canal Company or the Canal Zone government on or before October 1, 1979.

For native Panamanians, residency in Panama on April 1, 1979 is not a requirement. You also qualify as a special immigrant if you are a Panamanian by birth and were employed by the U.S. government in the Canal Zone for at least 15 years prior to October 1, 1979. Note that if you worked 15 years abroad for the U.S. government, this would also qualify you for the special immigrant class of former U.S. government workers described below. Canal Zone workers, however, do not need a U.S. government recommendation to qualify. A total of only 5,000 green cards may ever be issued in this category. Cards are still available at this time.

d. Former U.S. Government Workers

If you have been employed abroad by the U.S. government for at least 15 years, you may apply for a green card as a special immigrant. To qualify, you must have the recommendation of the principal officer-in-charge of the U.S. government foreign office in which you were employed. The U.S. Secretary of State must also approve the recommendation.

e. Retired Employees of International Organizations, Their Spouses and Unmarried Children

If you are a retired employee of an international organization, you qualify for a green card under the following conditions:

- you have resided in the U.S. for at least 15 years prior to your retirement on a G-4 or N visa
- you lived and were physically present in the U.S. for at least half of the seven years immediately before applying for a green card, and
- you apply to receive a green card within six months of your retirement.

If you are the unmarried child of an officer, employee, former officer or former employee of an international organization, you qualify for a green card if all of the following are true:

- you have a G-4 or N visa
- you lived and were physically present in the U.S. for at least half of the seven-year period before applying for a green card

- you lived in the U.S. for at least seven years while you were between the ages of five and 21, and
- you apply for a green card before your 25th birthday.

If you are the spouse of an officer or employee in this special immigrant class, you qualify for a green card as an accompanying relative. If you were married to a qualifying officer or employee who has died, you can still get a green card if you lived in the U.S. for at least 15 years on a G-4 or N visa before the death of your spouse.

f. Persons Employed at the United States Consulate in Hong Kong

If you are employed at the U.S. consulate in Hong Kong and have been so employed for at least three years, you may qualify for a green card as a special immigrant. To do this, you will need to get the recommendation of the U.S. consul general in Hong Kong. In addition, your welfare in Hong Kong must be threatened as a result of your consular employment. Green cards in this class must be applied for no later than January 1, 2002.

g. Persons Declared Dependent on a Juvenile Court

A foreign national who is a minor can qualify for a green card as a special immigrant if:

- he or she has been declared dependent on a juvenile court located in the U.S.
- he or she has been considered by that court to be eligible for long-term foster care, and
- the court has determined that it is in the minor's best interest to remain in the U.S.

A minor who gets a green card in this class will never be allowed to act as a green card sponsor for either natural or prior adoptive parents.

h. Accompanying Relatives

If you are married or have children below the age of 21 and you get a green card as a special immigrant, your spouse and children can automatically get green cards as accompanying relatives simply by providing proof of their family relationship to you.

3. Inadmissibility

If you have ever been arrested for a crime, lied on an immigration application, lied to an immigration officer or suffered certain physical or mental illness, you may be inadmissible from receiving a green card. In some cases, a Waiver of Inadmissibility may be available. See Chapter 25 to find out exactly who is inadmissible and how to get a waiver.

B. Getting a Green Card As a Special Immigrant

Getting a green card as a special immigrant is a two-step process. Each step will be explained below.

1. Step One: The Petition

The petition is filed by you. Most petitions are submitted to INS regional service centers in the U.S. The only exception is for persons qualifying as special immigrants through employment at the U.S. consulate in Hong Kong. In those cases, the Step One petition must be filed directly with that consulate. The object of the petition is to show that you meet the legal requirements of some special immigrant category as described above in Section A2.

Special immigrants are subject to annual quotas. The date on which you file the petition is called your priority date. The priority date is important because it marks the legally recognized moment when your waiting period for a green card under the quota starts to elapse.

If all goes well, your petition will eventually be approved, but be aware that an approved petition does not by itself give you any right to live or work in the U.S. It is only a prerequisite to Step Two, submitting the application for a green card. Your petition must be approved before you can submit the application.

2. Step Two: The Application

The application is filed by you and your accompanying relatives, if any. The application is your formal request for a green card. Step Two may be carried out in the U.S. at an INS service center or in your home country at a U.S. consulate there. You may not proceed with Step Two until after your Step One petition has been approved.

The majority of green card applications are filed at INS service centers inside the U.S., since usually the applicant is already in the country. If you are in the U.S. legally on a nonimmigrant visa with a current priority date, you apply for your green card either inside or outside the U.S., whichever you prefer. If you are in the U.S. illegally, overstayed prior visas, worked without authorization or entered illegally or without a visa under the Visa Waiver Program, you may be barred from getting your green card application inside the U.S., unless you had a visa petition or labor certification on file by January 14, 1998 and you pay a penalty fee which is currently $1,000. This is in addition to the regular filing fee for such applications. The only people not subject to this penalty are children under the age of 16 and immediate relatives of U.S. citizens. If you are subject to these penalties and want to avoid them, you may instead elect to apply for your green card at a U.S. consulate abroad, but in that case, you must make sure you are not ineligible to get a visa due to the three- to ten-year bars on one or more grounds of inadmissibility. (See Chapter 25.)

If you have an approved petition but your priority date is not yet current, you must wait until it is current to file your application. The consulate will advise you by mail when your priority date finally comes up, but if you want to check progress from time to time, you may do so by calling the U.S. State Department in Washington, D.C. at 202-663-1541 for the latest quota information.

3. Paperwork

There are two types of paperwork you must submit to get a green card as a special immigrant. The first consists of official government forms completed by you or your U.S. employer. The second is personal documents such as birth and marriage certificates. We will tell you exactly what forms and documents you need.

It is vital that forms are properly filled out and all necessary documents are supplied. You may resent the intrusion into your privacy and sizable effort it takes to prepare immigration applications, but you should realize the process is an impersonal matter to immigration officials. Your getting a green card is more important to you than it is to the U.S. government. This is not a pleasant thing to accept, but you are better off having a real understanding of your position. People from all over the world want green cards. There is no shortage of applicants. Take the time and trouble to prepare your papers properly. In the end it will pay off with a successful application.

The documents you supply to INS do not have to be originals. Photocopies of all documents are acceptable as long as you have the original in your possession and are willing to produce the originals at the request of INS. Documents submitted to U.S. consulates, on the other hand, must be either originals or official government certified copies. Government certified copies and notarized copies are not the same thing. Documents which have only been notarized are not acceptable. They must carry a government seal. In addition to any original or government certified copies of documents submitted to a consulate, you should submit plain photocopies of each document as well. After the consulate compares the copies with the originals, it will return the originals.

Documents will be accepted if they are in either English, or, with papers filed at U.S. consulates abroad, the language of the country where the documents are being filed. An exception exists for papers filed at the U.S. consulates in Japan, where all documents must be translated into English. If the documents are not in an acceptable language as just

explained, they must be accompanied by a full, word for word, written English translation. Any capable person may act as translator. It is not necessary to hire a professional. At the end of each translation, the following statement must appear:

I hereby certify that I translated this document from (language) to English. This translation is accurate and complete. I further certify that I am fully competent to translate from (language) to English.

The translator should sign this statement but it does not have to be witnessed or notarized.

Later in this chapter we describe in detail the forms and documents needed to get your green card as a special immigrant. A summary checklist of forms and documents appears at the end of the chapter.

C. Who's Who in Getting Your Green Card

Getting a green card will be easier if you familiarize yourself with the technical names used for each participant in the process. During Step One, you are the *beneficiary* and if there is a U.S. sponsor required (only in the case of non-clergy religious workers) that sponsor is called the *petitioner*. In Step Two, the application, you are called *applicant*. If you are bringing your spouse and children with you as accompanying relatives, they are known as *applicants* as well.

D. Step One: The Petition

This section includes the information you need to submit the petition.

1. General Procedures

You mail the petition, consisting of forms and documents, to the INS regional service center in the U.S. having jurisdiction over the place you will be living or working. INS regional service centers are not the same as INS local offices. There are four INS regional service centers spread across the U.S.

Within a week or two after mailing the petition, you should receive a written confirmation that the papers are being processed, together with a receipt for the fees. This notice will also give your immigration case file number and tell you approximately when to expect a decision. If INS wants further information before acting on your case, all petition papers, forms and documents will be returned to you together with another form known as an I-797. The I-797 tells you what corrections, additional pieces of information or additional documents are expected. You should make the corrections or supply the extra data and mail the whole package back to the INS regional service center.

The filing fee for each petition is currently $80. Checks or money orders are accepted. Regional service centers will not accept cash. We recommend sending the papers by certified mail, return receipt requested, and keeping a complete copy of everything sent for your records. Appendix II contains complete lists of all INS regional service centers with their addresses, telephone and fax numbers.

It generally takes one to three months to get a decision on the petition. Once your petition is approved, a Notice of Action Form I-797 will be sent to you, indicating the approval. If you plan to execute Step Two at a U.S. consulate abroad, INS will forward the file to the National Visa Center (NVC) located in Portsmouth, New Hampshire. NVC will then send a packet of forms and instructions to you so that you may proceed with Step Two.

Form I-360

The basic form for Step One, the petition, is immigration Form I-360. If a particular question on the form does not apply, it should be answered "None" or "N/A."

It is absolutely essential to answer each question truthfully, even if it means disclosing that you are in the U.S. illegally. (If you are in the U.S. out of status or have violated U.S. immigration or other laws, be sure to thoroughly understand the material in the chapter on inadmissibility (Chapter 25) before proceeding with your application.) Failure to reveal requested information may result in your being permanently barred from the U.S.

Part 1. The items under this part are self-explanatory. "A" numbers are usually issued only to people who previously held green cards or have made previous green card applications.

Part 2. Part 2 asks you to mark the category under which you are applying for special immigrant status and is self-explanatory.

Part 3. Part 3 is self-explanatory, asking questions about your current address and immigration status. If you are in the U.S., your current immigration status must be disclosed, even if you are in the U.S. illegally. If any of the boxes do not apply to you, answer "N/A."

In listing your address, you must put down the address where you really live, even if it means revealing an illegal U.S. residence. If you are in the U.S. illegally, read Chapter 26 discussing inadmissibility before departing the U.S. or proceeding with your application. INS offices during Steps One and Two and consular offices during Step Two will send correspondence to the address you put down in Part 3, so make sure it is correct.

Part 4. This part is self-explanatory.

Part 5. This part applies only to Amerasians, which is not a special immigrant category. Leave this blank.

Part 6. This part is filled in only if you are applying for special immigrant status for a juvenile declared dependent by a court. These questions are self-explanatory.

Part 7. This part only applies to widows or widowers of U.S. citizens, not a special immigrant category, and will therefore be left blank.

Part 8. This part asks for biographical information for your spouse and children and is self-explanatory.

2. Petition Documents

The documents required depend on the category of special immigrant.

a. Religious Workers

To prove you qualify as a special immigrant religious worker, you should submit all diplomas and certificates showing your academic and professional qualifications. In addition, submit a detailed letter from the religious organization in the U.S. explaining its organization, number of followers in both your home country and the U.S., details of your job offer in the U.S. including job title, duties, salary and qualification requirements. Finally, you should include written verification that you have been a member of and employed by that organization for at least two years.

b.   Foreign Medical Graduates

To prove you qualify as a special immigrant foreign medical graduate, you should submit your original I-94 card, even if it has expired, or passport with visa stamp showing you were admitted to the U.S. with a J or H visa prior to January 9, 1978. You will need to show your medical license issued by some U.S. state before January 9, 1978, or a letter from a medical board of a U.S. state verifying that you were licensed. You will also need evidence that you have been continuously employed as a physician since January 9, 1978. A letter from the employer or your personal income tax returns, including W-2 forms, for all years beginning with 1977 to the present, will provide such proof.

You must show that you have maintained continuous residence in the U.S. since your entry. Proof of this can include your personal income tax returns for each year, your children's school records, your utility bills, bank records, letters from employers, and the like. If you came to the U.S. on a J-1 visa, you should also submit a copy of the pink form, IAP-66 certificate, given to you so you could get your J visa. If the IAP-66 certificate indicated you were subject to the two-year foreign residence requirement, you will also need a No Objection Letter from the embassy of your home country. No Objection Letters are discussed more fully in Chapter 23.

c.   Former U.S. Government Workers

To prove that you qualify as a special immigrant former U.S. government worker, you must be able to verify at least 15 years of U.S. government employment outside of the U.S. You can do this by submitting copies of personal tax returns or a letter of verification from the U.S. government agency that employed you. The same agency will also need to provide you with a letter of recommendation for a green card from the principal officer-in-charge of the agency in which you were employed. Finally, you will need a letter of recommendation from the U.S. Secretary of State. The agency you worked for should be able to assist you in getting this.

d.   Former Employees of the Panama Canal Zone

To prove you are qualified as a special immigrant employee of the Panama Canal Zone, you should submit proof that you were employed by either the Canal Zone government or the Panama Canal Company on or before October 1, 1979. You can prove this by submitting copies of personal tax returns, past employment contracts or letters and affidavits from the employer stating that you were employed by them and for how long. Since the Canal Zone government

no longer exists, it may be impossible to obtain such letters or affidavits. As a last resort, you can try submitting affidavits from other people who worked with you, attesting to the fact that they personally observed you working, and for how long. There is really no perfect solution to this problem.

You must also submit evidence that you were a resident in the Canal Zone on April 1, 1979. This is usually shown with the same documents used to verify your employment. If you were not a resident in the Canal Zone on April 1, 1979, you may still qualify if you can document that you were employed by the Canal Zone Government for at least 15 years prior to October 1, 1979, and that at the time, you were a Panamanian national. Proof of this employment may be shown as stated above. Use your birth certificate, Panamanian passport, or Panamanian citizenship, naturalization or *cedula* certificates to prove your nationality.

e.   Retired Employees of International Organizations and Their Families

To prove your eligibility for this special immigrant category, you must have written documentation to show that you resided in the U.S. for at least 15 years on either a G-4 or N visa. Copies of your passports or I-94 cards covering the past 15 years, together with copies of U.S. income tax returns filed during that time, would be the best proof. If any of these are not available, then a detailed letter from the international organization in the U.S. stating your periods of employment and visa status should be acceptable. You must also prove that you were physically present in the U.S. for at least half of the seven-year period immediately prior to applying for a green card. Copies of your passport and I-94 cards during the past seven years would again be the best proof. You need to make a complete copy of your passport to show your entries and departures. If unavailable, other acceptable proofs of your physical presence in the U.S. are a letter from your employer stating the number of days you worked in the U.S. and bank statements showing regular deposits and withdrawals during this time. You must also present a letter from your employer stating your official retirement date. Remember that you must apply for your green card within six months after your retirement.

f.   Children of Retired Employees

If you are the unmarried child of an officer, employee, former officer or former employee of an international organization in the U.S., you must provide evidence that your parent was employed by an international organization in the U.S. through a letter from the organization verifying the position and dates of employment. Next you must prove you are his or her child. Normally, this will be shown on your birth certificate. You must also provide evidence that you were physically present in the U.S. for at least half of the seven-year period immediately before applying for the green card. This can be shown with a complete copy of your passport and all I-94 cards issued to you during that period, letters from employers, if any, stating the number of days you worked in the U.S. or school records.

g. Persons Employed at the U.S. Consulate in Hong Kong

To qualify as a special immigrant in this category, the consul general in Hong Kong must recommend your approval based on a belief that your welfare will be threatened if you remain in Hong Kong. Since a petition in this category may be filed only with the U.S. consulate in Hong Kong, it is possible that specific documentation of your employment there and of the consul general's recommendation will not be needed. You should, however, expect to provide a written letter from the consul general recommending the approval of your special immigrant petition, a written statement from you explaining how your welfare in Hong Kong will be threatened because you worked for the U.S. government there, and evidence that you were employed at the Hong Kong consulate for at least three years. Evidence of the three-year employment period could be in the form of tax returns or a letter from the consulate itself.

h. Persons Declared Dependent on a Juvenile Court

The documents required for this category are the formal findings and recommendations from a U.S. juvenile court judge. Ideally, the qualifying elements of this category should be stated in the judge's written order declaring the child dependent. Included in the order should be statements that the child is eligible for long-term foster care, and that it would not be in the child's best interest to be returned to his or her home country. If these findings are not specifically stated in the court decree, you should try to have the decree amended to include them. If that isn't possible, you will need a letter from the judge who heard the child's dependency case in which he does state these facts.

3. Petition Interviews

Interviews are rarely held on Step One petitions.

4. Petition Appeals

When you have poorly documented your eligibility for a special immigrant classification, the petition will probably be denied. You will then receive written notice of INS's unfavorable decision, a written statement of the reasons for the negative outcome and an explanation of how to make a formal appeal.

The best way to handle an appeal is to try avoiding it altogether. Filing an appeal means making an argument to INS that its reasoning was wrong. If you think you can eliminate the reason why the petition failed by improving the paperwork, it makes sense to disregard the appeals process and simply file a new petition, being careful to see that it is better prepared than the first.

If the petition was denied because you left out necessary documents that have since been located, the new documents should be sent together with a written request that the case be reopened to the same INS office that issued the denial. This is technically called a *Motion to Reopen*. There is a $110 fee for filing this motion. Appeals often take a long time. A Motion to Reopen can be concluded faster than an appeal.

If you do choose to file an appeal, it must be done within 30 days of the date on the Notice of Denial. The appeal should be filed at the same INS office with which you have been dealing. There is a $110 filing fee. INS will then forward the papers for consideration to the Administrative Appeals Unit of the central INS office in Washington, D.C. In six months or more you will get back a decision by mail. Few appeals are successful.

When an appeal to INS has been denied, the next step is to make an appeal through the U.S. judicial system. You may not file an action in court without first going through the appeals process available from INS. If your case has reached this stage and you are living illegally in the U.S., we strongly recommend seeking representation from a qualified immigration attorney, as you are now in danger of being deported.

E. Step Two: The Application (Consular Filing)

Anyone with an approved petition and a current priority date can apply for a green card at a U.S. consulate in his or her home country or last country of residence. You must be physically present in order to apply there. If you have been or are now working and living illegally in the U.S., you may be barred from getting a green card from a U.S. consulate if you have been out of status for over six months in the U.S. Be sure to read Chapter 25, *Inadmissibility*, to understand whether you qualify.

1. Benefits and Drawbacks of Consular Filing

Anyone with an approved petition and a current priority date can apply for a green card at the appropriate consulate. That is not the case with U.S. applications since you must be physically inside the U.S. to apply there. If you are a preference relative and are in the U.S. illegally, you may not be able to stay in the U.S. and get your green card. On the other hand, you may subject yourself to a three- or ten-year waiting period if you leave (after being out of status for six or ten months). (See Chapter 25 for a full discussion.)

A further plus to consular filing is that consulate offices may work more quickly to issue green cards than do some INS offices. Your waiting time for the paperwork to be finished may be months shorter at a U.S. consulate abroad than at U.S. INS offices. Remember, however, that the difference in waiting time between INS and consulate offices applies only to processing paperwork. Quotas move at the same rate of speed no matter where your application is filed.

One of two drawbacks to consular filing is the travel expense and inconvenience you will experience in returning to your home country if you are already in the U.S. The other problem is that should your consular application fail, you will have fewer ways to appeal than a U.S. filing would offer.

2. Application General Procedures: Consular Filing

The law states that only a U.S. consulate or embassy in your home country is required to accept your green card application. This is true for all except persons from countries without U.S. embassies. A complete list of U.S. consulates that process visa applications, with addresses and phone numbers may be found in Appendix I. You can ask a consulate located elsewhere to accept your application, but it has the option to say no, and in fact, many turn down most such requests. If you do wish to ask for this privilege, you should approach the consulate of your choice before filing the Step One petition. That is because Form I-360 in Step One asks where you will file your application and you must be prepared with an answer to this question.

You may not file an application for a green card at a consulate until after your petition has been approved. At that time, the INS office where your petition was originally submitted will forward your file to the National Visa Center in Portsmouth, New Hampshire. NVC will then forward your file to the U.S. consulate you have named on Form I-360 in Step One. At the same time, a Notice of Approval from Step One will be sent directly to you. NVC will send instructions and application forms to you within a month or two after petition approval. You will return all paperwork, however, directly to the consulate. If, after waiting a reasonable time, you have not heard from NVC, you should call and look into the matter.

NVC will send you Packet 3, containing forms and instructions. Complete and send Forms OF-230 I and OF-169 to the consulate as soon as possible. This will allow the consulate to begin a required security check into your background. Failure to return these forms promptly can significantly delay your green card.

The application for your green card is made in person by appointment. Once your quota number is current and the consulate is ready for your final processing, it will then send another group of papers known as Packet 4. Packet 4 includes an interview appointment letter, instructions for obtaining your medical examination and still more forms to be completed. Other than Form OF-230 I, which should be mailed in as soon as you receive it, and Form OF-169, which you will send in when you are ready for your interview, do not mail your paperwork to the consulate. Instead, bring the rest of your forms and all documents with you at the time of your appointment. The fee for filing an application is $200 per person.

3. Application Forms: Consular Filing

When you file at a U.S. consulate abroad, the consulate officials will provide you with certain optional forms, designated by an "OF" preceeding a number. Instructions for completing optional forms and what to do with them once they are filled out will come with the forms. We do not include copies of these forms in Appendix III. Copies of all non "OF" forms are in Appendix III.

Form I-134

It is necessary to convince the consulate that once you receive a green card you are not likely to go on public welfare. If your application is based on employment, that alone should be sufficient proof that you have a way to support yourself and an I-134 need not be filed for you. You should still, however, fill out Form-134, the Affidavit of Support, for any accompanying relatives. Because the consulate knows you will have an income, you must sign the I-134 forms and take financial responsibility for each of them.

Form I-134 is your guarantee that you will take care of your accompanying relatives. In signing the Affidavit of Support, you are not actually promising to support your accompanying relatives. What you do promise is to reimburse the U.S. government for the sum total of any government support payments they might receive should they go on welfare. The Affidavit of Support supposedly binds you to this obligation for three years. Your responsibility to the government then comes to an end.

4. Application Documents: Consular Filing

The most important document in your application is the Notice of Action showing approval of your petition. It is sent directly from the INS office in the U.S. to the consulate you named on Form I-360 in Step One. This is the only document you will not have to submit yourself. Do not mail in your other documents. Instead, bring them to your interview.

You must resubmit to the consulate all the documents first filed in Step One. Additionally, you must have your long form birth certificate and birth certificates of any unmarried minor children who are not immigrating with you.

It is also necessary to have in your possession a valid passport from your home country. The expiration date on the passport must leave enough time for the passport to remain valid at least six months beyond the date of your final application interview.

Unlike applications made in the U.S., you personally must collect police clearance certificates from each country you have lived in for one year or more since your 16th birthday. Additionally, you must have a police certificate from your home country or country of last residence, if you lived there for at least six months since the age of 16. You do not need to obtain police certificates from the U.S. Like

all other documents, you should be prepared to present the necessary police clearance certificates at your interview. If you go to your interview without the required certificates, you will be refused a green card and told to return after you get them.

OBTAINING POLICE CERTIFICATES

You should contact the local police department in your home country for instructions on how to get police certificates. To obtain police certificates from nations other than your home country, it is best to contact the nearest consulate representing that country for instructions. Some nations refuse to supply police certificates, or their certificates are not considered reliable, and so you will not be required to obtain them from those locations. At this writing, police certificates are not required from the following countries:

Afghanistan	Haiti	Saudi Arabia
Albania	Honduras	Sierra Leone
Angola	India	Somalia
Bangladesh	Indonesia	Sri Lanka
Brunei	Iran	Sudan
Bulgaria	Iraq	Syria
Cambodia	Jordan	Tanzania
Chad	Laos	Thailand
Colombia	Liberia	Turkey
Costa Rica	Libya	United Arab
Cuba	Malaysia	Emirates
Dominican Republic	Mexico	United Kingdom
El Salvador	Mongolia	United States
Equatorial Guinea	Mozambique	Venezuela
Ghana	Nepal	Vietnam
Guatemala	Pakistan	

For applicants who once lived in Japan but do not reside there at the time their green card applications are filed, the Department of State recognizes that police certificates are available from Japan only as far back as five years from the date of the green card application.

Other countries, including the Netherlands, North Korea, South Africa and South Korea, will send certificates directly to U.S. consulates but not to you personally. Before they send the certificates out, however, you must request that it be done. Usually this requires filing some type of request form together with a set of your fingerprints.

You and each accompanying relative must bring to the interview three photographs taken in compliance with the instruction sheet found in Appendix III. Additional photo instructions are provided in Packet 4. Often Packet 4 will also contain a list of local photographers who take this type of picture.

A few consulates require you to submit fingerprints, though most do not. Consulates wanting fingerprints will send you blank fingerprint cards with instructions.

5. Application Interviews: Consular Filing

Consulates hold interviews on all green card applications. A written notice of your interview appointment is included when you receive Packet 4. Immediately before the interview, you and your accompanying relatives will be required to have medical examinations. Some consulates conduct the medical exams up to several days before the interview. Others, including London, schedule the medical exam and the interview on the same day. You will be told where to go and what to do in your appointment letter.

The medical examinations are conducted by private doctors and you are required to pay the doctor a fee. The fees vary from as little as $50 to more than $150 per exam, depending on the country. The amount of the medical exam fee will be stated in your appointment letter. The exam itself involves the taking of a medical history, blood test and chest X ray, and verification or administering of vaccinations, if applicable. Pregnant women who do not want to be X-rayed may so advise the consulate and their appointments will be postponed until after the pregnancy. The requirement to have an X ray taken cannot be waived.

The main purpose of the medical exam is to verify that you are not medically inadmissible. The primary grounds of inadmissibility are tuberculosis and HIV (AIDS). Medical grounds of inadmissibility usually can be overcome with treatment. See Chapter 25, *Inadmissibility,* for more details. If you need a medical waiver, you will be given complete instructions by the consulate at the time of your interview.

After the medical exam, you and your accompanying relatives will report to the consulate for the interview. At that time, you must pay two more fees: $170 per person when your papers are submitted, and an additional $30 per person at the end of the interview when your applications are approved. Some consulates accept payment only by certified check, money order or traveler's check. Others accept cash. You will be told the proper method of payment in Packet 4.

Bring with you to the interview the completed forms, photographs, your passports and all of the required documents discussed here. The interview process involves verification of your application's accuracy and an inspection of your documents. If all is in order, you will be asked to return later in the day when you will be issued an immigrant visa. You are not yet a permanent resident.

The immigrant visa allows you to request entry to the U.S. You acquire the full status of green card holder at the moment of being inspected and admitted into the U.S. with your immigrant visa. At that time, your passport is stamped and you are immediately authorized to work. If you are bringing any accompanying relatives, they must enter at either the same time or after you do in order to become permanent residents. Permanent green cards for you and your accompanying relatives are then ordered. They will come to you by mail several months later.

6. Application Appeals: Consular Filing

When a consulate denies a green card application, there is no formal appeal available, although you are free to reapply as often as you like. When your green card is refused, the reasons will be explained. The most common reason for denial is failure to supply all the required documents. Sometimes presenting more evidence on an unclear fact can bring about a better result. If the denial was caused by a lack of evidence, this will be explained in a written notice sent to you by mail.

Another common reason for denial of a green card is that the consular officer believes you are inadmissible. If you are found to be inadmissible, you will be given an opportunity to apply for a Waiver of Inadmissibility, if one is available. See Chapter 25 for directions on how to apply.

When all these possibilities are exhausted, if the consulate still refuses you a green card, your opportunities for further appeals are severely limited. Historically, the courts have held that there is no right to judicial review and there is no formal appeal procedure through any U.S. government agency. The State Department in Washington, D.C. does offer an informal review procedure through the mail. This agency will look at the factual elements of your case and decide whether or not the consulate made a correct decision. Even if the State Department rules in your favor, the decision is only advisory and the consulate is free to ignore the State Department, letting its own decision stand. At present, there does appear to be a trend developing where courts in the U.S. are more frequently accepting jurisdiction over consular decisions, so a court appeal may be a possibility to consider. The jurisdiction of U.S. courts to review consular decisions, however, is still an unsettled legal issue.

Your denial may be based on a question of law rather than fact. The State Department offers the same informal review for legal questions with the difference that any decision it makes is binding on the consulate. Appeals of this kind are very technical and should be handled by a competent immigration attorney. Even with representation by an attorney, most such appeals fail.

Overall, the best way to handle an application that has been turned down is simply to wait awhile, reapply on a different basis and hope for better luck next time. The fact that you have been turned down once does not stop you from trying again.

F. Step Two: The Application (U.S. Filing)

If you are physically present in the U.S., you may apply for a green card without leaving the country on the following conditions:

- you have already received an approved petition
- a green card is currently available to you because your waiting period under the quota is up, and
- you are admissible to the U.S. and none of the grounds of inadmissibility apply to you (see Chapter 25).

Unless you can meet these terms, you may not file an application (Step Two) for a green card in the U.S.

1. Benefits and Drawbacks of U.S. Filing

The obvious benefit to applying for a green card in the U.S. is that if you are already in the country, you avoid the expense and inconvenience of overseas travel. Moreover, it is a rule of immigration that once you file Step Two, you must remain wherever you have filed. When you file in the U.S., should problems arise in your case, you will at least be able to wait for a decision in America, a circumstance most green card applicants prefer.

Another important benefit of U.S. filing is that you may receive permission to work while you wait for the results of your case. To obtain this benefit, you must file a separate application, by mail, at the INS service center where your Step Two application has been filed. You will receive the laminated work authorization card in the mail, several weeks later. If you do not need to work right away, but can wait until after getting your green card, you do not need to file this separate application, although the states are increasingly requiring a work permit to apply for benefits such as drivers' licenses.

If your application for a green card is turned down, you have greater rights of appeal inside the U.S. than you do at a U.S. consulate. INS offices have different procedures from consular offices because they are controlled by a different branch of the U.S. government.

There are some disadvantages to applying in the U.S. It may take longer to get results. Processing times at INS service centers may approach as long as one year in the future, even on cases where quotas are current. While your case is pending at an INS service center, you may not leave the U.S. without getting special permission. If you do leave without INS's permission, even for a genuine emergency, this will be regarded as a withdrawal of your application and you will have to start your application over again when you return.

PROCEDURES FOR ADVANCED WORK AUTHORIZATION

If you want to work before your application for a green card is approved, you should file an application for employment authorization. This can be done by completing Form I-765 and filing it with the same INS service center where you file the Step Two papers. Together with Form I-765, you must submit your I-94 card and pay a filing fee of $100. It is very important to keep the fee receipt INS gives you so you can prove that the I-765 was filed. Normally you will want to file the application for employment authorization at the same time as your Step Two application papers.

Legally, INS does not have to make a decision on your employment authorization application for up to 90 days. If for some reason you are not given a decision within 90 days, you will, at your request, be granted an interim employment authorization which will last 240 days.

If 240 days pass and you still have not received a final decision on the I-765, you must stop working. Interim work authorization cards cannot be renewed. However, if you reach this point, you have the option to file a new I-765 application and, if you do not get a decision on the new application within 90 days, you will then be entitled to another interim work authorization card.

---

2. Application General Procedures: U.S. Filing

You may not begin Step Two until you have an approved Step One petition. The application, consisting of both forms and documents, is submitted by mail to the INS service center designated for the place you are living. Appendix II contains a complete list of all U.S. immigration offices and service centers, with their telephone numbers and addresses.

For U.S. filings, the basic form used in Step Two, the application, is INS Form I-485, Application for Permanent Residence. Form I-485 is filed to adjust your status in the U.S. "Adjusting status" is a technical term used only in U.S. filings. It simply means that you are presently in the U.S. as a nonimmigrant and are in the process of acquiring a green card.

The filing fee for each application is $220 for applicants age 14 and over, and $160 for applicants under age 14. A separate application must be filed for you and each accompanying relative. (See the Chapter 25 section on the penalty provision to determine whether you are eligible or required to file the $1,000 penalty.) Checks and money orders are accepted. It is not advisable to send cash through the mail, but cash is satisfactory if you file in person. Cash is accepted only in the exact amount. INS offices will not make change. We recommend filing your papers in person if at all possible, as you will be given a written receipt from INS and your papers are likely to be processed right away. If you choose to mail in your application, you should do so by certified mail, return receipt requested. In either case, keep a complete copy of everything you send in.

Once your application has been filed, you should not leave the U.S. for any reason before your application has been approved. Any absence will be viewed as a termination of your application for a green card. If you must leave the U.S. (which you may do for any legitimate personal or business reason), you should file an "advance parole" application with your application, sending three passport-type photographs and proof of the reason for your trip (such as a short letter explaining the purpose of your trip) and ask for advance parole, by filing Form I-131 and paying a $95 filing fee. If approved, you will be allowed to leave the U.S. and return again with no break in the processing of your application.

Generally, after filing your application, you will not hear anything from INS for several months. Then you should receive a notice of your interview appointment. The interview notice will also contain instructions for getting the required medical exam and will tell you if any further documentation is needed.

If everything is in order at the end of your interview, your application will be approved at the conclusion of the interview. Your passport will be stamped to show that you have been admitted to the U.S. as a permanent resident, and your permanent green card will be ordered. The green card will come to you in the mail about two months after the interview.

3. Application Forms: U.S. Filing

Copies of all forms can be found in Appendix III.

Form I-485

While most of the form is self-explanatory, a few items typically raise concerns. If a particular question does not apply to you, answer it with "None" or "N/A." The questions on this form requiring explanation are as follows:

Part 1. Part 1 asks for general information about when and where you were born, your present address and immigration status. It also asks for an "A" number. Normally, you will not have an "A" number unless you previously applied for a green card or have been in deportation proceedings.

Part 2. In Part 2, you will mark Box A if you are the principal applicant. Box B is marked if your spouse or parent is the principal applicant.

Part 3. The questions in Sections A through C are self-explanatory. The nonimmigrant visa number is the number that appears on the very top of the visa stamp. It is not the same as your visa classification. The questions in Section C are meant to identify people who are inadmissible. With the exception of certain memberships in the Communist Party or similar organizations, you will not be deemed inadmissible simply because your joined an organization. However, if your answer to any of the other questions is "yes," you may be inadmissible. Read Chapter 25, which is intended to help you remove such obstacles. Don't lie on your answers because you will probably be found out, especially if you have engaged in criminal activity. Many grounds of inadmissibility can be legally overcome, but once a lie is detected, you will lose the legal right to correct the problem. In addition, a false answer is grounds to deny your application and may result in your being permanently barred from getting a green card.

Form I-485A

This form is required only if you are subject to a $1,000 penalty fee. The form is self-explanatory, and is intended only to determine if you are subject to the penalty. (You are only eligible to file it if you had a visa petition or labor certification on file by January 14, 1998 or your application was filed prior to November, 1997. See Chapter 25.)

Form G-325A

G-325A biographic data forms must be filled out for you and each accompanying relative. You need not file a G-325A for any child under the age of 14 or any adult over the age of 79. The G-325A form is meant to gather personal background information. The questions are self-explanatory.

Form I-134

It is necessary to convince INS that once you receive a green card, you are not likely to go on public welfare. If your application is based on employment, that alone should be sufficient proof that you have a way to support yourself and an I-134 need not be filed for you. You should still, however, fill out Form I-134, the Affidavit of Support, for any accompanying relative. Because INS knows you will have an income, you must sign the I-134 forms and take financial responsibility for each of them.

Form I-134 is your guarantee that you will take care of your accompanying relatives. In signing the Affidavit of Support, you are not actually promising to support your accompanying relatives. What you do promise is to reimburse the U.S. government for the sum total of any government support payments they might receive should they go on welfare. The I-134 Affidavit of Support binds you to this obligation for three years. Your responsibility to the government then comes to an end.

Form I-765

Block above Question 1. Mark the first box, "Permission to accept employment."

Questions 1–8. These questions are self-explanatory.

Question 9. This asks for your Social Security number, including all numbers you have ever used. If you have never used a Social Security number, answer "None." If you have a nonworking Social Security number, write down the number followed by the words "nonworking, for tax purposes only." If you have ever used a false number, give that number, followed by the words: "Not my valid number." (See Chapter 25 regarding the penalties for document fraud, before filing an application with any information about false social security cards.)

Question 10. You will not usually have an Alien Registration Number unless you previously applied for a green card, were in deportation proceedings, or have had certain types of immigration applications denied. All Alien Registration Numbers begin with the letter "A." If you have no "A" number but you entered the U.S. with a valid visa or without a visa under the Visa Waiver Program, you should have an I-94 card. In this case, answer Question 10 by putting down the admission number from the I-94 card.

If you are from Mexico, you may have entered the U.S. with a border crossing card, in which case you should put

down the number on the entry document you received at the border, if any. Otherwise simply put down the number of the border crossing card itself, followed with "BCC." If you are Canadian and you entered the U.S. as a visitor, you will not usually have any of the documents described here, in which case you should put down "None."

Questions 11–15. These questions are self-explanatory.
Question 16. Answer this question "(C)(9)."

4. Application Documents: U.S. Filing

You must submit the Notice of Action showing petition approval with the application. You and each of your accompanying relatives are required to submit two photographs. These photos should meet the specifications on the photo instruction sheet found in Appendix III. Additionally, you must submit your birth certificate or other record of birth, if married, a marriage certificate and your spouse's birth certificate, and birth certificates for all your children under age 21, even if not immigrating with you.

You must also submit a Medical Examination Report for each applicant. This is done on INS Form I-693, which must be taken to an INS authorized physician or medical clinic. The INS local office will provide you with the form as well as a list of approved physicians in your area. After completion of the medical exam and upon obtaining the test results, the doctor will give you the results in a sealed envelope. Do not open the envelope.

Each applicant must submit an I-94 card if one was issued. Failure to do so may result in a conclusion that you are not eligible. The I-94 is the small white or green card you received on entering the U.S.

The only other paperwork required is a fingerprint card. Beginning March 30, 1998, INS regulations changed so that all fingerprinting now takes place at an INS-run fingerprinting center. You will be notified where and when to appear after submitting your application forms. You will be required to pay INS $25 (often when you file your application papers) to cover the fingerprinting costs.

5. Application Interviews: U.S. Filing

Personal interviews are sometimes waived for special immigrant applications. If an interview is not waived, you and your accompanying relatives will be asked to come in to the INS local office for final processing. The INS officer will go over your application to make sure that everything is correct. He will also ask questions to convince himself that you are not inadmissible. (See Chapter 25, *Inadmissibility.*) A single fingerprint will then be taken and you will be asked to sign your application under oath. Accompanying relatives, all of whom must attend the interview with you, will go through the same procedure.

The interview normally takes about 30 minutes. If all goes well, your case should be approved on the spot. You will not be expected to wait for the results. Most INS offices will place a temporary stamp in your passport showing that you have become a U.S. permanent resident. With this stamp, you acquire all the rights of a green card holder including the right to work and freedom to travel in and out of the U.S. The stamp is not your green card. You will receive your permanent green card by mail several months later. If your fingerprints have not been cleared yet, your application will be approved only provisionally pending clearance. In those cases, no stamp will be placed in your passport at the interview. Instead, you will receive a written notice of approval within a month or two. That notice serves as your proof of U.S. residency until you receive your green card, which takes yet another two or three months. If you need to travel outside the U.S. before your green card arrives, however, you must go back to the INS office with your passport and the written notice of approval, and a temporary stamp will be placed in your passport, enabling you to return after your trip. Never leave the U.S. without either your green card or a temporary stamp in your passport.

6. Application Appeals: U.S. Filing

If your application is denied, you will receive a written decision by mail explaining the reasons for the denial. There is no way of making a formal appeal to INS when your application is turned down. If the problem is too little evidence, you may be able to overcome this obstacle by adding more documents and resubmitting the entire application to the same INS office you have been dealing with, together with a written request that the case be reopened. The written request does not have to be in any special form. This is technically called a *Motion to Reopen*. There is a $110 fee to file this motion. Alternatively, you may wait until INS begins deportation proceedings, in which case you may refile your application with the immigration judge.

If your application is denied because you are found inadmissible, you will be given the opportunity to apply for what is known as a *Waiver of Inadmissibility*, provided a waiver is available for your ground of inadmissibility. See Chapter 25 for directions on how to apply.

Although there is no appeal to INS for the denial of a green card application, you have the right to file an appeal in a U.S. district court. This requires employing an attorney at considerable expense. Such appeals are usually unsuccessful.

FORMS AND DOCUMENTS CHECKLIST

STEP ONE: PETITION

Forms

☐ Form I-360.

Documents

RELIGIOUS WORKERS

☐ Diplomas and certificates showing your academic and professional qualifications.

☐ Detailed letter from the U.S. religious organization, fully describing the operation of the organization both in and out of the U.S.

☐ Letter from the U.S. organization giving details of your U.S. job offer, including how you will be paid.

☐ Written verification that you have been a member of and worked outside the U.S. for that same organization for at least two years.

☐ Evidence that the religious organization in the U.S. qualifies as a tax-exempt organization under §501(c) of the Internal Revenue Code.

FOREIGN MEDICAL GRADUATES

☐ Original I-94 card (even if it has expired) or your passport with a visa stamp showing you were admitted to the U.S. with a J or H visa prior to January 9, 1978.

☐ Copy of your medical license issued by some U.S. state prior to January 9, 1978, or a letter from the medical board of a state verifying you were licensed.

☐ Evidence that you were employed as a physician on January 9, 1978.

☐ Evidence of your continuous residence in the U.S. since entry.

☐ If you had a J-1 visa, a copy of the IAP-66 and, if it indicated you were subject to the foreign residence requirement, a No Objection Letter from the embassy of your home country.

FORMER U.S. GOVERNMENT WORKERS

☐ Verification of at least 15 years of U.S. government employment.

☐ Letter of recommendation for a green card from the principal officer-in-charge of the agency where you worked.

☐ Letter of recommendation from the U.S. Secretary of State.

FORMER EMPLOYEES OF THE PANAMA CANAL ZONE

☐ Proof that the required employment with either the Canal Zone government or the Panama Canal Company took place on or before October 1, 1979.

☐ Work history and residence documents:

☐ evidence that you were a resident in the Canal Zone on April 1, 1979, or

☐ if you were not a resident in the Canal Zone on April 1, 1979 but are a Panamanian national, evidence that you worked for the Canal Zone government for at least 15 years prior to October 1, 1979.

RETIRED EMPLOYEES OF INTERNATIONAL ORGANIZATIONS

☐ Evidence you have lived in the U.S. on a G-4 or N visa for the past 15 years.

☐ Complete copy of your passport.

☐ Copies of all I-94 cards issued.

☐ Income tax returns or W-2 forms for the past 15 years.

☐ If any of the above are unavailable, a detailed letter from the international organization in the U.S. stating your periods of employment, visa status and period of actual physical presence in the U.S.

☐ A letter from the U.S. employer or other written verification of your retirement date.

CHILDREN OF INTERNATIONAL ORGANIZATION WORKERS

☐ Letter from the international organization in the U.S. employing your parent, verifying his or her position and period of employment.

☐ Your long-form birth certificate showing the names of your parents.

☐ A complete copy of your passport and all I-94 cards issued.

☐ If your passport and I-94 cards are unavailable or do not show your entries and departures for at least the past seven years, other evidence of your presence in the U.S. for the past seven years.

PERSONS EMPLOYED AT THE U.S. CONSULATE IN HONG KONG

- ☐ Written recommendation to grant you a green card from the consul general of the U.S. consulate in Hong Kong.
- ☐ Written statement explaining how your welfare in Hong Kong will be threatened because you are working for the U.S. government.
- ☐ Written evidence that you were employed at the U.S. consulate in Hong Kong for at least three years.

PERSONS DECLARED DEPENDENT ON A JUVENILE COURT

- ☐ Copy of a juvenile court decree declaring the child's dependency on the court.
- ☐ If it is not specifically stated in the court decree, a letter from the juvenile court judge stating the following:
    - ☐ that the child is eligible for long-term foster care, and
    - ☐ that it would not be in the child's best interest to return him or her to the home country.

STEP TWO: APPLICATION

Forms

- ☐ OF forms (available from U.S. consulate abroad for consular filings only).
- ☐ Form I-485 for you and each accompanying relative (U.S. filing only).
- ☐ Form I-485A (U.S. filing only).
- ☐ Form G-325A for you and each accompanying relative between the ages of 14 and 79 (U.S. filing only).
- ☐ Form I-134 (U.S. and consular filings).
- ☐ Form I-765, if advanced work authorization is needed (U.S. filing only).

Documents

- ☐ Copy of the petition approval notice.
- ☐ Long form birth certificate for you and each accompanying relative.
- ☐ Marriage certificate if you are married and bringing your spouse.
- ☐ If either you or spouse have ever been married, copies of divorce and death certificates showing termination of all previous marriages.
- ☐ Passports for you and each accompanying relative, valid for at least six months beyond the date of the final interview.
- ☐ I-94 card for you and each accompanying relative (U.S. filing only).
- ☐ Police certificates from every country in which you and each accompanying relative has lived for at least six months since age 16 (Consular filing only).
- ☐ Military records for you and each accompanying relative (Consular filing only).
- ☐ Fingerprints for you and each accompanying relative between the ages of 14 and 75. (U.S. filing only).
- ☐ Two photographs each of you and each accompanying relative.
- ☐ Proof of financial support:
    - ☐ Form I-134, Affidavit of Support, for you and each accompanying relative
    - ☐ written offer of employment from a U.S. employer, or
    - ☐ financial documents showing sufficient funds and investments to support the principal applicant and accompanying relatives without employment.
- ☐ Medical exam report for you and each accompanying relative.

CHAPTER 12

Special Statuses: Refugees, Political Asylees and Temporary Protected Status

Privileges

- You may come to the U.S. as a refugee to escape political, religious or racial persecution by the government or groups in your home country.

- If you are already in the U.S, you may be granted political asylum so you will not have to return to face political, religious or racial persecution.

- After one year as a refugee or political asylee, you may be eligible to apply for a green card.

- If you are in the U.S. and come from a country that is experiencing war or a natural disaster and so has been designated for special treatment by INS, you may be granted Temporary Protected Status (TPS) or Deferred Enforced Departure (DED) with permission to work.

- You may live anywhere in the U.S. and stay in the country until you either get a green card or it is safe to go home.

- You may work at any job for any company anywhere in the U.S. or you may choose not to work at all.

- Your spouse or unmarried children under the age of 21 may receive refugee or asylee status automatically as accompanying relatives and, like you, they may receive permission to work and travel.

Limitations

- You may not travel in and out of the U.S. without making a special request to do so by getting a special travel document, or you will lose your special status.

- TPS status must be renewed each year.

- You must wait five months after filing an application for political asylum before you can apply for a work permit.

- Political asylees (but not refugees) are subject to annual quotas on green cards which may result in delays of months or years before a green card is issued. If you are an asylee and the persecution in your home country ends before your wait for a green card under the quota is up, you may lose your political asylee status and you may have to leave the U.S.

- Temporary Protected Status never leads to a green card. If you are under TPS and want a green card, you must additionally fulfill the qualifications of one of the standard green card categories. Otherwise, when the temporary period is over, you must leave the U.S. or risk deportation.

A. How to Qualify

Qualifying for a green card through special status has some limitations.

1. Quota Restrictions

Refugees have an annual quota set each year by the president of the United States. The quota may vary by country. There are no quota restrictions on the number of individuals who may be granted asylum, TPS or DED.

The refugee quota cannot be accurately forecasted because the number of slots available each year changes. Some countries get many refugee numbers in a given year while others receive practically none. Both refugee and political asylum applications can take from several months to a year

or more for approval. TPS is generally approved within a few weeks.

2. Who Qualifies as a Refugee or Asylee?

To qualify as a refugee, you must have experienced persecution in the past or have a well-founded fear of persecution in the future in your home country. The fact that you are suffering economically is not considered a reason for granting refugee status. Persecution is defined generally as a serious threat to your life or freedom. To apply for refugee status you must be physically outside the U.S.

The number of people who can get refugee status is limited by an annual quota. The size of the quota is established each year by the president of the United States. The president also decides how the total will be divided among the various regions of the world such as Latin America, Southeast Asia, Eastern Europe and Africa. Recently, the annual quota has averaged around 90,000, with about half going to Eastern Europeans. Applications are approved on a first-come first-served basis. It is not unusual for qualified refugees to end up on a waiting list.

As a refugee applicant, you must have a financial sponsor inside the U.S. before your application can be approved. You must also show that you have not already been permanently resettled in another country.

Like refugee applicants, those seeking asylum must have suffered past persecution or have a well-founded fear of future persecution in their home country. Once again, economic problems in your country are not sufficient. While you must apply for refugee status before entering the U.S., you cannot qualify as an asylee until you have reached U.S. soil. Since asylees have already arrived in the U.S., they do not need financial sponsors to be granted asylum. The other major difference between qualifications for refugees and asylees is that there is no annual quota limiting the number of people granted asylum. Beyond these differences, the qualifying requirements for refugees and asylees are the same.

a.   Persecution or Well-founded Fear of Persecution

You may establish eligibility for asylum or refugee status by proving either past persecution or a fear of future persecution. In the case of past persecution, you must prove that you were persecuted in your home country or last country of residence. The persecution must be based on race, religion, nationality, political opinion or membership in a particular social group. It may in some cases also be based on persecution based on your gender, including fear of cultural practices such as female "circumcision." Once you have proven past persecution, your eligibility for asylum or refugee status will be approved unless INS can show that the conditions in your home country or last country of residence have changed since you were persecuted, so that there is no reasonable likelihood it will happen again or that you do not deserve asylum for another reason.

If you have not actually suffered persecution in the past, you can still qualify for political asylum or refugee status if you have a genuine fear of future persecution in your home country or last country of residence. Again, that persecution must be based on race, religion, nationality, membership in a particular social group or political opinion. You do not have to prove that you are likely to be singled out for persecution from the members of a generally persecuted group. You need only show a pattern or practice, where groups of persons who are similar to you are being persecuted. Then,

you must show that you either belong to or would be identified with the persecuted group.

b.   No Firm Resettlement in Another Country and Unavailability of Safe Haven Elsewhere

Though you may clearly be fleeing persecution, you generally cannot come to the U.S. as a refugee or asylee if you have already been granted or offered a permanent status in another country. You may prefer coming to the U.S., but that makes no difference if you have been offered a safe, permanent home elsewhere. The availability of permanent status in another country is known as *firm resettlement*.

Even if you do have an offer of permanent status elsewhere, you can still qualify for refugee or political asylum status in the U.S. if you entered the other country while fleeing persecution, stayed there only as long as was necessary to arrange your continued travel and did not establish significant ties to that country. In addition, if your rights there with respect to living conditions, employment, holding of property and travel were significantly less than those of actual citizens or full residents, you may still apply for refugee status or political asylum in the U.S. INS can deny an asylum application if you can be removed to a "safe third country" for temporary protection or asylum processing.

i. One Year Time Limit

Beginning April 1, 1997, you must file an asylum application within one year after you arrived in the U.S. to be eligible for asylum. If you arrived in the U.S. on or before April 1, 1997, you must have filed your asylum application by April 1, 1998 for the application to be considered under normal procedures.

There are a few exceptions. If you did not file your asylum application within the one-year filing deadline, you can still apply for asylum if you can show either changed circumstances which have a major effect on your eligibility for asylum or extraordinary circumstances for why your application wasn't filed on time. Changed circumstances can include changes in conditions in your country; extraordinary circumstances can include events or factors beyond your control that caused the late filing.

ii. Forms and Fingerprints

Submit your asylum application without fingerprints. All other requirements (described below) for filing an asylum application remain in effect. INS will notify you where and when to report to have your fingerprints taken. Fingerprints must be taken before your application can be considered; failure to report for a fingerprinting appointment may lead to dismissal of an your application or referral to an immigration judge.

Asylum applications are filed on Form I-589. There are several versions of this form. Before July 1, 1998, you can use either the April 1, 1997 version or the new 1998 version. Beginning July 1, 1998, you must use the new 1998 version of the Form I-589.

c. Financial Sponsorship—Refugees

Your refugee application will not be approved unless you can show that you have a way to pay for your transportation to the U.S. and a means of support once you arrive. This is usually done by finding a financial sponsor. Typically, promises of financial sponsorship come from relatives already in the U.S. or from private charitable groups such as churches and refugee-assistance organizations. Occasionally, the U.S. government itself allocates money for refugee assistance. Proof of financial sponsorship is not required for political asylum applications.

d. Parolees

If you qualify for refugee status but the quota has been exhausted for the year, you may be permitted to come to the U.S. as a parolee without a visa. Parolees are permitted to work and live indefinitely in the U.S., but their futures are less certain than those of refugees. Parolee status can be revoked at any time and does not lead to a green card. A parolee may apply for political asylum after arriving in the U.S., but there is no guarantee asylum will be granted.

3. Temporary Protected Status (TPS)

Temporary Protected Status (TPS) is granted to people from selected countries that the U.S. government has recognized as currently in turmoil and therefore unsafe. You must be in the U.S. when TPS is established for your country in order to qualify. TPS is very limited in time and does not lead to a green card. TPS is currently available for citizens of Bosnia-Herzegovina, Guinea-Bissau, Honduras, Kosovo, Montserrat, Nicaragua, Somalia and Sudan.

Whenever a new country is named, a notice will be published in the Federal Register, stating the time period for which the protection is granted, and the dates and procedures for registering.

4. Accompanying Relatives

If you are married or have children under the age of 21 and you get either refugee or political asylee status, your spouse and children can also be granted refugee or asylee status automatically by providing proof of their family relationship to you. Accompanying relative status allows your family not only to stay with you in the U.S., but also to work. Accompanying relatives are not recognized under TPS. Instead, each family member must qualify for TPS on his or her own.

5. Inadmissibility

If you have ever been convicted of a serious crime, lied on an immigration application, lied to an immigration officer or suffered certain physical or mental illnesses, you may be inadmissible from applying for permanent resident status after being given refugee status, political asylum or showing eligibility for TPS in the U.S. However, most grounds of inadmissibility can be waived for refugees, political asylees and persons seeking TPS, except those grounds concerning the commission of serious crimes, persecution of others or participation in subversive or terrorist activities such that you are considered a possible threat to U.S. security. (Unlike the normal waiver of inadmissibility, this waiver does not require you to have a family member who is already a permanent resident or U.S. citizen.)

B. Getting a Green Card

Refugees who get their statuses before entering the U.S. are entitled to apply for green cards one year after arriving in America.

Political asylees are also eligible to apply for green cards one year after their asylee status is granted. You will not automatically receive a notice to come in for a green card interview. You will have to keep track on your own of when you are eligible to apply.

After filing your green card application as an asylee, you may have to wait. Although there is no quota on the number of qualified applicants granted asylum, the number of asylees who may receive green cards each year is limited to 10,000. In the recent past, the small quota caused backlogs that led to waits of several years before political asylum applicants actually received green cards. This created potentially serious problems for asylees. If the persecution conditions in the asylee's home country end before the wait for a green card is over under the quota, the asylee status may be revoked and that person would have to leave the U.S.

Uncertainty and long waits for green cards cause many asylees to try to obtain green cards in other ways, such as through employment or marriage to a U.S. citizen. Remember that if you are an asylee, using your asylum status to get a green card is only one of your options. You may also try to qualify in any of the other green card categories. If you have the right qualifications, an alternative to applying for a green card as an asylee may be faster. If, however, you do manage to wait out the asylee quota, a green card application based on asylee status will almost certainly be successful, as long as the home country conditions on which your fear of persecution is based have not significantly improved and you are otherwise eligible.

As we have already stated, there is no specific method for those with TPS to get green cards. However, as one with TPS, all the standard ways to qualify for a green card, such as through family or a job with a U.S. employer, are open to you.

1.   The Application

Getting status as a refugee, political asylee or person with TPS is a one-step process. The one step is called the *application*. The object of the application is to show that you meet all the qualifications of a refugee, asylee or person entitled to TPS. You alone must file the application. Your accompanying relatives do not need separate applications, though additional copies of your own application must be filed for each relative. However, if your relatives qualify in their own right, they may want to do so to increase their chances of approval.

The application for political asylum is filed in the U.S., either at the INS regional service center or with an immigration judge. The application for status as a refugee must be filed outside the U.S. at an INS overseas office. INS overseas offices are not the same as U.S. embassies or consulates. There are only a few INS overseas offices. The cities in which these offices are located are listed in Section C, below.

2.   Paperwork

There are two types of paperwork you must submit to apply for special statuses. The first consists of official government forms. The second is personal documents such as birth and marriage certificates. We will tell you exactly what forms and documents you need.

The documents you supply to INS do not have to be originals. Photocopies of all documents are acceptable as long as you have the original in your possession and are willing to produce the originals at the request of INS.

Documents will be accepted if they are in either English, or, with papers filed at an overseas INS office, the language of the country where the documents are being filed. If the documents are not in an acceptable language as just explained, they must be accompanied by a full, word for word, written English translation. Any capable person may act as translator. It is not necessary to hire a professional. At the end of each translation, the following statement must appear:

I hereby certify that I translated this document from (language) to English. This translation is accurate and complete. I further certify that I am fully competent to translate from (language) to English.

The translator should sign this statement but it does not have to be witnessed or notarized.

Later in this chapter we describe in detail the forms and documents needed to get special statuses. A summary checklist of forms and documents appears at the end of this chapter.

C.   Application for Refugee Status: (Overseas Filing)

Anyone physically outside the U.S. who qualifies as a refugee may apply for refugee status at an INS overseas office. INS overseas offices are not the same as U.S. embassies or consulates, although most INS overseas offices are located within consulate or embassy buildings. It is important that you be aware there are very few INS overseas offices. By no means is there one located in every foreign country or even in every U.S. consulate. You cannot apply for refugee status by mail. You must do so in person. Therefore, to apply for refugee status you must first get to a city where an INS overseas office is located. At present, the places where you can file a refugee application are:

- Athens, Greece
- Bangkok, Thailand
- Belgrade, Serbia & Yugoslavia
- Buenos Aires, Argentina
- Cairo, Egypt
- Djibouti, Gulf of Aden
- Frankfurt, Germany
- Gaborne, Botswana
- Geneva, Switzerland
- Havana, Cuba
- Hong Kong, China
- Islamabad, Pakistan

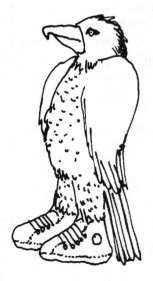

- Jakarta, Indonesia
- Karachi, Pakistan
- Khartoum, Sudan
- Kinshasa, Zaire
- Kuala Lumpur, Malaysia
- Lusaka, Zambia
- Madrid, Spain
- Manila, Philippines
- Mexico City, Mexico
- Mogadishu, Somalia
- Naha, Okinawa
- Nairobi, Kenya
- New Delhi, India
- Panama City, Panama
- Rio de Janeiro, Brazil
- Rome, Italy
- Seoul, South Korea
- San José, Costa Rica
- Singapore
- Tokyo, Japan, and
- Vienna, Austria.

U.S. consulates in other countries may be willing to take your application for review, but they will have to forward the application to one of the INS overseas offices listed above, and you will have to make an appearance wherever your file has been forwarded.

1. Benefits and Drawbacks of Filing for Refugee Status

If you are outside the U.S. and have no U.S. visa, there is no alternative to filing an application as a refugee at an INS overseas office. (But see the sidebar below on Summary Exclusion and Credible Fear.) A major benefit of a refugee application is that if it is approved, you qualify for a green card one year after arriving in the U.S.

There are two major drawbacks to applying overseas. First, there is a quota for getting refugee status. Each year, the president of the United States decides the maximum number of refugees to be allowed into the U.S. for the next year, distributing specific portions of the total to various parts of the world. If the quota is filled, once you apply, you may have to wait a year or more for a refugee number to become available. The other disadvantage is that you must remain outside the U.S. while your refugee paperwork is being processed. It is possible that you can overcome this disadvantage. INS has the power to admit you as a parolee for a year at a time, even though your refugee status has not yet been approved. Section 2, below, includes information on obtaining admission to the U.S. as a parolee.

SUMMARY EXCLUSION AND CREDIBLE FEAR

The immigration law changes of 1996 made it much easier for people entering the U.S. to be deported. In fact, someone requesting entry to the U.S. can now be quickly found inadmissible and deported for five years by an INS inspector at the airport. This can happen if an inspector believes that you are making a misrepresentation (committing fraud), or misrepresented the truth when you got your visa, or if you do not have the proper travel or visa documents at the time you request entry. This quick deportation procedure is known as "summary exclusion."

There is an exception to the summary exclusion process for people requesting asylum. So, even if you do not have the proper documents or you have made a misrepresentation, you could still be allowed to enter the U.S. if your reason is to apply for asylum and you can convince the immigration officer that you would be likely to win asylum. While the law does not require you to prove you would be granted asylum, you will need to be very clear about your reasons for wanting to apply in an effort to convince the immigration officer that what you are saying is true. Most importantly, the officer will want to be sure that your request for asylum protection is based on a fear of persecution as was described earlier in this section.

To determine if you meet this test, after you have said you want to apply for asylum, you would be given "credible fear" interview by an asylum officer. The purpose of this interview is to make sure you would have a significant possibility of winning your case. This interview is supposed to happen quickly, within one or two days, but it has been taking longer. If you fail the test, you must request a hearing before an immigration judge or you will be deported for five years. The judge may hold the hearing in person or by telephone. The hearing must be held within seven days.

If the judge finds that you have a credible fear of persecution, you will be scheduled for a full hearing. At that point, the proceeding will be a normal asylum proceeding as described in this chapter. Most asylum applicants are held in detention at this point, although you can and should request release. If you fail the credible fear test before the immigration judge, you will then be deported. INS has stated that it may (sometime in the future) allow individuals to withdraw their application for entry without being subject to the five year deportation bar.

2. General Procedures in Filing for Refugee Status

You may apply for refugee status at any INS overseas office in the cities and countries listed above, provided you are physically in one of those cities and able to remain there while your case is being processed. The U.S. consulates in these cities will be able to tell you where the INS overseas office is located, within the consulate building or elsewhere. See Appendix I for the addresses and telephone numbers of the U.S. consulates.

Since many refugees do not have passports, it is sometimes difficult to gain entry into a country where an INS overseas office is located. You may file your application at any INS overseas office you choose. Your choice of office should be based on how easily you can gain entry to the country where it is located and how the different offices operate. If you know that a particular INS overseas office approves more cases of your type than some others, you will probably want to apply there.

In most of the INS overseas offices, you can simply walk in and begin the application process. At some, you may be given a specific appointment to come back later. Procedures among INS overseas offices vary, so you should call in advance to find out the policies of the office where you intend to apply.

If your application for refugee status has been approved but receiving status is delayed because the quota is backlogged, you may, under certain conditions, be admitted to the U.S. immediately as a parolee. A request for parole

status must be made in writing to the INS central office in Washington, D.C. Such applications are most likely to be approved if you will be joining family already in the U.S., or if you cannot remain temporarily in the country where you filed your refugee application. There is no special form to file in requesting parole status. The INS overseas office that handles your refugee application can help you with the exact procedures.

On entering the U.S. as a refugee, you will be given an I-94 card. This is the small white card you are asked to fill out when you arrive. It will be stamped with a date showing for how long your refugee status has been approved. Normally, you are granted refugee status for one year, after which you will automatically be given a green card.

SPECIAL PROCEDURES FOR WORK AUTHORIZATION

If you want to work after you arrive in the U.S. as a refugee or parolee, you must file a separate application for an employment authorization card. This is done by completing Form I-765 and filing it by mail with the INS service center nearest the city where you are living. Together with Form I-765 you must submit your I-94 card. You can apply only after your application has been pending at least five months. There is no fee for the first work authorization application; extensions must be accompanied by a $70 check.

3. Forms Needed for Filing for Refugee Status

Copies of all forms can be found in Appendix III.

Form I-590

This form is self-explanatory. Question 19 asks for the name and address of your U.S. sponsor. You must have a financial sponsor in the U.S. or you will not qualify as a refugee.

Form I-765

Block above Question 1. Mark the first box, "Permission to accept employment."

Questions 1–8. These questions are self-explanatory.

Question 9. This asks for your Social Security number, including all numbers you have ever used. If you have never used a Social Security number, answer "None." If you have a nonworking Social Security number, write down the number followed by the words "Nonworking, for tax purposes only." If you have ever used a false number, give that number followed by the words "Not my valid number." (If you have used false documents or made misrepresentations to obtain employment or other benefits in the U.S., be sure you understand how this affects your application before you fill out your forms. See Chapter 25.)

Question 10. You will not usually have an Alien Registration Number unless you previously applied for a green card, were in deportation proceedings or have had certain types of immigration applications denied. All Alien Registration Numbers begin with the letter "A." If you have no "A" number, you should have an I-94 card. In this case, answer Question 10 by putting down the admission number from the I-94 card.

Questions 11–15. These questions are self-explanatory.

Question 16. If you were admitted as a refugee, answer this question "(A)(3)." If you were admitted as a parolee, answer this question "(A)(4)."

4. Documents Needed for Filing for Refugee Status

It is common for refugee applicants to have fled their home countries hurriedly, without time to gather many personal documents. Frequently, refugees also have been denied passports by their home countries. Therefore, INS does not insist on any specific documentation to support a refugee application. Some type of personal identification should be provided, however.

For each accompanying relative, you should bring documents proving their family relationship to you. You may verify a parent/child relationship by presenting the child's long form birth certificate. Many countries issue both short and long form birth certificates. Where both are available, the long form is needed because it contains the names of the parents while the short form does not. If you are accompanied by your spouse, you must show that you are lawfully married. This is best shown by a civil marriage certificate. If any of these documents are unavailable, the INS overseas office may, at its own discretion, accept other kinds of proof, including notarized affidavits from you or other people familiar with your family situation.

Additionally, you must provide documents to support your claim of persecution in your home country. Again, due to the varied circumstances under which refugees flee persecution, the INS requires no specific documents to prove this qualification, however, the burden is on you to show your eligibility. One important document proving persecution is your detailed sworn statement describing your fear and any past persecution. This statement should be in your own words and need not be in any special form.

Additional documents may include:

- newspaper articles describing the type of persecution you would encounter if you returned to your home country
- affidavits from people who know of or have personally experienced similar persecution in your home country, and
- written human-rights reports about your country supplied by organizations such as Amnesty International, Central American Resource Center, the Americas Watch Committee, or the State Department's Country Reports.

If the persecution is based on your membership in a particular social group, you must supply evidence that the group is experiencing persecution. You must also prove that you are a member of that group.

Finally, you must present documents showing you have a financial sponsor. If a relative is sponsoring you, the relative should fill out an Affidavit of Support, Form I-134. A copy of this self-explanatory form may be found in Appendix III. If you are being sponsored by an organization, the organization will supply you with a written sponsorship agreement.

Documenting your eligibility for refugee status can be extremely difficult. If, after reading this chapter, you believe you have a realistic chance of qualifying for refugee status, you may want to consider getting help with preparing your documents from one of the many refugee-assistance organizations that exist both in the U.S. and abroad. These organizations will help you without charge. Your church or synagogue can show you how to find such an organization.

5. Interviews Needed for Filing for Refugee Status

All refugee applications require personal interviews. Procedures vary from one INS overseas office to the next, but usually you will be told the time and place of your interview through an appointment letter sent by mail. Immediately before the interview, you and your accompanying relatives must have medical examinations. The procedures for these examinations will be explained in your appointment letter.

The medical examinations are conducted by private doctors for a fee. Fees vary from as little as $50 to more than $150 per exam, depending on the country. The amount of the medical exam fee will be stated in your appointment letter. The exam itself involves the taking of a medical history, blood test and chest X-ray, and if applicable, proof of vaccination. Pregnant women who do not want to be X-rayed may so advise the INS overseas office and their appointments will be postponed until after the pregnancy. The requirement to have an X-ray taken cannot be waived.

The main purpose of the medical exam is to verify that you are not medically inadmissible. The primary medical exclusions are HIV (AIDS) and tuberculosis. Medical grounds of inadmissibility usually can be overcome with treatment. See Chapter 25, *Inadmissibility*, for more details. If you need a medical waiver, you will be given complete instructions by INS at the time of your interview.

After the medical exam, you and your accompanying relatives will report to the INS overseas office for the interview. Your application will be reviewed, information verified and you will be questioned in detail about your claim of persecution in your home country.

If your application is approved, you will be issued what is known as a travel document. This document will allow you to enter the U.S. as a refugee. You must enter the U.S. within four months after the date your application was approved or you will lose your refugee status.

6. Appeals When Refugee Status Denied

When an INS overseas office denies a refugee application, there is no formal appeal available, although you are free to reapply as often as you like. When your application is denied, the reasons will be explained. The most common reason for denial is failure to establish that you have been either subject to persecution or have a reasonable fear of being persecuted if you remain in your home country. When a lack of evidence to support your claim of persecution is the problem, this will be explained to you at the INS overseas office. Sometimes presenting more evidence on an unclear fact can bring about a better result.

Another common reason for denial of a refugee application is that the INS officer believes you are inadmissible. If you are found to be inadmissible, you will be given the opportunity to apply for a Waiver of Inadmissibility. See Chapter 25 for directions on how to apply.

When all these possibilities are exhausted, if the INS overseas office still refuses to approve your refugee application, your chances for further appeals are severely limited. There is no right to appeal through the U.S. courts and there is no formal appeal procedure through any U.S. government agency.

D. Application for Political Asylum: U.S. Filing

If you are physically present in the U.S. in either a legal or undocumented status and you are otherwise qualified, you may apply for political asylum. If you are not presently in removal proceedings, applications must be filed by mail to one of the four INS regional service center offices. Appendix II contains a complete list of INS regional offices with their addresses and telephone numbers. If you are in proceedings, the application must be filed with the court and immigration judge presiding over your case.

1. Benefits and Drawbacks of Filing for Asylum

You rarely have a choice about whether to apply in the U.S. or overseas since you must apply wherever you are physically located; however, there are several benefits to applying in the U.S. First, the number of possible approved political asylum applications is not limited by the annual quota as are applications for refugee status. Therefore, you may still get political asylum through a U.S. filing even when a refugee number is not available to you through filing overseas. In addition, you are allowed to remain inside the U.S. while your asylum application is being considered. If your application is turned down, there are more avenues of appeal open in a U.S. filing. Furthermore, your application will be considered by a specialized asylum officer, trained in political asylum applications. This may result in a fairer decision than is sometimes made on refugee applications.

The biggest drawback to applying for political asylum inside the U.S. compared to applying for refugee status outside the U.S. is that you are no longer entitled to immediate work authorization. An applicant for political asylum inside the U.S. cannot apply for work authorization until either the application has been approved or it has been pending for at least five months. Also, although there is no quota on the number of people granted asylum, there is a quota when an asylee applies for a green card. If you are a political asylee, you may apply for a green card one year after your application is approved, but due to annual quotas, you may have to wait months or years after that before a green card becomes available. If the situation causing the fear of persecution in your home country should end, your asylee status may be revoked. If the conditions supporting your claim to asylee status end before your wait for a green card under the quota is over, you may never receive a green card and you may have to leave the U.S. Finally, if your case is denied, you will end up in removal proceedings, unless you are in a valid status at the time your application is denied (or referred to an immigration judge).

2. General Procedures in Filing for Asylum

The application, consisting of both forms and documents, is filed in triplicate, only by mail, at one of the four INS regional service centers. Regional service centers are given special jurisdictions that apply just for asylum cases. The proper regional service center jurisdiction for filing asylum cases is as follows:

California Service Center if you live in Arizona, Southern California or Southern Nevada.

Texas Service Center if you live in Maryland, Virginia, West Virginia, North Carolina, South Carolina, Georgia, Alabama, District of Columbia, Western Pennsylvania, Texas, Louisiana, Arkansas, Mississippi, Tennessee, Oklahoma, New Mexico, Colorado, Utah or Wyoming.

Vermont Service Center if you live in Maine, New Hampshire, Vermont, New York, Massachusetts, Rhode Island, New Jersey, eastern Pennsylvania, Connecticut or Delaware.

Nebraska Service Center if you live anywhere else in the U.S.

Appendix II contains a list of all INS regional service center offices and their addresses. The primary forms for a political asylum application are Form I-589 and work authorization application Form I-765. The November 1997 version of Form I-589 contains erroneous information regarding the one-year limit on applying for asylum after you have entered the U.S. The form states that this new one-year rule is in effect. In fact, INS' regulations state that it did not begin to apply the rule until April 1, 1998. Under these rules, you cannot file your application for work authorization until your case has been pending for five months after you have filed Form I-589 or your case has been approved, whichever comes first. The regional service center will initially review your application to determine if there is a legal prohibition to your application being approved, such as a serious criminal conviction. If that is the case, your application will be denied quickly and you will be placed in deportation proceedings.

If your application is not summarily denied, you will be asked to come to an asylum office for a personal interview. Asylum interviews are conducted at only a few locations so you may be required to travel for the interview. You will receive notice of the time of your interview in the mail. Many applications for political asylum are sent by INS for review to the U.S. Department of State, which makes a nonbinding recommendation on the application. This recommendation carries considerable weight with INS. New regulations require that you be told the decision on your application in person. If your case is not approved, instead of denying it, you are referred to removal proceedings where you can again apply for political asylum before a judge. If your case is approved, you will be given documentation to show that you have the status of an asylee.

SPECIAL PROCEDURES IF YOU ARE IN REMOVAL PROCEEDINGS

If you wish to apply for political asylum but removal proceedings have already been started against you, instead of a regional service center you must file your asylum application with the immigration judge who is presiding over your removal hearing. The procedures are similar to those for a standard asylum filing except everything is carried out through the immigration court. If you are in removal proceedings, we strongly advise hiring a competent immigration lawyer to assist you. If your application for asylum is turned down, you may be deported.

3. Forms Needed for Filing for Asylum

Copies of all forms can be found in Appendix III.

Form I-589 (three copies must be submitted)

Be sure to answer all questions as fully as possible. INS or an immigration judge will closely review your answers for inconsistencies and will be doubtful about new information that arises during an interview or hearing unless you can show good reasons why such information was not initially included in your written application.

Part A.

Question 1. Question 1 asks for your "A" number. Normally, you will not have an "A" number unless you have previously applied for a green card, were paroled into the U.S. or are already in deportation proceedings. If you do not have one, leave this question blank.

Questions 2–12. These questions are self-explanatory.

Question 13. This question asks for your nationality, or, if you are stateless, how you became stateless. You are not stateless unless your nationality has been taken away from you and you have no legal right to live in any country. The fact that you might be arrested if you return to your home country does not make you stateless.

Questions 14-16. These are self-explanatory. Be sure that this information is consistent with your asylum claim; if you are claiming persecution based on your religion, race or nationality, this section should reflect that fact.

Question 17. Check the box (a-d) that corresponds to the type of your court proceeding, if applicable. If you are in deportation proceedings, look at your Order to Show Cause or Notice to Appear to verify the type of proceeding. Boxes e-k ask for data on your status and dates of entry. Fill out the dates and describe the status (such as visitor or student) or the corresponding letter used for that status (B-2 or F-1).

If you entered without permission and without being inspected, write "entered without inspection." Box i asks for your I-94 number, which is the number on the white or green entry document you have if you were inspected and admitted. Box j asks for your most recent or current status—if you entered as B-2 but changed to F-1, put F-1 here. Box k asks for the date your status expires. This is usually indicated on your I-94 or on INS form I-797 if you requested an extension or change of status. If you are a student admitted for the duration of your studies, write "D/S."

Question 18. This is self-explanatory; however, if you check box c, be prepared to explain why you are applying again, in light of the prohibition on subsequent asylum applications discussed in this chapter.

Questions 19-24. These are self-explanatory. If your prior address was in a third country (not your home country) for an extended period of time, you will be required to show that you were not firmly resettled—that is, you were not granted permanent residence or otherwise entitled to substantial benefits and privileges in that country.

Part B. This section is self-explanatory. It asks for information about your family members. Be aware that you must be legally married to your current spouse for him or her to be granted asylum under your application. Your children will be included only if they are unmarried and under 21 years old at the time of the asylum grant.

Part C.

Questions 10–17. These questions are self-explanatory.

Question 1. This question asks why you are seeking asylum. Be as specific as possible. If your answer cannot fit in the space on the form, it is best to put down "see attached" and write your entire response on a separate sheet of paper to avoid the possibility of part of your answer getting misplaced.

Question 2. This question asks what you think will happen to you if you return to your home country. Be as specific as

you can, explaining how you will be arrested, tried by the military, sentenced to jail, put to death or whatever consequence you might suffer. You should also put down "see my affidavit and supporting documentation accompanying this application."

Questions 3–5. These questions all ask for the details supporting your claim of persecution in your home country. They are self-explanatory. It is vital to answer each of these questions in as much detail as possible. If there is not enough room on the form, write your answers on a separate sheet of paper, putting the question number on the top of each page. On the form itself put down "see attached sheet."

Question 6. This question requests information about your trip to the U.S. If, on your way to the U.S. you spent more than the normal travel time it takes to get through another country, INS may claim that you were firmly resettled there and not eligible for asylum in the U.S. You will need to establish that you were not granted permanent residence or otherwise entitled to substantial benefits and privileges in that other country. If you spent several months or years there before coming to the U.S., consult a knowledgeable attorney or asylum expert before filing your papers, as you may be found ineligible.

Question 7. This question asks whether you fear being tortured in your home country. The answer may be based on what happened to you in the past or what is happening to persons who are in similar circumstances.

Part D.

Questions 1-4. These questions request information about any prior asylum applications and whether you were firmly resettled in another country before coming to the U.S. If you answer "yes" to any of these questions, consult with an asylum expert or attorney before filing your form I-589.

Questions 5-6. If you answer "yes," consult with an asylum expert or attorney before filing your form I-589, as one or more of your family members may be ineligible for asylum.

Question 7. See the discussion of the time limits that apply to application for asylum, above. If you answer "yes" to this question, you are ineligible for asylum unless you fall under one of the exceptions discussed above. In that case, see an attorney or asylum expert before filing your application.

Parts E-G. This section requests information about you and the person who prepared the application. It is self-explanatory. Keep in mind that a person who files a fraudulent application may be subject to criminal penalties and barred from getting any applications or benefits approved by INS, in addition to being deported. There are also criminal penalties for failure to disclose one's role in helping to prepare and/or submit an application which contains false information. Finally, INS may use the information to deport a person, if the person is not granted asylum.

Form G-325A

G-325A Biographic Data forms must be filled out for you and each accompanying relative. You need not file a G-325A for any child under the age of 14 or any adult over the age of 79. The G-325A form is meant to gather personal background information. The questions are self-explanatory.

Form I-765

Block above Question 1. Mark the first box, "Permission to accept employment."

Questions 1–8. These questions are self-explanatory.

Question 9. This asks for your Social Security number, including all numbers you have ever used. If you have never used a Social Security number, answer "None." If you have a nonworking Social Security number, write down the number followed by the words "Nonworking, for tax purposes only." If you have ever used a false number, give that number followed by the words "Not my valid number." (Be aware that use of false documents for work authorization is a ground of inadmissibility. See Chapter 25.)

Question 10. You will not usually have an Alien Registration Number unless you previously applied for a green card, were in deportation proceedings, or have had certain types of immigration applications denied. All Alien Registration Numbers begin with the letter "A." If you have no "A" number but you entered the U.S. with a valid visa, you should have an I-94 card. In this case, answer Question 10 by putting down the admission number from the I-94 card. If you entered the U.S. without a visa, put down "None."

Questions 11–15. These questions are self-explanatory.

Question 16. Answer this question "(C)(8)."

4. Documents Needed for Filing for Asylum

It is common for asylum applicants to have fled their home countries hurriedly without time to gather many personal documents. Frequently, asylees also have been denied passports. Therefore, INS does not insist upon any specific documentation to support asylum applications. Some type of personal identification should be provided, however. If you entered the U.S. legally, you should present your I-94 card and a copy of your passport.

For each accompanying relative, you should bring documents showing their family relationship to you. You may prove a parent/child relationship by presenting the child's long form birth certificate. Many countries issue both short and long form birth certificates. Where both are available, the long form is needed because it contains the names of the parents while the short form does not. If you are accompanied by your spouse, you must prove that you are lawfully married. This is best shown by a civil marriage certificate. If any of these documents are unavailable, the INS office may, at its discretion, accept other kinds of proof, including notarized affidavits from you or other people familiar with your family situation.

Additionally, you must provide documents to support your claim of persecution by the government of your home country. Again, due to the varied circumstances under which asylees flee persecution, the INS requires no specific documents to prove this qualification; however, the burden is on you to prove your eligibility. One document proving fear of persecution is your own sworn statement explaining your persecution or fear of persecution. The statement should be in your own words and need not be in any special form. Additional documents may include:

- newspaper articles describing the type of persecution you would encounter if you returned to your home country
- affidavits from other people who know of or have personally experienced similar persecution in your home country, and
- written human-rights reports about your country supplied by organizations such as Amnesty International, Central American Resource Center, the Americas Watch Committee, or the State Department's Country Reports.

If the persecution is based on your membership in a particular social group, you must not only supply evidence that the group is experiencing persecution, but also you must offer proof that you are a member of that group.

Documenting your eligibility for asylee status can be extremely difficult. If, after reading this chapter, you believe you have a realistic chance of qualifying for asylum, you may want to consider getting help with preparing your documents from one of the many organizations that assist asylees, existing both in the U.S. and abroad. These organizations may help you without charge. Your church or synagogue can show you how to find such an organization.

The only other paperwork required is a fingerprint card. All fingerprinting takes place at an INS-run fingerprinting center. You will be notified where and when to appear after submitting your application forms. You will be required to pay INS $25 (often when you file your application papers) to cover the fingerprinting costs.

5. Interviews Needed for Filing for Asylum

All political asylum applications require personal interviews before they can be approved. You will receive a written notice from the appropriate INS office telling you the time and place of the interview and suggesting additional documentation you should bring. The interview itself will be long and detailed. Your application will be reviewed carefully and you will be questioned at great length concerning your fear of persecution in your home country. A decision might be made at the time of the interview or you may be asked to return at a later date to be given the decision in person.

PERMISSION TO WORK AFTER ASYLUM APPLICATION IS APPROVED

To continue working after you have been granted political asylum, you must apply for a new employment authorization card, by filing a new Form I-765 at an INS local office. Follow the instructions in Section D3, above, with one exception. Answer Question 16 by putting down "(A)(5)." You are not applying for permission to work. You already have permission. You are merely applying for your identification card.

---

6. Appeals When Filing for Asylum Is Denied

If your asylum application is not going to be approved, you will be personally given a written decision by mail explaining the reasons why it will not be approved. You will also be given a Notice to Appear, which is the start of a removal proceeding where your application may be reconsidered by an immigration judge. If your application is then turned down by the immigration judge, you may file an appeal with the Board of Immigration Appeals in Washington, D.C. If that appeal is unsuccessful, you may have your case reviewed in a U.S. Circuit Court of Appeals. You should not attempt such appeals without the assistance of an experienced immigration lawyer because you are in serious danger of being deported.

E. Application for Temporary Protected Status

Applying for Temporary Protective Status is a one-step process performed at the INS local office nearest your home in the U.S. Three Forms, I-104, I-765 and I-821 are required. Copies of these forms may be found in Appendix III. All are simple and self-explanatory. The I-104 is merely

an address card; the I-821 is a simple questionnaire asking your name, address, birth date, nationality and the date you began living in the U.S. The I-765 is an application for a work permit. You will mark box (A)(11) in Group A.

In addition to the above forms, you must also submit two fingerprint cards, three 1½" x 1½" photographs and documents showing you have lived in the U.S. for the time required under the TPS rules for your particular country. Evidence of your stay in the U.S. could include your passport and I-94 card, employment records and school records. Applicants must pay a $50 fee, which includes work authorization.

F. Deferred Enforced Departure

Another possible basis for remaining in U.S. for people from countries which are in the midst of political or civil conflicts is called Deferred Enforced Departure (DED). This temporary form of relief allows specified people to work and stay in the U.S. for a certain period of time, during which time INS will not try to deport them.

In December of 1997, President Clinton used his executive powers to provide DED protection to Haitian nationals, which delayed deportation if they had been paroled into the U.S., or filed for asylum, before December 31, 1995. Later, Congress enacted the Haitian Refugee and Immigration Fairness Act, which provided permanent residence to many of these people (see Chapter 13).

Under present INS policy, nationals of Liberia who have been in the U.S. since at least September 29, 1999, are protected from deportation. In addition, they can obtain employment authorization using Form I-765D (the normal filing fee of $100 has been waived for Liberians). They just also supply the following:

- Form I-94, Arrival-Departure Record
- their last Employment Authorization Document (EAD)
- documentation proving their residence in the United States as of September 29, 1999
- A photo ID, such as a passport, driver's license, identity card, or school identification card
- documentation to establish that they are a citizen or national of Liberia
- two photographs.

The application should be filed at the INS District Office nearest where the applicant lives. It is advisable for Liberian nationals to consult an attorney about whether to file for DED protection, political asylum or both.

This protection does not extend to anyone
- who has been convicted of an aggravated felony
- who is a persecutor of others

- whose removal, in the opinion of the Attorney General, is in the interest of the U.S.
- whose presence or activities in the U.S. is found by the Secretary of State to have potentially serious adverse foreign policy consequences for the U.S.
- who voluntarily returned or returns to Haiti or his or her country of last habitual residence outside the U.S.
- who was deported, excluded or removed before December 23, 1997, or
- who is subject to extradition.

In addition to being able to stay in the U.S. for one year, eligible Haitians can apply for one-year work permits.

If you are in removal proceedings, ask the immigration judge to defer action on your case. If your case is on appeal to the Board of Immigration Appeals, you should receive notice of the temporary suspension of your proceeding.

G. Application for Green Cards

If you are a political asylee or refugee, you may apply for a green card at the INS local office nearest your U.S. residence after one year. The application, consisting of both forms and documents, is submitted either by mail or in person. Appendix II contains a list of all INS offices with telephone numbers and addresses.

The basic form for asylees or qualifying parolees is INS Form I-485, Application for Permanent Residence. The filing fee for each application is $220 if you are age 14 or over, and $160 if you are under age 14. A separate application must be filed by each family member. Checks and money orders are accepted. It is not advisable to send cash through the mail but cash is satisfactory if you file in person. Cash is accepted only in the exact amount. INS offices will not make change. We recommend filing your papers in person if at all possible, as you will be given a written receipt from INS and your papers are likely to be processed right away. Also, in the case of asylees, the receipt will be proof of your priority date in the event that INS misplaces your paperwork. If you choose to mail in your application, you should do so by certified mail, return receipt requested. In either case, keep a complete copy of everything you send in.

Once your application has been filed, you should not leave the U.S. for any reason before your application has been approved. Any absence will be viewed as a termination of your application for a green card. If you must leave the U.S. on an emergency basis, you should go in person to the INS office processing your application, bringing three passport-type photographs and proof of the emergency (such as a telegram from relatives advising of a death in the family) and complete Form I-131, asking for advance parole. There is a filing fee of $95. If approved, you will be allowed to leave the U.S. and return again with no break in the processing of your application. However, if you return to your home country—even with advance parole—you seriously jeopardize your chances of being granted permanent residence.

Generally, after filing your application, you will not hear anything from INS for several months. Then you should receive a notice of your interview appointment. Applications cannot be approved without an interview. At the interview, your application will be reviewed, you will be fingerprinted, and asked to sign the application in front of an immigration officer. If everything is in order, your application should be approved at the conclusion of the interview. Your passport will be stamped to show that you have been admitted to the U.S. as a permanent resident and your permanent green card will be ordered. The green card will come to you in the mail about two to five months after the interview.

1. Forms

Copies of all forms can be found in Appendix III.

Form I-485

While most of the form is self-explanatory, a few items typically raise concerns. If a particular question does not apply to you, answer it with "None" or "N/A." The questions on this form requiring explanation are as follows:

Part 1. Part 1 asks for general information about when and where you were born, your present address and immigration status. It also asks for an "A" number. Everyone who enters the U.S. as a refugee or has applied for political asylum is given an "A" number.

Part 2. Mark box D.

Part 3. The questions in Sections A through C are self-explanatory. Questions concerning a visa do not apply. The questions in Section C are meant to identify people who are inadmissible. With the exception of certain memberships in the Communist Party or similar organizations, you will not be deemed inadmissible simply because you joined an organization. However, if your answer to any of the other questions is "yes," you may be inadmissible. See Chapter 25, which is intended to help you identify and overcome such obstacles. Don't lie on your answers because you will probably be found out, especially if you have engaged in criminal activity. Many inadmissible conditions can be legally overcome, but once a lie is detected, you will lose the legal right to correct the problem. In addition, a false answer is grounds to deny your application and may result in your being permanently barred from getting a green card.

Form G-325A

G-325A Biographic Data forms must be filled out for you and each accompanying relative. You need not file a G-325A for any child under the age of 14 or any adult over the age of 79. The G-325A form is meant to gather personal background information. The questions are self-explanatory.

2. Documents

Each applicant must submit an I-94 card or other immigration document showing your status as an asylee or parolee. You should also file, if available, birth certificates for each applicant, and if married, marriage certificates and proof that any previous marriages were terminated by death or divorce. You will also need two photographs for each applicant, taken in compliance with the special photograph instructions contained in Appendix III.

You must also submit a medical examination report for each applicant. This is done on INS Form I-693, which must be taken to an INS authorized physician or medical clinic. The INS local office will give you the form together with a list of approved physicians in your area. After completion of the medical exam and upon obtaining the test results, the doctor will give you the results in a sealed envelope. Do not open the envelope.

The only other paperwork required is a fingerprint card. Beginning March 30, 1998, INS regulations changed so that all fingerprinting now takes place at an INS-run fingerprinting center. You will be notified where and when to appear after submitting your application forms. You will be required to pay INS $25 (often when you file your application papers) to cover the fingerprinting costs.

3. Interviews

Personal interviews are normally held. You and your accompanying relatives will be asked to come in to the INS local office to verify your eligibility and may be asked questions about the conditions in your home country which are relevant to your persecution claim.

4. Appeals

If your application is denied, you will receive a written decision by mail explaining the reasons for the denial. There is no way of making a formal appeal to INS when your application is turned down. If the problem is too little evidence, you may be able to overcome this obstacle by adding more documents and resubmitting the entire application to the same INS office you have been dealing with, together with a written request that the case be reopened. The written request does not have to be in any special form. This is technically called a *Motion to Reopen*. If you believe the INS made a mistake, it is called a *Motion to Reconsider*. There is a $110 fee to file this motion. Alternatively, you may wait until INS begins removal proceedings, in which case you may refile your application with the immigration judge.

If your application is denied because you are ruled inadmissible, you will be given the opportunity to apply for what is known as a *Waiver of Inadmissibility* provided a waiver is available for your ground of inadmissibility. See Chapter 25 for directions on how to apply.

Although there is no appeal to INS for the denial of a green card application, you have the right to file an appeal in a U.S. district court. This requires employing an immigration attorney at considerable expense. Such appeals are usually unsuccessful.

FORMS AND DOCUMENTS CHECKLIST

REFUGEE STATUS

Forms

☐ Form I-590.

☐ Form I-765, if you want to work after you arrive in the U.S.

Documents

☐ Personal identification for each applicant.

☐ Long form birth certificate for you and each accompanying relative.

☐ Marriage certificate if you are married and bringing your spouse.

☐ If either you or your spouse have ever been married, copies of divorce and death certificates showing termination of all previous marriages.

☐ Personal sworn affidavit describing in detail your reasons for seeking refugee status.

☐ Newspaper articles describing the conditions of persecution in your home country.

☐ Affidavits from knowledgeable people describing the conditions of persecution in your home country.

☐ Three photographs each of you and each accompanying relative.

☐ Written human-rights reports about your country supplied by organizations such as Amnesty International, Central American Resource Center, the Americas Watch Committee, or the U.S. State Department's Country Reports.

☐ Documents showing you have a financial sponsor in the U.S., such as a completed Form I-134.

POLITICAL ASYLEE STATUS

Forms

☐ Form I-589.

☐ Form G-325A for you and each accompanying relative between the ages of 14 and 79.

☐ Form I-765, if advanced permission to work is needed.

DOCUMENTS

☐ Personal identification for you and each accompanying relative.

☐ Long form birth certificate for you and each accompanying relative.

☐ Marriage certificate if you are married and bringing your spouse.

☐ If either you or spouse have ever been married, copies of divorce and death certificates showing termination of all previous marriages.

☐ Personal sworn affidavit describing in detail your reasons for seeking political asylum.

☐ Newspaper articles describing the conditions of persecution in your home country.

☐ Affidavits from knowledgeable people describing the conditions of persecution in your home country.

☐ Written human-rights reports about your country supplied by organizations such as Amnesty International, Central American Resource Center, the Americas Watch Committee, or the U.S. State Department's Country Reports.

TEMPORARY PROTECTED STATUS

Forms

☐ Form I-104.

☐ Form I-821.

☐ Form I-765.

Documents

☐ Three $1^1/_2$" x $1^1/_2$" photographs of each applicant.

☐ Evidence of your presence during the necessary time period in the U.S.

GREEN CARD APPLICATION

Forms

☐ Form I-485.

☐ Form G-325A.

DOCUMENTS

☐ I-94 card.

☐ Birth certificates for each applicant.

☐ Marriage certificates.

☐ Two 1½" x 1½: photographs of each applicant.

☐ Medical examination report for each applicant.

Special Statuses: Amnesty and Special Agricultural Workers

A. Special Suspension of Deportation Rules

Congress passed legislation late 1997 which isn't exactly amnesty, but it affords relief to people from various countries. The law, called the Nicaraguan Adjustment and Central American Relief Act (NACARA), grants different relief depending on whether you are from Central America, Cuba or a former Soviet Bloc country.

1. Applicants From Nicaragua or Cuba

An individual from Cuba or Nicaragua who has been continually present in the U.S. since December 1, 1995 (total absences cannot amount to more than 180 days) is eligible for permanent residence. So is the individual's spouse or unmarried child under age 21, even if that person would not qualify on his or her own.

An unmarried son or daughter over 21 years old may also qualify for permanent residence if the parent was granted a green card under this part of the law, but only if the son or daughter shows continuous physical presence in the U.S. since December 1, 1995.

An applicant must also show that he or she is admissible to the U.S.—that is, that none of the grounds of inadmissibility apply (or if one applies, that a waiver is available). Certain grounds of inadmissibility which apply to most green card applicants do not apply to NACARA applicants: public charge, the need for labor certification, being present in the U.S. without having been admitted or paroled, failure to comply with certain documentary requirements and being unlawfully present. These grounds are more fully discussed in Chapter 25.

If an applicant must leave the United States for a family emergency or some other reason, she will have to get permission by requesting advance parole on Form I-131. It may be necessary to consult with an immigration attorney if you have questions about getting advance parole.

a. Deadline for Applying

Cuban and Nicaraguan nationals have until April 1, 2000 to apply.

b. Applicants In Removal Proceedings

An immigration judge cannot order an eligible applicant deported while he or she has a pending NACARA application on file. If you qualify for benefits but do not yet have an application on file, notify the immigration judge that you want to close your immigration court case to apply for a NACARA-based green card. If you cannot prove you would be eligible for NACARA status, your removal case will proceed.

The law requires that the principal applicant has been in the United States continuously since December 1, 1995. To prove this, the applicant will have to show evidence, which can include:

- an earlier application to the INS for asylum, dated before December 2, 1995
- an INS order to appear for a deportation hearing and proof that at that hearing the dates of entry were accepted by the immigration court, or that the applicant was issued a notice to appear at immigration court dated anytime before December 2, 1995
- an application for adjustment of status or employment authorization dated before December 2, 1995
- business or employment records that show the person was in the U.S. before December 2, 1995, including Social Security tax information, W-2 forms, wage statements, rental agreements or utility bills
- an earlier application for immigration benefits
- a passport, or
- any other evidence that can support your claim.

The law does not specify how you must prove your continuous physical presence in the United States. Some documents issued by state or local governments that contain the name of the primary applicant, a date, a signature and an official seal may also work. A college transcript or an employment record may show that an applicant attended school or worked in the United States from December 1, 1995, until the time of the application. An applicant would need to submit a number of monthly rent receipts or electric bills to establish the same continuity of presence.

The law does not require proof that an applicant was in the United States every single day since December 1, 1995, only that there are no significant chronological gaps in the documentation. Generally, a gap of three months or less in documentation will not be considered significant. If a person is relying on documents in the INS files, then all that is needed is to list the documents.

2. Applicants From Guatemala, El Salvador or Certain Eastern European Nations

NACARA allows certain Guatemalans, Salvadorans and nationals of former Soviet Bloc countries to apply for suspension of deportation or cancellation of removal under the rules that existed before the enactment of the 1996 immigration law changes.

⚠️ Do not go to the INS before making sure that you qualify for NACARA relief. If you are not part of the group intended to receive this benefit you could, in effect, cause your own deportation. In addition, due to the complexity of reopening your case to apply for NACARA benefits, it is highly recommended that you hire a qualified attorney or other person to represent you in this kind of proceeding.

a. Cancellation of Removal

Cancellation of removal is the granting of a green card based on ten years presence in the US., provided that the removal (deportation) of the applicant would result in extreme and unusual hardship to a qualifying family member (not the applicant) who is a permanent resident or U.S. citizen. An applicant must also not be inadmissible under the criminal or security grounds of inadmissibility, or deportable under the criminal or security grounds of deportability. Applicants who have persecuted others or are deportable under certain document fraud grounds are not eligible, unless INS grants a waiver. (See Chapter 25.)

A similar form of relief available before the 1996 immigration law changes was called suspension of deportation. That benefit required only seven years presence, and allowed an applicant to qualify upon showing extreme hardship to himself or herself, or a qualifying family member. The applicant must have had good moral character.

The old rules for suspension of deportation are clearly more flexible than the new ones; many asylum applicants from Central America and Eastern Europe do not have qualifying family members or ten years presence. For that reason, NACARA allows some people to apply under the old rules:

Salvadoran ABC or TPS registrants present since 1990. Salvadoran nationals who entered the U.S. on or before September 19, 1990, and who have registered for ABC (American Baptist Church) benefits under that class action lawsuit on or before October 31, 1991, or have registered for temporary protected status (TPS) on or before October 1, 1990.

Guatemalan ABC registrants. Guatemalan nationals who entered the U.S. on or before October 1, 1990 and who registered for ABC benefits on or before December 31, 1991.

Salvadoran or Guatemalan asylum applicants. Guatemalans or Salvadorans who applied for asylum on or before April 1, 1990.

Asylum applicants who are nationals of Eastern Bloc countries. Nationals of the Soviet Union, Russia, any Republic of the former Soviet Union, Estonia, Latvia, Lithuania, Poland, Czechoslovakia, Romania, Hungary, Bulgaria, Albania, East Germany, Yugoslavia, or any state of the former Yugoslavia who entered the U.S. before December 31, 1990 and who filed an application for asylum on or before December 31, 1991.

b. Spouses and Children of Qualifying Individuals

The spouse and minor children of an individual who is granted cancellation or suspension under NACARA also qualify for permanent residence under NACARA. Unmarried adult sons and daughters (over 21 years old when their parents were granted suspension or cancellation) must have entered the U.S. before October 1, 1990 in order to qualify on the basis of a grant of suspension of deportation to their parents.

3. Application Procedures for NACARA Applications

The application period for NACARA benefits began on June 22, 1998, and ends on March 31, 2000.

a. Application Procedure

Applicants are required to use Form I-881, Application for Suspension of Deportation or Special Rule Cancellation of Removal (see Appendix III). The application fee to the INS is $215, except the maximum fee per family (husband, wife, unmarried children under 21 years old) is $430. Applications submitted to the Immigration Court will be charged a single $100 for one applicant or for applications filed by two or more aliens in the same proceeding. The $100 fee will not be required if the Form I-881 is denied by the INS and referred to the Immigration Court. Every applicant over the age of 14 is required to complete a fingerprinting card for a $25 fee. A request to waive this fee can be made, but in the past this has caused long delays to the application. The applicant must include:

1. a birth certificate or other record of birth
2. two photographs
3. a completed Biographic Information Sheet (Form G-325A) if the applicant is between 14 and 79 years of age
4. a report of medical examination
5. a local police clearance from each jurisdiction where the alien has resided for six months or longer since arriving in the United States, if the applicant is at least 14 years of age
6. a copy of the applicant's Arrival-Departure Record (Form I-94) or other evidence of inspection and admission or parole into the United States, if applicable
7. one or more of the documents that prove continuous physical presence, as described earlier in this chapter
8. a statement showing all departures from and arrivals in the United States since Dec. 1, 1995, and
9. if the applicant is applying as the spouse, child or unmarried son or daughter of another NACARA beneficiary, the applicant must submit evidence of the relationship.

An applicant who has already used Form EOIR-40 (Application for Suspension of Deportation) in the Immigration Court before June 21, 1999, may apply to the INS by submitting a copy of that application attached to a completed first page of Form I-881. The application must be filed at the regional INS service center indicated on the form.

b.   Proving Your Case.

People who meet the requirements of ABC class members described above are automatically presumed to meet the requirement of "extreme hardship." All other applicants must show that they meet the extreme hardship standard. Even though ABC class members are presumed to meet the "extreme hardship" standard, it is best for all applicants to be prepared to present evidence to back up their claim. An applicant should prepare as much of the following evidence as possible about herself and her immediate family, remembering that deportation alone is not enough to establish "extreme hardship."

1. The age of the people involved, both at the time of entry to the United States and at the time of application
2. The age, number and immigration status of the people who face the possibility of deportation. If there are

children, then it would be helpful to show the extent to which their limited ability to speak the native language and to adjust to life in the country might make things more difficult for their adjustment to the new country

3. The health condition of the persons who might be required to leave the U.S. including the children, spouse or parents and the availability of any required medical treatment in the country to which the alien would be returned
4. The possibility of obtaining employment in the country to which the people would be returned
5. The length of residence in the United States
6. The existence of other family members who are or will be legally residing in the United States
7. The financial impact of the alien's departure
8. The impact of a disruption of educational opportunities
9. The psychological impact of the being forced to leave the United States
10. The current political and economic conditions in the country to which the person would be returned
11. Family and other ties to the country to which the people would be returned
12. Contributions to and ties to a community in the United States, including the degree of integration into society
13. Immigration history, including authorized residence in the United States, and
14. The availability of other means of adjusting to permanent resident status.

c. The application

Note: The NACARA application clearly states that the applicant who is denied could be deported based upon the information provided. Therefore, we caution anyone who is not sure of their eligibility to consult with a lawyer before filing this application.

Parts 1 and 2 are self-explanatory.

Part 3: Presence in the United States: Here the INS wants you to account for where you have lived for at least six months at a time over the last ten years. It is important that you be able to clearly document your residences during the dates set out in the law, depending on whether you are applying as a Nicaraguan or Eastern European or Central American.

Part 4, Question 1, seeks similar information as was asked in Part 3, but concerning your employment.

Part 4, Question 3, seeks to determine whether you have paid income taxes. If you have not it is recommended that you take steps to complete income tax returns for the years you have not filed.

Part 5 seeks to determine whether you may be entitled to permanent residency based upon marriage to a U.S. citizen or lawful permanent resident or possibly whether you may be ineligible for cancellation of removal due to an earlier fraudulent marriage, or for other reasons like failure to support your prior spouse or child.

Another reason for asking these questions is to compare your answers with any prior answers you might have given to the INS, to determine if you answered them differently. If you have, you should be prepared to explain why. Also, failure to include a child or spouse may make them ineligible to receive NACARA benefits later.

Part 7. While this question only asks for financial information regarding your parents, we recommend that you also include a supplement at the end of the questionnaire on page eight presenting other reasons for hardship to your children, spouse or parents, or because of a medical condition or simply because of the long residency in the U.S., which makes it difficult for either them or you to have to leave the U.S

Part 8. These questions are to determine whether there are any legal reasons why you should be denied cancellation of removal. The questions relate to specific legal grounds of inadmissibility. If you believe that any of the items in the boxes apply to you, you should check with an experienced lawyer. When considering if any of these items apply to you, consider whether you have:

- in any way encouraged or helped a family member to come to the U.S. illegally
- ever lied about anything related to an immigrant visa application
- been convicted of driving under the influence (DUI), or
- entered the U.S. under an exchange student visa (J visa).

Part 9. While these questions generally only allow you to answer yes or no, you should use additional pages to provide more information. These are some of the most important questions in the application. Remember in answering these questions that "hardship" includes everything from emotional to economic to the physical. It relates to each individual in different ways and so almost anything which you believe is important will be relevant here.

Note: The NACARA rules have been subject to many changes since the original law was passed. The INS has been very slow to decide on the procedures and rules that it will follow in deciding NACARA claims. It only issued "interim" rules in May of 1999. We suggest that you contact a non-profit immigration support organization in your area to find the latest news on NACARA.

4. Fast-Track NACARA Program for ABC and Other Asylum Applicants

Prior to NACARA, only an immigration judge could grant suspension or cancellation of removal. That meant that you could apply only if you were already in removal proceedings. Under the new program, however, INS asylum officers will decide cancellation of removal applications for certain NACARA applicants, including individuals who have asylum applications pending with the INS Asylum Office, such as registered class members of the ABC settlement agreement.

As mentioned, the new rules and procedures for applying for administrative suspension of deportation are not yet in place. Nevertheless, INS has stopped processing asylum applications filed by eligible class members of the ABC settlement and certain others included in the cancellation of removal provisions of the new law. It appears that INS process pending asylum applications which are NACARA eligible as suspension of deportation applications first, and as asylum applications if the suspension case is not granted.

If you have an asylum application pending with INS and may be eligible for NACARA benefits, you can request an expedited asylum interview if you do not want to apply for cancellation of removal with the INS Asylum Office. (If you have family members abroad, you might prefer to apply for asylum because your members would be included in an asylum grant but would not be included in a suspension of deportation grant.) It may take a long time to get such an interview, given the large number of cases and the time and staff constraints of INS.

5. If a Deportation Order Has Been Entered

Until November 18, 1999, a person facing deportation had the legal right to ask that their case be reopened and considered under the NACARA rules. If you believe this would help your case, but did not file under NACARA by the deadline, you should consult with an attorney right away. But you should also file a completed NACARA application before the final deadline of March 31, 2000. If you have been ordered deported and have not filed a NACARA petition by the final date, the immigration service could take steps to remove you from the United States without any further hearings.

6. Appeals of Denials Under NACARA

The text of the NACARA law specifically bars judicial appeals (appeals made to the federal District Courts, Courts of Appeals and the Supreme Court). This means that the only appeal available is to an immigration judge or the Board of Immigration Appeals.

B. Haitian Immigrant Relief Act

The Haitian Refugee Immigration Fairness Act of 1998 (HRIFA) allows certain citizens of Haiti to become lawful permanent residents, if they:

- were in the United States on December. 31, 1995
- had been living in the United States for a continuous period beginning not later than December 31, 1995, and ending not earlier than the date the application for adjustment is filed (the applicant cannot have been outside the U.S. for more than 180 days at a time)
- are a child with Haitian citizenship, arrived in the United States without parents and have remained without parents in the United States since arrival, or who became orphaned after their arrival or were abandoned by their parents or guardians prior to April 1, 1998, and have remained abandoned, and
- file an application for adjustment before April 1, 2000.

All the grounds for inadmissibility still apply to Haitians under this law, except they will not be excluded if they are likely to become a public charge, don't meet labor certification requirements, are illegal entrants or lack the required documentation. Should the person be ineligible based on other grounds of inadmissibility, they must be able to qualify for a waiver (see Chapter 25).

If the applicant is in removal proceedings, he or she should ask the immigration judge to consider the Haitian Adjustment Application. If the case is on appeal, a request should be made to the immigration judge or to the Board of Immigration Appeals to reopen the case. If the person is not in removal proceedings, he or she should submit the application to the INS. The application period began on June 11, 1999, and ends on March 31, 2000. According to regulations issued at the publishing of this book the normal adjustment application form is to be used (Form I-485).

Each application must be accompanied by the following evidence, where possible:

- a birth certificate or other record of birth
- a completed Biographic Information Sheet (Form G-325A) if the applicant is between 14 and 79 years of age
- a report of medical examination
- two photographs as described in the Form I-485 instructions
- a copy of the applicant's Arrival-Departure Record (Form I-94) or other evidence of inspection and admission or parole into the United States, if applicable
- if the applicant is at least 14 years of age, a local police clearance from each jurisdiction where the alien has resided for six months or longer since arriving in the United States (although the regulation does allow this particular requirement to be waived under certain circumstances)
- if the applicant is a principal applicant, or the unmarried son or daughter of a principal applicant, one or more of the documents described below to establish presence in the United States on December 31, 1995
- if the applicant is a principal applicant or the unmarried son or daughter of a principal applicant, a statement showing all departures from and arrivals in the United States since December 31, 1995
- if the applicant is a principal applicant, evidence that he or she falls within one of the groups described above as eligible for HRIFA adjustment
- if the alien is applying as the spouse or unmarried son or daughter of another HRIFA beneficiary, evidence of the relationship (for example, a marriage certificate), and
- if the applicant acquired Haitian nationality through naturalization in that country, a copy of his or her Haitian naturalization certificate.

Proof of physical presence in the U.S. may be established by submitting the following:

- a copy of the person's arrival-departure record (I-94)
- a copy of the Form I-122, Notice to Applicant for Admission Detained for Hearing before Immigration Judge or Form I-221, Order to Show Cause issued by the INS on or before December 31, 1995, placing the applicant in proceedings for removal
- a photocopy of any application or petition for a benefit under the immigration laws filed before December 31, 1995, or a fee receipt issued by the INS
- other documents issued by a federal, state or local authority provided that it has a signature, seal or other official notice dated before December 31, 1995.

You may also submit copies of any of the following documents, provided that they were issued before December 31, 1995:

- a state drivers license
- a state identification card issued instead of a driver's license to a non-driver
- a county or municipal hospital record
- a public college or public school transcript
- rental receipts, wage statements or utility bills in your name
- income tax records.

These are not the only documents that you may use. You should submit as many documents that you have that show you were in the U.S. on Dec. 31, 1995.

The application fee for this adjustment of status request is $220 for applicants 14 years old or older and $160 for applicants under 14 years old. There is an additional $25 fee for fingerprinting costs. If the application is submitted to an immigration court or the Board of Immigration Appeals, the fees must be submitted to the appropriate local office of the Service. If the application is submitted to the Nebraska Service Center, the $25 fee must accompany the application and be sent to USINS Nebraska Service Center, P.O. Box 87245, Lincoln, NE 68501-7245.

An applicant who does not have enough money to pay for the HRIFA adjustment may request a waiver of the filing fee. If the application is denied it may be renewed before an immigration judge.

C. Amnesty

The Immigration Reform and Control Act of 1986 (IRCA) created a legalization program that granted amnesty to persons who have lived in the U.S. illegally since the beginning of 1982. The last day for filing amnesty applications was officially May 4, 1988. However, two major class-action lawsuits have been filed challenging some of the amnesty regulations. (Class-action lawsuits are lawsuits affecting large numbers of people, all of whom have the same problem with one person or organization. The large group of people is called a "class." If a certain number of people who are in the class can be located, this relatively small number can file a lawsuit on behalf of everyone who falls into the class, even those who do not directly participate in the suit or are unaware of it.) The result of this is that anyone falling into one of the two classes named in the lawsuits was permitted to apply for amnesty, even though the final filing date has passed. Due to extensive appeals of these decisions, and new limitations on relief and appeals of the lawsuits which were brought by the 1996 immigration law reforms, the status of late applications for legalization is unclear. The following information is provided as general information and for reference. However, if you do not have any way of regularizing your status and you believe you qualify as a late legalization applicant, you should seek advice from a competent community organization or immigration attorney.

The first lawsuit is based on objections to an INS amnesty regulation stating that anyone who physically left the U.S. after January 1, 1982 and then returned with a valid visa was ineligible for amnesty. INS's reasoning was that since the once illegal immigrant had entered the U.S. with a legal visa during the necessary period of "illegal" residency, the requirement of illegality was broken.

Those who wanted to help amnesty applicants believed INS's interpretation of the law was wrong. These people said that in reality, anyone entering the U.S. with a temporary nonimmigrant visa while having the intent to stay in the U.S. permanently were in fact here illegally because they were not honest about their purpose in coming to the U.S. They were guilty of misrepresentation and were, therefore, illegal. INS at first refused to recognize illegality based on that type of misrepresentation for purposes of amnesty qualification. However, INS eventually withdrew the controversial regulation during the last months of the amnesty program. As a result, illegal immigrants who left the U.S. and returned with a visa after January 1, 1982, were no longer barred from filing for amnesty.

Many immigrants did not take advantage of this change in the regulations, however, and did not apply for amnesty, either because they didn't know about the change or had been given wrong information about their eligibility by legalization help groups, lawyers or even INS. Meanwhile, the time limit on filing amnesty applications ran out.

1. LULAC Case

A class-action lawsuit filed by the League of United Latin American Citizens, commonly known as LULAC, brought suit to force INS to accept late amnesty applications. To be considered part of the LULAC class, you must have lived in the U.S. illegally since before January 1, 1982. Then, you must have left the U.S. between January 1, 1982 and November 6, 1987, returning again and reentering with a visa or, if no visa was required, making an otherwise legal reentry. Aside from absences of this sort, you must have lived continuously in the U.S. as an illegal alien since January 1, 1982. Finally, to qualify for late filing under the LULAC class, you must have been unaware of or misinformed about the INS change in regulation that would have allowed you to file on time.

Due to limitations on judicial review and relief brought by the Immigration Reform Act of 1996, it is now doubtful that any pending or new LULAC cases will be approved, unless the person actually applied for legalization and had their application rejected by INS. This issue is on appeal in the courts. If you do not have any other way to immigrate and you believe you qualify under late amnesty, you should consult an immigration attorney who has specific experience in legalization, or a qualified community organization.

2. CSS Case

The second class-action lawsuit found fault with another INS amnesty regulation. The regulation states that any trip outside the U.S. after May 4, 1987, the first date amnesty applications could be filed, ended your eligibility to apply for amnesty unless INS had given you special permission to leave and return. Several suits were filed against INS challenging the validity of this regulation, including a class-action suit by Catholic Social Services. The suit is now known as the CSS case. Anyone who has lived in the U.S. illegally since January 1, 1982, left the U.S. without INS permission after May 4, 1987, and returned to the U.S. illegally sometime before May 4, 1988 initially qualified for inclusion in the CSS class. However, like the LULAC case, the right to have late applications and other relief granted under CSS was severely curtailed by the immigration reforms of 1996. Those changes attempt to limit late applications to those people who actually applied or tried to apply for legalization, but had the application refused by the INS. If you do not have any other way to immigrate and you believe you qualify as a late filing amnesty applicant, you should consult an immigration attorney who specializes in legalization to determine the status of these cases.

3. Applications Under LULAC and CSS

The LULAC and CSS suits were joined into one suit and won certain rights for applicants after being appealed in the courts. Specifically, it won the right of individuals to make late applications for amnesty if they did not actually apply during the filing period, if they were discouraged by INS' policies at the time requiring "advance parole" (readmission) permission. As discussed above, due to the Immigration Reform Act changes in 1996, it now appears that the only people who will be permitted to continue with amnesty applications are those who can demonstrate that they had actually gone to an INS office during the original application period but were erroneously told by an INS official that they did not qualify. A final decision, however, may not be made before 1998 or later. Until then, you should consult an attorney or community organization that does legalization work before you file a late application.

D. Special Agricultural Workers (SAW)

IRCA also granted legal status to special agricultural workers (SAWs) who performed certain types of agricultural field labor for at least 90 days between May 1, 1985 and May 1, 1986. The deadline for filing applications under the SAW program officially expired on November 30, 1988. However, some SAW applicants who missed the deadline were allowed to file late applications if INS forced them not to apply or forced them to withdraw their applications.

One of the requirements to qualifying as a SAW is that the labor performed must involve seasonal or perishable crops. There has been considerable court litigation over the Department of Agriculture's definition of seasonal or perishable crops. If you did not file for SAW status, but can

prove you performed 90 days of field labor between May 1, 1985 and May 1, 1986, check with a lawyer or immigration assistance group to see if you can file late. Likewise, if you did apply but were turned down because the crops you worked with did not qualify, you should contact someone who knows the law to see if there may be a chance to file a new application.

E. Family Unity: Spouses and Children

Many families were faced with special problems caused by amnesty. While one family member qualified for amnesty benefits, that person's spouse or children did not qualify. This occurred when some family members arrived in the U.S. before January 1, 1982, while others arrived after that date. In SAW applications, there were problems when not everyone in the family worked in the fields. Those who did not could not qualify for immigration benefits under amnesty.

The Immigration Act of 1990 created a family unity program to help out in these cases. To qualify, you must be the spouse or unmarried child under age 21 of an amnesty recipient. You must have entered the U.S. no later than May 5, 1988, and have been living in the U.S. continuously since that date, and have been eligible continuously since that time for a second preference family-based visa petition. Also, your qualifying relationship (such as marriage) to the amnesty recipient must have existed on May 5, 1988. Note that children will not lose their status when they turn 21, as long as they remain unmarried. Family unity benefits may be terminated if the applicant committed fraud to obtain the status, or becomes inadmissible as an immigrant or ineligible according to the family unity requirements, or the relationship to the legalization beneficiary ends. The 1996 Immigration Reform Law added an additional disqualification, for aliens who committed an act of juvenile delinquency, if it would be a felony offense if committed by an adult and if it included violence, threat of force, or possible violence, but only if committed after September 1996.

An additional benefit of family unity status is that it stops the running of time for both the three- and ten-year overstay bars. (See Chapter 25 for a discussion of the overstay bars.) Finally, persons in family unity status are allowed to request advance permission to leave and reenter the U.S. ("advance parole") so that they may travel abroad.

Family unity status does not turn into a green card automatically. An amnesty relative who already has a green card must eventually file a relative petition on behalf of the other family members. The family unity status will last until a green card can be obtained, however. ∎

Nonimmigrant Visas: An Overview

There are many kinds of nonimmigrant visas. Each is issued for a different purpose and each is known by a letter-number combination as well as a name. A lot of people are familiar with the more popular types of nonimmigrant visas such as B-2 visitors, E-2 investors or F-1 students. All of these fall into the general nonimmigrant group. When you get a nonimmigrant visa, the U.S. government assumes you will perform a specific activity while you are in America. You are therefore given a specialized visa authorizing that activity and no other.

While nonimmigrant visas come in many varieties, they all have one major feature in common: they are temporary. Probably the best way to describe nonimmigrant visas is by comparing them to green cards. Making this comparison is also a good idea because experience has shown us that there is in fact confusion about how the two differ.

The most basic difference between a nonimmigrant visa and a green card is that all green cards are permanent while all nonimmigrant visas are temporary. If you hold a green card, you are considered a permanent resident of the U.S. Your green card can be taken away if you act in a manner that suggests you do not intend to live in the U.S. permanently, or by violating certain laws or regulations. The exact opposite is true of nonimmigrant visas. If you travel to the U.S. on a nonimmigrant visa and INS thinks you do not plan to go home, the visa will be taken away. After you've held a green card for a certain length of time, you can become an American citizen; a nonimmigrant visa, however, will never lead to U.S. citizenship.

A. Types of Nonimmigrant Visas

Nonimmigrant visas come in a variety of types, while every green card is exactly the same. There are many different ways to get a green card, but once you have it, each card carries the same privileges. Nonimmigrant visas differ from each other in the kinds of privileges they offer, as well as how long they last. As we said earlier, every nonimmigrant visa is issued with a specific purpose in mind. Here is a complete list of nonimmigrant visas available.

A-1. Ambassadors, public ministers or career diplomats and their immediate family members.

A-2. Other accredited officials or employees of foreign governments and their immediate family members.

A-3. Personal attendants, servants or employees and their immediate family members of A-1 and A-2 visa holders.

B-1. Business visitors.

B-2. Tourist visitors. Tourists from certain countries are permitted to come to the U.S. without B-2 visas under what is known as the *Visa Waiver Program*. (See Chapter 15 for a description of this program and the countries included.)

C-1. Foreign travelers in immediate and continuous transit through the U.S.

D-1. Crewmen who need to land temporarily in the U.S. and who will depart aboard the same ship or plane on which they arrived.

E-1. Treaty traders.

E-2. Treaty investors.

F-1. Academic or language students.

F-2. Immediate family members of F-1 visa holders.

G-1. Designated principal resident representatives of foreign governments coming to the U.S. to work for an international organization, their staff members and immediate family members.

G-2. Other accredited representatives of foreign governments coming to the U.S. to work for an international organization and their immediate family members.

G-3. Representatives of foreign governments, and their immediate family members who would ordinarily qualify for G-1 or G-2 visas except that their governments are not members of an international organization.

G-4. Officers or employees of international organizations and their immediate family members.

G-5. Attendants, servants and personal employees of G-1 through G-4 visa holders and their immediate family members.

H-1B. Persons working in specialty occupations requiring at least a bachelor's degree or its equivalent in on-the-job experience, and distinguished fashion models.

H-2A. Temporary agricultural workers coming to the U.S. to fill positions for which a temporary shortage of American workers has been recognized by the U.S. Department of Agriculture.

H-2B. Temporary workers of various kinds coming to the U.S. to perform temporary jobs for which there is a shortage of available qualified American workers.

H-3. Temporary trainees.

H-4. Immediate family members of H-1, H-2 or H-3 visa holders.

I. Bona fide representatives of the foreign press coming to the U.S. to work solely in that capacity and their immediate family members.

J-1. Exchange visitors coming to the U.S. to study, work or train as part of an exchange program officially recognized by the United States Information Agency.

J-2. Immediate family members of J-1 visa holders.

K-1. Fiancé(e)s of U.S. citizens coming to the U.S. for the purpose of getting married.

K-2. Minor, unmarried children of K-1 visa holders.

L-1. Intracompany transferees who work in positions as managers, executives or persons with specialized knowledge.

L-2. Immediate family members of L-1 visa holders.

M-1. Vocational or other nonacademic students, other than language students.

M-2. Immediate families of M-1 visa holders.

N. Children of certain special immigrants.

NATO-1, NATO-2, NATO-3, NATO-4 and NATO-5. Associates coming to the U.S. under applicable provisions of the NATO Treaty and their immediate family members.

NATO-6. Members of civilian components accompanying military forces on missions authorized under the NATO Treaty and their immediate family members.

NATO-7. Attendants, servants or personal employees of NATO-1 through NATO-6 visas holders and their immediate family members.

O-1. Persons of extraordinary ability in the sciences, arts, education, business or athletics.

O-2. Essential support staff of O-1 visa holders.

O-3. Immediate family members of O-1 and O-2 visa holders.

P-1. Internationally recognized athletes and entertainers and their essential support staff.

P-2. Entertainers coming to perform in the U.S. through a government-recognized exchange program.

P-3. Artists and entertainers coming to the U.S. in a group for the purpose of presenting culturally unique performances.

P-4. Immediate family members of P-1, P-2 and P-3 visa holders.

Q-1. Exchange visitors coming to the U.S. to participate in international cultural-exchange programs.

Q-2. Immediate family members of Q-1 visa holders.

R-1. Ministers and other workers of recognized religions.

R-2. Immediate family members of R-1 visa holders.

S-1. People coming to the U.S. to supply critical information to federal or state authorities where it has been determined that their presence in the U.S. is essential to the success of a criminal investigation or prosecution.

S-2. People coming to the U.S. to provide critical information to federal authorities or a court, who will be in danger as a result of providing such information, and are eligible to receive a reward for the information.

S-3. Immediate family members of S-1 or S-2 visa holders.

By looking at these categories, you can probably see that some will apply to much larger groups of people than others. In this book, we have covered in detail those nonimmigrant visas utilized by the greatest majority of people. If you wish information on some of the lesser used nonimmigrant visas, call your INS local office for more information.

B. Difference Between a Visa and a Status

A nonimmigrant visa is something you can see and touch. It is a stamp placed on a page in your passport. A visa stamp cannot be issued inside the U.S. It can be obtained only at a U.S. embassy or consulate outside the U.S. Your nonimmigrant visa gives you certain privileges. One of them is the right to request entry to the U.S., and that is a primary feature of all visas. *Visas are entry documents.*

There are, however, other privileges that come with visas, such as permission to work, study or invest in the U.S. Different privileges are attached to different visas.

Status is the name given to the particular group of privileges you receive after being allowed to enter the U.S. with your visa. Again, different groups of privileges go with different types of statuses and visas. However, the ability to enter the U.S. is not part of the status. Only the visa itself will give you the right to enter the U.S.

C. Time Limits on Nonimmigrant Visas

Just as nonimmigrant visas vary in purpose, they also vary as to how long they last. Each nonimmigrant visa is given an expiration date according to what the law allows for that particular category. Most nonimmigrant visas can be extended a certain number of times. The number and length of these extensions also vary according to the visa category and this, too, is fixed by law. In the individual nonimmigrant visa profiles contained this book, we will tell you the length of time each visa lasts and how many extensions are available. Some general limits, however, affect the duration of all nonimmigrant visas.

- the expiration date of your petition or certificate of eligibility, if one is required
- the expiration date of your visa
- the number of entries permitted on your visa
- the date stamped on your I-94 card
- the expiration date of your passport (rules are different for Canadians—see Chapter 28), and
- the expiration date of your status.

1. Expiration Date of Your Visa Petition or Certificate of Eligibility

To get H, L, O, P and Q work visas, you must have a petition approved by INS. F student visas, M student visas and J exchange-visitors visas require certificates of eligibility issued by a U.S. school or employer. All nonimmigrant petitions and certificates of eligibility indicate the desired starting and expiration dates of the visa. These visas can be approved for maximum periods of three to five years, but you will receive only as much time as you request, and only for the specific period between the dates that are listed on the petition or certificate of eligibility form.

When you enter the U.S. with one of these visas, you should also bring the certificate of eligibility or Notice of Approval for the petition. The INS officer who admits you into the country will then know from the petition or certificate of eligibility, not the visa in your passport, how long you are permitted to stay. As you pass through Immigration at the port of entry or border-crossing checkpoint, you will receive an I-94 card. The officer there will write the date you must leave on the I-94 card.

2. Expiration Date of Your Visa

A visa serves two purposes: it allows you to request entry to the U.S., and it gives you the right to engage in certain activities once you are admitted. Permissible activities vary with the type of visa, but all visas function as U.S. entry documents. The expiration date on your visa does not show how long you can stay in the U.S. once you arrive, but it does indicate how long you have the right to enter the U.S. with visa privileges.

Nonimmigrant visas can be issued for any length of time up to a certain maximum allowed by law, depending on the type of visa. Visitor's visas, for example, can last indefinitely. (Remember, this means only that you have entry privileges

indefinitely, not that you can stay forever.) Many other nonimmigrant visas can be issued for up to five years.

Citizens of some countries can't get visas issued for the maximum period usually allowed by law. Countries whose citizens are frequently limited to visas with shorter expiration dates are:

Afghanistan*	Liberia*
Albania	Libya
Algeria	Madagascar
Angola	Mali
Bangladesh	Mauritania
Barbados	Mexico
Benin	Mozambique
Bosnia-Herzegovina*	Nepal
Brazil	Nicaragua
Brunei	Niger
Bulgaria	North Korea*
Burma*	Poland
Burundi	Romania
Cape Verde	Rwanda
Central African Republic	San Marino
Chad	São Tomé and Príncipe
China, People's Republic of	Senegal
Congo*	Serbia
Cuba*	Sierra Leone
Cyprus	Slovakia
Czech Republic	Somalia
Djibouti	South Africa
Equatorial Guinea	South Korea
Ethiopia	Sudan
Gabon	Syria
Gambia	Tanzania
Guinea	Uganda
Guinea-Bissau	United Arab Emirates
Indonesia	Yemen (Aden)
Iran*	Zaire
Laos	Zambia
Latvia	Zimbabwe

Note: Citizens of countries noted with an asterisk will find it difficult to get a visa under any category.

The shorter time limitation is placed on the nationality of the applicant, not the location of the consulate that issues the visa. For example, H-1B visas, which usually last three years, can be issued to citizens of Mexico for only six months. British nationals can get H-1B visas lasting the full three years. If a Mexican national applies for an H-1B visa at the embassy in Great Britain, it will still be issued for only six months.

Remember that the visa controls only how long you have the right to enter the U.S., not how long you can stay.

Even nationals of those countries who receive visas of shorter duration can have petitions or certificates of eligibility approved for the maximum time. Then, when they do make an entry, they may stay for the full length of time indicated on the approved petition or certificate of eligibility, and that date will be written on the I-94 card.

If you are from one of the countries listed above and if your visa expires before your petition or certificate of eligibility, you can renew your visa. In that way you can keep the ability to travel in and out of the U.S. for the entire time your petition or certificate of eligibility is in effect. You can also choose to stay in the U.S. without traveling for the full term of your petition or certificate of eligibility. Then the fact that your visa may expire doesn't really matter.

LIMITED TRAVEL WHEN YOUR VISA HAS EXPIRED

If you have an expired visa in your passport but a current I-94 card, you can still do some traveling on a limited basis. Specifically, you are permitted to go to Canada, Mexico or an island adjacent to the U.S. (such as the Bahamas or Bermuda) for up to 30 days, and return to the U.S. without getting a new visa. If you in fact want a new visa, this 30-day travel privilege is particularly useful because you are able to go to Canada or Mexico and apply for a new visa there. Then, even if the visa application is turned down, you can still return to the U.S., using the I-94 card as an entry document. However, some consuls have been known to confiscate the I-94 document. If your visa is denied and your I-94 is retained, your only option would be to proceed to your home country and apply there. The limited travel law is also very useful to Mexican nationals in the U.S. on work and study visas. This is because they are often hampered in simply visiting their homes by the fact that many types of visas to Mexican nationals are issued for only six months at a time.

3.   Number of U.S. Entries Permitted on the Visa

Most visas are the multiple entry type. This means that until the visa expires, you may use it to go in and out of the U.S. an unlimited number of times. Some visas are the single entry type. If you hold such a visa, you may use it to enter the U.S. only once. When you leave, you can't return again with that same visa, even if time still remains before its expiration date.

4.   Date Stamped on Your I-94 Card

When you enter the U.S. on a valid nonimmigrant visa, you will be given a small white or green card called an I-94 card. An INS officer will stamp the card with a date as you enter the country. We have already mentioned that the date you get will come from either the immigration laws, or the date on your petition or certificate of eligibility, if you have one. It is this date and not the expiration date of the visa which controls how long you can stay.

U.S. government regulations state that when you enter the U.S., you should be admitted for the full amount of time remaining on your petition, if you have one. Normally, this is also the expiration date of your visa. In practice, the date on your I-94 card, the final date on your petition and the expiration date of your visa will usually all be the same.

Occasionally, however, an INS inspector will stamp the I-94 card giving you a shorter stay than the dates on your petition indicate. Although this is technically improper, it is best not to argue with an INS inspector. In such cases, if the date on your I-94 card is about to pass and you still wish to remain in the U.S., you can apply for an extension. Directions on how to apply for extensions of nonimmigrant visas are in the specific chapters on these visas.

5.   Expiration Date of Your Passport

You can't get into the U.S. without a valid passport. Mexicans with border crossing cards and Canadians are the only

exceptions to this rule. Remember that visas are stamped inside your passport. When you are ready to receive the visa stamp, make sure you have a passport that is not about to expire. You will not normally be admitted to the U.S. with an expired passport, even if the visa inside is still current.

There is a simple solution to this problem. If your passport contains a visa that is still in effect but the passport itself has already expired, you should apply for a new passport but keep the old one with the current visa stamp. When entering the U.S, show both the new passport and the old one containing the valid visa. Then your visa will be honored for its full term.

6. Expiration of Your Status

If you are presently in the U.S. in valid nonimmigrant status, but want to switch to another nonimmigrant category, you can change your status without leaving the U.S. In that case, you will get a different nonimmigrant status but no new visa. Your new status will be written on a new I-94 card you receive when your request for change of status is approved. Your period of authorized stay will be extended to the time allowed in the new status category.

D. Effect of Nonimmigrant Visas on Green Cards

A question we are often asked is, "How does getting a non-immigrant visa affect my ability to get a green card?" The answer is that usually, there is no effect at all. From a strictly legal standpoint, getting a nonimmigrant visa will not help you to get a green card, nor will it hurt you. There is, however, a complexity in the law that creates a problem. The problem is called immigrant intent. To qualify for most nonimmigrant visas, you must have the intention to eventually leave the U.S. By applying for a green card, you are in effect admitting that you never want to leave, but would like to remain permanently. Since you are not eligible for most nonimmigrant visas if you have the intent to remain permanently in America, the U.S. government will not usually give you a nonimmigrant visa after you have filed for a green card.

This is another situation where you should carefully consider your needs. If you must have a nonimmigrant visa so you can go to the U.S. right away, you should probably not apply for a green card until you have less need to travel. When you can wait for the green card to come through without too much inconvenience, only then should you apply for one.

There are certain nonimmigrant visa categories that allow you to apply for a green card without worrying about immigrant intent. By law, immigrant intent is not a factor for consideration in H-1A, H-1B, L, O and P visa applications.

E. Nonimmigrant Visas and U.S. Taxes

Though nonimmigrants are, by definition, not permanent residents of the U.S., it is possible to become a *tax resident* simply by spending a certain amount of time in America each year. If you become a tax resident, your entire world-wide income must be reported to the U.S. government. It doesn't matter if a portion or all of that income was earned from investments or business activities carried on outside the U.S. It still must be reported.

Becoming a tax resident does not necessarily mean that the U.S. government will actually tax all of your worldwide income. International treaties control whether or not you must pay U.S. taxes on income earned elsewhere. However, if you stay in the U.S. long enough to become a tax resident, you will have to at least report all income you have earned worldwide.

At what point do you become a tax resident? If you have been present in the U.S. for 183 days or more of the current year, you are a tax resident for the year. If you have been in the U.S. for a weighted total of 183 days during the previous three years, you are also a tax resident unless you spend fewer than 30 days in the U.S. in the current year. For determining the "weighted" total number of days, each day in the current year counts as one, each day in the previous year counts as only one-third of a day, and each day in the second previous year counts as only one-sixth of a day. This latter rule does not apply to certain foreign government employees, certain teachers, students and professional athletes. Provided you spend fewer than 183 days of the current year in the U.S., you will also avoid being classified as a tax resident if you maintain a tax home in another country and have a closer connection to that country than to the U.S. There are other exceptions to these rules. A tax treaty between the U.S. and your home country may also alter these rules. If you are unsure of your situation, you may wish to consult with a tax accountant or lawyer.

If you do become a tax resident, you must file U.S. tax return Form 1040 each year by April 15th. Failure to follow U.S. tax laws may be considered a criminal offense. Failure to comply with U.S. tax laws can also make it more difficult for you to obtain permanent residency. To find out exactly how to comply with U.S. tax laws, consult a tax professional or the nearest office of the Internal Revenue Service. If you are found guilty of a tax crime, your nonimmigrant visa can be revoked and you may be deported.

F. Status Overstays and Automatic Cancellation of Visas

The 1996 immigration law changes limit a person's ability to obtain a nonimmigrant visa at a consulate other than one in their home country. Applying for a visa at a consulate which is not located in your home country is called "third country national," or TCN, processing.

TCN processing is prohibited if you have been unlawfully present in the U.S. under a prior visa status. Even if you overstayed your status by just one day, your visa will be automatically canceled, you will not be eligible for TCN processing and your will have to return to your home country to apply for a new visa.

If you were admitted on an A, F, G or J visa for duration of status (indicated as "D/S" on your Form I-94) and you remain in the U.S. beyond the time for which your status was conferred, you still may be eligible for TCN processing. You will be barred only if INS or an immigration judge has determined that you were unlawfully present. Six or more months of unlawful presence acquired after April 1, 1997 is

also a ground of inadmissibility if you leave the U.S. (See Chapter 25 for more details.)

G. Summary Exclusion

Another new law gives an INS inspector at the airport the power to deport someone requesting admission to the U.S. under two circumstances:

- The inspector believes you are making a misrepresentation about practically anything connected to your entering the U.S., such as your purpose in coming, intent to return or prior immigration history.
- You do not have the proper documentation to support your entry to the U.S. in the category you are requesting.

If the inspector excludes you, you may not request entry for five years, unless INS grants a special waiver. For this reason, it is extremely important to understand the terms of your requested status and to not make any misrepresentations. If you are found inadmissible, you can ask to withdraw your application to enter the U.S. to prevent having the five year ban on your record. INS may allow you to do so in some cases. ■

Business and Tourist Visitors: B-1 and B-2 Visas

Privileges

- You can come to the U.S. on a B-2 visa as a tourist visitor or on a B-1 visa as a business visitor. Often, B-1 and B-2 visas are issued together to allow flexibility on your U.S visits.

- B-1 and B-2 visas can be issued quickly in most countries.

- Visitor's visas are often issued for an indefinite period without an expiration date, meaning that one visitor's visa may last you a lifetime.

Limitations

- You may not be employed or operate your own business in the U.S. on a visitor's visa.

- Although you may make any number of trips into the U.S. on a visitor's visa, the length of each visit is limited to a maximum of six months. After six months, you must either leave or apply for an extension of stay.

- You may not legally use your visitor's visa to live permanently in the U.S.

A. How to Qualify

There are no quota restrictions for B-1 and B-2 visas. Most consulates approve and issue visitor's visas in one day.

1. Who Qualifies for a Visitor's Visa?

You qualify for a B-1 visa if you are coming to the U.S. as a visitor for a temporary business trip. You qualify for a B-2 visa if you are visiting the U.S. temporarily as a tourist. Most of the time these two visas are issued together in a combination form so you have all the options under both. Whether you have come for business or tourist activities, you must have the intent to return to your home country after your visit is over. Usually, you are required to have a home abroad to which you intend to return. Anyone who wishes to travel to the U.S. as a visitor is eligible to apply for a visitor's visa at a U.S. consulate. You must be physically present to apply there.

A B-1 visa allows you to be in the U.S. for business purposes. You may not, however, be employed or operate your own company. You may not be paid by a source inside the U.S. It is sometimes difficult to draw the line between permissible business activities and illegal employment on a B-1 visa, but generally your agenda must be limited to making investments, buying goods, attending seminars or performing other temporary work for an employer located outside the U.S.

Unlike the B-1 visitor, the B-2 tourist may not engage in business-related activities at all. A condition of being admitted on a B-2 visa is that you are in fact a tourist.

The immigration law reforms of 1996 brought severe penalties for persons who use fraudulent documents or make misrepresentations, or who attempt entry to the U.S. without proper documentation. Individuals who commit one of these acts can be quickly deported from the U.S. without the right to a hearing. If this happens, you will not be able to request entry for five years, unless you are granted permission to withdraw your application (request) to enter the U.S. Accordingly, it is extremely important to understand the requirements of the visa classification you are requesting, and that you not make any misrepresentations of your intent or qualifications for a particular visa.

If you enter the U.S. with a B visa, the law requires that your intention must be to come only as a visitor. Tourists are given stays of six months and business visitors may stay as necessary up to a maximum of one year. Theoretically, you may leave the U.S. at the end of the six months, return the next day and be readmitted for another six months. Alternatively, when the six months are up, you can apply for an extension of stay without leaving, usually for another six months. (See Section C.) However, when your travel history shows that you are spending most of your time in the U.S., INS will assume you have the intent to be more than just a temporary visitor. On this basis, you can be denied entry altogether, even though you do have a valid visa. Some people, thinking that they have found a loophole in the system, try to live in the U.S. permanently on a visitor's visa by merely taking brief trips outside the country every six months. Do not expect this tactic to work for very long. However, those who want to have vacation homes in the U.S. and live in them for about six months each year may do so legally.

a. Exception to the Visitor's Visa Requirement: The Visa Waiver Program

Visa Waivers are available for people from countries that do not have a history of illegal immigration to the U.S. Currently there are 29 participating countries in the Visa Waiver Program, including: Andorra, Argentina, Austria, Australia, Belgium, Brunei, Denmark, Finland, France, Germany, Iceland, Ireland, Italy, Japan, Liechtenstein, Luxembourg, Monaco, The Netherlands, New Zealand, Norway, Portugal, San Marino, Singapore, Slovenia, Spain, Sweden, Switzerland, the United Kingdom and Uruguay. The government has approved Greece for inclusion in the program in the near future. Nationals of these countries have the option of entering the U.S. for up to 90 days without a visa. Each visitor who enters under the program must arrive with a transportation ticket to leave the U.S. Those who come by land from Canada or Mexico must show evidence at the border of sufficient funds to live in the U.S. without working.

When you enter the U.S. under the Visa Waiver Program, you will not be allowed to change your status to another nonimmigrant classification without first leaving the country. Moreover, if you come to the U.S. under this program and wish to apply for a green card, you will be limited to making your application at a U.S. consulate abroad. (The only exception is for persons who marry a U.S. citizen.)

Participation in the Visa Waiver Program is optional, not a requirement. Nationals from those countries qualifying for visa waivers can still get standard visitor's visas and come to the U.S. conventionally. We advise you not to make use of this new program if you can avoid it. You will have more flexibility and rights once you enter the U.S. if you come with a visa.

b. Applying for a Green Card From B-1 or B-2 Status

If you have a B-1 or B-2 visa, you can file for a green card, but being in the U.S. on a B visa gives you no advantage in doing so. Many people believe that if they physically go to

the U.S. as a visitor, a way will somehow open up for them to stay. This is simply not a realistic expectation. In fact, even if you are fully qualified for a green card, unless your claim to it is through marriage to an American citizen (see Chapter 5), immigration law often requires you to leave the U.S. and make your application at a U.S. consulate or embassy in your home country.

Another problem for someone who applies for permanent residency after entering the U.S. on a B-1 or B-2 visa is that they may open themselves to a charge of having committed fraud or material misrepresentation in getting their nonimmigrant visa. This means that the INS or Consulate believes that the person gave false information to gain entry to the U.S. or to get the visa. An allegation of fraud can severely impact your chances of winning permanent residence.

2. Paperwork

There are two types of paperwork you must submit to get a visitor's visa. The first consists of official government forms. The second is personal documents such as birth and marriage certificates. We will tell you exactly what forms and documents you need.

It is vital that forms are properly filled out and all necessary documents are supplied. You may resent the intrusion into your privacy and sizable effort it takes to prepare immigration applications, but you should realize the process is an impersonal matter to immigration officials. Your getting a visa is more important to you than it is to the U.S. government. This is not a pleasant thing to accept, but you are better off having a real understanding of your position. People from all over the world want U.S. visas. There is no shortage of applicants. Take the time and trouble to prepare your papers properly. In the end it will pay off with a successful application.

Documents submitted to U.S. consulates must be either originals or official government certified copies. Government certified copies and notarized copies are not the same thing. Documents that have only been notarized are not acceptable. They must carry a government seal. In addition to any original or government certified copies of documents submitted to a consulate, you should submit plain photocopies of each document as well. After the consulate compares the copies with the originals, it will return the originals.

Documents will be accepted if they are in either English or the language of the country where the documents are being filed. An exception exists for papers filed at the U.S. consulates in Japan, where all documents must be translated into English. If the documents are not in an acceptable language as just explained, they must be accompanied by a full, word for word, written English translation. Any capable person may act as translator. It is not necessary to hire a professional. At the end of each translation, the following statement must appear:

I hereby certify that I translated this document from (language) to English. This translation is accurate and complete. I further certify that I am fully competent to translate from (language) to English.

The translator should sign this statement but it does not have to be witnessed or notarized.

Later in this chapter we describe in detail the forms and documents needed to get your visitor's visa. A summary checklist of forms and documents appears at the end of the chapter.

B. The Application

Applying for a B visa is a one-step process. You file only an application.

1. General Procedures

Technically, the law allows you to apply for a B visa at any U.S. consulate you choose. A complete list of all U.S. consulates that process visa applications, together with their addresses and phone numbers, may be found in Appendix I. From a practical standpoint your case will be given greatest consideration at the consulate in your home country. Applying in some other country creates suspicion in the minds of the consul officers about your motives for choosing their consulate. Often, when an applicant is having trouble at a home consulate, he will seek a more lenient office in some other country. This practice of consulate shopping is frowned on by officials in the system. Unless you have a very good reason for filing elsewhere (such as a temporary job assignment in some other nation), it is smarter to file your visa application in your home country.

Furthermore, if you have ever been present in the U.S. unlawfully, in general you cannot apply as a third country national. Even if you overstayed your status in the U.S. by just one day, you must return to your home country and apply for the visa from that consulate. There is an exception. If you were admitted to the U.S. for the duration of your status (indicated by a "D/S" on your I-94 form) and you remained in the U.S. beyond that time or purpose for which your status was conferred, you may still be able to apply as a third country national. The State Department's current regulations seem to imply that you will be barred from third country national processing only if an immigration judge or INS official has determined that you were unlawfully present. Because of the ambiguity, you may find that your success in applying as a third country national will depend on your country, the consulate and the relative seriousness of your offense.

In many consulates, you can simply walk in with your passport and supporting documents, fill out the application form while you are there, and get your B visa all on the same day. Other consulates insist on advance appointments. Most consulates in Canada and Mexico require you to come up to a week in advance to receive an appointment. A few, like London, will process visa applications by mail. Since procedures among the consulates vary, you should always telephone in advance to ask about local policies. (U.S. consulates in Canada require you to make an appointment by phone.)

While there is a definite difference between B-1 and B-2 visas, the two are frequently issued together. In fact, the machine used to print the visas in your passport groups both B-1 and B-2 on the same stamp. If the consulate wishes you to have only one, the other will be crossed out by hand in your passport.

On entering the U.S. with your new B visa, you will be given an I-94 card. It will be stamped with the dates showing your authorized stay. Normally, you are permitted to remain in the U.S. for six months. Each time you exit and reenter the U.S., you will get a new I-94 card with a new period of authorized stay.

If your visa was issued as both B-1 and B-2 together, you should make it clear to the immigration inspector which visa you are using. Your I-94 card will show whether you were admitted as a B-1 business visitor or a B-2 tourist.

2. Forms

When you file at a U.S. consulate abroad, the consulate officials will provide you with certain optional forms, designated by an "OF" preceeding a number. Instructions for completing optional forms and what to do with them once they are filled out will come with the forms. We do not include copies of these forms in Appendix III. Copies of all non "OF" forms are in Appendix III.

Form I-134

You must convince the consulate that once you arrive in the U.S. you are not likely to seek employment or go on public welfare. Form I-134, the Affidavit of Support, guarantees that someone is willing to take financial responsibility for you. There is a new affidavit of support, Form I-864, which contains many new legal requirements. It is not used for nonimmigrant visas, so you will want to use this older form.

In a visitor's visa application, the person you will be visiting in the U.S. should sign Form I-134 on your behalf, and that person must be a U.S. citizen or green card holder. If you can prove that you are financially independent or are employed in your home country, an I-134 need not be filed on your behalf.

When you request someone in the U.S. to sign an Affidavit of Support supposedly on your behalf, he or she will doubtless wish to know the legal extent of the financial obligation. In signing the Affidavit of Support, the person does not promise to support you. What he or she does promise to do is repay the U.S. government for the total of any government support payments you might receive should you go on welfare. The Affidavit of Support supposedly binds your relative to this obligation for three years. His or her responsibility to both you and the government is then at an end.

3. Documents

As an applicant for a visitor's visa, you must show a valid passport and one passport-type photograph. You will also need documents showing your intent to leave the U.S. when your visa expires. The consulate will want to see evidence that your ties to your home country are so strong you will be highly motivated to return. Proof of such ties can include deeds verifying ownership of a home or other real property, written statements from you explaining that close relatives are staying behind or a letter from a company in your home country.

A potential visitor must convince the consul officer that he or she will not need to work while in the U.S. Therefore, you should always bring proof of your income and assets. Bank statements or personal financial statements are the appropriate documents for this purpose. Alternatively, if you will be visiting a relative in the U.S. who is a U.S. citizen or green card holder and you will be dependent on that relative for support, you should have your relative complete INS Form I-134, Affidavit of Support. Additionally, a letter from your relative inviting you to visit and stating that you are welcome to stay with him or her is helpful.

If applying as a B-1 business visitor, you should bring with you a letter from your employer in your home country describing your job and telling what you will be doing for your employer in the U.S. It is important for the letter to explain that you will be paid only from sources outside the U.S. and to state when you will be expected to return from your U.S. business trip.

4. Interviews

The consulate frequently requires an interview before issuing a B visa. During the interview, a consul officer examines the application form for accuracy. Evidence of ties to your home country and the state of your financial resources are also checked. During the interview, you will surely be asked how long you intend to remain in the U.S. Any answer suggesting uncertainty about plans to return or an interest

in applying for a green card is likely to result in a denial of your B visa.

5. Appeals

When a consulate turns down a B visa application, there is no way to make a formal appeal, although you are free to reapply as often as you like. If your visa is denied, you will be told by the consul officer the reasons for the denial. Written statements of decisions are not normally provided in nonimmigrant cases. If a lack of evidence about a particular point is the problem, sometimes simply presenting more evidence on an unclear fact can bring a positive change in the result. The most common reasons for denial of a B visa are that the consul officer does not believe you intend to return to your home country when the time of your legal U.S. stay is up, or that the consul officer feels you will try to work illegally in the U.S.

Certain people who have been refused B visas reapply at a different consulate, trying to hide the fact that they were turned down elsewhere. If your application is denied, the last page in your passport will be stamped "Application Received" with the date and location of the rejecting consulate. A consul officer will recognize this notation as meaning some type of prior visa application has failed. It serves as a warning that your case merits close inspection. If what we have just told you makes you think it would be a good idea to overcome the problem by getting a new, unmarked passport, you should also know that permanent computer records are kept of all visa denials.

C. Extensions of Stay

Applications for extensions of stay must be filed before the date on your I-94 card passes. (Rules are different for Canadians. See Chapter 28.)

1. General Procedures

Your visit can be extended as long as you did not enter the U.S. on a visa waiver and your total stay does not exceed one year. Therefore, since you will be given a six-month stay when you first enter the U.S., you cannot usually get an extension of more than six additional months. You may apply for an extension of stay by mailing forms and documents to the INS regional service center having jurisdiction over the place you are visiting. Appendix II contains a list of all INS offices and their addresses. The filing fee for each application is currently $120 plus $10 for each accompanying spouse or child. Checks and money orders are accepted. It is not advisable to send cash. We recommend submitting all papers by certified mail, return receipt requested, and keeping a copy of everything sent in.

If INS wants further information before acting on your case, all papers, forms and documents will be returned together with another form known as an *I-797*. The I-797 tells you what additional pieces of information or documents are expected. You should supply the extra data and mail the whole package back to the INS regional service center.

Applications for extensions of stay for visitors are normally approved within two months. You must apply before the date on your I-94 card passes, but not more than 60 days before. If you file your application on time, you will be permitted to remain in the U.S. until receiving a decision, even if your authorized stay expires. When your application is approved, you will receive a blue Notice of Action Form I-797, indicating the approval with the new date. Your I-94 card, which you will have submitted as a document with your extension application, is returned to you, but it will not be stamped with a new date. You must keep Form I-797 together with your I-94 card at all times.

If your application for an extension of stay is denied, you will be sent a written notice explaining the reasons for the negative decision. The most common reason for denial is that INS feels you are merely trying to prolong your U.S. stay indefinitely. When your application is denied, you will normally be given a period of 30 days to leave the U.S. voluntarily. Failure to leave within that time may result in your being deported.

There is no way of making a formal appeal to INS if your extension is turned down. You may challenge the decision in a U.S. district court, but the time and expense required for this approach usually makes it impractical.

SPECIAL NOTE FOR VISA WAIVER PROGRAM
If you were admitted to the U.S. under the Visa Waiver Program, described in Section A1a, you may not apply for an extension of stay unless there is a genuine emergency that prevents you from leaving the U.S. on time. If such an extension is needed, you should apply for it in person, not by mail, and you will not get more than 30 days time to leave.

2. Extension Forms

Copies of all forms can be found in Appendix III.

Form I-539

Only one application form is needed for an entire family. If you have a spouse or children coming with you, you should also complete the I-539 supplement.

Part 1. These questions are self-explanatory. "A" numbers are usually given only to people who have previously applied for green cards or who have been in deportation proceedings.

Part 2, Question 1. Mark box "a."

Question 2. This question asks if you are also applying for a spouse or children. If so, you must complete the supplement, which asks for their names, dates of birth and passport information.

Part 3. In most cases, you will answer only the first item in this part, by putting in the date. You should put down a date not more than six months beyond the expiration of your current authorized stay, and not more than one year from the date you first entered the U.S. with a visitor's visa.

Part 4, Questions 1–2. These questions are self-explanatory.

Question 3. The different parts to this question are self-explanatory; however, items "a" and "b" ask if an immigrant visa petition or adjustment of status application has ever been filed on your behalf. If you are applying for a green card through a relative, this would be Step One, as described in Chapter 5, or if you are applying for a green card through employment, this would be Step Two as described in Chapter 8. If your relative or employer has filed the papers for either of these steps, the answer is "yes," and since you have therefore expressed a desire to live in the U.S. permanently, your extension application is very likely to be denied. If you have only begun the Labor Certification, the Step One of getting a green card through employment, this question should be answered "No."

Form I-134

You must convince INS that you can remain in the U.S. without working. Form I-134, the Affidavit of Support, guarantees that someone is willing to take financial responsibility for you. (In the event someone tells you that you should use the new Affidavit of Support, Form I-864, that is not true. The new form isn't applicable in nonimmigrant visa situations.) In the case of visitors, the person you are visiting in the U.S. should sign Form I-134 on your behalf. It is best if that person is either a U.S. citizen or a green card holder. If you can prove that you are financially independent or are employed in your home country, an I-134 need not be filed for you.

When you request someone in the U.S. to sign an Affidavit of Support on your behalf, he or she will doubtless wish to know the legal extent of the financial obligation. In signing the Affidavit of Support, the person does not promise to support you. Instead he or she promises to repay the U.S. government for the total of any government support payments you might receive should you go on welfare. The Affidavit of Support binds the signer to this obligation for three years. His or her responsibility to both you and the government is then at an end.

3. Extension Documents

You must submit I-94 cards for yourself and any family members you have brought with you. (Canadian visitors do not usually get I-94 cards, but the rest of the procedures, forms and documents are the same. See Chapter 28.) You should also submit proof of the relationship between you and accompanying family members. You may verify a parent/child relationship by presenting the child's long form birth certificate. Many countries, including Canada and England, issue both short and long form birth certificates. Where both are available, the long form is needed because it contains the names of the parents while the short form does not. If you are accompanied by your spouse, you must establish that you are lawfully married by showing a civil marriage certificate. Church certificates are generally unacceptable. (There are a few exceptions, depending on the laws of your particular country. Canadians, for example, may use church certificates if the marriage took place in Quebec Province, but not elsewhere. If a civil certificate is available, however, you should always use it.) You may have married in a country where marriages are not usually recorded. Tribal areas of Africa are an example. In such situations, call the nearest consulate or embassy of your home country for help with getting acceptable proof of marriage.

If you are a business visitor, you should include a letter from your foreign employer explaining why you need the extension of stay. If you are a tourist, you should, again, submit evidence that you do not need to work by showing proof of your own income and assets. Bank statements or personal financial statements are the best documents for this purpose. Alternatively, if you will be visiting a relative in the U.S. who is a U.S. citizen or green card holder, you may have your relative complete INS Form I-134, Affidavit of Support, discussed just above.

4. Extension Appeals

If your extension application is denied, you will receive a written decision by mail explaining the reasons for the denial. There is no way of making a formal appeal to INS for the denial of an extension of stay. If the problem is too little evidence, you can overcome this obstacle by adding more documents and resubmitting the entire application to the same INS office you have been dealing with, together with a written request that the case be reopened. The written request does not have to be in any special form. This is technically called a *Motion to Reopen*. There is a $110 fee to file this motion. You may not remain in the U.S. to wait for a decision on your Motion to Reopen.

Theoretically, when an extension of stay is denied you also have the option to file a legal action in a U.S. district court, but this does not give you the right to remain in the U.S. pending a decision either. Since extensions for visitor's visas are only granted for six months or less anyway, pursuing court action is not really practical.

If your application is denied, you should leave the U.S. within the period given to leave voluntarily. If you do this, you should be able to return without difficulty as a visitor at a later date. When you remain beyond your date of voluntary departure, you may have problems returning to the U.S. later. Recently, computers have been installed at each port of entry that tell INS of all your entries and departures.

FORMS AND DOCUMENTS CHECKLIST

STEP ONE: APPLICATION (the only step)

Form

☐ OF forms (available from U.S. consulates abroad).

☐ Form I-134.

☐ Form I-539, to apply for an extension.

Documents

☐ Your passport, valid for at least six months.

☐ One passport-type photo of you.

☐ Documents showing ownership of real estate in your home country.

☐ Documents showing that close family members or property are being left behind in your home country.

☐ Documents showing a job waiting on your return to your home country.

☐ Proof of financial support, such as:

    ☐ Form I-134, Affidavit of Support from U.S. relative, or

    ☐ letter from a relative inviting you to visit, stating you are welcome to stay with him or her.

☐ Bank statements.

☐ Personal financial statements.

☐ Evidence of your current sources of income.

☐ If you are coming to the U.S. on business, a letter from your foreign employer explaining the reason for your U.S. trip.

CHAPTER

16

Temporary Specialty Workers: H-1B Visas

Privileges

- You can work legally in the U.S. for your H-1B sponsor.

- H-1B visas can be issued quickly.

- You may travel in and out of the U.S. or remain here continuously until your H-1B visa status expires.

- Visas are available for accompanying relatives.

Limitations

- You are restricted to working only for the employer who acted as your H-1B sponsor. If you wish to change jobs, you must get new H-1B status.

- Employers must have an attestation on file with the U.S. Labor Department before they can sponsor you for H-1B status.

- H-1B status can be held for no more than six years. Then, you must return to your home country, unless you are eligible to change to another nonimmigrant category or apply for permanent residence.

- Accompanying relatives may stay in the U.S. with you, but they may not work, unless they qualify for a work visa in their own right.

UPDATE ON H-1A NURSING NONIMMIGRANT VISAS

As of September 1, 1995, the H-1A category for nonimmigrant nurses was eliminated. This visa category previously provided a way for nurses to work temporarily in the U.S. for up to five years, assuming that they had a job offer and had a nursing license, and even though they did not have a university degree. The H-1A visa was thus a streamlined and occupation-specific temporary visa for nurses.

With the elimination of the H-1A visa, a nurse can now only get a nonimmigrant H visa by satisfying the H-1B specialty occupation requirements, for which a bachelor's degree or the equivalent is the minimum entry requirement. Such applications will probably only be successful where the job actually requires a four-year nursing degree, because, for example, of the supervisory duties (head nurse), the need to conduct advanced procedures, or the industry's or employer's hiring standards and practices require a bachelor's degree. Nurses may also qualify under the TN category (Canadians and Mexican nationals—see Chapter 28), or in limited circumstances, under the H-3 trainee category (see Chapter 18).

In order to ease the burden of the elimination of the H-1A visa for nurses, some accommodations were made

for nurses already in the U.S. in H-1A status or for nurses where the status had lapsed. A nurse who was in H-1A status after September 1, 1995 was allowed to keep that status for one year, as long as the employer had a certain attestation (one of the requirements for the visa) on file. Later, in 1996, the INS announced an automatic temporary extension of the H-1A legal status of nurses who entered under an H-1A visa, were present in the U.S. on or after September 1, 1995 and were also present on October 11, 1996, if their stay would otherwise have expired. This benefit only extended the status through September 30, 1997 of the H-1A nurse in order to work for the same employer. It did not extend the visa itself (right to reenter the U.S.)

Accordingly, nurses must now try to qualify for temporary status through the H-1B specialty occupation category or obtain permanent resident status through the Schedule A green card application. Nurses who were previously in the U.S. in H-1A status and who have been out of status for over six months should thus be sure to understand the grounds of inadmissibility and bars to getting a green card, as discussed in Chapter 25, in order to devise a strategy for regularizing their status.

A. How to Qualify

Qualifying for a H-1B visa has some limitations.

1. Quota Restrictions

Until 1998, no more than 65,000 H-1B visa petitions were approved each year. Legislation enacted in 1998 expanded the numbers of available H-1B visas to 115,000 in fiscal year 1999/2000 and 107,500 for fiscal year 2000/2001. The number then is scheduled to return to 65,000 for each year after that. Even after Congress increased the number of visas, the quota was reached halfway through the year. Recently, there have been legislative efforts to further increase the number of H-1 visas. If the quota gets used up in a given year, no more H-1B petitions can be approved until the start of the next fiscal year, October 1.

Before the visa petition can be submitted, the employer must file a labor condition application concerning its offered wage and working conditions.

The labor condition attestation takes ten to thirty days for approval. Step One petitions are normally approved within three to eight weeks. Visas are usually issued within several weeks after petition approval.

2. Who Qualifies for an H-1B Visa?

To qualify for an H-1B visa, you must first have a job offer from a U.S. employer for duties to be performed in the U.S. The employer must have filed what is known as an "attestation" with the federal Department of Labor (DOL), which, among other things, certifies that the employer will be paying at least the average or "prevailing" wage for that type of job in the particular geographic area.

H-1B visas are available only to workers in occupations requiring highly specialized knowledge normally acquired through a college education, and to distinguished fashion models. To qualify for this visa, unless you are a fashion model, you need at least a bachelor's degree or substantial on-the-job experience that is the equivalent of a bachelor's degree. To use INS's words, you must be coming to the U.S. to perform services in a "specialty occupation." If a license to practice your particular occupation is required by the U.S. state in which you will be working, then, in addition to your educational credentials, you must also have the appropriate license.

To get an H-1B visa, not only do your job qualifications have to meet the standards mentioned above, it is also necessary to have the correct type of background for the job you are offered. If your academic and professional credentials are strong, but they do not match the job, then you are not eligible for an H-1B visa.

H-1B visas are specifically *not* given to prominent business people without college degrees, even though they may have substantial on-the-job experience. O-1 visas are available to this group. (See Chapter 24.) H-1B visas are likewise not given to athletes and entertainers, who should consider instead O or P visas, discussed in Chapter 24. Professional nurses are only eligible for H-1B visas if the position they will occupy actually requires an RN degree—usually because the job duties are complex or there are supervisory duties involved. (Nurses are no longer eligible for the H-1A visa, which has been discontinued.)

To summarize, there are five requirements for getting an H-1B visa:

- you must be coming to the U.S. to perform services in a specialty occupation with a college degree or its equivalent in work experience, or be a distinguished fashion model
- you must have a job offer from a qualified U.S. employer for work to be performed in the U.S., and you must be offered at least the prevailing wage that is paid in the same geographic area for that type of job (or the actual wage paid to similar workers at that employer—whichever is the higher of the two wages)
- you must have the correct background to qualify for the job you have been offered, and
- your employer must have filed an attestation with DOL.

Your job must meet one of the following criteria:

- A bachelor's degree or higher degree (or the equivalent) is the minimum requirement for entry into the position.
- The degree requirement is common to the industry in parallel positions among similar organizations or the duties of the position are so complex that it can be performed only by a person with a degree.
- The employer normally requires a degree or its equivalent for the position.
- The nature of the specific duties is so specialized and complex that knowledge required to perform the duties is usually associated with a bachelor's degree.

a. Job Criteria

Specialty occupations include but are not limited to accountants, computer systems analysts, physical therapists, chemists, pharmacists, medical technologists, hotel managers (large hotels) and upper-level business managers.

Some occupations requiring licenses do not usually fall into the H-1B category because college degrees are not normally needed. Such occupations include many types of medical technicians, real estate agents, plumbers and electricians. Unless a college degree is required, people in such occupations are limited to the more restrictive H-2B visa described in Chapter 17.

b.   Job Offer From a U.S. Employer for Work Performed Inside the U.S.

To get an H-1B visa, you need a specific job offer from a qualified employer for work to be performed inside the U.S. The employer will have to act as the petitioner in getting your H-1B visa.

Many people are surprised to learn that they require an employment offer before applying for a work visa. The idea behind it is that you are being granted an H-1B visa only because your services have been recognized as essential to an American enterprise. Put another way, the U.S. government is issuing the visa not for your benefit, but to help the American economy.

The petitioner may be a company or an individual. Whether or not you can form your own corporation and have that corporation act as your sponsoring employer is not completely clear under the law. When the company you own is a legitimate business corporation and is not dependent on your presence to operate, there should be no trouble in using the company as a petitioner. If, however, the corporation appears to be formed strictly for the purpose of getting you a visa, there are likely to be problems with the application.

The employer must also be offering you at least the prevailing wage that is paid for your type of job in that geographic area. Prevailing wage is defined as 5% below the "weighted average" salary. Labor attestation forms will

---

ACADEMIC CREDENTIAL EVALUATIONS

Unless you are a distinguished fashion model, to qualify for an H-1B visa you must always hold at least a bachelor's degree or have its equivalent in work experience. However, not every country in the world operates on the same academic degree and grade level systems found in the U.S. If you were educated in some other country, INS, as part of judging your H-1B eligibility, will often ask for an academic credential evaluation from an approved consulting service to determine the American equivalent of your educational level.

Evaluations from accredited credential evaluation services are not binding on INS, but they are very persuasive. When the results are favorable, they strengthen your case. If, on the other hand, the evaluation shows that your credentials do not equal at least an American bachelor's degree, this can mean you will not qualify for an H-1B visa.

We recommend getting a credential evaluation in every case where non-U.S. education is a factor. We also advise getting the evaluation before INS asks for it. The service charge for an evaluation is around $100. When the evaluation is favorable, you can automatically include it with your petition since it strengthens your case and saves time if INS decides to request it later.

There are several qualified credential evaluation services recognized by INS. Two of them are:

International Education Research Foundation
P.O. Box 66940
Los Angeles, CA 90066
Telephone: 310-390-6276
Fax: 310-397-7686
Website: http://www.ierf.org

Educational Credential Evaluators, Inc.
P.O. Box 514070
Milwaukee, WI 53203-3470
Telephone: 414-289-3400
Fax: 414-289-3411
Website: http://www.ece.org

The credential evaluation companies listed above evaluate only formal education. They do not rate job experience. American universities also offer evaluations of foreign academic credentials but, unlike the credential evaluation services, many are willing to recognize work experience as having an academic equivalent. Therefore, if you lack a university education but can show many years of responsible experience, you are better off trying to get an evaluation from a U.S. college or university.

When sending your credentials to a U.S. university, include documents showing your complete academic background, as well as all relevant career achievements. Letters of recommendation from former employers are the preferred proof of work experience. Evidence of any special accomplishments, such as awards or published articles, should also be submitted.

INS considers every three years of experience to be equivalent to one year of college. Therefore, it is possible to qualify for an H-1B visa if you have no college education but at least 12 years of experience. However, in all cases, the standard entry requirement for the position must be a bachelor's degree, or the job itself will not fit the H-1B category.

require the employer to state the amount of the prevailing wage. The local job service or state labor department office does periodic surveys of salaries and can provide you with prevailing wage information. If you elect to rely on your own or a different survey, however, you will be required to identify the source of your information.

c. Specialty Occupation

The job offered can't be for just any type of work. The position must really require the skills of a highly educated person. For example, you may be a certified public accountant holding an advanced college degree. Public accounting clearly qualifies as a professional occupation. However, if you are offered a job as a bookkeeper, you will not get an H-1B visa because it doesn't take a highly educated accountant to carry out standard bookkeeping tasks.

d. Correct Background

You must have the correct background for the job you have been offered. For example, if you are a qualified nuclear scientist, but are offered a position managing a U.S. automobile factory, you will not be granted an H-1B visa because you have no background in automobile-factory management. If, however, you are asked to manage a factory that produces the kinds of items where your nuclear science background is required to perform the job duties, you would be eligible for the H-1B visa.

It is irrelevant that your native intelligence and general knowledge of business may make you quite capable of handling the automobile factory job. Likewise, reliability or willingness to work hard, characteristics difficult to find and much in demand by real-world employers, are not an INS consideration.

e. Approved Attestation

A business cannot sponsor you for an H-1B petition unless it first files an attestation, also known as a *Labor Condition Application,* with DOL. The attestation is a document similar to a sworn declaration or written oath. It must include a number of statements insuring that both American and foreign workers are being treated fairly. These are discussed below in Section B.

3. Accompanying Relatives

When you qualify for an H-1B visa, your spouse and unmarried children under age 21 can get H-4 visas simply by providing proof of their family relationship to you. H-4 visas authorize your family members to stay with you in the U.S., but not to work there.

APPLYING FOR A GREEN CARD

Having an H-1B visa gives you no legal advantage in applying for a green card. Realistically, however, it is probably easier to get an employer to sponsor you for an H-1B visa than a green card, and coming to the U.S. first with an H-1B gives you the opportunity to decide if you really want to live in the U.S. permanently. Once you are in the U.S. with a work permit, it is also usually easier to find an employer willing to sponsor you for a green card.

B. Employer Requirements

No employer can sponsor you for an H-1B petition unless he first files an attestation with DOL.

1. Employer's Attestation

An attestation is similar to a sworn declaration or a written oath. It must include the following information and statements:

- a list of occupations for which H-1B workers are needed
- a statement of the number of foreign workers to be hired in that occupation
- a statement of the wages to be paid the foreign workers, what the prevailing wage is for each worker and where the employer obtained the prevailing wage information
- a written promise that foreign nationals will be paid the higher of the prevailing market wage for the position, or the actual wage paid to similarly situated workers working for the same employer
- a statement that there are no strikes or lockouts in progress involving the jobs to be filled by H-1B workers, and
- a statement that the employer has given notice of the filing of H-1B attestations to either the labor union representing the type of employee involved, or, if no union exists, that the employer has posted notice of the filing in a conspicuous place for other workers to see.

A separate attestation must be filed for each type of job the company wishes to fill with H-1B workers. Filing the attestation is a very simple matter. Form ETA-9035 is completed, in duplicate, and mailed or faxed to a regional office of the DOL. A list of all regional DOL offices, together with addresses, telephone and fax numbers is in

Appendix II. The form has all necessary statements already written out, with blanks to be filled in with the appropriate occupations, numbers of workers and salaries. DOL will accept for filing all complete attestations; however, anyone, including other employees at the petitioning company, can file a complaint. The primary objective here is to require employers to pay H-1B workers at least the "prevailing wage" or average ("weighted average") salary for that type of job in the particular geographic area.

When the attestation is accepted, one of the original ETA-9035 forms will be returned to the employer with a DOL endorsement. A copy of the endorsed ETA-9035 must then be submitted to INS as a supporting Step One document.

2. Employer's Additional Obligation

Frequently, before agreeing to sponsor a worker for an H-1B visa, prospective employers ask what their liability is in filing a petition. Any employer who dismisses an H-1B worker before his or her authorized stay expires must pay for the trip back to the worker's home country. This liability does not apply if the worker quits the job, but only if he or she is fired.

C. Obtaining an H-1B Visa

Once you have been offered a job and your U.S. employer has completed the preliminary attestation requirements, getting an H-1B visa is a two-step process. Some applicants expect their U.S. employers to handle the entire process for them and, indeed, many large companies have experienced staff specialists who will do this for highly desirable employees. Even smaller companies may be prepared to do whatever is necessary, including paying an immigration attorney's fees, to attract key employees. However, often it is the employee who is most interested in having the visa issued, and to U.S. employers, the red tape of hiring a foreign employee can be an unfamiliar nuisance.

As we give you step-by-step instructions for getting an H-1B visa, we will indicate that certain activities are to be performed by your employer and others are to be done by you. We will discuss each task according to who has legal responsibility for carrying it out. Though the law presumes your employer is performing a particular function, there is nothing to stop you from helping with the work. For example, you can fill out forms intended to be completed by your employer and simply ask him to check them over and sign them. Unless your employer volunteers to help or you are sure the company simply can't live without you, we recommend doing the paperwork yourself. The less your

U.S. employer is inconvenienced, the more the company will be willing to act as sponsor for your visa. An imposition on company time or money might cost you a job offer. With the help of this book, you will know how to do all that is required. It is completely legal as well as in your best interest to help whenever possible.

1. Step One: The Petition

The petition is filed by your U.S. employer. All H-1B visa petitions are submitted to INS regional service centers in the U.S. The object of the petition is to prove four things:
- that you personally qualify for H-1B status
- that your future job is of a high enough level to warrant someone with your advanced skills
- that you have the correct background and skills to match the job requirements, and
- that your U.S. employer has the financial ability to pay your salary.

Be aware that an approved petition does not by itself give you any immigration privileges. It is only a prerequisite to Step Two, submitting your application for an H-1B visa. The petition must be approved before you are eligible for Step Two.

2. Step Two: The Application

The application is filed by you and your accompanying relatives, if any. The application is your formal request for an H-1B visa or status. (If you are Canadian, your Step Two procedures will be different from those of other applicants. See Chapter 28, *Canadians: Special Rules*.) Step Two may be carried out in the U.S. at an INS service center or in your home country at a U.S. consulate there. If you file Step Two papers in the U.S., you will usually submit them together with those for Step One. When Step Two is dispatched at a U.S. consulate abroad, you must wait to file the application until the Step One petition is first approved.

The vast majority of nonimmigrant visa applications are filed at consulates. The major benefit is that an H-1B visa, which is stamped in your passport, can be issued only by American consulates. When you file Step Two at a consulate, your visa will be stamped in your passport at that time. INS offices inside the U.S. may issue statuses but not visas. (See Chapter 14, Section B.)

If you are already in the U.S. legally on some other type of nonimmigrant visa, you qualify to apply for an H-1B status at an INS office inside the U.S. using a procedure known as *change of nonimmigrant status*. (If you were admitted as a visitor without a visa under the Visa Waiver Program, you may not carry out Step Two in the U.S.

Currently there are 29 participating countries in the Visa Waiver Program, including: Andorra, Argentina, Austria, Australia, Belgium, Brunei, Denmark, Finland, France, Germany, Iceland, Ireland, Italy, Japan, Liechtenstein, Luxembourg, Monaco, The Netherlands, New Zealand, Norway, Portugal, San Marino, Singapore, Slovenia, Spain, Sweden, Switzerland, the United Kingdom and Uruguay. The government has approved Greece for inclusion in the program in the near future.) This is simply a technical term meaning you are switching from one nonimmigrant status to another. If a change of status is approved, you will then be allowed to assume H status in the U.S. without requesting an H visa at a consulate abroad. You can keep the status as long as you remain in the U.S. or until it expires, whichever comes first.

You will not, however, receive a visa stamp, which you need if your plans include traveling in and out of the U.S. Again, visa stamps are issued only at U.S. consulates abroad. Therefore, if you change your status and later travel outside the U.S., you will have to go to the U.S. consulate in your home country and repeat Step Two, obtaining the H-1B visa stamp in your passport before you can return. This extra procedure makes changing status an unattractive option for all but Canadians, who don't need visas to cross the U.S. border. (See Chapter 28, *Canadians: Special Rules*.)

3. Paperwork

There are two types of paperwork you must submit to get an H-1B visa. The first consists of official government forms completed by you or your U.S. employer. The second is personal documents, such as academic credentials and professional licenses. We will tell you exactly what forms and documents you need.

It is vital that forms are properly filled out and all necessary documents are supplied. You or your U.S. employer may resent the intrusion into your privacy and sizable effort it takes to prepare immigration applications, but you should realize the process is an impersonal matter to immigration officials. Your getting a visa is more important to you than it is to the U.S. government. This is not a pleasant thing to accept, but you are better off having a real understanding of your position. People from all over the world want U.S. visas. There is no shortage of applicants. Take the time and trouble to prepare your papers properly. In the end it will pay off with a successful application.

The documents you or your U.S. employer supply to INS do not have to be originals. Photocopies of all documents are acceptable as long as you have the originals in your possession and are willing to produce them at the request of INS. Documents submitted to U.S. consulates, on the other hand, must be either originals or official government certified copies. Government certified copies and notarized copies are not the same thing. Documents that have only been notarized are not acceptable. They must carry a government seal. In addition to any original or government certified copies of documents submitted to a consulate, you should submit plain photocopies of each document as well. After the consulate compares the copies with the originals, it will return the originals.

Documents will be accepted if they are in either English, or, with papers filed at U.S. consulates abroad, the language of the country where the documents are being filed. An exception exists for papers filed at U.S. consulates in Japan, where all documents must be translated into English. If the documents are not in an acceptable language as just explained, they must be accompanied by a full, word for word, written English translation. Any capable person may act as translator. It is not necessary to hire a professional. At the end of each translation, the following statement must appear:

I hereby certify that I translated this document from (language) to English. This translation is accurate and complete. I further certify that I am fully competent to translate from (language) to English.

The translator should sign this statement but it does not have to be witnessed or notarized.

Later in this chapter we describe in detail the forms and documents needed to get your H-1B visa. A summary checklist of forms and documents appears at the end of this chapter.

D. Who's Who in Getting Your H-1B Visa

Getting an H-1B visa will be easier if you familiarize yourself with the technical names used for each participant in the process. During Step One, the petition, you are known as either the *beneficiary* or the *employee* and your U.S. employer is called the *petitioner* or the *employer*. The petitioner may be either a business or a person but usually it is a business. In Step Two, the application, you are called *applicant*, but your employer remains the petitioner or employer. If you are bringing your spouse and children with you as accompanying relatives, each of them is known as *applicant* as well.

E. Step One: The Petition

This section includes the information you need to submit the petition.

1. General Procedures

The U.S. employer submits the petition, consisting of forms and documents, by mail, in duplicate, to the INS regional service center having jurisdiction over your intended employer's place of business. INS regional service centers are not the same as INS local offices. There are four INS regional service centers spread across the U.S. Appendix II contains a list of all INS regional service centers with their addresses.

The filing fee for each petition, if no change of status (Step Two, U.S. Filing) is being requested, is currently $100 plus $500, which is intended to go to a special training fund to create jobs for domestic workers. With a change of status request, there is an additional fee of $120. Institutions of higher learning, nonprofits and government organizations are exempt from this additional fee. Checks or money orders are accepted. It is not advisable to send cash. We recommend submitting all papers by certified mail, return receipt requested, and making a copy of everything sent in to keep in your records.

Within a week or so after mailing in the petition, your employer should get back a written confirmation that the papers are being processed, together with a receipt for the fee. This notice will also give your immigration file number and tell approximately when you should expect to have a decision. If INS wants further information before acting on your case, all petition papers, forms and documents will be returned to your employer with another form known as an *I-797*. The request for more information tells your employer what additional pieces of information or documents are expected. Your employer should supply the extra data and mail the whole package back to the INS regional service center.

H-1B petitions are normally approved within three to eight weeks. When this happens, a Notice of Action Form I-797 will be sent to your employer showing the petition was approved. If you plan to execute Step Two at a U.S. consulate abroad, INS will also notify the consulate of your choice, sending a complete copy of your file. Only the employer receives communications from INS about the petition because technically it is the employer who is seeking the visa on your behalf.

2. Petition Forms

Copies of all forms can be found in Appendix III.

Form I-129 and H Supplement

The basic form for Step One, the petition is immigration Form I-129 and H Supplement. The I-129 form is used for many different nonimmigrant visas. In addition to the basic part of the form that applies to all types of visas, it comes with several supplements for each specific nonimmigrant category. Simply tear out and use the supplement that applies to you. Your employer must file the petition form in duplicate. Send in two signed originals. Copies are not acceptable.

More than one foreign employee may be listed on a single I-129 petition. This is done if the employer has more than one opening to be filled for the same type of job. If more than one employee is to be included, Supplement-1, which is also part of Form I-129, should be completed for each additional employee.

Most of the questions on the I-129 form are straightforward. If a question does not apply to you, answer it with "None" or "N/A." Those questions requiring explanations are as follows:

Part 1. These questions concern the employer only and are self-explanatory.

Part 2, Question 1. Question 1 should be answered "H-1B."

Questions 2–3. These questions are self-explanatory.

Question 4. This question asks you to indicate what action is requested from INS. Normally you will mark box "a" which tells INS to notify a U.S. consulate abroad of the petition approval so that you may apply for a visa there. If you will be filing your Step Two application in the U.S., mark box "b." If this petition is being filed as an extension, mark box "c."

Question 5. This question is self-explanatory.

Part 3. These questions are self-explanatory. If you previously held a U.S. work permit and therefore have a U.S. Social Security number, put down that number where asked. If you have a Social Security number that is not valid for employment, put down that number followed by "not valid for employment." If you have never had a Social Security number, put down "None."

Alien Registration Numbers, which all begin with the letter "A," are given only to people who have applied for green cards, received political asylum or been in deportation proceedings. If you do have an "A" number, put that number down and also explain how you got it, such as "number issued from previous green card petition filed by my brother." If you do not have an "A" number, write down "None."

If your present authorized stay has expired, you must disclose that where asked. This should not affect your ability to get an H-1B visa at a U.S. consulate, but if you are out of status now, you cannot file Step Two inside the U.S.

Part 4. These questions are self-explanatory. Under recent changes in the law, the fact that you may have a green card petition or application in process does not prevent you from getting an H-1B visa.

Part 5. These questions are self-explanatory. The dates of intended employment should not exceed a total of three years, which is the maximum period of time for which an H-1B petition may be approved.

H Supplement, Top of Form. These questions are self-explanatory. Note, however, that there are a number of H-1B categories listed that we have not discussed, such as those for artists, entertainers and athletes. These occupations were eliminated from H-1B eligibility after the official government form was printed.

H Supplement, Section 1. Complete only the first four items, which are self-explanatory. The petitioner must sign this form in two places.

H Supplement, Sections 2–4. These do not apply to H-1B petitions and should be left blank.

3. Petition Documents

You must provide several documents with the petition.

a. Preliminary Attestation

Your employer must submit evidence that he has completed the attestation. This involves supplying a copy of the accepted Form ETA-9035.

b. Job Verification

Your employer must show that the job you have been offered really exists. To do this, he must produce either a written employment agreement with you or a written summary of an oral agreement. The terms of your employment, including job duties, hours, and salary, must be mentioned in the letter. It is acceptable that the employment be "at will" and not of any particular duration.

c. Proof of Professional Level Job

Next should come evidence that the job being offered really requires a person who meets one of the four criteria discussed above, that is to say, someone with a bachelor's degree or the equivalent. Sometimes, as with positions for physicians, accountants and similarly recognized professions, the high level of the work is common knowledge. In such cases, the employment agreement will serve to prove both the existence and the level of the job.

Where it is not evident that the position is a "specialty occupation," additional documents are required. Then your employer should write out and submit a detailed description of all job functions, with an explanation of how advanced knowledge and education are essential to their performance. If it is very unclear that the job requires a high level employee, still more job level proof can be obtained by asking for written affidavits from experts, such as educators in the field or other employers in similar businesses, stating that jobs of this kind are normally held by highly qualified and degreed individuals.

d. Proof of Employer's Ability to Pay Your Salary

Your employer must be able to prove its existence and financial viability. If the employer is large and well known, it is usually enough to state the annual gross receipts or income in the letter it submits which describes the job opportunity and duties. If the employer is very small, INS may request documents to verify the existence and financial solvency of the employer's business. In that case, INS will specifically list the documents it wishes to see, including tax returns, profit and loss statements, etc.

Publicly held companies do not have to produce tax returns, accounting records or bank statements. For them, annual reports of the past two years are accepted to prove ability to pay wages. Again, the larger the company, the less evidence INS demands of its ability to pay additional salaries. When a company is nationally known, INS may require no proof of this at all.

e. Proof That You Are a Professional

To qualify for an H-1B visa, you must show evidence that you have a bachelor's degree or otherwise meet the criteria discussed above concerning "specialty occupations." This evidence should include copies of diplomas and transcripts from the colleges and universities you attended. INS insists on both a diploma and a transcript from a school where you graduated. If you attended a school but did not graduate, the transcript is required. If you were educated outside the U.S., INS may request a credential evaluation from an approved evaluation service as explained in Section A2, above.

f. Special Documents for Physicians

Graduates of medical schools outside the U.S. or Canada may not get H-1B visas as practicing physicians unless they have passed the FLEX licensing exam or an equivalent exam and satisfy the state licensing requirements if they will provide direct patient care services. If patient care will be provided, the physician must also have an unrestricted license to practice in a foreign state, or have graduated from a U.S. medical school. Passing the exam, however, is not required of foreign medical graduates who come to the U.S. to work solely in teaching or research positions at a public or nonprofit institution. In those cases, any patient-care activities must be incidental to the teaching or research functions. Therefore, in addition to all other documents required from members of the professions, the petitioning employer must submit either a certificate showing you have passed the FLEX or an equivalent exam, or a statement certifying that you will be employed as either a teacher or researcher and that any patient care will be undertaken only as part of the teaching or research. This written statement does not have to be in any special form but simply in the petitioner's own words.

Foreign medical students attending medical school abroad may petition to be classified as an H-3 trainee if the hospital is approved by the American Medical Association or American Osteopathic Association. A hospital submits the petition, for either a residency or internship, if the alien will engage in employment as an extern during his or her medical school training.

4. Petition Interviews

INS rarely holds interviews on H-1B visa petitions. When it does, the interview is always with the employer. If you are in the U.S., you may be asked to appear as well. Interviews are requested only if INS doubts that the documents or information on Form I-129 and the H Supplement are genuine. Then the petition file is forwarded from the INS regional service center where it was submitted to the INS local office nearest your employer's place of business and your employer is notified to appear there. The employer may also be asked to bring additional documents at that time. If, after the interview, everything is in order, the petition will be approved. The best way to avoid an interview is to have the employer document the petition well from the beginning.

5. Petition Appeals

When your job qualifications or the ability of the employer to pay your salary have been poorly documented, the petition will probably be denied. Your employer will then get a notice of INS's unfavorable decision, a written statement of the reasons for the negative outcome and an explanation of how to appeal.

The best way to handle an appeal is to try avoiding it altogether. Filing an appeal means making an argument to INS that its reasoning was wrong. This is difficult to do successfully. If you think you can eliminate the reason your petition failed by improving your paperwork, it makes sense to disregard the appeals process and simply file a new petition, better prepared than the first.

If the petition was denied because your U.S. employer left out necessary documents that have since been located, the new documents should be sent together with a written request that the case be reopened to the same INS office that issued the denial. This is technically called a *Motion to Reopen*. There is a $110 fee to file this motion. Appeals often take a long time. A Motion to Reopen can be concluded faster than an appeal.

If your U.S. employer does choose to appeal, it must be done within 30 days of the date on the Notice of Denial. The appeal should be filed at the same INS office that issued the denial. There is a $110 filing fee. INS will then forward the papers for consideration to the Administrative Appeals Unit of the central INS office in Washington, D.C. In six to eighteen months or more your employer will get back a decision by mail. Fewer than 5% of all appeals are successful.

When an appeal to INS has been denied, the next step is to make an appeal through the U.S. judicial system. Your employer may not file an action in court without first going through the appeals process available from INS. If the case has reached this stage and you are in the U.S. illegally, we strongly recommend seeking representation from a qualified immigration attorney as you are now in danger of being deported.

F. Step Two: The Application (Consular Filing)

Anyone with an approved H-1B petition can apply for a visa at a U.S. consulate in his or her home country. You must be physically present to apply there. If you have been or are now working or living illegally in the U.S., you may still get an H-1B visa from a U.S. consulate if you otherwise qualify.

If you are Canadian, your Step Two procedures will be different from those of other applicants. See Chapter 28, *Canadians: Special Rules*, for details.

1.   Benefits and Drawbacks of Consular Filing

The most important benefit to consular filing, making it almost always preferable to U.S. filing, is that only consulates issue visas. When you go through a U.S. filing, you get a status, not a visa. (See Chapter 14, Section B, Difference Between a Visa and a Status.) H-1B status confers the same right to work as an H-1B worker has, but it does not give you the ability to travel out of the U.S. and get back in again. Therefore, if you want travel privileges, you will at some time have to go through the extra step of applying for a visa at a U.S. consulate, even though you have already applied for and received H-1B status in the U.S.

Moreover, anyone with an approved petition may apply for an H-1B visa at the appropriate consulate. That is not the case with U.S. applications for H-1B status. If you are in the U.S. illegally, consular filing is a must. See Chapter 25 on inadmissibility to make sure none of the grounds of inadmissibility or bars to change of status apply to you. You are not eligible to process a status application in the U.S. unless you are presently in status.

A further plus to consular filing is that consular offices work much more quickly to issue nonimmigrant visas than INS offices do to process nonimmigrant statuses. Your waiting time for the paperwork to be finished will be much shorter at a U.S. consulate abroad than at most U.S. INS offices.

A drawback to consular filing is that you must be physically present in the country where the consulate is located to file there. If your petition is ultimately turned down because of an unexpected problem, not only will you have to wait outside the U.S. until the problem is resolved, but other visas in your passport, such as a visitor's visa, may be canceled. It will then be impossible for you to enter the U.S. in any capacity. Consequently, if your H-1B visa case is not very strong and freedom of travel is not essential to you, it might be wise to apply in the U.S., make up your mind to remain there for the duration of the H-1B status, and skip trying to get a visa from the consulate.

2.   Application General Procedures: Consular Filing

Technically, the law allows you to apply for an H-1B visa at any U.S. consulate you choose. A complete list of all U.S. consulates that process visa applications, together with their addresses and phone numbers, is in Appendix I. However, from a practical standpoint, your case will be given the greatest consideration at the consulate in your home country. Applying in some other country creates suspicion in the minds of the consul officers there about your motives for choosing their consulate. Often, when an applicant is having trouble at a home consulate, he will seek a more lenient office in some other country. This practice of consulate shopping is frowned on by officials in the system. Unless you have a very good reason for being elsewhere (such as a temporary job assignment in some other nation), it is smarter to file your visa application in your home country.

3.   Overstays and Cancellation of Visas

If you have ever been present in the U.S. unlawfully, your visa will be automatically cancelled and you cannot apply as a third country national. Even if you overstayed your status in the U.S. by just one day, you must return to your home country and apply for the visa from that consulate. There is an exception. If you were admitted to the U.S. for the duration of your status (indicated by a "D/S" on your I-94 form) and you remained in the U.S. beyond that time for which your status was conferred, you may still be able to apply as a third country national. The State Department's current regulations seem to imply that you will be barred from third country national processing only if an immigration judge or INS officer has determined that you were unlawfully present. Because of the ambiguity, you may find that your success in applying as a third country national will depend on your country, the consulate and the relative seriousness of your offense. Being unlawfully present is also a ground of inadmissibility if the period of unlawful presence is six months or more. (See Chapter 25.)

You may not file an application for an H-1B visa at a consulate before your petition has been approved. Once this occurs, the INS regional service center where the petition was originally submitted will forward a complete copy of your file to the U.S. consulate designated on Form I-129 in Step One. At the same time, a Notice of Action Form I-797 indicating approval will be sent directly to your U.S. employer. When your employer receives this, you should telephone the consulate to see if the petition file has arrived from INS. If the file is slow in coming, ask the consulate to consider granting approval of your H-1B visa based only on the Notice of Action. Many U.S. consulates are willing to do so.

Once the petition is approved, you can simply walk into many consulates with your application paperwork and get your H-1B visa immediately. Others insist on advance appointments. Most U.S. consulates in Canada require you to schedule an appointment by telephone a week or more in advance of your interview to receive an appointment. Some, like London, prefer to process visa applications by mail. Since procedures among consulates vary, you should always telephone in advance to ask about local policies.

On entering the U.S. with your new H-1B visa, you will be given an I-94 card. It will be stamped with a date showing how long you can stay. Normally, you are permitted to remain up to the expiration date on your H-1B petition. Each time you exit and reenter the U.S., you will get a new I-94 card authorizing your stay up to the final date indicated on the petition.

4. Application Forms: Consular Filing

When you file at a U.S. consulate abroad, the consulate officials will provide you with certain optional forms, designated by an "OF" preceeding a number. Instructions for completing optional forms and what to do with them once they are filled out will come with the forms. We do not include copies of these forms in Appendix III.

5. Application Documents: Consular Filing

You must show a valid passport and present one passport-type photograph taken according to the photo instructions in Appendix III. If the consulate has not yet received your INS file containing the paperwork from the approved petition, you will then need to show the original Notice of Action, Form I-797, which your employer received from INS by mail. Most consulates will issue H-1B visas based only on the Notice of Action, although some, particularly in South America and Asia, insist on seeing the complete INS file. If the consulate wants to see your file and it is late (more than a month) in arriving, you should request that the consulate investigate the file's whereabouts. You, too, can write the INS regional service center where your petition was processed, asking for the file.

For each accompanying relative, you must present a valid passport and one passport-type photograph taken according to the photo instructions in Appendix III. You will also need documents verifying their family relationship to you. You may verify a parent/child relationship by pre-

senting the child's long form birth certificate. Many countries, including Canada and England, issue both short and long form birth certificates. Where both are available, the long form is needed because it contains the names of the parents while the short form does not. If you are accompanied by your spouse, you must prove that you are lawfully married by showing a civil marriage certificate. Church certificates are generally unacceptable. (There are a few exceptions, depending on the laws of your particular country. Canadians, for example, may use church marriage certificates if the marriage took place in Quebec Province, but not elsewhere. If a civil certificate is available, however, you should always use it.) You may have married in a country where marriages are not customarily recorded. Tribal areas of Africa are an example. In such situations, call the nearest consulate or embassy of your home country for help with getting acceptable proof of marriage.

There may or may not be a fee for the visa. H-1B visas are issued free to the citizens of most countries, but others may be charged fees that can be as high as $100. If the country of your nationality charges fees for visas to U.S. citizens who wish to work there, then the U.S. will charge people of your country a similar fee as well. Whether or not there is a fee is determined by your nationality, not by where you apply. Check with the nearest U.S. consulate to find out if there will be a fee in your case.

6. Application Interviews: Consular Filing

The consulate will frequently require an interview before issuing an H-1B visa. During the interview, a consul officer will examine the data you gave in Step One for accuracy, especially regarding facts about your own qualifications.

7. Application Appeals: Consular Filing

When a consulate turns down an H-1B visa application, there is no way to make a formal appeal, although you are free to reapply as often as you like. Some consulates, however, will make you wait several months before allowing you to file another application. If your visa is denied, you will be told by the consul officer the reasons for the denial. Written statements of decisions are not normally provided in non-immigrant cases. If a lack of evidence about a particular point is the problem, sometimes simply presenting more evidence on an unclear fact can bring a positive change in the result.

The most likely reasons for having an H-1B visa turned down are because you are found inadmissible or the consulate believes that you are not really qualified for an H-1B visa.

Certain people who have been refused visas reapply at a different consulate, attempting to hide the fact that they were turned down elsewhere. You should know that if your application is denied, the last page in your passport will be stamped "Application Received" with the date and location of the rejecting consulate. This notation shows that some type of prior visa application has failed. It serves as a warning to other consulates that your case merits close inspection. If what we have just told you makes you think it would be a good idea to overcome this problem by obtaining a new, unmarked passport, you should also know that permanent computer records are kept of all visa denials.

G. Step Two: The Application (U.S. Filing)

If you are physically present in the U.S., you may apply for H-1B status without leaving the country on the following conditions:

- you are simultaneously filing paperwork for or have already received an approved petition
- you entered the U.S. legally
- you have never worked in U.S. illegally, and
- the date on your I-94 card has not passed.

If you were admitted as a visitor without a visa under the Visa Waiver Program, currently available only to nationals of Andorra, Argentina, Australia, Austria, Belgium, Brunei, Denmark, Finland, France, Germany, Great Britain (including Scotland, Wales, Northern Ireland, the Channel Islands and the Isle of Man), Iceland, Italy, Japan, Liechtenstein, Luxembourg, Monaco, New Zealand, Netherlands, Norway, San Marino, Slovenia, Spain, Sweden and Switzerland, you may not carry out Step Two in the U.S.

If you cannot meet these terms, you may not file for H-1B status in the U.S. It is important to realize, however, that eligibility to apply in the U.S. has nothing to do with overall eligibility for an H-1B visa. Applicants who are barred from filing in the U.S. but otherwise qualify for H-1B status can apply successfully for an H-1B visa at U.S. consulates abroad. If you find you are not eligible for U.S. filing, read Section F, above.

1. Benefits and Drawbacks of U.S. Filing

Visas are never given inside the U.S. They are issued exclusively by U.S. consulates abroad. If you file in the U.S. and you are successful, you will get H-1B status but not the visa itself. This is a major drawback to U.S. applications. H-1B status allows you to remain in the U.S. with H-1B privileges until the status expires, but should you leave the country

for any reason before that time, you will have to apply for the visa itself at a U.S. consulate before returning to America. Moreover, the fact that your H-1B status has been approved in the U.S. does not guarantee that the consulate will also approve your visa. Some consulates may even regard your previously acquired H-1B status as a negative factor, an indication that you have deliberately tried to avoid the consulate's authority.

There is another problem which comes up only in U.S. filings. It is the issue of what is called *preconceived intent*. To approve a change of status, INS must believe that at the time you originally entered the U.S. as a visitor or with some other nonimmigrant visa, you did not intend to apply for a different status. If INS thinks you had a preconceived plan to change from the status you arrived with to a different status, INS may deny your application. The preconceived intent issue is one less potential hazard you will face if you apply at a U.S. consulate abroad.

On the plus side of U.S. filing is that when problems do arise with your U.S. application, you can stay in America while they are being corrected, a circumstance most visa applicants prefer. If you run into snags at a U.S. consulate, you will have to remain outside the U.S. until matters are resolved.

2. Application General Procedures: U.S. Filing

The general procedure for filing Step Two in the U.S. is to follow Step One as outlined in Section E, above, but to mark box "4b" in Part 2 of Form I-129, indicating that you will complete processing in the U.S. There is no separate application form for filing Step Two in the U.S. If you have an accompanying spouse or children, however, a separate Form I-539 must be filed for them.

When you apply for a change of status, the filing fee for a Step One petition is presently $155. If you are also applying for accompanying relatives, there is an additional fee of $75 for the first dependent and $10 more for each additional dependent. For example, if you are applying for yourself, your spouse and two children, the total filing fee is $155 for you plus $95, which covers all your family members. The $95 breaks down to $75 for the first of your three dependents and $10 each for the remaining two. Checks and money orders are accepted. It is not advisable to send cash. We recommend submitting all papers by certified mail, return receipt requested, and making a copy of everything sent in to keep for your records.

Within a week or two after mailing in the application, you should get back a written notice of confirmation that the papers are being processed, together with a receipt for the fees. This notice will also tell you your immigration file number and approximately when to expect a decision. If INS wants further information before acting on your case, all application papers, forms and documents will be returned together with another form known as an *I-797*. The I-797 tells you what additional pieces of information or documents are expected. You should supply the extra data and mail the whole package back to the INS regional service center.

Applications for an H-1B status are normally approved within two to eight weeks. When this happens, you will receive a Notice of Action Form I-797 indicating the dates for which your status is approved. A new I-94 card will be attached to the bottom of the form.

3. Application Forms: U.S. Filing

Copies of all forms can be found in Appendix III.

Form I-129

Follow the directions for Step One in Section E, above, except in Part 2, mark box "4b" instead of box "4a."

Form I-539 (for accompanying relatives only)

Only one application form is needed for an entire family, but if there is more than one accompanying relative, each additional one should be listed on the I-539 supplement.

Part 1. These questions are self-explanatory. "A" numbers are usually given only to people who have previously applied for green cards or who have been in deportation proceedings.

Part 2, Question 1. Mark box "b," and write in "H-4."

Question 2. This question is self-explanatory.

Part 3. In most cases, you will mark Item 1 with the date requested in the Step One petition. You will also complete Items 3 and 4, which are self-explanatory.

Part 4, Questions 1–2. These questions are self-explanatory.

Question 3. The different parts to this question are self-explanatory; however, items "a" and "b" ask if an immigrant visa petition or adjustment of status application has ever been filed on your behalf. If you are applying for a green card through a relative, this would be Step One, as described in Chapter 5. If you are applying for a green card through employment, this would be Step Two as described in Chapter 8. If you have only begun the Labor Certification, the first step of getting a green card through employment, this question should be answered "no."

4. Application Documents: U.S. Filing

Each applicant must submit an I-94 card, the small white card you received on entering the U.S. Remember, if the date stamped on your I-94 card has already passed, you are ineligible for U.S. filing. If you entered the U.S. under the Visa Waiver Program and have a green I-94 card, you are also ineligible for U.S. filing. Canadians who are just visiting are not expected to have I-94 cards. Canadians with any other type of nonimmigrant status should have them.

For each accompanying relative, send in an I-94 card. You will also need documents verifying their family relationship to you. You may prove a parent/child relationship by presenting the child's long form birth certificate. Many countries, including Canada and England issue both short and long form birth certificates. Where both are available, the long form is needed because it contains the names of the parents while the short form does not. If you are accompanied by your spouse, you must prove that you are lawfully married by showing a civil marriage certificate. Church certificates are usually unacceptable. (There are a few exceptions, depending on the laws of your particular country. Canadians, for example, may use church marriage certificates if the marriage took place in Quebec Province, but not elsewhere. If a civil certificate is available, however, you should always use it.) You may have married in a country where marriages are not customarily recorded. Tribal areas of Africa are an example. In such situations, call the nearest consulate or embassy of your home country for help with getting acceptable proof of marriage.

5. Application Interviews: U.S. Filing

Interviews on H-1B change of status applications are rarely held. When an interview is required, the INS regional service center where you filed will send your paperwork to the local INS office nearest the location of your U.S. employer's institution. This office will in turn contact you for an appointment. (If INS has questions on the Step One petition rather than the application, your employer will be contacted.) INS may ask you to bring additional documents at that time.

If you are called for an interview, the most likely reason is that INS either suspects some type of fraud or believes you may be subject to a ground of inadmissibility. Interviews are usually a sign of trouble and can result in considerable delays.

6. Application Appeals: U.S. Filing

If your application is denied, you will receive a written decision by mail explaining the reasons for the denial. There is no way of making a formal appeal to INS if your application to change status is turned down. If the problem is too little evidence, you may be able to overcome this obstacle by adding more documents and resubmitting the entire application to the same INS office you have been dealing with together with a written request that the case be reopened. The written request does not have to be in any special form. This is technically called a *Motion to Reopen*. There is a $110 fee to file this motion.

Remember that you may be denied the right to a U.S. filing without being denied an H-1B visa. When your application is turned down because you are found ineligible for U.S. filing, simply change your application to a consular filing.

Although there is no appeal to INS for the denial of an H-1B change of status application, you do have the right to file an appeal in a U.S. district court. It would be difficult to file such an appeal without employing an attorney at considerable expense. Such appeals are usually unsuccessful.

H. Extensions

H-1B visas can be extended for three years at a time, but you may not hold an H-1B visa for longer than a total of six years. Although an extension is usually easier to get than the H-1B visa itself, it is not automatic. INS has the right to reconsider your qualifications based on any changes in the facts or law, and your employer must maintain a valid attestation for your position. As always, however, good cases that are well prepared will be successful.

To extend your H-1B visa, the petition and visa stamp will both have to be updated. As with the original application, you can file either in the U.S. or at a consulate. However, contrary to our advice on the initial visa procedures, extensions are best handled in the U.S. That is because visa stamps, which can only be issued originally at consulates, may be extended in the U.S.

1. Step One: Extension Petition

Extension procedures are identical with the procedures followed in getting the initial visa, except that less documentation is required and the filing fee for the worker is only $125. In addition to a copy of the previous employer's attestation (if it is valid for the extension period requested—or a new LCA if the old one is expired), you need only submit your I-94 card, a letter from the employer requesting your visa be extended, and stating that you will continue to be employed in a specialty occupation as previously described, and a copy of your U.S. income tax returns for the previous two years, including the W-2 forms. (Be sure the tax returns reflect only H-1B employment before submitting them.)

WORKING WHILE YOUR EXTENSION PETITION IS PENDING

If you file your petition for an extension of H-1B status before your authorized stay expires, you are automatically permitted to continue working for up to 240 days while you are waiting for a decision. If, however, your authorized stay expires after you have filed for an extension but before you receive an approval, and more than 240 days go by without getting a decision on your extension petition, your work authorization ceases and you must stop working. You will not be able to continue working until your extension is finally approved.

---

a. Extension Petition Forms

Copies of all forms can be found in Appendix III.

Form I-129 and H Supplement

Follow the directions for this form in Section E, above. The only difference is that you will mark boxes "2b" and "4c" of Part 2.

Form I-539 (for accompanying relatives only)

Follow the directions for this form in Section G2, above, but mark box "1a" of Part 2.

b. Extension Petition Documents

You must submit your I-94 card. You should also submit the original Notice of Action I-797, a letter from your employer stating that your extension is required and a copy of your employer's labor condition application (attestation).

2. Step Two: Visa Revalidation

Visas can be revalidated either in the U.S. or at a consulate.

a. Visa Revalidation: U.S. Filing

If you are physically in the U.S. and your H-1B status extension has been approved by INS, you can have your visa revalidated by mail without leaving the country. To do this, you must fill out Form OF-156, following the directions in Section F3, above, and send it to the Department of State. With the form you should submit as documents your passport, current I-94 card, Notice of Action Form I-797 and a detailed letter from your employer describing your job duties. You should enclose a self-addressed, stamped envelope, or a completed Federal Express airbill. Send the entire package by certified mail to:

CA/VO/P/D
Department of State
Visa Services
2401 "E" Street, N.W., (SA-1 L-703)
Washington, DC 20522-0106
Telephone: 202-663-1213
Fax: 202-663-1608

The passport will be returned to you with a newly revalidated visa in a few weeks. Nationals of some countries like Mexico are charged a fee for revalidating a visa, while nationals of other countries receive this service at no charge. Whether or not there is a fee depends on the nationality of the applicant, not the place where the application for the visa was originally made. Call the State Department in Washington, D.C. to find out the amount of the revalidation fee, if any. If you send in your revalidation package without the correct fee, it will be returned to you, so check the amount in advance.

If your accompanying relatives are physically in the U.S., their H-4 visas may be revalidated by sending in their passports and I-94 cards together with yours. We strongly advise gathering your family together inside U.S. borders so you can take advantage of this simple revalidation procedure.

b.   Visa Revalidation: Consular Filing

If you must leave the U.S. after your extension has been approved but before you had time to get your visa revalidated, you must get a new visa stamp issued at a consulate. Reread the procedures in Section F, above. The procedures for consular extensions are identical.

We would like to reemphasize that it is much more convenient to apply for a revalidated visa by mail through the State Department in Washington, D.C. than it is to extend your H-1B visa through a consulate. If possible, you should try to schedule filing your extension application when you can remain in the U.S. until it is complete.

FORMS AND DOCUMENTS CHECKLIST

EMPLOYER ATTESTATION

Form
☐ Form ETA-9035.

STEP ONE: PETITION

Form
☐ Form I-129 and H Supplement.

Documents
☐ Copy of employer's attestation Form ETA-9035.
☐ Written employment contract or written summary of an oral agreement.
☐ College and university diplomas.
☐ If you do not have a degree, evidence that your combined education and experience is equivalent to a degree.

STEP TWO: APPLICATION

Forms
☐ OF forms (available at U.S. consulates for consular filing only).
☐ Form I-129 (U.S. filing only).
☐ Form I-539 (U.S. filing, accompanying relatives only).

Documents
☐ Notice showing approval of the H-1B petition.
☐ Valid passport for you and each accompanying relative.
☐ I-94 card for you and each accompanying relative (U.S. filing only).
☐ One passport-type photo of you and each accompanying relative (Consular filing only).

Temporary Nonagricultural Workers: H-2B Visas

Privileges

- You can work legally in the U.S. for your H-2B sponsor.
- You may travel in and out of the U.S. or remain here continuously until your H-2B visa expires.
- Visas are available for accompanying relatives.

Limitations

- You are restricted to working only for the U.S. employer who acted as your H-2B visa sponsor. If you wish to change jobs, you must get a new H-2B visa.
- H-2B visas can initially be approved for up to only one year. Additional one-year extensions are allowed. After a maximum of three years, you must return home and wait at least 12 months before applying for another H-2B visa, unless you qualify to change to another status.
- Accompanying relatives may stay in the U.S. with you, but they may not work.

A. How to Qualify

Qualifying for a H-2B visa has some limitations.

1. Quota Restrictions

No more than 66,000 H-2B visa petitions may be approved during the government year (fiscal year) which ends on September 30. The annual quota has not yet been exceeded and prospects are good that these visas will remain easily available in the future.

Temporary Labor Certification takes from two to four months. Petition approval takes an additional one to two months. After the petition is approved, visas are usually issued within several weeks.

2. Who Qualifies for an H-2B Visa?

You qualify for an H-2B visa if you are coming to the U.S. to accept a temporary or seasonal nonagricultural job from a U.S. employer and you have the correct background or skills or natural abilities needed by that employer. H-2B visas are aimed at skilled and unskilled workers, compared to H-1B visas, which are intended for college-educated workers. To get an H-2B visa, it must be shown that there are no qualified Americans available to take the job you have been offered.

The term "temporary" refers to the employer's need for the duties performed by the position, regardless of whether the underlying position is permanent or temporary. Seasonal laborers, workers on short-term business projects and those who come to the U.S. as trainers of other workers commonly get H-2B visas. H-2B visas are also frequently used for entertainers who cannot meet the criteria for O or P visas. H-2B visas enable such entertainers to come to the U.S. for specific bookings. These bookings are considered temporary positions. A job can be deemed temporary if it is a onetime occurrence, meets a seasonal or peak-load need or fulfills an intermittent but not regular need of the employer. Although we've just given you some examples of jobs that meet INS's definition of temporary, be aware that most jobs do not.

Finally, you are eligible for an H-2B visa only if you have the intention to return to your home county when the visa expires.

To summarize, there are four requirements for obtaining an H-2B visa:

- You must have a job offer from a U.S. employer to perform work that is either temporary or seasonal.
- You must have the correct background to qualify for the job you have been offered.
- There must be no qualified Americans willing or able to take the job. A Temporary Labor Certification is required.
- You must intend to return home when your visa expires.

TEMPORARY AGRICULTURAL WORKER: H-2A VISAS

Under the 1986 amendments to the U.S. immigration laws, temporary agricultural workers are now treated differently from all other types of temporary workers. Agricultural workers are now issued H-2A visas while all other temporary workers receive H-2B visas. The rules for getting temporary agricultural workers visas are extremely complex and beyond the scope of this book. The basic requirements are that before a non-U.S. agricultural worker may be granted an H-2A visa, the prospective employer must attempt to find U.S. agricultural workers. The employer must search for U.S. workers not just in his own immediate geographical area, but throughout the entire adjacent region of the country. The employer must do this by undertaking a multi-state recruitment effort. Moreover, H-2A visas will not, as a practical matter, be issued to foreign workers who are already in the U.S. illegally. Due to the great amount of effort involved in obtaining H-2A visas, they will be attractive only to employers who urgently need to bring in a large crew of foreign laborers at one time to work on a particular harvest. Again, from a practical standpoint, the employer will either have to travel abroad or use the services of a foreign labor contractor to find these crews of temporary foreign workers. H-2A visas are not practical for bringing one temporary agricultural worker at a time to the U.S.

a.   Job Offer From a U.S. Employer

You need a specific job offer from a U.S. employer to get an H-2B visa. The employer will have to act as the petitioner in getting your H-2B visa. Many people are surprised to learn that they require an employment offer before applying for a work visa. The idea behind it is that you are being granted an H-2B visa because your services are essential to an American company. Put another way, the U.S. government is issuing the visa not for your benefit, but to help your American employer.

The petitioner may be a company or an individual. Generally, you cannot act as your own employer. An agent who books your talents for a variety of jobs can be the source of the job offer, if the salary is paid to you directly by the agent and not by the individual places where you perform. This is a common arrangement for entertainers.

The job you are offered can't be just any position. It must be one that meets the legal definition of temporary or seasonal. It is easy to understand what kind of jobs are seasonal. Professional minor-league baseball players are a common example of employees who do seasonal work. (Major-league players will usually qualify for O visas. See Chapter 24.)

Job temporariness is a harder concept to grasp because it is viewed by the law in a very limited way. To be considered temporary, the period of the employer's need for services must be one year or less, absent unusual circumstances. The types of jobs INS usually thinks of as temporary are those tied to a specific project of the employer, such as building a housing development. Once the project is completed, the job will disappear. If, however, the employer is in the business of going continuously from one project to another, and if the position you have been offered is always available on one of the projects, INS will view the job as permanent. Another common job viewed as temporary for H-2B purposes is a training position. Training positions involve your spending a limited time teaching others how to carry out specific company procedures or use special company equipment. Jobs can also qualify if there is an unusually heavy demand for workers.

b.   Correct Background

You must have the correct background and abilities for the job you have been offered. For example, if you are a qualified insurance salesman but are offered a job supervising a catering project, you will not be granted an H-2B visa for that job because you have no background in catering. It is irrelevant that your native intelligence and general knowledge of business may make you quite capable of handling the catering job. Likewise, reliability or willingness to work hard, characteristics difficult to find and much sought after by real-world employers, are not an INS consideration. If you lack the required background in the job offered, the petition will fail.

H-2B visas can be issued to unskilled as well as skilled workers. If your job offer happens to be for employment as an unskilled worker, there are by definition no specific background qualifications for you to meet. Under these circumstances, your natural abilities may be a consideration, but you do not need to be concerned about having the correct background.

c.   No Qualified Americans

To obtain an H-2B visa, there must be no qualified Americans available to take the job you have been offered.

ENTERTAINMENT INDUSTRY WORKERS: SPECIAL CONSIDERATIONS

Entertainment industry workers, both the performers and the many diversified workers it takes to make a movie or stage a live performance, often need temporary U.S. work visas. H-1B visas are not available to entertainers or athletes. The better-known ones will qualify for O or P visas. (See Chapter 24.) The individual entertainment industry worker who is not well known, not part of a well-known group or not part of an international production team is limited to an H-2B visa.

In these cases, there is a problem with both the temporariness of the job and the availability of similarly qualified American workers. The definition of temporariness is narrow for entertainment industry jobs, as it is for positions in other occupations. If, for example, a Las Vegas nightclub wants to book an act for only one week, INS will still say that the job is *not* temporary because nightclubs are always employing acts to perform there. The conclusion is that the job is not temporary even if the booking is. On the other hand, jobs for performers on tour are considered temporary, as are jobs for workers on motion pictures. That is because tours and motion picture productions always end.

Even if the job is clearly temporary, your U.S. employer must still get a clearance from DOL acknowledging that no Americans are available to fill the job that is open. When such a clearance is requested, DOL will in turn contact the appropriate U.S. entertainment industry union to see if the union can find an American worker to fill the position or has some other objection to a non-American taking the job. Since there are many competent U.S. entertainment industry workers looking for employment, getting union approval on an H-2B case may be difficult.

The availability of competing American workers is not a problem in several situations. H-2B visas are readily available to all performing and non-performing members of lesser known troupes coming to the U.S. on tour. We have already explained that in the view of INS, the touring factor makes a job temporary. Moreover, U.S. entertainment industry unions are usually reluctant to break up performing units. Therefore, an entire touring group, from performers to technicians and stage hands, can all get H-2B visas.

The offer of employment must be from a U.S. employer. The workers cannot be self-employed nor may they be working in the U.S. for a foreign company. Individual performers, therefore, normally have to get their H-2B visas through a central booking agent. This is acceptable, provided the booking agent acts as the employer in every respect, including being responsible for paying the salary.

Foreign entertainment industry working units, such as film companies, who wish to get H-2B visas will need to do one of two things to supply themselves with the required U.S. employer. They can be sponsored for visas by an established U.S. company which will act as the employer of each individual foreign employee. Alternatively, the foreign group may form their own U.S. corporation and have it act as the employer. U.S. corporations are set up by state governments in the U.S. state where the business will be headquartered. Forming a U.S. corporation is extremely simple and in most states can be accomplished in a matter of days. Information on how to form a U.S. corporation is available from the office of the Secretary of State located in each state capital.

A Temporary Labor Certification must be successfully completed to prove the unavailability of U.S. workers. This condition may or may not be hard to meet, depending on the type of job. Where the jobs are meant for skilled and unskilled workers rather than professionals, the competition factor can be a problem. Many employers do go begging, however, for want of either qualified or willing U.S. applicants, especially jobs in businesses requiring unusual skills and those with odd working hours or other undesirable features.

d. Intent to Return to Your Home Country

H-2B visas are meant to be temporary. At the time of applying, you must intend to return home when the visa expires. If you have it in mind to take up permanent residence in the U.S., you are legally ineligible for an H-2B visa. The U.S. government knows it is difficult to read minds. Therefore, you can expect to be asked for evidence showing that when you go to America on an H-2B visa, you are leaving behind possessions, property or family members as incentive for your eventual return to your home country.

3. Accompanying Relatives

When you qualify for an H-2B visa, your spouse and unmarried children under age 21 can get H-4 visas simply by providing proof of their family relationship to you. H-4 visas authorize your accompanying relatives to stay with you in the U.S., but not to work there.

B. Applying for a Green Card From H-2B Status

If you have an H-2B visa, you can file to get a green card, but being in the U.S. on an H-2B visa gives you no advantage in doing so, and in fact will almost certainly prove to be a drawback. That is because H-2B visas, like most nonimmigrant visas, are intended only for those who plan to return home once their jobs or other activities in the U.S. are completed. However, if you apply for a green card, you are in effect making a statement that you never intend to leave the U.S. Therefore, INS will allow you to keep H-2B status while pursuing a green card, but only if you can convince INS that you did not intend to get a green card when you originally applied for the H-2B visa and that you will return home if you are unable to secure a green card before your H-2B visa expires. Doing this can be difficult. If you do not succeed, your H-2B status can be taken away. It is also important to understand that even if you argue successfully and keep your H-2B status, the visa and the petition each

carry an absolute maximum duration of one year and they will probably expire before you get a green card. Once you have made a green card application of your visa, you will be absolutely barred from receiving an extension of your status. Should you, for any reason, lose your H-2B status, it may affect your green card application. (See Chapter 25.)

Another problem comes up if it is your current H-2B sponsoring employer who also wants to sponsor you for a green card. INS regulations provide that if you have an approved permanent labor certification sponsored by the same employer who petitioned for your H-2B visa, the H-2B visa will automatically be revoked. The only way you can apply for a green card through employment and retain an H-2B visa, even until its expiration date, is to have a different sponsoring employer for the green card than you had for the H-2B visa.

If what you really want is a green card, apply for it directly and disregard H-2B visas. Although the green card is harder to get and may take several years, in the long run you will be happier with the results of a green card application. Also, relatively few jobs qualify as temporary for H-2B visa purposes and you may actually have a better chance of getting a green card through a given job than an H-2B visa.

C. Getting an H-2B Visa

Once you have been offered a job, getting an H-2B visa is a three-step process. Often applicants expect their employers to handle the entire procedure for them and indeed, a number of large companies are equipped with experienced staff specialists who will do this for highly desirable employees. Even smaller companies may be prepared to do whatever is necessary, including paying an immigration attorney's fees, in order to attract a key employee.

1. Step One: Temporary Labor Certification

Temporary Labor Certification is filed by your U.S. employer. The process may not begin more than 120 days before you are needed. The object of the Temporary Labor Certification is to satisfy the U.S. government that there are no qualified American workers available to take the specific job that has been offered to you, and to determine whether the job is temporary in nature and therefore suitable for an H-2B visa. These things must be proven first to DOL, and then to INS. Therefore, you will initially file Temporary Labor Certification papers with DOL.

If all goes well, your Temporary Labor Certification will eventually be approved, but be aware that an approved Temporary Labor Certification does not by itself give you any immigration privileges. It is only a prerequisite to Steps Two and Three, submitting your petition and application for an H-2B visa. The judgment of DOL on the Temporary Labor Certification is only advisory in nature. INS has the final word. However, INS gives great weight to DOL's opinion and if the Temporary Labor Certification is denied, it will be difficult to get an approval from INS in Step Two. In any event, without a response from DOL on the Temporary Labor Certification, whether it be an approval or a denial, you are not eligible to go on with Steps Two and Three.

2.   Step Two: The Petition

Step Two is called the petition. It is filed by your U.S. employer. All H-2B petitions are submitted to INS regional service centers in the U.S. The object of the petition is to prove four things:

- That the job is temporary or seasonal in nature. (Remember, DOL's decision is only advisory.)
- That no qualified Americans are available for the job. (Once again, DOL's decision is only advisory.)
- That you have the correct background, skills and abilities to match the job requirements.
- That your U.S. employer has the financial ability to pay your salary.

Like the Temporary Labor Certification, an approved petition does not by itself give you any immigration privileges. It is only a prerequisite to Step Three, submitting your application. The petition must be approved before you are eligible for Step Three.

3.   Step Three: The Application

Step Three is called the *application*. It is filed by you and your accompanying relatives, if any. The application is your formal request for an H-2B visa or status. (If you are Canadian, your Step Three procedures will be different from those of other applicants. See Chapter 28, *Canadians: Special Rules.*) Step Three may be carried out in the U.S. at an INS office or in your home country at a U.S. consulate there. If you file Step Three papers in the U.S., you will usually submit them at the same time as those for Step Two. When Step Three is dispatched at a U.S. consulate abroad, you must wait to file the application until the Step Two petition is first approved.

The vast majority of nonimmigrant visa applications are filed at consulates. The major benefit is that an H-2B visa, which is stamped in your passport, can be issued only by American consulates. When you file Step Three at a consulate, your visa will be stamped in your passport at that

time. INS offices inside the U.S. may issue statuses but not visas. (See Chapter 14, Section B, Difference Between a Visa and a Status).

If you are already in the U.S. legally on some other type of nonimmigrant visa, you qualify to apply for an H-2B status at an INS office inside the U.S., using a procedure known as change of nonimmigrant status. (If you are admitted as a visitor without a visa under the Visa Waiver Program, you may not carry out Step Three in the U.S. Currently there are 29 participating countries in the Visa Waiver Program, including: Andorra, Argentina, Austria, Australia, Belgium, Brunei, Denmark, Finland, France, Germany, Iceland, Ireland, Italy, Japan, Liechtenstein, Luxembourg, Monaco, The Netherlands, New Zealand, Norway, Portugal, San Marino, Singapore, Slovenia, Spain, Sweden, Switzerland, the United Kingdom and Uruguay. The government has approved Greece for inclusion in the program in the near future.) This is simply a technical term meaning you are switching from one nonimmigrant status to another. If a change of status is approved, you will then be treated as if you had entered the country with an H-2B visa and you can keep the status as long as you remain in the U.S. or until it expires, whichever comes first.

You will not, however, receive a visa stamp, which you need if your plans include traveling in and out of the U.S. Again, visa stamps are issued only at U.S. consulates abroad. Therefore, if you change your status and later travel outside the U.S., you will have to go to the U.S. consulate in your home country and repeat Step Three over again, obtaining the H-2B visa stamp in your passport before you can return. This extra procedure makes changing status an unattractive option for all but Canadians, who don't need visas to cross the U.S. border.

4.   Paperwork

There are two types of paperwork you must submit to get an H-2B visa. The first consists of official government forms completed by you or your U.S. employer. The second is personal documents such as academic credentials and evidence of previous job experience. We will tell you exactly what forms and documents you need.

It is vital that forms are properly filled out and all necessary documents are supplied. You or your U.S. employer may resent the intrusion into your privacy and sizable effort it takes to prepare immigration applications, but you should realize the process is an impersonal matter to immigration officials. Your getting a visa is more important to you than it is to the U.S. government. This is not a pleasant thing to accept, but you are better off having a real understanding of your position. People from all over the world want U.S. visas. There is no shortage of applicants.

Take the time and trouble to prepare your papers properly. In the end it will pay off with a successful application.

The documents you or your U.S. employer supply to INS do not have to be originals. Photocopies of all documents are acceptable as long as you have the originals in your possession and are willing to produce them at the request of INS. Documents submitted to U.S. consulates, on the other hand, must be either originals or official government certified copies. Government certified copies and notarized copies are not the same thing. Documents that have only been notarized are not acceptable. They must carry a government seal. In addition to any original or government certified copies of documents submitted to a consulate, you should submit plain photocopies of each document as well. After the consulate compares the copies with the originals, it will return the originals.

Documents will be accepted if they are in either English, or, with papers filed at U.S. consulates abroad, the language of the country where the documents are being filed. An exception exists for papers filed at U.S. consulates in Japan, where all documents must be translated into English. If the documents are not in an acceptable language as just explained, they must be accompanied by a full, word for word, written English translation. Any capable person may act as translator. It is not necessary to hire a professional. At the end of each translation, the following statement must appear:

> *I hereby certify that I translated this document from (language) to English. This translation is accurate and complete. I further certify that I am fully competent to translate from (language) to English.*

The translator should sign this statement but it does not have to be witnessed or notarized.

Later in this chapter we describe in detail the forms and documents needed to get your H-2B visa. A summary checklist of forms and documents appears at the end of this chapter.

D. Who's Who in Getting Your H-2B Visa

Getting an H-2B visa will be easier if you familiarize yourself with the technical names used for each participant in the process. During Steps One and Two, the Temporary Labor Certification and the petition, you are known as the *beneficiary* or the *employee* and your U.S. employer is known as the *petitioner* or the *employer*. In Step Three, the application, you are referred to as *applicant*, but your employer remains the petitioner or employer. If you are bringing your spouse and children with you as accompanying relatives, each of them is known as *applicant* as well.

E. Step One: Temporary Labor Certification

This section includes the information you need to get a Temporary Labor Certification.

1. General Procedures

Temporary Labor Certifications, consisting both of forms and documents, are filed in the U.S. at the local state employment agency office nearest the employer's place of business. We emphasize that this is an office of the state government, not DOL. State government employment agencies assist DOL in the Temporary Labor Certification process by monitoring employers' efforts to locate American workers. However, a regional office of DOL, where the file is sent after the state office finishes its work, makes the final decision on your Temporary Labor Certification. Unlike Labor Certifications for green cards, DOL's decision is only advisory. In Step Two, the petition, INS does not have to accept DOL's findings. However, INS weighs DOL's opinion heavily and it will be difficult to get an H-2B visa without an approved Temporary Labor Certification.

States differ about the exact place and procedures for filing Temporary Labor Certifications. Some designate a single office to accept applications for the entire state while others use a system of several regional offices around the state. A call to the nearest office of the state employment agency in your employer's area of the country will tell you where and how to file Step One papers.

There is no filing fee for a Temporary Labor Certification. If possible, it is better for the employer to file in person so you can be sure that the arrival of the papers is recorded. When filing the papers in person, ask for a dated written receipt. The receipt should be kept in a safe place together with a complete copy of everything submitted. Then your employer can prove when your Temporary Labor Certification was filed and help to locate the papers should they get lost or delayed in processing. When filing by mail, we recommend sending the papers by certified mail, return receipt requested, and again keeping a complete copy for your records.

Because there is no uniformity in operating methods among the various state employment agencies, the length of time it takes to get a Temporary Labor Certification approved varies greatly from one state to another; however, all offices are supposed to give priority to Temporary Labor Certification applications. The application cannot be filed more than 120 days before the worker is needed, and it is likely to take about three months to get approval. In some states, it may take longer. If you have good reason, most DOL offices will expedite the processing of a Temporary Labor Certification if you ask. Your employer must simply include a letter requesting expedited processing and explain why your presence on the job is needed immediately.

2. Advertising Procedures

The Temporary Labor Certification is similar to the Labor Certification process discussed in Chapter 8. State labor departments now monitor recruitment efforts for Labor Certifications. Prior to 1995 they did not.

In general, the procedure consists of efforts on the part of the U.S. employer to recruit American workers for the position that has been offered to a foreign national. It is crucial to the success of the H-2B application for the employer to fail at this attempt. To demonstrate that American workers are in fact unavailable, the job must be publicly advertised. The employer must then wait to see if any qualified U.S. candidates come forward. DOL has established a specific procedure for this advertising.

The procedure begins when the employer files Form ETA-750 with the state labor department. Once this form is submitted, the state labor department will send back a letter to the employer acknowledging receipt of the form and assigning an identification number known as a job-order number to the case. The letter will also give instructions on how to advertise.

It is mandatory that the employer carry out the advertising procedures exactly as required. There are specific guidelines on how and where the advertisements must be placed. Three separate types of advertisements are necessary. First, the state labor department will enter a description of the position, identified by the job-order number, in its state-wide computer bank. For ten days, anyone throughout the state who contacts the labor department will have an opportunity to apply for the job.

Second, the petitioning employer must prepare a written advertisement for the classified section of a newspaper or professional journal. The ad must state the job title, salary and working hours of the position as well as describe the duties and qualifications. It is important that the job descriptions in the ad match the one that appears in the ETA-750 form. The employer cannot reject an American job applicant for lacking any qualification not listed in both the ad and the form.

The advertisement should not give the name or address of the employer's company. Instead, it must contain the address of the state labor department and the job-order number. Prospective U.S. job candidates will be asked to contact the state labor department office and make reference to this number. By having all job candidates contact them directly, the labor department is able to monitor the results of the ad placed by the employer.

Normally, the employer should place the advertisement in the classified section of a standard newspaper circulated in the city where the employer's place of business is located. If the city has only one daily newspaper, the ad should be placed there. If there are two or more daily newspapers in the area, as is common in larger cities, the employer may choose whichever one he prefers. The same ad must be run for three consecutive days.

Sometimes the letter from the state labor department will suggest that the employer advertise in a professional journal, trade journal or national publication, instead of a local newspaper. The employer is not required to follow this suggestion, but unless there is a good business reason for not doing so, it is generally best to comply. When the ad is placed in a national newspaper or journal, it need appear only once instead of three times.

The third type of advertising required for Labor Certification is an official job notice posted at the employer's place of business. The notice must contain the identical language used in the newspaper or journal advertisement, but instead of giving the job-order number, prospective candidates should be asked to contact a specific person in the company. The notice must be posted for at least ten business days on an employee bulletin board or other suitable location on the company premises.

If the job being offered is one represented by a labor union or collective bargaining group, that union or group must also be sent a notice that a Labor Certification application has been filed. This gives the union an opportunity to refer union members for the job.

3. Handling Job Applications

If anyone applies for the job by responding to the advertisement or state labor department listing, the labor department will collect resumes from the candidates and forward them to the employer. The employer must then review the resumes and be prepared to state in writing why each candidate does not meet the *minimum* qualifications for the job as described in the advertisement and on Form ETA-750. The same must be done with candidates who respond directly to the employer from the posting of the in-house notice. Even if a single requested qualification is missing from the resume, that is enough reason for the employer to reject an American job candidate in favor of you, if he wishes to do so. However, when some acceptable resumes do turn up, the employer must interview those people. After the interview, if the employer is unsatisfied and still wishes to employ you, he should again put in writing why the U.S. job candidates were not suitable. Once an interview has been held, the employer is no longer limited to rejecting candidates only because they do not meet the job description as stated in the ad or the ETA-750 form. Poor work habits, lack of job stability, questionable character and similar business considerations, if legitimate, are also satisfactory reasons. In addition, it sometimes comes out in an interview that the prospective worker's qualifications are not in fact what they appeared to be on the resume. This provides still another reason to turn down the U.S. candidate.

DOL does not consider the fact that you may be more qualified than any other candidate to be a valid reason for rejecting an American worker. Being the most qualified is not enough. You must be the *only* one who is qualified. The employer cannot be forced to hire an American who happens to apply for the job as a result of the required advertising, but if a qualified American does turn up and your prospective employer cannot find a solid business reason to reject him, the Temporary Labor Certification application filed on your behalf will fail.

If no suitable American job candidates present themselves, the Temporary Labor Certification will be approved. Then the stamped certification will be sent to your U.S. employer. Only the employer receives communications from DOL because technically it is the company that is seeking Temporary Labor Certification in order to fill a staff need.

4. Temporary Labor Certification Form

A copy of this form can be found in Appendix III.

Form ETA-750, Part A Only

Form ETA-750, Part A, is the only form used in Step One, Temporary Labor Certification. It must be submitted in triplicate. Each of the three forms must be a signed original. Photocopies are not acceptable.

All questions on the ETA-750 should be answered truthfully, as on all government forms. Even if you reveal that you are in the U.S. illegally, that will not necessarily affect the outcome of the Temporary Labor Certification, but giving false information on a government form is a criminal offense and could lead to your deportation from the U.S. There is some risk that if the ETA-750 form discloses that you are presently in the U.S. illegally, DOL will notify INS. Normally, DOL disregards this information and even if INS knows, it usually will not try to deport you when a Tempo-

rary Labor Certification application is in process. Read Chapter 25, *Inadmissibility*, to understand how being out of status affects your ability to get a visa or green card.

The ETA-750 form is divided into Parts A and B. For a Temporary Labor Certification, use only Part A, which asks for a description of the job you are being offered. Be sure there are no qualifications listed in Part A that you, as the potential employee, cannot meet.

One of the questions asked in Part A is the number of years of work experience the job requires. You will eventually be asked to show that you have at least that much experience. When you count up how many years of relevant experience you have to offer, you may not include experience gained from working for your petitioning employer. You must be prepared to prove that you met the minimum experience and education requirements as stated in Part A of the ETA-750 before you started working for the petitioner, even if you have been employed there for some time.

You will remember that a purpose of Step One is to demonstrate to DOL's satisfaction that there are no qualified Americans available for the job in question. DOL does not normally evaluate your job fitness during Step One. By law, this judgment is made by INS in Step Two. Nonetheless, DOL will sometimes send your ETA-750 form back to your employer and ask for proof of your qualifications. This is not a proper request for DOL to make. However, when the demands are not too difficult to meet, giving DOL what it asks for is the easiest and quickest way to keep your case moving.

Although it is not mandatory to verify the employee's qualifications in Step One, don't lose sight of the fact that this will eventually have to be done in Step Two. In Step Two, it must be proven to INS that you can meet every qualification requested by the employer in Part A of Form ETA-750. A Temporary Labor Certification will be approved if no qualified American job candidates come forward, but that doesn't guarantee you will eventually get an H-2B visa. If you can't meet the job qualifications either, the approved Temporary Labor Certification will turn out to be wasted effort. We also reemphasize that you must not only meet the job qualification, you must be able to prove you meet them. Section E5, below explains how to do this.

Now we will look at the ETA-750 form question by question. Most of the questions are straightforward.

Top of the Form. Write in red ink on the top "Temporary Labor Certification." This should assist in expediting your application.

Part A. Questions 1–11. These questions are self-explanatory.

Question 12. DOL is concerned that a petitioning employer may offer a very low salary to discourage Americans from applying for the job. To insure that such a tactic can't work,

DOL has salary guidelines that must be followed. The salary offer listed in Question 12 can be no more than 5% below the average salary paid to workers in the same type of job in the same geographical area where the employer's company is located. This average salary is called the prevailing wage. To find out the prevailing wage for your job, the local state employment agency office makes a wage survey for similar jobs in the area. Most state employment offices have on file wage surveys for various occupations and, upon request, will tell the employer the prevailing wage in response to a faxed request. Before beginning advertising or submitting the ETA-750 form, the employer may wish to call and ask for the amount of the prevailing wage so that he can judge if the salary being offered is high enough to meet Temporary Labor Certification requirements. If the salary listed in Question 12 is more than 5% below the prevailing wage, the Temporary Labor Certification will be turned down.

Question 13. Question 13 asks the employer to describe the job being offered. This question should be answered with as much detail as possible. Daily duties, typical projects, supervisory responsibilities, the kinds and use of any machinery or equipment, foreign language skills needed and so forth should all be thoroughly explained. If there are special job conditions, such as the requirement to live in, or unusual physical demands, these too must be described. The employer should not fail to put down *any* skill or activity the job requires, no matter how obvious it may seem. The ability to reject U.S. workers will depend completely on how well the American job candidates match up to the job description in Question 13. The more detailed the job description, the more possible reasons for rejecting American candidates.

While the employer should do his best to describe the position and its demands fully, he should not invent aspects of the job that don't exist or seem ridiculous. For example, suppose the job opening is for a trainer of bakery managers but in the job description the employer states that all applicants must have a background in nuclear science. This sort of illogical requirement makes it clear to the state employment agency reviewer that the job description is not legitimate, but deliberately made up to discourage American workers from applying. When the job description lacks real-world credibility, the ETA-750 will be sent back and the employer will be asked to justify the more unusual requirements. If the state employment agency reviewer cannot be convinced that the job description reflects the employer's true needs, the Temporary Labor Certification will be denied.

The employer should also guard against asking for such a variety of requirements that the job seems more appropriate for two separate workers instead of one. For example, if the job is that of summer resort restaurant manager and the job description requires the applicant not only to manage the restaurant but to do the cooking as well, the reviewer might say the business really needs two people, a cook and a restaurant manager. Once again, this will result in the Temporary Labor Certification being denied.

Question 14. Question 14 asks for the minimum experience and education the job requires. The answer to this question should describe the demands of the job, not the personal qualifications of the potential H-2B visa recipient. For example, you may have a degree from a technical school representing two years of automotive mechanic's training, but if the position you have been offered is for a live-in housekeeper for the summer, being an automotive mechanic usually has nothing to do with being a housekeeper and therefore should not be mentioned in the answer to this question. Remember, it is the job offer that is being described, not you.

As with salary levels, DOL also has specific guidelines on what the minimum number of years of experience and education should be for a certain kind of job. If your employer calls and asks, the local state employment agency office can tell him exactly the number of years of education and experience they consider a normal minimum for the particular job you have been offered. This number comes from looking up the job in a book called the *Dictionary of Occupational Titles*, and it is available at government bookstores and most public libraries.

The number of years listed for each job in the *Dictionary of Occupational Titles* controls what you may put down in answer to Question 14. You and your employer need not concern yourselves with the *Dictionary of Occupational Titles* other than to know it exists. Keep in mind that the number of years of experience and education it lists for each job is the total allowable years of both experience and education. If you wish to learn more about the *Dictionary of Occupational Titles*, it can be found in most U.S. public libraries or ordered from the U.S. Government Printing Office. It is actually composed of two volumes that must be used together to determine the minimum number of years of background for each job. U.S. company personnel staff or others reading this book who may be working with Labor Certifications on a regular basis may find it useful to familiarize themselves with the *Dictionary of Occupational Titles* and its Specific Vocational Preparation classifications, which dictate the number of years of background presumed necessary for each job. The employer may divide up the years in any way he sees fit, as long as he doesn't go over the total. For example, if the *Dictionary of Occupational Titles* says the job you have been offered warrants a minimum of two years of background, your employer has a choice of requiring two years of education, two years of experience or one of each. He may even divide it by months, requiring, say, six months of training or education and 18 months of experience.

Suppose the employer genuinely feels he needs a person with more total years of education and experience than the *Dictionary of Occupational Titles* indicates. Then a letter from the employer should be submitted with the ETA-750 forms giving the reason he feels additional years of background are justified. DOL will normally respect the employer's judgment if it seems reasonable. In Question 14, if the employer puts down a higher number of years than the *Dictionary of Occupational Titles* allows, it must be supported with an explanatory letter, or the Temporary Labor Certification will be denied. This letter does not have to be in any special form. A simple explanation in your employer's own words will do.

When a certain number of years appears in the box marked "experience," it is understood that this means experience in the same occupation as the job being offered. If the experience is in a different but relevant field, it should go in the box marked "related occupations."

Once again, if, in Question 14, the employer asks for a background of specific education or experience, make sure you yourself can meet these requirements. In Step Two, the petition, you will be asked to prove that you can fulfill the job criteria established in the ETA-750. If you cannot do so, you will not get an H-2B visa.

Part A, Question 15. Question 15 asks the employer to state essential requirements for the job over and above years of formal education or work experience. Any special knowledge or skills detailed in Question 13, such as foreign language ability, familiarity with certain types of machinery or special physical capabilities (the strength to do heavy lifting, for example) should be repeated here. When you reach Step Two, you will have to prove in some way that you can perform the skills listed in Question 15, but you will not have to show an exact number of years of education or on-the-job experience as you will for the qualifications listed in Question 14.

Questions 16 and 17. These questions are self-explanatory.

Questions 18 and 19. These questions ask for the exact dates you wish to be able to work in the U.S. Keep in mind that the H-2B status cannot be approved for more than 12 months at a time and therefore you should not request more than 12 months. The petition will be approved only through the dates requested on the Temporary Labor Certification. Remember, the dates you ask for are the dates you will get, so choose a starting date three or four months after you

begin filing your papers to allow some lead time for visa processing.

Question 20. This question is self-explanatory.

Question 21. Question 21 asks your employer to describe past attempts to hire U.S. workers for the position being offered to you. At this stage, it is not essential that such efforts have already been made. If the U.S. employer has not yet tried to hire a worker for the job, he should write the following statement for Question 21:

"Advertisements and job posting to begin upon receipt of job-order number."

If, however, your employer has already made some attempt to hire a U.S. worker, the nature of these efforts (newspaper ads, use of employment agencies, etc.) and the results should be described here. Of course, we assume any prior efforts to fill the job have failed, or the employer would not be trying to hire you.

5. Temporary Labor Certification Documents

Your U.S. employer must submit to DOL proof and written results of the mandatory advertising procedure. A key document is the employer's written explanation of why each American who applied for the job was unsatisfactory. By far the most acceptable reason for turning down an applicant is failure to meet the requirements as stated on the Form ETA-750 and in the newspaper or journal advertisement, but other reasons are also considered adequate, as long as they reflect valid business concerns.

The pages from the publications where the advertisement appeared must be torn out and submitted. If the ad ran in a newspaper for three days, three pages must be presented, one for each day, even though the exact same ad was published on all three days. Photocopies of the ad are not acceptable. Your employer must obtain a copy of every publication in which the ad appeared and actually tear out the entire page so the date shows.

The submission of all these documents normally completes the Temporary Labor Certification procedure. Once your employer has sent them in, the forms and documents are eventually forwarded from the state employment agency to the regional certifying office of DOL for a decision. If the paperwork has been carefully prepared, the Temporary Labor Certification should be approved on the first try. Sometimes, papers are returned to the employer with a request for additional information or instructions to remedy a defect in the advertising. After mistakes and deficiencies have been corrected, the papers should be returned to DOL. When your employer has finally gotten the paperwork the way DOL wants it, he will get back a decision either granting or denying the Temporary Labor Certification.

FOREIGN LANGUAGE REQUIREMENTS

According to DOL, foreign language capability is not a valid requirement for most jobs, except perhaps the occupations of foreign language teacher or translator. By foreign language capability we mean the ability to speak English plus at least one other language. Many Temporary Labor Certification job descriptions contain a foreign language requirement because petitioning employers know it is a good way to decrease the chances that qualified Americans will apply for the job.

If your employer wants a foreign language capability in his job description, he must prove his need is real by preparing and submitting a signed statement explaining the business reasons for the foreign language requirement. The statement does not have to be in any particular form but it should answer obvious questions the language requirement might raise. What is it about the employer's business that makes knowledge of a foreign language necessary? Why does this position require knowledge of a foreign language if someone else in the company already speaks that language? Why couldn't the company simply hire a translator as a separate employee or use a translator on a part-time basis when the need arises? The statement prepared by the petitioning employer should provide good answers to questions like these. The employer must show that the need for the employee to speak a foreign language is very great and that no alternative arrangement will be an adequate substitute.

A good example of how to approach this problem is an employer who owns a restaurant in a resort and is trying to justify a foreign language requirement for a seasonal waiter. Here, the employer can explain that a large percentage of the restaurant's customers speak the particular foreign language in question and expect to be addressed in that language when they come in to eat. If the restaurant's clientele demand it, it is reasonable that all employees of this restaurant who have contact with the public be able to speak the language of the customers.

DOL doesn't like foreign language requirements because it is well aware that most people who apply for Temporary Labor Certifications have the ability to speak a language other than English. DOL regards this as a poor excuse to keep an American worker from taking a job. Therefore, it is usually best not to include a language requirement, especially if the Temporary Labor Certification is likely to be approved anyway. If, however, the occupation being certified is relatively unskilled, as in the case of the seasonal waiter, a language requirement supported by strong documents showing a real business need may mean the difference between success and failure of the Temporary Labor Certification.

6. Temporary Labor Certification Appeals

If DOL thinks the Temporary Labor Certification is unsatisfactory, it will be denied and the employer will receive a written decision explaining the reasons for the denial. The most common reason for denial is that the job is not temporary in nature. No appeal is available. The Temporary Labor Certification, however, is considered to be only advisory and therefore an H-2B visa petition may be filed with INS even though the Temporary Labor Certification is denied. You will have to convince INS, however, that DOL was wrong.

F. Step Two: The Petition

This section includes the information you need to complete the petition.

1. General Procedures

The U.S. employer submits the petition, consisting of forms and documents, by mail, in duplicate, to the INS regional service center having jurisdiction over your intended employer's place of business. INS regional service centers are not the same as INS local offices. There are four INS regional service centers spread across the U.S. Appendix II contains a list of all INS regional service centers with their addresses.

The filing fee for each petition, if no change of status is being requested, is currently $110. With a change of status request, the fee is an additional $70. Checks or money orders are accepted. It is not advisable to send cash. We recommend submitting all papers by certified mail, return receipt requested, and making a copy of everything sent in to keep in your records.

Within a week or so after mailing in the petition, your employer should get back a written confirmation that the papers are being processed, together with a receipt for the fees. This notice will also give your immigration file number and tell approximately when you should expect to have a decision. If INS wants further information before acting on your case, all petition papers, forms and documents will be returned to your employer with another form known as an I-797. The I-797 tells your employer what additional pieces of information or documents are expected. Your employer should supply the extra data and mail the whole package back to the INS regional service center, with the I-797 on top.

H-2B petitions are normally approved within two to eight weeks. When this happens, a Notice of Action Form I-797 will be sent to your employer showing the petition was approved. If you plan to execute Step Two at a U.S. consulate abroad, INS will also notify the consulate of your choice, sending a complete copy of your file. Only the employer receives communications from INS about the petition because technically it is the employer who is seeking the visa on your behalf.

2. Petition Forms

Copies of all forms can be found in Appendix III.

Form I-129 and H Supplement

The basic form for Step Two, the petition, is immigration Form I-129 and H Supplement. The I-129 form is used for many different nonimmigrant visas. In addition to the basic part of the form that applies to all types of visas, it comes with several supplements for each specific nonimmigrant category. Simply tear out and use the supplement that applies to you. Your employer must file the petition form in duplicate. Send in two signed originals. Copies are not acceptable.

More than one foreign employee may be listed on a single I-129 petition. This is done if the employer has more than one opening to be filled for the same type of job. If more than one employee is to be included, Supplement-1, which is also part of Form I-129, should be completed for each additional employee.

Most of the questions on the I-129 form are straight-forward. If a question does not apply to you, answer it with "None" or "N/A."

Part 1. These questions concern the employer only and are self-explanatory.

Part 2, Question 1. Question should be answered "H-2B."

Questions 2–3. These questions are self-explanatory.

Question 4. This question asks you to indicate what action is requested from INS. Normally you will mark box "a" which tells INS to notify a U.S. consulate abroad of the petition approval so that you may apply for a visa there. If you will be filing your Step Three application in the U.S., mark box "b." If this petition is being filed as an extension, mark box "c."

Question 5. This question is self-explanatory.

Part 3. These questions are self-explanatory. If you previously held a U.S. work permit and therefore have a U.S. Social Security number, put down that number where asked. If you have a Social Security number that is not valid for employment, put down that number followed by "not valid for employment." If you have never had a Social Security number, put down "None."

Alien Registration Numbers, which all begin with the letter "A," are given only to people who have applied for green cards, received political asylum or have been in deportation proceedings. If you have an "A" number, put that number down and also explain how you got it, such as

"number issued from previous green card petition filed by my brother." If you do not have an "A" number, write down "None."

If your present authorized stay has expired, you must disclose that where asked. This makes your ineligible to file Step Three inside the U.S. You may still apply for a visa at a U.S. consulate, but the fact that you remained in the U.S. illegally may affect your ability to get an H-2B visa at a U.S. consulate. You are required to have the intention to return to you home country when your status expires. If you have already lived in the U.S. illegally for a substantial period of time, it will be difficult to convince a consulate that you won't do it again. See Chapter 25 for other problems which may arise from having been out of status in the U.S.

Part 4. These questions are self-explanatory. The fact that you may have a green card petition or application in process makes it less likely your H-2B visa will be approved. If your H-2B employer is sponsoring you for a green card, you will not qualify for the H-2B visa.

Part 5. These questions are self-explanatory. The dates of intended employment should coincide with the dates shown on the Temporary Labor Certification. An H-2B petition cannot be approved beyond its expiration date.

H Supplement, Top of Form. These questions are self-explanatory.

H Supplement, Section 1. Do not complete this section.

H Supplement, Section 2. This question asks if the employment is seasonal or temporary, and asks for your employer to explain why the need is temporary. Temporary employment is defined in Section A2a, above.

H Supplement, Sections 3-4. These do not apply to H-2B petitions and should be left blank.

3.   Petition Documents

You must provide several documents with the Petition.

a.   Temporary Labor Certification

You must submit your approved Temporary Labor Certification. This is actually the ETA-750 Form, Part A, which has been returned to your employer with a red and blue approval stamp. You must submit the original approved form. A copy is not acceptable. If the Temporary Labor Certification was denied, the ETA-750 will be sent back without an approval stamp together with a letter from DOL stating that Temporary Labor Certification cannot be issued.

Whether the Temporary Labor Certification was approved or denied, all of the documentation submitted to the labor department with the ETA-750 will be returned to your employer. The approved Temporary Labor Certification or letter of denial together with all documentation submitted in Step One must be submitted again in Step Two.

b.   Employer's Statement of Need

Your employer must provide a detailed explanation of why the job is temporary, and if the need is seasonal or intermittent, whether the need is expected to occur again. If the job is temporary because it is tied into a specific project of the employer and will terminate upon completion of the project, a copy of the employer's contract for that project should be attached to his affidavit.

c.   Proof of Your Job Qualifications

Documents to prove your own qualifications for the job also go with the petition. There must be evidence that you have the minimum education and experience called for in the advertisements and job description on Form ETA-750. If special requirements were written in Question 15 of Part A of the form, you must prove you have those skills or abilities as well.

Evidence of job experience should include letters or notarized affidavits from previous employers. These do not have to be in any special form but simply in your former employer's own words. The letters should clearly indicate what your position was with the company, your specific job duties and the length of time you were employed. If letters from previous employers are unavailable, you may be able to prove your work experience with your personal tax returns or by affidavits from former coworkers. Proof of special knowledge or skills can be supplied through notarized affidavits, either from you or someone else who can swear you have the special ability (such as skill to use a

particular machine or speak a foreign language) required. These, too, need not be in any special form.

If your employer asked for a specific type or amount of education, diplomas and transcripts from schools attended must be shown to verify your education. INS insists on both a diploma and a transcript from each school where you graduated. (Keep in mind that if you have a college-level diploma in a major field of study related to the type of job you have been offered, you probably qualify for an H-1B visa. H-1B visas are more desirable in many ways than H-2B visas, so if you think you may qualify, read Chapter 17.) If you attended a school but did not graduate, the transcript is required. If you were educated outside the U.S., INS may request a credential evaluation.

d.   Special Documents for Entertainment Industry Workers

Frequently, entertainers will tour the U.S. instead of remaining in one location. If that is the case with your job, your employer must provide a copy of the touring route schedule, including cities and dates of performance.

4.   Petition Interviews

INS rarely holds interviews on H-2B visa petitions but when they do, the interview is always with the employer. If you are in the U.S., you may be asked to appear as well. Interviews are requested only if INS doubts that the documents or information on Form I-129 or H Supplement are genuine. Then the petition file is forwarded from the INS regional service center where it was submitted to the INS local office nearest your employer's place of business and your employer is notified to appear there. The employer may also be asked to bring additional documents at that time. If, after the interview, everything seems in order, the petition will be approved. The best way to avoid an interview is to have the employer document the petition well, from the beginning.

5.   Petition Appeals

When your job qualifications, the temporariness of the position or the ability of the employer to pay your salary have been poorly documented, the petition will probably be denied. Your employer will get a notice of INS's unfavorable decision, a written statement of the reasons for the negative outcome and an explanation of how to appeal.

The best way to handle an appeal is to try avoiding it altogether. Filing an appeal means making an argument to INS that its reasoning was wrong. This is difficult to do successfully. If you think you can eliminate the reason why your petition failed by improving your paperwork, it makes sense to disregard the appeals process and simply file a new petition, being careful to see that it is better prepared than the first.

If the petition was denied because your U.S. employer left out necessary documents that have since been located, the new documents should be sent, together with a written request that the case be reopened, to the same INS office that issued the denial. This is technically called a *Motion to Reopen*. There is a $110 fee to file this motion. Appeals often take a long time. A Motion to Reopen can be concluded faster than an appeal.

If your U.S. employer does choose to appeal, it must be done within 30 days of the date on the Notice of Denial. The appeal should be filed at the same INS office that issued the denial. There is a $110 filing fee. INS will then forward the papers for consideration to the Administrative Appeals Unit of the central INS office in Washington, D.C. In six months or more, your employer will get back a decision by mail. Few appeals are successful.

When an appeal to INS has been denied, the next step is to make an appeal through the U.S. judicial system. Your employer may not file an action in court without first going through the appeals process available from INS. If the case has reached this stage and you are illegally present in the U.S., we strongly recommend seeking representation from a qualified immigration attorney, as you are now in danger of being deported.

G. Step Three: The Application (Consular Filing)

Anyone with an approved H-2B petition can apply for a visa at a U.S. consulate in his or her home country. You must be physically present to apply there. If you have been or are now working or living illegally in the U.S., you may have problems or be ineligible to get an H-2B visa from a U.S. consulate, even if you otherwise qualify. (See Chapter 25.)

1. Benefits and Drawbacks of Consular Filing

The most important benefit to consular filing, making it almost always preferable to U.S. filing, is that only consulates issue visas. When you go through a U.S. filing you get a status, not a visa. (See Chapter 14, Section B, Difference Between a Visa and a Status.) An H-2B approval status by INS confers the same right to work as you receive after entering the U.S. on an H-2B visa, but it does not give you the ability to travel out of the U.S. and get back in again. Therefore, if you want travel privileges, you will at some time have to go through the extra step of applying for a visa at a U.S. consulate, even though you have already applied for and received H-2B status in the U.S.

Moreover, anyone with an approved petition may apply for an H-2B visa at the appropriate consulate. That is not the case with U.S. applications for H-2B status. If you are in the U.S. illegally, consular filing may be your only option. However, if you have been out of status over six or twelve months and depart the U.S. there will be a three- or ten-year wait, respectively, before you can be readmitted. See Chapter 25. You are not eligible to process a change of status application in the U.S. unless your presence and activities in the U.S. have always been legal.

A drawback to consular filing comes from the fact that you must be physically present in the country where the consulate is located to file there. If your petition is ultimately turned down because of an unexpected problem, not only will you have to wait outside the U.S. until the problem is resolved, but other visas in your passport, such as a visitor's visa, may be canceled. It will then be impossible for you to enter the U.S. in any capacity. Consequently, if your H-2B visa case is not very strong and freedom of travel is not essential to you, it might be wise to apply in the U.S., make up your mind to remain there for the duration of the H-2B status and skip trying to get a visa from the consulate.

2. Application General Procedures: Consular Filing

Technically, the law allows you to apply for an H-2B visa at any U.S. consulate you choose. However, if you have ever overstayed your visa status by even one day, you have to apply in your home country. A complete list of all U.S. consulates that process visa applications, together with their addresses and phone numbers, is in Appendix I. However, from a practical standpoint, your case will be given the greatest consideration at the consulate in your home country. Applying in some other country creates suspicion in the minds of the consul officers there about your motives for choosing their consulate. Often, when an applicant is having trouble at a home consulate, he will seek a more lenient office in some other country. This practice of consulate shopping is frowned on by officials in the system. Unless you have a very good reason for being elsewhere (such as a temporary job assignment in some other nation), it is smarter to file your visa application in your home country.

You may not file an application for an H-2B visa at a consulate before your petition has been approved. Once this occurs, the INS regional service center where the petition was originally submitted will forward a complete copy of your file to the U.S. consulate designated on Form I-129 in Step Two. At the same time, a Notice of Action Form

ACADEMIC CREDENTIAL EVALUATIONS

Every country in the world does not operate on the same academic degree and grade level systems found in the U.S. If you were educated in some other country, INS, as part of judging your H-2B eligibility, may ask for an academic credential evaluation from an approved consulting service to determine the American equivalent of your educational level. Evaluations from accredited credential evaluation services are binding on INS. When the results are favorable, that is, when they show you have the equivalent of the educational level required by your U.S. employer, credential evaluations strengthen your case.

We recommend obtaining a credential evaluation in every case where non-U.S. education is a factor. We also advise getting the evaluation before INS asks for it. When the evaluation is favorable, you can automatically include it with your petition since it strengthens your case and saves time in case INS decides to request it later. When the evaluation is unfavorable, and your credentials prove to be less than the equivalent of what your employer has asked for, you should not submit the results unless INS insists you do so. You should consider discussing this with your employer, who may decide to ask for less education when he fills out Form ETA-750, Part A. You should also note that if the credential evaluation shows that you have the educational equivalent of a U.S. university bachelor's degree or more, you are eligible for an H-1B visa and should apply for that instead. H-1B visas are explained in Chapter 16.

Before sending a credential evaluation service your academic documents, you may want to call in advance to discuss your prospects over the telephone. Usually you can then get some idea of the likelihood for receiving good results. If your prospects are truly bleak, you may decide not to order the evaluation and to save the service charge, which is typically around $100.

There are several qualified credential evaluation services recognized by INS. Two of them are:

International Education Research Foundation
P.O. Box 66940
Los Angeles, CA 90066
Telephone: 310-390-6276
Fax: 310-397-7686
Website: http://www.ierf.org

Educational Credential Evaluators, Inc.
P.O. Box 514070
Milwaukee, WI 53203-3470
Telephone: 414-289-3400
Fax: 414-289-3411
Website: http://www.ece.org

The credential evaluation companies listed above will evaluate only formal education. They will not evaluate job experience. American universities offer evaluations of foreign academic credentials and will recognize work experience as having an academic equivalent. Therefore, if you lack formal education but can show many years of responsible experience, you are better off trying to get an evaluation from a U.S. college or university.

When sending your credentials to a U.S. university, include documents showing your complete academic background, as well as all relevant career achievements. Letters of recommendation from former employers are the preferred proof of work experience. Evidence of any special accomplishments, such as awards or published articles, should also be submitted. INS can be influenced, but not bound by, academic evaluations from U.S. colleges and universities.

I-797 indicating approval will be sent directly to your U.S. employer. Once your employer receives this, you should telephone the consulate to see if the petition file has arrived from INS. If the file is slow in coming, ask the consulate to consider granting approval of your H-2B visa based only on the Notice of Action. Many U.S. consulates are willing to do so.

Once the petition is approved, you can simply walk into many consulates with your application paperwork and get your H-2B visa immediately. Others insist on advance appointments. Most U.S. consulates in Canada require you to phone at least two weeks in advance of your interview to receive an appointment. Some, like those in London, prefer to process visa applications by mail. Since procedures among consulates vary, you should always telephone in advance to ask about local policies.

On entering the U.S. with your new H-2B visa, you will be given an I-94 card. It will be stamped with a date showing how long you can stay. Normally, you are permitted to remain up to the expiration date on your H-2B petition. Each time you exit and reenter the U.S., you will get a new I-94 card authorizing your stay up to the final date indicated on the petition.

3. Application Forms: Consular Filing

When you file at a U.S. consulate abroad, the consulate officials will provide you with certain optional forms, designated by an "OF" preceeding a number. Instructions for completing optional forms and what to do with them once they are filled out will come with the forms. We do not include copies of these forms in Appendix III.

4. Application Documents: Consular Filing

You are required to show a valid passport and present one passport-type photograph taken in accordance with the photo instructions in Appendix III. If the consulate has not yet received your INS file containing the paperwork from the approved Temporary Labor Certification and petition, you will then need to show the original Notice of Action, Form I-797, which your employer received from INS by mail. Most consulates will issue H-2B visas based only on the Notice of Action, although some, particularly in Latin America and Asia, insist on seeing the complete INS file. If the consulate wants to see your file and it is late (more than a month) in arriving, you should request that the consulate investigate the file's whereabouts. You, too, can write the INS regional service center where your petition was processed, asking for the file.

For each accompanying relative, you must present a valid passport and one passport-type photograph taken in accordance with the photo instructions in Appendix III. You will also need documents verifying their family relationship to you. You may verify a parent/child relationship by presenting the child's long form birth certificate. Many countries, including Canada and England, issue both short and long form birth certificates. Where both are available, the long form is needed because it contains the names of the parents while the short form does not. If you are accompanied by your spouse, you must prove that you are lawfully married by showing a valid civil marriage certificate. Church marriage certificates are generally unacceptable. (There are a few exceptions, depending on the laws of your particular country. Canadians, for example, may use church marriage certificates if the marriage took place in Quebec Province, but not elsewhere. If a civil certificate is available, however, you should always use it.) You may have married in a country where marriages are not customarily recorded. Tribal areas of Africa are an example. In such situations, call the nearest consulate or embassy representing your home country for help with getting acceptable proof of marriage.

You will need documents establishing your intent to leave the U.S. when your status expires. The consulate will want to see evidence that ties to your home country are so strong you will be highly motivated to return. Proof of such ties can include deeds verifying ownership of a house or other real property, written statements from you explaining that close relatives are staying behind or letters from a company showing that you have a job waiting when you return from the U.S.

5. Application Interviews: Consular Filing

The consulate will frequently require an interview before issuing an H-2B visa. During the interview, a consul officer will examine the data you gave in Step One for accuracy, especially regarding facts about your own qualifications. Evidence of ties to your home country will also be checked. During the interview, you will surely be asked how long you intend to remain in the U.S. Any answer indicating that you are unsure about plans to return or have an interest in applying for a green card is likely to result in a denial of your H-2B visa.

6. Application Appeals: Consular Filing

When a consulate turns down an H-2B visa application, there is no way to make a formal appeal, although you are free to reapply as often as you like. If your visa is denied, you will be told by the consul officer the reasons for the denial. Written statements of decisions are not normally provided. If a lack of evidence about a particular point is the problem, sometimes simply presenting more evidence on an unclear fact can bring a positive change in the result.

The most common reason for denial of an H-2B visa is that the consul officer did not believe you intend to return to your home country when the visa expires. This is particularly common if you have previously lived in the U.S. illegally. The other most likely reasons for having an H-2B visa turned down are because you are found inadmissible or the consulate believes that you are not really qualified for the job.

Certain people who have been refused H-2B visas reapply at a different consulate, attempting to hide the fact that they were turned down elsewhere. You should know that if your application is denied, the last page in your passport will be stamped "Application Received" with the date and location of the rejecting consulate. This notation shows that some type of prior visa application has failed. It serves as a warning to other consulates that your case merits close inspection. If what we have just told you makes you think it would be a good idea to overcome this problem by obtaining a new, unmarked passport, you should also know that permanent computer records are kept of all visa denials.

H. Step Three: The Application (U.S. Filing)

If you are physically present in the U.S., you may apply for H-2B status without leaving the country on the following conditions:

- you have already obtained a Temporary Labor Certification
- you are simultaneously filing paperwork for or have already received an approved petition

- you entered the U.S. legally and not under the Visa Waiver Program
- you have never worked illegally in the U.S.
- the date on your I-94 card has not passed, and
- you are admissible (and not deportable) to the U.S..

If you are admitted as a visitor without a visa under the Visa Waiver Program, you may not carry out Step Three in the U.S. Currently there are 29 participating countries in the Visa Waiver Program, including: Andorra, Argentina, Austria, Australia, Belgium, Brunei, Denmark, Finland, France, Germany, Iceland, Ireland, Italy, Japan, Liechtenstein, Luxembourg, Monaco, The Netherlands, New Zealand, Norway, Portugal, San Marino, Singapore, Slovenia, Spain, Sweden, Switzerland, the United Kingdom and Uruguay. The government has approved Greece for inclusion in the program in the near future.

If you cannot meet these terms, you may not file for H-2B status in the U.S. It is important to realize, however, that eligibility to apply for change of status in the U.S. will not necessarily result in ineligibility for an H-2B visa. Applicants who are barred from filing in the U.S. but otherwise qualify for H-2B status can apply successfully for an H-2B visa at U.S. consulates abroad. To determine if you are eligible for U.S. filing, read Section G, above, and Chapter 25 on inadmissibility.

1. Benefits and Drawbacks of U.S. Filing

Visas are never given inside the U.S. They are issued exclusively by U.S. consulates abroad. If you file in the U.S. and you are successful, you will get H-2B status, but not a visa. This is a major drawback to U.S. applications. H-2B status allows you to remain in the U.S. with H-2B privileges until the status expires, but should you leave the country for any reason before that time, you will have to apply for the visa itself at a U.S. consulate before returning to America. Moreover, the fact that your H-2B status has been approved in the U.S. does not guarantee that the consulate will also approve your visa. Some consulates may even regard your previously acquired H-2B status as a negative factor, an indication that you have deliberately tried to avoid the consulate's authority.

There is another problem which comes up only in U.S. filings. It is the issue of what is called *preconceived intent*. In order to approve a change of status, INS must believe that at the time you originally entered the U.S. as a visitor or with some other nonimmigrant visa, you did not intend to apply for a different status. If INS thinks you had a preconceived plan to change from the status you arrived with to a different status, INS will deny your application. The preconceived intent issue is one less potential hazard you will face if you apply at a U.S. consulate abroad.

On the plus side of U.S. filing, if you come from a place where it is difficult to obtain U.S. visas, such as Latin America or India, your chances for success may be better in the U.S. Another benefit is that when problems do arise with your U.S. application, you can stay in America while they are being corrected, a circumstance most visa applicants prefer. If you run into snags at a U.S. consulate, you will have to remain outside the U.S. until matters are resolved.

2. Application General Procedures: U.S. Filing

The general procedure for filing Step Two in the U.S. is to follow Step One as outlined above, but to mark box "b" in Question 4 of Part 2 of Form I-129, indicating that you will complete processing in the U.S. There is no separate application form for filing Step Two in the U.S. If you have an accompanying spouse or children, however, a separate Form I-539 must be filed for them. When you apply for a change of status, the filing fee for a Step Two petition is presently $180. Checks and money orders are accepted. It is not advisable to send cash. We recommend submitting all papers by certified mail, return receipt requested, and making a copy of everything sent in to keep for your records.

Within a week or two after mailing in the application, you should get back a written notice of confirmation that the papers are being processed, together with a receipt for the fees. This notice will also tell you your immigration file number and approximately when to expect a decision. If INS wants further information before acting on your case, all application papers, forms and documents will be returned together with another form known as an *I-797*. The I-797 tells you what additional pieces of information or documents are expected. You should supply the extra data and mail the whole package back to the INS regional service center.

Applications for an H-2B status are normally approved within two to eight weeks. When this happens, you will receive a Notice of Action Form I-797 indicating the dates for which your status is approved. A new I-94 card will be attached to the bottom of the form.

3. Application Forms: U.S. Filing

Copies of all forms can be found in Appendix III.

Form I-129

Follow the directions for Step Two in Section F2, above, except in Part 2, Question 4, mark box "b" instead of box "a."

Form I-539 (for accompanying relatives only)

Only one application form is needed for an entire family, but if there is more than one accompanying relative, each additional one should be listed on the I-539 supplement.

Part 1. These questions are self-explanatory. "A" numbers are usually given only to people who have previously applied for green cards or who have been in deportation proceedings.

Part 2, Question 1. Mark box "b," and write in "H-4."

Question 2. This question is self-explanatory.

Part 3. In most cases, you will mark Item 1 with the date requested in the Step Two petition. You will also complete Items 3 and 4, which are self-explanatory.

Part 4, Questions 1–2. These questions are self-explanatory.

Question 3. The different parts to this question are self-explanatory; however, items "a" and "b" ask if an immigrant visa petition or adjustment of status application has ever been filed on your behalf. If you are applying for a green card through a relative, this would be Step One, as described in Chapter 5. If you are applying for a green card through employment, this would be Step Two as described in Chapter 8. If you have only begun the Labor Certification, the first step of getting a green card through employment, this question should be answered "no." Answering any of these questions "yes" may make you ineligible for an H-2B status.

4. Application Documents: U.S. Filing

Each applicant must submit an I-94 card, the small white card you received on entering the U.S. Remember, if the date stamped on your I-94 card has already passed, you are ineligible for U.S. filing. If you entered the U.S. under the Visa Waiver Program and have a green I-94 card, you are also ineligible for U.S. filing. Canadians who are just visiting are not expected to have I-94 cards. Canadians with any other type of nonimmigrant status should have them.

You are required to document your qualifications for H-2B status. When you file the application together with the H-2B petition, the documents you submitted as part of Step Two will do double duty as the documents for Step Three.

For each accompanying relative, send in an I-94 card. You will also need documents verifying their family relationship to you. You may verify a parent/child relationship by presenting the child's long form birth certificate. Many countries, including Canada and England, issue both short and long form birth certificates. Where both are available, the long form is needed because it contains the names of the parents while the short form does not. If you are accompanied by your spouse, you must establish that you are lawfully married by showing a valid civil marriage certificate. Church certificates are generally unacceptable. (There are a few exceptions, depending on the laws of your particular country. Canadians, for example, may use church marriage certificates if the marriage took place in Quebec Province, but not elsewhere. If a civil certificate is available, however, you should always use it.) You may have married in a country where marriages are not customarily recorded. Tribal areas of Africa are an example. In such situations, call the nearest consulate or embassy of your home country for help with getting acceptable proof of marriage.

We have emphasized that in order to qualify for an H-2B visa, you must have the intention of returning to your home country when your visa expires. We have explained how consulates will demand evidence that ties to your home country are strong enough to motivate your eventual return. In a U.S. filing, INS does not always ask for proof of this. However, we strongly advise you to submit such evidence anyway. Proof of ties to your home country can include deeds verifying ownership of a house or other real property, written statements from you explaining that close relatives are staying behind or a letter from a company in your home country showing that you have a job waiting when you return from the U.S.

5. Application Interviews: U.S. Filing

Interviews on H-2B change of status applications are rarely held. When an interview is required, the INS regional service center where you filed will send your paperwork to the local INS office nearest your U.S. employer's place of business. This office will in turn contact you for an appointment. (If INS has questions on the petition rather than the application, your employer will be contacted.) INS may ask you to bring additional documents at that time.

If you are called for an interview, the most likely reason is that INS either suspects some type of fraud or has doubts about your intent to return home after the H-2B visa expires. Interviews are a sign of trouble and can delay your application.

6. Application Appeals: U.S. Filing

If your application is denied, you will receive a written decision by mail explaining the reasons for the denial. There is no way of making a formal appeal to INS if your application is turned down. If the problem is too little evidence, you may be able to overcome this obstacle by adding more documents and resubmitting the entire application to the same INS office you have been dealing with, together with a written request that the case be reopened. The written request does not have to be in any special form. This is technically called a *Motion to Reopen*. There is a $110 fee to file this motion.

Remember that you may be denied the right to a U.S. filing without being denied an H-2B visa. When your application is turned down because you are found ineligible for U.S. filing, simply change your application to a consular filing.

Although there is no appeal to INS for the denial of an H-2B change of status application, you do have the right to file an appeal in a U.S. district court. It would be difficult to file such an appeal without employing an immigration attorney at considerable expense. Such appeals are usually unsuccessful.

I. Extensions

H-2B visas may be extended for one year at a time, but you may not hold H-2B status for longer than a total of three years. Therefore, if your visa was first issued for the one-year maximum, you will be allowed two one-year extensions. Extensions are not automatic, nor are they easier to get than the original visa. In fact, extensions are sometimes more difficult to obtain because the longer you remain on a particular job, the less likely DOL and INS are to believe that the job is truly temporary. Moreover, INS has the right to reconsider your qualifications based on any changes in the facts or law. When the original application for an H-2B visa was weak, it is not unusual for an extension request to be turned down. As always, however, good cases that are well prepared will be successful.

To extend your H-2B visa, the Temporary Labor Certification, petition and visa stamp will all have to be updated. As with the original application, you can file either in the U.S. or at a consulate. However, contrary to our advice on the initial visa procedures, in the case of extensions we highly recommend U.S. filing. That is because visa stamps, which can only be issued originally at consulates, may be extended in the U.S.

1. Step One: Temporary Labor Certification

The process for getting an extension of the Temporary Labor Certification is identical in every respect with the one used to obtain the original Temporary Labor Certification. See Section E, above.

2. Step Two: Extension Petition

Extension procedures are identical to the procedures followed in getting the initial visa. Fully document your application so that your case is not delayed if INS cannot locate your previous file.

WORKING WHILE YOUR EXTENSION PETITION IS PENDING

If you file your petition for an extension of H-2B status before your authorized stay expires, you are automatically permitted to continue working for up to 240 days while you are waiting for a decision. If, however, your authorized stay expires after you have filed for an extension but before you receive an approval, and more than 240 days go by without getting a decision on your extension petition, your work authorization ceases and you must stop working.

a. Extension Petition Forms

Copies of all forms can be found in Appendix III.

Form I-129 and H Supplement

Follow the directions for this form under Step Two in Section F2, above. The only difference is that you will mark boxes "2b" and "4c" of Part 2.

Form I-539 (for accompanying relatives only)

Follow the directions for this form under Step Three in Section H3, above, but mark box "1a" of Part 2.

b. Extension Petition Documents

Submit the new Temporary Labor Certification and Notice of Action indicating the approval that your employer received on the original petition. All your personal U.S. income tax returns and W-2 forms for the time period you have already been working in the U.S. on an H-2B visa are required as well. Once INS has these documents, it will notify the employer if any further data are needed.

3. Step Three: Visa Revalidation

This section includes information you need to complete the visa revalidation.

a. Visa Revalidation: U.S. Filing

If you are physically in the U.S. and your H-2B status extension has been approved by INS, you can have your visa revalidated by mail without leaving the country. To do this, you must fill out Form OF-156, following the directions in Section G3, and send it to the Department of State. With the form you should also submit as documents your passport, current I-94 card, Notice of Action Form I-797 and a detailed letter from your employer describing your job duties. You should enclose a self-addressed, stamped envelope, or a completed Federal Express airbill. Send the entire package by certified mail to:

CA/VO/P/D
Department of State
Visa Services
2401 "E" Street, N.W., (SA-1 L-703)
Washington, DC 20522-0106
Telephone: 202-663-1213
Fax: 202-663-1608

The passport will be returned to you with a newly revalidated visa in a few weeks. Nationals of some countries like Mexico are charged a fee for revalidating a visa, while nationals of other countries receive this service at no charge. Whether or not there is a fee depends on the nationality of the applicant, not the place where the application for the visa was originally made. Call the State Department in Washington, D.C. to find out the amount of the revalidation fee, if any. If you send in your revalidation package without the correct fee, it will be returned to you, so check the amount in advance.

If your accompanying relatives are physically in the U.S., their H-4 visas may be revalidated by sending in their passports and I-94 cards together with yours. We strongly advise gathering your family together inside U.S. borders so you can take advantage of this simple revalidation procedure.

b. Visa Revalidation: Consular Filing

If you must leave the U.S. after your extension has been approved but before you had time to get your visa revalidated, you must get a new visa stamp issued at a consulate. Read Section G, above. The procedures for consular extensions are identical.

We would like to reemphasize that it is much more convenient to apply for a revalidated visa by mail through the State Department in Washington, D.C. than it is to extend your H-2B visa through a consulate. If possible, you should try to schedule filing your extension application when you can remain in the U.S. until it is complete.

FORMS AND DOCUMENTS CHECKLIST

STEP ONE: TEMPORARY LABOR CERTIFICATION

Form

☐ Form ETA-750, Part A only.

Documents

☐ Tear sheets from newspapers or journals where advertisements were printed.

☐ Evidence employer posted notice of job opening within place of business.

☐ Employer's written statement of recruitment results.

☐ Employer's written statement explaining why the job is temporary or seasonal.

☐ If you are a touring entertainment industry worker, a written schedule of dates and cities where you will be working.

STEP TWO: PETITION

Form

☐ Form I-129 and H Supplement.

Documents

☐ Approved Temporary Labor Certification.

☐ All documents submitted to DOL in Step One.

☐ Written employment contract.

☐ Detailed written statement from the employer explaining why the position is temporary or seasonal.

☐ If the position is temporary because it is tied to a specific project, a copy of the U.S. employer's contract for that particular project.

☐ Employer's annual report, if it is a public company.

☐ Letters from banks or bank statements indicating the average account balance of the employer's business, if it is a private company.

☐ Accountant's financial statements, including profit and loss statements and balance sheets of the employer's company for the past two years, if available.

☐ Tax returns of the employer's company for the past two years (if it is a private company), if available.

☐ Diplomas from schools attended.

☐ Transcripts from schools attended.

☐ Letters from former employers describing previous experience in detail.

STEP THREE: APPLICATION

Forms

☐ OF forms (available at U.S. consulates abroad for consular filing only).

☐ Form I-129, and H Supplement (U.S. filing only).

☐ Form I-539 (U.S. filing only).

Documents

☐ Notice of approval of the H-2B visa petition.

☐ Valid passport for you and each accompanying relative.

☐ I-94 card for you and each accompanying relative (U.S. filing only).

☐ One passport-type photo of you and each accompanying relative (Consular filing only).

☐ Long form birth certificate for you and each accompanying relative.

☐ Marriage certificate if you are married and bringing your spouse.

☐ If either you or your spouse have ever been married, copies of divorce and death certificates showing termination of all previous marriages.

☐ Documents showing ownership of real estate in your home country.

☐ Documents showing that close family members or property are being left behind in your home country.

☐ Documents showing a job is waiting on your return to your home country.

Temporary Trainees: H-3 Visas

Privileges

- You can participate in a training program offered by a U.S. company and you can work legally in the U.S. for the company that is training you.

- Visas can be issued quickly.

- You may travel in and out of the U.S. or remain here continuously until your H-3 status expires.

- Visas are available for accompanying relatives.

Limitations

- Your primary activity in the U.S. must be receiving training. Any work you perform for the U.S. company must be incidental to the training program. You are restricted to working only for the employer who admitted you to the training program and acted as sponsor for your H-3 visa. If you wish to change training programs, you must get a different H-3 visa.

- Visas can initially be approved for the time needed to complete the training program, although there is usually a maximum of 18 months permitted. Extensions of a year at a time may be allowed, but only if the original training program has not yet been completed.

- Accompanying relatives may stay in the U.S. with you, but they may not work, unless they obtain permission to do so in their own right.

A. How to Qualify

There are no quota restrictions. Step One petitions are normally approved within one to three months. Visas are usually issued within several weeks after petition approval.

You qualify for an H-3 visa if you are coming to the U.S. for on-the-job training to be provided by an American company. Productive employment in the U.S. can be only a minor part of the total program. The purpose of the training should be to further your career in your home country. Similar training opportunities must be unavailable there.

Training programs supporting H-3 visas exist most often in two situations. A company with branches in foreign countries will often train foreign employees in their U.S. branches before sending them to work overseas. Another common training situation occurs when a U.S. company wishes to establish a beneficial business relationship with a foreign company. A good way to do this is by bringing in some of the foreign company's personnel and teaching them about the American business. These people then develop personal ties with the U.S. company.

To qualify for an H-3 visa, you must possess the necessary background in education and experience to complete the U.S. training program successfully. In addition, you are eligible for an H-3 visa only if you intend to return to your home country when the visa expires. Be aware that most people are unable to get H-3 visas because there are few training programs that meet INS's very strict qualifications for such programs.

1. Training Program

You need a specific offer to participate in a job training program from a U.S. company or U.S. government agency to get an H-3 visa. The job training slot you are invited to fill can't be in just any occupation. It must be one that will further your career abroad. The training program must be formal in structure with a curriculum, books and study materials. INS will look closely at the training program to see if it meets INS's standards.

2. Training Is Unavailable in Your Home Country

One of the more difficult requirements for getting an H-3 visa is that the training you will receive in the U.S. must be unavailable to you in your home country. This does not mean that the training cannot exist there, but only that you, personally, do not have access to it.

3. Productive Employment Is Only a Minor Part

Although you can work on an H-3 visa, employment must be merely incidental to the training activities. If the employment aspect takes up so much time that the company could justify hiring a full-time American worker to perform these duties, your H-3 visa will be denied. As a rule, if more than half of your time will be spent on productive employment, you will not qualify for an H-3 visa.

4. Correct Background

You must have the correct background for the training position you are offered. For example, if the training position is as an intern with a U.S. law firm, intended to further your career as an international lawyer, you will have to show that you have a law degree.

5. Intent to Return to Your Home Country

H-3 visas are meant to be temporary. At the time of applying, you must intend to return home when the visa expires. If you have it in mind to take up permanent residence in the U.S., you are legally ineligible for an H-3 visa. The U.S. government knows it is difficult to read minds. Therefore, you can expect to be asked for evidence showing that when you complete your American training, you will go back home and use it there. If you are training for work that doesn't exist in your home country, the nature of the training position itself will make it clear that you do not intend to return. For example, if you will be engaged in a training program for offshore oil drilling and you come from a country that is landlocked and has no oil, no one will believe you plan to take the skills learned in the U.S. back home. As proof that you intend to return home, you will also be asked for evidence that you are leaving behind possessions, property or family members as incentives for your eventual return.

6. Accompanying Relatives

When you qualify for an H-3 visa, your spouse and unmarried children under age 21 can get H-4 visas simply by providing proof of their family relationship to you. H-4 visas authorize your family members to stay with you in the U.S., but not to work there.

APPLYING FOR A GREEN CARD FROM AN H-3 STATUS

If you have an H-3 visa, you can file to get a green card, but being in the U.S. on an H-3 visa gives you no advantage in doing so, and in fact may prove to be a drawback. That is because H-3 visas, like most nonimmigrant visas, are intended only for those who plan to return home once their training or other activities in the U.S. are completed. If you apply for a green card, you are in effect making a statement that you never intend to leave the U.S. Therefore, INS will allow you to keep H-3 status while pursuing a green card only if you are able to convince INS that you did not intend to get a green card when you originally applied for the H-3 visa and that you will return home if you are unable to secure a green card before your H-3 visa expires. Proving these things can be difficult. If you do not succeed, your H-3 status may be taken away. Should this happen, it will in no way affect your green card application. You will simply risk being without your nonimmigrant visa until you get your green card. However, if you are out of status for over six or twelve months, or work without authorization, you may not be able to get your green card. Read Chapter 25 regarding inadmissibility and bars to adjustment of status before you overstay six months or depart the U.S.

If your method of applying for a green card is through employment, as discussed in Chapter 8, there is an even more difficult problem. The ultimate purpose of the H-3 visa is furtherance of your career abroad. By applying for a green card through employment you are making it clear that you are really utilizing the H-3 visa to establish a career in the U.S. and so are no longer qualified for H-3 status. Therefore, although you are permitted to apply for the green card, your H-3 status may be revoked.

B. H-3 Visa Overview

If what you really want is a green card, apply for it directly and disregard H-3 visas. Although it may be more difficult to get a green card, which frequently takes several years, in the long run you will be happier with the results of a green card application, not to mention the fact that you will be obeying the law by not trying to hide your true intentions.

Once you have been offered a training position by a U.S. company, getting an H-3 visa is a two-step process. We have already explained how having foreign trainees can be beneficial to U.S companies. When this is the case, H-3 applicants often expect their U.S. employers to handle the entire process for them and indeed, many large companies are equipped with staff specialists who will do this for highly desirable trainees. Even smaller companies may be prepared to do whatever is necessary, including paying an immigration attorney's fees, in order to attract a trainee who may later prove valuable to them. However, in many cases it is the trainee who is most interested in having the visa issued, and to U.S. employers, the red tape of taking on a foreign trainee can be an unfamiliar nuisance.

As we give you step-by-step instructions for getting an H-3 visa, we will tell you what certain activities are to be performed by your employer and which others are to be done by you. We will discuss each task according to who has legal responsibility for carrying it out. Though the law assumes your employer is performing a particular function, there is nothing to stop you from helping with the work. For example, you can fill out forms intended to be completed by your employer and simply ask him to check them over and sign them. Unless your employer volunteers to help or you are sure the company simply can't live without you, we recommend doing the paperwork yourself. The less your U.S. employer is inconvenienced, the more the company will be willing to act as sponsor for your visa. An imposition on company time or money might cost you a training offer. With the help of this book, you will know how to do all that is required. It is completely legal as well as in your best interest to help whenever possible.

1. Step One: The Petition

The petition is filed by your U.S. employer. All H-3 petitions are submitted to INS regional service centers in the U.S. The object of the petition is to prove four things:

- that a qualifying formal training position has been offered to you by a U.S. company
- that you have the correct background for the training
- that the training is unavailable to you in your home country, and
- that the training will further your career in your home country.

Be aware that an approved petition does not by itself give you any immigration privileges. It is only a prerequisite to Step Two, submitting your application for an H-3 visa. The petition must be approved before you are eligible for Step Two.

2. Step Two: The Application

The application is filed by you and your accompanying relatives, if any. The application is your formal request for an H-3 visa or status. (If you are Canadian, your Step Two procedure will be different from those of other applicants. See Chapter 28, *Canadians: Special Rules.*) Step Two may be carried out in the U.S. at an INS office or in your home country at a U.S. consulate there. If you file Step Two papers in the U.S., you will usually submit them together with those for Step One. When Step Two is dispatched at a U.S. consulate abroad, you must wait to file the application until the Step One petition is first approved.

The vast majority of nonimmigrant visa applications are filed at consulates. The major benefit is that an H-3 visa, which is stamped in your passport, can be issued only by American consulates. When you file Step Two at a consulate, your visa will be stamped in your passport at that time. INS offices inside the U.S. may issue statuses but not visas. (See Chapter 14, Section B, Difference Between a Visa and a Status.)

If you are already in the U.S. legally on some other type of nonimmigrant visa, you may qualify to apply for an H-3 status at an INS office inside the U.S. using a procedure known as *change of nonimmigrant status*. (If you are admitted as a visitor without a visa under the Visa Waiver Program, you may not carry out Step Two in the U.S. Currently there are 29 participating countries in the Visa Waiver Program, including: Andorra, Argentina, Austria, Australia, Belgium, Brunei, Denmark, Finland, France, Germany, Iceland, Ireland, Italy, Japan, Liechtenstein, Luxembourg, Monaco, The Netherlands, New Zealand, Norway, Portugal, San Marino, Singapore, Slovenia, Spain, Sweden, Switzerland, the United Kingdom and Uruguay. The government has approved Greece for inclusion in the program in the near future.) This is simply a technical term meaning you are switching from one nonimmigrant status to another. If a change of status is approved, you will then be treated as if you had entered the country with an H-3 visa and you can keep the status as long as you remain in the U.S. or until it expires, whichever comes first.

You will not, however, receive a visa stamp, which you need if your plans include traveling in and out of the U.S. Again, visa stamps are issued only at U.S. consulates abroad. Therefore, if you change your status and later travel outside the U.S., you will have to go to the U.S. consulate in your home country and repeat Step Two, getting the H-3 visa stamp in your passport, before you can return. This extra procedure makes changing status an unattractive option for all but Canadians, who don't need visas to cross the U.S. border.

3. Paperwork

There are two types of paperwork you must submit to get an H-3 visa. The first consists of official government forms completed by you or your U.S. employer. The second is personal documents such as academic credentials and professional licenses. We will tell you exactly what forms and documents you need.

It is vital that forms are properly filled out and all necessary documents are supplied. You or your U.S. employer may resent the intrusion into your privacy and sizable effort it takes to prepare an immigration applications but you should realize the process is an impersonal matter to immigration officials. Your getting a visa is more important to you than it is to the U.S. government. This is not a pleasant thing to accept, but you are better off having a real understanding of your position. People from all over the world want U.S. visas. There is no shortage of applicants. Take the time and trouble to prepare your papers properly. In the end it will pay off with a successful application.

The documents you or your U.S. employer supply to INS do not have to be originals. Photocopies of all documents are acceptable as long as you have the originals in your possession and are willing to produce them at the request of INS. Documents submitted to U.S. consulates, on the other hand, must be either originals or official government certified copies. Government certified copies and notarized copies are not the same thing. Documents which have only been notarized are not acceptable. They must carry a government seal. In addition to any original or government certified copies of documents submitted to a consulate, you should submit plain photocopies of each document as well. After the consulate compares the copies with the originals, it will return the originals.

Documents will be accepted if they are in either English, or, with papers filed at U.S. consulates abroad, the language of the country where the documents are being filed. An exception exists for papers filed at U.S. consulates in Japan, where all documents must be translated into English. If the documents are not in an acceptable language as just explained, they must be accompanied by a full, word for word, written English translation. Any capable person may act as translator. It is not necessary to hire a professional. At the end of each translation, the following statement must appear:

I hereby certify that I translated this document from (language) to English. This translation is accurate and complete. I further certify that I am fully competent to translate from (language) to English.

The translator should sign this statement but it does not have to be witnessed or notarized.

Later in this chapter we describe in detail the forms and documents needed to get your H-3 visa. A summary checklist of forms and documents appears at the end of this chapter.

C. Who's Who in Getting Your H-3 Visa

Getting an H-3 visa will be easier if you familiarize yourself with the technical names used for each participant in the process. During Step One, the petition, you are known as the *beneficiary* or the *trainee* and your U.S. employer is known as the *petitioner* or the *employer*. In Step Two, the application, you are referred to as *applicant*, but your employer remains the petitioner or employer. If you are bringing your spouse and children with you as accompanying relatives, each of them is known as *applicant* as well.

D. Step One: The Petition

This section includes the information you need to submit the petition.

1. General Procedures

The U.S. employer submits the petition, consisting of forms and documents, by mail, in duplicate, to the INS regional service center having jurisdiction over your intended employer's place of business. INS regional service centers are not the same as INS local offices. There are four INS regional service centers spread across the U.S. Appendix II contains a list of all INS regional service centers with their addresses.

The filing fee for each petition, if no change of status (Step Two, U.S. Filing) is being requested, is currently $85. With a change of status request, the fee is $155. Checks or money orders are accepted. It is not advisable to send cash. We recommend submitting all papers by certified mail, return receipt requested, and making a copy of everything sent in to keep in your records.

Within a week or so after mailing in the petition, your employer should get back a written confirmation that the papers are being processed, together with a receipt for the fees. This notice will also give your immigration file number and tell approximately when you should expect to have a decision. If INS wants further information before acting on your case, all petition papers, forms and documents will be returned to your employer with another form known as an I-797. The I-797 tells your employer what additional pieces of information or documents are expected. Your employer should supply the extra data and mail the whole package back to the INS regional service center, with the I-797 on top.

H-3 petitions are normally approved within three to eight weeks. When this happens, a Notice of Action Form I-797 will be sent to your employer showing the petition was approved. If you plan to execute Step Two at a U.S.

consulate abroad, INS will also notify the consulate of your choice, sending the consulate a complete copy of your file. Only the employer receives communications from INS about the petition because technically it is the employer who is seeking the visa on your behalf.

2. Petition Forms

Copies of all forms can be found in Appendix III.

Form I-129 and H Supplement

The basic form for Step One, the petition, is immigration Form I-129 and H Supplement. The I-129 form is used for many different nonimmigrant visas. In addition to the basic part of the form that applies to all types of visas, it comes with several supplements for each specific nonimmigrant category. Simply tear out and use the supplement that applies to you. Your employer must file the petition form in duplicate. Send in two signed originals. Copies are not acceptable.

More than one foreign employee may be listed on a single I-129 petition. This is done if the employer has more than one opening to be filled for the same type of training position. If more than one employee is to be included, Supplement-1, which is also part of Form I-129, should be completed for each additional employee.

Most of the questions on the I-129 form are straightforward. If a question does not apply to you, answer it with "None" or "N/A."

Part 1. These questions concern the employer only and are self-explanatory.

Part 2, Question 1. Question 1 should be answered "H-3."
Questions 2–3. These questions are self-explanatory.
Question 4. This question asks you to indicate what action is requested from INS. Normally you will mark box "a" which tells INS to notify a U.S. consulate abroad of the petition approval so that you may apply for a visa there. If you will be filing your Step Two application in the U.S., mark box "b." If this petition is being filed as an extension, mark box "c."
Question 5. This question is self-explanatory.
Part 3. These questions are self-explanatory. If you previously held a U.S. work permit and therefore have a U.S. Social Security number, put down that number where asked. If you have a Social Security number that is not valid for employment, put down that number followed by "not valid for employment." If you have never had a Social Security number, put down "None."

Alien Registration Numbers, which all begin with the letter "A," are given only to people who have applied for green cards, received political asylum or have been in deportation proceedings. If you have an "A" number, put that number down and explain how you got it, such as "number issued from previous green card petition filed by my brother." If you do not have an "A" number, write down "None."

If your present authorized stay has expired, you must disclose that where asked. This may affect your ability to get an H-3 visa at a U.S. consulate, especially if you have been out of status for a long time, but if you are out of status now, you cannot file Step Two inside the U.S.

Part 4. These questions are self-explanatory. If a green card petition has been filed on you behalf, you will probably not be able to get an H-3 visa since you are required to have the intention to return to your home country after the training program is completed.

Part 5. These questions are self-explanatory. The dates of intended training should not exceed a total of 18 months, which is the maximum period of time for which an H-3 petition may be approved.

H Supplement, Top of Form. These questions are self-explanatory.

H Supplement, Sections 1–3. These do not apply to H-3 petitions and should be left blank.

H Supplement, Section 4. Each question in this section is self-explanatory. Remember that the training should be unavailable to you in your home country and you must have the intention to return to your home country after it is completed. INS is very suspicious of most H-3 petitions. Therefore, Section 4 requires a written explanation of why the employer is willing to incur the cost of training you. There should be some logical way in which your training will financially benefit the U.S. employer, such as to help it with business abroad after you return to your home country.

3. Petition Documents

You must provide several documents with the petition.

a. Describing the Training Program

Your employer must submit a detailed statement describing the type of training and giving the number of hours that will be devoted to classroom instruction, on-the-job training, productive employment and unsupervised work or study. Also, include a description of the curriculum, giving the names of any textbooks to be used and the specific subjects to be covered.

b. Showing Training Is Unavailable in Your Home Country

Your employer must present some type of evidence to prove that you cannot receive the training in your home country. This is best shown by letters or affidavits from authorities in your home country who are leaders of industry, officials in government or administrators in universities. The letters should give the name and position of the writer. In these letters it should be stated that the writer is acquainted with the training program you intend to pursue in the U.S. and that similar training is not available in your home country. It may take a lot of effort to get

these statements, but without them, the H-3 visa stands little chance of approval.

c. Showing How Training Will Further Your Career

Ideally, the H-3 training program will be related to your current occupation at home. In that case, your U.S. employer can show the nature of your present job with a letter from your foreign employer explaining how the training will further your career in your home country. If you are not now employed in the occupation for which you hope to get U.S. training, it would be very helpful to your case to have a letter from a company in your homeland offering you a job based on the completion of your training in the U.S. If you can't get a letter containing a specific job offer for the future, you will have to present evidence that jobs in the field for which you are training are available. Your U.S. employer must then submit a general statement from a leader in the industry for which you will be trained or an official of the government department of labor in your home country, confirming that there is a demand for persons with the type of training you will receive in the U.S.

d. Proving You Are Qualified for the Training Program

If the nature of the training you will receive requires special background for entering the program, the U.S. employer must submit evidence with the petition showing that you have that background. For example, if the training is at a professional level, such as internships for lawyers or engineers, your employer must submit evidence that you are already qualified to practice law or engineering at home. He should also submit copies of your diplomas, and if you have previous professional work experience, letters from your foreign employers describing the nature and length of your previous employment.

4. Petition Interviews

INS rarely holds interviews on H-3 visa petitions but when it does, the interview is always with the employer. If you are in the U.S., you may be asked to appear as well. Interviews are requested only if INS doubts that the documents or information on Form I-129 or H Supplement are genuine. Then the petition file is forwarded from the INS regional service center where it was submitted to the INS local office nearest your employer's place of business and your employer is notified to appear there. The employer may also be asked to bring additional documents at that time. If, after the interview, everything seems in order, the petition will be approved. The best way to avoid an interview is to have the employer document the petition well from the beginning.

5. Petition Appeals

When the existence of a legitimate training position or the unavailability of such training in your home country has been poorly documented, the petition will probably be denied. Your employer will then get a notice of INS's unfavorable decision, a written statement of the reasons for the negative outcome and an explanation of how to appeal.

The best way to handle an appeal is to try avoiding it altogether. Filing an appeal means making an argument to INS that its reasoning was wrong. This is not something INS likes to hear. If you think you can eliminate the reason why your petition failed by improving your paperwork, it makes sense to disregard the appeals process and simply file a new petition, being careful to see that it is better prepared than the first.

If the petition was denied because your U.S. employer left out necessary documents that have since been located, the new documents should be sent together with a written request that the case be reopened to the same INS office that issued the denial. This is technically called a *Motion to Reopen.* There is a $110 fee to file this motion. Appeals often take a long time. A Motion to Reopen can be concluded faster than an appeal.

If your U.S. employer does choose to appeal, it must be done within 30 days of the date on the Notice of Denial. The appeal should be filed at the same INS office that issued the denial. There is a $110 filing fee. INS will then forward the papers for consideration to the Administrative Appeals Unit of the central INS office in Washington, D.C. In six months or more, your employer will get back a decision by mail. Only a small number of appeals are successful.

When an appeal to INS has been denied, the next step is to make an appeal through the U.S. judicial system. Your employer may not file an action in court without first going through the appeals process available from INS. If the case has reached this stage and you are illegally present in the U.S., we strongly recommend seeking representation from a qualified immigration attorney, as you are now in danger of being deported.

E. Step Two: The Application (Consular Filing)

If you are Canadian, your Step Two procedures will be different from those of other applicants. See Chapter 28, *Canadians: Special Rules,* for details.

Anyone with an approved H-3 petition can apply for a visa at a U.S. consulate in his or her home country. You must be physically present to apply there. If you have been or are now working or living illegally in the U.S., you may not be able to get an H-3 visa from a U.S. consulate even if you otherwise qualify. Read Chapters 14 and 25 to determine whether you are admissible to the U.S. as a nonimmigrant and otherwise qualified to apply for a visa.

1. Benefits and Drawbacks of Consular Filing

The most important benefit to consular filing, making it almost always preferable to U.S. filing, is that only consulates issue visas. When you go through a U.S. filing, you get a status, not a visa. (See Chapter 14, Section B, Difference Between a Visa and a Status.) An H-3 status does not give you the ability to travel out of the U.S. and get back in again. Therefore, if you want travel privileges, you will at some time have to go through the extra step of applying for a visa at a U.S. consulate, even though you have already applied for and received H-3 status in the U.S.

Moreover, anyone with an approved petition may apply for an H-3 visa at the appropriate consulate. That is not the case with U.S. applications for H-3 status. If you are in the U.S. illegally, consular filing may be the only option, but see Chapter 25 to make sure that you qualify. You may not be eligible to process a status application in the U.S. unless your presence and activities in the U.S. have been consistent with your immigration status.

A drawback to consular filing comes from the fact that you must be physically present in the country where the consulate is located to file there. If your petition is ultimately turned down because of an unexpected problem, not only will you have to wait outside the U.S. until the problem is resolved, but other visas in your passport, such as a visitor's visa, may be canceled. It will then be impossible for you to enter the U.S. in any capacity. Consequently, if your H-3 visa case is not very strong and freedom of travel is not essential to you, it might be wise to apply in the U.S., make up your mind to remain there for the duration of the H-3 status and skip trying to get a visa from the consulate.

2. Application General Procedures: Consular Filing

Technically, the law allows you to apply for an H-3 visa at any U.S. consulate you choose. A complete list of all U.S. consulates that process visa applications, together with their addresses and phone numbers, is in Appendix I. However, from a practical standpoint, your case will be given the greatest consideration at the consulate in your home country. Applying in some other country creates suspicion in the minds of the consul officers there about your motives for choosing their consulate. Often, when an applicant is having trouble at a home consulate, he will seek a more lenient office in some other country. This practice of consulate shopping is frowned on by officials in the system. Unless you have a very good reason for being elsewhere (such as a temporary job assignment in some other nation), it is smarter to file your visa application in your home country.

You may not file an application for an H-3 visa at a consulate before your petition has been approved. Once this occurs, the INS regional service center where the petition was originally submitted will forward a complete copy of your file to the U.S. consulate designated on Form I-129 in Step One. At the same time, a Notice of Action Form I-797 indicating approval will be sent directly to your U.S. employer. Once your employer receives this, you should telephone the consulate to see if the petition file has arrived from INS. If the file is slow in coming, ask the consulate to consider granting approval of your H-3 visa based only on the Notice of Action. Many U.S. consulates are willing to do so.

Once the petition is approved, you can simply walk into many consulates with your application paperwork and get your H-3 visa immediately. Others insist on advance appointments. Most U.S. consulates in Canada require you to make an appointment by telephone. Some, like the consulates in London and Germany, prefer to process visa applications by mail. Since procedures among consulates vary, you should always telephone in advance to ask about local policies.

On entering the U.S. with your new H-3 visa, you will be given an I-94 card. It will be stamped with a date showing how long you can stay. Normally, you are permitted to remain up to the expiration date on your H-3 petition. Each time you exit and reenter the U.S., you will get a new I-94 card authorizing your stay up to the final date indicated on the petition.

3. Application Forms: Consular Filing

When you file at a U.S. consulate abroad, the consulate officials will provide you with certain optional forms, designated by an "OF" preceeding a number. Instructions for completing optional forms and what to do with them once they are filled out will come with the forms. We do not include copies of these forms in Appendix III.

4. Application Documents: Consular Filing

You must show a valid passport and present one passport-type photograph taken in accordance with the photo instructions in Appendix III. If the consulate has not yet received your INS file containing the paperwork from the approved petition, you will then need to show the original Notice of Action, Form I-797, which your employer received from INS by mail. Most consulates will issue H-3 visas based only on the Notice of Action, although some, particularly in South America and Asia, insist on seeing the complete INS file. If the consulate wants to see your file and it is late (more than a month) in arriving, you should request that the consulate investigate the file's whereabouts. You, too, can write the INS regional service center where your petition was processed, asking them to look for the file.

For each accompanying relative, you must present a valid passport and one passport-type photograph taken in accordance with the photo instructions in Appendix III. You will also need documents verifying their family relationship to you. You may verify a parent/child relationship by presenting the child's long form birth certificate. Many countries, including Canada and England, issue both short and long form birth certificates. Where both are available,

the long form is needed because it contains the names of the parents while the short form does not. If you are accompanied by your spouse, you must prove that you are lawfully married by showing a valid civil marriage certificate. Church certificates are generally unacceptable. (There are a few exceptions, depending on the laws of your particular country. Canadians, for example, may use church marriage certificates if the marriage took place in Quebec Province, but not elsewhere. If a civil certificate is available, however, you should always use it.) You may have married in a country where marriages are not customarily recorded. Tribal areas of Africa are an example. In such situations, call the nearest consulate or embassy of your home country for help with getting acceptable proof of marriage.

You will need documents establishing your intent to leave the U.S. when your visa expires. The consulate will want to see evidence that ties to your home country are so strong you will be highly motivated to return. Proof of such ties can include deeds verifying ownership of a house or other real property, written statements from you explaining that close relatives are staying behind or letters from a company showing that you have a job waiting when you return from the U.S.

5. Application Interviews: Consular Filing

The consulate will frequently require an interview before issuing an H-3 visa. During the interview, a consul officer will examine the data you gave in Step One for accuracy, especially regarding facts about your own qualifications. Evidence of ties to your home country will also be checked. During the interview, you will surely be asked how long you intend to remain in the U.S. Any answer indicating that you are unsure about plans to return or have an interest in applying for a green card is likely to result in a denial of your H-3 visa.

6. Application Appeals: Consular Filing

When a consulate turns down an H-3 visa application, there is no way to make a formal appeal, although you are free to reapply as often as you like. If your visa is denied, you will be told by the consul officer the reasons for the denial. Written statements of decisions are not normally provided in nonimmigrant cases. If a lack of evidence about a particular point is the problem, sometimes simply presenting more evidence on an unclear fact can bring a positive change in the result.

The most common reason for denial of an H-3 visa is that the consul officer does not believe you intend to return to your home country when the visa expires. Another likely reason for having an H-3 visa turned down is because you

are found inadmissible or the consulate believes that you are not really qualified for the training position.

Certain people who have been refused H-3 visas reapply at a different consulate, attempting to hide the fact that they were turned down elsewhere. You should know that if your application is denied, the last page in your passport will be stamped "Application Received" with the date and location of the rejecting consulate. This notation shows that some type of prior visa application has failed. It serves as a warning to other consulates that your case merits close inspection. If what we have just told you makes you think it would be a good idea to overcome this problem by obtaining a new, unmarked passport, you should also know that permanent computer records are kept of all visa denials.

F.   Step Two: The Application (U.S. Filing)

If you are physically present in the U.S., you may apply for H-3 status without leaving the country on the following conditions:

- you are simultaneously filing paperwork for or have already received an approved petition
- you entered the U.S. legally
- you have never worked illegally in the U.S., and
- the date on your I-94 card has not passed.

If you were admitted as a visitor without a visa under the Visa Waiver Program, you may not carry out Step Two in the U.S. Currently there are 29 participating countries in the Visa Waiver Program, including: Andorra, Argentina, Austria, Australia, Belgium, Brunei, Denmark, Finland, France, Germany, Iceland, Ireland, Italy, Japan, Liechtenstein, Luxembourg, Monaco, The Netherlands, New Zealand, Norway, Portugal, San Marino, Singapore, Slovenia, Spain, Sweden, Switzerland, the United Kingdom and Uruguay. The government has approved Greece for inclusion in the program in the near future.

If you cannot meet these terms, you may not file for H-3 status in the U.S. It is important to realize, however, that eligibility to apply in the U.S. has nothing to do with overall eligibility for an H-3 visa. Applicants who are barred from filing in the U.S. but otherwise qualify for H-3 status can often apply successfully for an H-3 visa at U.S. consulates abroad. If you find you are not eligible for U.S. filing, read Section E, above, and be sure to understand Chapter 25's discussion of overstays and inadmissibility before departing the U.S.

1.   Benefits and Drawbacks of U.S. Filing

Visas are never given inside the U.S. They are issued exclusively by U.S. consulates abroad. If you file in the U.S. and you are successful, you will get H-3 status but not a visa. This is a major drawback to U.S. applications. H-3 status allows you to remain in the U.S. with H-3 privileges until the status expires, but should you leave the country for any reason before that time, you will have to apply for the visa itself at a U.S. consulate before returning to America. Moreover, the fact that your H-3 status has been approved in the U.S. does not guarantee that the consulate will also approve your visa. Some consulates may even regard your previously acquired H-3 status as a negative factor, an indication that you have deliberately tried to avoid the consulate's authority.

There is another problem which comes up only in U.S. filings. It is the issue of what is called *preconceived intent*. To approve a change of status, INS must believe that at the time you originally entered the U.S. as a visitor or with some other nonimmigrant visa, you did not intend to apply for a different status. If INS thinks you had a preconceived plan to change from the status you arrived with to a different status, INS may deny your application. The preconceived-intent issue is one less potential hazard you will face if you apply at a U.S. consulate abroad.

On the plus side of U.S. filing is that when problems do arise with your U.S. application, you can stay in America while they are being corrected, a circumstance most visa applicants prefer. If you run into snags at a U.S. consulate, you will have to remain outside the U.S. until matters are resolved.

2. Application General Procedures: U.S. Filing

The general procedure for filing Step Two in the U.S. is to follow Step One as outlined above, but to mark box "b" in Part 2, Question 4 of Form I-129, indicating that you will complete processing in the U.S. There is no separate application form for filing Step Two in the U.S. If you have an accompanying spouse or children, however, a separate Form I-539 must be filed for them.

When you apply for a change of status, the filing fee for a Step One petition is presently $180. Checks and money orders are accepted. It is not advisable to send cash. We recommend submitting all papers by certified mail, return receipt requested, and making a copy of everything sent in to keep for your records.

Within a week or two after mailing in the application, you should get back a written notice of confirmation that the papers are being processed, together with a receipt for the fees. This notice will also tell you your immigration file number and approximately when to expect a decision. If INS wants further information before acting on your case, all application papers, forms and documents will be returned together with another form known as an I-797. The I-797 tells you what additional pieces of information or documents are expected. You should supply the extra data and mail the whole package back to the INS regional service center.

Applications for an H-3 status are normally approved within one to three months. When this happens, you will receive a Notice of Action Form I-797 indicating the dates for which your status is approved. A new I-94 card is attached to the bottom of the form.

3. Application Forms: U.S. Filing

Copies of all forms can be found in Appendix III.

Form I-129

Follow the directions in Section D2, above, except in Part 2, Question 4, mark box "b" instead of box "a."

Form I-539 (for accompanying relatives only)

Only one application form is needed for an entire family, but if there is more than one accompanying relative, each additional one should be listed on the I-539 supplement.

Part 1. These questions are self-explanatory. "A" numbers are usually given only to people who have previously applied for green cards or who have been in deportation proceedings.

Part 2, Question 1. Mark box "b," and write in "H-4."

Question 2. This question is self-explanatory.

Part 3. In most cases, you will mark Item 1 with the date requested in the Step One petition. You will also complete Items 3 and 4, which are self-explanatory.

Part 4, Questions 1–2. These questions are self-explanatory.

Question 3. The different parts to this question are self-explanatory; however, items "a" and "b" ask if an immigrant visa petition or adjustment of status application has ever been filed on your behalf. If you are applying for a green card through a relative, this would be Step One, in Chapter 5. If you are applying for a green card through employment, this would be Step Two in Chapter 8. If you have only begun the Labor Certification, the first step of getting a green card through employment, this question should be answered "no." Answering any of these questions "yes" may make you ineligible for H-3 status.

4. Application Documents: U.S. Filing

Each applicant must submit an I-94 card, the small white card you received on entering the U.S. Remember, if the date stamped on your I-94 card has already passed, you are ineligible for U.S. filing. If you entered the U.S. under the Visa Waiver Program and have a green I-94 card, you are also ineligible for U.S. filing. Canadians who are just visiting are not expected to have I-94 cards. Canadians with any other type of nonimmigrant status should have them.

You must document your qualifications for H-3 status. When you file the application together with the H-3 petition, the documents you submitted as part of Step One will do double duty as the documents for Step Two. If the petition was submitted first and then approved, you can simply submit a copy of Form I-797, Notice of Action instead.

For each accompanying relative, send in an I-94 card. You will also need documents verifying their family relationship to you. You may verify a parent/child relationship by presenting the child's long form birth certificate. Many countries, including Canada and England, issue both short and long form birth certificates. Where both are available, the long form is needed because it contains the names of the parents while the short form does not. If you are accompanied by your spouse, you must prove that you are lawfully married by showing a civil marriage certificate. Church marriage certificates are generally unacceptable. (There are a few exceptions, depending on the laws of your particular country. Canadians, for example, may use church marriage certificates if the marriage took place in Quebec Province, but not elsewhere. If a civil certificate is available, however, you should always use it.) You may have married in a country where marriages are not customarily recorded. Tribal areas of Africa are an example. In such situations call the nearest consulate or embassy of your home country for help with getting acceptable proof of marriage.

We have emphasized that to qualify for an H-3 visa, you must have the intention of returning to your home country when your visa expires. We have explained how consulates will demand evidence that ties to your home country are strong enough to motivate your eventual return. In a U.S. filing, INS does not always ask for proof of this. However, we strongly advise you to submit such evidence anyway. Proof of ties to your home country can include deeds verifying ownership of a house or other real property, written statements from you explaining that close relatives are staying behind or letters from a company in your home country showing that you have a job waiting when you return from the U.S.

5. Application Interviews: U.S. Filing

Interviews on H-3 change of status applications are rarely held. When an interview is required, the INS regional service center where you filed will send your paperwork to the INS local office nearest your U.S. employer's place of business. This office will in turn contact you for an appointment. (If INS has questions on the petition rather than the application, your employer will be contacted.) INS may ask you to bring additional documents at that time.

If you are called for an interview, the most likely reason is that INS either suspects some type of fraud or has doubts about your intent to return home after the H-3 visa expires. Because they are not common and usually a sign of trouble, these interviews can result in considerable delays.

6. Application Appeals: U.S. Filing

If your application is denied, you will receive a written decision by mail explaining the reasons for the denial. There is no way of making a formal appeal to INS if your application is turned down. If the problem is too little evidence, you may be able to overcome this obstacle by adding more documents and resubmitting the entire application to the same INS office you have been dealing with together with a written request that the case be reopened. The written request does not have to be in any special form. This is technically called a *Motion to Reopen*. There is a $110 fee to file this motion.

Remember that you may be denied the right to a U.S. filing without being denied the right to eventually take up that status after getting an H-3 visa. When your application is turned down because you are found ineligible for U.S. filing, simply change your application to a consular filing. (See Chapter 25, however, before departing the U.S. to make sure you are not subject to the three- or ten-year waiting periods.)

Although there is no appeal to INS for the denial of an H-3 change of status application, you do have the right to file an appeal in a U.S. district court. It would be difficult to file such an appeal without employing an immigration attorney at considerable expense. Such appeals are usually unsuccessful.

G. Extensions

H-3 visas can be extended for up to a total of two years' time in H-3 status. Although an extension is usually easier to get than the status itself, it is not automatic. INS has the right to reconsider your qualifications based on any changes in the facts or law. When the original application for an H-3 visa was weak, it is not unusual for an extension request to be turned down. As always, however, good cases that are well prepared will be successful.

To extend your H-3 visa, the petition, I-94 card and visa stamp will all have to be updated. As with the original application, you can file either in the U.S. or at a consulate. However, contrary to our advice on the initial visa procedures, for extension we highly recommend U.S. filing. That is because visa stamps, which can only be issued originally at consulates, may be extended in the U.S.

1. Step One: Extension Petition

Extension procedures are identical to the procedures followed in getting the initial visa. The petition should be fully documented in the same manner as it was prepared for the initial petition, including a letter from the employer requesting your status be extended with an explanation of why the training has not yet been completed and a copy of your U.S. income tax returns for the previous year, including W-2 forms.

WORKING WHILE YOUR EXTENSION PETITION IS PENDING

If you file your petition for an extension of H-3 status before your authorized stay expires, you are automatically permitted to continue working for up to 240 days while you are waiting for a decision. If, however, your authorized stay expires after you have filed for an extension but before you receive an approval, and more than 240 days go by without getting a decision on your extension petition, work authorization ceases.

---

a. Extension Petition: Forms

Copies of all forms can be found in Appendix III.

Form I-129 and H Supplement

Follow the directions in Section D2, above. The only difference is that you will mark boxes "2b" and "4c" of Part 2.

Form I-539 (for accompanying relatives only)

Follow the directions in Section E3, above, but mark box "a" of Part 2, Question 1.

b. Extension Petition: Documents

You must submit your I-94 card. You should also submit the original Notice of Action I-797, a letter from your employer stating that your extension is required and the reason why your training is not yet completed and a copy of your personal U.S. income tax returns for the past year, including form W-2. (Be sure no employment other than that for your H-3 employer is reflected in your tax documents.)

2. Step Two: Visa Revalidation

This section includes information you need to complete the extension petition.

a. Visa Revalidation: U.S. Filing

If you are physically in the U.S. and your H-3 status extension has been approved by INS, you can have your visa revalidated by mail without leaving the country. To do this, you must fill out Form OF-156, following the directions in Section E3, above, and send it to the Department of State. With the form you should also submit as documents your passport, current I-94 card, Notice of Action Form I-797 and a detailed letter from your employer describing your training and job duties. You should enclose a self-addressed, stamped envelope, or a completed Federal Express airbill. Send the entire package by certified mail to:

CA/VO/P/D
Department of State
Visa Services
2401 "E" Street, N.W., (SA-1 L-703)
Washington, DC 20522-0106
Telephone: 202-663-1213
Fax: 202-663-1608

The passport will be returned to you with a newly revalidated visa in a few weeks. Nationals of some countries like Mexico are charged a fee for revalidating a visa, while nationals of other countries receive this service at no charge. Whether or not there is a fee depends on the nationality of the applicant, not the place where the application for the visa was originally made. You may call the State Department in Washington, D.C. to find out the amount of the revalidation fee, if any. If you send in your revalidation package without the correct fee, it will be returned to you, so check the amount in advance.

If your accompanying relatives are physically in the U.S., their H-4 visas may be revalidated by sending in their passports and I-94 cards together with yours. We strongly advise gathering your family together inside U.S. borders so you can take advantage of this simple revalidation procedure.

b. Visa Revalidation: Consular Filing

If you must leave the U.S. after your extension has been approved but before you had time to get your visa revalidated, you must get a new visa stamp issued at a consulate. Reread Section E, above. The procedures for consular extensions are identical.

We would like to reemphasize that it is much more convenient to apply for a revalidated visa by mail through the State Department in Washington, D.C. than it is to extend your H-3 visa through a consulate. If possible, you should try to schedule filing your extension petition when you can remain in the U.S. until it is complete.

FORMS AND DOCUMENTS CHECKLIST

STEP ONE: PETITION

Form

- ☐ Form I-129 and H Supplement.

Documents

- ☐ Detailed statement from the U.S. employer describing the training program.
- ☐ Documents proving previous, relevant experience.
- ☐ Diplomas showing the completion of any necessary education.
- ☐ Letters or affidavits from companies in your home country or from your own government stating that similar training is unavailable in your home country.
- ☐ Proof of opportunities to use your training at home:
  - ☐ letter from a foreign employer explaining how the training will further your career in your home country, or
  - ☐ letter from your home country's labor department describing job opportunities for persons with the type of training you will receive in the U.S.

STEP TWO: APPLICATION

Forms

- ☐ OF forms (available from U.S. consulates abroad for consular filing only).
- ☐ Form I-129 (U.S. filing only).
- ☐ Form I-539 (U.S. filing only for accompanying relatives).

Documents

- ☐ Notice of approval of the H-3 visa petition.
- ☐ Valid passport for you and each accompanying relative.
- ☐ I-94 card for you and each accompanying relative (U.S. filing only).
- ☐ One passport-type photo of you and each accompanying relative (Consular filing only).
- ☐ Long form birth certificate for you and each accompanying relative.
- ☐ Marriage certificate if you are married and bringing your spouse.
- ☐ Documents showing ownership of real estate in your home country.
- ☐ Documents showing that close family members or property are being left behind in your home country.
- ☐ Documents showing a job is waiting on your return to your home country.

Intracompany Transfers: L-1 Visas

Privileges

- You can be transferred to the U.S. and work legally for a U.S. company that is a branch, subsidiary, affiliate or joint venture partner of a company that already employs you outside of the U.S.

- Visas can be issued quickly.

- You may travel in and out of the U.S. or remain there continuously until your L-1 status expires.

- Visas are available for accompanying relatives.

- If you have an L-1 visa for an executive or managerial level position in the U.S. company and want to apply for a green card through employment (see Chapter 8), you can do so and skip a major step of that process.

Limitations

- You are restricted to working only for the U.S. employer who acted as your L-1 visa sponsor, and the U.S. company must be a branch, subsidiary, affiliate or joint venture partner of the company that currently employs you outside the U.S.

- Visas can initially be approved for only up to three years. Extensions of two years at a time may be allowed until you have been in the U.S. for a total of seven years if you are a manager or executive. Persons with specialized knowledge can get extensions totaling only five years.

- Accompanying relatives may stay in the U.S. with you, but they may not work, unless they get work authorization through their own work.

A. How to Qualify

There are no quota restrictions. Petitions are normally approved within four to eight weeks. Visas are usually issued within several weeks after petition approval.

You qualify for an L-1 visa if you have been employed outside the U.S. as a manager, executive or person with specialized knowledge for at least one out of the past three years, and you are transferred to the U.S. to be employed in a similar position. The U.S. company to which you are transferring must be a branch, subsidiary, affiliate or joint venture partner of your non-U.S. employer. The non-U.S. company must remain in operation while you have the L-1 visa. When we use the term non-U.S. company we mean only that it is physically located outside the U.S. Such a company may well be a foreign division of an American-based business or it may have originated in a country outside the U.S. Either one fits our definition of non-U.S. company.

To get an L-1 visa, it is not necessary that either your non-U.S. or prospective U.S. employer be operating in a particular business structure. Many legal forms of doing business are acceptable, including, but not restricted to,

corporations, limited corporations, partnerships, joint ventures and sole proprietorships.

1. Manager, Executive or Person With Specialized Knowledge

To be eligible for an L-1 visa, the job you hold with the non-U.S. company must be that of manager, executive or person with specialized knowledge. You must have worked in that position a total of at least one year out of the past three years. For immigration purposes, the definitions of manager, executive and specialized knowledge are more restricted than their everyday meanings.

a. Managers

A manager is defined as a person who has all four of the following characteristics:

- He or she manages the organization or a department of the organization.
- He or she supervises and controls the work of other supervisory, professional or managerial employees or manages an essential function of the organization.

- He or she has the authority to hire and fire those persons supervised. If none are supervised, the manager must work at a senior level within the organization.
- He or she has the authority to make decisions concerning the day-to-day operations of the portion of the organization which he or she manages.

First-line supervisors are lower management personnel who directly oversee nonmanagement workers. A first-line supervisor is not normally considered a manager unless the employees supervised are professionals. The word "professional" here means a worker holding a university degree.

A manager coming to work for a U.S. office that has been in operation for at least one year also qualifies for a green card as a priority worker. See Chapter 8 for details.

b. Executives

An executive is defined as a person who has all four of the following characteristics:

- He or she directs the management of the organization or a major part of it.
- He or she sets the goals or policies of the organization or a part of it.
- He or she has extensive discretionary decision-making authority.
- He or she receives only general supervision or direction from higher level executives, a board of directors or the stockholders of the organization.

An executive coming to work for a U.S. office that has been in operation for at least one year also qualifies for a green card as a priority worker. Again, see Chapter 8 for details.

c. Persons With Specialized Knowledge

The knowledge that is referred to in the term "specialized knowledge" covers any knowledge that specifically concerns the employer company, its procedures, products or international marketing methods.

2. Branch, Subsidiary, Affiliate or Joint Venture Partner

L-1 visas are available only to employees of companies outside the U.S. that have related U.S. branches, subsidiaries, affiliates or joint venture partners. There is also a special category of international accounting firms. For visa purposes, these terms have specific definitions.

a. Branches

Branches are simply different operating locations of the same company. The clearest example of this is a single international corporation that has branch offices in many countries.

b. Subsidiaries

In a subsidiary relationship, one company must own a controlling percentage of the other company, that is, 50% or more. For L-1 purposes, when two companies are in the same corporate or limited form and at least 50% of the stock of a company in the U.S. is owned by a non-U.S. company, or vice versa, this is a classic subsidiary relationship.

c. Affiliates

Affiliate business relationships are more difficult to demonstrate than those of branches or subsidiaries because there is no direct ownership between the two companies. Instead, they share the fact that both are controlled by a common third entity, either a company, group of companies, individual or group of people.

There are two methods of ownership that will support an L-1 visa based on an affiliate relationship. The first is for one common person or business entity to own at least 50% of the non-U.S. company and 50% of the U.S. company. If no single entity owns at least 50% of both companies, the second possibility is for each owner of the non-U.S. company to also own the U.S. company, and in the same percentages. For example, if five different people each own 20% of the stock of the non-U.S. company, then the same five people must each own 20% of the U.S. company for an affiliate relationship to exist.

d. Joint Venture Partners

A joint venture exists when there is no common ownership between the two companies, but they have jointly undertaken a common business operation or project. To qualify for L-1 purposes, each company must have veto power over decisions, take an equal share of the profits and bear the losses on an equal basis.

In a situation where both the U.S. and non-U.S. companies are in the corporate or limited form and the majority of the stock of both is publicly held, unless they are simply branches of the same company that wish to transfer employees between them, the joint venture relationship is the only one that is practical for L-1 qualifying purposes. The ownership of a publicly held company is too vast and diverse to prove any of the other types of qualifying business relationships.

e. International Accounting Firms

The Immigration Act of 1990 made it clear that L-1 visas are available to employees and partners of international accounting firms. In the case of big accounting firms, the partnership's interests between one country and another are not usually close enough for them to qualify as affiliates under normal L-1 visa rules. For this reason, the managers of such companies that could not, in the past, be transferred to U.S. international accounting firms, are now considered qualified to support L-1 visa petitions for their employees. This is provided the firm is part of an international accounting organization with an internationally recognized name. These rules are intended to apply only to a limited number of very large and prominent firms.

3. Blanket L-1 Visas: Privileges for Large Companies

Large U.S. companies that are branches, subsidiaries or affiliates of non-U.S. companies may obtain what is known as a blanket L-1 status. Blanket L-1 status enables qualified U.S. companies that require frequent transferring of non-U.S. employees to their related U.S. companies to do so easily. Instead of applying individually for each transferee, the company itself gets a general approval for transferring employees, which eliminates much of the time and paperwork in each individual case. A company's blanket L-1 status can last for an indefinite period. If a non-U.S. company has more than one U.S. branch, subsidiary or affiliate, it need obtain only one blanket L-1 petition for all of its related American companies.

It is the company itself and not the individual employee that qualifies for this program. Although this procedure is not used often, there are enormous benefits when a company obtains blanket L-1 status. The company need apply only once to receive a blanket L-1 status, and when the company does so, it may easily bring key employees into the U.S. as needed, bypassing the INS individual petition process and the inevitable delays that come with it. We wish to make clear that although a U.S. company must be a branch, subsidiary or affiliate of a non-U.S. company to qualify, it is the U.S. company that petitions for and receives the blanket L-1 status.

Initially, a blanket L-1 petition can be approved for only three years. However, if the company continues to qualify, at the end of three years it can obtain an indefinite renewal. L-1 visas are available under the blanket program to executives and managers of the blanket L-1 status company as well as those employees considered to be specialized knowledge professionals. The definitions for manager and executives wanting blanket L-1 visas are the same as for those who apply for individual L-1 visas. However, this specialized knowledge category differs from the one for individual L-1 applicants. Individual L-1 visas may be given to those who simply have specialized knowledge. For the blanket visa, they must be considered professionals as well.

If a company has the need and meets the following requirements, it should obtain a blanket L-1 petition:

- The petitioning U.S. company to which employees may be transferred must be a branch, subsidiary or affiliate of a company outside the U.S. (Note that a joint venture partnership is not a qualifying business relationship for blanket L-1 status purposes.)
- Both the U.S. company and its related non-U.S. company must be engaged in actual trade or rendering of services.
- The U.S. company must have been engaged in business for at least one year.
- The U.S. company must have a total of at least three branches, subsidiaries or affiliates, although all three need not be located in the U.S.
- The company and any related U.S. companies must have:
  - successfully obtained L-1 visas for at least ten of its employees during the past 12 months
  - combined annual sales of at least $25 million, irrespective of the related company outside the U.S., or
  - a total of at least 1,000 employees actually working in the U.S.

4. Specialized Knowledge Professionals

This category is only for employees of companies with blanket L-1 status. It is a more stringent substitute for the specialized knowledge category available to individual L-1 applicants. The INS' regulations require that an individual have specialized knowledge, as defined above, and that he or she further be a member of the professions as that term is defined in immigration law. The immigration law specifically includes architects, engineers, lawyers, physicians, surgeons, teachers in elementary and secondary schools, colleges, academies or seminaries. However, the term profession has been more liberally interpreted in other contexts, to include any occupation that requires theoretical and practical knowledge to perform the occupation in such fields as architecture, physical and social sciences, business specialties and the arts, requiring completion of a university education reflected by at least a bachelor's degree in a specific occupational specialty, as long as that degree is the minimum requirement for entry to that occupation.

Under this definition, the following occupations have been found to be professional: registered nurse, accountant, computer systems analyst, physical therapist, chemist, pharmacist, medical technologist, hotel manager, fashion designer, commercial airline pilot of 747s or other large aircraft and upper-level business managers.

Other occupations may also be considered professional, as long as they meet the criteria discussed above

5. Accompanying Relatives

When you qualify for an L-1 visa, your spouse and unmarried children under age 21 can get L-2 visas simply by providing proof of their family relationship to you. L-2 visas authorize your accompanying relatives to stay with you in the U.S., but not to work there.

B. Applying for a Green Card From L-1 Status

If you are eligible for or now have an L-1 visa as either a manager or an executive, you may also be eligible for a green card through employment as explained in Chapter 8. In addition to your eligibility, you also have the benefit of being able to get the green card without going through the rigorous procedures of Labor Certification, which is usually the first step required for those seeking green cards through employment. The purpose of the Labor Certification procedure is to show that there are no American workers available to take the U.S. job that has been offered to you. However, if you qualify for L-1 status as a manager or executive, you also fall under a green card preference category called *priority workers*. This category is exempt from Labor Certification requirements.

We wish to stress that in order to use L-1 eligibility to qualify for a green card, you need not have actually gotten an L-1 visa. Showing that you are eligible to get one is sufficient. Chapter 8, *Getting a Green Card Through Employment*, will give you full instructions on how to get a green card using an L-1 visa or L-1 visa eligibility.

C. Applying for an L-1 Status

Once you have been offered a job transfer to the U.S., getting an L-1 visa is a two-step process. Often applicants expect their U.S. employers to handle the entire process for them and indeed, a number of large companies are equipped with staff specialists who will do this for highly

desirable employees. Even smaller companies may be prepared to do whatever is necessary, including paying an immigration attorney's fees, in order to transfer a key employee. However, in many cases it is the employee who is most interested in the U.S. transfer, and to a U.S.-based company, the red tape of transferring a foreign employee can be an unfamiliar nuisance.

As we give you step-by-step instructions for getting an L-1 visa, we will indicate that certain activities are to be performed by the U.S. company and others are to be done by you. We will discuss each task according to who has legal responsibility for carrying it out. Even though the law presumes the U.S. company is performing a particular function, there is nothing to stop you from helping with the work. For example, you can help fill out forms intended to be completed by the U.S. company and ask the appropriate official in the company to check them over and sign them. Unless the U.S. company volunteers to help or you are sure the company has a pressing need to transfer you to the U.S., we recommend assisting in the paperwork as much as possible. The less the U.S. employer is inconvenienced, the more the company will be willing to act as sponsor for your visa. An imposition on company time or money might cost you a job transfer to the U.S. With the help of this book, you will know how to do all that is required. It is completely legal as well as in your best interest to assist whenever possible.

1. Step One: The Petition

The petition is filed by your U.S. employer company. All L-1 petitions, both individual and blanket, are submitted to INS regional service centers in the U.S. The object of the individual L-1 petition is to prove three things:

- that you have been employed outside the U.S. for at least one of the past three years as an executive, manager or person with specialized knowledge
- that the company you worked for outside the US. has a branch, subsidiary, affiliate or joint venture partner company in the U.S., and
- that the U.S. entity requires your services to fill a position of the same or similar level as the one you presently hold outside of the U.S.

The object of the blanket L-1 petition is to prove five things:

- that the petitioning U.S. company is in a branch, subsidiary or affiliate relationship with a company outside of the U.S.
- that the U.S. company has been engaged in actual trade or the rendering of services

- that the U.S. company has been in business for at least one year
- that the U.S. company has a total of at least three U.S. branches, subsidiaries or affiliates, and
- that the U.S. company and its other U.S. related businesses entities have:
  - successfully obtained L-1 visas for at least ten employees in the past year
  - combined total annual sales of at least $25 million, or
  - a combined total of at least 1,000 employees working in the U.S.

An approved petition, either individual or blanket, does not by itself give the transferee any immigration privileges. It is only a prerequisite to Step Two, submitting the application for an L-1 visa. The petition must be approved before you are eligible for Step Two.

2. Step Two: The Application

The application is filed by you and your accompanying relatives, if any. The application is your formal request for an L-1 visa or status. (If you are Canadian, your Step Two procedures will be different from those of other applicants. See Chapter 28, *Canadians: Special Rules.*) Step Two may be carried out in the U.S. at an INS office or in your home country at a U.S. consulate there. If you file Step Two papers in the U.S., you will usually submit them at the same time as those for Step One. When Step Two is dispatched at a U.S. consulate abroad, you must wait to file the application until the Step One petition is first approved. When the case is based on your employer company having blanket L-1 status, under no circumstances can Step Two be carried out before the employer has completed Step One and obtained approval of the blanket L-1 petition.

The vast majority of nonimmigrant visa applications are filed at consulates. The major benefit is that an L-1 visa, which is stamped in your passport, can be issued only by American consulates. When you file Step Two at a consulate, your visa will be stamped in your passport at that time. INS offices inside the U.S. may issue petition approvals that result in "status" but not visas. (See Chapter 14, Section B, Difference Between a Visa and a Status.)

If you are already in the U.S. legally on some other type of nonimmigrant visa, you qualify to apply for an L-1 status at an INS office inside the U.S. using a procedure known as *change of nonimmigrant status.* (If you were admitted as a visitor without a visa under the Visa Waiver Program, you may not carry out Step Two in the U.S. Currently there are 29 participating countries in the Visa Waiver Program, including: Andorra, Argentina, Austria,

Australia, Belgium, Brunei, Denmark, Finland, France, Germany, Iceland, Ireland, Italy, Japan, Liechtenstein, Luxembourg, Monaco, The Netherlands, New Zealand, Norway, Portugal, San Marino, Singapore, Slovenia, Spain, Sweden, Switzerland, the United Kingdom and Uruguay. The government has approved Greece for inclusion in the program in the near future.) This is simply a technical term meaning you are switching from one nonimmigrant status to another. If a change of status is approved, you will then be treated as if you had entered the country with an L-1 visa and you can keep the status as long as you remain in the U.S. or until it expires, whichever comes first.

You will not, however, receive a visa stamp, which you need if your plans include traveling in and out of the U.S. Again, visa stamps are issued only at U.S. consulates abroad. Therefore, if you change your status and later travel outside the U.S., you will have to go to the U.S. consulate in your home country and repeat Step Two, obtaining the L-1 visa stamp in your passport, before you can return. This extra procedure makes changing status an unattractive option for all but Canadians who don't need visas to cross the U.S. border.

3. Paperwork

There are two types of paperwork you must submit to get an L-1 visa. The first consists of official government forms completed by you or your employer. The second is personal and business documents such as birth certificates, marriage certificates, school transcripts, diplomas, company financial statements and company tax returns. We will tell you exactly what forms and documents you need.

It is vital that forms are properly filled out and all necessary documents are supplied. You or your U.S. employer may resent the intrusion into your privacy and sizable effort it takes to prepare immigration applications, but you should realize the process is an impersonal matter to immigration officials. Your getting a visa is more important to you than it is to the U.S. government. This is not a pleasant thing to accept, but you are better off having a real understanding of your position. People from all over the world want U.S. visas. There is no shortage of applicants. Take the time and trouble to prepare your papers properly. In the end it will pay off with a successful application.

The documents you or your U.S. employer supply to INS do not have to be originals. Photocopies of all documents are acceptable as long as you have the originals in your possession and are willing to produce them at the request of INS. Documents submitted to U.S. consulates, on the other hand, must be either originals or official government certified copies. Government certified copies

ACADEMIC CREDENTIAL EVALUATIONS

Because it is almost always necessary that you hold at least a bachelor's degree, evidence that you are personally eligible as a specialized knowledge professional should include copies of diplomas and transcripts from the colleges and universities you attended. However, every country in the world does not operate on the same academic degree and grade level systems found in the U.S. If you were educated in some other country, INS or the U.S. consulate, as part of judging your eligibility, will often ask for an academic credential evaluation from an approved consulting service to determine the American equivalent of your educational level.

When the results of a credential evaluation are favorable, they strengthen your case. If, however, the evaluation shows that your credentials do not equal at least an American bachelor's degree, this can mean you will not qualify as a specialized knowledge professional.

We recommend obtaining a credential evaluation in every case where non-U.S. education is a factor. In addition, we advise getting the evaluation before INS or the consulate has the opportunity to ask for it. When the evaluation is favorable, you can automatically include it with your application since it strengthens your case and saves time if INS or the consulate decides to request it later. You should also reconsider applying for an L-1 visa under the blanket program as you probably will not qualify.

Before sending a credential evaluation service your academic documents, you may want to call in advance to discuss your prospects over the telephone. Usually, you can get some idea of the likelihood for receiving good results. If your prospects are truly bleak, you may decide not to order the evaluation and to save the service charge, which is typically around $100.

There are several qualified credential evaluation services recognized by INS. Two of them are:

International Education Research Foundation
P.O. Box 66940
Los Angeles, CA 90066
Telephone: 310-390-6276
Fax: 310-397-7686
Website: http://www.ierf.org

Educational Credential Evaluators, Inc.
P.O. Box 514070
Milwaukee, WI 53203-3470
Telephone: 414-289-3400
Fax: 414-289-3411
Website: http://www.ece.org

The credential evaluation companies listed above will evaluate only formal education. They will not evaluate job experience. American universities also offer evaluations of foreign academic credentials but will recognize work experience as having an academic equivalent. Therefore, if you lack a university education but can show many years of responsible experience, you are better off trying to get an evaluation from a U.S. college or university.

When sending your credentials to a U.S. university, include documents showing your complete academic background, as well as all relevant career achievements. Letters of recommendation from former employers are the preferred proof of work experience. Evidence of any special accomplishments, such as awards or published articles, should also be submitted.

INS and the U.S. consulates can be influenced but not bound by academic evaluations from U.S. colleges and universities.

and notarized copies are not the same thing. Documents that have only been notarized are not acceptable. They must carry a government seal. In addition to any original or government certified copies of documents submitted to a consulate, you should submit plain photocopies of each document as well. After the consulate compares the copies with the originals, it will return the originals.

Documents will be accepted if they are in either English, or, with papers filed at U.S. consulates abroad, the language of the country where the documents are being filed. An exception exists for papers filed at U.S. consulates in Japan, where all documents must be translated into English. If the documents are not in an acceptable language as just explained, they must be accompanied by a full, word for word, written English translation. Any capable person may act as translator. It is not necessary to hire a professional. At the end of each translation, the following statement must appear:

I hereby certify that I translated this document from (language) to English. This translation is accurate and complete. I further certify that I am fully competent to translate from (language) to English.

The translator should sign this statement but it does not have to be witnessed or notarized.

Later in this chapter we describe in detail the forms and documents needed to get your L-1 visa. A summary checklist of forms and documents appears at the end of the chapter.

D. Who's Who in Getting Your L-1 Visa

Getting an L-1 visa will be easier if you familiarize yourself with the technical names used for each participant in the process. During Step One, the petition, you are known as either the *beneficiary* or the *employee* and the U.S. company to which you are being transferred is called the *petitioner* or the *employer*. In Step Two, the application, you are referred to as *applicant*, but your U.S. employer remains the petitioner or employer. If you are bringing your spouse and children with you as accompanying relatives, they are known as *applicants* as well.

E. Step One: The Petition

There are two different types of L-1 visa petitions, individual and blanket. Individual L-1 petitions are used when a company wishes to transfer one or just a few employees on an infrequent basis. Blanket L-1 petitions are reserved for large corporations that transfer many employees to the U.S.

each year. We have already discussed the advantages to a blanket L-1 status. Remember that blanket L-1 petitions are filed to get blanket L-1 status for the U.S. company, while individual petitions are filed for each potential transferee.

If your non-U.S. employer wants to transfer you to the U.S. and regularly transfers others, ask if the company already has an approved blanket petition. If so, ask your potential U.S. employer to issue you three copies of a document known as a Certificate of Eligibility, INS Form I-129S and one copy of the Notice of Action Form I-797, indicating approval of the blanket L-1 petition. These items will prove that the company does indeed have an approved blanket L-1 petition. Once you have these papers, you may skip Step One, go directly to Step Two, the application, and follow the directions for applicants in blanket L-1 cases.

If the U.S. company does transfer many employees to the U.S. but has not obtained a blanket L-1 visa, you may wish to suggest that it look into getting one. Instructions for getting blanket L-1 petitions are in Section A3, above.

1. General Procedures

The U.S. employer submits the petition, consisting of forms and documents, by mail, in duplicate, to the INS regional service center having jurisdiction over your intended employer's place of business. INS regional service centers are not the same as INS local offices. There are four INS regional service centers spread across the U.S. Appendix II contains a list of all INS regional service centers with their addresses.

The filing fee for each petition is currently $110, if no change of status (Step Two, U.S. Filing) is being requested, and $180 if it is. Checks or money orders are accepted. It is not advisable to send cash. We recommend submitting all papers by certified mail, return receipt requested, and making a copy of everything sent in to keep in your records.

Within a week or so after mailing in the petition, your employer should get back a written confirmation that the papers are being processed, together with a receipt for the fee. This notice will also give your immigration file number and tell approximately when you should expect to have a decision. If INS wants further information before acting on your case, all petition papers, forms and documents will be returned to your employer with another form known as an *I-72*. The I-72 tells your employer what additional pieces of information or documents are expected. Your employer should supply the extra data and mail the whole package back to the INS regional service center.

L-1 petitions are normally approved within two to eight weeks. When this happens, a Notice of Action Form I-797 will be sent to your employer showing the petition was approved. If you plan to execute Step Two at a U.S. consulate abroad, INS will also notify the consulate of your choice, sending a complete copy of your file. Only the employer receives communications from INS about the petition because technically it is the employer who is seeking the visa on your behalf.

2. Petition Forms

Copies of these forms can be found in Appendix III.

Form I-129 and L Supplement

The basic form for Step One, the petition, is immigration Form I-129 and L Supplement. The I-129 form is used for many different nonimmigrant visas. In addition to the basic part of the form that applies to all types of visas, it comes with several supplements for each specific nonimmigrant category. Simply tear out and use the supplement that applies to you. Your employer must file the petition form in duplicate. Send in two signed originals. Copies are not acceptable.

Most of the questions on the I-129 form are straight-forward. If a question does not apply to you, answer it with "None" or "N/A."

Part 1. These questions concern the employer only and are self-explanatory.

Part 2, Question 1. Question 1 should be answered "L-1."

Questions 2–3. These questions are self-explanatory.

Question 4. This question asks you to indicate what action is requested from INS. Normally you will mark box "a" which tells INS to notify a U.S. consulate abroad of the petition approval so that you may apply for a visa there. If you will be filing your Step Two application in the U.S., mark box "b." If this petition is being filed as an extension, mark box "c."

Question 5. This question is self-explanatory.

Part 3. These questions are self-explanatory. If you previously held a U.S. work permit and therefore have a U.S. Social Security number, put down that number where asked. If you have a Social Security number that is not valid for employment, put down that number followed by "not valid for employment." If you have never had a Social Security number, put down "None."

Alien Registration Numbers, which all begin with the letter "A," are given only to people who have applied for green cards, received political asylum or have been in deportation proceedings. If you do have an "A" number, put that number down and explain how you got it, such as "number issued from previous green card petition filed by my brother." If you do not have an "A" number, write down "None."

If your present authorized stay has expired, you must disclose that where asked. This should not affect your ability to get an L-1 visa at a U.S. consulate, but if you are out of status now, you cannot file Step Two inside the U.S. (See Chapter 25.)

If this is a blanket petition, Part 3 does not apply. On the top line, write "N/A, Blanket petition, see L Supplement for individual employee details."

Part 4. These questions are self-explanatory. The fact that you may have a green card petition or application in process does not prevent you from getting an L-1 visa.

If you are filing a blanket petition, Part 4 does not apply. Write in "N/A, Blanket petition."

Part 5. These questions are self-explanatory. The dates of intended employment should not exceed a total of three years. This is the maximum period of time for which an L-1 petition may be approved.

L Supplement

This supplement is self-explanatory. Section 1 is completed for all individual petitions. Section 2 is completed for blanket petitions.

3. Petition Documents

You must provide several documents with the petition.

a. Proof of Employment Abroad

Your U.S. employer must supply documents proving that you were employed outside the U.S. by the non-U.S. company for at least one of the past three years. The best way to prove this is by providing copies of any wage statements you may have received. In Canada this is the T-4, in England, the P.A.Y.E. You should also submit your personal income tax return filed in your home country for the most recent year. If this is unavailable, a notarized statement from the bookkeeping department or accountant of your non-U.S. employer may be used; however, you should also submit a statement explaining why the tax returns are unavailable. For example, you might state that tax returns are not required in your home country or that the returns haven't been prepared yet.

b. Proof That You Are a Manager, Executive or Person With Specialized Knowledge

Your U.S. employer must submit evidence that your employment abroad fits the INS definition of manager, executive or person with specialized knowledge, and that your employment in the U.S. will be of a similar type. To prove this, detailed statements from both the U.S. and non-U.S. employers explaining your specific duties as well as the number and kind of employees you supervise must be presented. If the petition is based on specialized knowledge, the statements should also describe the nature of the specialized knowledge and how it will be used in your U.S. job. These statements may be in your employer's own words and do not have to be in any special form.

c. Proof That the U.S. and Non-U.S. Companies Are Engaged in Trade or the Rendering of Services

The petitioning U.S. employer should submit as many documents as possible to show that both the U.S. and non-U.S. companies are financially healthy and presently engaged in trade or the rendering of services. Such documents would include:

- copies of the articles of incorporation or other legal charters
- any business registration certificates
- company tax returns for the past two years
- company annual reports or financial statements for the past two years, including balance sheets and profit/loss statements
- payroll records for the past two years, letters of reference from chambers of commerce
- promotional literature describing the nature of the company
- letters from banks indicating average account balances, and
- copies of leases or deeds for business premises.

d. Proof of a Qualifying Business Relationship Between the U.S. and Non-U.S. Companies

The U.S. employer must submit documents showing that the U.S. and non-U.S. companies are in a branch, subsidiary,

affiliate or joint venture relationship. There are many different types or business organizations that may qualify to support L-1 visa petitions, ranging from privately owned companies to large corporations whose stocks are publicly traded. The types of documents that are submitted will differ from case to case depending on the legal structure of the companies involved as well as the nature of the relationship. Business documents will also vary greatly from one country to another, as some types of business structures are unique to a particular country and cannot be found elsewhere. Therefore, it is impossible to list all the documents that can be used to show the existence of one of the four qualifying business relationships, as they differ with each case. The petitioning employer must simply keep the elements of the four types of relationship in mind and produce all documents possible to demonstrate that one of them applies to his company.

If a company is in the corporate or limited company form, whether privately or publicly held, articles of incorporation, stock certificates showing ownership of the companies and statements from the secretaries of the corporations explaining the percentages of stock ownership are required to prove any of the four qualifying business relationships. Remember that in subsidiary and affiliate relationships, at least 50% of the stock must be involved for the relationship to qualify. If the corporations are privately held, notarized affidavits from the secretary or other record keeper of each company verifying the names of the officers and directors, as well as copies of minutes of shareholder meetings appointing the officers and directors should be submitted.

If one or both companies are not in the corporate form, other proof of who owns the company such as business registration certificates, business licenses and affidavits from company officials attesting to the identity of the owners should be submitted. The purpose of identifying the owners is to show commonality of ownership between the U.S. and non-U.S. companies.

In the case of joint venture partnerships, the U.S. employer must submit a copy of the joint venture agreement together with as much of the above mentioned documentation concerning each company as possible.

e. Additional Documents for Blanket L-1 Petitions

All documents for blanket L-1 petitions concern the U.S. and non-U.S. companies, establishing that they have one of the three necessary business relationships (joint venture partnerships cannot qualify for blanket L-1 status) and meet the other specific criteria for blanket L-1 status. No documents are necessary concerning the individual employees who will be transferred. In addition to the above company documents, the following items must be provided:

- documents showing the U.S. company and any related companies have successfully obtained L-1 visas for at least ten of its employees during the past 12 months
- documents showing the U.S. company and any related U.S. companies have combined annual sales of at least $25 million, or
- documents showing the U.S. company and any related U.S. companies have a total of at least 1,000 employees actually working in the U.S.

If the U.S. company is claiming eligibility for a blanket L-1 petition because in the past year it has obtained ten L-1 visas for employees, this may be documented by supplying copies of the Notice of Action forms I-797 for each approved employee.

If the U.S. company is claiming eligibility for a blanket L-1 visa petition because all of its related U.S. companies had combined sales of at least $25 million in the past year, this may be documented by company income tax returns, audited accountant's financial statements or the annual report to the shareholders.

If the U.S. company is claiming eligibility for a blanket L-1 visa petition because it has more than 1,000 U.S. employees, this may be documented by presenting the most recent quarterly state unemployment tax return and federal employment tax return Form 940.

4. Petition Interviews

INS rarely holds interviews on L-1 visa petitions. When it does, the interview is always with the employer. If you are in the U.S., you may be asked to appear as well. Interviews are requested only if INS doubts that the documents or information on Form I-129 and the L supplement are genuine. Then the petition file is forwarded from the INS regional service center where it was submitted to the INS local office nearest your employer's place of business and your employer is notified to appear there. The employer may also be asked to bring additional documents at that time. If, after the interview, everything is in order, the petition will be approved. The best way to avoid an interview is to have the employer document the petition well from the beginning.

5. Petition Appeals

When your job qualifications or the ability of the employer to pay your salary have been poorly documented, the petition will probably be denied. Your employer will then get a notice of INS's unfavorable decision, a written statement of the reasons for the negative outcome and an explanation of how to appeal. In the alternative, INS may request additional

information by sending you a form I-797 and a list of information and/or documents it needs to determine your eligibility. You must respond to such a request within the specified time period (usually about three months) or your petition will be decided on the basis of the already submitted documentation.

The best way to handle an appeal is to try avoiding it altogether. Filing an appeal means making an argument to INS that its reasoning or facts were wrong. This is difficult to do successfully. If you think you can eliminate the reason your petition failed by improving your paperwork, it makes sense to disregard the appeals process and simply file a new petition, better prepared than the first.

If the petition was denied because your U.S. employer left out necessary documents that have since been located, the new documents should be sent, together with a written request that the case be reopened, to the same INS office that issued the denial. This is technically called a *Motion to Reopen*. There is a $110 fee to file this motion. Appeals often take a long time. A Motion to Reopen can be concluded faster than an appeal.

If your U.S. employer does choose to appeal, it must be done within 30 days of the date on the Notice of Denial. The appeal should be filed at the same INS office that issued the denial. There is a $110 filing fee. INS will then forward the papers for consideration to the Administrative Appeals Unit of the central INS office in Washington, D.C. In six months or more your employer will get back a decision by mail. Less than 5% of all appeals are successful.

When an appeal to INS has been denied, the next step is to make an appeal through the U.S. judicial system. Your employer may not file an action in court without first going through the INS appeals process. If the case has reached this stage and you are in the U.S. illegally, we strongly recommend seeking representation from a qualified immigration attorney, as you are now in danger of being deported.

F. Step Two: The Application (Consular Filing)

If you are Canadian, your Step Two procedures will be different from those of other applicants. See Chapter 28, *Canadians: Special Rules,* for details.

Anyone with an approved L-1 petition or any qualified employee of a company holding an approved blanket L-1 petition can apply for a visa at a U.S. consulate in his or her home country. You must be physically present in order to apply there. Even if you have been or are now working or living illegally in the U.S., you can still get an L-1 visa from a U.S. consulate if you otherwise qualify.

1. Benefits and Drawbacks of Consular Filing

The most important benefit to consular filing, making it almost always preferable to U.S. filing, is that only consulates issue visas. When you go through a U.S. filing, you get a status, not a visa. (See Chapter 14, Section B, Difference Between a Visa and a Status.) An L-1 status confers the same right to work as an L-1 visa, but it does not give you the ability to travel out of the U.S. and get back in again. Therefore, if you want travel privileges, you will at some time have to go through the extra step of applying for a visa at a U.S. consulate, even though you have already applied for and received L-1 status in the U.S.

Moreover, anyone with an approved petition may apply for an L-1 visa at the appropriate consulate. That is not the case with U.S. applications for L-1 status. If you are in the U.S. illegally, consular filing is a must. You are not eligible to process a status application in the U.S. unless you are presently in status.

A further plus to consular filing is that consular offices work much more quickly to issue nonimmigrant visas than INS offices do to process nonimmigrant statuses. Your waiting time for the paperwork to be finished may be much shorter at a U.S. consulate abroad than at most U.S. INS offices.

A drawback to consular filing comes from the fact that you must be physically present in the country where the consulate is located to file there. If your petition is ultimately turned down because of an unexpected problem, not only will you have to wait outside the U.S. until the problem is resolved, but other visas in your passport, such as a visitor's visa, may be canceled. It will then be impossible for you to enter the U.S. in any capacity. Consequently, if your L-1 visa case is not very strong and freedom of travel is not essential to you, it might be wise to apply in the U.S., make up your mind to remain there for the duration of the L-1 status and skip trying to get a visa from the consulate.

2. Application General Procedures: Consular Filing

Technically the law allows you to apply for an L-1 visa at any U.S. consulate you choose. A complete list of all U.S. consulates that process visa applications, together with their addresses and phone numbers, is in Appendix I. However, from a practical standpoint, your case will be given the greatest consideration at the consulate in your home country. Applying in some other country creates suspicion in the minds of the consul officers there about your motives for choosing their consulate. Often, when an applicant is having trouble at a home consulate, he will seek a more lenient office in some other country. This practice of consulate shopping is frowned on by officials in the system. Unless you have a very good reason for being elsewhere (such as a temporary job assignment in some other nation), it is smarter to file your visa application in your home country.

Furthermore, if you have been present in the U.S. unlawfully, in general you cannot apply as a third country national. Even if you overstayed your status in the U.S. by just one day, you must return to your home country and apply for the visa from that consulate. Overstaying will also result in the automatic cancellation of your visa. There is an exception. If you were admitted to the U.S. for the duration of your status (indicated by a "D/S" on your I-94 form) and you remained in the U.S. beyond that time, you may still be able to apply as a third country national. The State Department's current regulations seem to imply that you will be barred from third country national processing only if an immigration judge has determined that you were unlawfully present. Because of the ambiguity, you may find that your success in applying as a third country national will depend on your country, the consulate and the relative seriousness of your offense. Because unlawful presence for over six months may also be a ground of inadmissibility (if it happened after April 1, 1997), be sure to understand how this could affect your application. (See Chapter 25.)

You may not file an application for an L-1 visa at a consulate before your petition has been approved. Once this occurs, the INS regional service center where the petition was originally submitted will forward a complete copy of your file to the U.S. consulate designated on Form I-129 in Step One. At the same time, a Notice of Action Form I-797 indicating approval will be sent directly to your U.S. employer. Once your employer receives this, you should telephone the consulate to see if the petition file has arrived from INS. If the file is slow in coming, ask the consulate to consider granting approval of your L-1 visa based only on the Notice of Action. Many U.S. consulates are willing to do so. If your U.S. employer has approved L-1 blanket status, the U.S. company will issue a Certificate of Eligibility directly to you. This is used as a substitute for the Notice of Action in individual L-1 cases.

Once the petition is approved, in a large number of consulates you can simply walk in with your application paperwork and get your L-1 visa immediately. Others insist on advance appointments. Most U.S. consulates in Canada now require you to make an appointment by telephone a week or more in advance of your interview. Some, like those in London and Germany, will only process visa applications by mail. Since procedures among consulates vary, you should always telephone in advance to ask about local policies.

On entering the U.S. with your new L-1 visa, you will be given an I-94 card. It will be stamped with a date indicating for how long you can stay. Normally, you are permitted to remain up to the expiration date on your L-1 petition or, in a blanket L-1 case, the Certificate of Eligibility. If you are coming to the U.S. on a blanket L-1 visa, your U.S. employer will provide you with Certificate of Eligibility Forms I-129S in triplicate and a copy of the Notice of Action indicating approval of the blanket L-1 petition. In addition to the I-94 card, upon your entry the I-129S will be stamped by an immigration inspector and you will be required to keep one copy, together with your I-94 card. Each time you exit and reenter the U.S., you will get a new I-94 card authorizing your stay up to the final date indicated on the petition or Certificate of Eligibility.

3. Application Forms: Consular Filing

When you file at a U.S. consulate abroad, the consulate officials will provide you with certain optional forms, designated by an "OF" preceding a number. Instructions for completing optional forms and what to do with them once they are filled out will come with the forms. We do not include copies of these forms in Appendix III.

4. Application Documents: Consular Filing

You are required to show a valid passport and present one passport-type photograph taken in accordance with the photo instructions in Appendix III. If the consulate has not yet received your INS file containing the paperwork from the approved petition, you will then need to show the original Notice of Action, Form I-797, which your employer received from INS by mail, or your Certificate of Eligibility Form I-129S. Most consulates will issue L-1 visas based only on the Notice of Action or Certificate of Eligibility, although some, particularly in South America, insist on seeing the complete INS file. If the consulate wants to see your file and it is late (more than a month) in arriving, you should request that the consulate investigate the file's whereabouts. You, too, can write the INS regional service center where the petition was processed, requesting that they look for the file.

For each accompanying relative, you must present a valid passport and one passport-type photograph taken in accordance with the photo instructions in Appendix III. You will also need documents verifying their family relationship to you. You may verify a parent/child relationship by presenting the child's long form birth certificate. Many countries, including Canada and England, issue both short and long form birth certificates. Where both are available, the long form is needed because it contains the names of the parents while the short form does not. If you are accompanied by your spouse, you must prove that you are

lawfully married by showing a civil marriage certificate. Church marriage certificates are generally unacceptable. (There are a few exceptions, depending on the laws of your particular country. Canadians, for example, may use church marriage certificates if the marriage took place in Quebec Province, but not elsewhere. If a civil certificate is available, however, you should always use it.) You may have married in a country where marriages are not customarily recorded. Tribal areas of Africa are an example. In such situations, call the nearest consulate or embassy of your home country for help with getting acceptable proof of marriage.

5. Additional Application Documents for Blanket L-1 Visas: Consular Filing

In addition to all those documents listed above for applicants in individual L-1 cases, applicants having U.S. employers with approved blanket L-1 visa petitions must submit some extra documents. The first of these is the Notice of Action showing approval of the blanket petition, Form I-797. Your U.S. employer will give this form directly to you and you will, in turn, submit it with your application. This document is a substitute for the Notice of Action sent to the consulate by INS in individual L-1 cases.

Since your own eligibility for an L-1 classification is not proven in the Step One portion of a blanket L-1 petition case as it is with individual L-1 cases, you must now document your own eligibility.

a. Proof of Employment Abroad

You must present documents proving that you were employed outside of the U.S. by the non-U.S. company for at least one of the past three years. The best way to prove this is by providing copies of any wage statements you may have received. In Canada this is the T-4, in England, the P.A.Y.E. You should also submit your personal income tax return filed in your home country for the most recent year. If this is unavailable, a notarized statement from the bookkeeper or accountant of the non-U.S. employer may be used; however, you should also submit a statement explaining why the tax returns are unavailable. For example, you might state that tax returns are not required in your home country or that the returns haven't been prepared yet.

b. Proof That You Are a Manager, Executive or Specialized Knowledge Professional

You must submit evidence that your employment abroad fits the INS definition of manager, executive or specialized knowledge professional, and that your employment in the U.S. will be of a similar type. To prove this, detailed statements from both the U.S. and non-U.S. employers explaining your specific duties as well as the number and kind of employees you supervise must be presented. If the application is based on specialized knowledge, the statements should also describe the nature of the specialized knowledge you possess, the reason why only you have that knowledge and how it will be used in your U.S. job. Specialized knowledge must have the characteristic of being special to the individual company. It cannot be knowledge that is available from others in the open job market. The statements your employer submits should be in his own words and do not have to be in any special form.

Because you must be a specialized knowledge professional, you must submit documents showing you meet INS's definition of professional. This usually requires you to show that you have a degree from a college or university. Therefore, evidence that you are a member of a profession should include copies of diplomas and transcripts from the colleges and universities you attended. The consulate insists on both a diploma and a transcript from a school where you graduated. If you attended a school but did not graduate, the transcript is required. If you were educated outside of the U.S., the consulate may request a credential evaluation from an approved evaluation service as explained in Section A4, above.

6. Application Interviews: Consular Filing

The consulate will frequently require an interview before issuing an L-1 visa. During the interview, a consul officer will examine the data you gave in Step One for accuracy, especially regarding facts about your own qualifications.

7. Application Appeals: Consular Filing

When a consulate turns down an L-1 visa application, there is no way to make a formal appeal, although you are free to reapply as often as you like. If your visa is denied, the reasons for the denial will be explained by the consul officer. Written statements of decisions are not normally provided in nonimmigrant cases. If a lack of evidence about a particular point is the problem, sometimes simply presenting more evidence on an unclear fact can bring a positive change in the result. The most common reason for denial of an L-1 visa is that you are found inadmissible.

Certain people who have been refused L-1 visas reapply at a different consulate, attempting to hide the fact that they were turned down previously. You should know that if your application is denied, the last page in your passport will be stamped "Application Received" with the date and location of the rejecting consulate. This notation shows that some type of prior visa application has failed. It serves as a

warning to other consulates that your case merits close inspection. If what we have just told you makes you think it would be a good idea to overcome this problem by obtaining a new, unmarked passport, you should also know that permanent computer records are kept of all visa denials.

G. Step Two: The Application (U.S. Filing)

If you are physically present in the U.S., you may apply for L-1 status without leaving the country on the following conditions:

- you are simultaneously filing paperwork for or have already received an approved petition for an individual L-1, or you have a Certificate of Eligibility for a blanket L-1
- you entered the U.S. legally
- you have never worked illegally in the U.S., and
- the date on your I-94 card has not passed.

If you are admitted as a visitor without a visa under the Visa Waiver Program, you may not carry out Step Two in the U.S. Currently there are 29 participating countries in the Visa Waiver Program, including: Andorra, Argentina, Austria, Australia, Belgium, Brunei, Denmark, Finland, France, Germany, Iceland, Ireland, Italy, Japan, Liechtenstein, Luxembourg, Monaco, The Netherlands, New Zealand, Norway, Portugal, San Marino, Singapore, Slovenia, Spain, Sweden, Switzerland, the United Kingdom and Uruguay. The government has approved Greece for inclusion in the program in the near future.

If you cannot meet these terms, you may not file for L-1 status in the U.S. It is important to realize, however, that eligibility to apply in the U.S. has nothing to do with overall eligibility for an L-1 visa. Applicants who are barred from filing in the U.S. but otherwise qualify for L-1 status can apply successfully for an L-1 visa at U.S. consulates abroad. If you find you are not eligible for U.S. filing read Section F, above.

1. Benefits and Drawbacks of U.S. filing

Visas are never given inside the U.S. They are issued exclusively by U.S. consulates abroad. If you file in the U.S. and you are successful, you will get L-1 status but not the visa itself. This is a major drawback to U.S. applications. L-1 status allows you to remain in the U.S. with L-1 privileges until the status expires, but should you leave the country for any reason before that time, you will have to apply for the visa itself at a U.S. consulate before returning to America. Moreover, the fact that your L-1 status has been approved in the U.S. does not guarantee that the consulate will also approve your visa.

There is another problem which comes up only in U.S. filings. It is the issue of what is called *preconceived intent*. To approve a change of status, INS must believe that at the time you originally entered the U.S. as a visitor or with some other nonimmigrant visa, you did not intend to apply for a different status. If INS thinks you had a preconceived plan to change from the status you arrived with to a different status, INS may deny your application. The preconceived intent issue is one less potential hazard you will face if you apply at a U.S. consulate abroad.

On the plus side of U.S. filing is that when problems do arise with your U.S. application, you can stay in America while they are being corrected, a circumstance most visa applicants prefer. If you run into snags at a U.S. consulate, you will have to remain outside the U.S. until matters are resolved.

2. Application General Procedures: U.S. Filing

The general procedure for filing Step Two in the U.S. is to follow Step One as outlined in Section E, above, but to mark box "b" in Part 2 of Form I-129, indicating that you will complete processing in the U.S. There is no separate application form for filing Step Two in the U.S. If you have an accompanying spouse or children, however, a separate Form I-539 must be filed for them.

When you apply for a change of status, the filing fee for a Step One petition is presently $180. Checks and money orders are accepted. It is not advisable to send cash. We recommend submitting all papers by certified mail, return receipt requested, and making a copy of everything sent in to keep for your records.

Within a week or two after mailing in the application, you should get back a written notice of confirmation that the papers are being processed, together with a receipt for the fees. This notice will also tell you your immigration file number and approximately when to expect a decision. If INS wants further information before acting on your case, all application papers, forms and documents will be returned together with another form known as an *I-797*. The I-797

tells you what additional pieces of information or documents are expected. You should supply the extra data and mail the whole package back to the INS regional service center by the deadline given, usually 12 weeks.

Applications for an L-1 status are normally approved within two to eight weeks. When this happens, you will receive a Notice of Action Form I-797 indicating the dates for which your status is approved, and a new I-94 card, which is attached to the bottom of the form.

3. Application Forms: U.S. Filing

Copies of all forms can be found in Appendix III.

Form I-129

Follow the directions in Section E2, except in Part 2, Question 4, mark box "b" instead of box "a."

Form I-539 (for accompanying relatives only)

Only one application form is needed for an entire family, but if there is more than one accompanying relative, each additional one should be listed on the I-539 supplement.

Part 1. These questions are self-explanatory. "A" numbers are usually given only to people who have previously applied for green cards or who have been in deportation proceedings.

Part 2, Question 1. Mark box "b," and write in "L-2."

Question 2. This question is self-explanatory.

Part 3. In most cases, you will mark Item 1 with the date requested in the Step One petition. You will also complete Items 3 and 4, which are self-explanatory.

Part 4, Questions 1–2. These questions are self-explanatory.

Question 3. The different parts to this question are self-explanatory; however, items "a" and "b" ask if an immigrant visa petition or adjustment of status application has ever been filed on your behalf. If you are applying for a green card through a relative, this would be Step One, as described in Chapter 5. If you are applying for a green card through employment, this would be Step Two as described in Chapter 8. If you have only begun the Labor Certification, the first step of getting a green card through employment, this question should be answered "no."

4. Application Documents: U.S. Filing

Each applicant must submit an I-94 card, the small white card you received on entering the U.S. Remember, if the date stamped on your I-94 card has already passed, you are ineligible for U.S. filing. Canadians who are just visiting are not expected to have I-94 cards. Canadians with any other type of nonimmigrant status should have them.

For each accompanying relative, send in an I-94 card. You will also need documents verifying their family relationship to you. You may verify a parent/child relationship by presenting the child's long form birth certificate. Many countries, including Canada and England, issue both short and long form birth certificates. Where both are available, the long form is needed because it contains the names of the parents while the short form does not. If you are accompanied by your spouse, you must prove that you are lawfully married by showing a valid civil marriage certificate. Church marriage certificates are generally unacceptable. (There are a few exceptions, depending on the laws of your particular country. Canadians, for example, may use church marriage certificates if the marriage took place in Quebec Province, but not elsewhere. If a civil certificate is available, however, you should always use it.) You may have married in a country where marriages are not customarily recorded. Tribal areas of Africa are an example. In such situations call the nearest consulate or embassy representing your home country for help with getting acceptable proof of marriage.

5. Additional Application Documents for Blanket L-1 Visa: U.S. Filing

In addition to all those documents listed above for applicants in individual L-1 cases, applicants having U.S. employers with approved blanket L-1 visa petitions must submit some extra documents. The first of these is the Notice of Action indicating approval of the blanket petition, Form I-797. Your U.S. employer will give this form directly to you and you will in turn submit it with your application. This document is a substitute for the Notice of Action sent by INS in individual L-1 cases.

Since your own eligibility for an L-1 classification is not proven in the Step One portion of a blanket L-1 petition case as it is in individual L-1 cases, you must document your own eligibility as part of Step Two.

a. Proof of Employment Abroad

You must supply documents proving that you were employed outside the U.S. by the non-U.S. company for at least one of the past three years. The best way to prove this is by providing copies of any wage statements you may have received. In Canada this is the T-4, in England, the P.A.Y.E. You should also submit your personal income tax return filed in your home country for the most recent year. If this is unavailable, a notarized statement from the bookkeeper or accountant of the non-U.S. employer may be used. However, you should also submit a statement explaining why the tax returns are unavailable. For example, you might state that tax returns are not required in your home country or that the returns haven't been prepared yet.

b. Proof You Are a Manager, Executive or Specialized Knowledge Professional

You must submit evidence that your employment abroad fits the INS definition of manager, executive or specialized knowledge professional, and that your employment in the U.S. will be of a similar type. To prove this, submit detailed statements from both the U.S. and non-U.S. employers explaining your specific duties as well as the number and kind of employees you supervise. If the application is based on specialized knowledge you possess, the statements should also describe the nature of the specialized knowledge, the reason why only you have that knowledge and how it will be used in your U.S. job. The specialized knowledge must have the characteristic of being special to the individual company. It cannot be knowledge that is available from others in the open job market. The statements your U.S. employer submits may be in his own words and do not have to be in any special form.

Because you must be a specialized knowledge professional, you must submit documents showing you meet INS's definition of professional. This usually requires you to show that you have a degree from a college or university. Therefore, evidence that you are a member of a profession should include copies of diplomas and transcripts from the colleges and universities you attended. INS insists on both a diploma and a transcript from a school where you graduated. If you attended a school but did not graduate, the transcript is required. If you were educated outside of the U.S., INS may request a credential evaluation from an approved evaluation service as explained in Section A4, above.

6. Application Interviews: U.S. Filing

Interviews on L-1 change of status applications are rarely held. When an interview is required, the INS regional service center where you filed will send your paperwork to the local INS office nearest your U.S. employer's place of business. This office will in turn contact you for an appointment. (If INS has questions on the petition rather than the application, your employer will be contacted.) INS may ask you to bring additional documents at that time.

If you are called for an interview, the most likely reason is that INS either suspects some type of fraud, doubts the existence of the company or believes you may be subject to a ground of inadmissibility. Interviews are usually a sign of trouble and can result in considerable delays.

7. Application Appeals: U.S. Filing

If your application is denied, you will receive a written decision by mail explaining the reasons for the denial. There is no way of making a formal appeal to INS if your application to change status is turned down. If the problem is too little evidence, you may be able to overcome this obstacle by adding more documents and resubmitting the entire application to the same INS office you have been dealing with, together with a written request that the case be reopened. The written request does not have to be in any special form. This is technically called a *Motion to Reopen*. There is a $110 fee to file this motion.

Remember that you may be denied the right to a U.S. filing without being denied an L-1 visa. When your application is turned down because you are found ineligible for U.S. filing, simply change your application to a consular filing. But before you depart the U.S., be sure that none of the bars to change of status (such as being out of status in the U.S. for a long time before departing) or grounds of inadmissibility, apply. If you depart and one of these problems exists, you may be stuck outside the U.S. for a long time before you can reenter.

Although there is no appeal to INS for the denial of an L-1 change of status application, you do have the right to file an appeal in a U.S. district court. It would be difficult to file such an appeal without employing an attorney at considerable expense. Such appeals are usually unsuccessful.

H. Extensions

L-1 visas can be extended for three years at a time, but you may not hold an L-1 visa for longer than a total of seven years. Although an extension is usually easier to get than the L-1 visa itself, it is not automatic. INS has the right to reconsider your qualifications based on any changes in the facts or law. As always, however, good cases that are well prepared will usually be successful.

To extend your L-1 visa, the petition and visa stamp will both have to be updated. Like the original application procedures, you can file either in the U.S. or at a consulate. However, contrary to our advice on the initial visa procedures, extensions are best handled in the U.S. That is because visa stamps, which can only be issued originally at consulates, may be extended in the U.S.

1. Step One: Extension Petition

Extension procedures are identical to the procedures followed in getting the initial visa, except that less documentation is generally required. However, the best practice is to fully document an extension application as well as the initial request, since INS will probably not have the original file and papers onsite, and it could cause a long delay if they have to request the old file to decide the extension request. In addition to the same documents you filed the first time, also submit your attestation, I-94 card, a letter from the employer requesting your visa be extended and a copy of U.S. income tax returns from both you and your employer for the previous two years, including the W-2 forms.

a. Extension Petition Forms

Copies of all forms can be found in Appendix III.

Form I-129 and L Supplement

Follow the directions in Section E2. The only difference is that you will mark boxes "2b" and "4c" of Part 2.

Form I-539 (for accompanying relatives only)

Follow the directions for Section G3, but mark box "1a" of Part 2.

b. Extension Petition Documents

You must submit your I-94 card. You should also submit the original Notice of Action I-797 (approval notice), a letter from your employer stating that your extension is required, a copy of your personal U.S. income tax returns for the past two years, including W-2 forms and a copy of your employer's most recent U.S. income tax return.

WORKING WHILE YOUR EXTENSION PETITION IS PENDING

If you file your petition for an extension of L-1 status before your authorized stay expires, you are automatically permitted to continue working under the same terms of your L-visa, for up to eight months (240 days) while you are waiting for a decision. If, however, your authorized stay expires after you have filed for an extension but before you receive an approval, and more than eight months (240 days) go by without getting a decision on your extension petition, you do not have continued work authorization and you must stop working.

2.   Step Two: Visa Revalidation

Visas can be revalidated either in the U.S. or at a consulate.

a.   Visa Revalidation: U.S. Filing

If you are physically in the U.S. and your L-1 status extension has been approved by INS, you can have your visa revalidated by mail without leaving the country. To do this, you must fill out Form OF-156, following the directions in Section F3, above, and send it to the Department of State. With the form you should also submit as documents your passport, current I-94 card, Notice of Action Form I-797 and a detailed letter from your employer describing your job duties. You should enclose a self-addressed, stamped envelope, or a completed Federal Express airbill. Send the entire package by certified mail to

CA/VO/P/D
Department of State
Visa Services
2401 "E" Street, N.W., (SA-1 L-703)
Washington, DC 20522-0106
Telephone: 202-663-1213
Fax: 202-663-1608

The passport will be returned to you with a newly revalidated visa in a few weeks. Nationals of some countries like Mexico are charged a fee for revalidating a visa, while nationals of other countries receive this service at no charge. Whether or not there is a fee depends on the nationality of the applicant, not the place where the application for the visa was originally made. You may call the State Department in Washington, D.C. to find out the amount of the revalidation fee, if any. If you send in your revalidation package without the correct fee, it will be returned to you, so check the amount in advance.

If your accompanying relatives are physically in the U.S., their L-2 visas may be revalidated by sending in their passports and I-94 cards together with yours. We strongly advise gathering your family together inside U.S. borders so you can take advantage of this simple revalidation procedure.

b.   Visa Revalidation: Consular Filing

If you must leave the U.S. after your extension has been approved but before you had time to get your visa revalidated, you must get a new visa stamp issued at a consulate. Read Section F, above. The procedures for consular extensions are identical.

We would like to reemphasize that it is much more convenient to apply for a revalidated visa by mail through the State Department in Washington, D.C. than it is to extend your L-1 visa through a consulate. If possible, you should try to schedule filing your extension petition when you can remain in the U.S. until it is complete.

3.   Blanket L-1 Extensions

This refers to the extension of the blanket status itself that is given to the company. This is not an explanation of how you may extend your own visa if you arrived in the U.S. under your company's blanket L-1 visa. Extensions for individual L-1 visa holders and those who obtained visas under the blanket program are handled in the same manner as explained above, except that a Certificate of Eligibility Form I-129S must also be submitted.

A company holding an approved blanket L-1 petition will have to extend that petition only one time. After the initial three-year approval period, the blanket L-1 visa petition can be extended with indefinite validity.

a.   Blanket L-1 Extension Forms

A new Form I-129 and L Supplement has to be filed. For instructions on filling out this Form, see Section E2, above.

b.   Blanket L-1 Extension Documents

The only documents required to extend the blanket L visa petition are as follows:

- a copy of the previous Notice of Action, Form I-797, and
- a written list of the names of all transferees admitted under the blanket L-1 petition for the previous three years; for each person, include the position held, name of the specific company where the person worked, the date of initial admission and the date of final departure.

FORMS AND DOCUMENTS CHECKLIST

STEP ONE: PETITION

Forms

- [ ] Form I-129 and L Supplement.

Documents

- [ ] Documents proving one year of employment outside the U.S.
- [ ] Documents proving employment outside of U.S. as an executive, manager or person with specialized knowledge.
- [ ] Articles of incorporation or other legal charter or business license of the non-U.S. company.
- [ ] Articles of incorporation or other legal charter or business license of the U.S. company.
- [ ] Legal business registration certificate of the non-U.S. company.
- [ ] Legal business registration certificate of the U.S. company.
- [ ] Tax returns of the non-U.S. company for the past two years.
- [ ] Tax returns of the U.S. company for the past two years, if available.
- [ ] Copies of all outstanding stock certificates, if the business is a corporation.
- [ ] Notarized affidavit from the secretary of the corporation, or, if the business is not a corporation, from the official record keeper of the business, stating the names of each owner and percentages of the company owned.
- [ ] If the business relationship is a joint venture, a copy of the written joint venture agreement.
- [ ] Annual shareholder reports of the U.S. and non-U.S. companies, if publicly held.
- [ ] Accountant's financial statements, including profit and loss statements and balance sheets of the non-U.S. company for the past two years.
- [ ] Accountant's financial statements, including profit and loss statements and balance sheets of the U.S. company for the past two years, if available.
- [ ] Payroll records of the non-U.S. company for the past two years.
- [ ] Payroll records of the U.S. company for the past two years, if available.

- [ ] Letters of reference from Chambers of Commerce for the non-U.S. company.
- [ ] Promotional literature describing the nature of U.S. employer's business.
- [ ] Letters from banks or bank statements indicating the average account balance of the U.S. business.
- [ ] Copy of a business lease or deed for business premises of the U.S. business.
- [ ] If more than half the stock of either the U.S. or non-U.S. company is publicly held, statements from the secretary of the corporation describing how the companies are related.

Additional Documents for Blanket Petitions

- [ ] Copies of the Notice of Action Forms I-797 showing at least ten L-1 approvals during the past year
- [ ] Company income tax returns, audited accountant's financial statements or the annual shareholders' report showing combined annual sales for all of the related U.S. employer companies totaling at least $25 million, or
- [ ] The most recent quarterly state unemployment tax return and federal employment tax return Form 940 showing at least 1,000 employees for all of the related U.S. employer business locations.

STEP TWO: APPLICATION

Forms

- [ ] OF forms (available at U.S. consulates abroad for consular filing only).
- [ ] Form I-129 (U.S. filing only).
- [ ] Form I-539 (U.S. filing only for accompanying relatives).

Documents

- [ ] Form I-797 indicating approval of the L-1 petition.
- [ ] Valid passport for you and each accompanying relative.
- [ ] I-94 card for you and each accompanying relative (U.S. filing only).
- [ ] One passport-type photo of you and each accompanying relative (Consular filing only).

Treaty Traders: E-1 Visas

Privileges

- You can work legally in the U.S. for a U.S. company for whom more than 50% of its business is trade between the U.S. and your home country.

- Visas can be issued quickly.

- You may travel in and out of the U.S. or remain here continuously until your E-1 visa expires.

- There is no legal limitation on the number of extensions that may be granted. Because of the initial duration of an E-1 visa (two years) as well as the limitless extensions, E-1 visas can allow you to live in the U.S. on a prolonged basis, provided you continue to maintain E-1 qualifications.

- Visas are available for accompanying relatives.

Limitations

- Visas are available only to nationals of countries having trade treaties with the U.S.

- You are restricted to working only for the specific employer or self-owned business that acted as your E-1 visa sponsor.

- Visas can initially be approved for up to two years. Extensions of up to two more years at a time may be allowed.

- Accompanying relatives may stay in the U.S. with you, but they may not work, unless they qualify to do so in their own right.

A. How to Qualify

There are no quota restrictions for E-1 visas. U.S. filed applications are usually approved within one to three months. Applications made at U.S. consulates are usually approved and visas issued within two to four weeks. There are several requirements for qualifying for an E-1 visa.

1. Citizen of a Treaty Country

E-1 visas are available to citizens of only selected countries which have trade treaties with the U.S. Those countries with treaties currently in effect are:

Argentina, Australia, Austria, Belgium, Bolivia, Brunei, Canada, Colombia, Costa Rica, Denmark, Estonia, Ethiopia, Finland, France, Georgia, Greece, Honduras, Iran, Ireland, Israel, Italy, Japan, Latvia, Liberia, Luxembourg, Mexico, Netherlands, Norway, Oman, Pakistan, Paraguay, Philippines, Spain, Suriname, Sweden, Switzerland, Taiwan, Thailand, Togo, Turkey, United Kingdom, Yugoslavia.

Treaties are also being contemplated or negotiated with Barbados, Hong Kong, Hungary, Nigeria, Uruguay and

Venezuela. Because treaty provisions are subject to change, be sure your country has one in force before proceeding with your application.

2. Company Owned by Citizens of a Qualifying Country

To qualify for an E-1 visa, you must be coming to the U.S. to work for a business, at least 50% of which is owned by citizens of your treaty country. The company may be owned by you or others. If the company is owned in part or in whole by others, and some or all of them already live in the U.S., those people may need to have E-1 visas themselves before the company can act as an E-1 sponsor for you. Specifically:

- at least 50% of the company must be owned by citizens of a single trade treaty country, and
- the owners from the single trade treaty country must either live outside the U.S. and be classifiable for E-1 status or live inside the U.S. with E-1 visas.

This second condition can be a little confusing. Some examples may help to make it clearer.

EXAMPLE 1: The company is owned 100% by one person. The owner is a citizen of a trade treaty country and lives outside the U.S. in his home country. He would qualify for E-1 status if he sought to enter the U.S.

In this case the owner does not need an E-1 visa for the company to support your E-1 visa application. He has already fulfilled the alternative condition by living outside the U.S. and being eligible for such status.

EXAMPLE 2: The company is owned in equal shares by two individuals. Each owner is a citizen of the same trade treaty country. One owner lives in the U.S. on a green card. The other still lives in his home country and is classifiable as an E-1.

In this case, neither owner needs an E-1 visa for the company to support your E-1 application because 50% of the owners have fulfilled the qualifying conditions. If, however, we changed this example so that both owners lived in the U.S., at least one of them would need an E-1 visa to fulfill the required conditions. (Green card holders do not qualify as E-1 principals.)

EXAMPLE 3: The company is owned in equal shares by 100 people. Thirty owners are citizens of a particular trade treaty country but live in the U.S. Thirty other owners are citizens of the same trade treaty country and they are living in their home country, but are eligible as E-1 visa holders. The remaining 40 owners are U.S. citizens.

In this situation, if the company is to act as an E-1 sponsor for others, 20 of the 30 owners who are citizens of the trade treaty country but live in the U.S. must hold E-1 visas. Remember that only 50 of the owners need to be citizens of the treaty country. Of those 50, each must either live outside the U.S. and be classifiable as E-1's or live in the U.S. on an E-1 visa. In our example, 30 live outside the U.S. Therefore, only 20 of the trade treaty country citizens living inside the U.S. need have E-1 visas to make up the necessary 50% total of qualifying owners.

Additionally, INS' regulations allow a different test in the case of large multinational corporations in which it is difficult to determine ownership by stock ownership. Therefore, in the situation where a corporation's stock is sold exclusively in the country of incorporation, it may be presumed to have the nationality of the country where the stocks are exchanged.

3. You Must Be a 50% Owner or Key Employee

E-1 visas may be issued only to the principal owners or key employees of the qualifying business, provided all have the same treaty nationality. To qualify as a principal owner, you must control at least 50% of the company, possess operational control through a managerial position or similar corporate device, or be in a position to control the enterprise by other means. To qualify as a key employee you must be considered an executive, supervisor, supervisory role executive or person whose skills are essential to the enterprise.

a. Executives and Supervisors

For E-2 classification purposes, the main thrust of the position must be executive or supervisory, and give the employee ultimate control and responsibility for the operation of at least a major part of the enterprise. INS will examine the following to determine whether a given position fits the bill:

- an "executive" position is normally one that gives the employee great authority in determining policy and direction of the enterprise;
- "supervisory" positions normally entail responsibility for supervising a major portion of an enterprise's operations and do not usually involve direct supervision of low-level employees, and
- whether the individual applicant's skills, experience, salary and title are on a par with executive or supervisory positions, and whether the position carries overall authority and responsibility in the overall context of the enterprise, such as discretionary decision making, policy-setting, direction and management of business operations, and supervision of other professional and supervisory personnel.

b. Essential Employees

INS' regulations are vague on what constitutes the essentiality of an employee. The employee's skills do not have to be unique or "one of a kind" but they should be indispensable to the success of the investment. They will be evaluated on a case-by-case basis; however, if the skills possessed by the employee are commonplace or readily available in the U.S. labor market, it will be difficult to show that the employee is essential.

Specifically, INS will consider the following to determine whether an individual who is a non-executive, non-supervisor and who is not at least a 50% owner, should be classified as an E-2 employee because of the essentiality of his or her skills:

- the degree of expertise in the area of operations involved; the degree of experience and training with the enterprise
- whether U.S. workers possess the individual's skills or aptitude

- the length of the applicant's specific skill or aptitude
- the length of time required to train an individual to perform the job duties of the position
- the relationship of the individual's skills and talents to the overall operations of the entity, and
- the salary the special qualifications can command.

Knowledge of a foreign language and/or culture will not by themselves constitute the degree of essentiality required.

4. Fifty-One Percent of the Company's Trade Must Be Between the U.S. and Your Home Country

More than 50% of the company's trade must be between the U.S. and the treaty nation citizen's home country. For example, if you are from the U.K. and are in the business of importing English antiques to the U.S., more than 50% of your inventory, as measured by its cash value, must have been imported directly from the U.K. If some other company does the importing and your business simply buys the British goods once they reach the U.S., you will not qualify for the visa because your company is not directly engaged in trade with the U.K.

The law is liberal in its definition of what constitutes trade. The most straightforward example is the import or export of a tangible product. The transfer of technology through scientifically knowledgeable employees or the rendering of services are also considered trade. Activities other than the sale of goods that have been officially recognized by the U.S. Department of State as trade for E-1 purposes include international banking, the practice of law, the sale of insurance, the provision of international transportation, the sale of communications services, some news gathering activities and the sale of tickets by tourist agencies.

5. Substantial Trade

A company must be carrying on a substantial amount of trade between the U.S. and the home country in order for the company to successfully support your E-1 application. The term "substantial" is not defined in the law by a strict numerical measure. In fact it is not specifically defined at all. What is considered substantial depends on the type of business. For example, a business that imports heavy machinery will have to show a greater dollar volume of business than one importing candy bars to meet the requirement of substantial trade.

There are three general tests—dollars, volume, and frequency— that, in our experience, can normally be relied on to measure substantiality. The company must be able to meet the minimum standards of all three.

a. Dollar Amount of Trade

The dollar amount (not the retail value) of the inventory, services or other commodities purchased from or sold to the treaty country should exceed $200,000 per year. However, some consulates require the sales or purchases to equal or exceed as much as $500,000, while others may accept as little as $50,000. A specific sum is not written into the law. The individual consul officer has the authority to require varying amounts in different cases. Still, experience shows that anything under the $200,000 mark is a weak case.

b. Volume

If the company sells products, to satisfy the volume test import or export trade must be enough to create full-time business in the U.S. The company's initial shipment must fill at least an entire warehouse or retail store. If the company sells services, the volume should be large enough to support the E-1 visa holder and at least one other worker. Some businesses do not meet the volume test when they are first starting up but grow to the required size as time goes on. Purchasing a growing business may be one way to fulfill the volume requirement immediately.

c. Frequency

The company must import to or export from the U.S. with sufficient frequency to maintain a full inventory at all times. One shipment is not enough. Importation or exportation must be ongoing.

We emphasize that these tests have been derived from our own experience and are not part of the immigration laws. It is possible for an E-1 visa to be approved with a smaller amount of trade than we have described in our three tests. With E-1 visas, a great deal is left to the judgment of the INS or consul officer evaluating the application. However, the results from cases we have filed suggest that E-1 visas will usually not be issued unless the three conditions outlined above are satisfied.

6. Intent to Leave the U.S.

E-1 visas are meant to be temporary. At the time of application, you must intend to depart the U.S. when your business there is completed. As previously mentioned, you are not required to maintain a foreign residence abroad. Furthermore, if you are applying as a representative of foreign media, the State Department's rules specify that the consul should first consider your application under the "I" visa rules, under which you must show a definitive intent to depart and not pursue permanent residence.

Remember, all nonimmigrant visas are intended to be temporary. The U.S. government knows it is difficult to read minds. Therefore, you can expect to be asked for evidence showing that when you go to America on an E-1 visa, you eventually plan to leave. In many nonimmigrant categories, you are asked to show proof that you keep a house or apartment outside the U.S. as an indication that you eventually intend to go back to your home country. You do not need to keep a home outside the U.S. to qualify for an E-1 visa, but this does not mean that you are freed from the requirement of having the intent to leave. You are not. It simply means that when you apply for an E-1 visa, maintaining a residence abroad is not an essential element of proving that intent. You will, however, be asked to show that you do have some family members, possessions or property elsewhere in the world as an incentive for your eventual departure from the U.S.

7. Accompanying Relatives

When you qualify for an E-1 visa, your spouse and unmarried children under age 21 can also get E-1 visas simply by providing proof of their family relationship to you. E-1 visas for dependents authorize your accompanying relatives to stay with you in the U.S., but not to work there.

APPLYING FOR A GREEN CARD FROM E-1 STATUS

If you have an E-1 visa, you can file to get a green card, but being in the U.S. on an E-1 visa gives you no advantage in doing so, and in fact may prove to be a drawback. That is because E-1 visas, like all nonimmigrant visas, are intended only for those who plan on leaving the U.S. once their jobs or other activities there are completed. However, if you apply for a green card, you are in effect making a statement that you never intend to leave the U.S. Therefore, the U.S. government will allow you to keep E-1 status while pursuing a green card, but only if you can convince the government that you did not intend to get a green card when you originally applied for the E-1 visa, and that you will leave the U.S. if you are unable to secure a green card before your E-1 visa expires. Proving these things can be difficult. If you do not succeed, your E-1 visa may be taken away. Should this happen, it may affect your green card application, since being out of status or working without authorization may be a bar to getting a green card in the U.S., or may create a waiting period if you depart the U.S. and apply for a visa. (See Chapter 25.)

B. E-1 Visa Overview

Getting an E-1 visa is a one-step process.

1. The Application

Once you have opened a qualifying company engaged in trade between your home country and the U.S., or been offered a job as a key employee of a qualifying company owned by others from your country, getting an E-1 visa is a one-step process. Some applicants seeking E-1 visas as key employees expect their sponsoring employers to handle the entire process for them and indeed, a number of large companies are equipped with experienced workers who will do this for highly desirable employees. Other companies are prepared to pay an immigration attorney's fees as an expense of trying to attract a key staff member. However, in many cases it is the employee who is most interested in having the visa issued, and, to employers, the red tape of having a foreign employee can be an unfamiliar nuisance.

As we give you step-by-step instructions for getting an E-1 visa, we will indicate that certain activities are to be performed by your employer and others are to be performed by you, recognizing that in the case of an E-1 visa you yourself may be the principal owner of the qualifying business. We will discuss each task according to who has the legal responsibility for carrying it out. Even if you are being hired as a key employee, though the law presumes your employer is performing a particular function, there is nothing to stop you from helping with the work. For example, you can fill out forms intended to be completed by your employer and simply ask him to check them over and sign them. Unless your employer volunteers to help or you are sure the company simply can't live without you, we recommend that you assist as much as possible in the preparation of the paperwork. The less your sponsoring employer is inconvenienced, the more the company will be willing to act as sponsor for your E-1 visa. An imposition on company time or money might cost you a job offer. With the help of this book, you will know how to do all that is required. It is completely legal, as well as in your best interest, to assist whenever possible. Of course if you are the principal owner of a qualifying business, all the paperwork responsibilities will fall on you.

The one step required to get an E-1 visa is called the application. The object of the application is to show that the conditions to getting an E-1 visa discussed earlier in this chapter have been met. It is filed by you and your accompanying relatives, if any. The application is your formal request for an E-1 visa or status. The application may be carried out in the U.S. at an INS office or in your home country at a U.S. consulate there. The vast majority of nonimmigrant visa applications are filed at consulates. That is because most cases don't qualify for U.S. filing and besides, consular filing usually brings better results. The major benefit is that an E-1 visa, which is stamped in your passport, can be issued only by American consulates. When you file the application at a consulate, your visa will be stamped in your passport at that time. INS offices inside the U.S. may issue statuses but not visas. (See Chapter 14, Section B, Difference Between a Visa and a Status).

If you are already in the U.S. legally on some other type of nonimmigrant visa, you qualify to apply for an E-1 status at an INS office inside the U.S., using a procedure known as *change of nonimmigrant status.* (If you were admitted as a visitor without a visa under the Visa Waiver Program, you may not carry out the application step in the U.S. Currently there are 29 participating countries in the Visa Waiver Program, including: Andorra, Argentina, Austria, Australia, Belgium, Brunei, Denmark, Finland, France, Germany, Iceland, Ireland, Italy, Japan, Liechtenstein, Luxembourg, Monaco, The Netherlands, New Zealand, Norway, Portugal, San Marino, Singapore, Slovenia, Spain, Sweden, Switzerland, the United Kingdom and Uruguay. The government has approved Greece for inclusion in the program in the near future.) This is simply a technical term meaning you are switching from one nonimmigrant status to another. If a change of status is approved, you will then be treated as if you had entered the country with an E-1 visa and you can keep the status as long as you remain in the U.S. or until it expires, whichever comes first.

You will not, however, receive a visa stamp, which is what you need if your plans include traveling in and out of the U.S. To repeat, visa stamps are issued only at U.S. consulates abroad. Therefore, if you change your status and later travel outside the U.S., you will have to go to the U.S. consulate in your home country and repeat the application over again, obtaining the E-1 visa stamp in your passport before you can return. This extra procedure may make changing status an unattractive option.

Although it is not a requirement, one item you or your sponsoring employer may wish to add to the paperwork package is a cover letter. Cover letters act as a summary and index to the forms and documents, and are often used by immigration attorneys or U.S. companies that process many visas for their employees. Cover letters begin with a statement summarizing the facts of the case and explaining why the particular applicant is eligible for the visa. This statement is followed by a list of the forms and documents submitted. If it is carefully written, a cover letter can make the case clearer and easier to process for the consular or INS officer evaluating it. This is particularly important in an E-1 visa case where the documentation by itself may require explanation. Cover letters must be individually tailored to each case, so if you don't think you can write a good one on your own, just leave it out and submit only your forms and documents.

2. Paperwork

There are two types of paperwork you must submit to get an E-1 visa. The first consists of official government forms completed by you or your employer. The second is personal and business documents such as birth and marriage certificates, school transcripts and diplomas, and company financial statements and tax returns. We will tell you exactly what forms and documents you need.

It is vital that forms are properly filled out and all necessary documents are supplied. You or your U.S. employer may resent the intrusion into your privacy and sizable effort it takes to prepare immigration applications but you should realize the process is an impersonal matter to immigration officials. Your getting a visa is more important to you than it is to the U.S. government. This is not a pleasant thing to accept, but you are better off having a real understanding of your position. People from all over the world want U.S. visas. There is no shortage of applicants. Take the time and trouble to prepare your papers properly. In the end it will pay off with a successful application.

The documents you or your U.S. employer supply to INS do not have to be originals. Photocopies of all documents are acceptable as long as you have the originals in your possession and are willing to produce them at the request of INS. Documents submitted to U.S. consulates, on the other hand, must be either originals or official government certified copies. Government certified copies and notarized copies are not the same thing. Documents that have only been notarized are not acceptable. They must carry a government seal. In addition to any original or government certified copies of documents submitted to a consulate, you should submit plain photocopies of each document as well. After the consulate compares the copies with the originals, it will return the originals.

Documents will be accepted if they are in either English, or, with papers filed at U.S. consulates abroad, the language of the country where the documents are being filed. An exception exists for papers filed at U.S. consulates in Japan, where all documents must be translated into English. If the documents are not in an acceptable language as just explained, they must be accompanied by a full, word for word, written English translation. Any capable person may act as translator. It is not necessary to hire a professional. At the end of each translation, the following statement must appear:

I hereby certify that I translated this document from (language) to English. This translation is accurate and complete. I further certify that I am fully competent to translate from (language) to English.

The translator should sign this statement but it does not have to be witnessed or notarized.

Later in this chapter, we describe in detail the forms and documents needed to get your E-1 visa. A summary checklist of forms and documents appears at the end of the chapter.

C. Who's Who in Getting Your E-1 Visa

Getting an E-1 visa will be easier if you familiarize yourself with the technical names used for each participant in the process. You are known as the *applicant*. The applicant can be either the owner or a key employee, depending on whether or not it is you who owns the company. The business is known as the *qualifying business* or *qualifying company*, the *employer* or the *sponsoring business*. If you are bringing your spouse and children with you as accompanying relatives they are known as *applicants* as well.

D. The Application: Consular Filing

Anyone who owns a qualifying business or who has been offered a job in the U.S. as a key employee by a qualifying business can apply for an E-1 visa at a U.S. consulate in his or her home country. You must be physically present in order to apply there. If you have been or are now working or living illegally in the U.S., you may be ineligible to get an E-1 visa from a U.S. consulate even if you otherwise qualify. Read Chapter 25 to understand the issues and risks involved.

1. Benefits and Drawbacks of Consular Filing

The most important benefit to consular filing, making it almost always preferable to U.S. filing, is that only consulates issue visas. When you go through a U.S. filing you get a status, not a visa. (See Chapter 14, Section B, Difference Between a Visa and a Status). An E-1 status confers the same right to work as an E-1 visa, but it does not give you the ability to travel in and out of the U.S. Therefore, if you want travel privileges, you will at some time have to go through the extra step of applying for a visa at a U.S. consulate, even though you have already applied for and received E-1 status in the U.S.

Moreover, anyone with a qualifying business may apply for an E-1 visa at the appropriate consulate, without waiting for action from INS. That is not the case with U.S.

applications for E-1 status. If you are in the U.S. illegally, consular filing is a must, although you may not be eligible (see Chapter 25). You are not eligible to process a status application in the U.S. unless you are presently in status.

A further plus to consular filing is that consular offices may work more quickly to issue nonimmigrant visas than INS service centers may to process nonimmigrant statuses. Your waiting time for the paperwork to be finished will be much shorter at a U.S. consulate abroad than at most U.S. INS offices.

A drawback to consular filing comes from the fact that you must be physically present in the country where the consulate is located to file there. If your petition is ultimately turned down because of an unexpected problem, not only will you have to wait outside the U.S. until the problem is resolved, but other visas in your passport, such as a visitor's visa, may be canceled. It will then be impossible for you to enter the U.S. in any capacity. Consequently, if your E-1 visa case is not very strong and freedom of travel is not essential to you, it might be wise to apply in the U.S., make up your mind to remain there for the duration of the E-1 status and skip trying to get a visa from the consulate.

2. Application General Procedures: Consular Filing

Technically, the law allows you to apply for an E-1 visa at any U.S. consulate you choose, although if you have even overstayed your status by as little as one day, you are required to apply at your home consulate. A complete list of all U.S. consulates that process visa applications, together with their addresses and phone numbers, is in Appendix I. However, from a practical standpoint your case will be given greatest consideration at the consulate in your home country. Applying in some other country creates suspicion in the minds of the consul officers there about your motives for choosing their consulate. Often, when an applicant is having trouble at a home consulate he will seek a more lenient office in some other country. This practice of consulate shopping is frowned upon by officials in the system. Unless you have a very good reason for being elsewhere (such as a temporary job assignment in some other nation), it is smarter to file your visa application in your home country.

In some consulates you can simply walk in with your application paperwork and get your E-1 visa immediately. Most insist that you submit your forms and documents in advance, and then give you an appointment for a personal interview several weeks later. Since procedures among consulates vary, you should always telephone in advance to ask about local policies.

On entering the U.S. with your new E-1 visa, you will be given an I-94 card. It will be stamped with a date indicating how long you can stay. Normally you are permitted to remain for two years at a time, without regard to when your visa actually expires. Each time you exit and reenter the U.S., you will get a new I-94 card authorizing your stay for an additional one- or two-year period, or if you do not wish to leave the U.S. after that time, you can apply for extensions of stay which are issued in two-year increments for as long as you maintain your E-1 status qualifications.

3. Application Form: Consular Filing

When you file at a U.S. consulate abroad, the consulate officials will provide you with certain optional forms, designated by an "OF" preceding a number. Instructions for completing optional forms and what to do with them once they are filled out will come with the forms. We do not include copies of these forms in Appendix III.

4. Application Documents: Consular Filing

All E-1 applicants must show a valid passport and present one passport-type photograph taken in accordance with the photo instructions in Appendix III. For each accompanying relative, you must present a valid passport and one passport-type photograph taken in accordance with the photo instructions in Appendix III. You will also need documents verifying their family relationship to you. You may verify a parent/child relationship by presenting the child's long form birth certificate. Many countries, including Canada and England, issue both short and long form birth certificates. Where both are available, the long form is needed because it contains the names of the parents while the short form does not. If you are accompanied by your spouse, you must establish that you are lawfully married by showing a civil marriage certificate. Church marriage certificates are generally unacceptable. (There are a few exceptions, depending on the laws of your particular country. Canadians, for example, may use church marriage certificates if the marriage took place in Quebec Province, but not elsewhere. If a civil certificate is available, however, you should always use it.) You may have married in a country where marriages are not customarily recorded. Tribal areas of Africa are an example. In such situations, call the nearest consulate or embassy of your home country for help with getting acceptable proof of marriage.

You will need documents establishing your intent to leave the U.S. when your business in the U.S. is completed. The consulate will want to see evidence of ties to some other country so strong that you will be highly motivated to return there. Proof of such ties can include deeds verifying ownership of a house or other real property, written statements from you explaining that close relatives live elsewhere, or letters from a company outside the U.S. showing that you have a job waiting when you return from America. We have already explained that technically you should not be required to prove that you are maintaining a residence outside the U.S. in order to get an E-1 visa. As a practical matter, however, a consul officer may ask for evidence that you do have assets of some kind located outside the U.S. If you want your visa to be approved you will have to produce this evidence.

Some additional documents are necessary.

i.   Proof of Your Nationality

You must prove that you are a citizen of one of the trade treaty countries. Your passport showing your nationality must therefore be presented.

ii.   Proof of the Nationality of the Qualifying Business Owners

You must show that the qualifying business is owned by citizens of one of the trade treaty countries. If you are not the owner yourself, you will need to show that both you and those who do own the company are citizens of the same treaty country. If the owners are presently living in the U.S., you must show that they hold E-1 visas. If you are the majority owner of the business, your passport showing that you are a national of one of the E-1 treaty countries must be presented. If you are applying for the visa not as an owner, but as a key employee, you must also submit passports or other proof of the citizenship of each owner who is a national of your treaty country. Remember that although you will be doing work for the qualifying company in the U.S., the company and its owners may or may not be located there. Therefore, documents must be presented showing where each of the owners is living currently. Affidavits from each of these owners stating their places of residence will serve this purpose. If any are living in the U.S., copies of their passports and I-94 cards are also needed to demonstrate that they hold valid E-1 visas. Remember, if the owners of the company live in the U.S., at least 50% must also hold E-1 visas for the business to support your own E-1 application.

You will need to prove that you or other nationals of your country own not just a small part, but a majority of the qualifying business. If the qualifying business is a corporation, you should submit copies of all stock certificates, together with a notarized affidavit from the secretary of the corporation listing the name of each shareholder and the number of shares each owns. The affidavit must account for all the shares issued to date. Remember, at least 50% must be owned by nationals of your treaty country.

If the qualifying business is not incorporated, instead of copies of stock certificates you will need to present legal papers proving the existence and ownership of the company. These may be partnership agreements, business registration certificates or business licenses, together with a notarized affidavit from an official of the company certifying who owns the business and in what percentages.

iii.   Proof That You are a Key Employee

If you are not the majority owner of the company, you must submit evidence that your job in the U.S. will fit the INS definition of executive or supervisor or supervisory role essential employee. To prove this, detailed statements from the sponsoring business explaining your specific duties as well as the number and kind of employees you will supervise must be presented. If the application is based on your special position as an employee, the statements should also describe the nature of the essential knowledge or experience and how it will be used and why it is essential in your U.S. job. These required statements may be in your employer's own words and do not have to be in any special form.

iv.   Proof of the Existence of an Active Business

You should submit as many documents as possible to show that your E-1 visa application is based on a real, ongoing business. Such evidence should include:
- articles of incorporation or other business charter of the qualifying company
- bank statements from the qualifying company
- credit agreements with suppliers
- letters of credit issued
- leases or deeds for business premises and warehouse space
- tax returns filed in the past two years, if any, including payroll tax returns, and
- promotional literature or advertising.

If the business is newly formed, there will be no tax returns yet. You should then submit a detailed business plan including financial projections for the next five years.

v.   Proof That a Majority of the Company's Trade Is Between the U.S. and Your Home Country

More than 50% of the company's total trade must consist of commerce between your treaty home country and the U.S. This is best shown by presenting copies of all import or export documents from the previous 12 months, including purchase or sale orders, bills of lading and customs entry documents, contracts with suppliers outside of the U.S, and a balance sheet from the qualifying company showing the total amount of inventory for the same period. Comparison of the balance sheet with the import or export documents will show the percentage of the company's trade devoted to commerce between the U.S. and the trade treaty country. The dollar amount of the imports or exports between the U.S. and your home country must total more than 50% of the entire inventory.

vi. Proof That the Trade Is Substantial

The qualifying company's trade between the U.S. and your home treaty country must be substantial, meeting the three tests previously described: dollar, volume, and frequency. The same documents presented to prove that the majority of the company's trade is between the U.S. and your home treaty country will also serve to show that the trade is substantial.

5. Application Interviews: Consular Filing

Most consulates will require an interview before issuing an E-1 visa. A major exception to this is the U.S. embassy in London, which approves E-1 visa applications entirely by mail. During the interview, a consul officer will examine the forms and documents for accuracy, especially regarding facts about the substantiality of the business and the nationality of the owners. Evidence of ties to your home country will also be checked. During the interview, you will surely be asked how long you intend to remain in the U.S. Any answer indicating uncertainty about plans to return or an interest in applying for a green card may result in a denial of your E-1 visa. (See the "Intent to Leave the U.S." section at page 4.)

6. Application Appeals: Consular Filing

When a consulate turns down an E-1 visa application, there is no way to make a formal appeal, although you are free to reapply as often as you like. Some consulates, however, will make you wait several months before allowing you to file another application. If your visa is denied, you will be told by the consul officer the reasons for the denial. Written statements of decisions are not normally provided in non-immigrant cases. If a lack of evidence about a particular point is the problem, sometimes simply presenting more evidence on an unclear fact can bring a positive change in the result.

The most likely reasons for having an E-1 visa turned down are because the consul officer does not believe that your trade is substantial enough, or you are found inadmissible.

Certain people who have been refused visas reapply at a different consulate, attempting to hide the fact that they were turned down elsewhere. If your application is denied, the last page in your passport will be stamped "Application Received" with the date and location of the rejecting consulate. This notation shows that some type of prior visa application has failed. It serves as a warning to other consulates that your case merits close inspection. If what we have just told you makes you think it would be a good idea to overcome this problem by obtaining a new, unmarked passport, you should also know that permanent computer records are kept of all visa denials.

E. The Application: U.S. Filing

If you are physically present in the U.S., you may apply for E-1 status without leaving the country on the following conditions:

- you entered the U.S. legally and not on a visa waiver
- you have never worked illegally
- the date on your I-94 card has not passed, and
- you are admissible and none of the bars to changing status apply to you (see Chapter 25).

If you were admitted as a visitor without a visa under the Visa Waiver Program, you may not carry out the application step in the U.S. Currently there are 29 participating countries in the Visa Waiver Program, including: Andorra, Argentina, Austria, Australia, Belgium, Brunei, Denmark, Finland, France, Germany, Iceland, Ireland, Italy, Japan, Liechtenstein, Luxembourg, Monaco, The Netherlands, New Zealand, Norway, Portugal, San Marino, Singapore, Slovenia, Spain, Sweden, Switzerland, the United Kingdom and Uruguay. The government has approved Greece for inclusion in the program in the near future.

⚠️ If you cannot meet these terms, you may not file for E-1 status in the U.S. It is important to realize, however, that eligibility to apply in the U.S. has nothing to do with overall eligibility for an E-1 visa. Applicants who are barred from filing in the U.S. but otherwise qualify for E-1 status can sometimes apply successfully for an E-1 visa at U.S. consulates abroad. If you find you are not eligible for U.S. filing, see Section D, above, and read Chapter 25 before devising a strategy.

1. Benefits and Drawbacks of U.S. Filing

Visas are never given inside the U.S. They are issued exclusively by U.S. consulates abroad. If you file in the U.S. and you are successful, you will get E-1 status but not the visa itself. This is a major drawback to U.S. applications. E-1 status allows you to remain in the U.S. with E-1 privileges until the status expires, but should you leave the country for any reason before that time, you will have to apply for the visa itself at a U.S. consulate before returning to America. Moreover, the fact that your E-1 status has been approved in the U.S. does not guarantee that the consulate will approve your visa. Some consulates may even regard your previously acquired E-1 status as a negative factor, an indication that you have deliberately tried to avoid the consulate's authority.

There is another problem which comes up only in U.S. filings. It is the issue of what is called "preconceived intent." To approve a change of status, INS must believe that at the time you originally entered the U.S. as a visitor or with some other nonimmigrant visa, you did not intend to apply for a different status. If INS thinks you had a preconceived plan to change from the status you arrived with to a different status, it may deny your application. The preconceived intent issue is one less potential hazard you will face if you apply at a U.S. consulate abroad.

On the plus side of U.S. filing is that when problems do arise with your U.S. application, you can stay in America while they are being corrected, a circumstance most visa applicants prefer. If you run into snags at a U.S. consulate, you will have to remain outside the U.S. until matters are resolved.

2. Application General Procedures: U.S. Filing

The application, consisting of both forms and documents, is sent by mail to the INS regional service center having jurisdiction over the intended place of business. INS regional service center are not the same as INS local offices. There are four INS regional service centers spread across the U.S. Appendix II contains a list of all INS regional service centers and their addresses.

The filing fee for applying to change status is $120 (Form I-539) and an additional $110 for the request for E Status (Form I-129). Checks or money orders are accepted. It is not advisable to send cash. We recommend submitting all papers by certified mail, return receipt requested, and making a copy of everything sent in to keep in your records.

Within a week or two after mailing in the application, you should get back a written notice of confirmation that the papers are being processed, together with a receipt for the fees. This notice will also tell you your immigration file number and approximately when to expect a decision. If INS wants further information before acting on your case, all application papers, forms and documents, will be returned together with another form known as an *I-797*. The I-797 tells you what additional pieces of information or

documents are expected. You should supply the extra data and mail the whole package back to the INS regional service center.

Applications for an E-1 status are normally approved within two to eight weeks. When this happens, you will receive a Notice of Action Form I-797 indicating the dates for which your status is approved. A new I-94 card will be attached to the bottom of the form.

3. Application Forms: U.S. Filing

Copies of all forms can be found in Appendix III.

Form I-129 and E Supplement

The basic form for the application is Form I-129 and E Supplement. A new form is being developed. Until it is released, continue to use the old forms. The I-129 form is used for many different nonimmigrant visas. In addition to the basic part of the form that applies to all types of visas, it comes with several supplements for each specific nonimmigrant category. Simply tear out and use the supplement that applies to you. Your employer must file the form in duplicate. Send in two signed originals. Copies are not acceptable.

Most of the questions on the I-129 form are straightforward. If a question does not apply to you, answer it with "None" or "N/A." Those questions requiring explanations are as follows:

Part 1. These questions are self-explanatory.

Part 2, Question 1. Question 1 should be answered "E-1."

Questions 2–3. These questions are self-explanatory.

Question 4. This question asks you to indicate what action is requested from INS. Normally you will mark box "b."

Question 5. This question is self-explanatory

Part 3. These questions are self-explanatory. If you previously held a U.S. work permit and therefore have a U.S. Social Security number, put down that number where

asked. If you have a Social Security number that is not valid for employment, put down that number followed by "not valid for employment." If you have never had a Social Security number, put down "None." (Read Chapter 25 before listing a false number.)

Alien Registration Numbers, which all begin with the letter "A," are given only to people who have applied for green cards, received political asylum or been in deportation proceedings. If you do have an "A" number, put that number down and also explain how you got it, such as "number issued from previous green card petition filed by my brother." If you do not have an "A" number, write down "None."

If your present authorized stay has expired, you cannot file your application inside the U.S. You must use consular processing.

Part 4. These questions are self-explanatory. Having a green card petition or application in process may affect your ability to get an E-1 status. To qualify for an E-1 status, you must intend to return to your home country after your business needs are completed in the U.S.

Part 5. These questions are self-explanatory. The dates of intended employment should not exceed one year, which is the maximum period of time for which an initial E-1 status may be approved. Extensions may be approved for two years at a time.

E Supplement

This form is self-explanatory. Fill in all parts except Section 4.

Form I-539 (for accompanying relatives only)

Only one application form is needed for an entire family, but if there is more than one accompanying relative, each additional one should be listed on the I-539 supplement.

Part 1. These questions are self-explanatory. "A" numbers are usually given only to people who have previously applied for green cards or who have been in deportation proceedings.

Part 2, Question 1. Mark box "b," and write in "E-1."

Question 2. This question is self-explanatory.

Part 3. In most cases you will mark Item 1. You will also complete Items 3 and 4, which are self-explanatory.

Part 4, Questions 1–2. These questions are self-explanatory.

Question 3. The different parts to this question are self-explanatory, however, Items "a" and "b" ask if an immigrant visa petition or adjustment of status application has ever been filed on your behalf. If you are applying for a green card through a relative, this would be Step One, as described in Chapter 5. If you are applying for a green card through

employment, this would be Step Two as described in Chapter 8. If you have only begun the Labor Certification, the first step of getting a green card through employment, this question should be answered "no."

4. Application Documents: U.S. Filing

Each applicant must submit an I-94 card, the small white card you received on entering the U.S. Remember, if the date stamped on your I-94 card has already passed, you are ineligible for U.S. filing. Canadians who are just visiting are not expected to have I-94 cards. Canadians with any other type of nonimmigrant status should have them.

For each accompanying relative, send in an I-94 card. You will also need documents verifying their family relationship to you. You may verify a parent/child relationship by presenting the child's long form birth certificate. Many countries, including Canada and England, issue both short and long form birth certificates. Where both are available, the long form is needed because it contains the names of the parents while the short form does not. If you are accompanied by your spouse, you must establish that you are lawfully married by showing a civil marriage certificate. Church marriage certificates are generally unacceptable. (There are a few exceptions, depending on the laws of your particular country. Canadians, for example, may use church marriage certificates if the marriage took place in Quebec Province, but not elsewhere. If a civil certificate is available, however, you should always use it.) You may have married in a country where marriages are not customarily recorded. Tribal areas of Africa are an example. In such situations call the nearest consulate or embassy of your home country for help with getting acceptable proof of marriage.

We have emphasized that in order to qualify for an E-1 you must have the intent to eventually leave the U.S. when your business is completed and we have explained how consulates will demand proof that ties to your home country or some other place outside the U.S. are strong enough to motivate your eventual departure. In a U.S. filing, INS does not always ask for proof of this. However, we strongly advise you to submit such evidence anyway. Proof of ties to some other country can include deeds verifying ownership of a house or other real property, written statements from you explaining that close relatives are living elsewhere, or letters from a company outside the U.S. showing that you have a job waiting when you leave America.

Some additional documents are necessary.

i. Proof of Your Nationality

You must prove that you are a citizen of one of the trade treaty countries. Your passport showing your nationality must therefore be presented.

ii.   Proof of the Nationality of the Qualifying Business Owners

You must show that the qualifying business is owned by citizens of one of the trade treaty countries. If you are not the owner yourself, you will need to show that both you and those who do own the company are citizens of same treaty country. If the owners are presently living in the U.S., you must show that they hold E-1 visas. If you are the majority owner of the business, your passport showing that you are a national of one of the E-1 treaty countries must be presented. If you are applying for the visa not as an owner but as a key employee, you must also submit passports or other proof of the citizenship of each owner who is a national of your treaty country. Remember that although you will be doing work for the qualifying company in the U.S., the company and its owners may or may not be located there. Therefore, documents must be presented showing where each of the owners is living currently. Affidavits from each of these owners stating their places of residence will serve this purpose. If any are living in the U.S., copies of their passports and I-94 cards are also needed to demonstrate that they hold valid E-1 visas. Remember, if the owners of the company live in the U.S. at least 50% must also hold E-1 visas for the business to support your own E-1 application.

You will need to prove that you or other nationals of your country own not just a small part, but a majority of the qualifying business. If the qualifying business is a corporation, you should submit copies of all stock certificates together with a notarized affidavit from the secretary of the corporation listing the name of each shareholder and the number of shares each owns. The affidavit must account for all the shares issued to date. Remember, at least 50% must be owned by nationals of your treaty country.

If the qualifying business is not incorporated, instead of copies of stock certificates you will need to present legal papers proving the existence and ownership of the company. These may be partnership agreements, business registration certificates or business licenses together with a notarized affidavit from an official of the company certifying who owns the business and in what percentages.

iii.   Proof That You Are a Key Employee

If you are not the majority owner of the company, you must submit evidence that your job in the U.S. will fit the INS definition of executive, supervisor, supervisory role or essential employee. To prove this, detailed statements from the sponsoring business explaining your specific duties, as well as the number and kind of employees you will supervise, must be presented. If the application is based on your being

an essential employee, the statements should also describe the nature of the essential knowledge or experience, the reason why only you have that knowledge and how it will be used in your U.S. job. Remember that the essential expertise/knowledge must be generally unavailable from anyone else either inside or outside the company. These required statements may be in your employer's own words and do not have to be in any special form.

iv.   Proof of the Existence of an Active Business

You should submit as many documents as possible to show that your E-1 visa application is based on a real, ongoing and active business. Such evidence should include

- articles of incorporation or other business charter of the qualifying company
- bank statements from the qualifying company
- credit agreements with suppliers
- letters of credit issued
- leases or deeds for business premises and warehouse space
- tax returns filed in the past two years, if any, including payroll tax returns, and
- promotional literature or advertising.

If the business is newly formed, there will be no tax returns yet. You should then submit a detailed business plan including financial projections for the next five years.

v.   Proof That a Majority of the Company's Trade Is Between the U.S. and Your Home Country

More than 50% of the company's total trade must consist of commerce between your treaty home country and the U.S. This is best shown by presenting copies of all import or export documents from the previous 12 months, including purchase or sale orders, bills of lading and customs entry documents, contracts with suppliers outside of the U.S, and a balance sheet from the qualifying company showing the total amount of inventory for the same period. Comparison of the balance sheet with the import or export documents will show the percentage of the company's trade devoted to commerce between the U.S. and the trade treaty country. The dollar amount of the imports or exports between the U.S. and your home country must total more than 50% of the entire inventory.

vi.   Proof That the Trade Is Substantial

The qualifying company's trade between the U.S. and your home treaty country must be substantial, meeting the three tests previously described: dollar, volume and frequency. The same documents presented to prove that the majority of the company's trade is between the U.S. and your home treaty country will also serve to show that the trade is substantial.

5. Application Interviews: U.S. Filing

Interviews on E-1 change of status applications are rarely held. When an interview is required, the INS regional service center where you filed will send your paperwork to the INS local office nearest your U.S. place of business. This office will in turn contact you for an appointment. INS may ask you to bring additional documents at that time.

If you are called for an interview, the most likely reason is that INS either suspects some type of fraud or has doubts about your intent to leave the U.S. after the E-1 status expires. Because they are not common and usually a sign of trouble, these interviews can result in considerable delays.

6. Application Appeals: U.S. Filing

If your application is denied, you will receive a written decision by mail explaining the reasons for the denial. There is no way of making a formal appeal to INS if your application to change status is turned down. If the problem is too little evidence, you may be able to overcome this obstacle by adding more documents and resubmitting the entire application to the same INS office you have been dealing with, together with a written request that the case be reopened. The written request does not have to be in any special form. This is technically called a *Motion to Reopen*. There is a $110 fee to file this motion.

You may be denied the right to a U.S. filing without being denied an E-1 visa. When your application is turned down because you are found ineligible for U.S. filing, simply change your application to a consular filing. (Read Chapter 25 to make sure you qualify.)

Although there is no appeal to INS for the denial of an E-1 change of status application, you do have the right to file an appeal in a U.S. district court. It would be difficult to file such an appeal without employing an immigration attorney at considerable expense. Such appeals are usually unsuccessful.

F. Extensions

E-1 visas can be extended for up to five years at a time and E-1 status stays can be extended for two years at a time. When you enter the U.S. with an E-1 visa, your authorized stay as indicated on your I-94 card, which is limited to two years at a time, may elapse before the expiration date of

your visa. Therefore, depending on your situation, you may need to extend just your I-94 card, your visa or both. Although an extension is usually easier to get than the E-1 visa itself, it is not automatic. INS or the consulate has the right to reconsider your qualifications based on any changes in the facts or law. When the original application for an E-1 visa or status was weak, it is not unusual for an extension request to be turned down. As always, however, good cases that are well prepared will be successful.

You can file for an extension of your visa either in the U.S. or at a consulate. However, contrary to our advice on the initial application, if your visa needs to be extended we highly recommend U.S. filing. That is because visa stamps, which can only be issued originally at consulates, may be extended in the U.S. If you have received an E-1 status but never applied for a visa, U.S. extensions of your status as indicated on your I-94 card are also advisable. However, if you have an E-1 visa that is still valid but your I-94 card is about to expire, it is generally better to leave the U.S. and return again instead of trying to extend your I-94 card in the U.S. When you return to the U.S. on your valid E-1 visa, you will automatically receive a new I-94 card and a new one- or two-year period of authorized stay. By leaving and reentering, no extension application will be needed and there will be no reevaluation of your qualifications.

1. Extension Applications: U.S. Filing

The general procedures for an E-1 extension are the same as those described in Section E, above. The forms and documents are identical. As with the original application, the paperwork, together with a $120 filing fee, should be mailed to the INS regional service center nearest your place of business. Appendix II contains a complete list of all INS regional service centers and their addresses.

WORKING WHILE YOUR EXTENSION APPLICATION IS PENDING

If you file your application for an extension of E-1 status before your authorized stay expires, you are automatically permitted to continue working for up to 240 days while you are waiting for a decision. If, however, your authorized stay expires after you have filed for an extension but before you receive an approval, and more than 240 days go by without getting a decision on your extension application, your work authorization ends.

2. Extension Application Forms

Copies of all forms can be found in Appendix III.

Form I-129 and E Supplement

Follow the directions in Section E3, above. The only difference is that you will mark boxes "2b" and "4c" of Part 2.

Form I-539 (for accompanying relatives only)

Follow the directions in Section E3, above, but mark box "1a" of Part 2.

3. Extension Application Documents

You must submit your I-94 card. You should also submit the original Notice of Action I-797, if your status was previously approved or extended in the U.S., or a copy of your complete passport including the E-1 visa stamp if you have an actual visa, a letter from your employer stating that your extension is required and a copy of your personal and business U.S. income tax returns for the past two years, including payroll tax returns.

G. Visa Revalidation: U.S. Filing

If you are physically in the U.S. and have been granted an extension on your I-94 card, you can have your visa revalidated by mail without leaving the country. To do this, you must fill out Form OF-156, following the directions in Section D3, above, and send it to the Department of State. With the form, you should submit your passport, current I-94 card, updated evidence of continuing trade between the U.S. and your home treaty country, a detailed letter from your employer describing your job duties and explaining why you are needed in the U.S. and a written statement from you declaring that you intend to leave the U.S. when your E-1 status ends. You should enclose a self-addressed, stamped envelope, or a completed Federal Express airbill. Send the entire package by certified mail to:

CA/VO/P/D
Department of State
Visa Services
2401 "E" Street, N.W., (SA-1 L-703)
Washington, DC 20522-0106
Telephone: 202-663-1213
Fax: 202-663-1608

The passport will be returned to you with a newly revalidated visa in about a month. Nationals of some countries like the U.K. are charged a fee for revalidating a visa, while nationals of other countries receive this service at no charge. Whether or not there is a fee depends on the nationality of the applicant, not the place where the application for the visa was originally made. You may call the State Department in Washington, D.C. to find out the amount of the revalidation fee, if any. If you send in your revalidation package without the correct fee, it will be returned to you, so check the amount in advance.

If your accompanying relatives are physically in the U.S., their E-1 visas may be revalidated by sending in their passports and I-94 cards, together with yours. Again, there may be a charge for each visa revalidated. If your E-1 visa has expired, we strongly advise gathering your family together inside U.S. borders so you can take advantage of this simple revalidation procedure.

H. Visa Revalidation: Consular Filing

If you are outside of the U.S. when your visa stamp expires, you must have a new visa stamp issued at a consulate. Reread procedures for the application, consular filing, in Section D. The procedures for consular visa extensions are identical. If you are outside the U.S. with a valid visa, you need only reenter and a new I-94 card authorizing your stay for one year will be given to you.

FORMS AND DOCUMENTS CHECKLIST

STEP ONE: APPLICATION (THE ONLY STEP)

Forms

☐ OF forms (available at U.S. consulates abroad for consular filing only).

☐ Form I-129 and E Supplement (U.S. filing only).

☐ Form I-539 (U.S. filing only for accompanying relatives).

Documents

☐ Valid passport for you and each accompanying relative.

☐ One passport-type photo of you and each accompanying relative (Consular filing only).

☐ I-94 card for you and each accompanying relative (U.S. filing only).

☐ Long form birth certificate for you and each accompanying relative.

☐ Marriage certificate if you are married and bringing your spouse.

☐ If either you or your spouse have ever been married, copies of divorce and death certificates showing termination of all previous marriages.

☐ Documents showing ownership of real estate in your home country.

☐ Documents showing that close family members or property are being left behind in your home country.

☐ Documents showing that a job is waiting on your return to your home country.

☐ If trade involves the import or export of goods, copies of shipping documents and customs invoices for all shipments during the past two years.

☐ If trade involves the sale of services, a detailed statement and itemized breakdown showing that the trade is between the U.S. and your home country.

☐ Copies of all outstanding stock certificates, if the qualifying business is a corporation.

☐ Notarized affidavit from the secretary of the qualifying corporation, or, if the business is not a corporation, from the official record keeper of the business, stating the names of each owner and percentages of company owned.

☐ Passport or proof of citizenship for each owner of the qualifying business.

☐ Articles of incorporation or other legal charter or business license of the qualifying company.

☐ Tax returns of the qualifying company for the past two years, if available.

☐ Accountant's financial statements, including profit and loss statements and balance sheets, of the qualifying company for the past two years, if available.

☐ Payroll records of the qualifying company for the past two years, if available.

☐ Promotional literature describing the nature of the qualifying business.

☐ Letters from banks or bank statements indicating the average account balance of the qualifying business.

☐ Copy of a business lease or deed for U.S. business premises of the qualifying business.

☐ If the qualifying company is a new business, a comprehensive business plan with financial projections for the next five years.

☐ If you are not a majority owner of the qualifying business, evidence that your position in the U.S. will be as an executive, supervisor or essential employee.

Treaty Investors: E-2 Visas

Privileges

- You can work legally in the U.S. for a U.S. business in which a substantial cash investment has been made by you or other citizens of your home country.

- Visas can be issued quickly.

- You may travel in and out of the U.S. or remain here continuously until your E-2 visa and status expire.

- There is no legal limitation on the number of extensions that may be granted. Because of the two-year initial duration of an E-2 visa, as well as the limitless extensions, E-2 visas can allow you to live in the U.S. on a prolonged basis, provided you continue to maintain E-2 qualifications.

- Visas are available for accompanying relatives.

Limitations

- Visas are available only to nationals of countries having trade treaties with the U.S.

- You are restricted to working only for the specific employer or self-owned business that acted as your E-2 visa sponsor.

- Visas can initially be approved for up to two years. Extensions of up to two more years at a time may be allowed.

- Accompanying relatives may stay in the U.S. with you, but they may not work (unless they obtain their own status and visa to do so).

A. How to Qualify

There are no quota restrictions on E-2 visas. U.S. filed applications are usually approved within one to three months. Applications made at U.S. consulates are usually approved and visas issued within two to four weeks.

You qualify for an E-2 visa if you are a citizen of a country that has an investor treaty with the U.S. and you are coming to America to work for a U.S. business supported by a substantial cash investment from nationals of your home country. You can own the business yourself or you may be a key employee of a business which is at least 50% owned by other nationals of your home country. The investment must be made in a U.S. business that is actively engaged in trade or the rendering of services. Investment in stocks, land speculation or holding companies does not qualify. Do not confuse E-2 treaty investor nonimmigrant visas with green cards through investment discussed in Chapter 10. The E-2 visa is a completely different type of visa with completely different requirements. Remember, all nonimmigrant visas are temporary while green cards are permanent. Moreover, a green card through investment requires a dollar investment of $1 million or more, while an

E-2 visa can possibly be obtained with an investment of around $200,000. Again, see Chapter 10 to compare.

Citizenship in a country having an investor treaty with the U.S. is an E-2 visa requirement. Legal residence is not enough. In fact, with the exception of E-2 applicants from the U.K., you need not be presently residing in your country of citizenship in order to qualify for an E-2 visa. When you are a citizen of more than one nation, you may qualify for an E-2 visa if at least one of them has an investor treaty with the U.S.

Finally, in order to get an E-2 visa, you must plan to leave the U.S. when your business is completed, although you are not required to maintain a foreign residence abroad. Furthermore, INS' regulations state that as long as you intend to depart the U.S. at the end of your stay, the fact that you have an approved permanent labor certification or have filed or received approval of an immigrant visa petition should not by itself be used as a reason to deny your application. Note, however, that the State Department's regulations merely state that the intent to depart the U.S. at the end of E-2 status is required without specifically referring to the allowance for permanent residence petitions. This may mean that E-2 applications requested at a foreign consulate will demand a higher standard of proof that you will depart, and may still deny visas where permanent residence is contemplated. Furthermore, if you are applying as a representative of foreign media, the State Department's rules specify that the consul should first consider your application under the "I" visa rules, under which you must show a definitive intent to depart and not pursue permanent residence. Remember, all nonimmigrant visas are intended to be temporary.

To summarize, there are six requirements for getting an E-2 visa:

1. You must be a citizen of a country that has an investor treaty with the U.S.
2. You must be coming to work in the U.S. for a company you own or one that is at least 50% owned by other nationals of your home country.
3. You must be either the owner or a key employee of the U.S. business.
4. You or the company must have made a substantial cash investment in the U.S. business.
5. The U.S. business must be actively engaged in trade or the rendering of services.
6. You must intend to leave the U.S. when your business there is completed.

1. Citizen of a Treaty Country

E-2 visas are available to citizens of only selected countries that have investor treaties with the U.S. Those countries with treaties currently in effect, or pending final implementation are:

Albania (pending)	Germany	Philippines
Argentina	Grenada	Poland
Armenia	Haiti (pending)	Romania
Australia	Honduras	Russia (pending)
Austria	Iran	Senegal
Bangladesh	Ireland	Slovak Republic
Belarus (pending)	Italy	Spain
Belgium	Jamaica	Sri Lanka
Bulgaria	Japan	Suriname
Cameroon	Kazakhstan	Sweden
Canada	Latvia	Switzerland
Colombia	Liberia	Taiwan
Congo (Brazzaville)	Luxembourg	Thailand
Congo (Democratic	Mexico	Togo
Republic)	Moldova	Trinidad &
Costa Rica	Mongolia	Tobago (pending)
Czech Republic	Morocco	Tunisia
Ecuador	Netherlands	Turkey
Egypt	Norway	Ukraine
Estonia	Oman	United Kingdom
Ethiopia	Pakistan	(Great Britain &
Finland	Panama	No. Ireland only)
France	Paraguay	Yugoslavia
Georgia		

Those countries listed above as "pending" have treaties that have already been signed by both countries, but have not yet taken effect. These treaties will go into effect within the next several years. Treaties are also being contemplated or negotiated with Barbados, Bolivia, Hong Kong, Hungary, Nigeria, Uruguay and Venezuela. Check with the appropriate consulate to make sure a treaty is in force before you apply.

2. Company Owned by Citizens of a Qualifying Country

To get an E-2 visa, you must be coming to the U.S. to work for a business that is at least 50% owned by citizens of your treaty country. The company may be owned by you or others. If the company is owned in part or in whole by others, and some or all of them already live in the U.S., those people may need to have E-2 visas themselves before the company can act as an E-2 sponsor for you. Specifically:

• at least 50% of the company must be owned by citizens of a single investor treaty country, and

• the owners from the single investor treaty country must either live outside the U.S. and be able to be classified as treaty investors or live inside the U.S. with E-2 visas.

This second condition can be a little confusing. Some examples may help to make it clearer.

EXAMPLE 1: The company is owned 100% by one person. The owner is a citizen of an investor treaty country and lives outside the U.S. in his home country.

In this case the owner does not need an E-2 visa for the company to support your E-2 visa application, but he must be able to satisfy the criteria for an E-2 visa if he were to apply.

EXAMPLE 2: The company is owned in equal shares by two individuals. Each owner is a citizen of the same investor treaty country. One owner lives in the U.S. on a green card. The other still lives in his home country.

In this case, the owner living abroad must be classifiable for E-2 status. If, however, we changed this example so that both owners lived in the U.S., the owner who is a green card holder would be prohibited by regulations from being a qualifying employer, so the other owner would have to be in E status.

EXAMPLE 3: The company is owned in equal shares by 100 people. Thirty owners are citizens of a particular investor treaty country but live in the U.S. Thirty other owners are citizens of the same investor treaty country and they are living in their home country. The remaining 40 owners are U.S. citizens.

In this situation, if the company is to act as an E-2 visa sponsor for others, 20 of the 30 owners who are citizens of the investor treaty country but live in the U.S. must hold E-2 visas. Remember that only 50 of the owners need to be citizens of the treaty country. Of those 50, each must either live outside the U.S. and be classifiable for E-2 status or live in the U.S. on an E-2 visa. In our example, 30 live outside the U.S. Therefore, only 20 of the investor treaty country citizens living inside the U.S. need to have E-2 visas to make up the necessary 50% total of qualifying owners.

Additionally, INS' regulations allow a different test in the case of large multinational corporations in which it is difficult to determine ownership by stock ownership. Therefore, in the situation where a corporation's stock is sold exclusively in the country of incorporation, it may be presumed to have the nationality of the country where the stocks are exchanged.

3. You Must Be a 50% Owner or Supervisor, Executive or "Key Employee"

E-2 visas may be issued only to the principal owners or key employees of the qualifying business, provided all have the same treaty nationality. To qualify as a principal owner, you must own at least 50% of the company, possess operational control through a managerial position or similar corporate device, or be in a position to control the enterprise by other means. To qualify as a key employee you must be considered an executive, supervisor, supervisory role or person whose skills are essential to the enterprise.

a. Executives and Supervisors

For E-2 classification purposes, the main thrust of the position must be executive or supervisory, and give the employee ultimate control and responsibility for the operation of at least a major part of the enterprise. INS will examine the following to determine whether a given position fits the bill:

- an "executive" position is normally one that gives the employee great authority in determining policy and direction of the enterprise;

- "supervisory" positions normally entail responsibility for supervising a major portion of an enterprise's operations and do not usually involve direct supervision of low-level employees, and

- whether the individual applicant's skills, experience, salary and title are on a par with executive or supervisory positions, and whether the position carries overall authority and responsibility in the overall context of the enterprise, such as discretionary decision-making, policy-setting, direction and management of business operations, and supervision of other professional and supervisory personnel.

b. Essential Employees

INS regulations are somewhat vague on what constitutes the essentiality of an employee. The employee's skills do not have to be unique or "one of a kind" but they should be indispensable to the success of the investment. They will be evaluated on a case-by-case basis; however, if the skills possessed by the employee are commonplace or readily available in the U.S. labor market, it will be difficult to show that the employee is essential.

Specifically, INS will consider the following to determine whether an individual who is a non-executive, non-supervisor and who is not at least a 50% owner, should be classified as an E-2 employee because of the essentiality of his or her skills:

- the degree of expertise in the area of operations involved; the degree of experience and training with the enterprise

- whether U.S. workers possess the individual's skills or aptitude

- the length of the applicant's specific skill or aptitude

- the length of time required to train an individual to perform the job duties of the position

- the relationship of the individual's skills and talents to the overall operations of the entity, and

- the salary the special qualifications can command.

Knowledge of a foreign language and/or culture will not by themselves constitute the degree of essentiality required.

4. Substantial Investment

A substantial cash investment must be made in the U.S. business in order for the business to successfully support an E-2 visa application. The term substantial is not defined in the law by a strict numerical measure. In fact it is not specifically defined at all. What is considered substantial depends on the type of business. For example, an automobile manufacturer will have to show a greater dollar amount of investment than a retail toy store in order to meet the requirement of substantial investment.

There are three general tests—dollars, capitalization, and jobs—that, in our experience, can normally be relied on to measure substantiality. The investment must be able to meet the minimum standards of all three.

a.   Dollar Amount of Investment

The dollar amount of the cash business investment should normally exceed $200,000. However, some consulates require as much as $500,000 or more, while others may accept an investment of less than $100,000. A specific sum is not written into the law. The individual consul officer has the authority to require varying amounts in different cases depending on the type of business. Still, experience shows that anything under the $200,000 mark is a weak case.

In order for investment dollars to be counted into the total amount, they must be spent on the U.S. business. Money invested in a house to be used as the investor's residence will not be considered when a decision is made on whether or not the investment meets the dollar requirement. Mortgage values and other borrowed money can be included in the dollar totals. If borrowed funds make up the investment, the investor must be personally liable for the debt or it must be secured by personal assets. Capital investment must be irrevocably committed to the venture, although the investor may utilize escrow as a way of protecting him or herself against loss of capital in case the visa is not issued.

b.   Capitalization

To satisfy the capitalization test, the investment must be large enough to start and operate a business of the type in which the investment is made. This means that different dollar amounts of capitalization will be considered sufficient in different cases. A restaurant, for example, needs a large enough investment to furnish the restaurant, buy,

build or lease the actual restaurant building, pay wages until the business generates enough income to support its staff, purchase food, and pay for initial advertising. The $200,000 minimum dollar amount mentioned above may or may not be enough, depending on the size and type of restaurant. On the other hand, if the business will be the construction and management of a shopping center or office complex, several million dollars may be necessary to adequately capitalize such a project. An investment is not considered substantial unless it is large enough to capitalize the venture properly, so that it has a realistic chance of success.

The investment amount must also be substantial in proportion to the overall cost of the enterprise. INS uses an "inverted sliding scale" for this determination: the lower the total cost of the enterprise, the higher the investment must be in order to qualify, and vice versa.

The Investment Must Not Constitute a "Marginal Enterprise" and Job Creation

A business investment will not be considered substantial for E-2 visa purposes if the business is likely to generate only enough income to support the owners and their families. The business should operate at a sufficient volume to make hiring Americans necessary and the cash flow should be large enough to pay their salaries. Regardless of the dollars invested, a small family-operated business, such as a retail store, will rarely qualify to support E-2 visa applications if jobs are created only for the owners.

INS' new regulations impose this requirement by placing a burden on the investor to show a business plan that indicates that the business will provide more than a subsistence living for the investor starting five years after the onset of normal business activities.

We emphasize that these three tests have been derived from our own experience and are not part of immigration law. It is possible for an E-2 visa to be approved with a less substantial business investment than we have described in our tests. With E-2 visas, a great deal is left to the judgment of the INS or consul officer evaluating the application. However, the results from cases we have filed suggest that E-2 visas will usually not be issued unless the three conditions outlined above are satisfied.

Active Business

The investment must be in a for-profit business that is actively engaged in trade or the rendering of services, which meets the applicable legal requirements for doing business in the state or region. Investment in holding companies, stocks, bonds and land speculation will not support an E-2 visa application, since they are not considered "active."

The test is whether or not the business requires active supervisory or executive oversight on a day-to-day basis. Clearly, retail, wholesale and manufacturing operations require such supervision, while stock purchases and land speculation do not. There are some types of investments, especially in real estate, where the line between a qualifying and non-qualifying business investment is difficult to draw. For example, if you purchase and rent out a single home or duplex, this is not the type of investment that will support an E-2 visa application, even if the dollar amount is adequate. If you purchase and rent out an eight- or ten-unit apartment building, that is probably a marginal case. As the number of rental units becomes greater, the need for daily management increases and the case for an E-2 visa becomes stronger.

6. Intent to Leave the U.S.

E-2 visas are meant to be temporary. At the time of application, you must intend to depart the U.S. when your business there is completed. As previously mentioned, you are not required to maintain a foreign residence abroad. Furthermore, INS' regulations state that as long as you intend to depart the U.S. at the end of your stay, the fact that you have an approved permanent labor certification or have filed or received approval of an immigrant visa petition should not by itself be used as a reason to deny your application. Note, however, that the State Department's regulations merely state that the intent to depart the U.S. at the end of E-2 status is required without specifically referring to the allowance for permanent residence petitions. This may mean that E-2 applications requested at a foreign consulate will demand a higher standard of proof that you will depart, and may still deny visas where permanent residence is contemplated. Furthermore, if you are applying as a representative of foreign media, the State Department's rules specify that the consul should first consider your application under the "I" visa rules, under which you must show a definitive intent to depart and not pursue permanent residence. Remember, all nonimmigrant visas are intended to be temporary.

The U.S. government knows it is difficult to read minds. Therefore, you can expect to be asked for evidence showing that when you go to America on an E-2 visa, you eventually plan to leave. In many nonimmigrant categories, you are asked to show proof that you keep a house or apartment outside the U.S. as an indication of your intent to eventually go back to your home country. You do not need to keep a home outside the U.S. to qualify for an E-2 visa, but this does not mean that you are freed from the requirement of having the intent to leave. You are not. It simply means that when you apply for an E-2 visa, maintaining a residence abroad is not an essential element of proving that intent. You will, however, be asked to show that you do have some family members, possessions or property elsewhere in the world as an incentive for your eventual departure from the U.S.

7. Accompanying Relatives

When you qualify for an E-2 visa, your spouse and unmarried children under age 21 can also get E-2 visas simply by providing proof of their family relationship to you. E-2 visas for dependents authorize your accompanying relatives to stay with you in the U.S. but not to work there.

APPLYING FOR A GREEN CARD FROM E-2 STATUS

If you have an E-2 visa, you can file to get a green card, but being in the U.S. on an E-2 visa gives you no advantage in doing so, and in fact may prove to be a drawback. That is because E-2 visas, like all nonimmigrant visas, are intended only for those who plan on leaving the U.S. once their jobs or other activities there are completed. However, if you apply for a green card, you are in effect making a statement that you never intend to leave the U.S. Therefore, the U.S. government will allow you to keep E-2 status while pursuing a green card, but only if you can convince the government that you did not intend to get a green card when you originally applied for the E-2 visa, and that you will leave the U.S. if you are unable to secure a green card before your E-2 visa expires. Proving those things can be difficult. If you do not succeed, your E-2 visa may be taken away. Should this happen, it may affect your green card application, since being out of status or working without authorization may be a bar to getting a green card in the U.S., or may create a waiting period if you depart the U.S. and apply for a visa. (See Chapter 25.)

B. E-2 Visa Overview

Getting an E-2 visa is a one-step process.

1. The Application

Once you have made a qualifying investment in the U.S. or have been offered a job as a key employee of a qualifying company owned by people from your country, getting an E-2 visa is a one-step process. Some applicants seeking E-2 visas as key employees expect their sponsoring employers to handle the entire process for them and indeed, a number of large companies are equipped with experienced workers who will do this for highly desirable employees. Other companies are prepared to pay an immigration attorney's fees as an expense of trying to attract a key staff member. However, in many cases it is the employee who is most interested in having the visa issued and to employers, the red tape of having a foreign employee can be an unfamiliar nuisance.

As we give you step-by-step instructions for getting an E-2 visa, we will indicate that certain activities are to be performed by your employer and others are to be performed by you, recognizing that in the case of an E-2 visa you yourself may be the principle owner of the qualifying business. We will discuss each task according to who has the legal responsibility for carrying it out. Even if you are being hired as a key employee, though the law presumes your employer is performing a particular function, there is nothing to stop you from helping with the work. For example, you can fill out forms intended to be completed by your employer and simply ask him to check them over and sign them. Unless your employer volunteers to help or you are sure the company simply can't live without you, we recommend that you assist as much as possible in the preparation of the paperwork. The less your sponsoring employer is inconvenienced, the more the company will be willing to act as sponsor for your E-2 visa. An imposition on company time or money might cost you a job offer. With the help of this book, you will know how to do all that is required. It is completely legal, as well as in your best interest, to assist whenever possible. Of course if you are the principal owner of a qualifying business, all the paperwork responsibilities will fall on you.

The one step required to get an E-2 visa is called the application. The object of the application is to show that the conditions to getting an E-2 visa discussed earlier in this chapter have been met. It is filed by you and your accompanying relatives, if any. The application is your formal request for an E-2 visa or status. The application may be carried out in the U.S. at an INS office or in your home country at a U.S. consulate there. The vast majority of nonimmigrant visa applications are filed at consulates. That is because most cases don't qualify for U.S. filing and besides, consular filing usually brings better results. The major benefit is that an E-2 visa, which is stamped in your passport, can be issued only by American consulates. When you file the application at a consulate, your visa will be stamped in your passport at that time. INS offices inside the U.S. may issue statuses but not visas. (See Chapter 14, Section B, Difference Between a Visa and a Status.)

If you are already in the U.S. legally on some other type of nonimmigrant visa, you may qualify to apply for an E-2 status at an INS office inside the U.S. using a procedure known as change of nonimmigrant status. If you have been admitted as a visitor without a visa under the Visa Waiver Program, currently available only to nationals of Andorra, Argentina, Australia, Austria, Belgium, Brunei, Denmark, Finland, France, Germany, Great Britain (including Scotland, Wales, Northern Ireland, the Channel Islands and the Isle of Man), Iceland, Ireland, Italy, Japan, Liechtenstein, Luxembourg, Monaco, Netherlands, New Zealand, Norway, Portugal, San Marino, Singapore, Slovenia, Spain, Sweden, Switzerland and Uruguay, you may not carry out the application step in the U.S. This is simply a technical term meaning you are switching from one nonimmigrant status to another. If a change of status is approved, you will then be treated as if you had entered the country with an E-2 visa and you can keep the status as long as you remain in the U.S. or until it expires, whichever comes first.

You will not, however, receive a visa stamp, which is what you need if your plans include traveling in and out of the U.S. To repeat, visa stamps are issued only at U.S. consulates abroad. Therefore, if you change your status and later travel outside the U.S., you will have to go to the U.S. consulate in your home country and repeat the application over again, obtaining the E-2 visa stamp in your passport before you can return. This extra procedure may make changing status an unattractive option.

Although it is not a requirement, one item you or your sponsoring employer may wish to add to the paperwork package is a cover letter. Cover letters act as a summary and index to the forms and documents, and are often used by immigration attorneys or U.S. companies that process many visas for their employees. Cover letters begin with a statement summarizing the facts of the case and explaining why the particular applicant is eligible for the visa. This statement is followed by a list of the forms and documents submitted. If it is carefully written, a cover letter can make the case clearer and easier to process for the consular or INS officer evaluating it. This is particularly important in an E-2 visa case where the documentation by itself may require explanation. Cover letters must be individually tailored to each case, so if you don't think you can write a good one on your own, just leave it out and submit only your forms and documents.

2. Paperwork

There are two types of paperwork you must submit to get an E-2 visa. The first consists of official government forms completed by you or your employer. The second is personal and business documents such as birth and marriage certificates, school transcripts and diplomas, and company financial statements and tax returns. We will tell you exactly what forms and documents you need.

It is vital that forms are properly filled out and all necessary documents are supplied. You or your U.S. employer may resent the intrusion into your privacy and sizable effort it takes to prepare immigration applications but you should realize the process is an impersonal matter to immigration officials. Your getting a visa is more important to you than it is to the U.S. government. This is not a pleasant thing to accept, but you are better off having a real understanding of your position. People from all over the world want U.S. visas. There is no shortage of applicants. Take the time and trouble to prepare your papers properly. In the end it will pay off with a successful application.

The documents you or your U.S. employer supply to INS do not have to be originals. Photocopies of all documents are acceptable as long as you have the originals in your possession and are willing to produce them at the request of INS. Documents submitted to U.S. consulates, on the other hand, must be either originals or official government certified copies. Government certified copies and notarized copies are not the same thing. Documents that have only been notarized are not acceptable. They must carry a government seal. In addition to any original or government certified copies of documents submitted to a consulate, you should submit plain photocopies of each document as well. After the consulate compares the copies with the originals, it will return the originals.

Documents will be accepted if they are in either English, or, with papers filed at U.S. consulates abroad, the language of the country where the documents are being filed. An exception exists for papers filed at U.S. consulates in Japan, where all documents must be translated into English. If the documents are not in an acceptable language as just explained, they must be accompanied by a full, word for word, written English translation. Any capable person may act as translator. It is not necessary to hire a professional. At the end of each translation, the following statement must appear:

I hereby certify that I translated this document from (language) to English. This translation is accurate and complete. I further certify that I am fully competent to translate from (language) to English.

The translator should sign this statement but it does not have to be witnessed or notarized.

Later in this chapter we describe in detail the forms and documents needed to get your E-2 visa. A summary checklist of forms and documents appears at the end of this chapter.

C. Who's Who in Getting Your E-2 Visa

Getting an E-2 visa will be easier if you familiarize yourself with the technical names used for each participant in the process. You are known as the applicant. The applicant can be either the owner or a key employee, depending on whether or not it is you who owns the company. The business is known as the qualifying business or qualifying company, the employer or the sponsoring business. If you are bringing your spouse and children with you as accompanying relatives they are known as applicants as well.

D. The Application: Consular Filing

Anyone who has made a qualifying investment or who has been offered a job in the U.S. as a key employee by a qualifying business can apply for an E-2 visa at a U.S. consulate in his or her home country. You must be physically present in order to apply there. If you have been or are now working or living illegally in the U.S., you may be ineligible to get an E-2 visa from a U.S. consulate even if you otherwise qualify. Read Chapter 25 to understand the issues and risks involved.

1. Benefits and Drawbacks of Consular Filing

The most important benefit to consular filing, making it almost always preferable to U.S. filing, is that only consulates issue visas. When you go through a U.S. filing you get a status, not a visa. (See Chapter 14, Section B, Difference Between a Visa and a Status). An E-2 status confers the same right to work as an E-2 visa, but it does not give you the ability to travel in and out of the U.S. Therefore, if you want travel privileges, you will at some time have to go through the extra step of applying for a visa at a U.S. consulate, even though you have already applied for and received E-2 status in the U.S.

Moreover, anyone with a qualifying business may apply for an E-2 visa at the appropriate consulate, without waiting for action from INS. That is not the case with U.S. applications for E-2 status. If you are in the U.S. illegally, consular filing is a must, although you may not be eligible (see Chapter 25). You are not eligible to process a status application in the U.S. unless your presence and activities in the U.S. have always been legal.

A further plus to consular filing is that some consular offices may work more quickly to issue nonimmigrant visas than INS service centers may to process nonimmigrant statuses. Your waiting time for the paperwork to be finished may be much shorter at a U.S. consulate abroad than at most U.S. INS offices.

A drawback to consular filing comes from the fact that you must be physically present in the country where the consulate is located to file there. If your application is ultimately turned down because of an unexpected problem, not only will you have to wait outside the U.S. until the problem is resolved, but other visas in your passport, such as a visitor's visa, may be canceled. It will then be impossible for you to enter the U.S. in any capacity. Consequently, if your E-2 visa case is not very strong and freedom of travel is not essential to you, it might be wise to apply in the U.S., make up your mind to remain there for the duration of the E-2 status, and skip trying to get a visa from the consulate.

2. Application General Procedures: Consular Filing

Technically, the law allows you to apply for an E-2 visa at any U.S. consulate you choose, although if you have even overstayed your status by as little as one day, you are required to apply at your home consulate. Because unlawful presence in the U.S. may also constitute a ground of inadmissibility, be sure to read Chapters 14 and 25 before proceeding. A complete list of all U.S. consulates that process visa applications together with their addresses and phone numbers is in Appendix I. However, from a practical standpoint your case will be given greatest consideration at the consulate in your home country. Applying in some other country creates suspicion in the minds of the consul officers there about your motives for choosing their consulate. Often, when an applicant is having trouble at a home consulate he will seek a more lenient office in some other country. This practice of consulate shopping is frowned upon by officials in the system. Unless you have a very good reason for being elsewhere (such as a temporary job assignment in some other nation), it is smarter to file your visa application in your home country.

In some consulates you can simply walk in with your application paperwork and get your E-2 visa immediately. Most insist that you submit your forms and documents in advance, and then give you an appointment for a personal interview several weeks later. Since procedures among consulates vary, you should always telephone in advance to ask about local policies.

On entering the U.S. with your new E-2 visa, you will be given an I-94 card. It will be stamped with a date indicating how long you can stay. Normally you are permitted to remain for two years at a time, without regard to when your visa actually expires. Each time you exit and reenter the U.S., you will get a new I-94 card authorizing your stay for an additional one- or two-year period, or if you do not wish to leave the U.S. after that time, you can apply for extensions of stay which are issued in two-year increments for as long as you maintain your E-2 status qualifications.

3. Application Forms: Consular Filing

When you file at a U.S. consulate abroad, the consulate officials will provide you with certain optional forms, designated by an "OF" preceeding a number. Instructions for completing optional forms and what to do with them once they are filled out will come with the forms. We do not include copies of these forms in Appendix III.

4. Application Documents: Consular Filing

All E-2 applicants must show a valid passport and present one passport-type photograph taken in accordance with the photo instructions in Appendix III. For each accompanying relative you must present a valid passport and one passport-type photograph taken in accordance with the photo instructions in Appendix III. You will also need documents verifying their family relationship to you. You may verify a parent/child relationship by presenting the child's long form birth certificate. Many countries, including Canada and England, issue both short and long form birth certificates. Where both are available, the long form is needed because it contains the names of the parents while the short form does not. If you are accompanied by your spouse, you must establish that you are lawfully married by showing a civil marriage certificate. Church marriage certificates are generally unacceptable. (There are a few exceptions, depending on the laws of your particular country. Canadians, for example, may use church marriage certificates if the marriage took place in Quebec Province, but not elsewhere. If a civil certificate is available, however, you should always use it.) You may have married in a country where marriages are not customarily recorded. Tribal areas of Africa are an example. In such situations, call the nearest consulate or embassy of your home country for help with getting acceptable proof of marriage.

You will need documents establishing your intent to leave the U.S. when your business in the U.S. is completed. The consulate will want to see evidence of ties to some other country so strong that you will be highly motivated to return there. Proof of such ties can include deeds verifying ownership of a house or other real property, written statements from you explaining that close relatives live elsewhere, or letters from a company outside the U.S. showing that you have a job waiting when you return from America. We have already explained that technically you should not be required to prove that you are maintaining a residence outside the U.S. in order to get an E-2 visa. As a practical matter, however, a consul officer may ask for evidence that you do have assets of some kind located outside the U.S. and if you want your visa to be approved you will have to produce this evidence.

i. Proof of Your Nationality

You must prove that you are a citizen of one of the investment treaty countries. Your passport showing your nationality must therefore be presented.

ii. Proof of the Nationality of the Qualifying Business Owners

You must show that the qualifying business is owned by citizens of one of the investment treaty countries. If you are not the owner yourself, you will need to show that both you and those who do own the company are citizens of the same treaty country. If the owners are presently living in the U.S., you must show that they hold E-2 visas. If you are the majority owner of the business, your passport showing that you are a national of one of the E-2 treaty countries must be presented. If you are applying for the visa not as an owner, but as a key employee, you must also submit passports or other proof of the citizenship of each owner who is a national of your treaty country. Remember that although you will be doing work for the qualifying company in the U.S., the company and its owners may or may not be located there. Therefore, documents must be presented showing where each of the owners is living currently. Affidavits from each of these owners stating their places of residence will serve this purpose. If any are living in the U.S., copies of their passports and I-94 cards are also needed to demonstrate that they hold valid E-2 visas. Remember, if the owners of the company live in the U.S., at least 50% must also hold E-2 visas for the business to support your own E-2 application.

You will need to prove that you or other nationals of your country own not just a small part, but a majority of the qualifying business. If the qualifying business is a corporation, you should submit copies of all stock certificates, together with a notarized affidavit from the secretary of the corporation listing the name of each shareholder and the number of shares each owns. The affidavit must account for all the shares issued to date. Remember, at least 50% must be owned by nationals of your treaty country.

If the qualifying business is not incorporated, instead of copies of stock certificates you will need to present legal papers proving the existence and ownership of the company. These may be partnership agreements, business registration certificates or business licenses, together with a notarized affidavit from an official of the company certifying who owns the business and in what percentages.

iii. Proof That You Are a Key Employee

If you are not the majority owner of the company, you must submit evidence that your job in the U.S. will fit the INS definition of supervisor, executive, essential employee or person with predominantly supervisory job duties. To prove this, detailed statements from the sponsoring business explaining your specific duties, as well as the number and kind of employees you will supervise must be presented. If the application is based on your essentiality as an employee, the statements should also describe the nature of the essential knowledge or experience and how it will be used and why it is essential in your U.S. job. These required statements may be in your employer's own words and do not have to be in any special form.

iv. Proof of the Existence of an Active Business

You should submit as many documents as possible to show that your E-2 visa application is based on a real, ongoing business. Such evidence should include:

- articles of incorporation or other business charter of the qualifying company
- bank statements from the qualifying company
- credit agreements with suppliers
- letters of credit issued
- leases or deeds for business premises and warehouse space
- tax returns filed in the past two years, if any, including payroll tax returns, and
- promotional literature or advertising.

If the business is newly formed, there will be no tax returns yet. You should then submit a detailed business plan including financial projections for the next five years.

v. Documents Showing That U.S. Business Investment Is Substantial

The business investment made in the U.S. qualifying company must be substantial, meeting the three tests previously described: dollars, capitalization, and jobs. Documents to prove this will include:

- bank wire transfer memos showing money sent to the U.S. from abroad
- contracts and bills of sale for purchase of capital goods and inventory
- leases, deeds or contracts for purchase of business premises
- construction contracts and blueprints for building a business premise, comprehensive business plans with cash flow projections for the next five years, showing how the enterprise will support more than you (and your family) by then
- U.S. employment tax returns showing the number of employees on the qualifying company's payroll (if any)
- and accountant's financial statements for the business, including balance sheets.

If the business in the U.S. is new, you may not have tax returns or employment records but you must present evidence that the investment which has been made will provide sufficient capitalization for that type of business. Documents such as market surveys, written summaries of trade association statistics or written reports from qualified business consultants will serve this purpose.

5. Application Interviews: Consular Filing

The consulate will usually require an interview before issuing an E-2 visa. During the interview, a consul officer will examine the forms and documents for accuracy, especially regarding facts about the substantiality of the business and the nationality of the owners. Evidence of ties to your home country will also be checked. During the interview, you will surely be asked how long you intend to remain in the U.S. Any answer indicating uncertainty about plans to return or an interest in applying for a green card may result in a denial of your E-2 visa.

6. Application Appeals: Consular Filing

When a consulate turns down an E-2 visa application, there is no way to make a formal appeal, although you are free to reapply as often as you like. Some consulates, however, will make you wait several months before allowing you to file another application. If your visa is denied, you will be told by the consul officer the reasons for the denial. Written statements of decisions are not normally provided in nonimmigrant cases. If a lack of evidence about a particular point is the problem, sometimes simply presenting more evidence on an unclear fact can bring a positive change in the result.

The most likely reasons for having an E-2 visa turned down are because the consul officer does not believe that your investment is substantial enough, or you are found inadmissible.

Certain people who have been refused visas reapply at a different consulate, attempting to hide the fact that they were turned down elsewhere. If your application is denied, the last page in your passport will be stamped "Application Received" with the date and location of the rejecting consulate. This notation shows that some type of prior visa application has failed. It serves as a warning to other consulates that your case merits close inspection. If what we have just told you makes you think it would be a good idea to overcome this problem by obtaining a new, unmarked passport, you should also know that permanent computer records are kept of all visa denials.

E. The Application: U.S. Filing

If you are physically present in the U.S., you may apply for E-2 status without leaving the country on the following conditions:

- you entered the U.S. legally and not under the Visa Waiver Program
- you have never worked illegally
- the date on your I-94 card has not passed, and
- you are admissible and none of the bars to changing status apply to you (see Chapter 25).

If you were admitted as a visitor without a visa under the Visa Waiver Program, you may not carry out the application step in the U.S. Currently there are 29 participating countries in the Visa Waiver Program, including: Andorra, Argentina, Austria, Australia, Belgium, Brunei, Denmark, Finland, France, Germany, Iceland, Ireland, Italy, Japan, Liechtenstein, Luxembourg, Monaco, The Netherlands, New Zealand, Norway, Portugal, San Marino, Singapore, Slovenia, Spain, Sweden, Switzerland, the United Kingdom and Uruguay. The government has approved Greece for inclusion in the program in the near future.

If you cannot meet these terms, you may not file for E-2 status in the U.S. It is important to realize, however, that eligibility to apply in the U.S. has nothing to do with overall eligibility for an E-2 visa. Applicants who are barred from filing in the U.S. but otherwise qualify for E-2 status can sometimes apply successfully for an E-2 visa at U.S. consulates abroad. If you find you are not eligible for U.S. filing, see Section D, above, and read Chapter 25 before devising a strategy.

1. Benefits and Drawbacks of U.S. Filing

Visas are never given inside the U.S. They are issued exclusively by U.S. consulates abroad. If you file in the U.S., and you are successful, you will get E-2 status but not the visa itself. This is a major drawback to U.S. applications. E-2 status allows you to remain in the U.S. with E-2 privileges until the status expires, but should you leave the country for any reason before that time, you will have to apply for the visa itself at a U.S. consulate before returning to America. Moreover, the fact that your E-2 status has been approved in the U.S. does not guarantee that the consulate will approve your visa. Some consulates may even regard your previously acquired E-2 status as a negative factor, an indication that you have deliberately tried to avoid the consulate's authority.

There is another problem which comes up only in U.S. filings. It is the issue of what is called "preconceived intent." To approve a change of status, INS must believe that at the time you originally entered the U.S. as a visitor or with some other nonimmigrant visa, you did not intend to apply for a different status. If INS thinks you had a preconceived plan to change from the status you arrived with to a different status, they may deny your application. The preconceived intent issue is one less potential hazard you will face if you apply at a U.S. consulate abroad.

On the plus side of U.S. filing is that when problems do arise with your U.S. application, you can stay in America while they are being corrected, a circumstance most visa applicants prefer. If you run into snags at a U.S. consulate, you will have to remain outside the U.S. until matters are resolved.

2. Application General Procedures: U.S. Filing

The application, consisting of both forms and documents, is sent by mail to the INS regional service center having jurisdiction over the intended place of business. INS regional service centers are not the same as INS local offices. There are four INS regional service centers spread across the U.S. Appendix II contains a list of all INS regional service centers and their addresses.

The filing fee for each application is $155. Checks or money orders are accepted. It is not advisable to send cash. We recommend submitting all papers by certified mail, return receipt requested, and making a copy of everything sent in to keep in your records.

Within a week or two after mailing in the application, you should get back a written notice of confirmation that the papers are being processed, together with a receipt for the fees. This notice will also tell you your immigration file number and approximately when to expect a decision. If

INS wants further information before acting on your case, all application papers, forms and documents, will be returned together with another form known as an I-797. The I-797 tells you what additional pieces of information or documents are expected. You should supply the extra data and mail the whole package back to the INS regional service center, with the I-797 form on top.

Applications for an E-2 status are normally approved within two to eight weeks. When this happens, you will receive a Notice of Action Form I-797 indicating the dates for which your status is approved. A new I-94 card will be attached to the bottom of the form.

3. Application Forms: U.S. Filing

Copies of all forms are in Appendix III.

Form I-129 and E Supplement

The basic form for the application is Form I-129 and E Supplement. As mentioned previously, a new form is being developed. Until it is released, continue to use the old forms. The I-129 form is used for many different nonimmigrant visas. In addition to the basic part of the form that applies to all types of visas, it comes with several supplements for each specific nonimmigrant category. Simply tear out and use the supplement that applies to you. Your employer must file the form in duplicate. Send in two signed originals. Copies are not acceptable.

Most of the questions on the I-129 form are straightforward. If a question does not apply to you, answer it with "None" or "N/A." Those questions requiring explanations are as follows:

Part 1. These questions are self-explanatory.

Part 2, Question 1. Question 1 should be answered "E-2."

Questions 2–3. These questions are self-explanatory.

Question 4. This question asks you to indicate what action is requested from INS. Normally you will mark box "b."

Question 5. This question is self-explanatory.

Part 3. These questions are self-explanatory. If you previously held a U.S. work permit and therefore have a U.S. Social Security number, put down that number where asked. If you have a Social Security number that is not valid for employment, put down that number followed by "not valid for employment." If you have never had a Social Security number, put down "None." (Read Chapter 25 before listing a false number.)

Alien Registration Numbers, which all begin with the letter "A," are given only to people who have applied for green cards, received political asylum or been in deportation proceedings. If you do have an "A" number, put that number down and also explain how you got it, such as "number issued from previous green card petition filed by my brother." If you do not have an "A" number, write down "None."

If your present authorized stay has expired, you cannot file your application inside the U.S. You must use consular processing.

Part 4. These questions are self-explanatory. Having a green card petition or application in process may affect your ability to get an E-2 status. To qualify for an E-2 status, you must intend to return to your home country after your business needs are completed in the U.S.

Part 5. These questions are self-explanatory. The dates of intended employment should not exceed one year, which is the maximum period of time for which an initial E-2 status may be approved. Extensions may be approved for two years at a time.

E Supplement

This form is self-explanatory. Fill in all parts except Section 3.

Form I-539 (for accompanying relatives only)

Only one application form is needed for an entire family, but if there is more than one accompanying relative, each additional one should be listed on the I-539 supplement.

Part 1. These questions are self-explanatory. "A" numbers are usually given only to people who have previously applied for green cards or who have been in deportation proceedings.

Part 2. Question 1. Mark box "b," and write in "E-2."

Question 2. This question is self-explanatory.

Part 3. In most cases you will mark Item 1. You will also complete Items 3 and 4, which are self-explanatory.

Part 4. Questions 1–2. These questions are self-explanatory.

Question 3. The different parts to this question are self-explanatory; however, Items "a" and "b" ask if an immigrant visa petition or adjustment of status application has ever been filed on your behalf. If you are applying for a green card through a relative, this would be Step One, as described in Chapter 5. If you are applying for a green card through employment, this would be Step Two as described in Chapter 8. If you have only begun the Labor Certification, the first step of getting a green card through employment, this question should be answered "no."

4. Application Documents: U.S. Filing

Each applicant must submit an I-94 card, the small white card you received on entering the U.S. Remember, if the date stamped on your I-94 card has already passed, you are ineligible for U.S. filing.

For each accompanying relative, send in an I-94 card. You will also need documents verifying their family relationship to you. You may verify a parent/child relationship by presenting the child's long form birth certificate. Many countries, including Canada and England, issue both short and long form birth certificates. Where both are available, the long form is needed because it contains the names of the parents while the short form does not. If you are accompanied by your spouse, you must establish that you are lawfully married by showing a civil marriage certificate. Church marriage certificates are generally unacceptable. (There are a few exceptions, depending on the laws of your particular country. Canadians, for example, may use church marriage certificates if the marriage took place in Quebec Province, but not elsewhere. If a civil certificate is available, however, you should always use it.) You may have married in a country where marriages are not customarily recorded. Tribal areas of Africa are an example. In such situations call the nearest consulate or embassy of your home country for help with getting acceptable proof of marriage.

We have emphasized that in order to qualify for an E-2 you must have the intent to eventually leave the U.S. when your business is completed, and we have explained how consulates will demand proof that ties to your home country or some other place outside the U.S. are strong enough to motivate your eventual departure. In a U.S. filing, INS does not always ask for proof of this. However, we strongly advise you to submit such evidence anyway. Proof of ties to some other country can include deeds verifying ownership of a house or other real property, written statements from you explaining that close relatives are living elsewhere, or letters from a company outside the U.S. showing that you have a job waiting when you leave America.

Some additional documents are necessary.

i. Proof of Your Nationality

You must prove that you are a citizen of one of the investment treaty countries. Your passport showing your nationality must therefore be presented.

ii. Proof of the Nationality of the Qualifying Business Owners

You must show that the qualifying business is owned by citizens of one of the investment treaty countries. If you are not the owner yourself, you will need to show that both you and those who do own the company are citizens of the same treaty country. If the owners are presently living in the U.S., you must show that they hold E-2 visas. If you are the majority owner of the business, your passport, showing that you are a national of one of the E-2 treaty countries, must be presented. If you are applying for the visa not as an owner but as a key employee, you must also submit passports or other proof of the citizenship of each owner who is a national of your treaty country. Remember that although you will be doing work for the qualifying company in the U.S., the company and its owners may or may not be located there. Therefore, documents must be presented showing where each of the owners is living currently. Affidavits from each of these owners stating their places of residence will serve this purpose. If any are living in the U.S., copies of their passports and I-94 cards are also needed to demonstrate that they hold valid E-2 visas. Remember, if the owners of the company live in the U.S. at least 50% must also hold E-2 visas for the business to support your own E-2 application.

You will need to prove that you or other nationals of your country own not just a small part, but a majority of the qualifying business. If the qualifying business is a corporation, you should submit copies of all stock certificates, together with a notarized affidavit from the secretary of the corporation listing the name of each shareholder and the number of shares each owns. The affidavit must account for all the shares issued to date. Remember, at least 50% must be owned by nationals of your treaty country.

If the qualifying business is not incorporated, instead of copies of stock certificates you will need to present legal papers proving the existence and ownership of the company. These may be partnership agreements, business registration certificates or business licenses, together with a notarized affidavit from an official of the company certifying who owns the business and in what percentages.

iii. Proof That You Are a Key Employee

If you are not the majority owner of the company, you must submit evidence that your job in the U.S. will fit the INS definition of executive, supervisor, supervisory role or essential employee. To prove this, detailed statements from the sponsoring business explaining your specific duties, as well as the number and kind of employees you will supervise must be presented. If the application is based on your being an essential employee, the statements should also describe the nature of the essential knowledge or experience, the reason why only you have that knowledge and how it will be used in your U.S. job. Remember that the essential expertise/knowledge must be generally unavailable from anyone else either inside or outside the company. These required statements may be in your employer's own words and do not have to be in any special form.

iv. Proof of the Existence of an Active Business

You should submit as many documents as possible to show that your E-2 visa application is based on a real, ongoing and active business. Such evidence should include:
- articles of incorporation or other business charter of the qualifying company
- bank statements from the qualifying company
- credit agreements with suppliers
- letters of credit issued
- leases or deeds for business premises and warehouse space
- tax returns filed in the past two years, if any, including payroll tax returns, and
- promotional literature or advertising.

If the business is newly formed, there will be no tax returns yet. You should then submit a detailed business plan, including financial projections for the next three years.

v. Proof That U.S. Business Investment Is Substantial

The business investment made in the U.S. qualifying company must be substantial, meeting the three tests previously described: dollars, capitalization and jobs. Documents to prove this will include:
- bank wire-transfer memos showing money sent to the U.S. from abroad
- contracts and bills of sale for purchase of capital goods and inventory
- leases, deeds or contracts for purchase of business premises
- construction contracts and blueprints for building a business premise, comprehensive business plans with cash flow projections for the next three years
- U.S. employment tax returns showing the number of employees on the qualifying company's payroll, and
- accountant's financial statements for the business, including balance sheets.

If the business in the U.S. is new, you may not have tax returns or employment records but you must present evidence that the investment which has been made will provide sufficient capitalization for that type of business. Documents such as market surveys, written summaries of trade-association statistics or written reports from qualified business consultants will serve this purpose.

5. Application Interviews: U.S. Filing

Interviews on E-2 change of status applications are rarely held. When an interview is required, the INS regional service center where you filed will send your paperwork to the

INS local office nearest your U.S. place of business. This office will in turn contact you for an appointment. INS may ask you to bring additional documents at that time.

If you are called for an interview, the most likely reason is that INS either suspects some type of fraud or has doubts about your intent to leave the U.S. after the E-2 status expires. Because they are not common and usually a sign of trouble, these interviews can result in considerable delays.

6. Application Appeals: U.S. Filing

If your application is denied, you will receive a written decision by mail explaining the reasons for the denial. There is no way of making a formal appeal to INS if your application to change status is turned down. If the problem is too little evidence, you may be able to overcome this obstacle by adding more documents and resubmitting the entire application to the same INS office you have been dealing with, together with a written request that the case be reopened. The written request does not have to be in any special form. This is technically called a Motion to Reopen. There is a $110 fee to file this motion.

You may be denied the right to a U.S. filing without being denied an E-2 visa. When your application is turned down because you are found ineligible for U.S. filing, simply change your application to a consular filing. (Read Chapter 25 to make sure you qualify.)

Although there is no appeal to INS for the denial of an E-2 change of status application, you do have the right to file an appeal in a U.S. district court. It would be difficult to file such an appeal without employing an immigration attorney at considerable expense. Such appeals are usually unsuccessful.

F. Extensions

E-2 visas can be extended for up to five years at a time and E-2 status stays can be extended for two years at a time. When you enter the U.S. with an E-2 visa, your authorized stay as indicated on your I-94 card, which is limited to two years at a time, may elapse before the expiration date of your visa. Therefore, depending on your situation, you may need to extend just your I-94 card, your visa or both. Although an extension is usually easier to get than the E-2 visa itself, it is not automatic. INS or the consulate has the right to reconsider your qualifications based on any changes in the facts or law. When the original application for an E-2 visa or status was weak, it is not unusual for an extension request to be turned down. As always, however, good cases that are well prepared will be successful.

You can file for an extension of your visa either in the U.S. or at a consulate. However, contrary to our advice on the initial application, if your visa needs to be extended we highly recommend U.S. filing. That is because visa stamps, which can only be issued originally at consulates, may be extended in the U.S. If you have received an E-2 status but never applied for a visa, U.S. extensions of your status as indicated on your I-94 card are also advisable. However, if you have an E-2 visa that is still valid but your I-94 card is about to expire, it is generally better to leave the U.S. and return again instead of trying to extend your I-94 card in the U.S. When you return to the U.S. on your valid E-2 visa, you will automatically receive a new I-94 card and a new one- or two-year period of authorized stay. By leaving and reentering, no extension application will be needed and there will be no reevaluation of your qualifications.

1. Extension Application: U.S. Filing

The general procedures for an E-2 extension are the same as those described in Section E, above. The forms and documents are identical. As with the original application, the paperwork, together with a $120 filing fee, should be mailed to the INS regional service center nearest your place of business. Appendix II contains a complete list of all INS regional service centers and their addresses.

WORKING WHILE YOUR EXTENSION APPLICATION IS PENDING

If you file your application for an extension of E-2 status before your authorized stay expires, you are automatically permitted to continue working for up to 240 days while you are waiting for a decision. If, however, your authorized stay expires after you have filed for an extension, but before you receive an approval, and more than 240 days go by without getting a decision on your extension application, your work authorization ceases and you must stop working.

2. Extension Application Forms

Copies of all forms are in Appendix III.

Form I-129 and E Supplement

Follow the directions in Section E3, above. The only difference is that you will mark boxes "2b" and "4c" of Part 2.

Form I-539 (for accompanying relatives only)

Follow the directions in Section E3, above, but mark box "1a" of Part 2.

3. Extension Application Documents

You must submit your I-94 card. You should also submit the original Notice of Action I-797, if your status was previously approved or extended in the U.S., or a copy of your complete passport, including an E-2 visa stamp if you have an actual visa, a letter from your employer stating that your extension is required and a copy of your personal and business U.S. income tax returns for the past two years, including payroll tax returns.

G. Visa Revalidation: U.S. Filing

If you are physically in the U.S. and have been granted an extension on your I-94 card, you can have your visa revalidated by mail without leaving the country. To do this, you must fill out Form OF-156, following the directions in Section D3, above, and send it to the Department of State. With the form, you should submit as documents your passport, current I-94 card, updated evidence of continuing investment, a detailed letter from your employer describing your job duties and explaining why you are needed in the U.S., and a written statement from you declaring that you intend to leave the U.S. when your E-2 status ends. You should enclose a self-addressed, stamped envelope, or a completed Federal Express airbill. Send the entire package by certified mail to:

CA/VO/P/D
Department of State
Visa Services
2401 "E" Street, N.W., (SA-1 L-703)
Washington, DC 20522-0106
Telephone: 202-663-1213
Fax: 202-663-1608

The passport will be returned to you with a newly revalidated visa in about a month. Nationals of some countries like the U.K. are charged a fee for revalidating a visa, while nationals of other countries receive this service at no charge. Whether or not there is a fee depends on the nationality of the applicant, not the place where the application for the visa was originally made. You may call the State Department in Washington, D.C., to find out the amount of the revalidation fee, if any. If you send in your revalidation package without the correct fee, it will be returned to you, so check the amount in advance.

If your accompanying relatives are physically in the U.S., their E-2 visas may be revalidated by sending in their passports and I-94 cards together with yours. Again, there may be a charge for each visa revalidated. If your E-2 visa has expired, we strongly advise gathering your family together inside U.S. borders so you can take advantage of this simple revalidation procedure.

H. Visa Revalidation: Consular Filing

If you are outside of the U.S. when your visa stamp expires, you must have a new visa stamp issued at a consulate. Reread procedures for the application, consular filing, in Section D. The procedures for consular visa extensions are identical. If you are outside the U.S. with a valid visa, you need only reenter and a new I-94 card authorizing your stay for one year will be given to you.

FORMS AND DOCUMENTS CHECKLIST

STEP ONE: APPLICATION (THE ONLY STEP)

Forms

- ☐ OF forms (available from U.S. consulates abroad for consular filing only).
- ☐ Form I-129 and Supplement E (U.S. filing only).
- ☐ Form I-539 (U.S. filing only for accompanying relatives).

Documents

- ☐ Valid passport for you and each accompanying relative.
- ☐ One passport-type photo of you and each accompanying relative (Consular filing only).
- ☐ I-94 card for you and each accompanying relative (U.S. filing only).
- ☐ Long form birth certificate for you and each accompanying relative.
- ☐ Marriage certificate if you are married and bringing your spouse.
- ☐ If either you or your spouse have ever been married, copies of divorce and death certificates showing termination of all previous marriages.
- ☐ Documents showing ownership of real estate in your home country.
- ☐ Documents showing that close family members or property are being left behind in your home country.
- ☐ Documents showing that a job is waiting on your return to your home country.
- ☐ Copies of all outstanding stock certificates, if the qualifying business is a corporation.
- ☐ Notarized affidavit from the secretary of the qualifying corporation, or, if the business is not a corporation, from the official record keeper of the business, stating the names of each owner and percentages of the company owned.

- ☐ Passport or proof of citizenship for each owner of the qualifying business.
- ☐ Articles of incorporation or other legal charter or business license of the qualifying company.
- ☐ Tax returns of the qualifying company for the past two years, if available.
- ☐ Accountant's financial statements, including profit and loss statements and balance sheets, of the qualifying company for the past two years, if available.
- ☐ Payroll records of the qualifying company for the past two years, if available.
- ☐ Promotional literature describing the nature of the qualifying business.
- ☐ Letters from banks or bank statements indicating the average account balance of the qualifying business.
- ☐ Copy of a business lease or deed for the U.S. business premises of the qualifying business.
- ☐ If the qualifying company is a new business, a comprehensive business plan with financial projections for the next five years.
- ☐ If you are not majority owner of the qualifying business, evidence that your position in the U.S. will be as an executive, supervisor or essential employee.
- ☐ Bank wire-transfer memos showing money sent to the U.S. from abroad.
- ☐ Contracts for purchase and bills of sale for purchase of capital goods and inventory.
- ☐ Lease agreements for the business premises, or contracts to purchase or deeds for business real estate, or construction contracts and blueprints for building the business premises.
- ☐ If the qualifying company is a new business, documents showing that the investment is large enough to capitalize the business, such as market surveys, written trade-association statistics or written reports from qualified business consultants.

Students: F-1 and M-1 Visas

There are two different types of student visas: F-1 and M-1. F-1 visas are issued to full-time academic or language students. M-1 visas are issued to vocational or other nonacademic students. Both visas are obtained in exactly the same manner. However, the privileges and limitations of the two visas differ.

F-1 Privileges

- You may come to the U.S. as a full-time academic or language student enrolled in a program leading to a degree or certificate. (Students not requiring student visas include tourists who are taking a class or two for recreational purposes, those who have a spouse or parent in the U.S. with an A, E, G, H, J, L or NATO visa or status, or a worker in H status, as long as it does not interfere with his or her nonimmigrant status.)

- Visas can be issued quickly.

- You can transfer from one school to another or switch academic programs by going through a simple procedure to notify INS of the change.

- You may work legally in a part-time job on campus. Also, you may get special permission to work off campus if it is economically necessary or if the job provides practical training for your field of study.

- You may travel in and out of the U.S. or remain there until the completion of your studies.

- Visas are available for accompanying relatives.

F-1 Limitations

- You must first be accepted as a student by an approved school in the U.S. before you can apply for an F-1 visa. (Once accepted by the school, you can apply for your student status without leaving the U.S.)

- You may not work legally off campus without special permission.

- You are restricted to attending only the specific school for which your visa currently has been approved.

- Accompanying relatives may stay in the U.S. with you, but they may not work.

- You may not obtain an F visa to study at a public elementary school, a publicly funded adult education program or a public secondary school unless you prepay the full cost of such program for a maximum of one year (applies to public secondary schools only).

- You may not obtain F status to study at a private elementary or secondary school, or private adult education program, and then transfer to or attend publicly funded elementary, secondary or adult education programs.

- An individual who, in violation of the above regulations, obtains F status in order to study at a public elementary, secondary or publicly funded adult education program or changes such enrollment from such a private school or program to such a public program (without receiving prior approval and paying the full cost for a period not to exceed one year) will be inadmissible to the U.S. for five years. (This limitation is only applicable to applications made on or after November 30, 1996.)

M-1 Privileges

- You may come to the U.S. as a full-time vocational or nonacademic student enrolled in a program leading to a degree or certificate.

- You can transfer from one school to another.

- You may work legally in a part-time job on campus. You may also get permission to work off campus in a job that is considered practical training for your field of study.

- You may travel in and out of the U.S. or remain there until the completion of your studies, up to a maximum of one year. If you have not completed your program in a year or by the time indicated on your I-20M form, whichever is less, you must apply for an extension.

- Visas are available for accompanying relatives.

M-1 Limitations

- You are restricted to attending only the specific school for which your visa has been currently approved. You can transfer from one school to another only if you apply for and receive permission from INS to do so. Once you are six months into the program of studies, you are prohibited from transferring or changing your course of study at all except under truly exceptional circumstances.

- You are never permitted to change your course of study.

- You may not work legally off campus without special permission.

- Accompanying relatives may stay in the U.S. with you, but they may not work, unless they receive work permission in their own right.

A. How to Qualify

There are no quota restrictions. Applications filed at consulates are usually approved within one or two days. Applications filed in the U.S. are approved within one to three months.

1. Student Time Limits

Privileges and limitations of time spent by students in the U.S. are measured in a special way. As we explained in Chapter 14, Section B, Difference Between a Visa and a Status, a visa serves two purposes: it allows you to travel to and request entry to the U.S. Status (given to you upon lawful entry), gives you the right to engage in certain activities once you arrive. Permissible activities vary with the type of visa, but all visas share the characteristic of functioning as U.S. entry documents. The expiration date on your student *visa* indicates how long you have the right to request entry to the U.S. in order to assume student privileges. It doesn't tell how long you may stay once you arrive. This is controlled by the duration of your student status.

Duration of status is the period of time it is expected to take for you to complete your studies. When you enter the U.S. using a valid student visa, you will be given a small white card called an I-94 card. With all other types of nonimmigrant visas, an INS officer normally stamps the I-94 card with a date as you enter the country and it is this date, not the expiration date of the visa, which controls how long you can stay. However, student I-94 cards are not stamped with a specific date. Instead, the I-94 card is marked "D/S" for duration of status. This means that you may remain in the U.S. in a student status for as long as it takes to complete your educational objectives, provided you finish within what INS considers a reasonable period of time. The following specific rules control the time you may spend in the U.S. as a student:

- Both F-1 and M-1 visas are issued for the estimated length of time it will take to complete your proposed program of studies. M-1 students will receive a maximum period of one year. Consulates will use their judgment in deciding the expiration date of the visa. Normally it is expected that academic programs for F-1 students will last longer than vocational or nonacademic programs for M-1 students. Therefore, M-1 visas will generally not be approved for a program lasting longer than a total of 12 months.
- Once you arrive in the U.S., you may remain in student status without requesting an extension for up to the date indicated on your Form I-20, plus a 60-day grace period provided that you remain enrolled in an approved program of studies, and you maintain your full-time student status and do not become inadmissible or deportable.
- If your student status expires because your maximum stay (time indicated on I-20 for F students; time indicated on I-20M for M students) is up, you can apply to your designated school official for an extension of stay. To receive an extension, you will have to show that you are still enrolled in an approved program, you are still eligible for nonimmigrant student status, and that there is a good reason why it is taking you extra time to complete your studies. You must do so within 30 days of the I-20 expiration date. If that date passes, you are out of status and will have to petition the INS for reinstatement of your status.
- If you have completed or otherwise terminated your studies, you must leave the U.S. You have 60 days to leave if your status is F-1 and 30 days if your status is M-1. The school you attended is required to report to INS that you are no longer enrolled.

COMING TO THE U.S. TO LOOK FOR A SCHOOL

As a prospective student, you can come to the U.S. as a tourist for the purpose of locating a school you want to attend. If you do this, however, be sure to tell the consul at your interview that this is your intent so that s/he can make the appropriate annotation in your passport (such as "Prospective Student—school not yet selected"); otherwise, under the "30/60 day rule" the consul will (and the INS may) presume that you committed fraud by applying for a visitor visa when you intended to come to the U.S. to study. Under this rule, there is an unrebuttable presumption during the first 30 days, and a rebuttable presumption up to 61 days after entry, that any conduct such as requesting an I-20 form or submitting a request for a change of status (from B2 to F1 or M1) reflects your "preconceived intent" to get around INS rules by using a visitor visa for the improper purpose of being a full-time student in the U.S. (After day 61, there is no presumption at all.)

2. Who Qualifies for a Student Visa?

If you are coming to the U.S. to study full-time in a program leading to a degree, diploma or certificate, you must be a student at a U.S. government-approved school to qualify for a student visa. Academic and language students get F-1 visas while vocational and technical school students get M-1 visas. The primary differences are that F-1 visas may be held for a much longer time than M-1 visas, and F-1 students have greater opportunities to get work permits.

To qualify for a student visa, you must already be accepted by the school of your choice and have enough money to study full-time without working. You must be able to speak, read and write English well enough to understand the course work or, alternatively, the school can offer special tutoring or instruction in your native tongue to help overcome any language barriers. In addition to your academic and financial qualifications, you are eligible for a student visa only if you intend to return to your home country when your program of studies is over.

When you are dealing with student visas, you should be aware that at every government-approved school there is a person on the staff known as the designated school official. The designated school official is the person who is recognized by INS and the consulates as having primary responsibility for dealing with foreign students.

To summarize, there are six requirements for obtaining a student visa:

- you must be coming to the U.S. as a full-time student
- you must be enrolled in a program which leads to the attainment of a specific vocational or educational objective.
- you must have been accepted by a U.S. government-approved school
- you must have sufficient knowledge of English to be able to understand the course work. Alternatively, the school can offer you either instruction in your native language or special English tutoring
- you must have enough money or financial support to study full-time without working, and
- you must intend to return home when your studies are completed.

Now we will explain each of these requirements in detail.

a. Full-Time Student

The qualifications you must meet to be considered a full-time student depend on what kind of program you are pursuing. The different types of programs are classified for immigration purposes as:
- undergraduate college or university programs
- postgraduate college or university programs
- programs of specialized college-level schools
- high school and primary school programs, and
- technical, vocational or other nonacademic programs.

The time requirements of full-time enrollment vary for each one.

Undergraduate college or university programs. If you are an undergraduate at a U.S. college or university, you must be enrolled in at least 12 semester or quarter hours of instruction per term. An exception to this is if you are in your last term and need fewer than 12 semester hours to graduate.

Postgraduate college or university programs. If you are a graduate student, full-time studies are whatever the designated school official says they are. For example, a graduate student may be working on a dissertation and taking no classes at all, but still be considered a full-time student, if the designated school official approves.

Programs of specialized college-level schools. When your course of studies is at a specialized school offering recognized college-level degrees or certificates in language, liberal arts, fine arts or other nonvocational programs, you must be attending at least 12 hours of class per week. This means 12 hours by the clock, not 12 semester hours.

High school and primary school programs. Primary school or high school students must attend the minimum number of class hours per week required by the school for normal progress toward graduation. However, the school may recommend a lesser load for a foreign student with a limited understanding of English.

Technical, vocational or other nonacademic programs. To be classified as a full-time student in a technical, vocational or other type of nonacademic program, you must attend at least 18 clock hours per week, if the courses consist mostly of classroom study. If the courses are made up primarily of laboratory work, 22 clock hours per week is the minimum.

PERMISSION TO TAKE A REDUCED LOAD

When you are unable to carry a full-time course load due to health problems, you may be permitted to keep your student status even though you are not going to school full-time. You may also maintain your status while taking less than a full-time course load if the designated school official thinks it is academically necessary. No special application is made in either of these circumstances. However, when you take a reduced load, INS has the right to challenge your status at a later date. Therefore, it is advisable to get a written statement from your designated school official explaining that he or she believes it is medically or academically necessary for you to reduce your course load, and giving the reasons why.

b.   Program Leading to the Attainment of a Specific Educational or Vocational Objective

In order to qualify for a student visa, you must be enrolled in a program that leads to the attainment of a specific educational or vocational objective. You must also maintain a full-time course load, as described above.

c.   Government-Approved School

Student visas are issued only to students who attend U.S. schools that have received prior approval from INS for enrollment of foreign students. While virtually all public and accredited private colleges, universities and vocational schools have been approved, INS does not make an independent effort to qualify these institutions. To become approved, the school must take the initiative and file a formal application with INS. If you do not plan to attend a public school or a fully accredited college or university, before you apply for either an F-1 or M-1 visa you should check to be sure that the school you have selected has been approved by INS to accept foreign students.

d.   Knowledge of English

To qualify for a student visa, you must know the English language well enough to pursue your studies effectively. Most U.S. colleges and universities will not admit students whose native language is not English until they first pass an English proficiency test. Tests can be arranged in your home country. Your chosen school in the U.S. will tell you if such a test is required and how to go about taking it.

Usually, consul officials let each school decide for itself who is and is not qualified to study there. Still, occasionally even when a school is willing to admit you without a strong knowledge of English, the U.S. consulate may refuse to issue a student visa based on its own judgment that your English is not good enough. Should you have this problem, you may still be able to satisfy the consulate if the school you plan to attend is willing to supply English language tutoring or, alternatively, offer a course of studies in your native tongue.

e.   Adequate Financial Resources

You must show that you have adequate financial resources to complete your entire course of studies without working. At the time you apply for a student visa, you must have enough cash on hand to cover all first-year expenses. In addition, you must be able to show a reliable source of money available to pay for subsequent years. This is normally accomplished by having your parents or other close relatives promise in writing to finance your education and submit proof of their ability to do so.

f.   Intent to Return to Your Home Country

Student visas are meant to be temporary. At the time of applying, you must intend to return home when your studies are completed. If you have it in mind to take up permanent residence in the U.S., you are legally ineligible for a student visa. The U.S. government knows it is difficult to read minds. Therefore, you can expect to be asked for evidence showing that when you go to America on a student visa, you are leaving behind possessions, property or family members as an incentive for your eventual return. It is also helpful if you can show that you have a job waiting at home after graduation.

If you are studying to prepare yourself for an occupation where no jobs are available in your home country, neither INS nor the U.S. consulate will believe that you are planning to return there. To avoid trouble with getting a student visa, be sure to choose a field of study that will give you career opportunities in your home country when you graduate.

g.   Accompanying Relatives

When you qualify for an F-1 or M-1 visa, your spouse and unmarried children under age 21 can get F-2 or M-2 visas merely by providing proof of their family relationship to you and by showing that you have sufficient financial resources to support them in the U.S. so that they will have no need to work. F-2 and M-2 visas authorize your accompanying relatives to stay with you in the U.S., but not to work there.

APPLYING FOR A GREEN CARD FROM STUDENT STATUS

If you have an F-1 or M-1 visa, you can file for a green card, but being in the U.S. on a student visa gives you no direct advantage in doing so. Earning a degree may, however, help you indirectly, especially when you happen to be studying in a field where there is a shortage of qualified U.S. workers. If after graduating you eventually apply for a green card through employment, it may improve your chances of success because a key element is proving that there are not enough American workers available to fill a position for which you are qualified. College graduates also have a number of other advantages in applying for a green card through employment. See Chapter 8 for details.

Keep in mind, however, that student visas, like all nonimmigrant visas, are meant to be temporary. They are intended only for those who plan on returning home once their studies in the U.S. are completed. Therefore, should you decide to apply for a green card before your studies are finished, the U.S. government will allow you to maintain student status while pursuing a green card, but only if you are able to convince them of two things: first, that you did not intend to get a green card when you originally applied for the F-1 or M-1 visa and second, that you will return home if you are unable to secure a green card before your student status expires. Proving these things can be difficult. If you do not succeed, your student visa may be taken away. Should this happen, it will not directly affect your green card application. You will simply risk being without a nonimmigrant visa until you get your green card.

However, being out of status for even six or twelve months and then departing the U.S. may result in a three- or ten-year bar to your green card eligibility. Current INS interpretations state that a student who goes out of status does not begin to accumulate time toward these six- or twelve-month periods until an INS official or an immigration judge makes a ruling that such an individual is out of status. This means that if you stop attending school for some reason you will not begin to accrue time toward the overstay bars unless you come to the government's attention. This could happen, for example, if you request reinstatement of student status and the INS denies it. Then you would begin to accrue time toward the six- or twelve-month "overstay bars" as of the date of INS' decision. (See Chapter 25 for a discussion of how being out of status can affect your ability to get a green card.)

B. Student Visa Overview

Getting either an F-1 or M-1 visa is a one-step process.

1. The Application

Certain portions of the application are technically the responsibility of the school you will be attending. Some applicants expect their schools to handle the entire procedure for them, but this rarely happens. The only part of the student visa application you should expect your school to complete is a form known as the Certificate of Eligibility. You will use this certificate in preparing your application for a student visa.

The application is your formal request for a student visa or status. (If you are Canadian, your application procedures will be different from those of other applicants. See Chapter 28, *Canadians: Special Rules.*) It is filed by you and your accompanying relatives, if any. The application process may be carried out in the U.S. at an INS office, or in your home country at a U.S. consulate there.

The vast majority of nonimmigrant visa applications are filed at consulates. That is because most cases don't qualify for U.S. filing. You are not eligible for U.S. filing if you planned to file for a student status before you entered the U.S. on some other type of visa, unless your visitor visa was so annotated or you waited at least 61 days before requesting school documents such as the I-20 and filing your change of status application. Such a preplanned change is technically called *preconceived intent.* If an INS officer believes you had a preconceived intent to become a student when you entered the U.S., your application will be turned down. In recent years, INS has become especially strict about preconceived intent in student cases. That is why an overwhelming percentage of student cases filed in the U.S. are not approved.

Aside from the preconceived intent problem, consular filing usually brings better results than U.S. filings in still another way. A major benefit is that a student visa, which is stamped in your passport, can be issued only by American consulates. When you file your application at a consulate, your visa will be stamped in your passport at that time. INS offices inside the U.S. may issue statuses but not visas. (See Chapter 14, Section B, *Difference Between a Visa and a Status*).

If you are already in the U.S. legally on some other type of nonimmigrant visa, you may qualify to apply for a student status at an INS office inside the U.S. using a procedure known as change of nonimmigrant status. (If you were admitted as a visitor without a visa under the Visa Waiver Program, you may not carry out the application step in the U.S. Currently there are 29 participating countries in the Visa Waiver Program, including: Andorra, Argentina, Austria, Australia, Belgium, Brunei, Denmark, Finland,

France, Germany, Iceland, Ireland, Italy, Japan, Liechtenstein, Luxembourg, Monaco, The Netherlands, New Zealand, Norway, Portugal, San Marino, Singapore, Slovenia, Spain, Sweden, Switzerland, the United Kingdom and Uruguay. The government has approved Greece for inclusion in the program in the near future.) This is simply a technical term meaning you are switching from one nonimmigrant status to another. If a change of status is approved, you will then be treated as if you had entered the country with a student visa and you can keep the status as long as you remain in the U.S. or until it expires, whichever comes first.

You will not, however, receive a visa stamp, which is what you need if your plans include traveling in and out of the U.S. To repeat, visa stamps are issued only at U.S. consulates abroad. Therefore, if you change your status and later travel outside the U.S., you will have to go to the U.S. consulate in your home country and repeat the application process over again, obtaining the student visa stamp in your passport before you can return. This extra procedure makes changing status an unattractive option for all but Canadians who don't need visas to cross the U.S. border. (See Chapter 28, *Canadians: Special Rules*).

2. Paperwork

There are two types of paperwork you must submit to get a student visa. The first consists of official government forms completed by you or your U.S. school. The second is personal and financial documents such as school transcripts and diplomas, bank statements and guarantees of support. We will tell you exactly what forms and documents you need.

It is vital that forms are properly filled out and all necessary documents are supplied. You may resent the intrusion into your privacy and sizable effort it takes to prepare immigration applications, but you should realize the process is an impersonal matter to immigration officials. Your getting a visa is more important to you than it is to the U.S. government. This is not a pleasant thing to accept, but you are better off having a real understanding of your position. People from all over the world want U.S. visas. There is no shortage of applicants. Take the time and trouble to prepare your papers properly. In the end it will pay off with a successful application.

The documents you supply to INS do not have to be originals. Photocopies of all documents are acceptable as long as you have the originals in your possession and are willing to produce them at the request of INS. Documents submitted to U.S. consulates, on the other hand, must be either originals or official government certified copies. Government certified copies and notarized copies are not the same thing. Documents that have only been notarized are not acceptable. They must carry a government seal. In addition to any original or government certified copies of documents submitted to a consulate, you should submit plain photocopies of each document as well. After the consulate compares the copies with the originals, it will return the originals.

Documents will be accepted if they are in either English, or, with papers filed at U.S. consulates abroad, the language of the country where the documents are being filed. An exception exists for papers filed at U.S. consulates in Japan, where all documents must be translated into English. If the documents are not in an acceptable language as just explained, they must be accompanied by a full, word for word, written English translation. Any capable person may act as translator. It is not necessary to hire a professional. At the end of each translation, the following statement must appear:

I hereby certify that I translated this document from (language) to English. This translation is accurate and complete. I further certify that I am fully competent to translate from (language) to English.

The translator should sign this statement, but it does not have to be witnessed or notarized.

Later in this chapter we describe in detail the forms and documents needed to get your student visa. A summary checklist of forms and documents appears at the end of this chapter.

C. Who's Who in Getting Your Student Visa

Getting an F-1 or M-1 visa will be easier if you familiarize yourself with the technical names used for each participant in the process. You are known as the *student* or the *applicant*. Your U.S. government-approved school is referred to as the *school*. Each government-approved school is required by INS to appoint at least one individual who has responsibility for visa processing and other school-related immigration matters of foreign students. That individual is known as the *designated school official*. If you are bringing your spouse and children with you as accompanying relatives, they are known as *applicants* as well.

D. The Application: Consular Filing

Anyone with a Certificate of Eligibility from a U.S. school indicating acceptance by the school into a full-time program can apply for an F-1 or M-1 visa at a U.S. consulate in his or her home country. You must be physically present in order to apply there. If you have been or are now working or living illegally in the U.S., you may not be eligible. Be sure to read and understand Chapter 25 before your out of status period exceeds six or twelve months, before you depart the U.S., or file any applications with INS.

1. Benefits and Drawbacks of Consular Filing

The most important benefit to consular filing, making it almost always preferable to U.S. filing, is that only consulates issue visas. When you go through a U.S. filing you get a status, not a visa. (See Chapter 14, Section B, Difference Between a Visa and a Status) An F-l or M-1 status confers the same right to attend school as an F-l or M-1 visa, but it does not give you the ability to travel in and out of the U.S. Therefore, if you want travel privileges, you will at some time have to go through the extra step of applying for a visa at a U.S. consulate, even though you have already applied for and received student status in the U.S. However, if you had an immigrant visa petition filed on your behalf after entering in F or M status, you may be denied a nonimmigrant visa if you depart the U.S., as the consul may not believe you will leave the U.S. In that case you may be better off staying in the U.S. until you get your green card.

Moreover, anyone with a Certificate of Eligibility indicating acceptance into a full-time program by a U.S. government-approved school may apply for an F-l or M-1 visa at the appropriate consulate. That is not the case with U.S. applications for F-l or M-1 status. If you are in the U.S. illegally, consular filing is a must. You are not eligible to process a status application in the U.S. unless you have maintained your nonimmigrant status since your last entry.

A further advantage to consular filing is that some consular offices work more quickly to issue nonimmigrant visas than some INS offices do to process nonimmigrant statuses. Your waiting time for the paperwork to be finished may be much shorter at a U.S. consulate abroad than at most U.S. INS offices. Know the reputation and track record of a foreign U.S. consulate before applying for a visa there.

A drawback to consular filing comes from the fact that you must be physically present in the country where the consulate is located in order to apply there. If your petition is ultimately turned down because it is suspected you are not going to return home when your studies are completed, it is the duty of the consul officer also to stop you from entering the U.S. on any nonimmigrant visa. Therefore, in addition to refusing your student visa, he may at the same time cancel some other nonimmigrant visa you already have, including a visitor's visa. It will then be impossible for you to enter the U.S. in any capacity. Consequently, if your F-l or M-1 visa case is not very strong and freedom of travel is not essential to you, it might be wise to apply in the U.S., make up your mind to remain there for the duration of the student status and skip trying to get a visa from the consulate.

TCN PROCESSING AND SUMMARY EXCLUSIONS

The immigration law amendments of 1996 made changes concerning obtaining a nonimmigrant visa at a consulate other than one in your home country. Applying for a visa at a consulate which is not located in your home country is called "third country national," or TCN, processing.

TCN processing is prohibited when you have been unlawfully present in the U.S. under a prior visa status. Even if you overstayed your status by just one day, the visa will be automatically canceled, you will be ineligible for TCN processing and you will have to return to your home country to apply for a new visa at the consulate there.

If you were admitted for duration of status (indicated as "D/S" on your forms I-94), however, you still may be able to do TCN processing even though you remained in the U.S. beyond the time for which your status was conferred. This applies to individuals in A, F, G and J status. In this situation, you will be barred from TCN processing only if INS or an immigration judge has determined that you were unlawfully present. (In general though, unlawful presence need not be determined by a judge or INS officer if you overstayed your I-94 date.) Unlawful presence of six months or more after April 1, 1997, is also a ground of inadmissibility, if you left the U.S. and are requesting reentry. (See Chapter 25.)

Another new law may have an impact on people requesting entry to the U.S. This law empowers an INS inspector at the airport to summarily (without allowing judicial review) bar entry to someone requesting admission to the U.S. if either of the following are true:

- The inspector thinks you are making a misrepresentation about practically anything connected with entering the U.S., including your purpose in coming, intent to return and prior immigration history. This includes the use or suspected use of false documents
- You do not have the proper documentation to support your entry to the U.S. in the category you are requesting.

If the inspector excludes you, you cannot be readmitted to the U.S. for five years, unless INS grants a special waiver. For this reason it is extremely important to understand the terms of your requested status, and to not make any misrepresentations. If you are found to be inadmissible, you may request to withdraw your application to enter the U.S. in order to prevent having the five year deportation order on your record. INS may allow this in some exceptional cases.

2. Application General Procedures: Consular Filing

Technically, the law allows you to apply for an F-1 or M-1 visa at any U.S. consulate you choose. A complete list of all U.S. consulates that process visa applications, together with their addresses and phone numbers, is in Appendix I.

You may not file an application for an F-l or M-1 visa at a consulate until a U.S. government-approved school has given you a Certificate of Eligibility (Form I-20). Once you have obtained the Certificate of Eligibility, in a large number of consulates you can simply walk in with your application paperwork and get your F-l or M-1 visa immediately. Others insist on advance appointments. Most U.S. consulates in Canada require you to appear at least a week in advance of your interview to receive an appointment. Some, like the consulate in London, will only process visa applications by mail. Since procedures among consulates vary, you should always telephone in advance to ask about local policies.

On entering the U.S. with your new F-1 or M-1 visa, you will be given an I-94 card. This will be stamped showing you have been admitted for duration of status (D/S). Also shown is the name of the school you have been authorized to attend. Each time you exit and reenter the U.S., you will get a new I-94 card authorizing your stay for duration of status. When you have stayed in the U.S. on an M-1 visa for a year (or whatever time you were given) and you wish to remain longer, you will have to apply for an extension of your I-20 to your designated school official. You can apply for extensions of stay as long as you continue to maintain your eligibility for the status, and your DSO grants an extension of your I-20 time to complete studies.

3. Application Forms: Consular Filing

When you file at a U.S. consulate abroad, the consulate officials will provide you with certain optional forms, designated by an "OF" preceding a number. Instructions for completing optional forms and what to do with them once they are filled out will come with the forms. We do not include copies of these forms in Appendix III. In addition to the optional forms, the consulate will need a copy of Form I-20, which is completed by your school. You must have been accepted, met any special requirements for foreign students (such as proficiency in English) and proven you have the ability to pay for your education without working before the school will be authorized to complete its part of this form on your behalf. Ask your school to provide you with the completed form.

4. Application Documents: Consular Filing

You are required to show a valid passport and present one passport-type photograph taken in accordance with the photo instructions in Appendix III. For each accompanying relative, you must present a valid passport and one passport-type photograph. You will also need documents verifying their family relationship to you. You may verify a parent/child relationship by presenting the child's long form birth certificate. Many countries, including Canada and England, issue both short and long form birth certificates. Where both are available, the long form is needed because it contains the names of the parents while the short form does not. If you are accompanied by your spouse, you must establish that you are lawfully married by showing a civil marriage certificate. Church certificates are generally unacceptable. (There are a few exceptions, depending on the laws of your particular country. Canadians, for example, may use church marriage certificates if the marriage took place in Quebec Province, but not elsewhere. If a civil certificate is available, however, you should always use it.) You may have married in a country where marriages are not customarily recorded. Tribal areas of Africa are an example. In such situations, call the nearest consulate or embassy of your home country for help with getting acceptable proof of marriage.

You will need documents establishing your intent to leave the U.S. when your studies in the U.S. are completed. The consulate will want to see evidence of ties to some other country so strong that you will be highly motivated to return there. Proof of such ties can include deeds verifying ownership of a house or other real property, written statements from you explaining that close relatives live elsewhere or letters from a company outside the U.S. showing that you have a job waiting when you return from America.

If you will be attending a U.S. college or university, some consul officers will require you to prove that you are academically qualified to pursue the program, even though the school itself has already accepted you. Therefore, you should present evidence of all of your previous education in the form of official transcripts and diplomas from schools you attended. If these documents are not available, you should submit detailed letters written by officials of the schools you previously attended describing the extent and nature of your education.

Most important, you must submit documents showing you presently have sufficient funds available to cover all tuition and living costs for your first year of study. The Certificate of Eligibility, Form I-20, gives the school's estimate of what your total annual expenses will be. Specifically, you must show you have that much money presently available. You must also document that you have a source of funds to cover expenses in future years without your having to work. The best evidence of your ability to pay educational expenses is a letter from a bank or a bank statement, either in the U.S. or abroad, showing an account in your name with a balance of at least the amount of money it will take to pay for your first year of education. Alternatively, you can submit a written guarantee of support signed by an immediate relative, preferably a parent, together with your relative's bank statements. Unless your relative can show enough assets to prove he or she is able to support you without additional income, you should also show that your relative is presently employed. You can document this by submitting a letter from the employer verifying your relative's work situation.

Although the guarantee of support may be in the form of a simple written statement in your relative's own words, we suggest you use INS Form I-134, called an *Affidavit of Support*. A copy of this form is in Appendix III. The questions on Form I-134 are self-explanatory. However, you should be aware that the form was designed to be filled out by someone living in the U.S. Since it is quite likely that the person who will support you is living outside the U.S., any questions that apply to U.S. residents should be answered "N/A."

5. Application Interviews: Consular Filing

The consulates will frequently require an interview before issuing a student visa. During the interview, a consul officer will examine the forms and documents for accuracy. Documents proving your ability to finance your education will be carefully checked as will evidence of ties to your home country. During the interview you will surely be asked how long you intend to remain in the U.S. Any answer indicating uncertainty about plans to return home or an interest in applying for a green card is likely to result in a denial of your student visa.

6. Application Appeals: Consular Filings

When a consulate turns down an F-1 or M-1 visa application, there is no way to make a formal appeal, although you are free to reapply as often as you like. If your visa is denied, you will be told by the consul officer the reasons for the denial. Written statements of decisions are not normally provided in nonimmigrant cases. If a lack of evidence about a particular point is the problem, sometimes simply presenting more evidence on an unclear fact can bring a positive change in the result. The most common reasons for denial of a student visa are that the consul officer does not believe you intend to return home when your studies are completed or you have failed to prove an ability to pay for your education without working.

Certain people who have been refused student visas reapply at a different consulate, attempting to hide the fact that they were turned down elsewhere. You should know that if your application is denied, the last page in your passport will be stamped "Application Received" with the date and location of the rejecting consulate. This notation shows that some type of prior visa application has failed. It serves as a warning to other consulates that your case merits close inspection. If what we have just told you makes you think it would be a good idea to overcome this problem by obtaining a new, unmarked passport, you should also know that permanent computer records are kept of all visa denials.

E. Applying for a Student Visa When You Have Not Yet Been Accepted by a U.S. School

The requirement that you must first be accepted by a school in the U.S. before applying for a student visa sometimes creates a problem. It is very possible that you may need to travel to the U.S. before being accepted in order to make a final selection of schools or complete the school application. Under these circumstances you may enter the U.S. on a visitor's visa (see Chapter 15); however, you should advise the U.S. consulate issuing the visitor's visa that you are a prospective student. The consulate will then ask for proof of your ability to pay for your education as well as evidence that you are otherwise qualified for a student visa. If you are found qualified, the visitor's visa will be marked with the notation "prospective student." This notation will enable you to enter the U.S. as a visitor and, after being accepted into school, apply for student status without leaving the country. The fact that you have made your plans clear to the consulate from the beginning serves to overcome the problem of preconceived intent discussed earlier, and your student status should be issued in the U.S. without difficulty. The procedure for a U.S. filing is discussed next.

F. The Application: U.S. Filing

If you are physically present in the U.S., you may apply for F-1 or M-1 status without leaving the country on the following conditions:

- you have been accepted as a student by a U.S. government-approved school and in recognition of your acceptance, the school has given you a Certificate of Eligibility, Form I-20
- you entered the U.S. legally and not under the Visa Waiver Program
- you have never worked in the U.S. illegally
- the date on your I-94 card has not passed, and
- you are not inadmissible.

If you are admitted as a visitor without a visa under the Visa Waiver Program, you may not carry out the application step in the U.S. Currently there are 29 participating countries in the Visa Waiver Program, including: Andorra, Argentina, Austria, Australia, Belgium, Brunei, Denmark, Finland, France, Germany, Iceland, Ireland, Italy, Japan, Liechtenstein, Luxembourg, Monaco, The Netherlands, New Zealand, Norway, Portugal, San Marino, Singapore, Slovenia, Spain, Sweden, Switzerland, the United Kingdom and Uruguay. The government has approved Greece for inclusion in the program in the near future.

If you cannot meet these terms, you may not file for F-l or M-1 status in the U.S. It is important to realize, however, that eligibility to apply in the U.S. has nothing to do with overall eligibility for an F-l or M-1 visa. Applicants who are barred from filing in the U.S. but otherwise qualify for student status can apply successfully for an F-l or M-1 visa at U.S. consulates abroad. If you find you are not eligible for U.S. filing, read Section D, above, and Chapter 25 (*Inadmissibility* and bars to change and adjustment of status) before filing an application or departing the U.S.).

1.   Benefits and Drawbacks of U.S. Filing

Visas are never given inside the U.S. They are issued exclusively by U.S. consulates abroad. If you file in the U.S. and are successful, you will get student status but not the visa itself. This is a major drawback to U.S. applications. Student status allows you to remain in the U.S. with student privileges until the status expires, but should you leave the country for any reason before that time, you will have to apply for the visa itself at a U.S. consulate before returning to America. Moreover, the fact that your F-1 or M-1 status has been approved in the U.S. does not guarantee that the consulate will also approve your visa. Some consulates may even regard your previously acquired F-1 or M-1 status as a negative factor, an indication that you have deliberately tried to avoid the consulate's authority.

There is another problem which comes up only in U.S. filings. It is the issue of what is called *preconceived intent.* To approve a change of status, INS must believe that at the time you originally entered the U.S. as a visitor or with some other nonimmigrant visa, you did not intend to apply for a different status. If INS thinks you had a preconceived plan to change from the status you arrived with to a different status, it may deny your application. The preconceived intent issue is one less potential hazard you will face if you apply at a U.S. consulate abroad.

On the plus side of U.S. filing is that when problems do arise with your U.S. application, you can stay in America

while they are being corrected, a circumstance most visa applicants prefer. If you run into snags at a U.S. consulate, you will have to remain outside the U.S. until matters are resolved.

Overall, INS offices do not favor change of status applications. Your student application will stand a better chance of approval at most consulates than it will if filed in the U.S. But understand the pitfalls involved in departing the U.S. (discussed in Chapter 25) before making your decision.

2.   Application General Procedures: U.S. Filing

The application, Form I-539, consisting of both forms and documents, is sent by mail to the INS regional service center having jurisdiction over the intended school. INS regional service centers are not the same as INS local offices. There are four INS regional service centers spread across the U.S. Appendix II contains a list of all INS regional service centers and their addresses.

The filing fee for each application is currently $120. Checks and money orders are accepted. It is not advisable to send cash. We recommend submitting all papers by certified mail, return receipt requested, and making a copy of everything sent in to keep for your records.

Within a week or two after mailing in the application, you should get back a written notice of confirmation that the papers are being processed, together with a receipt for the fees. This notice will also tell you your immigration file number and approximately when to expect a decision. If INS wants further information before acting on your case, all application papers, forms and documents will be returned together with another form known as an *I-797.* The I-797 tells you what additional pieces of information or documents are expected. You should supply the extra data and mail the whole package back to the INS regional service center.

Applications for an F-1 or M-1 status are normally approved within two to eight weeks. When this happens, you will receive a Notice of Action Form I-797 indicating the dates for which your status is approved. A new I-94 card will be attached to the bottom of the form. You will also be issued an I-20 Student ID.

3.   Application Forms: U.S. Filing

Copies of all forms you must complete are in Appendix III.

Form I-20

You must submit a completed Form I-20, called Certificate of Eligibility. It is completed by your school. You must have been accepted, met any special requirements for foreign students (such as proficiency in English) and proven you have the ability to pay for your education without working before the school will be authorized to complete its part of this form on your behalf. Ask your school to provide you with a completed copy.

Form I-539

Only one application form is needed for an entire family. If you have a spouse or children coming with you, you should also complete the I-539 supplement.

Part 1. These questions are self-explanatory. "A" numbers are usually given only to people who have previously applied for green cards or who have been in deportation proceedings.

Part 2. Question 1. Mark box "b" followed by "F-1" or "M-1."

Question 2. This question asks if you are also applying for a spouse or children. If so, you must complete the supplement, which asks for their names, dates of birth and passport information.

Part 3. In most cases you will answer only the first item in this part, by putting in the date. You should put down the date shown on your I-20 as the anticipated completion time of your studies.

Part 4, Questions 1–2. These questions are self-explanatory.

Question 3. The different parts to this question are self-explanatory; however, items a and b ask if an immigrant visa petition or adjustment of status application has ever been filed on your behalf. If you are applying for a green card through a relative, this would be Step One, as described in Chapter 5. If you are applying for a green card through employment, this would be Step Two, as described in Chapter 8. If your relative or employer has filed the papers for either of these steps, the answer is "yes," and since you have therefore expressed a desire to live in the U.S. permanently, your application is very likely to be denied. If you have only begun the Labor Certification, the Step One of getting a green card through employment, this question should be answered "no."

4. Application Documents: U.S. Filing

Each applicant must submit an I-94 card, the small white card you received on entering the U.S. Remember, if the date stamped on your I-94 card has already passed, you are ineligible for U.S. filing. Canadians who are just visiting are not expected to have I-94 cards. Canadians with any other type of nonimmigrant status should have them.

For each accompanying relative, send in an I-94 card. You will also need documents verifying their family

relationship to you. You may verify a parent/child relationship by presenting the child's long form birth certificate. Many countries, including Canada and England, issue both short and long form birth certificates. Where both are available, the long form is needed because it contains the names of the parents while the short form does not. If you are accompanied by your spouse, you must prove that you are lawfully married by showing a civil marriage certificate. Church certificates are generally unacceptable. (There are a few exceptions, depending on the laws of your particular country. Canadians, for example, may use church marriage certificates if the marriage took place in Quebec Province, but not elsewhere. If a civil certificate is available, however, you should always use it.) You may have married in a country where marriages are not customarily recorded. Tribal areas of Africa are an example. In such situations, call the nearest consulate or embassy of your home country for help with getting acceptable proof of marriage.

We have emphasized that in order to qualify for either an F-1 or M-1 visa, you must have the intention of returning to your home country when your studies are completed and we have explained how consulates will demand evidence that ties to your home country are strong enough to motivate your eventual return. In a U.S. filing, INS does not always ask for proof of this. However, we strongly advise you to submit such evidence anyway. Proof of ties to your home country can include deeds verifying ownership of a house or other real property, written statements from you explaining that close relatives are staying behind or letters from a company in your home country showing that you have a job waiting when you return from the U.S.

If you will be attending a U.S. college or university, some consul officers will require you to prove that you are academically qualified to pursue the program, even though the school itself has already accepted you. Therefore, you should present evidence of all of your previous education in the form of official transcripts and diplomas from schools you attended. If these documents are not available, you should submit detailed letters written by officials of the schools you previously attended, describing the extent and nature of your education.

Most important, you must submit documents showing you presently have sufficient funds available to cover all tuition and living costs for your first year of study. The Certificate of Eligibility, Form I-20, gives the school's estimate of what your total annual expenses will be. Specifically, you must show you have that much money presently available. You must also document that you have a source of funds to cover expenses in future years without your having to work. The best evidence of your ability to pay educational expenses is a bank statement or letter from a bank, either in the U.S. or abroad, showing an account in your name with a balance of at least the amount of money it will take to pay for your first year of education. Alternatively, you can submit a written guarantee of support signed by an immediate relative, preferably a parent, together with your relative's bank statements. Unless your relative can show enough assets to prove he or she can support you without additional income, you should also show that your relative is presently employed. You can document this by submitting a letter from the employer verifying your relative's work situation.

Although the guarantee of support may be in the form of a simple written statement in your relative's own words, we suggest you use INS Form I-134 called an Affidavit of Support. (Do not use the new Form I-864.) A copy of this form is in Appendix III. The questions on Form I-134 are self-explanatory. However, you should be aware that the form was designed to be filled out by someone living in the U.S. Since it is quite likely that the person who will support you is living outside the U.S., any questions that apply to U.S. residents should be answered "N/A."

5. Application Interviews: U.S. Filing

Interviews on student change of status applications are rarely held. When an interview is required, the INS regional service center where you filed will send your paperwork to the INS local office nearest your intended school. This office will in turn contact you for an appointment. INS may ask you to bring additional documents at that time.

If you are called for an interview, the most likely reason is that INS either suspects some type of fraud or has doubts about your intent to leave the U.S. after the student status expires. Because they are not common and usually a sign of trouble, these interviews can result in considerable delays.

6. Application Appeals: U.S. Filing

If your application is denied, you will receive a written decision by mail explaining the reasons for the denial. There is no way of making a formal appeal to INS if your application is turned down. If the problem is too little evidence, you may be able to overcome this obstacle by adding more documents and resubmitting the entire application to the same INS office you have been dealing with, together with a written request that the case be reopened. The written request does not have to be in any special form. This is technically called a *Motion to Reopen*. There is a $110 fee to file this motion.

Remember that you may be denied the right to a U.S. filing without being denied a student visa. When your application is turned down only because you are found

ineligible for U.S. filing (change of status), simply change your application to a consular filing. However, be sure you are eligible for a consular filing and not subject to the overstay bars—see Chapter 25.

Although there is no appeal to INS for the denial of a student change of status application, you do have the right to file an appeal in a U.S. district court. It would be difficult to file such an appeal without employing an immigration attorney at considerable expense. Such appeals are usually unsuccessful.

G. Extensions

Student visas and student statuses can be extended to allow necessary continuation of your studies. F-1 statuses as written on the Form I-20M must be extended if your studies exceed the time limits stated on that form. F-1 I-20's can be extended. The new period will extend to the end of the revised estimated completion date of your academic program. All M-1 I-94 card statuses must be extended after one year.

Your authorized stay as indicated on your Form I-20 may last longer than the expiration date of your visa or it may expire before your visa expires. Therefore, depending on your situation, you may need to extend your I-20 date, your visa, or both. Statuses as written on the Forms I-20 can be extended only by your designated school official in the U.S. Student visas can be extended only at consulates. Extensions are not automatic. Your DSO or the consul officers have the right to reconsider your qualifications based on any changes in the facts or law. When it appears you are not making progress toward your academic or vocational objectives, it is not unusual for an extension request to be turned down. As always, however, good cases that are well prepared will be successful.

For those who must extend the duration of status as shown on the I-20 ID student copy, contact your DSO, who is responsible for making the extension and forwarding the information and paperwork to INS.

It is possible for your visa to expire before your duration of status period (as indicated on your I-20) is up. Even though you may be maintaining your student qualification and your duration of status is still in force, if you should leave the U.S. for any reason after your visa has expired, you must have a new visa issued at a consulate in order to return. If you do not leave the U.S., you do not need to have a valid *visa*; your I-20 and I-94 control your status period while in the U.S. See Section D, above. The procedures for visa extensions are identical. Extension requests by students are done through the Designated School Official on the I-539 form, which requires a fee of $70.

H. Work Permission for Students

When you have student status, you can work only under limited circumstances. In many cases these work privileges do not come automatically with the visa. You are often expected to file a separate application. There are a number of different types of work situations recognized as permissible for those with student status, and different rules apply to each one. Each situation is described in this section.

1. On-Campus Employment

You are permitted to work in an on-campus job for up to 20 hours per week when school is in session. During vacation periods, you can work on campus full-time. No special permission or application is required. Students working on campus can be employed by the school itself or any independent companies serving the school's needs, such as cafeteria suppliers providing food on campus premises, as long as it does not displace U.S. residents.

2. Employment As Part of a Scholarship

If you are given a job as part of the terms of a scholarship, fellowship or assistantship, and the job duties are related to your field of study, again, no special work permission or application is required. This is true even when the actual location of the job is off campus.

3. Off-Campus Employment With Special Employers

F-1 students may get permission to work off-campus for certain employers who have elected to participate in a pilot student employment program. Employers wanting to hire foreign students under this program are first required to submit an attestation to the U.S. Department of Labor. The attestation is required to contain statements that the employer has, for at least 60 days, attempted without success to recruit American workers for the jobs available. The employer must also attest that foreign students will be paid the same wage as other workers similarly employed.

Students who have been enrolled in a U.S. school for at least nine months and are in good academic standing may request permission to work for a pilot employer by applying to the designated school official. Permission from INS is not required. Permission to work can be approved only for the specific employer. A copy of the employer's attestation should be part of the application. Approval is given in increments of one year. Renewals are available indefinitely, provided the student remains in good academic standing. If the student transfers to another school, a new work request must be filed with the designated school official there.

Employers wishing to participate in this program have a significant burden placed on them to qualify. As a result, only a small number of companies have filed attestations, and this program is of limited value to most students.

4. Practical Training

Both F-1 and M-1 students are eligible to apply for work permission on the basis of practical training. Practical training can be either curricular or post-completion. Curricular practical training occurs before graduation, while post-completion takes place afterward.

Curricular practical training is available only to F-1 students who have been enrolled in school for at least nine months. The nine-month enrollment requirement can be waived for graduate students requiring immediate participation in curricular practical training. All requests for curricular practical training are approved by the designated school official, not INS.

Only the following types of work situations qualify as curricular practical training:
- alternate work/study programs
- internships, whether required or not required by the curriculum
- cooperative education programs, and
- required practicums offered though cooperative agreements with the school.

Both F-1 and M-1 students can get permission to work in post-completion practical training after graduating. F-1 students, however, are not eligible for post-completion practical training if they have already worked for more than one year in curricular practical training.

Post-completion practical training can be approved for up to one year (six months for M students), and part-time practical training taken is deducted from the total period available at one-half the full-time rate. Both the designated school official and INS must approve all applications for post-completion practical training.

5. Economic Necessity

Only F-1 students are eligible for work permission based on economic necessity. You will remember that in order to obtain a student visa, you were required to show that you had enough money on hand to cover all of your first-year costs. Therefore, work permission on the basis of economic necessity will never be granted during your first year of studies.

As an F-1 student, you can request work permission after the first year if there has been an unforeseen change in your financial situation and if your employment plans meet the following conditions:

- you have maintained an F-1 student status for at least one academic year
- you are in good standing at your school
- you are a full-time student
- you will continue to be a full-time student while working
- you will not work for more than 20 hours per week while school is in session, and
- you have tried but failed to find on-campus employment or employment under the pilot program with special employers.

INS recognizes as unforeseen circumstances such things as losing a scholarship, unusually large devaluation of your home country's currency, unexpected new restrictions enacted by your government that prevent your family from sending money out of the country, large increases in your tuition or living expenses, unexpected changes in the ability of your family to support you or other unanticipated expenses such as medical bills that are beyond your control. Work permission can be granted for one year at a time, and must be renewed each year. Instructions on how to apply for work permission are given later in this chapter.

You should consider your situation carefully before deciding to file a request for employment authorization based on economic necessity. If the application is denied, the INS may decide that you do not have enough financial backing to continue in your student status, since you are basically telling the INS that you don't have sufficient funds to support yourself.

6. Applications for Work Permission Based on Economic Need

Work permission based on economic need is available only to F-1 students who have completed their first year of studies. Check with your DSO or the local INS whether it is filed in your district INS office or the service center. Before bringing your application to INS, your designated school official will first review the paperwork to decide whether or not you meet all the requirements for work permission. If you appear to qualify, you will be given a written recommendation for employment, endorsed by the designated school official on Form I-20 ID. You should submit the endorsed form to INS with your other work application papers. The filing fee is currently $100. It is very important to keep the fee receipt INS will give you so you can prove that the I-765 was filed.

INS is required to make a decision on your employment authorization application within 90 days. If the decision is in your favor, you will receive a work authorization identification card. Most INS offices will attempt to decide your application within a few weeks.

If, for some reason, you are not given a decision within 90 days, you will, at your request, be granted an interim employment authorization which will last for 240 days. To receive an interim card, you must return in person to the INS local office where you filed your I-765 and show your fee receipt. Then your interim work authorization card will be issued.

If 240 days pass and you still have not received a final decision on the I-765, you must stop working. Interim work authorization cards cannot be renewed. However, if you reach this point, you have the option to file a new I-765 application and, if you do not get a decision on the new application within 90 days, you will then be entitled to another interim work authorization. You may not begin to work before receiving some sort of INS approval.

If your request for work permission is denied, you will receive a written decision by mail explaining the reason for the denial. There is no way of making a formal appeal to INS if your request is turned down. If you have new evidence of why you should be allowed to work, you may submit it to the same INS office that made the original decision and request that your case be reconsidered. This is technically called a *Motion to Reopen* and you must pay a $110 filing fee. You may also challenge the decision in U.S. district court but the time and expense required for this approach usually makes it impractical.

a. Work Application Forms

Copies of all forms are in Appendix III.

Form I-765

Block above Question 1. Mark the first box, "Permission to accept employment."

Questions 1–9. These questions are self-explanatory.

Question 10. You will not usually have an Alien Registration Number unless you previously applied for a green card, were in deportation proceedings or have had certain types of immigration applications denied. All Alien Registration Numbers begin with the letter "A." If you have no "A" number but you entered the U.S. with a valid visa, you should have an I-94 card. In this case, answer Question 10 by putting down the admission number from the I-94 card.

Questions 11–15. These questions are self-explanatory.

Question 16. Answer this question "(C))(3)(iii)."

b. Work Application Documents

You will need to submit as a document your I-20 ID student copy. You will also need documents to support your claim that there has been an unexpected change in circumstances that is creating your economic need. Such proof might include letters from government officials of your home country stating that there has been an unusual devaluation of the national currency or that your country's laws have changed and prevent your family from sending money out of the country to help support you as they once did. Depending on the situation, other items you might present are documents from your school showing a substantial tuition increase or bills from hospitals and doctors evidencing a costly family illness or birth of a child. If someone who has been supporting you is no longer able to do so, you can present a statement from a doctor or a death certificate showing that the person has become ill or died. You can also show documents demonstrating that the person who has been supporting you is having financial problems and so is unable to continue with your support.

7. Application for Work Permission Based on Practical Training

Both F-1 and M-1 foreign students may apply for work permission to accept practical training employment. Practical training employment is any position where the work is directly related to the student's course of studies.

a. General Procedures for F-1 Students

As an F-1 student, you can apply for permission to take practical training either during or immediately following completion of your study program. You may not apply until you have been enrolled as a student for at least nine months. If you apply before your course work is completed, you may be granted permission to take practical training only if it is necessary to fulfill a specific requirement of your particular academic program or if the work will be scheduled exclusively during regular school vacations. If the practical training will begin after you graduate, you may work simply because you wish to do so.

When practical training is to start after your studies are completed, an application for work permission must be filed not more than 60 days before or 30 days after your graduation. You can be granted permission to work in a practical training position for a total of no more than 12 months. You must have an offer of employment.

The application, consisting of both forms and documents, should be submitted in person at the INS service center designated for where you are attending school. Before mailing your application to INS, first your designated school official will review the paperwork to decide whether or not you meet all the requirements for work permission. If you appear to qualify, you will be given a written recommendation for employment, endorsed by the designated school official on Form I-20 ID. You should submit the endorsed form to INS with your other work application papers. The filing fee is currently $100. It is very important to keep the fee receipt INS will give you so you can prove that the I-765 was filed.

If INS wants further information before acting on your case, INS may send you a form known as an I-797. The I-797 tells you what additional pieces of information or documents are expected. You should supply the extra data and mail the whole package back to the INS office that is processing your application.

Most INS offices will make a decision on your application within a few weeks. The law requires INS to make a decision on your employment authorization application within 90 days. If the decision is in your favor, you will receive a work authorization card.

If, for some reason, you are not given a decision within 90 days, you will, at your request, be granted an interim employment authorization which will last for 240 days. To receive an interim card, you must return in person to the INS local office near where you live and show your fee receipt. Then your interim work authorization card will be issued.

If 240 days pass and you still have not received a final decision on the I-765, you must stop working. Interim work authorization cards cannot be renewed. However, if you reach this point, you have the option to file a new I-765 application and, if you do not get a decision on the new application within 90 days, you will then be entitled to another interim work authorization card.

If your request for work permission is denied, you will receive a written decision by mail explaining the reason for the denial. There is no way of making a formal appeal to INS if your request is turned down. If you have new evidence, you may submit it to the same INS office that made the original decision and request that your case be reconsidered. This is technically called a *Motion to Reopen* and you must pay a $110 filing fee. You may also challenge the decision in U.S. district court but the time and expense required for this approach usually make it impractical.

SPECIAL RULES FOR F-1 STUDENTS WHO TAKE PRACTICAL TRAINING AS A REQUIRED PART OF THEIR STUDIES PRIOR TO GRADUATION

If, prior to graduation, you accept practical training employment that is a required part of your studies, as is frequently done by students on fellowships, only 50% of your employment time will be deducted from the allotted 12-month total. Practical training in this special situation is called curricular practical training and has the effect of allowing you to work for a total of 24 months prior to graduation instead of only 12. If you work for six months in curricular practical training, you are required to deduct only three months from your allotment, meaning you may still accept nine months of additional practical training employment prior to graduation and the full 12 months after graduation. If, however, you work more than 20 hours per week, you lose the benefit of this special rule. Under these circumstances, once again you must deduct the whole amount of time you worked, meaning you are limited to a maximum of 12 months of practical training prior to graduation.

b. General Procedures for M-1 Students

As an M-1 student, you can apply for permission to take practical training only after you have completed your entire program of studies. Applications for work permission must be filed not more than 60 days before or 30 days after your graduation. M-1 students can be granted permission to work in a practical training position only for a period of one month for each four months of study, with a total overall maximum of six months. While the time periods for getting practical training work permission for F-1 students differ from those for M-1 students, the procedures, forms and documents are exactly the same.

The application, consisting of both forms and documents, should be submitted by mail to the INS service center responsible for your school's location. Before mailing your

application to INS, first your designated school official will review the paperwork to decide whether or not you meet all the requirements for work permission. If you appear to qualify, you will be given a written recommendation for employment, endorsed by the designated school official on Form I-20 ID. You should submit the endorsed form to INS with your other work application papers. The filing fee is currently $70. It is very important to keep the fee receipt INS will give you so you can prove that the I-765 was filed.

Most INS offices will make a decision on your application within a few weeks. The law requires INS to make a decision on your employment authorization application within 90 days. If the decision is in your favor, you will receive a work authorization card.

If, for some reason, you are not given a decision within 90 days, you will, at your request, be granted an interim employment authorization which will last for 240 days. To receive an interim card, you must return in person to the INS local office where you filed your I-765 and show your fee receipt. Then your interim work authorization card will be issued.

If 240 days pass and you still have not received a final decision on the I-765, you must stop working. Interim work authorization cards cannot be renewed. However, if you reach this point, you have the option to file a new I-765 application and, if you do not get a decision on the new application within 90 days, you will then be entitled to another interim work authorization card.

If your request for work permission is denied, you will receive a written decision by mail explaining the reason for the denial. There is no way of making a formal appeal to INS if your request is turned down. If you have new evidence, you may submit it to the same INS office that made the original decision and request that your case be reconsidered. This is technically called a *Motion to Reopen* and you must pay a $110 filing fee. You may also challenge the decision in U.S. district court but the time and expense required for this approach usually make it impractical.

c. Work Application Forms

Copies of all forms are in Appendix III.

Form I-765

Block above Question 1. Mark the first box, "Permission to accept employment."

Questions 1–9. These questions are self-explanatory.

Question 10. You will not usually have an Alien Registration Number unless you previously applied for a green card, were in deportation proceedings, or have had certain types of immigration applications denied. All Alien Registration Numbers begin with the letter "A." If you have no "A" number but you entered the U.S. with a valid visa, you should have an I-94 card. In this case, answer Question 10 by putting down the admission number from the I-94 card.

Questions 11–15. These questions are self-explanatory.

Question 16. If you are an F-1 student, answer this question "(C))(3)(i)." If you are an M-1 student, answer this question "(C)(6)."

d. Work Application Documents

You must submit as documents your I-94 card and I-20 ID student copy. If your practical training is post-completion, you must have a job offer. You should therefore submit as an application document a letter from your U.S. employer explaining the details of the work you will perform. The job description should show clearly that the work is in the same field as your course of studies.

For off-campus employment under the pilot program (described above) you may work only for those employers who have filed an attestation with both the Department of Labor and your school. Employers wanting to participate must first attempt to find sufficient American workers to fill the positions. Attestation Form ETA-9034 must be filed with both the U.S. Department of Labor and the designated school official at each school from which the employer wants to hire foreign students. Applications for this type of work authorization are made directly to the designated school official at your school, not to INS. Contact your DSO for more information, as these requirements may have changed.

I. Transfers

Requirements for transfers are different for F-1 students and M-1 students.

1. Applications for Transfers of F-1 Students

As an F-1 student, you may transfer from one school to another following a specific procedure. You must be a full-time student at the time—otherwise you will have to request reinstatement to student status. You must notify INS of the change, as well as the designated school officials at both your old and new schools. Applications to transfer are made by submitting Form I-20, together with your I-20 ID copy, to the designated school official at your new school who will, in turn, forward the paperwork to INS. You must submit the paperwork to the designated school official no more than 15 days after enrolling in the new school. A letter must be sent to the designated school official at the school you are leaving, telling him or her that you have transferred. This letter should be sent by certified mail. A copy of the letter should also be included when you submit Form I-20. Your I-20 ID student copy, which you have submitted as a document, will eventually be returned to you by INS (not the designated school official). On it will be written a notation showing that you have been authorized to transfer schools.

Transfers are denied only if it is discovered that you have in some way violated your student status. You cannot appeal a refusal of permission to transfer through INS. In fact, because your request will be refused only if a violation of your status has been discovered, in addition to denying you permission to transfer, INS may also order you to leave the U.S. or face deportation. If this occurs, it is at this point (under current INS interpretations) that you will begin to accrue time out of status toward the three- or ten-year bars. (See Chapter 25.) If you have new evidence to prove that you have not in fact been out of status, you may submit it to the same INS office that made the original decision and request that your case be reconsidered. This is technically called a *Motion to Reopen* and with it you must pay a $110 filing fee. You may also challenge the decision in U.S. district court but the time and expense required for this approach usually make it impractical.

2. Applications for Transfers of M-1 Students

As an M-1 student, you can transfer from one school to another, but only during your first six months of study, unless the transfer is required by circumstances beyond the M-1 student's control. You may transfer by following a specific procedure to request permission for the transfer from INS.

Applications to transfer are made by submitting Form I-20, issued by the school to which you will transfer, together with your I-20 ID student copy, to the INS local office having jurisdiction over the location of your new school. Appendix I contains a complete list of INS local offices with their addresses and phone numbers. You must apply at least 60 days before you wish to transfer. Provided you file your application on time, you may enroll in the new school 60 days after filing, even if you have not yet received INS's decision. If you transfer schools without following these procedures, you are considered out of status.

Transfer applications are normally approved in one or two months. When this happens, the I-20 ID, which you have submitted as a document, will be returned directly to you. On it will be written a notation showing that you have been authorized to transfer to the new school. If your request to transfer is denied, you will receive a written decision by mail explaining the reason for the denial. INS has discretion to deny your application to transfer for any legitimate reason. There is no way of making a formal appeal to INS if your request is turned down. If you have new evidence, you may submit it to the same INS office that made the original decision and request that your case be reconsidered. This is technically called a *Motion to Reopen* and you must pay a $110 filing fee. You may also challenge the decision in U.S. district court but the time and expense required for this approach usually make it impractical.

J. Changes in Course of Studies

F-1 students can change their courses of studies within the same school as long as they remain in qualifying programs. No formal permission from INS is required to change major areas of studies. M-1 students are never permitted to change courses of studies. If an M-1 student wishes to make such a change, he or she will have to return to a consulate and apply for a completely new student visa.

FORMS AND DOCUMENTS CHECKLIST

STEP ONE: APPLICATION (THE ONLY STEP)

Forms

☐ Form I-20 (available from your school).

☐ OF forms (available at U.S. consulates abroad for consular filing only).

☐ Form I-539 (U.S. filing only).

Documents

☐ Valid passport for you and each accompanying relative.

☐ I-94 card for you and each accompanying relative (U.S. filing only).

☐ One passport-type photo of you and each accompanying relative (Consular filing only).

☐ Long form birth certificate for you and each accompanying relative.

☐ Marriage certificate if you are married and bringing your spouse.

☐ If either you or your spouse have ever been married, copies of divorce and death certificates showing termination of all previous marriages.

☐ Transcripts and diplomas showing your previous education.

☐ Proof of financial support:

  ☐ Form I-134, Affidavit of Support, for you and each accompanying relative, or

  ☐ financial documents showing sufficient funds to attend school for at least one year without working.

☐ Documents showing that close family members or property are being left behind in your home country.

☐ Documents showing ownership of real estate in your home country.

☐ Documents showing a job is waiting on your return to your home country.

APPLICATION FOR PERMISSION TO WORK

ECONOMIC NECESSITY

Form

☐ Form I-765.

Documents

☐ I-20 ID student copy.

☐ I-94 card.

☐ Evidence of change in financial circumstances.

PRACTICAL TRAINING

Form

☐ Form I-765.

Documents

☐ I-20 ID student copy.

☐ I-94 card.

☐ Letter from prospective employer (post-completion).

APPLICATION FOR TRANSFER

Forms

None.

Documents

☐ I-20 from new school and I-20 ID student copy.

☐ If F-1, notice of transfer sent to old school.

☐ If M-1, new evidence of financial resources.

■

Exchange Visitors: J-1 Visas

Privileges

- You may come to the U.S. to participate in a specific exchange visitor program approved by the United States Information Agency (USIA). USIA has approved a large array of such special programs, sponsored by schools, businesses and a variety of organizations and institutions, which are meant to foster international cooperation through exchange of information. The programs are intended for students, scholars, trainees in business and industry, teachers, research assistants and international visitors on cultural missions.

- J-1 visas can be issued quickly.

- You may work legally in the U.S. if work is part of your approved program or if you receive permission to work from the official program sponsor.

- You may travel in and out of the U.S. or remain there until the completion of your exchange visitor program.

- Visas are available for accompanying relatives.

- Your accompanying relatives may work in the U.S. if they receive special permission from INS and the money is not needed to support you.

Limitations

- Your activities are restricted to studying, working or otherwise participating in the specific exchange visitor programs for which your visa has been approved.

- You must first be accepted as a participant in an exchange visitor program approved by the USIA before you can apply for a J-1 visa.

- Exchange visitors participating in certain types of programs may be required to return to their home countries for at least two years before they are permitted to get a green card or change to another nonimmigrant status or to have an "L" or "H" visa petition approved on their behalf.

A. How to Qualify

There are no quota restrictions for J-1 visas. Applications filed at consulates are usually approved in one or two days. Applications filed in the U.S. are approved within one to three months.

1. Exchange Visitor Time Limits

In seeking a J-1 visa, you will be asked to present a Certificate of Eligibility, known as Form IAP-66. This form is provided to you by the sponsor of the exchange visitor program in which you will take part. The form will list the specific dates you are expected to be participating in the program. Upon entering the U.S. with a J-1 visa, you will be authorized to remain only up to the final date indicated on the Certificate of Eligibility.

The Certificate of Eligibility is usually issued for the period of time needed to complete the particular exchange visitor program for which your J-1 visa is approved. INS regulations, however, place some maximum time limits on J-1 visas according to the type of program.

a. Students

Students may remain in the U.S. for the duration of their programs plus an additional 18 months of practical training employment (the student must apply for practical training). Practical training is any employment directly related to the subject matter of the student's major field of study. Remaining in the U.S. for the additional 18 months of practical training is at the student's discretion.

b.   Teachers, Professors, Research Scholars and People With Specialized Skills

Exchange visitors in any of these categories may be issued J-1 visas for no more than three years.

c.   International Visitors

International visitors whose purpose it is to promote cultural exchange, such as those working in the cultural/ethnic pavilions of Disney's Epcot Center, may be issued J-1 visas for only one year. Persons qualifying under this category may also be eligible for Q visas.

d.   Foreign Medical Graduate Students

Foreign medical graduates may be issued J-1 visas for the length of time necessary to complete their training programs, up to a maximum of seven years.

e.   Other Medically Related Programs

Participants in any medically related programs other than those for foreign medical graduates may be issued J-1 visas for the duration of their educational programs plus 18 months of practical training, however, the total time of both program participation and practical training may not be more than three years.

f.   Business and Industrial Trainees

Business and industrial trainees may be issued J-1 visas for a maximum of 18 months.

g.   Employees of the International Communications Agency

Participants in this particular exchange visitor program may be issued J-1 visas for up to ten years or even longer if the director of the International Communications Agency makes a special request to INS.

h.   Research Assistants Sponsored by the National Institute of Health

Participants in this particular exchange visitor program may be issued J-1 visas for a period of up to five years.

i.   Au Pairs

A trial exchange program bringing au pairs to the U.S. to live in and work with U.S. families has been in effect for several years. Under a June 1997 INS rule, au pairs may work up to ten hours a day, for no more than 45 hours per week, and the au pair must attend at least six hours of academic course work. As of this writing, only a few agencies have been approved to issue Form IAP-66 for bringing au pairs to the U.S. Stays are limited to only one year and cannot be extended. If this program interests you, check with the United States Information Agency for the names of approved au pair agencies, by phoning (202) 401-9810.

j.   Exceptions to the General Rules

Any exchange visitor may be allowed to remain in the U.S. beyond the limitations stated above if exceptional circumstances that are beyond the exchange visitor's control, such as illness, warrant an extension.

2.   Who Qualifies for a J-1 Visa?

You qualify for a J-1 exchange visitor visa if you are coming to the U.S. as a student, scholar, trainee, teacher, professor, research assistant, medical graduate or international visitor who is participating in a program of studies, training, research or cultural enrichment specifically designed for such individuals by the United States Information Agency (USIA). You must already be accepted into the program before you can apply for the visa. Some common programs for which J-1 visas are issued include the Fulbright Scholarship program, specialized training programs for foreign medical graduates and programs for foreign university professors teaching or doing research in the U.S.

You must have enough money to cover your expenses while you are in the U.S. as an exchange visitor. Those funds may come from personal resources, or when the J-1 visa is based on work activities, the salary may be your means of support. If you are a J-1 student, the money may also come from a scholarship.

You must be able to speak, read and write English well enough to participate effectively in the exchange program of your choice. In addition to all other qualifications, you are eligible for a J-1 visa only if you intend to return to your home country when the program is over.

To summarize, there are five requirements for getting a J-1 visa:

- you must be coming to the U.S. to work, study, teach, train or observe U.S. culture in a specific exchange visitor program approved by the USIA
- you must already have been accepted into the program
- you must have enough money to cover your expenses while in the U.S.
- you must have sufficient knowledge of English to be able to participate effectively in the exchange visitor program you have chosen, and
- you must intend to return home when your status expires.

a.   An Exchange Visitor Program Approved by the USIA

J-1 visas allow you to study, teach, do research or participate in cultural activities in the U.S. as part of any program specifically approved by the USIA. Sponsors of acceptable programs may be foreign or U.S. government agencies, private foreign and U.S. organizations or U.S. educational institutions. Such groups wanting program approval must apply to the USIA on Form IAP-37. Those making successful applications will be authorized to issue what are known as Certificates of Eligibility to J-1 visa applicants. They indicate that the applicant has been accepted into an approved program. Each approved program appoints an administrator known as the *responsible officer*. The responsible officer plays a formal part in dealing with the immigration process for program applicants.

There are over 1,500 USIA-approved programs in existence. A current list of exchange visitor programs is available from:

United States Information Agency
Office of the General Counsel
301 4th St., SW, Room 700
Washington, DC 20547
Telephone: 202-619-4979
Fax: 202-619-4573
Website: http://198.67.74.222/gc/

b.   Acceptance Into the Program

Before applying for a J-1 visa, you must first apply for acceptance into the USIA-approved program of your choice. Application is made directly to the program sponsor. Until you have been accepted, you do not qualify for a J-1 visa.

c.   Financial Support

You must establish that you have enough money to cover all expenses while you are in the U.S. The money may come from you, your family or scholarships and salaries that are part of the program itself. Since most exchange visitor programs involve either employment or scholarships, this particular requirement is usually easy to meet.

d.   Knowledge of English

To qualify for an exchange visitor visa you must know English well enough to participate effectively in the exchange visitor program. If your program is for students, you should know that most U.S. colleges and universities will not admit people whose native language is not English unless they first pass an English proficiency test. Tests can sometimes be arranged in your home country. The school will tell you if such a test is required and how to go about taking it.

Consul officials usually let each school decide for itself who is and is not qualified to study there. Still, occasionally, even though a particular U.S. school is willing to admit you without a strong knowledge of English, the consulate may refuse to issue an exchange visitor visa based on its own judgment that you do not know enough English to function well as a U.S. student.

e.   Intent to Return to Your Home Country

Exchange visitor visas are meant to be temporary. At the time of applying, you must intend to return home when your program in the U.S. is completed. If you have it in mind to take up permanent residence in the U.S., you are legally ineligible for an exchange visitor visa. The U.S. government knows it is difficult to read minds. Therefore, you can expect to be asked for evidence showing that when you go to America on a J-1 visa, you are leaving behind possessions, property or family members as incentives for your eventual return. It is also helpful to show that you have a job waiting at home when your program is completed. If you are studying or training to prepare yourself for an occupation where no jobs are available in your home country, neither INS nor the U.S. consulate will believe that you are planning to return there. If you want to avoid trouble in getting a J-1 visa, be sure to choose a field of study that will give you career opportunities at home when you are finished.

f.   Foreign Medical Graduates: Additional Qualifications

In addition to the above qualifications, if you are coming to the U.S. as a foreign medical graduate for the purpose of continuing your medical training or education, there are some added requirements. First, you must have passed Parts I and II of the U.S. National Board of Medical Examiners examination or its equivalent. At present, the only equivalent is the foreign Medical Graduate examination. Information on taking the exam is available from:

Educational Commission for Foreign Medical
  Graduates
3624 Market Street
Philadelphia, PA 19104-2685
Telephone: 215-386-5900
Fax: 215-387-9963

The exam is given twice a year, in July and January. The application deadline is 13 weeks prior to each exam date.

Like all J-1 visa applicants, foreign medical graduates must prove they will return home when their status expires. However, in such cases there is a specific piece of evidence needed to prove this. You must get a written guarantee from the government in your home country verifying that employment will be available to you when your U.S. medical training is completed.

Foreign medical graduates applying for J-1 visas should understand that they are legally required to return home for at least two years before becoming eligible to apply for green cards. Pay especially close attention to Section B1, below.

g. Accompanying Relatives

When you qualify for a J-1 visa, your spouse and unmarried children under age 21 can get J-2 visas simply by providing proof of their family relationship to you. J-2 visas authorize your accompanying relatives to stay with you in the U.S., but not to work there unless they first obtain special permission from INS.

B. Students: Comparing J-1 Visas to F-1 and M-1 Visas

Students coming to the U.S. often have a choice between J-1 exchange visitor visas and M-1 or F-1 student visas. Student visas are discussed in Chapter 22. J-1 programs for students are very limited as to the level of education and types of subjects that can be studied, while F-1 and M-1 visas can be issued for almost any type of education program imaginable, including vocational, secondary and high school programs as well as all courses of study at colleges and universities. Assuming there is an exchange visitor program that will fit

your needs as a student, there are certain advantages to holding a J-1 visa. It is much easier to get work permission as an exchange visitor than it is on a student visa. With a J-1 visa you may remain in the U.S. for up to 18 months after you graduate for the purpose of working in a practical training position. F-1 student visa holders are limited to 12 months of practical training employment and M-1 students are limited to only six months.

F-1 and M-1 student visas, however, are more flexible than exchange visitor visas in several ways. With a student visa, you may transfer from one school to another or change courses of study quite freely, and after graduation you may enroll in a new educational program without having to obtain a new visa. On a J-1 visa, you must remain in the exact program for which your visa was issued. Most important, certain J-1 visa programs *automatically make you subject to a two-year home residency requirement*, which will cause problems should you later want to apply for a green card or change to another nonimmigrant status, or have a nonimmigrant worker "L" or "H" visa petition approved.

1. Applying for a Green Card From J-1 Status

Keep in mind that J-1 visas, like all nonimmigrant visas, are meant to be temporary. They are intended only for those who plan on returning home once the exchange program in the U.S. is completed. Should you decide to apply for a green card before your program is finished, the U.S. government will allow you to keep J-1 status while pursuing a green card, but only if you are able to convince them that you did not intend to get a green card when you originally applied for the J-1 visa and that you will return home if you are unable to secure a green card before your exchange visitor status expires. Proving these things can be difficult. If you do not succeed, your J-1 visa may be taken away. Some program sponsors have been known to withdraw J-1 privileges after an exchange visitor has applied for a green card.

2. The Home Residency Requirement

The most serious drawback to applying for a green card from J-1 status is that many J-1 visas are granted subject to a two-year home residency requirement. If you choose an exchange visitor program that carries this requirement, it means that you must return to your home country and remain there for at least two years before you are eligible to apply for a green card, be approved for change of status, or have an "L" or "H" visa petition approved for yourself, even if you leave the U.S. and attempt consular processing.

It is possible to apply for a waiver of the home residency requirement. Although the procedures for filing waiver applications are simple, getting approval can be extremely difficult, especially for foreign medical graduates. Most exchange visitors can get waivers if the governments of their home countries consent to it. If not, and in the case of all foreign medical graduates as well as most Fulbright scholars, even if the home government does consent, waiver applications are approved only under compelling circumstances. Most are simply denied.

The reason for this is that many J-1 visa programs are set up and financed by foreign governments for the specific purpose of getting U.S. training for their citizens. The foreign governments hope that those who are trained will eventually return and use their new skills to benefit their homeland. Were the U.S. government to interfere with these goals by allowing J-1 visa holders to remain in America, there would be political discord between the U.S. and the other nations involved. Therefore, the U.S. makes every effort to see that J-1 exchange visitors keep their bargains and fulfill the home residency requirements.

Not all J-1 visa holders are subject to a home residency requirement. It applies only to participants in the following types of exchange visitor programs:

- programs for foreign medical graduates coming to the U.S. to receive additional medical training
- programs where the expenses of the participants are paid by the U.S., a foreign government or international organization, and
- programs for teaching individuals certain skills that are in short supply in their home countries. The USIA maintains a list of such skills and the countries where they are especially needed.

The Certificate of Eligibility, Form IAP-66, which you will receive when you are accepted into an approved J-1 program, has a space on it showing whether or not your J-1 visa is subject to a home residency requirement. If it is, the U.S. consulate issuing the visa will have you sign a declaration stating that you understand your obligation to return to your home country for at least two years before being allowed to apply for a green card or other U.S. visa. The consulate will also make a notation of the home residency requirement in your passport.

Be aware that the consulate does not have the power to decide who will or won't be subject to a home residency requirement. The facts of your situation, not the consulate's notation on your visa or IAP-66, determine whether you must meet this requirement. Some consulates routinely mark all J-1 visas subject to the home residency requirement, no matter what the facts. The consulate's notation is a strong indication that you are probably subject to the home residency requirement, but it is not the final word. If you have doubts about the correctness of the consulate's notation it is worth checking into the matter.

HOME RESIDENCY REQUIREMENT WAIVERS FOR CHINESE NATIONALS

On April 11, 1990, the president of the United States issued an executive order granting home residency waivers to all citizens of mainland China holding J-1 visas who were present in the U.S. sometime between June 5, 1989 and April 11, 1990. To be eligible for this special waiver, you are not required to have been present for the entire period between those dates. You need only have been in the U.S. sometime during the period.

C. J-1 Overview

Getting a J-1 visa is a one-step process.

1. The Application

Certain portions of the application are technically the responsibility of the sponsor of the particular exchange visitor program in which you will participate. Some applicants expect the responsible officer of their program sponsors to handle the entire procedure for them, but this rarely happens. The only part of the J-1 visa application you should expect your program sponsor to complete is the Certificate of Eligibility. You will use this certificate in preparing your application for a J-1 visa or status.

The application is your formal request for a J-1 visa or status. (If you are Canadian, your application procedures will be different from those of other applicants. See Chapter 28, *Canadians: Special Rules*.) It is filed by you and your accompanying relatives, if any. The application process may be carried out in the U.S. at an INS office or in your home country at a U.S. consulate there.

The vast majority of nonimmigrant visa applications are filed at consulates. That is because most cases don't qualify for U.S. filing. You are not eligible for U.S. filing if you planned to file for a J-1 status before you entered the U.S. on some other type of visa. Such a preplanned change is technically called *preconceived intent*. If an INS officer believes you had a preconceived intent to become an exchange visitor when you entered the U.S., your application will be turned down. In recent years, INS has become especially strict about preconceived intent in student exchange visitor cases. That is why an overwhelming percentage of student exchange visitor applications filed in the U.S. are not approved. (See Section F1, below.)

Aside from the preconceived intent problem, consular filings usually bring better results than U.S. filings in still another way. A major benefit is that a J-1 visa, which is stamped in your passport, can be issued only by American consulates. When you file your application at a consulate, your visa will be stamped in your passport at that time. INS offices inside the U.S. may issue statuses but not visas. (See Chapter 14, Section B, Difference Between a Visa and a Status). If you are already in the U.S. legally on some other type of nonimmigrant visa, you do qualify to apply for a J-1 visa status at an INS office inside the U.S. using a procedure known as *change of nonimmigrant status*. (If you are admitted as a visitor without a visa under the Visa Waiver Program, you may not carry out the application step in the U.S. Currently there are 29 participating countries in the Visa Waiver Program, including: Andorra, Argentina, Austria, Australia, Belgium, Brunei, Denmark, Finland, France, Germany, Iceland, Ireland, Italy, Japan, Liechtenstein, Luxembourg, Monaco, The Netherlands, New Zealand, Norway, Portugal, San Marino, Singapore, Slovenia, Spain, Sweden, Switzerland, the United Kingdom and Uruguay. The government has approved Greece for inclusion in the program in the near future.) This is simply a technical term meaning you are switching from one nonimmigrant status to another. If a change of status is approved, you will then be treated as if you had entered the country with a J-1 visa and you can keep the status as long as you remain in the U.S. or until it expires, whichever comes first.

You will not, however, receive a visa stamp, which is what you need if your plans include traveling in and out of the U.S. To repeat, visa stamps are issued only at U.S. consulates abroad. Therefore, if you change your status and later travel outside the U.S., you will have to go to the U.S. consulate in your home country and repeat the application process over again, obtaining the J-1 visa stamp in your passport before you can return. This extra procedure makes changing status an unattractive option for all but Canadians, who in many instances don't need visas to cross the U.S. border.

2. Paperwork

There are two types of paperwork you must submit to get a J-1 visa. The first consists of official government forms completed by you or your program sponsor. The second is personal documents, such as birth and marriage certificates, school transcripts and diplomas. We will tell you exactly what forms and documents you need.

It is vital that forms are properly filled out and all necessary documents are supplied. You may resent the intrusion into your privacy and sizable effort it takes to prepare immigration applications, but you should realize the process is an impersonal matter to immigration officials. Your getting a visa is more important to you than it is to the U.S.

government. This is not a pleasant thing to accept, but you are better off having a real understanding of your position.

People from all over the world want U.S. visas. There is no shortage of applicants. Take the time and trouble to prepare your papers properly. In the end it will pay off with a successful application.

The documents you supply to INS do not have to be originals. Photocopies of all documents are acceptable as long as you have the originals in your possession and are willing to produce them at the request of INS. Documents submitted to U.S. consulates, on the other hand, must be either originals or official government certified copies. Government certified copies and notarized copies are not the same thing. Documents that have only been notarized are not acceptable. They must carry a government seal. In addition to any original or government certified copies of documents submitted to a consulate, you should submit plain photocopies of each document as well. After the consulate compares the copies with the originals, it will return the originals.

Documents will be accepted if they are in either English, or, with papers filed at U.S. consulates abroad, the language of the country where the documents are being filed. An exception exists for papers filed at U.S. consulates in Japan, where all documents must be translated into English. If the documents are not in an acceptable language as just explained, they must be accompanied by a full, word for word, written English translation. Any capable person may act as translator. It is not necessary to hire a professional. At the end of each translation, the following statement must appear:

I hereby certify that I translated this document from (language) to English. This translation is accurate and complete. I further certify that I am fully competent to translate from (language) to English.

The translator should sign this statement but it does not have to be witnessed or notarized.

Later in this chapter we describe in detail the forms and documents needed to get your J-1 visa. A summary checklist of forms and documents appears at the end of this chapter.

D. Who's Who in Getting Your J-1 Visa

Getting a J-1 visa will be easier if you familiarize yourself with the technical names used for each participant in the process. You are known as the *exchange visitor* or the *applicant*. Your U.S. employer or school is referred to as the *exchange visitor program sponsor* and the individual at the employer or school responsible for J-1 visa processing is known as the *responsible official*. If you will be bringing your spouse and children with you as accompanying relatives, they are known as *applicants* as well.

E. The Application: Consular Filing

Anyone with a Certificate of Eligibility, Form IAP-66, from an exchange visitor program sponsor can apply for a J-1 visa at a U.S. consulate in his or her home country. You must be physically present in order to apply there. Even if you have been or are now working or living illegally in the U.S., you can still get a J-1 visa from a U.S. consulate if you otherwise qualify.

1. Benefits and Drawbacks of Consular Filing

The most important benefit of consular filing, making it almost always preferable to U.S. filing, is that only consulates issue visas. When you go through a U.S. filing you get a status, not a visa. (See Chapter 14, Section B, Difference Between a Visa and a Status.) A J-1 status confers the same right to work or attend school as a J-1 visa, but it does not give you the ability to travel in and out of the U.S. Therefore, if you want travel privileges, you will at some time have to go through the extra step of applying for a visa at a U.S. consulate, even though you have already applied for and received exchange visitor status in the U.S.

Moreover, anyone with a Certificate of Eligibility indicating acceptance into an exchange visitor program approved by the USIA may apply for a J-1 visa at the appropriate consulate. That is not the case with U.S. applications for J-1 status. If you are in the U.S. illegally, consular filing may be your only option. You are usually not eligible to process a status application in the U.S. unless you are currently maintaining legal status.

A further plus to consular filing is that consular offices may work more quickly to issue nonimmigrant visas than INS offices do to process nonimmigrant statuses. Your waiting time for the paperwork to be finished may be shorter at a U.S. consulate abroad than at certain U.S. INS offices.

A drawback to consular filing comes from the fact that you must be physically present in the country where the consulate is located in order to file there. If your application is ultimately turned down because it is suspected you are not going to return home when your participation in the exchange visitor program is completed, it is also the duty of the consul officer to stop you from entering the U.S. on any nonimmigrant visa. Therefore, in addition to refusing your J-1 visa, he may at the same time cancel some other nonimmigrant visa you already have, including a visitor's visa. It will then be impossible for you to enter the U.S. in any capacity. Consequently, if your J-1 visa case is not very strong and freedom of travel is not essential to you, it might be wise to apply in the U.S., make up your mind to remain there for the duration of the exchange visitor status and skip trying to get a visa from the consulate.

2. Application General Procedures: Consular Filing

Technically the law allows you to apply for a J-1 at any U.S. consulate you choose. A complete list of all U.S. consulates that process visa applications, together with their addresses and phone numbers, is in Appendix I. However, from a practical standpoint your case will be given greatest consideration at the consulate in your home country. Applying in some other country creates suspicion in the minds of the consul officers there about your motives for choosing their consulate. Often, when an applicant is having trouble at a home consulate he will seek a more lenient office in some other country. This practice of consulate shopping is frowned on by officials in the system. Unless you have a very good reason for being elsewhere (such as a temporary job assignment in some other nation), it is smarter to file your visa application in your home country.

Furthermore, if you have been present in the U.S. unlawfully, in general you cannot apply as a third country national. Even if you overstayed your status in the U.S. by just one day, your visa will be automatically cancelled and you must return to your home country and apply for the visa from that consulate. There is an exception. If you were admitted to the U.S. for the duration of your status (indicated by a "D/S" on your I-94 form) and you remained in the U.S. beyond the authorized period of stay, you may still be able to apply as a third country national. The State Department's current regulations seem to imply that you will be barred from third country national processing only if an immigration judge or INS officer has determined that you were unlawfully present. Because of the ambiguity, you may find that your success in applying as a third country national will depend on your country, the consulate and the relative seriousness of your offense.

You may not file an application for a J-1 visa at a consulate until a USIA-approved exchange visitor program sponsor has given you a Certificate of Eligibility, Form IAP-66. Once you have obtained the Certificate of Eligibility, in a large number of consulates you can simply walk in with your application paperwork and get your J-1 visa immediately. Others insist on advance appointments. Some, like the consulate in London, will only process visa applications by mail. Since procedures among consulates vary, you should always telephone in advance to ask about local policies.

On entering the U.S. with your new J-1 visa, you will be given an I-94 card. It will be stamped with a date indicating how long you can stay. Normally, you are permitted to remain up to the expiration date on your Form IAP-66 Certificate of Eligibility. Each time you exit and reenter the U.S., you will get a new I-94 card authorizing your stay up to the final date indicated on the IAP-66.

3. Application Forms: Consular Filing

When you file at a U.S. consulate abroad, the consulate officials will provide you with certain optional forms, designated by an "OF" preceding a number. Instructions for completing optional forms and what to do with them once they are filled out will come with the forms. We do not include copies of these forms in Appendix III. In addition to the optional forms, the consulate will need a copy of Form IAP-66, which is prepared by the exchange visitor program sponsor. You do not fill out or sign any part of it. After your program sponsor completes the form, it will give the form to you for you to submit, together with your other forms and documents, to the consulate for processing.

4. Application Documents: Consular Filing

You are required to show a valid passport and present one passport-type photograph taken in accordance with the photo instructions in Appendix III. For each accompanying relative, you must present a valid passport and one passport-type photograph. You will also need documents verifying their family relationship to you. You may verify a parent/child relationship by presenting the child's long form birth certificate. Many countries, including Canada and England, issue both short and long form birth certificates. Where both are available, the long form is needed because it contains the names of the parents while the short form does not. If you are accompanied by your spouse, you must establish that you are lawfully married by showing a civil marriage certificate. Church certificates are generally unacceptable. (There are a few exceptions depending on the laws of your particular country. Canadians, for example, may use church marriage certificates if the marriage took place in Quebec Province, but not elsewhere. If a civil certificate is available, however, you should always use it.) You may have married in a country where marriages are not customarily recorded. Tribal areas of Africa are an example. In such situations, call the nearest consulate or embassy of your home country for help with getting acceptable proof of marriage.

You will need documents establishing your intent to leave the U.S. when your visa expires. The consulate will want to see evidence that ties to your home country are so strong you will be highly motivated to return. Proof of such ties can include deeds verifying ownership of a house or other real property, written statements from you explaining that close relatives are staying behind or letters from a company outside the U.S. showing that you have a job waiting when you return from America.

If you will be attending school in the U.S. and neither employment nor a scholarship is part of your exchange visitor program, you must present evidence that you have sufficient funds available to cover all of your costs for the first year of study and that you also have a source of funds to cover your expenses in future years so that you will be able to study full time without working. If your particular exchange visitor program provides you with a scholarship or employment, evidence of such support in the form of a letter from the program sponsor will satisfy this requirement. If the exchange visitor program sponsor will not be furnishing you with financial support, you will have to show either that you can meet your own expenses without working or that a close relative is willing to guarantee your support. The best evidence of your ability to pay educational expenses is a bank statement or letter from a bank, either in the U.S. or abroad, showing an account in your name with a balance of at least one year's worth of expenses in it. Alternatively, you can submit a written guarantee of support signed by an immediate relative, preferably a parent, together with your relative's bank statements. Unless your relative can show enough assets to prove he or she is able to support you without additional income, you should also show that your relative is presently employed. You can document this by submitting a letter from the employer verifying your relative's work situation.

Although the guarantee of support may be in the form of a simple written statement in your relative's own words, we suggest you use INS Form I-134, called an Affidavit of Support. A copy of this form is in Appendix III. The questions on Form I-134 are self-explanatory. However, the form was designed to be filled out by someone living in the U.S. Since it is quite likely that the person who will support you is living outside the U.S., any questions that apply to U.S. residents should be answered "N/A."

5. Application Interviews: Consular Filing

The consulates will frequently require an interview before issuing an exchange visitor visa. During the interview, a consul officer will examine the forms and documents for accuracy. Documents proving your ability to support yourself while you are in the U.S. will be carefully checked as will evidence of ties to your home country. During the interview, you will surely be asked how long you intend to remain in the U.S. Any answer indicating uncertainty about plans to return home or an interest in applying for a green card is likely to result in a denial of your J-1 visa. If you are subject to the two-year home residency requirement, the consul officer will probably discuss this with you to make certain you understand what it means. Keep in mind that if you want a green card, a home residency requirement can significantly delay your reaching this goal.

6. Application Appeals: Consular Filings

When a consulate turns down a J-1 visa application, there is no way to make a formal appeal, although you are free to reapply as often as you like. If your visa is denied, you will be told by the consul officer the reasons for the denial. Written statements of decisions are not normally provided in nonimmigrant cases. If a lack of evidence about a particular point is the problem, sometimes simply presenting more evidence on an unclear fact can bring a positive change in the result. The most common reasons for denial of an exchange visitor visa are that the consul officer does not believe you intend to return home upon the completion of your program or, if you will be a student, that you have failed to prove an ability to pay for your education without working.

Certain people who have been refused J-1 visas reapply at a different consulate, attempting to hide the fact that they were turned down elsewhere. You should know that if your application is denied, the last page in your passport will be stamped "Application Received" with the date and location of the rejecting consulate. This notation shows that some type of prior visa application has failed. It serves as a warning to other consulates that your case merits close inspection. If what we have just told you makes you think it would be a good idea to overcome this problem by obtaining a new, unmarked passport, you should also know that permanent computer records are kept of all visa denials.

F. The Application: U.S. Filing

If you are physically present in the U.S., you may apply for J-1 status without leaving the country on the following conditions:

- you have been accepted as an exchange visitor by a USIA-approved exchange visitor program sponsor and in recognition of your acceptance, the program sponsor has given you a Certificate of Eligibility, Form IAP-66
- you entered the U.S. legally and not under the Visa Waiver Program
- you have never worked illegally in the U.S.
- the date on your I-94 card has not passed, and
- you are not subject to any grounds of inadmissibility or bars to changing status (see Chapter 25).

If you are admitted as a visitor without a visa under the Visa Waiver Program, you may not carry out the application step in the U.S. Currently there are 29 participating countries in the Visa Waiver Program, including: Andorra, Argentina, Austria, Australia, Belgium, Brunei, Denmark, Finland, France, Germany, Iceland, Ireland, Italy, Japan, Liechtenstein, Luxembourg, Monaco, The Netherlands, New Zealand, Norway, Portugal, San Marino, Singapore, Slovenia, Spain, Sweden, Switzerland, the United Kingdom and Uruguay. The government has approved Greece for inclusion in the program in the near future.

⚠ If you cannot meet these terms, you may not file for J-1 status in the U.S. It is important to realize, however, that eligibility to apply in the U.S. has nothing to do with overall eligibility for a J-1 visa. Applicants who are barred from filing in the U.S. but otherwise qualify for exchange visitor status can apply successfully for a J-1 visa at U.S. consulates abroad. If you find you are not eligible for U.S. filing, read Section E. However, be sure to read and understand the issues and problems involving inadmissibility, discussed in Chapter 25, before proceeding.

1. Benefits and Drawbacks of U.S. Filing

Visas are never given inside the U.S. They are issued exclusively by U.S. consulates abroad. If you file in the U.S. and you are successful, you will get J-1 status but not the visa itself. This is a major drawback to U.S. applications. J-1 status allows you to remain in the U.S. with J-1 privileges until the status expires, but should you leave the country for any reason before that time, you will have to apply for the visa itself at a U.S. consulate before returning to

America. Moreover, the fact that your exchange visitor status has been approved in the U.S. does not guarantee that the consulate will approve your visa. Some consulates may even regard your previously acquired status as a negative factor, an indication that you have deliberately tried to avoid the consulate's authority.

There is another problem which comes up only in U.S. filings. It is the issue of what is called *preconceived intent*. We already defined preconceived intent earlier in this chapter and explained how INS is especially strict in this area on student program applications. In order to approve a change of status, INS must believe that at the time you originally entered the U.S. as a visitor or with some other nonimmigrant visa, you did not intend to apply for a different status. If INS thinks you had a preconceived plan to change from the status you arrived with to a different status, INS will deny your application. The preconceived intent issue is one less potential hazard you will face if you apply at a U.S. consulate abroad.

On the plus side of U.S. filing, if you come from a place where it is difficult to obtain U.S. visas, such as Latin America or Asia, your chances for success may be better in the U.S. Another benefit is that when problems do arise with your U.S. application, you can stay in America while they are being corrected, a circumstance most visa applicants prefer. If you run into snags at a U.S. consulate you will have to remain outside the U.S. until matters are resolved.

Overall, INS offices disfavor change of status applications if they are submitted or if other action is taken too soon after you received your nonimmigrant visa and entered the U.S. consulate. Many INS offices use a 30/60 day rule to charge applicants with fraud or "preconceived intent" if they behave in a way which is inconsistent with their visitor visa within 30 or 60 days. For example, if you are admitted in visitor status on June 1, 1998, and you commence unauthorized employment or seek to change to F or J status on June 15, 1998, INS will presume that you already had that intent to change status or commence employment at the time you entered. That presumption is conclusive for 30 days; from 31-60 days it is rebuttable, which means a consulate or INS office may or may not deny your application, depending on what your circumstances are. At day 61 after entry, the presumption no longer operates.

2. Application General Procedures: U.S. Filing

The application, consisting of both forms and documents, is sent by mail to the INS regional service center having jurisdiction over the location of the USIA-approved program that has accepted you. INS regional service centers are not the same as INS local offices. There are four INS regional service centers spread across the U.S. Appendix II contains a list of all INS regional service centers and their addresses.

The filing fee for each application is currently $75, plus $10 for each accompanying relative. Checks and money orders are accepted. It is not advisable to send cash. We recommend submitting all papers by certified mail, return receipt requested, and making a copy of everything sent in to keep for your records.

Within a week or so after mailing in the application, you should get back a written notice of confirmation that the papers are being processed, together with a receipt for the fees. The notice will also tell you your immigration file number and approximately when to expect a decision. If INS wants further information before acting on your case, INS will send a form known as an *I-797* (Request for Evidence). The I-797 tells you what additional pieces of information or documents are expected. You should supply the extra data and mail the package back to the INS regional service center, with the I-797 form on top.

Applications for a J-1 status are normally approved within one to two months. When this happens, the I-94 card which you will have submitted as a document is returned directly to you. On the back of the I-94 card will be written your new status and a date indicating how long you can remain in the U.S. Normally, this will be 30 days later than the last date shown on the IAP-66, Certificate of Eligibility.

3. Application Forms: U.S. Filing

Copies of all forms you must complete are in Appendix III.

Form IAP-66

This form is prepared by the exchange visitor program sponsor. You do not fill out or sign any part of it. After your program sponsor completes the form, it will give the form to you for you to submit, together with your other forms and documents, to INS for processing.

Form I-539

Only one application form is needed for an entire family. If you have a spouse or children coming with you, you should also complete the I-539 supplement.

Part 1. These questions are self-explanatory. "A" numbers are usually given only to people who have previously applied for green cards or who have been in deportation proceedings.

Part 2. Question 1. Mark box "b" followed by "J-1."

Question 2. This question asks if you are also applying for a spouse or children. If so, you must complete the supplement, which asks for their names, dates of birth and passport information.

Part 3. In most cases you will answer only the first item in this part, by putting in the date. You should put down the date shown on your IAP-66 as the anticipated completion time of your exchange visitor program.

Part 4, Questions 1–2. These questions are self-explanatory.

Question 3. The different parts to this question are self-explanatory; however, items a and b ask if an immigrant visa petition or adjustment of status application has ever been filed on your behalf. If you are applying for a green card through a relative, this would be Step One, as described in Chapter 5. If you are applying for a green card through employment, this would be Step Two as described in Chapter 8. If your relative or employer has filed the papers for either of these steps, the answer is "yes," and since you have therefore expressed a desire to live in the U.S. permanently, your application is very likely to be denied. If you have only begun the Labor Certification, the Step One of getting a green card through employment, this question should be answered "no."

4. Application Documents: U.S. Filing

Each applicant must submit an I-94 card, the small white card you received on entering the U.S. Remember, if the date stamped on your I-94 card has already passed, you are ineligible for U.S. filing. Canadians who are just visiting are not expected to have I-94 cards. Canadians with any other type of nonimmigrant status should have them.

For each accompanying relative, send in an I-94 card. You will also need documents verifying their family relationship to you. You may verify a parent/child relationship by presenting the child's long form birth certificate. Many countries, including Canada and England, issue both short and long form birth certificates. Where both are available, the long form is needed because it contains the names of the parents while the short form does not. If you are accompanied by your spouse, you must establish that you are lawfully married by showing a civil marriage certificate. Church certificates are generally unacceptable. (There are a few exceptions, depending on the laws of your particular country. Canadians, for example, may use church marriage certificates if the marriage took place in Quebec Province, but not elsewhere. If a civil certificate is available, however, you should always use it.) You may have married in a country where marriages are not customarily recorded. Tribal areas of Africa are an example. In such situations, call the nearest consulate or embassy of your home country for help with getting acceptable proof of marriage.

We have emphasized that in order to qualify for a J-1 visa, you must have the intention of returning to your home country upon the completion of your exchange visitor program and we have explained how consulates will demand evidence that ties to your home country are strong enough to motivate your eventual return. In a U.S. filing, INS does not always ask for proof of this. However, we strongly advise you to submit such evidence anyway. Proof of ties to your home country can include deeds verifying ownership of a house or other real property, written statements from you explaining that close relatives are staying behind or letters from a company in your home country showing that you have a job waiting when you return from the U.S.

If you will be attending school in the U.S. and neither employment nor a scholarship is part of your exchange visitor program, you must present evidence that you have sufficient funds available to cover all of your costs for the first year of study and that you also have a source of funds to cover your expenses in future years so that you will be able to study full-time without working. If your particular exchange visitor program provides you with a scholarship or employment, evidence of such support in the form of a letter from the program sponsor will satisfy this requirement. If the exchange visitor program sponsor will not be furnishing you with financial support, you will have to show either that you can meet your own expenses without working or that a close relative is willing to guarantee your support. The best evidence of your ability to pay educational expenses is a bank statement or letter from a bank, either in the U.S. or abroad, showing an account in your name with a balance of at least one year's worth of expenses in it. Alternatively you can submit a written guarantee of support signed by an immediate relative, preferably a parent, together with your relative's bank statements. Unless your relative can show enough assets to prove he or she is able to support you without additional income, you should also show that your relative is presently employed. You can document this by submitting a letter from the employer verifying your relative's work situation.

Although the guarantee of support may be in the form of a simple written statement in your relative's own words, we suggest you use INS Form I-134, called an Affidavit of Support. A copy of this form is in Appendix III. The questions on Form I-134 are self-explanatory; however, you should be aware that the form was designed to be filled out by someone living in the U.S. Since it is quite likely that the person who will support you is living outside the U.S., any questions that apply to U.S. residents should be answered "N/A."

5. Application Interviews: U.S. Filing

Interviews on exchange visitor change of status applications are rarely held. When an interview is required, the INS regional service center where you originally filed your application will send your paperwork to the INS local office nearest the location of your exchange visitor program. This office will in turn contact you for an appointment. INS may ask you to bring additional documents at that time.

If you are called for an interview, the most likely reason is that INS either suspects some type of fraud or has doubts about your intent to return home after you complete your exchange visitor program. Because they are not common and are usually a sign of trouble, these interviews can result in considerable delays.

6. Application Appeals: U.S. Filing

If your application is denied, you will receive a written decision by mail explaining the reasons for the denial. There is no way of making a formal appeal to INS when your application is turned down. If the problem is too little evidence, you may be able to overcome this obstacle by adding more documents and resubmitting the entire application to the same INS office you have been dealing with, together with a written request that the case be reopened. The written request does not have to be in any special form. This is technically called a *Motion to Reopen*. There is a $110 fee to file this motion.

Remember that you may be denied the right to a U.S. filing without being denied a J-1 visa. When your application is turned down because you are found ineligible for U.S. filing, simply change your application to a consular filing.

Although there is no appeal to INS for the denial of a J-1 change of status application, you do have the right to file an appeal in a U.S. district court. It would be difficult to file such an appeal without employing an immigration attorney at considerable expense. Such appeals are usually unsuccessful.

G. Extensions

J-1 visas and statuses can be extended in the U.S. as needed to enable you to complete your particular exchange visitor program. However, since J-1 statuses are usually granted for the period of time considered reasonable for the type of exchange visitor program in which you are participating, extensions are not easy to get. INS has the right to reconsider your qualifications based on any changes in the facts or law, and will want to hear a compelling reason why you have been unable to complete your exchange visitor program within normal time limits. As always, however, good cases that are well prepared will be successful.

When you enter the U.S. on a J-1 visa, your authorized stay as indicated on your I-94 card is granted for the time period on your Certificate of Eligibility. However, if you come from a country where J-1 visa time privileges are especially limited, your visa may expire before your I-94 card date. In such a situation, if you wish to leave the U.S. and then reenter to complete your exchange visitor program, you will have to extend your visa. To extend the visa that is stamped in your passport, you must apply at a U.S. consulate abroad.

1. I-94 Card Extension General Procedures

There is no special application form to extend your stay in a J-1 status as written on your I-94 card. Application is made informally, either verbally or in writing, to the INS local office having jurisdiction over the place where you are living in the U.S. Appendix II contains a complete list of all INS local offices with their addresses and phone numbers. The application must be filed before your current I-94 card expires. Many INS offices respond to J-1 extension requests immediately, but in some of the busier locations it may take several months for you to receive an answer. As long as you have applied before your I-94 card has expired, you may continue in your exchange visitor program until a decision is made. When your application is approved, your I-94 card, which you will have submitted as a document with your extension application, is returned to you, either by mail or in person, with a new date shown on the reverse side.

If your application for an extension of status is denied, you will be sent a written notice explaining the reasons for the negative decision. The most common reason for denial is that INS does not believe you have been diligently pursuing your exchange visitor program and you have not adequately explained why you couldn't have completed the program within the time of the stay you were originally granted. When your application is denied, you will normally be given a period of 30 days to leave the U.S. voluntarily. Failure to leave within that time may result in your being deported.

There is no way of making a formal appeal to INS if your extension is turned down. You may challenge the decision in U.S. district court but the time and expense required for this approach usually make it impractical.

WORKING WHILE YOUR EXTENSION APPLICATION IS PENDING

If you file your application for extension of J-1 status before your authorized stay expires, you are automatically authorized to continue working for up to 240 days while waiting for a decision. If, however, your authorized stay expires after you have filed for an extension but before you receive an approval, and more than 240 days go by without getting a decision on your extension application, you must stop working.

2. I-94 Card Extension Forms

These forms are not in Appendix III.

Form IAP-66

The only form required for an I-94 extension of status is the IAP-66, Certificate of Eligibility. This is the same form required to obtain the original visa or status. You will have to get a new IAP-66 from your exchange visitor program sponsor, reflecting the new dates of your participation.

Form I-644 (special form for foreign medical graduates)

Foreign medical graduates who wish to extend their J-1 statuses must also complete immigration Form I-644, Annual Report for Foreign Medical Graduates. This form is available from your program sponsor.

3. I-94 Card Extension Documents

You must submit your I-94 card. If the extension is granted, the card will eventually be returned to you with an approval and the dates of the extension period written on the back. You should also submit a letter written in your own words, addressed to the INS local office requesting the extension, stating how long the extension is needed, and explaining in as much detail as possible why you were unable to complete your exchange visitor program within the normal period of time. Discuss this with your designated school official before contacting the INS.

4. Visa Extensions

When you extend your status as discussed above, your I-94 card is returned to you with the approval and the dates of the extension period written on the back. You need do nothing further if you do not wish to travel outside the U.S. before your extension expires. However, if your visa has expired and you need to be able to travel in and out of the U.S., you must have a new visa stamp issued at a consulate. See Section E, above. The procedures for visa extensions are identical. If you are outside the U.S. with a valid visa, you need only reenter and a new I-94 card authorizing your stay for the period of time remaining on your present Certificate of Eligibility will be given to you.

H. Waivers of Foreign Home Residency Requirements

You may be participating in the type of exchange visitor program that makes it mandatory for you to spend two years residing in your home country after completing your program before you are eligible to apply for a green card or other U.S. visa. If you wish to escape this obligation and apply for a green card immediately, you will first have to apply for a waiver of the home residency requirement.

There are special procedures which must be followed in applying for a waiver of the home residency requirement. Although the presence of this requirement is considered a ground of inadmissibility in green card cases, you should not follow the standard procedures for waivers of inadmissibility as discussed in Chapter 25.

Unless you are a foreign medical graduate, the easiest way to obtain a waiver is by having your home government consent to it through what is known as a *No Objection Letter*. A No Objection Letter is a written document issued by the government of your home country stating that it does not oppose your applying immediately for a green card or other U.S. visa. You can contact your home country's embassy in Washington, D.C. to request such a letter. Embassies of many countries grant them freely.

There are, however, many foreign embassies that refuse to grant No Objection Letters to J-1 exchange visitors. Moreover, in the case of foreign medical graduates a No Objection Letter is not by itself sufficient grounds for a waiver to be issued. For those without No Objection Letters and for involving foreign medical graduates, waivers will be issued only if:

- granting your waiver has been especially requested by an interested U.S. government agency, or in the case of foreign medical graduates, an interested state governmental agency
- your absence from the U.S. for two years will cause an exceptional hardship to a U.S. citizen or green card holder, or
- you anticipate persecution if you return to your home country.

If your waiver request is based on a No Objection Letter from your home government, then no separate waiver application form is required. You need only make a written request for the waiver to the service center with jurisdiction over your place of residence before you make your formal application for a green card. You then file or submit in person a copy of the approval, Form I-612, to INS. A copy of the No Objection Letter must also be presented at that time. The original No Objection Letter is sent directly to the U.S. government by the government of your home country through diplomatic channels. Waiver requests based on No Objection Letters are almost always approved unless your exchange visitor program was financed by the U.S. government.

If your waiver application is to be based on the request of an interested U.S. or state government agency, once again, no specific INS waiver application form is required. However, some of the U.S. government agencies do have their own special forms or questionnaires. You must contact the particular agency and ask for assistance. If the agency agrees to help, then normally they will handle everything for you. If you are unable to find an appropriate agency to assist you, the USIA will sometimes act on your behalf as an interested agency of the U.S. government. Whether or not your waiver will be granted on the basis of a U.S. government agency request depends on how important your continued presence is to the U.S. government and to the particular exchange visitor program sponsor. In the case of foreign medical graduates, however, waivers are not normally granted unless the majority of your time in the U.S. has been spent in teaching or research as opposed to the actual practice of medicine.

Your application for the waiver may be based on a claim of exceptional hardship or political persecution in your home country. Applications on either of these two grounds require that INS Form I-612 be filled out and submitted to the INS local office having jurisdiction over the place where you currently live in the U.S. or, if you do not live in the U.S., over the place where the green card petitioner is located. In these cases, INS makes a preliminary decision on whether or not exceptional hardship or possible persecution exist and then forwards your application to the USIA in Washington, D.C. USIA then makes its recommendation and returns your file to INS, who in turn will notify you by mail of the final result. INS almost always abides by the USIA recommendation, even if it is contrary to its own preliminary decision.

There are no formal appeals available if your waiver is denied. Not long ago, USIA established a waiver review board to reconsider denials. In recent years, U.S. courts have held that you may not bring an action in federal district court challenging USIA's decision in a waiver case. Therefore, whatever USIA decides concerning your waiver is final. Before you attempt to apply for a waiver of the home residency requirement, we strongly advise you to get help from an experienced immigration lawyer.

1. Waiver Application Forms

A copy of this form is in Appendix III.

Form I-612

This is the only official form used for waiver application and it is submitted only in cases where the application is based on a claim of exceptional hardship to a U.S. citizen or green card holder, or political persecution to you if you return to your home country.

Questions 1–3. These questions are self-explanatory.

Question 4. This question asks why you believe that you are subject to the home residency requirement. If your exchange visitor program was financed by the U.S. government or the government of your home country, check box A. If as part of your program you received a grant or scholarship paid for by the U.S. government or a foreign government, check box B and put down the name of the foreign country or U.S. government agency that sponsored the financial aid. If the skills you have acquired in the U.S. are on the list of occupations that have few qualified workers in your home country, called the skills list, check box C. If you came to the U.S. as a foreign medical graduate for the purpose of receiving medical training, check box D.

Question 5. If returning to your home country for two years will result in an exceptional hardship to your spouse or child who is a U.S. citizen or U.S. permanent resident, mark box A. If you are afraid to return to your home country because you fear possible racial, religious or political persecution, check box B. If you are eligible for a waiver for any other reason, such as having received a No Objection Letter from the government of your home country, this form is not required.

Questions 6–14. These questions are self-explanatory.

Questions 15 and 16. These questions are self-explanatory and apply only to those requesting waivers based on a claim of exceptional hardship to a U.S. citizen or U.S. permanent resident spouse or child. If you are seeking a waiver on some other grounds, answer these questions "N/A."

2. Waiver Application Documents

Several documents are necessary to obtain a foreign home residency waiver.

a. No Objection Letters

If at all possible, you should seek a No Objection Letter from the government of your home country. If your exchange visitor program was paid for by the U.S. government, you can request a similar letter from your sponsoring agency. When such a letter is issued, it goes directly from your home country or the U.S. agency to USIA and you will receive a copy. A No Objection Letter will usually mean an approval on your waiver application except in those cases

involving foreign medical graduates. However, even they should get No Objection Letters if possible, because it greatly strengthens their waiver cases. If the government of your home country is not opposed to your remaining, there is less pressure on the U.S. government to force your return.

b. Documents From Interested U.S. or State Government Agencies

Each government agency uses its own criteria in determining whether or not to act on your behalf and each has its own procedures. Clearly, if you are rendering vital services directly to a government agency, that agency will probably agree to assist you. If you are unable to find such an agency, the USIA will frequently act as the interested party. Because there are no standard procedures, you should contact the particular agency directly. If the agency does decide to assist you, it will create any necessary documents and submit them directly to USIA. In all likelihood, the agency will want to issue a statement in writing clearly explaining to USIA why you are important to them. Remember that state government agencies can only recommend waivers for foreign medical graduates. U.S. government agencies can recommend waivers for anyone.

c. Documents Showing Exceptional Hardship to a U.S. Citizen or Green Card Holder

Under these circumstances, it is you who must submit the documents. For a waiver application based on a claim of hardship to succeed, the hardship must be unanticipated and unavoidable. For example, if you came to the U.S. with a J-1 visa and while here married a U.S. citizen who is now sponsoring you for a green card, the hardships that your U.S. spouse may suffer if you return to your home country for two years will not normally support a waiver application. That is because the U.S. government feels you should have anticipated these problems at the time of your marriage and so the hardship is self-imposed.

If your family is in fact subject to a hardship that will support a waiver, you should prepare a notarized affidavit in your own words describing the exceptional hardship and explaining why that hardship is beyond your control. Successful hardship cases should be based on one or more of the following situations:

- Your U.S. spouse or child has serious medical problems and his or her health may be jeopardized by returning with you to your home country.
- The education of your U.S. spouse or child will be harmfully disrupted by returning with you to your home country.

- Your U.S. spouse or child will have to endure serious financial difficulties, language barriers or unhealthy living conditions by returning with you to your home country.
- You are unable to locate employment in your home country.
- Your spouse has elderly or ill parents living in the U.S. who would be deprived of necessary care if he or she returned with you to your home country.

d. Documents Showing Danger of Racial, Religious or Political Persecution

Under these circumstances, it is you who must submit the documents. You must be able to show that, should you return to your home country, you will be singled out for or have good reason to fear persecution. The persecution that you anticipate must be based on race, religion or political beliefs. If you have been persecuted in the past and can produce evidence of that, such as newspaper reports showing you were jailed or affidavits from people in your home country who personally witnessed your persecution, your case probably stands a reasonable chance of success. If you cannot prove that you have been persecuted previously, you will have to present evidence that you are a member of a certain group of people that is routinely persecuted in your home country. Such evidence should be in the form of newspaper articles, human rights reports about your home country from organizations such as Amnesty International or affidavits from experts knowledgeable in the affairs of your home country, describing the nature of the persecution. Before applying for a waiver based on persecution, you should see an experienced immigration attorney. It may be more advantageous for you to apply for political asylum if you have a good case.

I. Working As an Exchange Visitor

Special rules apply for you to be able to work.

1. Without Special Permission

Exchange visitors are permitted to work in the U.S. if the job is part of the particular exchange program in which they are participating. Many J-1 programs, such as those for college and university professors or graduate medical students, are specifically created to engage the exchange visitor in employment. Others, like those for graduate students, often involve part-time employment in the form of teaching or research assistantships. The job may be located on or off the school premises. As long as the employment is part of the program, no special work permission is required.

2. With Special Permission

Working often requires special permission.

a. Practical Training

If your J-1 visa was issued for a study program, you may accept work that is not specifically part of the program but is related to the subject matter of your studies. Such employment is called practical training. You must have written permission from the responsible officer of your exchange visitor program to accept a practical training position. INS plays no role in granting permission for practical training.

b. Economic Necessity

Remember that in order to get a J-1 visa you must show that you have sufficient financial resources to support yourself while participating in an exchange visitor program. As we discussed earlier, such resources may be in the form of scholarships or salary earned for work that is part of or related to the program. However, if unforeseen financial problems arise after you arrive in the U.S., you may get work permission for employment that is unrelated to your exchange visitor program if the employment will not adversely affect your ability to be a full-time participant in the exchange visitor program. There is no special application but you must have written approval from the responsible officer of your exchange visitor program.

3. Employment for Accompanying Relatives

Your accompanying spouse or minor children may apply to INS for permission to work. However, they cannot get work permission if the money earned helps to support you, or is needed to support you.

If your accompanying spouse or children want to work, they must file separate applications for employment authorization. This can be done by completing Form I-765 and filing it with the INS service center nearest to where your program in the U.S. is being carried out. Together with Form I-765 they must submit their I-94 cards and pay a filing fee of $70 each. It is very important to keep the fee receipt INS will send them so they can prove that the I-765 was filed.

INS is required to make a decision on employment authorization applications within 90 days. If the decision is in your accompanying relative's favor, he or she will receive a work authorization card.

If, for some reason, a decision on the application is not made within 90 days, your relative will, at his or her request, be granted an interim employment authorization which will last for 240 days. To receive an interim card, your relative must contact the INS office where the I-765 was filed and show the fee receipt. Then an interim work authorization card will be issued.

If 240 days pass and your relative still hasn't received a final decision on the I-765, he or she must stop working. Interim work authorization cards cannot be renewed. However, if this point is reached, your relative has the option to file a new I-765 application and, if a decision on the new application is not made within 90 days, another interim work authorization card will be issued.

Form I-765 (needed for your accompanying relatives to get work authorization)

Block above Question 1. Mark the first box, "Permission to accept employment."

Questions 1–8. These questions are self-explanatory.

Question 9. This asks for your relative's Social Security number, including all numbers he or she has ever used. If he or she has never used a Social Security number, answer "None." If your relative has a nonworking Social Security number, write down the number followed by the words "Nonworking, for tax purposes only." If he or she has ever used a false number, give that number followed by the words "Not my valid number," but see Chapter 25 before proceeding.

Question 10. Your relative will not usually have an Alien Registration Number unless he or she previously applied for a green card, was in deportation proceedings or had certain types of immigration applications denied. All Alien Registration Numbers begin with the letter "A." If your relative has no "A" number but entered the U.S. with a valid visa, he or she should have an I-94 card. In this case, answer Question 10 by putting down the admission number from the I-94 card.

Questions 11–15. These questions are self-explanatory.

Question 16. Answer this question "(C)(5)."

J. Annual Reports for Foreign Medical Graduates

All foreign medical graduates training in the U.S. on J-1 visas are required to file annual reports with the INS local office having jurisdiction over their places of training. The reports are filed on INS Form I-644, which is self-explanatory. A copy of this form is in Appendix III. A complete list of INS local offices with their addresses and phone numbers is in Appendix II. Failure to file this report each year will result in your visa being canceled.

FORMS AND DOCUMENTS CHECKLIST

STEP ONE: APPLICATION (THE ONLY STEP)

Forms

☐ Form IAP-66 (available from exchange visitor program sponsor).

☐ OF forms (available from U.S. consulates abroad for consular filing only).

☐ Form I-539 (U.S. filing only).

Documents

☐ Valid passport for you and each accompanying relative.

☐ One passport-type photo of you and each accompanying relative (Consular filing only).

☐ I-94 card for you and each accompanying relative (U.S. filing only).

☐ Long form birth certificate for you and each accompanying relative.

☐ Marriage certificate if you are married and bringing your spouse.

☐ If either you or your spouse have ever been married, copies of divorce and death certificates showing termination of all previous marriages.

☐ If attending school, transcripts and diplomas showing your previous education.

☐ If employment is not part of the program, proof of financial support:

　☐ Form I-134, Affidavit of Support, for you and each accompanying relative, or

　☐ financial documents showing sufficient funds to participate in the exchange program for at least one year without working.

☐ Documents showing that close family members or property are being left behind in your home country.

☐ Documents showing a job is waiting on your return to your home country.

☐ Documents showing ownership of real estate in your home country.

APPLICATION FOR EXTENSIONS OF STAY

Forms

☐ Form IAP-66 (available from exchange visitor program sponsor).

☐ Form I-644 (available from exchange visitor program sponsor, for foreign medical graduates only).

Documents

None.

APPLICATION FOR WAIVER OF TWO-YEAR HOME RESIDENCY BASED ON EXCEPTIONAL HARDSHIP OR POLITICAL PERSECUTION

Form

☐ Form I-612.

Documents

☐ No Objection Letter from your home government.

☐ Notarized affidavit explaining the nature of the hardship your family will suffer.

☐ Documents showing you have a spouse or child who is a U.S. citizen or green card holder.

☐ Documents to support the existence of the hardship.

☐ If application for waiver is based on likely persecution if you return to your home country:

　☐ documents showing you were previously persecuted

　☐ documents explaining the nature of the persecution in your home country, or

　☐ documents verifying that you belong to a group of people that will be singled out for persecution.

Temporary Workers in Selected Occupations: O, P and R Visas

Privileges

- You can work legally in the U.S. for your O, P or R sponsor.

- O, P and R visas can be issued quickly.

- You may travel in and out of the U.S. or as long as your visa stamp and status are valid. You may remain in the U.S. only as long as your status remains valid.

- Visas are available for accompanying relatives.

Limitations

- You are restricted to working only for the employer who acted as your visa sponsor. If you wish to change jobs, you must get a new visa.

- Accompanying relatives may stay in the U.S. with you but they may not work.

A. How to Qualify

There are no quota restrictions for O, P and R visas. Step One petitions are normally approved within two to eight weeks. Visas are usually issued within several weeks after petition approval.

The Immigration Act of 1990 created a number of highly specialized temporary work visa categories. O and P visas are for certain outstanding workers in the sciences, arts, education, business, entertainment and athletics. R visas are for religious workers. A job offer from a U.S. employer is a basic requirement for all these visas. The O, P and R visa categories are quite narrow in scope.

1. O-1 Visas: Persons of Extraordinary Ability in the Arts, Athletics, Science, Business and Education

O-1 visas are available to persons of proven extraordinary ability in the sciences, arts, education, business or athletics. To be considered a person of extraordinary ability, you must have sustained national or international acclaim, or, if you work in motion pictures or television productions, you must have a demonstrated record of extraordinary achievement. O-1 visas can be given only on the basis of individual qualifications. Membership in a group or team is not by itself enough to get you the visa. In addition, the alien must be coming to work in the area of extraordinary ability.

a. Extraordinary Ability in Science, Education, Business or Athletics

To meet O-1 standards, you must be able to show that you are coming to work in the area of extraordinary ability and that you have received sustained national or international recognition. This can be demonstrated if you have gotten a major, internationally recognized award, such as a Nobel Prize, or if you have accomplished at least three of the following:

- receipt of a nationally recognized prize or award for excellence
- membership in associations that require outstanding achievements of their members in your field of expertise
- publication of material in professional or major trade publications or major media about you and your work
- participation on a panel or individually as a judge of the work of others in your field
- making an original scientific, scholarly or business-related contribution that is of major significance in the field
- authorship of scholarly articles
- previous employment in a critical or essential capacity for an organization with a distinguished reputation, or
- commanding or having commanded a high salary or other outstanding remuneration for your services.

Or, if the above criteria do not readily apply to the occupation, the petitioner may submit comparable evidence in order to show that the applicant is "extraordinary" even though the above evidence is not available. Be sure to explain why the above criteria do not apply.

b. Motion Picture or Television Industry Workers

If you work in the motion picture or television industry, you must meet a different set of requirements. You must still be coming to work in the area of extraordinary ability. You must also have received, or at least been nominated for, a significant national or international award, such as an Academy Award, Emmy, Grammy or Director's Guild Award. If you have not been recognized in this way, then alternatively you must present evidence of at least three of the following achievements:

- performing, past, present or future, in a lead or starring role in a production or event having a distinguished reputation
- acquiring national or international recognition as shown in critical reviews or other published materials
- performing, past present or future, in a lead, starring or critical role for a distinguished organization
- performing in major commercial or critically acclaimed successes, as evidenced by good box office receipts or television ratings
- attaining significant recognition for accomplishments from organizations, critics, government agencies or recognized experts, or
- commanding a high salary or other significant remuneration.

If the above criteria do not lend themselves to the applicant's situation, the employer may submit alternative but comparable evidence to show the required extraordinary ability.

C. Alien of Extraordinary Ability in the Arts

If the applicant is applying as an O-1 alien of extraordinary ability in the arts (defined as any field of creative activity, including but not limited to fine, visual, culinary and performing arts), she must be coming to U.S. to perform in the area of extraordinary ability and must be recognized as being prominent in her field of endeavor. She can demonstrate her recognition with documents showing that she has been nominated for or has received significant national or international awards or prizes in the particular field, such as an Oscar, Emmy, Grammy or Director's Guild Award, or at least three of the following forms of documentation:

- Evidence that she has performed, and will perform, services as a lead or starring participant in productions or events that have a distinguished reputation as evidenced by critical reviews, advertisements, publicity releases, publications contracts or endorsements.
- Evidence that she has achieved national or international recognition for achievements evidenced by critical reviews or other published materials by or about her in major newspapers, trade journals, magazines or other publications.
- Evidence that she has performed, and will perform, in a lead, starring or critical role for organizations and establishments that have a distinguished reputation evidenced by articles in newspapers, trade journals, publications or testimonials.
- Evidence that she has a record of major commercial or critically acclaimed successes as evidenced by such indicators as title, rating, standing in the field, box office receipts, motion pictures or television ratings, and other occupational achievements reported in trade journals, major newspapers or other publications.
- Evidence that she has received significant recognition for achievements from organizations, critics, government agencies or other recognized experts in the field in which she is engaged. Such testimonials must be in a form that clearly indicates the author's authority, expertise and knowledge of her achievements.
- Evidence that she has either commanded a high salary or will command a high salary or other substantial remuneration for services in relation to others in the field, as evidenced by contracts or other reliable evidence.

If the above criteria do not lend themselves to the applicant's situation, the employer may submit alternative but comparable evidence in order to establish the applicant's eligibility.

Although O-1 principal and O-3 aliens are permitted to pursue permanent residence while in nonimmigrant O status, this is not true of O-2s, who must have the intent to depart and maintain a residence abroad during their stay.

2. O-2 Visas: Support Staff for Those With O-1 Visas

O-2 visas are available to those who work as essential support personnel of O-1 athletes and entertainers. O-2 visas are not available in the fields of science, business or education. O-2 workers must be accompanying O-1 artists or athletes and be an integral part of the actual performance. The O-2 worker must also have critical skills and experience with the particular O-1 worker that is not general in nature and cannot be performed by a U.S. worker. In the case of motion picture or television productions, there must be a preexisting, long-standing working relationship between the O-2 applicant and the O-1 worker. If significant portions of the production will take place both in and out of the U.S., O-2 support personnel must be deemed necessary for the achievement of continuity and a smooth, successful production. O-2 visa holders are not allowed to pursue permanent residence in the U.S. while on their nonimmigrant visa.

3. O-3 Visas: Accompanying Relatives of Those With O-1 and O-2 Visas

O-3 visas are available to accompanying spouses and unmarried children under age 21 of O-1 or O-2 visa holders. O-3 visas allow relatives to remain in the U.S., but they may not work. They may seek permanent residence while in O-3 status.

4. P-1 Visas: Outstanding Athletes, Athletic Teams and Entertainment Companies

P-1 visas are available to athletes or athletic teams that have been internationally recognized as outstanding for a long and continuous period of time. Entertainment companies that have been nationally recognized as outstanding for a long time also qualify. A written statement from an appropriate labor union or peer group confirming the group's stature in the industry is a required document in these cases. Unlike O visas, which always rest on the capabilities of individuals, P-1 visas can be issued based on the expertise of a group. However, don't be surprised to find a lot of overlap between uses and qualifications for O and P visas.

In the case of entertainment companies, each performer who wishes to qualify for a P-1 visa must have been an integral part of the group for at least one year, although up to 25% of them can be excused from the one-year requirement, if necessary. This requirement may also be waived in exceptional situations, where due to illness or other unanticipated circumstances, a critical performer is unable to travel. The one-year requirement is for performers only. It does not apply to support personnel. It also does not apply to anyone at all who works for a circus, including performers.

Like O-1 visas, P-1 visas are issued only for the time needed to complete a particular event, tour or season. Individual athletes, however, may remain in the U.S. for up to ten years.

a. Athletes

To qualify as a P-1 athlete, you or your team must have an internationally recognized reputation in the sport. Evidence of this must include a contract with a major U.S. sports league, team or international sporting event, and at least two of the following:

- proof of your, or your team's, previous significant participation with a major U.S. sports league
- proof of your participation in an international competition with a national team
- proof of your previous significant participation with a U.S. college in intercollegiate competition
- written statement from an official of a major U.S. sports league or the governing body of the sport, detailing how you or your team is internationally recognized
- other evidence that you or your team is internationally ranked, or
- proof that you or your team has received a significant honor or award in the sport.

b. Entertainers

P-1 visas are not available to individual entertainers, but only to members of groups with international reputations. Evidence of that reputation must be shown with the following:

- proof that your group has been performing regularly for at least one year
- a statement listing each member of your group and the exact dates each has been regularly employed by that group, and
- proof of your group's nomination for, or receipt of, significant international awards or prizes, or at least three of the following:
  - proof that your group has or will star or take a leading role in productions or events with distinguished reputations
  - reviews or other published material showing that your group has achieved international recognition and acclaim for outstanding achievement in the field
  - proof that your group has and will star or take a leading role in productions or events for organizations with distinguished reputations
  - proof of large box office receipts or ratings showing your group has a record of major commercial or critically acclaimed successes, or
  - proof that your group commands a high salary or other substantial remuneration.

c. Circuses

Circus personnel do not need to have been part of the organization for one year to get a P-1 visa provided the particular circus itself has a nationally recognized reputation.

d. Nationally Known Entertainment Groups

INS may waive the international recognition requirement for groups that only have outstanding national reputations, if special circumstances would make it difficult for your group to prove its international reputation. Such circumstances could include your group having only limited access to news media, or problems based on your group's geographical location.

e. Waiver of One-Year Group Membership

INS may waive the one-year group membership requirement for you if you are replacing an ill or otherwise unexpectedly absent but essential member of a P-1 entertainment group. This requirement may also be waived if you will be performing in any critical role of the group's operation.

5. P-2 Visas: Participants in Reciprocal Exchange Programs

P-2 visas are available to artists or entertainers, either individually or as part of a group, who come to the U.S. to perform under a reciprocal exchange program between the U.S. and one or more other countries. All essential support personnel are included. The legitimacy of the program must be evidenced by a formal, written exchange agreement. In addition, a labor union in the U.S. must have either been involved in the negotiation of the exchange or have agreed to it. The U.S. individual or group being exchanged must have skills and terms of employment comparable to the person or group coming to the U.S.

6. P-3 Visas: Culturally Unique Groups

P-3 visas are available to artists or entertainers who come to the U.S., either individually or as part of a group, to develop, perform, teach or coach in a program that is considered culturally unique. The program may be of either a commercial or non-commercial nature.

A P-3 alien must be coming to the U.S. to participate in a cultural event or events that will further the understanding or development of his art form. In addition, the individual will have to submit:

- Evidence showing the authenticity of his or his group's skills in performing, presenting, coaching or teaching the unique or traditional art form and giving credentials showing the basis of his knowledge of his or his group's skill, or
- Evidence that his or the group's performance is culturally unique, as shown by reviews in newspapers, journals or other published materials, and that their performance will be culturally unique.

Essential support personnel of P-3 aliens should also request classification under the P-3 category. The documentation for P-3 support personnel should include:

- A consultation from a labor organization with expertise in the area of the alien's skill
- A statement describing why the support person has been essential in the past, critical skills and experience with the principal alien, and
- A copy of the written contract or a summary of the terms of the oral agreement between the alien and the employer.

7. P-4 Visas: Accompanying Relatives of Those With P-1, P-2 and P-3 Visas

P-4 visas are issued to the accompanying relatives of any P visa workers. The accompanying relatives are permitted to remain in the U.S., but they cannot work unless granted work authorization in their own right.

8. R-1 Visas: Religious Workers

An R-1 visa is available to a person who has been a member of a legitimate religious denomination for at least two years and has a job offer in the U.S. to work for an affiliate of that same religious organization. R-1 visas may be issued to both members of the clergy and lay religious workers. The criteria for qualifying are the same as those for religious workers applying for special immigrant green cards discussed in Chapter 11, with one big difference. Unlike the green card category, it is not necessary that R-1 visa workers were employed by the religious organization before getting the visa. They need only have been members.

Usually, people qualifying for R-1 visas also qualify for green cards as special immigrants and in most cases will probably prefer to apply directly for a green card.

9. R-2 Visas: Accompanying Relatives of Those With R-1 Visas

Accompanying relatives of R-1 visa holders can get R-2 visas. This allows them to stay in the U.S., but not to work.

APPLYING FOR A GREEN CARD FROM O, P OR R STATUS

Having an O, P or R visa gives you no legal advantage in applying for a green card. Realistically, however, it is probably easier to get an employer to sponsor you for an O, P or R visa than a green card, and coming to the U.S. first with a temporary work visa gives you the opportunity to decide if you really want to live in the U.S. permanently. Once you are in the U.S. with a work permit, it is also usually easier to find an employer willing to sponsor you for a green card.

O and P visa holders are not required to have the intention of returning to their home countries. Accordingly, applying for a green card while in the U.S. on an O or P visa will not jeopardize your status. R visa holders are required to have the intention of returning home once the visa or status expires. Therefore, if you apply for a green card, it may be difficult to obtain or renew an R visa. Many religious workers qualify for green cards as special immigrants. If you are a religious worker and want to remain in the U.S. permanently, you should read Chapter 11 before applying for an R visa.

B. O, P and R Visa Overview

Once you have been offered a job, getting an O, P or R visa is a two-step process. Some applicants expect their U.S. employers to handle the entire process for them and, indeed, many large companies and institutions have experienced staff specialists who will do this for highly desirable employees. This is particularly likely in the case of a large sports or entertainment organization. Even smaller companies may be prepared to do whatever is necessary, including paying an immigration attorney's fees, to attract key employees. However, often it is the employee who is most interested in having the visa issued, and to U.S. employers, the red tape of hiring a foreign employee can be an unfamiliar nuisance.

As we give you step-by-step instructions for getting a visa, we will indicate that certain activities are to be performed by your employer and others are to be done by you. We will discuss each task according to who has legal responsibility for carrying it out. Though the law presumes your employer is performing a particular function, there is nothing to stop you from helping with the work. For example, you can fill out forms intended to be completed by your employer and simply ask him to check them over and sign them. Unless your employer volunteers to help or you are sure the company simply can't live without you, we recommend helping your employer with the paperwork. The less your U.S. employer is inconvenienced, the more the company will be willing to act as sponsor for your visa. An imposition on company time or money might cost you a job offer. With the help of this book, you will know how to do all that is required. It is completely legal as well as in your best interest to help whenever possible.

1. Step One: The Petition

Step One is called the petition. It is filed by your U.S. employer. All O, P and R visa petitions are submitted to INS regional service centers in the U.S. The object of the petition is to prove four things:

- that you qualify for O, P or R status
- that your future job is of a high enough level or appropriate nature to warrant someone with your advanced or specialized skills
- that you have the correct background and skills to match the job requirements, and
- in the case of O and P visas, that appropriate labor unions or similar organizations have been consulted concerning your eligibility.

Be aware that an approved petition does not by itself give you any immigration privileges. It is only a prerequisite to Step Two, submitting your application for an O, P or R visa. The petition must be approved before you are eligible for Step Two.

2. Step Two: The Application

Step Two is called the application. It is filed by you and your accompanying relatives, if any. The application is your formal request for an O, P or R visa or status. (If you are

Canadian, your Step Two procedures will be different from those of other applicants. See Chapter 28, *Canadians: Special Rules.*) Step Two may be carried out in the U.S. at an INS office or in your home country at a U.S. consulate there. If you file Step Two papers in the U.S., you will usually submit them together with those for Step One. When Step Two is dispatched at a U.S. consulate abroad, you must wait to file the application until the Step One petition is first approved.

The vast majority of nonimmigrant visa applications are filed at consulates. The major benefit is that a visa, which is stamped in your passport, can be issued only by American consulates. When you file Step Two at a consulate, your visa will be stamped in your passport at that time. INS offices inside the U.S. may issue statuses but not visas. (See Chapter 14, Section B, Difference Between a Visa and a Status).

If you are already in the U.S. legally on some other type of nonimmigrant visa, you qualify to apply for an O, P or R status at an INS office inside the U.S. using a procedure known as *change of nonimmigrant status.* (If you are admitted as a visitor without a visa under the Visa Waiver Program, you may not carry out Step Two in the U.S. Currently there are 29 participating countries in the Visa Waiver Program, including: Andorra, Argentina, Austria, Australia, Belgium, Brunei, Denmark, Finland, France, Germany, Iceland, Ireland, Italy, Japan, Liechtenstein, Luxembourg, Monaco, The Netherlands, New Zealand, Norway, Portugal, San Marino, Singapore, Slovenia, Spain, Sweden, Switzerland, the United Kingdom and Uruguay. The government has approved Greece for inclusion in the program in the near future.) This is simply a technical term meaning you are switching from one nonimmigrant status to another. If a change of status is approved, you will then be treated as if you had entered the country with an O, P or R visa. You can keep the status as long as you remain in the U.S. or until it expires, whichever comes first.

You will not, however, receive a visa stamp, which you need if your plans include traveling in and out of the U.S. Again, visa stamps are issued only at U.S. consulates abroad. Therefore, if you change your status and later travel outside the U.S., you will have to go to the U.S. consulate in your home country and repeat Step Two, obtaining the O, P or R visa stamp in your passport before you can return. This extra procedure makes changing status an unattractive option for all but Canadians, who don't need visas to cross the U.S. border.

3. Paperwork

There are two types of paperwork you must submit to get an O, P or R visa. The first consists of official government forms completed by you or your U.S. employer. The second is personal documents such as professional credentials and critical reviews. We will tell you exactly what forms and documents you need.

It is vital that forms are properly filled out and all necessary documents are supplied. You or your U.S. employer may resent the intrusion into your privacy and sizable effort it takes to prepare immigration applications, but you should realize the process is an impersonal matter to immigration officials. Your getting a visa is more important to you than it is to the U.S. government. This is not a pleasant thing to accept, but you are better off having a real understanding of your position. People from all over the world want U.S. visas. There is no shortage of applicants. Take the time and trouble to prepare your papers properly. In the end it will pay off with a successful application.

The documents you or your U.S. employer supply to INS do not have to be originals. Photocopies of all documents are acceptable as long as you have the originals in your possession and are willing to produce them at the request of INS. Documents submitted to U.S. consulates, on the other hand, must be either originals or official government certified copies. Government certified copies and notarized copies are not the same thing. Documents that have only been notarized are not acceptable. They must carry a government seal. In addition to any original or government certified copies of documents submitted to a consulate, you should submit plain photocopies of each document as well. After the consulate compares the copies with the originals, it will return the originals.

Documents will be accepted if they are in either English, or, with papers filed at U.S. consulates abroad, the language of the country where the documents are being filed. An exception exists for papers filed at U.S. consulates in Japan, where all documents must be translated into English. If the documents are not in an acceptable language as just explained, they must be accompanied by a full, word for word, written English translation. Any capable person may act as translator. It is not necessary to hire a professional. At the end of each translation, the following statement must appear:

I hereby certify that I translated this document from (language) to English. This translation is accurate and complete. I further certify that I am fully competent to translate from (language) to English.

The translator should sign this statement but it does not have to be witnessed or notarized.

Later in this chapter we describe in detail the forms and documents needed to get your O, P or R visa. A summary checklist of forms and documents appears at the end of this chapter.

C. Who's Who in Getting Your O, P or R Visa

Getting an O, P or R visa will be easier if you familiarize yourself with the technical names used for each participant in the process. During Step One, the petition, you are known as either the *beneficiary* or the *employee* and your U.S. employer is called the *petitioner* or the *employer*. The petitioner may be a business, an institution, or a person but usually it is a business or institution. In Step Two, the application, you are called *applicant*, but your employer remains the *petitioner* or *employer*. If you are bringing your spouse and children with you as accompanying relatives, each of them is known as an *applicant* as well.

D. Step One: The Petition

The U.S. employer submits the petition, consisting of forms and documents, by mail, in duplicate, to the INS regional service center having jurisdiction over your intended employer's place of business. INS regional service centers are not the same as INS local offices. There are four INS regional service centers spread across the U.S. Appendix II contains a list of all INS regional service centers with their addresses.

The filing fee for each petition, if no change of status is being requested, is currently $85. With a change of status request, the fee is $155. Checks or money orders are accepted. It is not advisable to send cash. We recommend submitting all papers by certified mail, return receipt requested, and making a copy of everything sent in to keep in your records.

Within a week or so after mailing in the petition, your employer should get back a written confirmation that the papers are being processed, together with a receipt for the fees. This notice will also give your immigration file number and tell approximately when you should expect to have a decision. If INS wants further information before acting on your case, INS may send you a request for information on Form I-797. The I-797 tells your employer what additional pieces of information or documents are expected. Your employer should supply the extra data and mail the whole package back to the INS regional service center.

O, P and R petitions are normally approved within two to eight weeks. When this happens, a Notice of Action Form I-797 will be sent to your employer showing the petition was approved. If you plan to execute Step Two at a U.S. consulate abroad, INS will also notify the consulate of your choice, sending them a complete copy of your file. Only the employer receives communications from INS about the petition because technically it is the employer who is seeking the visa on your behalf.

1. Petition Forms

Copies of all forms are in Appendix III.

Form I-129 and O/P/Q/R Supplement

The basic form for Step One, the petition, is immigration Form I-129 and O/P/Q/R Supplement. The I-129 form is used for many different nonimmigrant visas. In addition to the basic part of the form that applies to all types of visas, it comes with several supplements for each specific nonimmigrant category. Simply tear out and use the supplement that applies to you. Your employer must file the petition form in duplicate. Send in two signed originals. Copies are not acceptable.

More than one foreign employee may be listed on a single I-129 petition. This is done if the employer has more than one opening to be filled for the same type of job or if it is a group petition. If more than one employee is to be included, Supplement-1, which is also part of Form I-129, should be completed for each additional employee.

Most of the questions on the I-129 form are straightforward. If a question does not apply to you, answer it with "None" or "N/A." Those questions requiring explanations are as follows:

Part 1. These questions concern the employer only and are self-explanatory.

Part 2. Question 1. Question 1 should be answered "O-1, O-2, P-1, P-2, P-3 or R-1" as appropriate.

Questions 2–3. These questions are self-explanatory.

Question 4. This question asks you to indicate what action is requested from INS. Normally you will mark box "a" which tells INS to notify a U.S. consulate abroad of the petition approval so that you may apply for a visa there. If you will be filing your Step Two application in the U.S., mark box "b." If this petition is being filed as an extension, mark box "c."

Question 5. This question is self-explanatory.

Part 3. These questions are self-explanatory. If you previously held a U.S. work permit and therefore have a U.S. Social Security number, put down that number where asked. If you have a Social Security number that is not valid for employment, put down that number followed by "not valid for employment." If you have never had a Social Security number, put down "None."

Alien Registration Numbers, which all begin with the letter "A," are given only to people who have applied for green cards, received political asylum or been in deportation proceedings. If you have an "A" number, put that number down and also explain how you got it, such as "number issued from previous green card petition filed by my brother." If you do not have an "A" number, write down "None."

If your present authorized stay has expired, you must disclose that where asked. This may affect your ability to get an O, P or R visa at a U.S. consulate (see Chapter 25), but if you are out of status now, you cannot file Step Two inside the U.S.

Part 4. These questions are self-explanatory. Under recent changes in the law, the fact that you may have a green card petition or application in process does not prevent you from getting a visa if you are an O-1 or O-3 or P-1, but it will bar related categories such as O-2.

Part 5. These questions are self-explanatory. The dates of intended employment for O and P visas should not exceed the period of your employment contract. If you are applying for an R visa, put no more than three years, which is the maximum period of time for which an R petition may be approved.

O & P Supplement (for O and P petitions only)

Most of this form is self-explanatory. It asks if the required written consultations with labor unions have been provided. See Section 2b, just below.

Q & R Supplement (for R petitions only)

Section 1 of this form applies only to Q visas, a very limited category that is not covered here. Section 2 is for R visas and should be completed in full and is self-explanatory.

2. Petition Documents

You must submit several documents with the petition.

a. Job Verification

Your employer must show that the job you have been offered really exists. To do this, he must produce either a written employment contract with you or a written summary of an oral contract. The terms of your employment, including job duties, hours, salary and other benefits, must be mentioned in the document. If you will be going on tour, a tour schedule should be included. For O and P visas, the employer should also submit a detailed written statement explaining the nature of the employer, the specific events or activities in which you will be participating, and why your participation is needed.

b. O & P Visas

Documents for O and P visas should include:
- certificates showing prizes or awards won
- certificates of membership in associations
- copies of articles published about you and your work
- publications written by you
- letters from leaders in your field explaining your significant accomplishments, and
- letters from previous employers, showing your salary and explaining your importance to them.

If you are part of a group, documents explaining the prestige and accomplishments of your group and details about each of its members should also be provided.

All O and P visa petitions must be accompanied by a consultation report or written opinion from an appropriate peer group, labor union and/or management organization, concerning the nature of the work to be done and your qualifications. Alternatively, you may request INS to obtain a consultation report for you, but this will significantly delay your case. For O-1 petitions, the consultation report can simply be a letter stating that the organization has no objection to your getting an O-1 visa. In P-1 petitions, the consultation report must explain the reputation of either you or your team and the nature of the event in the U.S. The consultation report in all O-2 cases and for P-1 visa support personnel must contain an explanation of why you are essential to the performance and the nature of your working relationship with the principal performer. It must also state whether or not U.S. workers are available or assert that significant production activities will take place both in and out of the U.S. and, therefore, your presence is required for continuity. P-2 consultation reports must verify the existence of a viable exchange program. P-3 reports must evaluate the cultural uniqueness of the performances, state that the events are mostly cultural in nature and give the reason why the event or activity is appropriate for P-3 classification.

INS maintains a list of organizations willing to supply consultation reports. So far, the following organizations have agreed to do this:

- **Instrumental musicians:** American Federation of Musicians, New York, NY.
- **Other musical performers:** American Guild of Musical Artists, New York, NY.
- **Stage managers and all nonmusical performers in live productions:** Actors Equity Association, New York, NY.
- **All nonmusical performers in film and electronic media:** Screen Actors Guild, Hollywood, CA and New York, NY; American Federation of Television & Radio Artists, New York, NY.
- **All directors of photography, technical and craft personnel:** International Alliance of Theatrical State Employees and Moving Picture Machine Operators, New York, NY and Hollywood, CA; International Brotherhood of Electrical Workers, Washington, DC; National Association of Broadcast Employees and Technicians, Bethesda, MD.
- **Writers in film and electronic media:** Writers Guild of America, New York, NY and West Hollywood, CA.

c. R Visas

Documents required for an R visa petition are identical to those required to get a green card as a special immigrant in the religious worker category (see Chapter 11), except you need not show that you previously worked for the religious organization. It is only necessary that you have been a member of the organization. You should submit all diplomas and certificates showing your academic and professional qualifications. In addition, submit a detailed letter from the religious organization in the U.S. explaining its structure and number of followers in both your home country and the U.S., as well as the details of your job offer in the U.S. including job title, duties, salary and qualification demands. Finally, you should include written verification that you have been a member of that organization for at least two years.

3. Petition Interviews

INS rarely holds interviews on O, P or R visa petitions. When it does, the interview is always with the employer. If you are in the U.S., you may be asked to appear as well. Interviews are requested only if INS doubts that the documents or information on Form I-129 and the O, P, Q, R supplement are genuine. Then, the petition file is forwarded from the INS regional service center where it was submitted to the INS local office nearest your employer's place of business and your employer is notified to appear there. The employer may also be asked to bring additional documents at that time. If, after the interview, everything is in order, the petition will be approved. The best way to avoid an interview is to have the employer document the petition correctly from the beginning.

4. Petition Appeals

If you have poorly documented your qualifications, the petition will probably be denied. Your employer will then get a notice of INS's unfavorable decision, a written statement of the reasons for the negative outcome and an explanation of how to appeal, or a request for evidence (I-797) specifically requesting information or documentation.

The best way to handle an appeal is to try avoiding it altogether. Filing an appeal means making an argument to INS that its reasoning was wrong. This is difficult to do successfully. If you think you can eliminate the reason your petition failed by improving your paperwork, it makes sense to disregard the appeals process and simply file a new petition, better prepared than the first.

If the petition was denied because your U.S. employer left out necessary documents that have since been located, the new documents should be sent together with a written request that the case be reopened to the same INS office that issued the denial. This is technically called a *Motion to Reopen.* There is a $110 fee to file this motion. Appeals often take a long time. A Motion to Reopen can be concluded faster than an appeal.

If your U.S. employer does choose to appeal, it must be done within 30 days of the date on the Notice of Denial. The appeal should be filed at the same INS office that issued the denial. There is a $110 filing fee. INS will then forward the papers for consideration to the Administrative Appeals Unit of the central INS office in Washington, D.C. In six months or more your employer will get back a decision by mail. Fewer than 5% of all appeals are successful.

When an appeal to INS has been denied, the next step is to make an appeal through the U.S. judicial system. Your employer may not file an action in court without first going through the appeals process available from INS. If the case has reached this stage and you are in the U.S. illegally, we strongly recommend seeking representation from a qualified immigration attorney, as you are now in danger of being deported.

E. Step Two: The Application (Consular Filing)

If you are Canadian, your Step Two procedures will be different from those of other applicants. See Chapter 28, *Canadians: Special Rules,* for details.

Anyone with an approved O, P or R petition can apply for a visa at a U.S. consulate in his or her home country. You must be physically present to apply there. Even if you have been or are now working or living illegally in the U.S., you may still be able to get a visa from a U.S. consulate if you otherwise qualify. Be sure to read and understand the grounds of inadmissibility and bars to change of status, discussed in Chapter 25.

1. Benefits and Drawbacks of Consular Filing

The most important benefit to consular filing, making it almost always preferable to U.S. filing, is that only consulates issue visas. When you go through a U.S. filing you get a status, not a visa. (See Chapter 14, Section B, Difference Between a Visa and a Status). An O, P or R status confers the same right to work as an O, P or R visa, but it does not give you the ability to travel in and out of the U.S. Therefore, if you want travel privileges, you will at some time have to go through the extra step of applying for a visa at a U.S. consulate, even though you have already applied for and received status in the U.S.

Moreover, anyone with an approved petition may apply for a visa at the appropriate consulate. That is not the case with U.S. applications for status. If you are in the U.S. illegally, consular filing is a must. You are not eligible to process a change of status application in the U.S. unless your presence and activities in the U.S. have always been legal.

A further plus to consular filing is that consular offices may work more quickly to issue nonimmigrant visas than some INS offices do to process nonimmigrant statuses. Your waiting time for the paperwork to be finished may be much shorter at a U.S. consulate abroad than at most INS offices.

A drawback to consular filing comes from the fact that you must be physically present in the country where the consulate is located to file there. If your application is ultimately turned down because of an unexpected problem, not only will you have to wait outside the U.S. until the problem is resolved, but other visas in your passport, such as a visitors visa, may be canceled. It will then be impossible for you to enter the U.S. in any capacity. Consequently, if your case is not very strong and freedom of travel is not essential to you, it might be wise to apply in the U.S., make up your mind to remain there for the duration of the O, P or R status, and skip trying to get a visa from the consulate.

2. Application General Procedures: Consular Filing

Technically, the law allows you to apply for an O, P or R visa at any U.S. consulate you choose. A complete list of all U.S. consulates that process visa applications, together with their addresses and phone numbers, is in Appendix I.

TCN PROCESSING AND SUMMARY EXCLUSIONS

The immigration law amendments of 1996 made changes concerning obtaining a nonimmigrant visa at a consulate other than one in your home country. Applying for a visa at a consulate which is not located in your home country is called "third country national," or TCN, processing.

TCN processing is prohibited when you have been unlawfully present in the U.S. under a prior visa status. Even if you overstayed your status by just one day, the visa will be automatically canceled, you will be ineligible for TCN processing and you will have to return to your home country to apply for a new visa at the consulate there.

If you were admitted for duration of status (indicated as "D/S" on your forms I-94), however, you still may be able to do TCN processing even though you remained in the U.S. beyond the time for which your status was conferred. This applies to individuals in A, F, G and J status. In this situation, you will be barred from TCN processing only if INS or an immigration judge has determined that you were unlawfully present. (In general though, unlawful presence need not be determined by a judge or INS officer if you overstayed your I-94 date.) Unlawful presence of six months or more after April 1, 1997 is also a ground of inadmissibility, provided you leave the U.S. and request reentry. (See Chapter 25.)

Another new law may have an impact on people requesting entry to the U.S. This law empowers an INS inspector at the airport to summarily (without allowing judicial review) bar entry to someone requesting admission to the U.S. if either of the following are true:

- The inspector thinks you are making a misrepresentation about practically anything connected with entering the U.S., including your purpose in coming, intent to return and prior immigration history. This includes the use or suspected use of false documents
- You do not have the proper documentation to support your entry to the U.S. in the category you are requesting.

If the inspector excludes you, you cannot request entry for five years, unless INS grants a special waiver. For this reason it is extremely important to understand the terms of your requested status, and to not make any misrepresentations. If you are found to be inadmissible, you may request to withdraw your application to enter the U.S. in order to prevent having the five year deportation order on your record. INS may allow this in some exceptional cases.

You may not file an application for an O, P or R visa at a consulate before your petition has been approved. Once it is approved, the INS regional service center where the petition was originally submitted will forward a complete copy of your file to the U.S. consulate designated on Form I-129 in Step One. At the same time, a Notice of Action Form I-797 indicating approval will be sent directly to your U.S. employer. Once your employer receives this, you should telephone the consulate to see if the petition file has arrived from INS. If the file is slow in coming, ask the consulate to consider granting approval of your visa based only on the Notice of Action. Many U.S. consulates are willing to do so.

Once the petition is approved, you can simply walk into many consulates with your application paperwork and get your O, P or R visa immediately. Others insist on advance appointments. Most U.S. consulates in Canada require you to make a telephone appointment at least two weeks in advance of your interview to receive an appointment. Some, like the consulate in London, prefer to process visa applications by mail. Since procedures among consulates vary, you should always telephone in advance to ask about local policies.

On entering the U.S. with your new visa, you will be given an I-94 card. It will be stamped with a date showing how long you can stay. Normally, you are permitted to remain up to the expiration date on your Step One petition. Each time you exit and reenter the U.S., you will get a new I-94 card authorizing your stay up to the final date indicated on the petition.

3. Application Forms: Consular Filing

When you file at a U.S. consulate abroad, the consulate officials will provide you with certain optional forms, designated by an "OF" preceding a number. Instructions for completing optional forms and what to do with them once they are filled out will come with the forms. We do not include copies of these forms in Appendix III.

4. Application Documents: Consular Filing

You must show a valid passport and present one passport-type photograph taken according to the photo instructions in Appendix III. If the consulate has not yet received your INS file containing the paperwork from the approved petition, you will then need to show the original Notice of Action, Form I-797 which your employer received from INS by mail. Most consulates will issue O, P and R visas based only on the Notice of Action, although some, particularly in South America and Asia, insist on seeing the complete INS file. If the consulate wants to see your file and

it is late (more than a month) in arriving, you should request that the consulate investigate the file's whereabouts. You, too, can write the INS regional service center where your petition was processed, asking them to look for the file.

For each accompanying relative, you must present a valid passport and one passport-type photograph taken according to the photo instructions in Appendix III. You will also need documents verifying their family relationship to you. You may verify a parent/child relationship by presenting the child's long form birth certificate. Many countries, including Canada and England, issue both short and long form birth certificates. Where both are available, the long form is needed because it contains the names of the parents while the short form does not. If you are accompanied by your spouse, you must prove that you are lawfully married by showing a civil marriage certificate. Church certificates are generally unacceptable. (There are a few exceptions, depending on the laws of your particular country. Canadians, for example, may use church marriage certificates if the marriage took place in Quebec Province, but not elsewhere. If a civil certificate is available, however, you should always use it.) You may have married in a country where marriages are not customarily recorded. Tribal areas of Africa are an example. In such situations call the nearest consulate or embassy of your home country for help with getting acceptable proof of marriage.

There may or may not be a fee for the visa. O, P and R visas are issued free to the citizens of most countries, but others may be charged fees that can be as high as $100. If the country of your nationality charges fees for visas to U.S. citizens who wish to work there, then the U.S. will charge people of your country a similar fee as well. Whether or not there is a fee is determined by your nationality, not by where you apply. Check with the nearest U.S. consulate to find out if there will be a fee in your case.

5. Application Interviews: Consular Filing

The consulate will frequently require an interview before issuing an O, P or R visa. During the interview, a consul officer will examine the data you gave in Step One for accuracy, especially regarding facts about your own qualifications. In the case of R-1 visas, evidence of ties to your home country will also be checked. During the interview, you will surely be asked how long you intend to remain in the U.S. Any answer indicating uncertainty about plans to return or an interest in applying for a green card is likely to result in a denial of your R-1 visa. Note that O-1/O-3 and P-1 visas do not require you to have the intention to return home.

6. Application Appeals: Consular Filing

When a consulate turns down an O, P or R visa application, there is no way to make a formal appeal, although you are free to reapply as often as you like. Some consulates, however, will make you wait several months before allowing you to file another application. If your visa is denied, you will be told by the consul officer the reasons for the denial. Written statements of decisions are not normally provided in nonimmigrant cases. If a lack of evidence about a particular point is the problem, sometimes simply presenting more evidence on an unclear fact can bring a positive change in the result.

The most likely reasons for having an O or P visa turned down are because you are found inadmissible. The most likely reason for having an R visa turned down is that the consulate does not believe you intend to return to your home country.

Certain people who have been refused visas reapply at a different consulate, attempting to hide the fact that they were turned down elsewhere. You should know that if your application is denied, the last page in your passport will be stamped "Application Received" with the date and location of the rejecting consulate. This notation shows that some type of prior visa application has failed. It serves as a warning to other consulates that your case merits close inspection. If what we have just told you makes you think it would be a good idea to overcome this problem by obtaining a new, unmarked passport, you should also know that permanent computer records are kept of all visa denials.

F. Step Two: The Application (U.S. Filing)

If you are physically present in the U.S., you may apply for O, P or R status without leaving the country on the following conditions:

- you are simultaneously filing paperwork for or have already received an approved petition
- you entered the U.S. legally and not under the Visa Waiver Program
- you have never worked illegally in the U.S.
- the date on your I-94 card has not passed, and
- you are not inadmissible and none of the bars to change of status apply (see Chapter 25).

If you were admitted as a visitor without a visa under the new Visa Waiver Program, you may not carry out Step Two in the U.S. Currently there are 29 participating countries in the Visa Waiver Program, including: Andorra, Argentina, Austria, Australia, Belgium, Brunei, Denmark, Finland, France, Germany, Iceland, Ireland, Italy, Japan, Liechtenstein, Luxembourg, Monaco, The Netherlands, New Zealand, Norway, Portugal, San Marino, Singapore, Slovenia, Spain, Sweden, Switzerland, the United Kingdom and Uruguay. The government has approved Greece for inclusion in the program in the near future.

If you cannot meet these terms, you may not file for O, P or R status in the U.S. It is important to realize, however, that eligibility to apply in the U.S. has nothing to do with overall eligibility for an O, P or R visa. Applicants who are barred from filing in the U.S. but otherwise qualify for O, P or R status can apply successfully for a visa at U.S. consulates abroad. If you find you are not eligible for U.S. filing, read Section E. Read Chapter 25 to make sure you are not subject to any waiting periods or ground of inadmissibility.

1. Benefits and Drawbacks of U.S. Filing

Visas are never given inside the U.S. They are issued exclusively by U.S. consulates abroad. If you file in the U.S. and you are successful, you will get O, P or R status but not the visa itself. This is a major drawback to U.S. applications. O, P or R status allows you to remain in the U.S. with O, P or R privileges until the status expires, but should you leave the country for any reason before that time, you will have to apply for the visa itself at a U.S. consulate before returning to America. Moreover, the fact that your status has been approved in the U.S. does not guarantee that the consulate will also approve your visa. Some consulates may even regard your previously acquired status as a negative factor, an indication that you have deliberately tried to avoid the consulate's authority.

There is another problem which comes up only in U.S. filings. It is the issue of what is called *preconceived intent*. To approve a change of status, INS must believe that at the time you originally entered the U.S. as a visitor or with some other nonimmigrant visa, you did not intend to apply for a different status. If INS thinks you had a preconceived plan to change from the status you arrived with to a different status, it may deny your application. The preconceived intent issue is one less potential hazard you will face if you apply at a U.S. consulate abroad.

On the plus side of U.S. filing is that when problems do arise with your U.S. application, you can stay in America while they are being corrected, a circumstance most visa applicants prefer. If you run into snags at a U.S. consulate, you will have to remain outside the U.S. until matters are resolved.

2. Application General Procedures: U.S. Filing

The general procedure for filing Step Two in the U.S. is to follow Step One as outlined above, but to mark box "4b" in Part 2 of Form I-129, indicating that you will complete processing in the U.S. There is no additional application form for filing Step Two in the U.S. If you have an accompanying spouse or children, however, a separate Form I-539 must be filed for them.

When you apply for a change of status, the filing fee for a Step One petition is presently $180. Checks and money orders are accepted. It is not advisable to send cash. We recommend submitting all papers by certified mail, return receipt requested, and making a copy of everything sent in to keep for your records.

Within a week or two after mailing in the application, you should get back a written notice of confirmation that the papers are being processed, together with a receipt for the fees. This notice will also tell you your immigration file number and approximately when to expect a decision. If INS wants further information before acting on your case, it will send a request for evidence on a form known as an I-797. The I-797 tells you what additional pieces of information or documents are expected. You should supply the extra data and mail the whole package back to the INS regional service center, with the I-797 on top.

Applications for O, P and R status are normally approved within two to eight weeks. When this happens, you will receive a Notice of Action Form I-797 indicating the dates for which your status is approved. A new I-94 card is attached to the bottom of the form.

3. Application Forms: U.S. Filing

Copies of all forms are in Appendix III.

Form I-129

Follow the directions in Section D1, above, except in Part 2, mark box "4b" instead of box "4a."

Form I-539 (for accompanying relatives only)

Only one application form is needed for an entire family, but if there is more than one accompanying relative, each additional one should be listed on the I-539 supplement.

Part 1. These questions are self-explanatory. "A" numbers are usually given only to people who have previously applied for green cards or who have been in deportation proceedings.

Part 2. Question 1. Mark box "b," and write in "O-3," "P-4," or ""R-2," as appropriate.

Question 2. This question is self-explanatory.

Part 3. In most cases you will mark Item 1 with the date requested in the Step One petition. You will also complete Items 3 and 4, which are self-explanatory.

Part 4. Questions 1–2. These questions are self-explanatory.

Question 3. The different parts to this question are self-explanatory, however, items "a" and "b" ask if an immigrant visa petition or adjustment of status application has ever been filed on your behalf. If you are applying for a green card through a relative, this would be Step One, as described in Chapter 5. If you are applying for a green card through employment, this would be Step Two as described in Chapter 8. If you have only begun the Labor Certification, the first step of getting a green card through employment, this question should be answered "no." An answer of "yes" to any of these questions will not effect your ability to get an O or P visa, but may make you ineligible for an R visa, which requires you to have the intention of returning to your home country after the visa expires.

4. Application Documents: U.S. Filing

Each applicant must submit an I-94 card, the small white card you received on entering the U.S. Remember, if the date stamped on your I-94 card has already passed, you are ineligible for U.S. filing. If you entered the U.S. under the

Visa Waiver Program and have a green I-94 card, you are also ineligible for U.S. filing. Canadians who are just visiting are not expected to have I-94 cards. Canadians with any other type of nonimmigrant status should have them.

For each accompanying relative, send in an I-94 card. You will also need documents verifying their family relationship to you. You may prove a parent/child relationship by presenting the child's long form birth certificate. Many countries, including Canada and England, issue both short and long form birth certificates. Where both are available, the long form is needed because it contains the names of the parents while the short form does not. If you are accompanied by your spouse, you must prove that you are lawfully married by showing a civil marriage certificate. Church certificates are usually unacceptable. (There are a few exceptions, depending on the laws of your particular country. Canadians, for example, may use church marriage certificates if the marriage took place in Quebec Province, but not elsewhere. If a civil certificate is available, however, you should always use it.) You may have married in a country where marriages are not customarily recorded. Tribal areas of Africa are an example. In such situations call the nearest consulate or embassy of your home country for help with getting acceptable proof of marriage.

5. Application Interviews: U.S. Filing

Interviews on change of status applications are rarely held. When an interview is required, the INS regional service center where you filed will send your paperwork to the local INS office nearest the location of your U.S. employer's place of business or institution. This office will in turn contact you for an appointment. (If INS has questions on the Step One petition rather than the application, your employer will be contacted.) INS may ask you to bring additional documents at that time.

If you are called for an interview, the most likely reason is that INS either suspects some type of fraud or believes you may be subject to a ground of inadmissibility. Interviews are usually a sign of trouble and can result in considerable delays.

6. Application Appeals: U.S. Filing

If your application is denied, you will receive a written decision by mail explaining the reasons for the denial. There is no way of making a formal appeal to INS if your application is turned down. If the problem is too little evidence, you may be able to overcome this obstacle by adding more documents and resubmitting the entire application to the same INS office you have been dealing with together with a written request that the case be re-opened. The written request does not have to be in any special form. This is technically called a *Motion to Reopen*. There is a $110 fee to file this motion.

Remember that you may be denied the right to a U.S. filing without being denied an O, P or R visa. When your application is turned down because you are found ineligible for U.S. filing, simply change your application to a consular filing.

Although there is no appeal to INS for the denial of a change of status application, you do have the right to file an appeal in a U.S. district court. It would be difficult to file such an appeal without employing an immigration attorney at considerable expense. Such appeals are usually unsuccessful.

G. Extensions

O and P visas can be extended for the time needed, without limitation. R visas are limited to a total of five years, however. Although an extension is usually easier to get than the O, P or R visa itself, it is not automatic. INS has the right to reconsider your qualifications based on any changes in the facts or law. As always, however, good cases that are well prepared will be successful.

To extend your O, P or R visa, the petition and visa stamp will both have to be updated. As with the original application, you can file either in the U.S. or at a consulate. However, contrary to our advice on the initial visa procedures, O and P extensions are best handled in the U.S. That is because visa stamps, which can only be issued originally at consulates, may be extended in the U.S. R extensions must be issued at consulates.

1. Extension Petition

Extension procedures are identical with the procedures followed in getting the initial visa, except that less documentation is generally required and the filing fee for the worker is only $125. However the best practice is to fully document the extension request with all of the documents submitted with the initial petition, as the INS will probably not have the file on-site. In addition to the employer's attestation, you should also submit your I-94 card, a letter from the employer requesting your visa be extended and a copy of your U.S. income tax returns for the previous two years, including W-2 forms.

WORKING WHILE YOUR EXTENSION PETITION IS PENDING

If you file your petition for an extension of O, P or R status before your authorized stay expires, you are automatically permitted to continue working for up to 240 days while you are waiting for a decision. If, however, your authorized stay expires after you have filed for an extension but before you receive an approval, and more than 240 days go by without getting a decision on your extension petition, continued employment is not authorized and you must stop working.

a. Extension Petition Forms

Copies of all forms are in Appendix III.

Form I-129 and Supplement

Follow the directions in Section D1, above. The only difference is that you will mark boxes "2b" and "4c" of Part 2.

Form I-539 (for accompanying relatives only)

Follow the directions in Section F3, above, but mark box "1a" of Part 2.

b. Extension Petition Documents

You must submit your I-94 card. You should also submit the original Notice of Action I-797, a letter from your employer stating that your extension is required, and a copy of your personal U.S. income tax returns for the past two years, including Form W-2. Be sure that only authorized employment is reflected on your tax documents before submitting them.

2. Visa Revalidation

Visas can be revalidated either in the U.S. or at a consulate.

a. Visa Revalidation: U.S. Filing

If you are physically in the U.S. and your O or P status extension has been approved by INS, you can have your visa revalidated by mail without leaving the country. To do this, you must fill out Form OF-156, following the directions in Section E3, above, and send it to the Department of State. With the form you should also submit as documents your passport, current I-94 card, Notice of Action Form I-797 and a detailed letter from your employer describing your job duties. Enclose a self-addressed, stamped envelope or a completed Federal Express airbill. Send the entire package by certified mail to:

Department of State
Visa Services
2401 "E" Street, N.W., Room 1306
Washington, DC 20520
Telephone: 202-647-0510

The passport will be returned to you with a newly revalidated visa in a few weeks. Nationals of some countries like Mexico are charged a fee for revalidating a visa, while nationals of other countries receive this service at no charge. Whether or not there is a fee depends on the nationality of the applicant, not the place where the application for the visa was originally made. You may call the State Department in Washington, D.C. to find out the amount of the revalidation fee, if any. If you send in your revalidation package without the correct fee, it will be returned to you, so check the amount in advance.

If your accompanying relatives are physically in the U.S., their O-3 and P-4 visas may be revalidated by sending in their passports and I-94 cards together with yours. We strongly advise gathering your family together inside U.S. borders so you can take advantage of this simple revalidation procedure.

R visa holders cannot revalidate their visas in the U.S.

b. Visa Revalidation: Consular Filing

If you must leave the U.S. after your extension has been approved but before you had time to get your visa revalidated, you must get a new visa stamp issued at a consulate. Read Section E, above. The procedures for consular extensions are identical.

We would like to reemphasize that it is much more convenient to apply for a revalidated visa by mail through the State Department in Washington, D.C. than it is to extend your O or P visa through a consulate. If possible, you should try to schedule filing your extension application when you can remain in the U.S. until it is complete. Again, R visas do not qualify for this special procedure.

FORMS AND DOCUMENTS CHECKLIST

STEP ONE: PETITION

Form

☐ Form I-129 and O/P/Q/R Supplement.

Documents

☐ Written employment contract or written summary of an oral contract.

☐ College and university diplomas.

☐ Employer's written statement explaining the nature of the employer, the specific events or activities you will be participating in, and why your participation is needed.

Additional Documents for O & P Visas

☐ Consultation report.

☐ Certificates showing prizes or awards won.

☐ Certificates of membership in associations.

☐ Copies of articles published about you and your work.

☐ Publications written by you.

☐ Letters from leaders in your field explaining your significant accomplishments.

☐ Letters from previous employers showing your salary and explaining your importance to them.

☐ If part of a group:

    ☐ documentation explaining the prestige and accomplishments of your group, and

    ☐ details about each of its members.

Additional Documents for R Visas

☐ Diplomas and certificates showing your academic and professional qualifications.

☐ Detailed letter from the U.S. religious organization, fully describing the operation of the organization both in and out of the U.S.

☐ Letter from the U.S. organization giving details of your U.S. job offer, including how you will be paid.

☐ Written verification that you have been a member of that same organization outside the U.S. for at least two years.

☐ Evidence that the religious organization in the U.S. qualifies as a tax-exempt organization under §501(c) of the Internal Revenue Code.

STEP TWO: APPLICATION

Forms

☐ OF forms (available at U.S. consulates abroad for consular filing only).

☐ Form I-129 (U.S. filing only).

☐ Form I-539 (U.S. filing only for accompanying relatives).

Documents

☐ Notice showing approval of the visa petition.

☐ Valid passport for you and each accompanying relative.

☐ I-94 card for you and each accompanying relative (U.S. filing only).

☐ One passport-type photo of you and each accompanying relative (Consular filing only).

Inadmissibility

A. Grounds of Inadmissibility

There are conditions or characteristics which the U.S. government has decided are undesirable and therefore people who have these conditions should not be allowed to enter the country. These people are called *inadmissible*. Inadmissibility creates problems in green card applications. Technically, those who want nonimmigrant visas can also be inadmissible. In reality, inadmissibility is often not as closely checked in nonimmigrant applications.

There are many reasons why someone may be unwanted in the U.S. Each of these reasons represents a different category of inadmissibility. The list of such grounds includes affliction with various physical and mental disorders, commission of crimes and participation in subversive activity.

Just because you fall into one of the categories of inadmissibility does not mean you are absolutely barred from getting a green card or otherwise entering the U.S. Some grounds of inadmissibility may be legally excused or waived. Others may not. But determining how to appeal for a waiver is complicated and you should consult with an attorney if you are in this situation. Recent rulings by the Board of Immigration Appeals make it difficult to clear a crime off your record for immigration purposes, even if, under state law, the record of criminal conviction has been "expunged" or removed. Below is a complete chart showing all the grounds of inadmissibility, whether or not a waiver is available, and the special conditions you must meet in order to get a waiver.

B. Reversing an Inadmissibility Finding

You may be judged inadmissible at any time after you have filed an application for a green card, nonimmigrant visa or status. If you are found inadmissible, your application will be denied. The notice of denial will be issued in the same manner as denials for any other reason. Even if you manage to hide your inadmissibility long enough to receive a green card or visa and be admitted into the U.S., if the problem is ever discovered later, you can be deported.

There are four ways to overcome a finding of inadmissibility:

- In the case of physical or mental illness only, you can correct the condition. Some criminal grounds of inadmissibility can be removed through a court proceeding that can set aside the criminal conviction.
- You can prove that you really don't fall into the category of inadmissibility INS believes you do.
- You can prove that the accusations of inadmissibility against you are false.
- You can apply for a waiver of inadmissibility.

1. Correcting Grounds of Inadmissibility

If you have had a physical or mental illness that is a ground of inadmissibility and you have been cured of the condition by the time you submit your green card application, you will no longer be considered inadmissible for that reason. If the condition is not cured by the time you apply, with certain illnesses you can still get a waiver of inadmissibility.

2. Proving Inadmissibility Does Not Apply

Proving inadmissibility does not apply in your case is a method used mainly to overcome criminal and ideological grounds of inadmissibility. When dealing with criminal grounds of inadmissibility, it is very important to consider both the type of crime committed and the nature of the punishment to see whether your criminal activity really constitutes a ground of inadmissibility. For example, with some criminal activity, only actual convictions are grounds of inadmissibility. If you have been charged with a crime and the charges were then dropped, you may not be inadmissible.

Another example involves crimes of moral turpitude. Crimes of moral turpitude are those showing dishonesty or basically immoral conduct. Commission of acts that constitute a crime of moral turpitude can be a ground of inadmissibility, even with no conviction. Crimes with no element of moral turpitude, however, are often not considered grounds of inadmissibility. Laws differ from state to state on which crimes are considered to involve moral turpitude and which are not. Still other factors that may help you are the brevity of any prison terms, how long ago the crime was committed, the number of convictions in your background,

GROUNDS OF INADMISSIBILITY

Grounds of Inadmissibility	Waivers Available	Conditions of Waiver
Health Problems		
Persons with communicable diseases. The most common diseases are tuberculosis and HIV (AIDS).	Yes	A waiver is available to an individual who is the spouse or the unmarried son or daughter or the unmarried minor lawfully-adopted child of a U.S. citizen or permanent resident, or of an alien who has been issued an immigrant visa; or to an individual who has a son or daughter who is a U.S. citizen, or a permanent resident, or an alien issued an immigrant visa, upon compliance with INS' terms and regulations.
Persons with physical or mental disorders which threaten the safety of others.	Yes	Special conditions required by INS, at its discretion.
Drug abusers or addicts.	No	
Persons who fail to show that they have been vaccinated against certain vaccine-preventable diseases.	Yes	The applicant must show that he or she subsequently received the vaccine; that the vaccine is medically inappropriate as certified by a civil surgeon; or that having the vaccine administered is contrary to the applicant's religious beliefs or moral convictions.
Criminal and Related Violations		
Persons who have committed crimes involving moral turpitude.	Yes	Waivers are not available for commission of crimes such as attempted murder or conspiracy to commit murder or murder, torture or drug crimes, except for simple possession of less than 30 grams of marijuana, or for persons previously admitted as permanent residents, if they have been convicted of aggravated felony since such admission or if they have less than seven years of lawful continuous residence before deportation proceedings are initiated against them. Waivers for all other offenses are available only if the applicant is a spouse, parent or child of a U.S. citizen or green card holder; or the only criminal activity was prostitution or the actions occurred more than 15 years before the application for a visa or green card is filed and the alien shows that he or she is rehabilitated and is not a threat to U.S. security.
Persons with multiple criminal convictions.	Yes	
Prostitutes.	Yes	
Criminals involved in serious criminal activity who have received immunity from prosecution.	Yes	
Drug offenders.	No	However there may be an exception for a first and only offense or for juvenile offenders.
Drug traffickers.	No	
National Security and Related Violations		
Spies or governmental saboteurs.	No	
Persons intending to overthrow the U.S. government.	No	
Terrorists and representatives of foreign terrorist organizations.	No	

GROUNDS OF INADMISSIBILITY

Grounds of Inadmissibility	Waivers Available	Conditions of Waiver
Persons whose entry would endanger U.S. foreign policy, unless the applicant is an official of a foreign government, or the applicant's activities or beliefs would normally be lawful in the U.S., under the constitution.	No	
Voluntary members of totalitarian parties.	Yes	Waiver is available if the membership was involuntary, or is or was when the application was under 16 years old, by operation of law, or for purposes of obtaining employment, food rations, or other "essentials" of living. Waiver is also possible for past membership if the membership ended at least two years prior to the application (five years if the party in control of a foreign state is considered a totalitarian dictatorship). If neither applies, a waiver is available only for an immigrant who is the parent, spouse, son, daughter, brother or sister of a U.S. citizen, or a spouse, son or daughter of a permanent resident.
Nazis	No	
People Likely to Become Dependent on Public Welfare	No	
Family sponsored immigrants and employment-sponsored immigrants where a family member is the employment sponsor (or such a family member owns 5% of the petitioning business) whose sponsor has not executed an Affidavit of Support (Form I-864).	No	But an applicant may cure the ground of inadmissibility by subsequently satisfying affidavit of support requirements.
Nonimmigrant public benefit recipients (where the individual came as nonimmigrant and applied for benefits when he or she was not eligible or through fraud). Five year bar to admissibility.	No	But ground of inadmissibility expires after five years.
Labor Certifications and Employment Qualifications	No	
Persons without approved labor certifications, if one is required in the category under which the green card application is made.	No	But see Chapter 8, for a discussion of the national interest waiver.
Graduates of unaccredited medical schools, whether inside or outside of the U.S., immigrating to the U.S. in a category based on their profession, who have not both passed the foreign medical graduates exam and shown proficiency in English. (Physicians qualifying as special immigrants, who have been practicing medicine in the U.S., with a license, since January 9, 1978 are not subject to this exclusion.)	No	
Uncertified foreign healthcare workers (not including physicians).	No	But applicant may show qualifications by submitting a certificate from the Commission on Graduates of Foreign Nursing Schools or the equivalent.

GROUNDS OF INADMISSIBILITY

Grounds of Inadmissibility	Waivers Available	Conditions of Waiver
Immigration Violators		
Persons who are present in the U.S. without proper paperwork ("Admission or parole.")	Yes	Available for certain battered women and children who came to the U.S. escaping such battery or who qualify as self-petitioners. Also available for individuals who had visa petitions or labor certifications on file before January 14, 1998 ($1,000 penalty required for latter waiver.) Does **not** apply to applicants outside of the U.S.
Persons who were previously deported.	Yes	Discretionary with INS.
Persons who have failed to attend removal (deportation) proceedings (unless they had reasonable cause for doing so). Five-year bar to inadmissibility.	Yes	Advance permission to apply for readmission. Discretionary with INS.
Persons who made misrepresentations during the immigration process.	Yes	The applicant must be the spouse or child of a U.S. citizen or green card holder. A waiver will be granted if the refusal of admission would cause extreme hardship to that relative.
Persons who made a false claim to U.S. citizenship.	No	
Individuals subject to a final removal (deportation) order under the Immigration and Naturalization Act §274C (Civil Document Fraud Proceedings)	Yes	Available to permanent residents who voluntarily left the U.S., and for those applying for permanent residence as immediate relatives or other family-based petitions, if the fraud was committed solely to assist the person's spouse or child and provided that no fine was imposed as part of the previous civil proceeding.
Student visa abusers (person who improperly obtains F-1 status to attend a public elementary school or adult education program, or transfers from a private to a public program except as permitted.) Five-year bar to admissibility.	No	
Certain individuals previously removed (deported). Twenty-year bar to admissibility. Five-year bar to admissibility for aggravated felons and for second and subsequent removal.	Yes	Discretionary with INS (advance permission to apply for readmission).
Individuals unlawfully present (time counted only after April 1, 1997). Presence for 180-364 days, results in three-year bar to admissibility. Presence for 365 or more days creates ten-year bar to admissibility. Bars kick in only if the individual departs the U.S. and seeks reentry after a period of unlawful presence.	Yes	One is not considered "unlawfully present" for up to 120 days if, after a lawful admission, an individual filed a valid change or extension of status before the end of the authorized stay (but then subsequently fell out of status) as long as the individual did not work without authorization. Similarly, time spent as a minor, as an asylum applicant (provided the person had a bona fide asylum claim and did not work without authorization), beneficiaries of family unity legislation and claimants under the battered spouse/child provisions do not accrue time in unlawful presence. Individuals admitted for "duration of status" are not unlawfully present until INS or an immigration judge makes such a determination. A waiver is provided for an immigrant who has a U.S. citizen or permanent resident spouse or parent to whom

GROUNDS OF INADMISSIBILITY

Grounds of Inadmissibility	Waivers Available	Conditions of Waiver
Individuals unlawfully present after previous immigration violations. (Applies to individuals present unlawfully for an aggregate period over one year, who subsequently reenter without being properly admitted. Also applies to anyone ordered removed who subsequently attempts entry without admission.)	No	refusal of the application would cause extreme hardship.
Stowaways.	No	Is a permanent ground of inadmissibility. However, after being gone for ten years an applicant can apply for advance permission to reapply for admission.
Smugglers of illegal aliens.	Yes	Waivable if the applicant was smuggling in persons who were immediate family members at the time, and either is a permanent resident or is immigrating under a family or employment-based visa petition.

Document Violations

Persons without required current passports or visas.	Yes	Discretionary with INS. Under new "summary removal" procedures, INS may quickly deport for five years persons who arrive without proper documents or make misrepresentations during the inspection process.

Draft Evasion and Ineligibility for Citizenship

Persons who are permanently ineligible for citizenship.	No	
Persons who are draft evaders, unless they were U.S. citizens at the time of evasion or desertion.	No	

Miscellaneous Grounds

Practicing polygamists.	No	
Guardians accompanying excludable aliens.	No	
International child abductors. (The exclusion does not apply if the applicant is a national of a country that signed the Hague Convention on International Child Abduction.)	No	
Unlawful voters (voting in violation of any federal, state, or local law or regulation).	No	
Former U.S. citizens who renounced citizenship to avoid taxation.	No	

conditions of plea bargaining and available pardons. Sometimes a conviction can be "vacated" if you can show it was unlawfully obtained or you were not advised of its immigration consequences.

As you can see, proving that a criminal ground of inadmissibility does not apply in your case is a complicated business. You need to have a firm grasp not only of immigration law, but the technicalities of criminal law as well. If you have a criminal problem in your past, you may be able to get a green card, but not without the help of an experienced immigration lawyer. We strongly suggest you find one and hire him or her to help you.

3. Proving a Finding of Inadmissibility Is Factually Incorrect

When your green card or nonimmigrant visa application is denied because you are found inadmissible, you can try to prove that the finding of inadmissibility is factually incorrect. For example, if an INS medical examination shows that you have certain medical problems, you can present reports from other doctors stating that the first diagnosis was wrong and that you are free of the problem condition. If you are accused of lying on a visa application, you can present evidence proving you told the truth, or that any false statements were made unintentionally.

C. New Grounds of Inadmissibility

The 1996 Immigration Reform law made many changes to the Immigration Code, most of them restrictive. Below is a discussion of some of the grounds which will have the most significant impact on those planning to immigrate and/or obtain nonimmigrant visas.

1. New Affidavit of Support Required for Family Based Petitions

All family-based immigrants (and employment-based immigrants where the applicant's relatives submitted the visa petition or own at least 5% of the petitioning company) must a new affidavit of support, Form I-864, filed by the petitioner to apply for permanent residence. This form also satisfies or helps satisfy the requirement that an immigrant show he or she is not likely to become a public charge. Note that this form is not required for other employment based petitions or nonimmigrant visas.

The requirements for this affidavit of support are very different from those of its predecessor, Form I-134. The new form is legally enforceable by the government for any means tested public benefits utilized by the sponsored immigrant. It is also enforceable by the immigrant-family

member against the sponsor for support. And it requires that the sponsor show that he or she has at least 125% of income for a similar family size, according to the federal poverty level.

All family-based immigrants who file adjustment of status or immigrant visa applications on or after December 19, 1997 are required to have the new I-864 filed by the person who is sponsoring their immigrant petition. However, another person (a "joint sponsor") may add her income to the sponsors if she meets the 125% income requirement for her own household and she is:

- willing to be jointly liable
- an legal permanent resident or citizen
- over 18 years old, and
- residing in the U.S.

The joint sponsor files a separate affidavit of support. Other household members may join their income to help reach the 125% level, but only if they have been living with the sponsor for six months and they agree to be jointly liable by filing form I-864 ("contract between sponsor and household member").

Personal assets of the sponsor or the immigrant (such as property, bank account deposits and personal property such as automobiles) may also be used supplement the sponsor's income, if the primary sponsor's actual income does not add up to 125% of the federal income poverty guidelines. To use assets, however, the assets will have to add up to five times the difference between 125% of the poverty income guidelines level for an equivalent family and the sponsors' actual income.

The sponsors must also notify INS within 30 days of the sponsor's change of address, using Form I-865. Failure to do so is punishable by fines of $250-$5,000. The requirements and paperwork burden of the new affidavit are complicated and substantial; most of the requirements are spelled out on the forms. If you have questions about meeting the eligibility or the scope of your legal responsibility (which may be ten or more years for sponsors, or until the immigrant permanently leaves the country, dies or naturalizes) you may want to consult an immigration attorney.

2. Summary Exclusion Law

Another new law which may have an impact on individuals requesting to enter the U.S. is the summary exclusion law. This law empowers an INS inspector at the airport to summarily (without allowing judicial review) exclude and deport someone requesting admission to the U.S. if either of the following are true:

- The inspector thinks you are making a misrepresentation about practically anything connected to your right to enter the U.S., such as your purpose in coming, intent to return or prior immigration history. This includes the use or suspected use of false documents.

- You do not have the proper documentation to support your entry to the U.S. in the category you are requesting.

If the inspector excludes you, you may not request entry for five years, unless a special waiver is granted. For this reason it is extremely important to understand the terms of your requested status and to not make any misrepresentations. If you are found to be inadmissible, you may request to withdraw your application to enter the U.S. in order to prevent having the five year deportation order on your record. The INS may allow you to do so in some cases.

3.   Bars to Getting Your Green Card in the U.S. ("Adjusting Status")

The rules concerning adjustment of status (getting your green card in the U.S.) are somewhat complicated. In general, if you entered the U.S. properly—by being inspected by an INS official—and maintained your nonimmigrant status, you can probably get your green card without leaving the U.S. Most persons who marry U.S. citizens can adjust their status even if they have fallen out of status or worked without authorization, as long as they did not enter without being properly inspected, as a crewman or stowaway. Persons who marry U.S. citizens and who entered without inspection or as crewmen or stowaways need to use the penalty and grandfather clause.

a.   The Penalty and Grandfather Clause

Individuals may be barred from getting their green cards in the U.S., even though they have an approved petition saying a visa number is available. For example, an individual may not apply for adjustment of status as a second preference alien until their priority date is current. Once your priority date is current, you may apply for adjustment of status. If you met the requirements in Section 3 above, then you will be required to pay a filing of $220 for each applicant 14 years of age or older and $160 for those under age 14.

If, however, you are out of status, have worked without authorization or entered without inspection, you are eligible to apply for adjustment only if you are grandfathered, or included within the old penalty rule which allowed adjustment of otherwise ineligible applicants upon paying the $1,000 penalty fee. The old penalty law expired in the fall of 1997. Presently, the only people who may still use the penalty provision are those that had a visa petition or labor certification on file by January 14, 1998. (Exempted from penalty fees are unmarried children younger than 17 years old and the spouse or unmarried child younger than 21 years old of a legalized alien who is qualified for and have applied for voluntary departure under the family unity program.)

b.   Special Exception for Certain Employment Based Green Card Applicants

Except for immediate relatives—children, parents and spouses of U.S. citizens—and those persons grandfathered under the old penalty law, other persons must maintain their nonimmigrant status and not work without valid authorization in order to do their permanent residence processing in the U.S.

There is a new exception to this rule for persons who are getting their green cards through employment. If you are getting your green card through the first, second or third preference employment categories (as priority workers, advanced degree or exceptional ability, or skilled workers, professionals and other workers) or as a special immigrant, you can have worked without authorization or fallen out of status for no more than 180 days.

This exception applies only if at the time of filing the green card application, your last entry to the U.S. was legal, you have maintained continuous legal status and have not violated the terms of your status or other terms of admission, other than during a 180 day aggregate period.

4.   Unlawful Presence and the Overstay Bars

A new ground of inadmissibility applies to persons who were unlawfully present in the U.S. for six months after April 1, 1997, who subsequently left the U.S. and who now seek admission through adjustment of status or by applying for an immigrant or nonimmigrant visa. Such persons are subject to a three year waiting period; the period is ten years if they were unlawfully present for one year after April 1, 1997.

a.   What is Unlawful Presence?

It is actually easier to say what unlawful presence isn't. You will not be found to be unlawfully present for purposes of the three and ten year bars:

- for time spent under the age of 18
- for time spent as a bona fide asylum applicant (including time while administrative or judicial review is pending), unless you were employed without authorization
- for time spent under family unity protection
- for time spent as a battered spouse or child who shows a substantial connection between the status violation or unlawful entry, and the abuse, or

• if you were lawfully admitted and filed a valid and timely application for change or extension of status, as long as you have not been employed without authorization, but only for 120 days.

Furthermore, the following persons present in the U.S. under a period of stay authorized by the Attorney General, will not have time counted as unlawful presence:

• persons with properly filed applications for adjustment of status who have their applications pending with INS
• aliens admitted to the U.S. as refugees
• aliens granted asylum
• certain aliens granted withholding of deportation/removal
• aliens present under a current grant of Deferred Enforced Departure (DED) pursuant to an order by the President
• certain aliens under a current grant of Temporary Protected Status (TPS), and
• certain Cuban-Haitian entrants.

b. Special Rules About Unlawful Presence

No period of time prior to April 1, 1997, counts toward unlawful presence for overstay bar purposes. For those who entered without inspection (EWI's), unlawful presence begins to be counted as of the date the alien entered the U.S. without admission or parole.

An alien admitted for "duration of status" (such as a student or exchange visitor) will begin to accrue unlawful presence only if either an immigration judge finds the alien has violated status and is deportable, or, INS, in the course of adjudicating an application for a benefit determines that a status violation has occurred.

An alien admitted until a specified date will begin to accrue unlawful presence either when the date on the I-94 (or any extension) has passed, or if INS or an immigration judge makes a finding of a status violation, whichever comes first.

Where the unlawful presence determination is based on an INS or immigration judge finding of a status violation, the unlawful presence clock starts to run from the date determined to be when the status violation began.

A grant of voluntary departure (V/D) constitutes a period of authorized stay. This includes the period between the date of the V/D order and the date by which the alien must depart. If the alien fails to depart by the date specified in the V/D order, the clock starts running.

Periods of unlawful presence are not counted in the aggregate for purposes of the three and ten year bars—in order words, you have to be present for a block of time which constitutes six or twelve months; INS will not add up

three months during one stay and three months during another stay to find that you were unlawfully present for six months.

c. Aliens Not Considered to be in a Period of Stay

Under current INS rules, and for purposes of the unlawful presence/overstay bars, the following classes of aliens are not considered to be present in the U.S. pursuant to a period of stay authorized by the Attorney General:

• aliens under an order of supervision
• aliens granted deferred action status
• aliens with pending applications for cancellation of removal
• aliens with pending applications for withholding of removal
• aliens issued voluntary departure prior to, during, or following proceedings
• aliens granted satisfactory departure, and
• aliens in federal court litigation.

These persons are thus unlawfully present for overstay bar purposes.

d. Waiver of Three or Ten Year Waiting Periods

There is a waiver available for persons who are the spouse or son or daughter of a U.S. citizen or permanent resident, if the applicant can show it would cause that spouse or son or daughter extreme hardship. Extreme hardship usually means more hardship than is normally experienced by having to return to one's home country; economic hardship is not usually sufficient to meet this requirement.

e. Changes in Availability of the Fraud Waiver

Prior to the enactment of the Immigration Reform Act of 1996, children could serve as qualifying relatives for parents who needed a waiver for having made misrepresentations or used false documents. The fraud waiver is now only available to applicants who have a spouse or parent to whom, if the waiver were denied, extreme hardship would result.

f. False Citizenship Claims and Illegal Voting

Congress has also added new inadmissibility categories for which there is no waiver at all. This includes making a false claim that one is a U.S. citizen for the purpose of obtaining immigration benefits or to get benefits under any state or federal law, or voting illegally in federal, state or local elections.

For these reasons, it is extremely important to understand when a ground of inadmissibility is present and to see whether it can be overcome with a waiver before filing any papers with INS.

g. Special Rules in Asylum-Based Green Card Applications

The rules and grounds of inadmissibility are different for asylum than for other green card applications. Some grounds of inadmissibility, including public charge, affidavit of support, labor certification and documentary requirements, do not even apply to a refugee or asylee applicant for permanent residence.

Most other grounds of inadmissibility are waivable if the person can show INS that it would be in public interest, humanitarian interests or would assure family unity to grant the waiver. This means that the asylee or refugee applicant does not need to have one of the special qualifying relatives (spouse or parent) to get a green card, assuming that there is a ground of inadmissibility which requires a waiver.

D. Applying for a Waiver

In many circumstances you may be able to get a waiver of inadmissibility. By obtaining a waiver, you don't eliminate or disprove the ground of inadmissibility. Instead you ask INS to overlook the problem and give you a green card or visa anyway.

You may not apply for a waiver of inadmissibility until the consulate or INS office makes a judgment that you are in fact inadmissible. There is no way of knowing at what point after you have filed your green card application the government will reach that decision.

All green card and visa application forms ask questions designed to find out if any grounds of inadmissibility apply in your case. When the answers to the questions on these forms clearly show that you are inadmissible, you may be authorized to begin applying for a waiver immediately on filing your application. You will be notified by mail if you are so authorized. In most cases, however, the consulate or INS office insists on having your final visa interview before ruling that you are inadmissible. If the INS office or consulate handling your case decides to wait until your final interview before finding you inadmissible, it will delay your ability to file for a waiver. This may in turn greatly delay your getting a green card or visa. Waivers can take many months to process.

Once it is determined that a waiver is necessary, you will be given Form I-601 to complete and file with a $170 filing fee. Note that if you file this with a U.S. consulate abroad, you will have to wait for the consulate to send your application to an INS office. The consulate cannot approve the waiver.

Once again, there are many technical factors that control whether or not a waiver of inadmissibility is granted. If you want to get one approved, you stand the best chance of success by hiring a good immigration lawyer. ■

Naturalization: Becoming a U.S. Citizen

Privileges

- You acquire U.S. citizenship.

- As a U.S. citizen, you cannot be deported or lose your citizenship even if you commit a crime or choose to live elsewhere in the world, unless you misrepresented yourself to get citizenship or were ineligible at the time.

- As a U.S. citizen, you can petition for the green cards of close relatives.

- You can pass on U.S. citizenship to your children, both those who are already born and those born after your naturalization.

Limitations

- If, after you have become a naturalized citizen, it is discovered that you were not eligible for naturalization or that you were not really eligible for a green card when you acquired it, then your citizenship will be revoked and you may be subject to deportation.

- You may renounce the citizenship of your home country when taking the citizenship oath, depending on the laws of your home country regarding dual citizenship.

A. Who Qualifies?

Except in rare cases, no one can become a naturalized U.S. citizen without first getting a green card. To qualify for citizenship, you must have held the green card and been physically present in the U.S. for a certain period of time. You should also be a person of good moral character, have a knowledge of the English language and be familiar with American government and history. In addition, you must be at least 18 years of age.

Children under age 18 who hold green cards may be naturalized if petitioned for by a U.S. citizen parent. No specific period of residency is required. (This provision is used mostly for adopted children.)

Most people, in order to qualify for naturalization, are required to have held green cards a minimum of five years. At least one-half of that time must be spent physically inside U.S. boundaries. You must also show that your five-year period of permanent residence has not been interrupted by substantial time spent abroad. If you leave the country and remain absent for a year or more, this wipes out any time counted toward the five-year total and you must start adding up your time all over again. Absences of fewer than six months do not affect the five-year waiting period.

Absences of less than one year but more than six months may also wipe out your accrued time, unless you can prove that your absence does not interrupt your continuous residence. You can show that you did not interrupt your

continuous residence by submitting documents which show, for example: that you maintained your employment in the U.S. during the absence; that your immediate family remained in the U.S.; that you maintained full access to your U.S. home; or that you did not obtain employment while abroad. If INS believes such documents show that you in fact maintained continuous residence, you will be able to count that time toward the five-year period.

If you are married to a U.S. citizen, you need only have held a green card for a minimum of three years to qualify for naturalization. At least half that time must have been spent physically inside U.S. boundaries. The rules about long absences that apply to those with five-year waiting periods apply to those with three-year waiting periods as well.

If your American-citizen spouse is employed abroad by the U.S. government, and you will be leaving to join him or her abroad, there is no waiting period and no required residency period to get U.S. citizenship. You may apply for naturalization as soon as you receive your green card.

The decision to file for naturalization is not a simple one. An applicant should consider first whether there could be a problem of inadmissibility or a defect in their original permanent resident status. Filing an application for naturalization could cause the discovery of legal problems in permanent residency status, causing the INS to start deportation or removal proceedings.

1. Local Residence Requirement

To qualify for naturalization, in addition to having lived in the U.S. for the necessary time period, you must have resided for at least three months within the state or INS district where you file your application. If you should move out of the state or district while your naturalization application is pending, the application may be transferred to your new district.

2. When Can You File?

Because of long delays in naturalization processing at many INS offices, immigration experts used to advise filing your application many months before you were eligible. They reasoned that you would be eligible by the time your application was processed. The Immigration Act of 1990 partially limited this practice. Now you may file a naturalization application no more than three months before any required period of U.S. residency has been completed. If you file early, INS may not notify you until you are called for your interview, perhaps a year after filing. But they will tell you at that time that you have to start all over again by filing a new application.

3. Special Benefits for Former Members of the U.S. Armed Forces

Special laws often apply to non-Americans who once actively served in the U.S. armed forces. In some cases, these laws eliminate the residence and waiting period requirements applicable to most green card holders. In certain situations, ex-military personnel may even be able to become naturalized U.S. citizens without first getting green cards.

The types of naturalization benefits available to you as a former member of the U.S. armed forces are controlled by the particular war in which you fought and the time period during which you served in that war. The list of wars and military units that qualify you for special citizenship benefits is long. If you ever served in a U.S. military unit, check with a consulate to see what benefits are available to you based on your former U.S. military activities.

4. Special Naturalization for Filipino World War II Veterans

An old law passed during World War II stated that Philippine nationals who served during that war in either American or Filipino military units in the Pacific were eligible to be naturalized, even though they had no green cards or periods of U.S. residence. The law expired after World War II ended, and very few Filipinos were actually naturalized. Numerous court actions have been filed in recent years challenging the legality of the way this law was terminated and attempting to revive it. Most of these legal efforts failed.

In response to this problem, the Immigration Act of 1990 specifically granted naturalization rights to anyone born in the Philippines who served honorably in an active-duty status with any branch of the U.S. armed forces in the Far East, the Philippine army, the Philippine scouts or a recognized guerrilla unit, at any time between September 1, 1939 and December 31, 1946. The application period has expired.

5. Ineligibility

People believed to have demonstrated bad moral character within the last five years are ineligible to become naturalized U.S. citizens. The definition of "moral character" is a complicated one, but certain individuals are barred from showing good moral character during the five-year period preceeding the application, if the individual:

- committed one or more crimes of moral turpitude (such as theft or involving dishonesty, fraud or malice),
- was convicted of an aggravated felony after November 20, 1990,
- was convicted of murder at any time,
- was convicted of two or more offenses and the combined sentences added up to at least five years,
- violated any law relating to a controlled substance, except for a single offense for posession of marijuana of 30 grams or less,
- was confined to a jail or prison a total of 180 days ore more, or
- has given false testimony or to obtain any benefits under immigration laws, if made under oath and with the purpose of obtaining those benefits.

Various other acts also serve to bar the application for naturalization if they were committed during the five-year period, including involvement in prostitution or commercialized vice, practicing polygamy, illegal gambling, habitual alcoholism and in most cases, willful failure to support dependents, or having an extramarital affair that destroyed an existing marriage.

INS may use other acts or information not included in this list to find that an applicant lacks "good moral character." INS will not approve an application where the applicant is on probation or parole, but that does not in itself serve as a bar to eligibility. Finally, if an applicant falls into one of the above moral turpitude categories but it is outside the five-year period before the application, INS may still consider it in deciding the moral character issue. If the applicant can show he or she has reformed since the act or conviction, and there are no new bad acts during the five-year period, the application can be approved.

While not necessarily indicative of moral character, the 1996 changes added a new ground of ineligibility for applicants who received public benefits under any "means tested" public benefit program. The new law requires that any such amounts of money owed back to the government under an affidavit of support must be repaid before a naturalization application will be approved.

Applicants who have one or more of these issues should see an immigration attorney before filing a naturalization application, since by applying for naturalization you bring yourself to the attention of INS. If you are ineligible, you risk being deported, in addition to having your application denied.

B. The Application

Naturalization is a one-step application process. The papers for this application are filed at the INS local office having jurisdiction over your place of residence in the U.S. If you are one of those people entitled to naturalization without fulfilling a U.S. residency requirement and you live outside the U.S., you may apply at any INS office in the U.S. you choose.

After your application is processed, you will be called for an interview. Depending on where in the U.S. you filed your application, you may have to wait from a few months to more than a year before your interview is scheduled. At the interview you will be tested on your knowledge of U.S. history and government. You must also be able to show that you can read, write and speak English. The requirements of reading and writing English are waived for anyone who is over the age of 50 and has been a permanent resident of the U.S. for at least 20 years. The English requirements are also waived for anyone who has been a permanent resident of the U.S. for at least 15 years and is over the age of 55. If you are over 65 and have lived in the U.S. as a permanent resident for at least 20 years, you are exempt from the English language requirement as well as the history and government test.

1. General Procedures

Your completed application, consisting of forms and documents, is filed at the INS local office or service center having jurisdiction over your place of residence. Although all naturalization applications were previously filed at local INS offices or suboffices, INS is changing this procedure so that applications will be filed by mail at the regional Service Center designated for your place of residence. If the local office is still the proper place to file your papers, most offices will accept them in person or by mail. If the Service Center procedures are in effect for your city, then the forms must be filed with the Service Center by mail.

With Service Center filings, you will be called to the local INS office for fingerprinting and for an interview. You will be required to visit the local INS office at least twice; after you are fingerprinted, INS will send the prints to the FBI and will schedule your interview only after the FBI check is completed.

Once your local office begins its transition to Regional Service Center filing, you will have a 60 day grace period. This means that during the first 60 days of the transition, if you file your application with the local INS office, it will forward the form to the Service Center. After the 60 days expire, if you file your application with the local INS office, it will return the form to you and you will have to refile it at the Service Center. You don't want to lose this time. For that reason, be sure you file in the right place before you send in your application. Check with your local INS office or a community organization in your city.

The current filing fee for the application is $225 plus $25 for fingerprint processing. If you file in person, ask for a receipt so that you can later prove on what date your application was submitted. The receipt number will also help to locate your file should it get lost or delayed in processing. When filing by mail, send the papers by certified mail, return receipt requested. In either case, keep a complete copy of everything sent or filed for your records. Appendix II contains a list of all INS offices with their current addresses and phone numbers.

SERVICE CENTER FILING

Applicants for naturalization residing within the New Orleans District Office and the Louisville and Memphis suboffices must mail the Form N-400 directly to the Texas Service Center at USINS Texas Service Center, Attention: N-400 Unit, P.O. Box 851204, Mesquite, TX 75185-1204.

Applicants for naturalization residing within the San Francisco District Office and the Fresno, Oakland, Sacramento and San Jose suboffices must mail the Form N-400 directly to the California Service Center at USINS California Service Center, Attention: N-400 Unit, P.O. Box 10400, Laguna Nigel, CA 92607-0400.

Applicants for naturalization residing within the jurisdiction of the Dallas, El Paso, Harlingen, Houston and San Antonio District Offices, and the Albuquerque and Oklahoma City suboffices must mail the Form N-400 directly to the Texas Service Center at the above Texas address.

2. Forms

Copies of all forms can be found in Appendix III.

Form N-400

The application for naturalization is initiated by filing Form N-400. All questions on this form are self-explanatory. You will remember that in order to become a naturalized citizen, you must be at least 18 years of age. Therefore, your minor children cannot be naturalized with you. They are, however, eligible for citizenship without going through naturalization. This means that instead of a naturalization certificate, they will receive what are known as certificates of citizenship.

This form also asks for a complete history of all absences from the U.S. since getting your green card. If you have made a great number of brief trips, such as might be the case if you live near the Canadian or Mexican borders, you may put down "numerous brief trips." You can expect detailed questions about the length of your trips at your naturalization interview. If you have been away from the U.S. for more than six months at a time, there is a presumption that you gave up your U.S. residence for naturalization purposes. If you were away at any time for one year or more, you normally lose your U.S. residency for naturalization purposes. This does not necessarily mean that you lost your green card, but it does mean that the three- or five-year residency requirement starts over again.

Form G-325A

Form G-325A biographic data form must be filled out. This form is meant to gather personal background information. The questions are all self-explanatory.

3. Documents

You will be required to submit a copy of your green card and three color immigration-type photographs. Instructions for photographs may be found in Appendix III. No other specific documentation is required. When you go to the INS office for the personal interview, you may be asked to bring your green card and sometimes the marriage certificate and divorce decrees of you and your spouse and previous spouses, if any. INS offices differ in their policies concerning what documents you are expected to bring with you. You will be told exactly what is expected on your notice to appear for the interview.

The only other paperwork required is a fingerprint card. Beginning March 30, 1998, INS regulations changed so that all fingerprinting now takes place at an INS-run fingerprinting center. You will be notified where and when to appear after submitting your application forms. You will be required to pay INS $25 (often when you file your application papers) to cover the fingerprinting costs.

4. The Naturalization Test and Interview

Several months to a year or more after you file your naturalization application, INS will send you a written notice to appear for an interview. If you have not already passed an approved U.S. citizenship examination, either as a participant in the amnesty program or as a student of an INS accredited school, you will be tested on your knowledge of U.S. government and history at your interview. You may want to consider enrolling in an accredited citizenship class, frequently given by local high schools or community colleges. If you pass their test, INS cannot test you again. If you are over age 65 and have held a green card for at least 20 years, you do not have to meet this requirement.

INS uses a standardized test for naturalization, but you may be asked only some of the questions. The INS officer can exercise discretion on what to ask. Here are some typical questions:

- When did the U.S. declare its independence from England?
- What do the stripes on the U.S. flag represent?
- What is the name of the form of government used in the U.S.?
- What are the three branches of the U.S. government and the function of each?
- What special name is given to the first ten amendments to the U.S. Constitution, and what are some of the special rights granted by these amendments?
- How many members are there in the U.S. House of Representatives and in the U.S. Senate? How long are each of their terms of office?
- Who are the U.S. senators from your state?
- Who is the secretary of state?
- Where is the capital of your state?
- Who is the governor of your state?
- Who is the U.S. representative from your congressional district?
- Who elects the president of the United States?
- How long is the term of office of the president?
- If both the president and vice president should die in office, who becomes president?
- How many justices sit on the Supreme Court?
- What is the name of the national anthem and who wrote it?
- What were some of the reasons for the American Civil War?

At your naturalization interview, INS may also look into any other factors that might indicate that you are ineligible for naturalization. Technically, INS is required to investigate your eligibility prior to your interview date so any problem issues can be discussed at that time. However, some INS offices put off this investigation until after you have taken the naturalization test. If the procedure at the INS office where you filed your application is to delay the investigation until after the test, and some ground of ineligibility is then discovered, you will be called back for a second interview on the question of your eligibility. Current procedures require INS to make a decision on your application within four months after your interview.

Once you have passed your test and it has been established that you are eligible for naturalization, your application will be approved. If you do not pass the exam, you will be given an opportunity to take it again a few months later.

5.   Swearing-In Ceremony

To finally become a citizen you must be sworn in. This involves taking an oath to maintain allegiance to the United States and uphold the U.S. Constitution. Most ceremonies are administrative, meaning you will not go before a judge. In certain circumstances, however, judicial naturalizations take place.

The swearing-in ceremony is normally a happy occasion. When it is completed, you will be a U.S. citizen. Any of your children under the age of 18 who hold green cards, although they are not old enough to be sworn in themselves, will automatically become U.S. citizens too, as long as both parents are naturalized.

6.   Appeals

If your application is denied, you will be given a written decision stating the reasons. You may file an appeal directly with INS. Previously, appeals were handled by the courts rather than administratively through INS. If your application is denied, INS will provide you with instructions and necessary forms for filing an appeal.

If your administrative appeal is unsuccessful, you may file another appeal with a federal court. It is highly recommended that you do not attempt a naturalization appeal without a lawyer. Unless your naturalization is being denied only because you failed the exam or did not have the required residence in the U.S., denial could jeopardize your green card status as well.

The judge handling your appeal case will make a decision either at the conclusion of the hearing or by means of a written opinion issued at a later date. Whether or not you are given an immediate decision depends on the judge's personal preference and the complexity of your case. Some judges take several months to reach a decision. If, after a court hearing, your application is denied, you may file an appeal. Complex appeals are beyond the scope of this book and, quite frankly, cannot be handled properly without extensive legal training and experience in immigration matters. Unless you wish to take a real gamble with your future, you should hire an experienced immigration attorney to represent you for any appeal. ■

Discovering Claims to U.S. Citizenship

A. Who Qualifies for U.S. Citizenship?

U.S. citizenship can be acquired in one of four ways:
- birth in the U.S
- birth to U.S. citizen parents
- naturalization, or
- naturalization of parents.

If you were born on U.S. soil, became a naturalized U.S. citizen or were born to U.S. citizen parents, and you have been living in the U.S., the fact that you have U.S. citizenship is clear-cut. In our experience, however, we have found that there are many people born or living outside the U.S. who are already U.S. citizens but don't know it. Some of these people were born in the U.S. but have lived most of their lives in other countries. They now believe that their long absence from the U.S. and voting or military activities elsewhere have stripped them of U.S. citizenship. Another group is made up of people who have American citizens in their direct line of ancestry. These people don't realize that even though they were born elsewhere and their American ancestors have not lived in the U.S. for a long time, U.S. citizenship has still been passed down the line. The members of still another group do live in the U.S. They are children of naturalized U.S. citizens but they themselves were never naturalized because one cannot normally become naturalized while still a minor. However, when parents become naturalized, minor children with green cards acquire citizenship automatically without naturalization. Again, many people are unaware of this.

1. Birth in the U.S.

Under U.S. law, a child born on U.S. soil automatically acquires American citizenship unless the child is born to a foreign government official who is in the U.S. as a recognized diplomat. Anyone born with U.S. citizenship will retain it for life unless he or she performs some act to intentionally lose it, such as filing an oath of renunciation.

2. Birth to U.S. Citizen Parents

In many circumstances, even though a child is born outside the U.S., if at least one parent was a U.S. citizen at the time of the child's birth, he or she automatically acquires U.S. citizenship. When this child marries and has children, those children may also acquire U.S. citizenship at birth. The laws governing whether or not a child born outside U.S. boundaries acquires U.S. citizenship from his or her parents have changed several times. The law that was in effect on the date of the child's birth determines whether he or she acquired U.S. citizenship from a parent or grandparent. Many people are pleasantly surprised to find their quest for a green card ended by the unexpected discovery that they are already U.S. citizens. If there is anyone in your direct line of ancestry whom you believe may be a U.S. citizen, it is worth your time to read what the U.S. laws were on the date of your birth and theirs.

Most laws controlling the passage of U.S. citizenship from parent to child require that the parent, the child, or both have a period of residence in the U.S. Sometimes the residence is required to be for a specified length of time and sometimes it is not. When the law doesn't say exactly how long the residence period must be, you can assume that even a brief time, such as a week or a month, might be enough. The key element is often not the amount of time but whether or not INS or the consulate believes it was a residence and not a visit. If the period of stay has the character of a residence, the length of time doesn't matter.

a. Prior to May 24, 1934

Originally, the law provided that only U.S. citizen fathers could pass citizenship on to their children. The rules were very simple. In order to pass on U.S. citizenship, the father must have resided in the U.S. at some time before the child's birth. The length of the residence and the time it took place were not specified. Technically, a day or a week would be enough if it could be regarded as a residence and not just a visit. Once a child obtained U.S. citizenship at birth through a U.S. citizen father, under the law at this time there were no conditions to retaining it. These rules also applied to illegitimate children, provided the U.S. citizen father had at some time, legally legitimated the child. U.S. citizenship was then acquired at the time of legitimation, without regard to the child's age.

This law has been challenged several times as discriminatory, with some courts holding that citizenship could also be passed by the mother to the children. Congress finally addressed this issue in 1994 and amended the law, retroactively, to provide that either parent could pass his or her U.S. citizenship to children.

Consider that if you were born before May 24, 1934 and either of your parents was a U.S. citizen, that citizenship might have been passed on to you. Consider also, that if either of your parents was born before May 24, 1934, they may have acquired U.S. citizenship from either of their parents which they then passed on to you under laws in existence at a later date. A check of the family tree may well be worth your while.

b.   May 25, 1934 to January 12, 1941

If you were born between May 25, 1934 and January 12, 1941, you acquired U.S. citizenship at birth on the conditions that both your parents were U.S. citizens and at least one had resided in the U.S. prior to your birth. The law at this time placed no additional conditions on retaining U.S. citizenship acquired in this way.

You could also get U.S. citizenship if only one of your parents was a U.S. citizen, as long as that parent had a prior U.S. residence. If your U.S. citizenship came from only one parent, you too would have been required to reside in the U.S. for at least two years between the ages of 14 and 28 in order to retain the citizenship you got at birth. Otherwise, your citizenship would be lost. If the one U.S. citizen parent was your father and your birth was illegitimate, the same rules applied provided your father legally legitimated you. Citizenship was passed at the time of legitimation without regard to your age, provided you had met the retention requirements.

c.   January 13, 1941 to December 23, 1952

If you were born between January 13, 1941 and December 23, 1952, both your parents were U.S. citizens and at least one had a prior residence in the U.S., you automatically acquired U.S. citizenship at birth with no conditions to retaining it.

If only one parent was a U.S. citizen, that parent must have resided in the U.S. at least ten years prior to your birth and at least five of those years must have been after your parent reached the age of 16. With a parent thus qualified, you then acquired U.S. citizenship at birth, but with conditions for retaining it. To keep your citizenship, you must have resided in the U.S. for at least two years between the ages of 14 and 28. As a result of a U.S. Supreme Court decision, if you were born after October 9, 1952, your parent still had to fulfill the residence requirement in order to confer citizenship on you, but your own residence requirements for retaining U.S. citizenship were abolished. If your one U.S. citizen parent was your father and your birth was illegitimate, the same rules applied provided you were legally legitimated prior to your 21st birthday and you were unmarried at the time of legitimation.

d.   December 24, 1952 to November 13, 1986

If at the time of your birth both your parents were U.S. citizens and at least one had a prior residence in the U.S., you automatically acquired U.S. citizenship with no other conditions for retaining it.

If only one parent was a U.S. citizen at the time of your birth, that parent must have resided in the U.S. for at least ten years and at least five of those years must have been after your parent reached the age of 16. Even with only one U.S. citizen parent there are still no conditions to retaining your citizenship. If your one U.S. citizen parent is your father and your birth was illegitimate, the same rules apply provided you were legally legitimated prior to your 21st birthday and you were unmarried at the time of legitimation. If legitimation occurred after November 14, 1986, your father must have established paternity prior to your 18th birthday, either by acknowledgment, or by court order, and must have stated, in writing, that he would support you financially until your 18th birthday.

e.   November 14, 1986 to Present

If at the time of your birth, both your parents were U.S. citizens and at least one had a prior residence in the U.S., you automatically acquired U.S. citizenship with no conditions for retaining it.

If only one parent was a U.S. citizen at the time of your birth, that parent must have resided in the U.S. for at least five years and at least two of those years must have been after your parent reached the age of 14. Even with only one U.S. citizen parent there are still no conditions to retaining your citizenship. If your one U.S. citizen parent is your father and your birth was illegitimate, the same rules apply provided you were legally legitimated prior to your 18th birthday. Additionally, your father must have established paternity prior to your 18th birthday, either by acknowledgment, or by court order, and must have stated, in writing, that he would support you financially until your 18th birthday.

3. Exception to Requirements for Retaining Citizenship

It is not unusual for a child born and raised outside the U.S. to have acquired U.S. citizenship at birth from parents or grandparents without knowing it. The child, ignorant of the laws and circumstances affecting his birthright, then proceeds to lose U.S. citizenship by failing to fulfill U.S. residency requirements. Courts have held that U.S. citizenship is too valuable a right to lose by accident. Therefore, if you did get U.S. citizenship by birth under one of the laws described above, but you did not meet a U.S. residency requirement because you were unaware of the situation, you may still be able to claim U.S. citizenship if you can establish that you lost it due to lack of knowledge. The ability to be legally excused from inadvertently failing to fulfill a residency requirement is called the Doctrine of Constructive Retention. To establish citizenship under this doctrine:

- you have a parent who is a U.S. citizen
- you didn't know about your claim to U.S. citizenship or any residency requirement necessary to retain it, and
- you would have fulfilled the residence requirement had you known the facts.

HOW CONSTRUCTIVE RETENTION WORKS

Suppose one of your grandparents—your father's mother let us say—was a U.S. citizen at the time of your father's birth. Your father, who automatically received U.S. citizenship from his mother at birth, was born in 1942, a date when the law required him to have a U.S. residency in order to keep his U.S. citizenship. Your father never knew he was a U.S. citizen, but learned of it later as an adult. By then, the time for fulfilling his residence requirement under the law in effect at his birth had passed.

Your father had always wanted to live in the U.S. He once tried to get a visa but he was turned down. Now realizing what has been lost, he wants to establish that he is a U.S. citizen. He now attempts to prove to INS or a consulate that he didn't know about the U.S. citizenship he received through his mother until it was too late to meet the legal requirements for retaining it. It is helpful that he had already made an effort to move to the U.S., because this helps to prove that had he been aware of the situation, he would have acted to retain his U.S. citizenship. If your father can establish that he didn't know and had he known he would have taken steps to fulfill the residency requirements, he can claim U.S. citizenship through the Doctrine of Constructive Retention. You, in turn, can claim that at the time of your birth your father had the necessary qualifications to confer U.S. citizenship on you. Then, if you were also subject to residency requirements, you too should be excused from fulfilling them because you were obviously unaware of a claim to U.S. citizenship. You could not, after all, be expected to know your father had a claim to U.S. citizenship through your grandfather when your father himself was unaware. This situation is called the Doctrine of Double Constructive Retention. Although this logic could be used to trace citizenship back even further, such as through great grandparents, the Department of State and INS will not recognize more than a double constructive retention.

The practical meaning of this complex-sounding term is simply that if you had a grandparent who was a U.S. citizen, there is always a chance that U.S. citizenship passed from your grandparent, through your parent, to you, even though none of you ever lived in the U.S. Once again, we urge you to check thoroughly if you think such circumstances may apply to you. You can get information on how to establish a claim to U.S. citizenship from the U.S. consulate in your home country. Procedures differ from consulate to consulate but the factors you are asked to prove are the same everywhere.

4. Automatic U.S. Citizenship Through Naturalized Parents

When parents become naturalized U.S. citizens, the children become U.S. citizens automatically, provided they have green cards and are under age 18 at the time. Becoming a U.S. citizen in this way has a special benefit because a child who automatically gets U.S. citizenship through the naturalization of either or both parents does not have to participate in a naturalization ceremony and can thereby avoid taking an oath renouncing allegiance to any country but the U.S. This allows the child to keep the citizenship of the country in which he or she was born while also gaining U.S. citizenship.

There are a number of people whose parents have been naturalized who do not realize they are U.S. citizens because they never went through a naturalization ceremony themselves. The laws on automatic naturalization of children have varied over the years. Once again, whether or not you achieved U.S. citizenship in this manner is determined by the laws as they were when your parents' naturalization took place.

a. Parents Naturalized Before May 24, 1934

If either parent became naturalized prior to your 21st birthday and you held a green card at the time, you automatically acquired U.S. citizenship. This applied to you if you were an illegitimate child of your father and had been legally legitimated or an illegitimate child of your mother, whether legitimated or not. Adopted children did not qualify.

b. Parents Naturalized From May 24, 1934 to January 12, 1941

If both parents became naturalized prior to your 21st birthday and you held a green card at the time, you automatically acquired U.S. citizenship. This applied to you if you were an illegitimate child of your father and had been legally legitimated or an illegitimate child of your mother, whether legitimated or not. Adopted children did not qualify.

If only one parent became naturalized prior to your 21st birthday, you acquired U.S. citizenship automatically if you held a green card for at least five years. The five years could have taken place before or after your parent was naturalized, so if you hadn't held a green card that long when the naturalization occurred, you automatically became a U.S. citizen whenever you finally accumulated the five-year total.

c. Parents Naturalized From January 13, 1941 to December 23, 1952

You acquired U.S. citizenship if you held a green card at the time and both parents were naturalized prior to your 18th birthday (or if your parents were legally separated, the parent having legal custody was naturalized). At this time, the law did not permit either illegitimate or adopted children to acquire citizenship in this manner.

d. Parents Naturalized From December 24, 1952, to October 4, 1978

You acquired U.S. citizenship if you were unmarried, held a green card at the time and both parents were naturalized, prior to your 16th birthday. This applied to you if you were an illegitimate child of your father and had been legally legitimated or an illegitimate child of your mother, whether legitimated or not. Adopted children did not qualify.

e. Parents Naturalized October 5, 1978 to Present

You acquired U.S. citizenship if one of your parents was a U.S. citizen when you were born and never ceased to be a citizen, and your other parent was naturalized prior to your 18th birthday, and you were unmarried at the time or the naturalization of both parents occurred while you are unmarried. You must be lawfully admitted as a permanent resident under both of these scenarios. This applies to all children, including those who are illegitimate and adopted. However, adopted children born prior to December 29, 1981 or after November 14, 1986, derived U.S. citizenship only if the adoption occurred prior to their 16th birthday.

B. Obtaining Proof of U.S. Citizenship

If you have a legitimate claim to U.S. citizenship, in order to establish that claim you must apply for some kind of citizenship document. When you were born on U.S. soil and there is a record of your birth, a standard U.S. birth certificate issued by a state government is your primary proof of U.S. citizenship. Birth certificates issued by hospitals are not official records and do not serve as proof of citizenship. If you were naturalized, you have a naturalization certificate. However, when your birth took place outside the territorial U.S, and you acquired U.S. citizenship at birth from your parents or automatically through your parents' naturalization as we have been discussing in this chapter, you will have neither of these documents and so you must try to acquire a substitute. Three other types of documents may be obtained which will be recognized as proof of U.S. citizenship. They are:

- U.S. passports
- certificates of citizenship, or
- certificates of consular registration of birth.

1. U.S. Passports

If you were born abroad to U.S. citizen parents, you can apply for a U.S. passport in the same way as someone born in the U.S. However, you will have the added requirement of establishing your citizenship claim. Passports are available from either passport offices in the U.S. or at U.S. consulates abroad, but our experience shows that you have a better chance for success in making your case when it is handled by a U.S. consulate abroad. Wherever you apply, you will be required to present proof of your parents' U.S. citizenship and evidence that they complied with any applicable U.S. residency requirements. If you needed to fulfill residency requirements in order to retain U.S. citizenship, you will need evidence that you did so. If you are excused from compliance under the Doctrine of Constructive Retention, you will also need proof of this. Review the sections on birth to a U.S. citizen for what you must prove under these circumstances. You will need to present documents such as birth or citizenship records of your parent or grandparent, documents such as work or tax records establishing U.S. residency for your parent or grandparent, and affidavits from you and, if possible, from your parent or grandparent explaining why you were unaware of your claim to U.S. citizenship.

2. Certificates of Citizenship

Certificates of citizenship are issued only inside the U.S. by INS offices. Anyone with a claim to U.S. citizenship can apply for a certificate of citizenship. In most cases it is more difficult and takes much longer to prove your citizenship through a certificate of citizenship application than it is through applying for a U.S. passport. However, in situations where your U.S. citizenship was obtained automatically through the naturalization of a parent, certificates of citizenship applications are the best choice. Certificates of citizenship and certificates of naturalization are not the same thing. If you were born outside the U.S. and acquired U.S. citizenship through birth to a U.S. citizen parent you are entitled to a certificate of citizenship, not a naturalization certificate. If you were born to parents who became naturalized citizens and under the law in effect at the time, you

became a U.S. citizen automatically, your parents will have naturalization certificates but you are entitled to a certificate of citizenship. In fact, at the time a parent is naturalized, the children can, upon the parent's request, be issued certificates of citizenship simultaneously with their naturalization certificates.

Certificates of citizenship not requested simultaneously with a parent's naturalization must be applied for later, on Form N-600. The current fee is $100. A copy of this form is in Appendix III. Most of the questions on the N-600 are self-explanatory. We offer the following suggestion in answering Question 14.

Question 14. Question 14 asks you to list all documents being submitted. We recommend you answer this question "See Cover Letter." Then prepare a letter explaining the basis of your claim to U.S. citizenship and describing the documents you are offering as proof. Evidence of your claim to U.S. citizenship should include your parents' birth certificates, marriage certificates and citizenship or naturalization certificates. You should also present your own birth certificate, marriage certificates and any divorce decrees to show legal changes in your name since birth. If you are not applying as the child of a naturalized citizen, your letter should also list whatever evidence you will be presenting to show that you have met any residency requirements as described in the section in this chapter on birth to a U.S. citizen.

Form N-600 and the documents together with the cover letter should be submitted to the INS local office having jurisdiction over your place of residence in the U.S. Appendix II contains a list of INS local offices with their current addresses and phone numbers. Interviews on your application are usually required. In many of the busier INS offices, it takes well over a year to get a decision on an application for certificate of citizenship. It is for this reason that we recommend an application for a U.S. passport as preferable to an application for certificate of citizenship.

3. Certificates of Consular Registration of Birth

Certificates of consular registration of birth are issued by a U.S. consulate abroad. If your parents were U.S. citizens but were not physically in the U.S. when you were born, they may have registered your birth with a U.S. consulate to establish your right to U.S. citizenship and create an official birth record. For you to have acquired a certificate of consular registration of birth, your parents must have registered your birth at a consulate within five years after you were born. Multiple copies can be issued at the time of registration but duplicates cannot be obtained later. Therefore, parents should request at least several copies. In issuing the certificate, the consulate asks to see evidence that any residence requirements the law placed on your parents were fulfilled. The consular registration is conclusive proof of U.S. citizenship, but if your parents did not take the steps to get one when you were a child, there is no way of obtaining one now.

If your parents did not register your birth in time, you may either apply for a passport through a passport office in the U.S. or at a U.S. consulate abroad, or you may apply for a certificate of citizenship through INS in the U.S. Again, we strongly recommend that you apply for the U.S. passport, as you can get it much faster than a certificate of citizenship.

C. Dual Citizenship

If a child is born on U.S. soil and either or both parents are citizens of another country, it is quite possible that the child may have dual citizenship. Whether or not a dual citizenship is created depends on the laws of the parents' country. A child born in the U.S. is always a U.S. citizen in the eyes of the U.S. government no matter what the laws of the parents' homeland. (The only exception to this rule is children born of foreign diplomats.) However, if the foreign country involved recognizes the child as a citizen, the U.S. will recognize the non-U.S. citizenship as well.

Whenever a child is born to U.S. citizen parents but the birth takes place outside U.S. territory, again, the child may acquire dual citizenship. In this situation, the child will, depending on the laws of the country where the birth took place, usually have the nationality of the country in which he or she was actually born, in addition to U.S. citizenship through the nationality of the parents. U.S. law recognizes dual citizenship under these circumstances and if you have acquired dual citizenship in this manner, under U.S. law you will be entitled to maintain dual status for your lifetime. ■

Canadians: Special Rules

Many Canadians believe they are disfavored by the American immigration system. Actually, the exact opposite is true, as the following description of rules for Canadians show. Some of the special rules also apply to Mexican citizens.

A. Visitors and Other Nonimmigrants

Canadian citizens, Canadian landed immigrants who have a common nationality with Canadian nationals (such as those from the United Kingdom) do not require visas to enter the U.S. For the casual tourist or business visitor, this is a big benefit. With the exception of E-1 and E-2 treaty traders and investors, Canadians have no need to go to a U.S. consulate and get nonimmigrant visas. If a Canadian is coming to the U.S. directly from Canada, no passport is required either, although some proof of Canadian citizenship must be shown at the border. E-1 and E-2 treaty traders and investors, however, require both visas and passports.

B. Tourists and Business Visitors

Even though a nonimmigrant visa is not required, Canadians still must show that they are eligible to enter the U.S. For visitors, this may mean something as simple as answering a few questions from an immigration inspector at a U.S. port of entry. On other occasions, a Canadian visitor might be asked to prove that he or she has enough money to last during the U.S. trip. Visitors may also have to show that they still keep Canadian residences to which they can return.

Canadian visitors are not normally issued I-94 cards as are people from all other countries. This is another advantage. Canadians are not expected to have this document on hand for purposes of proving status in the U.S.

C. Special Work Privileges for Canadian and Mexican Visitors

Canadians and Mexicans are granted some special work privileges.

1. Working Without a Visa

The North American Free Trade Agreement (NAFTA) includes a program permitting Canadian and Mexican visitors who are coming to the U.S. to do certain kinds of work in the U.S. without having work visas. There are no other countries whose citizens are afforded these privileges. To take advantage of this opportunity, you must show written proof that you are engaging in one of the occupations included in the program. A letter from your employer verifying the work to be done will serve this purpose. If relevant, you should also offer evidence that you are qualified for the job, such as copies of diplomas or licenses. These documents are presented to a U.S. immigration officer on your entry to the U.S. No fee or special application is needed for Canadians. (However, Mexican nationals must obtain a valid entry document [Form I-186 or Form I-586] prior to arriving at the port of entry.). The types of work that Canadians may do in the U.S. without work visas are:

- Performing research and design functions for a company located in Canada or Mexico.
- Supervising a crew harvesting agricultural crops; only the owner of the company qualifies.
- Purchasing for a company located in Canada or Mexico.
- Conducting other commercial transactions for a company located in Canada or Mexico.
- Doing market research for a company located in Canada or Mexico.
- Attending trade fairs.
- Taking sales orders and negotiating contracts for a company located in Canada or Mexico.
- Transporting goods or passengers into the U.S.
- Picking up goods and passengers in the U.S., only for direct transport back to Canada or Mexico.
- Performing normal duties as a customs broker. The goods must be exports from the U.S. to Canada or Mexico.
- Servicing equipment or machinery after sales.
- Performing any professional services, provided no salary is paid from within the U.S.
- Performing financial services for a company located in Canada.

- Consulting in the fields of public relations and advertising.
- Conducting tours that originate or have significant portions taking place in Canada.
- Performing language translation and acting as an interpreter for a company located in Canada.

2. Simplified Procedures and Substitutes for H and L Visas

Canadians entering the U.S. to take jobs with American companies as H-1 and H-2 temporary workers or L-1 intracompany transferees must have approved visa petitions. To get such a petition, you must follow the Step One procedures for these visas described in earlier chapters of this book. Once the petition is approved, however, as a Canadian you need not perform Step Two. Instead, you can simply go to a port of entry, present the petition approval, and be admitted. (Be sure to have your passport stamped to show your entry.) You will also need proof of your Canadian citizenship, such as a passport or birth certificate.

Your accompanying spouse and children will be admitted on showing proof of their family relationship to you. This requires presenting a marriage certificate for your spouse and long form birth certificates for your children.

When you enter the U.S., you will be given an I-94 card. This will indicate your immigration status and give the dates of the time period for which you may remain in the country. If you leave and return again before this period expires, you need only present the I-94 card together with your petition approval or Certificate of Eligibility, and you will be allowed to reenter.

a. L-1 Visa Alternative

Instead of going through the INS petition process, you can choose to take all your L-1 paperwork, both forms and documents, along with the required fee, directly to a port of entry. There, an immigration officer will decide on the spot if you qualify for L-1 status. When your status is approved, you will be given an I-94 card and admitted to the U.S. immediately. The petition is then forwarded to the appropriate service center in the U.S. and the final decision on the petition is made in about 60 days, and mailed to you.

Although this method is much faster than going through normal INS petition procedures, if you are denied entry, your rights of appeal are limited. In addition, border inspectors are usually less experienced in deciding cases than INS office personnel, and therefore, may be reluctant to approve a more difficult case. When your situation is complicated, you are probably better off having your petition

approved in advance at the service center and not using this alternative procedure.

b. H-1 Visa Alternative: TN Status

For people who practice certain professional occupations, an alternative to filing an INS petition is available for H-1 cases as well. This is called TN status. At present, only the occupations listed below qualify for TN status. A bachelor's or licensure degree from a college or university is required, unless an alternative is shown in parentheses. TN status is not available for self-employment in the U.S. For some professions, there are requirements in addition to a degree. These too are shown in parentheses. Whenever a license is required, either a Federal Canadian or Mexican, or a U.S. licensing agency from any province or state is acceptable. The occupations are:

- Accountant
- Architect (degree or license)
- Computer systems analyst
- Disaster relief claims adjuster (degree or three years experience)
- Economist
- Engineer (degree or license)
- Forester (degree or license)
- Graphic designer (degree and three years experience)
- Hotel manager (licensure degree or diploma or certificate plus three years experience)
- Industrial designer (degree or certificate or diploma plus 3 years experience)
- Interior designer (degree or certificate or diploma plus 3 years experience)
- Land surveyor (degree or license)
- Landscape architect
- Lawyer (member of Canadian, Mexican or U.S. bar)
- Librarian (master's degree)
- Management consultant (degree or five years experience)
- Mathematician
- Medical professions:
    - Clinical lab technologist
    - Dentist (professional degree or license)
    - Dietitian (degree or license)
    - Medical lab technologist
    - Medical technologist (degree or certificate or diploma plus 3 years experience)
    - Nutritionist
    - Occupational therapist (degree or license)
    - Pharmacist (degree or license)
    - Physician (teaching or research position only)

- Physio/physical therapist (degree or license)
- Psychologist
- Recreational therapist
- Registered nurse (license)
- Veterinarian (professional degree or license)
- Range manager
- Research assistant (for colleges or universities only)
- Scientific technician (degree not required if you are working with professionals in: agricultural sciences, astronomy, biology, chemistry, engineering, forestry, geology, geophysics, meteorology, physics)
- Scientist working as:
  - Agronomist
  - Agriculturist
  - Animal breeder
  - Animal scientist
  - Apiculturist
  - Astronomer
  - Biochemist
  - Biologist
  - Chemist
  - Dairy scientist
  - Entomologist
  - Epidemiologist
  - Geneticist
  - Geochemist
  - Geologist
  - Geophysicist
  - Horticulturist
  - Meteorologist
  - Pharmacologist
  - Physicist
  - Plant breeder
  - Poultry scientist
  - Soil scientist
  - Zoologist
- Social worker
- Silviculturist
- Teacher (at a college, university or seminary only)
- Technical publications writer (degree, or diploma or certificate plus three years experience)
- Urban planner
- Vocational counselor

In short, the person seeking TN status must be coming temporarily, to engage in business activities at a professional level, and he or she must meet the minimum requirements for the profession or occupation in question, as set forth in Appendix 1603.D.1 to Annex 1603 of NAFTA. Furthermore, the person must not be self-employed in the U.S. Although the basic requirements are the same for Canadians and Mexicans, the procedures are distinct.

Procedures for Canadians

There is no annual limit for Canadian TNs. A Canadian professional worker may be admitted to the U.S. without advance petition approval or labor certification. In order to apply, the applicant merely proceeds directly to any U.S. port of entry, where an immigration or NAFTA officer will adjudicate the application. Although no formal application form is required, you must pay a fee. A Canadian applicant will need to present the following documents to be given TN status:

- evidence of Canadian citizenship, such as a birth certificate, passport or certificate of naturalization
- description of proposed employment activity at a professional level (described in the job offer letter)
- evidence of the qualifications to perform at a professional level, as demonstrated by degrees, licenses, memberships or other relevant credentials that establish professional status, and a resume (optional), and
- evidence of the particular profession as one listed in Appendix 1603.D.1 to Annex 1603 of NAFTA.

The application should include a letter from the prospective employer which confirms that the applicant will perform the professional activity for the employer, states that the duration will be temporary but describes in sufficient detail the need for professional services and the job duties, salary and other essential terms; and describes how the applicant's educational and work experience confirm his or her professional status. The letter should also state and describe how the applicant complies with any state licensing or other requirements.

When admitted, the TN professional will be given an I-94 card indicating authorized status for one year. This period can be extended in one year increments without leaving the U.S. An extension may be requested on form I-129, filed at the Northern Service Center (regardless of where you live) or it may be requested by departing the U.S. prior to the first status expiration and reentering at the port of entry by presenting the above listed documents.

Procedures for Mexicans

There is currently an annual cap of 5,500 TNs from Mexico. A Mexican professional worker must have Form 9035, a labor condition application, or LAC, filed and approved by the Department of Labor as the first step. After approval of the LCA, he or she must file a Form I-129 petition with the Northern Service Center, accompanied by the approved labor condition application and a check for the proper filing fee. The I-129 must also be accompanied by the same documents described above for Canadian TN applications, except that the citizenship documents are of course Mexican.

Upon receipt of Form I-797, the approval notice, the Mexican TN applicant then applies at a U.S. consular post for a TN visa to present him or herself for admission to the U.S. Extensions are done by filing form I-129 at the Northern Service Center, like the initial application.

The advantages of the treaty professional procedure are that you avoid potentially long delays from filing a petition in the U.S. The main disadvantage is that professional workers using the TN instead of a standard H-1 visa must intend to return to Canada or Mexico when their work in the U.S. is finished, and receive only one-year period of status at a time. Therefore, if you plan to apply for a green card, you should get a standard H-1 visa, which does not have these restrictions. In addition, if you have a difficult case and you are denied entry as a treaty professional, there is no avenue of appeal. When a standard H-1 visa petition is denied, or if you apply for TN status extension or change of status by filing an application with the service center, you have the ability to appeal the decision through both INS and, eventually, the U.S. courts.

3. Treaty Traders and Treaty Investors

NAFTA allows Canadians to obtain E-1 and E-2 visas. Canadians wishing to get E-1 or E-2 status are treated exactly like persons of all other nationalities. This means that you must obtain an actual visa stamp in your passport before you can enter the U.S. with an E-1 or E-2 status. Therefore, you should follow all of the procedures discussed in Chapters 20 and 21. This is the only nonimmigrant category where a visa is required of Canadians.

D. Simplified Procedures for Students and Exchange Visitors

Canadians entering the U.S. as F-1 students, M-1 students or J-1 exchange visitors also have a simplified way of getting a status. First you must get an approved Certificate of Eligibility form. The Certificate of Eligibility for F-1 and M-1 students is Form I-20. For J-1 exchange visitors it is form IAP-66. These are described in Chapters 22 and 23.

Once you have a Certificate of Eligibility, you may go directly to a port of entry and present it to a U.S. immigra-

tion inspector together with proof of your Canadian citizenship. You should also have available evidence of how you will be supported financially while in the U.S. On showing these documents, you will be admitted as a student or exchange visitor. Your accompanying spouse and children will be admitted on showing proof of their family relationship to you. This requires presenting a marriage certificate for your spouse and long form birth certificates for your children.

When you enter the U.S., you will receive an I-94 card indicating your immigration status and giving the dates of the period for which you may remain in the country. Your stay will usually be for duration of status, marked "D/S" on the I-94 card. This means you can stay until your studies are completed. If you leave the U.S. before your status expires and want to return, you need only present the I-94 card and Certificate of Eligibility at the port of entry and you will be admitted again.

E. Pre-Flight Inspections

Another benefit Canadians enjoy is access to the procedure known as "preflight inspection." There are U.S. immigration offices located at most of the Canadian international airports. When Canadians fly to the U.S., they clear U.S. immigration and customs before boarding the plane. This service is considered to be a timesaving advantage.

There is a negative side to preflight inspection. In situations where a Canadian's eligibility to enter the U.S. is questionable, if the U.S. immigration inspector does not believe the Canadian traveler should be admitted, the inspector can prevent the Canadian from boarding the plane. Without preflight inspection, travelers to the U.S. can at least land on U.S. soil and are usually granted enough time in the country to stay and argue their case with INS. However, a new law punishes those individuals who arrive without the proper documentation and those who make a misrepresentation to an INS inspector, by making them inadmissible for a visa or to request entry for five years. Because of this you should be extremely cautious about presenting yourself for inspection. (See Chapters 14 and 25 for more details.) ∎

Directory of U.S Embassies & Consulates

(Updated August 1999)

Afghanistan
U.S. Embassy
Closed

Albania
U.S. Embassy
Rruga E. Labinoti 103
PSC 59 Box 100 (A)
APO AE 09624
Tirana
Telephone: 355-42-32875
Fax: 355-42-32222

Algeria
U.S. Embassy
4 Chemin Cheich Bachir
El-ibrahimi
B.P. Box 549 (Alger-Gare)
16000 Algiers
Telephone: 213-2-69-11-86
Fax: 213-2-69-39-79

Angola
U.S. Embassy
Consular Section
Rua Major Kanhangula
No. 132/135
Luanda
Telephone: 244-2-396-927
Fax: 244-2-390-515

Argentina
U.S. Embassy
4300 Colombia, 1425
Buenos Aires
Telephone: 777-453334
Fax: 777-4576

Armenia
U.S. Embassy
18 Marshal Bagramian St.
Yerevan
Telephone: 3742-52-46-61
Fax: 3742-15-15-50 (Mark for Consular Section)

Australia
U.S. Embassy
Moonah PL
Yaralumla, Canberra
ACT 2600
Telephone: 61-2-6214-5600
Fax: 61-2-6214-5970

U.S. Consulate (No visa services)
553 St. Kilda Road
South Melbourne, Victoria 3004
Telephone: 03-9526-5900
Fax: 03-9525-0769

U.S. Consulate
59th Floor
MLC Centre
19-29 Martin Place
Sydney, NSW 2000
Telephone: 61-2-9373-9188/9
Fax: 61-2-9373-9184

U.S. Consulate
16 St. George's Terrace
Perth, WA 6000
Telephone: 61-8-9231-9400
Fax: 61-8-9231-9444

Austria
U.S. Embassy
Gartenbaupromenade 2
A-1010 Vienna
Telephone: 313-39-0
Fax: 513 43 51

Azerbaijan
U.S. Embassy
Azadlig Prospekti 83
Baku
Telephone: 9-9412-98-03-35/6/7
Fax: 9-9412-98-37-55

Bahamas
U.S. Embassy
Mosmar Building
Queen Street
Nassau
Telephone: 809-322-1181
Fax: 809-356-0222

Bahrain
U.S. Embassy
Building 979
Road 3119
Zinj District
Manama
Telephone: 973-273-300
Fax: 973-275-418

Bangladesh
U.S. Embassy
Diplomatic Enclave
Madani Avenue
Baridhara
Dhaka, 1212
Telephone: 880-2-884700-22
Fax: 880-2-883744-22

Barbados
U.S. Embassy
P.O. Box 302
Bridgetown
Telephone: 246-431-0225
Fax: 246-431-0179

Belarus
U.S. Embassy
46 Starovilenskaya Ilitsa
Minsk
Telephone: 375-172-31-50-00
Fax: 375-172-34-78-53

Belgium
U.S. Embassy
27 Boulevard du Regent
B-1000 Brussels
Telephone: 32-2-508-2111
Fax: 32-2-511-2725

Belize
U.S. Embassy
Gabourel Lane & Hutson Streets
Belize City
Telephone: 501-2-77161/2/3
Fax: 501-2-30802

Benin
U.S. Embassy
Rue Caporal Anani Bernard
Cotonou
Telephone: 229-30-06-50
Fax: 229-30-14-39

Bermuda
U.S. Consulate
Crown Hill
16 Middle Road
Devonshire, DV03
Hamilton
Telephone: 441-295-1342
Fax: 441-295-1592

Bhutan
(See India)

Bolivia
U.S. Embassy
Ave. Arce No. 2780
La Paz
Telephone: 591-2-433812
Fax: 591-2-433710

Bosnia-Herzegovina
43 Ul. Dure Dakovica
Sarajevo
Telephone: 387-71-445-700
or 387-71-667-391
Fax: 387-71-659-722

Botswana
U.S. Embassy
P.O. Box 90
Gaborone
Telephone: 267-353-982
Fax: 267-356-947

Brazil
U.S. Embassy
Avenida das Nocoes
Quadra 801, Lote 3
70403-900
Brasilia, DF
Telephone: 55-61-321-7272
Fax: 55-61-225-9136

U.S. Consulate
Avenida Presidente Wilson, 147
Castelo 20030-020
Rio de Janeiro, RJ
Telephone: 55-21-292-7117
Fax: 55-21-220-0439

U.S. Consulate
Rua Padre Joao Manoel, 933
Cerqueira Cesar 01411-001
Sao Paulo, SP
Telephone: 55-11-881-6511
Fax: 55-11-852-5154

U.S. Consulate
Rua Goncalves Maia, 163
Boa Vista 50070-060
Recife, PE
Telephone: 55-81-421-2441
Fax: 55-81-231-1906

Brunei
U.S. Embassy
3rd Floor
Teck Guan Plaza
Jalan Sultan
Bandar Seri Begawan
Telephone: 673-2-229-670
Fax: 673-2-225-293

Bulgaria
U.S. Embassy
Consular Section
1 Kapitan Andreev Street
Sofia, 1421
Telephone: 395-2-963-12-50
Fax: 395-2-963-28-59

Burkina Faso
U.S. Embassy
01 B.P. 35
Ouagadougou
Telephone: 226-30-67-23
Fax: 226-30-38-90

Burma (Myanmar)
U.S. Embassy
581 Merchant Street
Rangoon
Telephone: 95-1-282-055
Fax: 95-1-280-409

Burundi
U.S. Embassy
B.P. 1720
Avenue des Etats-Unis
Bujumbura
Telephone: 257-22-29-86
Fax: 257-22-29-26

Cambodia
U.S. Embassy
16, Street 228
(between Streets 51 and 63)
Phnom Penh
Telephone: 885-23-216-436
Fax: 885-23-216-437

Cameroon
U.S. Embassy
Rue Nachtigal
B.P. 817
Yaounde
Telephone: 237-23-40-14
Fax: 237-23-07-53

Canada
U.S. Embassy
100 Wellington St
Ottawa K1P 5T1
Telephone: 613-238-5335
Fax: 613-238-5720

U.S. Consulate
615 Macleod Trail S.E.
Calgary, Alberta T2G 4T8
Telephone: 403-266-8962
Fax: 403-264-6630

U.S. Consulate
Suite 910, Cogswell Tower
Scotia Square
Halifax, NS B3J 3K1
Telephone: 902-429-2480
Fax: 902-423-6861

U.S. Consulate
P.O. Box 65
Postal Station
Desjardins, H5B 1G1
Telephone: 514-398-9695
Fax: 514-398-0973

U.S. Consulate
2 Place Terrasse Dufferin
Quebec City, Quebec G1R 4T9
Telephone: 418-692-2095
Fax: 418-692-4640

U.S. Consulate
360 University Ave.
Toronto, Ontario M5G 1S4
Telephone: 416-595-1700
Fax: 416-595-0051

U.S. Consulate
1095 West Pender St.
Vancouver, B.C. V6E 2M6
Telephone: 604-685-4311
Fax: 604-685-5285

Cape Verde
U.S. Embassy
Rua Abilio Macedo 81
C.P. 201
Praia
Telephone: 238-61-56-16/17
Fax: 238-61-13-55

Central African Republic
U.S. Embassy
Avenue David Dacko
Bangui
Telephone: 236-61-02-00
Fax: 236-61-44-94

Chad
U.S. Embassy
Ave. Felix Eboue
N'Djamena
Telephone: 235-51-70-09
Fax: 235-51-56-54

Chile
U.S. Embassy
Ave. Andres Bello 2800
Santiago
Telephone: 56-2-232-2600
Fax: 56-2-330-3710

China, Mainland
U.S. Embassy
2 Xiu Shui Dong Jie
Beijing, 100600
Telephone: 86-10-6532-3431
Fax: 86-10-6532-4153

U.S. Consulate
4 Lingshiguan Road
Section 4, Renmin Nanlu
Chengdu 610041
Telephone: 86-28-558-3992, 555-3119
Fax: 86-28-558-3520.

U.S. Consulate
No. 1 Shamian St. South
Shamian Island 200S1
Guangzhou, 510133
Telephone: 86-20-8188-8911
Fax: 86-20-8186-2341

U.S. Consulate
1469 Huai Hai Zhong Lu
Shanghai
Telephone: 86-21-6433-6880
Fax: 86-21-6433-4122

U.S. Consulate
52 14th Wei Road
Heping District, 110003
Shenyang
Telephone: 86-24-2322-1198
Fax: 86-24-2322-2374

China, Taiwan
American Institute in Taiwan
7 Lane 134
Hsin Yi Road
Section 3
Taipei
Telephone: 886-2-2709-2000
Fax: 886-2-2702-0908

American Institute in Taiwan
2 Chung Cheng 3rd Road,
5th Floor
Kaohsiung
Telephone: 886-7-224-0154
Fax: 886-7-223-8237

Colombia
U.S. Embassy
Calle 22D-BIS No. 47-51
Apartado Aero 3831
Bogota
Telephone: 57-1-315-0811
Fax: 57-1-315-2197

U.S. Consulate
Calle 77 Number 68-15
Barranquilla
Telephone: 95-353-0970
Fax: 95-353-5216

Comoro Islands
(See Mauritius)

Congo, Democratic Republic of the
(Formerly Zaire)
U.S. Embassy
Consular Section
Avenue d-Isiro
Mobil Building
Kinshasa
Telephone: 243-88-43609
Fax: 243-88-43605

Congo, Republic of
U.S. Embassy
(closed due to civil unrest)
Contact:
U.S. Embassy
Democratic Republic of Congo
310 Avenue des Aviateurs
Kinshasa
Telephone: 243-88-43608
Fax: 243-88-43605

Costa Rica
U.S. Embassy
Calle 120/Avenida 0
Pavas
San Jose
Telephone: 506-220-3939
Fax: 506-220-2305

Cote d'Ivoire
(Formerly Ivory Coast)
U.S. Embassy
5 Rue Jesse Owens
Abidjan
Telephone: 225-21-09-79
Fax: 225-22-32-59

Croatia
U.S. Embassy
Andrije Hebranga 2
Zagreb
Telephone: 385-1-455-55-00
Fax: 385-1-455-85-85

Cuba
U.S. Interest, Swiss Embassy
Calzada entre L & M
Vedado Seccion
Havana
Telephone: 53-7-33-4401/2/3
Fax: 53-7-33-3700

Cyprus
U.S. Embassy
Metochiou and Ploutarchou
Streets
Engomi, Nicosia
Telephone: 357-2-776-400
Fax: 357-2-776-841 or 780-944
http://
www.americanembassy.org.cy

U.S. Consulate
#6 Saran St
Lefkosa, Nicosia
Telephone: 90-392-225-2440

Czech Republic
U.S. Embassy
Trziste 15
11801 Prague
Telephone: 420-2-5732-0663
Fax: 420-2-5732-0614

Denmark
U.S. Embassy
Dag Hammarskjolds Alle 24
Copenhagen 2100
Telephone: 45-31-42-31-44
Fax: 45-35-43-02-23

Djibouti
U.S. Embassy
Plateau de Serpent
Blvd. Marechal Joffre
Djibouti
Telephone: 253-35-3995
Fax: 253-35-3940

Dominican Republic
U.S. Embassy
Consular Section
Calle Cesar Nicolas Penson &
Maximo Gomez
Santo Domingo
Telephone: 809-221-5030
Fax: 809-686-7437

Consular Agency
Calle Beller 51 #2
Puerto Plata
Telephone: 809-586-4202

Ecuador
U.S. Embassy
Avenida 12 de Octubre y
Avenida Patria
Quito
Telephone: 593-2-562-890
Fax: 593-2-502-052

U.S. Consulate
9 de Octubre y Garcia Moreno
Guayaquil
Telephone: 593-4-323-570
Fax: 593-4-324-558

Egypt
U.S. Embassy
8, Kamal El-Din Salah St.
Garden City
Cairo
Telephone: 20-2-357-2301
Fax: 20-2-357-2472
Email: cacairo@cairod.us-state.gov
Website: http://
www.usis.egnet.net

U.S. Consulate
3 El Faroana Street
Alexandria
Telephone: 20-3-472-1009
Fax: 20-3-483-3811

El Salvador
U.S. Embassy
Final Blvd. Santa Elena
Urbanizacion Santa Elena
Antiguo Cuscatlan
San Salvador
Telephone: 503-278-4444
Fax: 503-278-6011

Equatorial Guinea
Contact: U.S. Embassy in
Cameroon
B.P. 817
Yaounde
Telephone: 237-23-40-14
Fax: 237-23-07-53

Eritrea
U.S. Embassy
Franklin D. Roosevelt St.
P.O. Box 211
Asmara
Telephone: 291-1-12-00-04
Fax: 291-1-12-75-84

Estonia
U.S. Embassy
Kentmanni 20, EE 0001
Tallinn
Telephone: 372-6-312-021
or 646-6521
Fax: 372-6-312-025
Website: http://www.estnet.ee/
usislib

Ethiopia
U.S. Embassy
Entoto Street
Addis Ababa
Telephone: 251-1-550-666
Fax: 251-1-551-094

Fiji
U.S. Embassy
31 Loftus Street
Suva, Fiji
Telephone: 679-314-466
Fax: 679-300-081

Finland
U.S. Embassy
Itainen Puistotie 14A
Helsinki
Telephone: 358-9-171931
Fax: 358-9-652057
Email: consular@usembassy.fi
Web page: http://
www.usembassy.fi

France
U.S. Embassy
Consular Section
2, rue St. Florentin
75001 Paris
Telephone: 33-1-4312-22-22
Fax: 33-1-4261-6140
Website: http://www.amb-usa.fr

U.S. Consulate
Boulevard Paul Peytral 12
13086 Marseille
Telephone: 33-4-91-54-92-00
Fax: 33-4-91-55-09-47

U.S. Consulate
5 Avenue d'Alsace
67082 Strasbourg
Telephone: 33-3-88-35-31-04
Fax: 33-3-88-24-06-95

Gabon
U.S. Embassy
Blvd. de la Mer
Libreville
Telephone: 241-762-003/4
Fax: 241-745-507

The Gambia
U.S. Embassy
Fajara East-Kairaba Ave.
Banjul
Telephone: 220-392-856
Fax: 220-392-475

Georgia
U.S. Embassy
25 Atoneli Street
Tbilisi
Telephone: 995-3298-9967/68
Fax: 995-3293-3759

Germany
U.S. Embassy
Consular Section
Clayallee 170
Berlin
Telephone: 49-30-832-9233
Fax: 49-30-831-4926

U.S. Embassy
Deichmanns Aue
53170 Bonn
Telephone: 49-228-3391
Fax: 49-228-332-712

U.S. Consulate
Kennedydamm 15-17
40476 Dusseldorf
Telephone: 49-211-470-6123
Fax: 49-211-431-448

U.S. Consulate
Siesmayerstrasse 21
60323 Frankfurt
Telephone: 49-69-75350
Fax: 49-69-7535-2304

U.S. Consulate
Alsterufer 27/28
20354 Hamburg
Telephone: 49-40-41171351
Fax: 49-40-443-004

U.S. Consulate
Wilhelm-Seyfferth-Strasse 4
04107 Leipzig
Telephone: 49-341-213-8418
Fax: 49-341-213-8417

U.S. Consulate
Koeniginstrasse 5
80539 Muenchen
Telephone: 49-89-288-8722
Fax: 49-89-280-9998
Website: http://
www.usembassy.de (or http://
www.us-botschaft.de)

Ghana
U.S. Embassy
Consular Section
10th and 11th Lanes
Near Danquah Circle, OSU
Accra
Telephone: 233-21-77-66-01/2
Fax: 233-21-77-57-47

Greece
U.S. Embassy
91 Vasilissis Sophias Blvd.
10160 Athens
Telephone: 30-1-721-2951
Fax: 30-1-725-3025

U.S. Consulate
Plateia Commercial Center
43 Tsimiski Street, 7th Floor
54623 Thessaloniki
Telephone: 30-31-242-905

Email: consul@ibm.net (Athens) or cons@hol.gr
(Thessaloniki)
Website http://
www.usisathens.gr.

Grenada
U.S. Embassy
Green Building
Lance aux Epines
P.O. Box 54
St. Georges
Telephone: 473044401173/4/
5/6
Fax: 473-444-4820
Email:
usemb_gd@caribsurf.com

Guatemala
U.S. Embassy
7-01 Avenida de la Reforma
Zone 10
Guatemala City
Telephone: 502-331-1541
Fax: 502-2-32-04-95

Guinea
U.S. Embassy
2nd Blvd. and 9th Ave.
Conakry
Telephone: 224-41-15-20/1/3
Fax: 224-41-15-22

Guinea-Bissau
U.S. Embassy temporarily
closed

Contact:
U.S. Embassy
Avenue Jean XXIII
Dakar, Senegal
Telephone: 221-8-23-42-96

Guyana
U.S. Embassy
99-100 Duke St.
Kingston, Georgetown
Telephone: 592-2-54900-9
Fax: 592-2-58497

Haiti
U.S. Embassy
Consular Section
Rue Oswald Durand
Telephone: 509-223-7011
Fax: 509-223-1641.

The Holy See
U.S. Embassy
Villa Domiziana
Via Delle Terme Deciane 26
00153 Rome, Italy
Telephone: 396-46741
Fax: 396-575-8346
or 396-573-0682

Honduras
U.S. Embassy
Avenida La Tegucigalpa
Tegucigalpa
Telephone: 504-236-9320
Fax: 504-238-4357
Website: http://www.usia.gov/
abtusia/posts/HO1/
wwwhmain.html

Hong Kong
U.S. Consulate
26 Garden Road
Central, Hong Kong
Telephone: 852-2523-9011
Fax: 852-2845-4845
Website: http://
www.usconsulate.org.hk

Hungary
U.S. Embassy
V. Szabadsag Ter 12
Budapest
Telephone: 36-1-267-4400
Fax: 36-1-269-9326

Iceland
U.S. Embassy
Laufasvegur 21
Reykjavik
Telephone: 354-562-9100
Fax: 354-562-9118

India
U.S. Embassy
Shanti Path
Chanakyapuri 110021
New Delhi
Telephone: 91-11-611-3033
Fax: 91-11-419-0017

U.S. Consulate
Lincoln House
78 Bhulabhai Desai Rd.
Mumbai 400026
Telephone: 91-22-363-3611
Fax: 91-22-363-0350

U.S. Consulate
5/1 Ho Chi Minh Sarani
Calcutta 700071
Telephone: 91-33-282-3611-15
Fax: 91-33-242-2335

U.S. Consulate
220 Mount Road
600006 Chennai (Madras)
Telephone: 91-44-827-3040
Fax: 91-44-825-0204
Website: http://www.usia.gov/
posts/delhi.html

Indonesia
U.S. Embassy
Medan Merdeka Selatan 5
Jakarta
Telephone: 62-21-344-2211
Fax: 62-21-386-2259

U.S. Consular Agency
Jalan hayam Wuruk 188
Denpasar
Bali
Telephone: 62-361-233-605
Fax: 62-361-222-426
Email:
tabuh@denpasar.wasantara.net.id

U.S. Consulate
Jalan Raya Dr. Sutomo 33
Surabaya
Telephone: 62-31-567-2287/8
Fax: 62-31-567-4492
Email: amconsby@rad.net.id
Website: http://
www.usembassyjakarta.org

Iran
No Embassy or Consular Services

Iraq
No Embassy or Consular Services

Ireland
U.S. Embassy
42 Elgin Road
Ballsbridge
Dublin
Telephone: 353-1-668-7122
Fax: 353-1-668-9946
Website: http://www.indigo.ie/
usembassy-usis/

Israel
U.S. Embassy
71 Hayarkon St.
Tel Aviv
Telephone: 972-3-519-7575
Fax: 972-3-516-0315
Email: amctelaviv@state.gov
Website: http://www.usis-
israel.org.il/publish/
citserv.htm.

U.S. Consulate
Consular Section
27 Nablus Road
Jerusalem
Telephone: 972-22622-7000
Fax: 972-2-627-2233
Website: http://www.usis-
jerusalem.org/visas.htm

Italy
U.S. Embassy
Via Veneto 119/A
00187 Rome
Telephone: 39-06-46741
Fax: 39-06-4674-2217
Website: http://www.usis.it

U.S. Consulate
Via Principe Amedeo 2/10
20121 Milano
Telephone: 39-02-290-351
Fax: 39-02-290-35-273

U.S. Consulate
Piazza della Repubblica
80122 Naples
Telephone: 39-081-583-8111
Fax: 39-081-761-1804

U.S. Consulate
Lungarno Amerigo Vespucci
38
Florence 50123
Telephone: 39-055-239-8276/
7/8/9
Fax: 39-055-284-088

U.S. Consular Agents
Via Dante 2
Genoa
Telephone: 39-010-584-492
Fax: 39-010-553-3033

Via Vaccarini 1
Palermo
Telephone: 39-091-305-857
Fax: 39-091-625-6026

Via Roma 15
Trieste 34132
Telephone: 39-0-040-660-177
Fax: 39-0040-631-240

Ivory Coast
(See Cote d'Ivoire)

Jamaica
U.S. Embassy
Consular Section
16 Oxford Road
Kingston
Telephone: 876-935-6044
Fax: 876-935-6018

U.S. Consulate
St. James Place, 2nd Floor
Gloucester Ave.
Montego Bay
Telephone: 876-952-0160
Fax: 876-952-5050

Japan
U.S. Embassy
10-5 Akasaka 1-chome
Minato-ku
107 Tokyo
Telephone: 81-3-3224-5000
Fax: 81-3-3505-1862

U.S. Consulate
2564 Nishihara
Urasoe City, Okinawa 90121
Telephone: 81-98-876-4211
Fax: 81-98-876-4243

U.S. Consulate
11-5 Nishitenma 2-chome
Kita-Ku
Osaka 530
Telephone: 81-6-315-5900
Fax: 81-6-315-5930

U.S. Consulate
5-26 Ohori 2-chome, Chuo-ku
Fukuoka 810
Telephone: 81-92-751-9331
Fax: 81-92-713-9222

U.S. Consulate
Nishiki SIS Building 6F 10-33
Nishiki 3-chome
Nagoya 460
Telephone: 81-52-203-4011
Fax: 81-52-201-4612

U.S. Consulate
Kita I-Jo
Nishi 28-chome
Chuo-ku
Sapporo 061
Telephone: 81-11-641-1115/7
Fax: 81-11-643-1283

Jordan
U.S. Embassy
Box 354
Amman 11118
Telephone: 962-6-592-0101
Fax: 962-6-592-4102
Website: http://
www.usembassy-amman.org.jo

Kazakhstan
U.S. Embassy
99/97 Furmanova St.
Almaty
Republic of Kazakhstan
480012
Telephone: 7-3272-63-39-05
Fax: 7-3272-63-38-83

Kenya
U.S. Embassy
USAID Building
The Crescent
Nairobi
Telephone: 254-2-583-586
Fax: 254-2-340838

Kiribati
See Marshall Islands

Korea
U.S. Embassy
82 Sejong-Ro
Chongro-Ku
Seoul
Telephone: 82-2-397-4114
Fax: 82-2-738-8845

Kuwait
U.S. Embassy
Al-Masjid Al-Aqsa Street
Plot 14, Block 14
Bayan
Telephone: 965-539-5307/8
Fax: 965-538-0282
Website: http://
www.kuwait.net/~usiskwt/
wwwhusis.htm

Kyrgyzstan
U.S. Embassy
Erkindik Prospect #66
Bishkek 720002
Telephone: 7-3312-22-32-89
Fax: 7-3312-22-35-51

Laos
U.S. Embassy
Rue Bartholonie
B.P. 114
Vientiane
Telephone: 856-21-212-581
Fax: 856-21-212-584

Latvia
U.S. Embassy
Raina Boulevard 7, LV-1510
Riga
Telephone: 371-2-721-0005
Fax: 371-2-782-0047

Lebanon
U.S. Embassy
P.O. Box 70-840
Antelias
Beirut
Telephone: 961-1-402-200
Fax: 961-1-407-112

Lesotho
U.S. Embassy
P.O. Box 333
254 Kingsway
Maseru West 100
Telephone: 266-312-666
Fax: 266-310-116

Liberia
U.S. Embassy
111 United Nations Drive
Mamba Point
Monrovia
Telephone: 231-226-370
Fax: 231-226-154

Lithuania
U.S. Embassy
Akmenu 6
Vilnius 2600
Telephone: 370-2-223-031
Fax: 370-670-6084

Luxembourg
U.S. Embassy
22 Blvd Emmanuel-Servais
2535 Luxembourg
Telephone: 352-46-01-23
Fax: 352-461401

Macau
See Hong Kong

Macedonia
(Former Yugoslav Republic)

U.S. Embassy
Ilindenska BB
91000 Skopje
Telephone: 389-91-116-180
Fax: 389-91-117-103

Madagascar
U.S. Embassy
14 and 16 Rue Raintovo
Antsahavola
Antananarivo
Telephone: 261-20-22-212-57
Fax: 2612-20-22-345-39

Malawi
U.S. Embassy
Area 40
City Center
P.O. Box 30016
Lilongwe
Telephone: 265-783-166
Fax: 265-780-471

Malaysia
U.S. Embassy
376 Jalan Tun Razak
50400 Kuala Lumpur
Telephone: 603-248-9011
Fax: 603-248-5801
Website: http://www.jaring.my/
usiskl/embassy/klcons.html

Mali
U.S. Embassy
Rue Rochester NY and Rue
Mohamed V, B.P.34
Bamako
Telephone: 223-22-38-33
Fax: 223-22-37-12
Website: http://
www.usa.org.ml

Malta
U.S. Embassy
3rd Floor, Development House
St. Anne Street
Floriana, Valletta
Telephone: 356-235-960
Fax: 356-243-229
Email:
U.S.Embassy@kemmunet.net.mt

Marshall Islands
U.S. Embassy
P.O. Box 1379
Majuro, Republic of the
Marshall Islands, 96960-1379
Telephone: 692-247-4011
Fax: 692-247-4012

Mauritania
U.S. Embassy
B.P. 222
Nouakchott
Telephone: 222-25-26-60
Fax: 222-25-15-92

Mauritius
U.S. Embassy
Rogers Building, 4th Floor
John F. Kennedy Street
Port Louis
Telephone: 230-208-9764/9
Fax: 230-208-9534
Website: http://usis.intnet.mu
Email: usembass@intnet.mu.

Mexico
U.S. Embassy
Paseo de la Reforma 305
Mexico City
Telephone: 525-5209-9100
Fax: 525-551-9980

U.S. Consulate
924 Avenue Lopez Mateos
Ciudad Juarez
Telephone: 52-16-11300
Fax: 52-16-169056

U.S. Consulate
Progreso 175
Guadalajara, Jalisco, 44100
Telephone: 52-3-825-2998
Fax: 52-3-826-6549

U.S. Consulate
Monterrey 141 Pre;
Hermosillo 83260, Sonora
Telephone: 52-62-17-2375
Fax: 52-62-17-2578

U.S. Consulate
Tapachula 96
Tijuana, B.C., 22420
Telephone: 52-66-81-7400
Fax: 52-66-81-8016

U.S. Consulate
Paseo Montejo 453
Merida, Yucatan, 97000
Telephone: 52-99-25-5011
Fax: 52-99-25-6219

U.S. Consulate
Avenida Constitucion
411 Poniente
Monterrey, N.L.
Telephone: 52-8-345-2120
Fax: 52-8-342-0177

U.S. Consulate
Calle Allende 3330
Col. Jardin
88260 Nuevo Laredo, Tamps.
Telephone: 52-87-14-0152
Fax: 52-87-14-7984

U.S. Consulate
Ave. Primera 2002
87330 Matamoros, Tamps.
Telephone: 52-88-12-44-02
Fax: 52-88-12-21-71

Micronesia
U.S. Embassy
P.O. Box 1286
Kasalehlie Street
Kolonia
Telephone: 691-320-2187
Fax: 691-320-2186

Moldova
U.S. Embassy
Strada Alexei Mateevicie #103
277014 Chisinau
Telephone: 373-2-23-37-72
Fax: 373-223-30-44

Mongolia
U.S. Embassy
Micro Region 11
Big Ring Road
Ulaanbaatar
Telephone: 976-1-329-095
Fax: 976-1-320-776

Morocco
U.S. Embassy
2 Ave de Marrakech
Rabat
Telephone: 212-7-76-2265
Fax: 212-7-76-5621

U.S. Consulate
8 Blvd. Moulay Youssef
Casablanca
Telephone: 212-2-264-550
Fax: 212-2-204-127

Mozambique
U.S. Embassy
193 Avenida Kenneth Kaunda
Maputo
Telephone: 258-1-49-27-97
Fax: 258-1-49-01-14

Namibia
U.S. Embassy
14 Lossen St.
Private Bag 12029
Ausspannplatz
Windhoek
Telephone: 264-61-22-1601
Fax: 264-61-22-9792

Nepal
U.S. Embassy
Pani Pokhari
Kathmandu
Telephone: 977-1-411-179
Fax: 977-1-419-963
Website: http://www.south-asia.com/usa

Netherlands
U.S. Embassy
Lange Voohout 102
2514 EJ
The Hague
Telephone: 31-70-310-9209
Fax: 31-70-361-4688

U.S. Consulate
Museumplein 19
Amsterdam
Telephone: 31-20-5755-309
Fax: 31-20-5755-310

Netherlands Antilles
U.S. Consulate
J.B. Gorsiraweg #1
Willemstad
Curacao
Telephone: 599-9-461-3066
Fax: 599-9-461-6489
Email: ConGenCura@guestwpoa.us-state.gov

New Zealand
U.S. Embassy
29 Fitzherbert Ter.
Thorndon
Wellington
Telephone: 64-4-472-2068
Fax: 64-4-478-1701

U.S. Consulate
4th Floor Yorkshire
General Bldg.
Shortland and O'Connel Sts.
Auckland
Telephone: 64-9-303-2724
Fax: 64-9-379-3722

Nicaragua
U.S. Embassy
Km. 4-1/2 Carretera Sur
Managua
Telephone: 505-268-0123
Fax: 505-2-669074

Niger
U.S. Embassy
Rue Des Ambassades
B.P. 11201
Niamey
Telephone: 227-72-26-61/4
Fax: 227-73-31-67, 72-31-46
Email: usemb@intent.ne

Nigeria
U.S. Embassy
2 Eleke Crescent
Victoria Island
Lagos
Telephone: 234-1-261-0097
Fax: 234-1-261-0257
Email: lagoscons@lagoswpoa.us-state.gov

U.S. Embassy Office
9 Mambilla
Maitama District
Abuja
Telephone: 234-9-523-0916

Norway
U.S. Embassy
Drammensveien 18
Oslo 2
Telephone: 47-22-44-85-50
Fax: 47-22-56-27-51

Oman
U.S. Embassy
P.O. Box 202, Code 15
Mediuat Al-Sultan Qaboos
Muscat
Telephone: 968-698-989
Fax: 968-699-189

Pakistan
U.S. Embassy
Diplomatic Enclave
Ramna 5
Islamabad
Telephone: 92-51-823-480
Fax: 92-51-276-427

U.S. Consulate
8 Abdullah Haroon Rd
Karachi
Telephone: 92-21-568-5170
Fax: 92-21-568-3089

U.S. Consulate
50 Empress Road
Lahore
Telephone: 92-42-636-5530
Fax: 92-42-636-5177

U.S. Consulate
11 Hospital Road
Peshawar
Telephone: 92-521-279801
Fax: 92-521-276712

Palau
P.O. Box 6028
Koror, 96940
Telephone: 680-488-2920
Fax: 680-488-2911

Panama
U.S. Embassy
Calle 37, Avenida Balboa
Apartado
6959 Panama City
Telephone: 507-227-1777
Fax: 507-227-1964

Papua New Guinea
U.S. Embassy
Douglas St.
Port Moresby
Telephone: 675-321-1455
Fax: 675-321-1593

Paraguay
U.S. Embassy
1776 Mariscal Lopez Ave.
Asuncion
Telephone: 595-21-213-715
Fax: 595-21-213-728

Peru
U.S. Embassy
Avenida Encalada
Cuadra 17
Surco, Lima
Telephone: 51-1-434-3000
Fax: 51-1-434-3037

Philippines
U.S. Embassy
1201 Roxas Blvd.
Manila
Telephone: 63-2-523-1001
Fax: 63-2-522-4361

U.S. Consulate
3rd Floor
PCI Bank
Gorordo Avenue
Lahug, Cebu City
Telephone: 63-32-231-1261
Fax: 63-32-310-174

Poland
U.S. Embassy
Aleje Ujazdowskie 29/31
Warsaw 00504
Telephone: 48-22-628-3041
Fax: 48-22-628-8298

U.S. Consulate
Ulica Stolarska 9
31043 Krakow
Telephone: 48-12-423-2044
Fax: 48-12-421-8212

Portugal
U.S. Embassy
Avenida das Forcas Armadas
1600 Lisbon
Telephone: 351-1-727-3300
Fax: 351-1-726-9109

U.S. Consulate
Avenida D. Henrique
Ponta Delgada, Sao Miguel
Azores
Telephone: 351-96-22216/7/8/9
Fax: 351-96-27216

Qatar
U.S. Embassy
149 Ali Bin Ahmed St.
Fariq Bin Omran
Doha
Telephone: 974-864701
Fax: 974-861-669

Romania
U.S. Embassy
Strada Tudor Arghezi 7-9
Bucharest
Telephone: 40-1-210-40-42
Fax: 40-1-210-0395

Russia
U.S. Embassy
Novinskiy Bul'var 19/23
Moscow 121099
Telephone: 7-095-252-2451
Fax 7-095-956-4261

U.S. Consulate
Ulitsa/Furshtadskaya 15
St. Petersburg
Telephone: 7-812-275-1701
Fax: 7-812-110-7022

U.S. Consulate
Ulitsa Pushkinskaya 32
Vladivostok
Telephone: 7-4232-268-458
Fax: 7-4232-300-091

Ulitsa Gogolya 15a, 4th floor
Yekaterinburg
Telephone: 7-3432-564-619
Fax: 7-3432-564-515

Rwanda
U.S. Embassy
Blvd de la Revolution
B.P. 28
Kigali
Telephone: 250-75601/2
Fax: 250-72128

Samoa
U.S. Embassy
John Williams Building,
5th floor
Beach Road
Apia
Telephone: 685-21-631
Fax: 685-22-030

Saudi Arabia
U.S. Embassy
Collector Road M
Riyadh Diplomatic Quarter
Riyadh
Telephone: 966-1-488-3800
Fax: 966-1-488-7275

U.S. Consulate
Between Aramco Headquarters
& Dhahran Int'l Airport
Dhahran
Telephone: 966-3-891-3200
Fax: 933-3-891-6816

U.S. Consulate
Palestine Rd.
Ruwais
Jeddah
Telephone: 966-2-667-0080
Fax: 966-2-669-3078

Senegal
U.S. Embassy
B.P. 49
Avenue Jean XXIII
Dakar
Telephone: 221-823-42-96
Fax: 221-822-29-91

Serbia-Montenegro
U.S. Embassy
Kneza Milosa 50
11000 Belgrade
Telephone: 381-11-645-655
Fax: 381-11-644-053

Seychelles
(See Mauritius)

Sierra Leone
U.S. Embassy
Walpole & Siaka Stevens Sts.
Freetown
Telephone: 232-22-226-481
Fax: 232-22-225-471

Singapore
U.S. Embassy
27 Napier Road
Singapore 258508
Telephone: 65-476-9100
Fax: 65-476-9340

Slovak Republic
U.S. Embassy
Hviezdoslavovo Namestie 4
81102 Bratislava
Telephone: 421-7-5443-3338
Fax: 421-7-5443-0096

Slovenia
U.S. Embassy
Box 254
Prazakova 4
1000 Ljubljana
Telephone: 386-61-301-427
Fax: 386-61-301-401

South Africa
U.S. Embassy
877 Pretorius St.
Pretoria
Telephone: 27-12-342-1048
Fax: 27-12-342-2244

U.S. Consulate
1 River Street
Killarney
Johannesburg
Telephone: 27-11-646-6900/
09
Fax: 27-11-646-6916

U.S. Consulate
7th Floor
Monte Carlo Bldg.
Heerengracht, Foreshore
Cape Town
Telephone: 27-21-21-4280
Fax: 27-21-25-3014

U.S. Consulate
Durban Bay House, 29th Floor
333 Smith Street
Durban 4000
Telephone: 27-31-304-4737
Fax: 27-31-301-0265

South Korea
(See Korea)

Spain
U.S. Embassy
Serrano 75
Madrid 28006
Telephone: 34-91-577-4000
Fax: 34-91-587-2266
Website: http://www.embusa.es
U.S. Consulate
Po. Reina Elisenda de
Montacada 23
Barcelona 08034
Telephone: 34-93-280-2227
Fax: 34-93-205-5206

Sri Lanka
U.S. Embassy
210 Galle Rd.
Colombo 3
Telephone: 94-1-448-007
Fax: 94-1-437-345

Sudan
U.S. Embassy
(Temporarily Closed)

Suriname
U.S. Embassy
Dr. Sophie Redmondstraat 129
Paramaribo
Telephone: 597-477-881
Fax: 597-477-42800

Swaziland
U.S. Embassy
Central Bank Building
P.O. Box 199, Warner Street
Mbabane
Telephone: 268-40-46441/5
Fax: 268-40-45959

Sweden
U.S. Embassy
Strandvagen 101
Stockholm
Telephone: 46-8-783-5300
Fax: 46-8-661-1964

Switzerland
U.S. Embassy
Jubilaeumstrasse 93
3001 Bern
Telephone: 41-31-357-7011
Fax: 41-31-357-7344

U.S. Consulate
American Center of Geneva
World Trade Center
IBC-Building
29 Rte de Pre-Bois
Geneva
Telephone: 41-22-749-1605
Fax: 41-22-749-1630

Syria
U.S. Embassy
Abu Roumaneh
Al Mansur St. No. 2
Damascus
Telephone: 963-11-333-2814
Fax: 963-11-331-9678

Tajikistan
U.S. Embassy (Temporarily
Closed)
Contact:
U.S. Embassy
99/97A Furmanov Street
Almaty, Kazakhstan
Telephone: 7-3272-63-39-05
Fax: 7-3272-63-38-83

Tanzania
U.S. Embassy
140 Msese Road
Kinondoni District
P.O. Box 9123
Dar es Salaam
Telephone: 255-51-666010
Fax: 255-51-666701

Thailand
U.S. Embassy
Consular Section
95 Wireless Rd.
Bangkok
Telephone: 66-2-205-4000
Fax: 66-2-205-4103
Website: http://www.usa.or.th/
embassy/embassyindex.htm
U.S. Consulate
Widchayanond Rd.
Chiang Mai
Telephone: 66-53-252-629
Fax: 66-53-252-633
Website: http://www.usa.or.th/
consulcm/consulcm.htm

Togo
U.S. Embassy
Rue Pelletier Caventou &
Rue Vauban
Lome
Telephone: 228-21-29-91
Fax: 228-21-79-52

Trinidad and Tobago
U.S. Embassy
15 Queens Park West
Port of Spain
Telephone: 868-622-6371
Fax: 809-628-5462

Tunisia
U.S. Embassy
144 Ave. de la Liberte
1002 Tunis-Belvedere
Telephone: 216-1-782-566
Fax: 216-1-789-719

Turkey
U.S. Embassy
110 Ataturk Blvd.
Kavaklidere
Ankara 06100
Telephone: 90-312-468-6110
Fax: 90-312-468-6131

U.S. Consulate
Ataturk Caddesi/Vali Yolu
Adana
Telephone: 90-322-453-9106
Fax: 90-322-457-6591

U.S. Consulate
104-108 Mesrutiyet Cadesi
Tepebasi
Istanbul
Telephone: 90-212-251-3602
Fax: 90-212-251-3218

Turkmenistan
U.S. Embassy
9 Pushkin Street
Ashgabat
Telephone: 9-9312-51-13-06
Fax: 9-9312-51-13-05

Uganda
U.S. Embassy
10-12 Parliament Avenue
Kampala
Telephone: 256-41-259792/3/5
Fax: 256-41-259794

Ukraine
U.S. Embassy
Vulitsa Yuria Kotsubinskoho
10
254053 Kiev 53
Telephone: 380-44-246-9750
Fax: 380-44-244-7350
Website: http://
www.usemb.kiev.ua

United Arab Emirates
U.S. Embassy
Al-Sudan St.
Abu Dhabi
Telephone: 971-2-436-691
Fax: 971-2-435-786

U.S. Consulate
Dubai International Trade Ctr
P.O. Box 9343
Dubai
Telephone: 971-2-314-043
Fax: 971-2-434-771

United Kingdom
U.S. Embassy
24 Grosvenor Square
London, W1A 1AE
Telephone: 44-171-499-9000
Fax: 44-171-409-1637

U.S. Consulate
Queen's House
14 Queen Street
Belfast, Northern Ireland, BT1
6EQ
Telephone: 44-1232-328-239
Fax: 44-1232-248-482

U.S. Consulate
3 Regent Terrace
Edinburgh, Scotland
Telephone: 44-131-556-8351
Fax: 44-131-557-6023

Uruguay
U.S. Embassy
Lauro Muller 1776
Montevideo 11100
Telephone: 598-2-203-6061
Fax: 592-2-408-8611

Uzbekistan
U.S. Consulate
82 Ulitsa Chilanzarskaya
Tashkent 700115
Telephone: 7-3712-77-22-31

Vanuatu
See Papua New Guinea

Venezuela
U.S. Embassy
Calle F con Calle Suapure
Colinas de Valle Arriba
Caracas 1060
Telephone: 58-2-975-9998
Fax: 58-2-975-8991

Vietnam
U.S. Embassy
7 Lang Ha Road
Ba Dinh District
Hanoi
Telephone: 84-4-843-1500
Fax: 84-4-835-0484

U.S. Consulate
51 Nguyen Dinh Chieu
District 3
Ho Chi Minh City
Telephone: 84-8-822-9433
Fax: 84-8-822-9434

(Tourist and Immigrant visas
handled by the Orderly Departure Program at the U.S. Embassy in Bangkok, Thailand)

Western Samoa
U.S. Embassy
P.O. Box 3430
Apia
Telephone: 685-21-631
Fax: 685-22-030

Yemen, Republic of
U.S. Embassy
Dhahr Himyar Zone
Sheraton Hotel District
Sanaa
Telephone: 967-1-238-843/52
Fax: 967-1- 251-563

Zaire
(See Congo, Democratic
Republic of the)

Zambia
U.S. Embassy
Independence & United
Nations Avenues
Lusaka
Telephone: 260-1-250-955
Fax: 260-1-252-225

Zimbabwe
U.S. Embassy
172 Herbert Chitepo Ave.
Harare
Telephone: 263-4-794-521
Fax: 263-4-796-488

∎

II

Directory of INS and DOL Offices

INS Central Office

IImmigration & Naturalization Service
Justice Department
425 Eye St. NW
Washington, DC 20536
Information: 202-514-2648
Form Requests: 800-870-3676
Fax: 202-514-3296

INS Regional Offices

CALIFORNIA SERVICE CENTER

Immigration & Naturalization Service
24000 Avila Road
P.O. Box 30080
Laguna Niguel, CA 92677-8080
Telephone: 949-360-2995
Fax: 714-306-3081

NEBRASKA SERVICE CENTER

Immigration & Naturalization Service
850 S Street
Lincoln, NE 68508
Telephone: 402-437-5218

TEXAS SERVICE CENTER

Immigration & Naturalization Service
Room 2300
7701 N. Stemmons Freeway
Dallas, TX 75247
Telephone: 214-767-7020
Fax: 214-767-7477

VERMONT SERVICE CENTER

Immigration & Naturalization Service
75 Lower Weldon St.
St. Albans, VT 05479-0001
Telephone: 802-660-5000
Fax: 802-660-5114

INS District Offices

Anchorage, Alaska
620 E. 10th Avenue
Suite 102
Anchorage, AK
907-271-4953

Atlanta, Georgia
77 Forsythe Street, SW
Room G-85
Atlanta, GA 30303-3427
404-331-5158

Baltimore, Maryland
100 S. Charles St.
Baltimore, MD 21201-8628
410-962-2065

Boston, Massachusetts
John F. Kennedy Federal Bldg.
Government Center, Room 1700
Boston, MA 02203-0701
617-565-3879

Buffalo, New York
Federal Center
130 Delaware Ave.
Buffalo, NY 14202-2404
716-849-6760

Chicago, Illinois
10 W. Jackson St., Rm. 610
Chicago, IL 60604
312-385-1900

Cleveland, Ohio
1240 E. 9th St., Room 1917
Cleveland, OH 44199-2085
800-375-5283

Dallas, Texas
8101 N. Stemmons Freeway
Dallas, TX 75247
214-905-5800

Denver, Colorado
4730 Paris Street
Denver, CO 80239
303-371-0986

Detroit, Michigan
333 Mount Elliott St.
Detroit, MI 48207-4381
313-259-8560

El Paso, Texas
1545 Hawkins Blvd.
El Paso, TX 79925
915-225-1745

Harlingen, Texas
2102 Teege Road
Harlingen, TX 78550
956-427-8592

Helena, Montana
2800 Skyway Drive
Helena, MT 59601
406-449-5220

Honolulu, Hawaii
595 Ala Moana Blvd.
Honolulu, HI 96813
808-532-3721

Houston, Texas
126 Northpoint
Houston, TX 77060
281-774-4610

Kansas City, Missouri
9747 North Conant Ave.
Kansas City, MO 64153
816-891-0684

Los Angeles, California
300 N. Los Angeles Street
Los Angeles, CA 90012
213-894-0528

Miami, Florida
7880 Biscayne Blvd.
Miami, FL 33138-4797
305-536-5741

New Orleans, Louisiana
701 Loyola Avenue
Room T-8011
New Orleans, LA 70113-1912
504-589-6533

New York, New York
Jacob K. Javits Federal Building
26 Federal Plaza
New York, NY 10278-0127
212-264-5650

Newark, New Jersey
Federal Building
970 Broad Street
Newark, NJ 07102-2506
973-645-4400

Omaha, Nebraska
3736 S. 132nd Street
Omaha, NE 68144
402-697-0049

Philadelphia, Pennsylvania
1600 Callowhill St.
Philadelphia, PA 19130-4106
800-375-5283

Phoenix, Arizona
2035 N. Central Ave.
Phoenix, AZ 85004
602-379-3122

Portland, Maine
176 Gannett Dr.
So. Portland, ME 04106-6909
207-780-3352

Portland, Oregon
Federal Building
511 N.W. Broadway
Portland, OR 97209
503-326-3006

St. Paul, Minnesota
2901 Metro Drive, Suite 100
Bloomington, MN 55425
612-313-9001

San Antonio, Texas
8940 Four Winds
San Antonio, TX 78230
210-967-7109

San Diego, California
880 Front Street
San Diego, CA 92101
619-557-5570

San Francisco, California
Appraisers Building
630 Sansome Street
San Francisco, CA 94111
415-705-4411

San Juan, Puerto Rico
Carlos E. Chardon Street
Room 359
Hato Rey, PR 00918
787-766-5000

Seattle, Washington
815 Airport Way South
Seattle, WA 98134
206-553-0070

Washington, D.C.
4420 N. Fairfax Drive
Arlington, VA 22003-1611
202-307-1501

Regional Department of Labor Offices

Region	States
Atlanta Atlanta Federal Center Room 6M12 61 Forsyth Street, SW Atlanta, GA 30303 Tel: 404-562-2092 Fax: 404-562-2149	Alabama, Florida, Georgia, Kentucky, Mississippi, North Carolina, South Carolina, Tennessee
Boston JFK Federal Building Room E-350 Boston, MA 02203 Tel: 617-565-3630 Fax: 617-565-2229	Connecticut, Maine, Massachusetts, New Hampshire, Rhode Island, Vermont
Chicago 230 South Dearborn St. 6th Floor Chicago, IL 60604 Tel: 312-353-0313 Fax: 312-353-4474	Ilinois, Indiana, Michigan, Minnesota, Ohio, Wisconsin
Dallas 525 Griffin Street Room 317 Dallas, TX 75202 Tel: 214-767-8263 Fax: 214-767-5113	Arkansas, Louisiana, New Mexico, Oklahoma, Texas
Denver 1999 Broadway Suite 1780 Denver, CO 80202-5716 Tel: 303-844-1650 Fax: 303-844-1685	Colorado, Montana, North Dakota, South Dakota, Utah, Wyoming

Region	States
Kansas City 110 Main St., Suite 1050 City Center Square Kansas City, MO 64105 Tel: 816-426-3796 Fax: 816-426-2729	Iowa, Kansas, Missouri, Nebraska
New York 201 Varick Street Room 755 New York, NY 10014 Tel: 212-337-2139 Fax: 212-337-2144	New York, New Jersey, Puerto Rico, Virgin Islands

Philadelphia
3535 Market St.
Philadelphia, PA 19101
Tel: 215-596-6363
Alien Certification
  Fax: 215-596-0480
Administrator Fax:
  215-596-0329
	Delaware, District of Columbia, Maryland, Pennsylvania, Virginia, West Virginia

San Francisco P.O. Box 193767 San Francisco, CA 94119-3767 Tel: 415-975-4610 Fax: 415-975-4612	Arizona, California, Guam, Hawaii, Nevada
Seattle 1111 Third Avenue Suite 900 Seattle, WA 98101-3212 Tel: 206-553-7700 Fax: 206-553-0098	Alaska, Idaho, Oregon, Washington

APPENDIX

III

Tear-Out Immigration Forms

I-765	Application for Employment Authorization
I-821	Application for Temporary Protected Status
I-829	Petition by Entrepreneur to Remove the Conditions
I-864	Affidavit of Support Under Section 213A of the Act
I-864A	Contract Between Sponsor and Household Member
I-864P	Minimum Income Requirements for Form 864
I-865	Sponsor's Notice of Change of Address
I-881	Application for Suspension of Deportation or Special Rule Cancellation of Removal
M-378	Color Photograph Specifications
N-400	Application for Naturalization
N-565	Application for Replacement Naturalization/Citizenship Document
N-600	Application for Certificate of Citizenship
N-600/ N-643	Supplement A, Application for Transmission of Citizenship Through a Grandparent
N-643	Certificate of Citizenship of Behalf of Adopted Child
N-644	Application for Posthumous Citizenship
N-648	Medical Certification for Disability Exception
9003	Additional Questions to be Completed by All Applicants for Permanent Residence in the United States

U.S. DEPARTMENT OF LABOR
Employment and Training Administration

APPLICATION
FOR
ALIEN EMPLOYMENT CERTIFICATION

IMPORTANT: READ CAREFULLY BEFORE COMPLETING THIS FORM

PRINT legibly in ink or use a typewriter. If you need more space to answer questions on this form, use a separate sheet. Identify each answer with the number of the corresponding question. SIGN AND DATE each sheet in original signature.

To knowingly furnish any false information in the preparation of this form and any supplement thereto or to aid, abet, or counsel another to do so is a felony punishable by $10,000 fine or 5 years in the penitentiary, or both (18 U.S.C. 1001).

PART A. OFFER OF EMPLOYMENT

1. Name of Alien *(Family name in capital letters, First, Middle, Maiden)*

2. Present Address of Alien *(Number, Street, City and Town, State, ZIP Code or Province, Country)*

3. Type of Visa *(If in U.S.)*

The following information is submitted as evidence of an offer of employment.

4. Name of Employer *(Full name of organization)*

5. Telephone *(Area Code and Number)*

6. Address *(Number, Street, City or Town, County, State, ZIP Code)*

7. Address Where Alien Will Work *(if different from item 6)*

8. Nature of Employer's Business Activity	9. Name of Job Title	10. Total Hours Per Week		11. Work Schedule *(Hourly)*	12. Rate of Pay	
		a. Basic	b. Overtime		a. Basic	b. Overtime
				a.m.	$	$
				p.m.	per	per hour

13. Describe Fully the Job to be Performed *(Duties)*

14. State in detail the MINIMUM education, training, and experience for a worker to perform satisfactorily the job duties described in Item 13 above.

15. Other Special Requirements

EDU-CATION *(Enter number of years)*	Grade School	High School	College	College Degree Required *(specify)*
				Major Field of Study

TRAIN-ING	No. Yrs.	No. Mos.	Type of Training

EXPERI-ENCE	Job Offered		Related Occupation		Related Occupation *(specify)*
	Number				
	Yrs.	Mos.	Yrs.	Mos.	

16. Occupational Title of Person Who Will Be Alien's Immediate Supervisor ► ►

17. Number of Employees Alien will Supervise ►

Date Forms Received	
L.O.	S.O.
R.O.	N.O.
Ind. Code	Occ. Code
Occ. Title	

Replaces MA 7-50A, B and C (Apr. 1970 edition) which is obsolete.

ETA 750 (Oct. 1979)

18. COMPLETE ITEMS ONLY IF JOB IS TEMPORARY			19. IF JOB IS UNIONIZED *(Complete)*	
a. No. of Openings To Be Filled By Aliens Under Job Offer	b. Exact Dates You Expect To Employ Alien		a. Number of Local	b. Name of Local
	From	To		
				c. City and State

20. STATEMENT FOR LIVE-AT-WORK JOB OFFERS   *(Complete for Private Household Job ONLY)*

a. Description of Residence		b. No. Persons Residing at Place of Employment				c. Will free board and private room not shared with anyone be provided?	*("X" one)*
("X" one)	Number of Rooms	Adults	Children		Ages		☐ YES ☐ NO
☐ House		BOYS					
☐ Apartment		GIRLS					

21. DESCRIBE EFFORTS TO RECRUIT U.S. WORKERS AND THE RESULTS. *(Specify Sources of Recruitment by Name)*

22. Applications require various types of documentation. Please read **PART II** of the instructions to assure that appropriate supporting documentation is included with your application.

23. EMPLOYER CERTIFICATIONS

By virtue of my signature below, I HEREBY CERTIFY the following conditions of employment.

a. I have enough funds available to pay the wage or salary offered the alien.

b. The wage offered equals or exceeds the prevailing wage and I guarantee that, if a labor certification is granted, the wage paid to the alien when the alien begins work will equal or exceed the prevailing wage which is applicable at the time the alien begins work.

c. The wage offered is not based on commissions, bonuses, or other incentives, unless I guarantee a wage paid on a weekly, bi-weekly or monthly basis.

d. I will be able to place the alien on the payroll on or before the date of the alien's proposed entrance into the United States.

e. The job opportunity does not involve unlawful discrimination by race, creed, color, national origin, age, sex, religion, handicap, or citizenship.

f. The job opportunity is not:

(1) Vacant because the former occupant is on strike or is being locked out in the course of a labor dispute involving a work stoppage.

(2) At issue in a labor dispute involving a work stoppage.

g. The job opportunity's terms, conditions and occupational environment are not contrary to Federal, State or local law.

h. The job opportunity has been and is clearly open to any qualified U.S. worker.

24. DECLARATIONS

DECLARATION OF EMPLOYER ➤ *Pursuant to 28 U.S.C. 1746, I declare under penalty of perjury the foregoing is true and correct.*

SIGNATURE	DATE
NAME *(Type or Print)*	TITLE

AUTHORIZATION OF AGENT OF EMPLOYER ➤ *I HEREBY DESIGNATE the agent below to represent me for the purposes of labor certification and I TAKE FULL RESPONSIBILITY for accuracy of any representations made by my agent.*

SIGNATURE OF EMPLOYER	DATE
NAME OF AGENT *(Type or Print)*	ADDRESS OF AGENT *(Number, Street, City, State, ZIP Code)*

PART B. STATEMENT OF QUALIFICATIONS OF ALIEN

FOR ADVICE CONCERNING REQUIREMENTS FOR ALIEN EMPLOYMENT CERTIFICATION: *If alien is in the U.S., contact nearest office of Immigration and Naturalization Service. If alien is outside U.S., contact nearest U.S. Consulate.*

IMPORTANT: READ ATTACHED INSTRUCTIONS BEFORE COMPLETING THIS FORM.

Print legibly in ink or use a typewriter. If you need more space to fully answer any questions on this form, use a separate sheet. Identify each answer with the number of the corresponding question. Sign and date each sheet.

1. Name of Alien *(Family name in capital letters)*	First name	Middle name	Maiden name

2. Present Address *(No., Street, City or Town, State or Province and ZIP Code*	Country	3. Type of Visa *(If in U.S.)*

4. Alien's Birthdate *(Month, Day, Year)*	5. Birthplace *(City or Town, State or Province)*	Country	6. Present Nationality or Citizenship *(Country)*

7. Address in United States Where Alien Will Reside

8. Name and Address of Prospective Employer if Alien has job offer in U.S.	9. Occupation in which Alien is Seeking Work

10. "X" the appropriate box below and furnish the information required for the box marked

a. ☐ Alien will apply for a visa abroad at the American Consulate in ⟶	City in Foreign Country	Foreign Country
b. ☐ Alien is in the United States and will apply for adjustment of status to that of a lawful permanent resident in the office of the Immigration and Naturalization Service at ⟶	City	State

11. Names and Addresses of Schools, Colleges and Universities Attended *(Include trade or vocational training facilities)*	Field of Study	FROM		TO		Degrees or Certificates Received
		Month	Year	Month	Year	

SPECIAL QUALIFICATIONS AND SKILLS

12. Additional Qualifications and Skills Alien Possesses and Proficiency in the use of Tools, Machines or Equipment Which Would Help Establish if Alien Meets Requirements for Occupation in Item 9.

13. List Licenses *(Professional, journeyman, etc.)*

14. List Documents Attached Which are Submitted as Evidence that Alien Possesses the Education, Training, Experience, and Abilities Represented

Endorsements	DATE REC. DOL
	O.T. & C.
(Make no entry in this section — FOR Government Agency USE ONLY)	

(Items continued on next page)

15. WORK EXPERIENCE. *List all jobs held during past three (3) years. Also, list any other jobs related to the occupation for which the alien is seeking certification as indicated in item 9.*

a. NAME AND ADDRESS OF EMPLOYER

NAME OF JOB	DATE STARTED Month Year	DATE LEFT Month Year	KIND OF BUSINESS

DESCRIBE IN DETAILS THE DUTIES PERFORMED, INCLUDING THE USE OF TOOLS, MACHINES, OR EQUIPMENT	NO. OF HOURS PER WEEK

b. NAME AND ADDRESS OF EMPLOYER

NAME OF JOB	DATE STARTED Month Year	DATE LEFT Month Year	KIND OF BUSINESS

DESCRIBE IN DETAIL THE DUTIES PERFORMED, INCLUDING THE USE OF TOOLS, MACHINES, OR EQUIPMENT	NO. OF HOURS PER WEEK

c. NAME AND ADDRESS OF EMPLOYER

NAME OF JOB	DATE STARTED Month Year	DATE LEFT Month Year	KIND OF BUSINESS

DESCRIBE IN DETAIL THE DUTIES PERFORMED, INCLUDING THE USE OF TOOLS, MACHINES, OR EQUIPMENT	NO. OF HOURS PER WEEK

16. DECLARATIONS

DECLARATION OF ALIEN ▶ ▶ *Pursuant to 28 U.S.C. 1746, I declare under penalty of perjury the foregoing is true and correct.*

SIGNATURE OF ALIEN	DATE

AUTHORIZATION OF AGENT OF ALIEN ▶ ▶ *I hereby designate the agent below to represent me for the purposes of labor certification and I take full responsibility for accuracy of any representations made by my agent.*

SIGNATURE OF ALIEN	DATE

NAME OF AGENT *(Type or print)*	ADDRESS OF AGENT *(No., Street, City, State, ZIP Code)*

U.S. Department of Labor
Employment and Training Administration
U.S. Employment Service

1. Full Legal Name of Employer	5. Employer's Address (No., Street, City, State, and ZIP Code)

OMB Approval No.: 1205-0310
Expiration Date: 11-30-97

2. Federal Employer I.D. Number

3. Employer's Telephone No.

(   )

6. Address Where Documentation is Kept (If different than item 5)

4. Employer's FAX No.

(   )

7. OCCUPATIONAL INFORMATION (Use attachment if additional space is needed)

(a) Three-digit Occupational Group Code (From Appendix 2): _____   (b) Job Title (Check Box if Part-Time): _____ ☐

(c) No. of H-1B Nonimmigrants   (d) Rate of Pay   (e) Prevailing Wage Rate and its Source (see instructions)   (f) Period of Employment From   To   (g) Location(s) Where H-1B Nonimmigrants Will Work (see instructions)

_____ $_____ $_____ ☐SESA ☐Other:_____ _____ _____ _____

_____ $_____ $_____ ☐SESA ☐Other:_____ _____ _____ _____

8. EMPLOYER LABOR CONDITION STATEMENTS (Employers are required to develop and maintain documentation supporting labor condition statements 8(a) and 8(d). Employers are further required to make available for public examination a copy of the labor condition application and necessary supporting documentation within one (1) working day after the date on which the application is filed with DOL. Check **each** box to indicate that the employer will comply with **each** statement.)

☐ (a)   H-1B nonimmigrants will be paid at least the actual wage level paid by the employer to all other individuals with similar experience and qualifications for the specific employment in question <u>or</u> the prevailing wage level for the occupation in the area of employment, whichever <u>is higher</u>.

☐ (b)   The employment of H-1B nonimmigrants will not adversely affect the working conditions of workers similarly employed in the area of intended employment.

☐ (c)   On the date this application is signed and submitted, there is not a strike, lockout or work stoppage in the course of a labor dispute in the occupation in which H-1B nonimmigrants will be employed at the place of employment. If such a strike or lockout occurs after this application is submitted, I will notify ETA within 3 days of the occurrence of such a strike or lockout and the application will not be used in support of petition filings with INS for H-1B nonimmigrants to work in the same occupation at the place of employment until ETA determines the strike or lockout has ceased.

☐ (d)   A copy of this application has been, or will be, provided to each H-1B nonimmigrant employed pursuant to this application, and, as of this date, notice of this application has been provided to workers employed in the occupation in which H-1B nonimmigrants will be employed: (check appropriate box)

    ☐ (i)   Notice of this filing has been provided to the bargaining representative of workers in the occupation in which H-1B nonimmigrants will be employed; or

    ☐ (ii)   There is no such bargaining representative; therefore, a notice of this filing has been posted and was, or will remain, posted for 10 days in at least two conspicuous locations where H-1B nonimmigrants will be employed.

9. DECLARATION OF EMPLOYER. Pursuant to 28 U.S.C. 1746, I declare under penalty of perjury that the information provided on this form is true and correct. In addition, I declare that I will comply with the Department of Labor regulations governing this program and, in particular, that I will make this application, supporting documentation, and other records, files and documents available to officials of the Department of Labor, upon such official's request, during any investigation under this application or the Immigration and Nationality Act.

Name and Title of Hiring or Other Designated Official   Signature   Date

Complaints alleging misrepresentation of material facts in the labor condition application and/or failure to comply with the terms of the labor condition application may be filed with any office of the Wage and Hour Division of the United States Department of Labor.

AN APPLICATION CERTIFIED BY DOL MUST BE FILED IN SUPPORT OF AN H-1B VISA PETITION WITH THE INS.

FOR U.S. GOVERNMENT AGENCY USE ONLY: By virtue of my signature below, I acknowledge that this application is hereby certified and will be valid from _____ through _____.

Signature and Title of Authorized DOL Official   ETA Case No.   Date

Subsequent DOL Action: Suspended _____ (date)   Invalidated _____ (date)   Withdrawn _____ (date)

The Department of Labor is not the guarantor of the accuracy, truthfulness or adequacy of a certified labor condition application.

Public reporting burden for this collection of information is estimated to average 1½ hour per response, including the time for reviewing instructions, searching existing data sources, gathering and maintaining the data needed, and completing and reviewing the collection of information. Send comments regarding this burden estimate or any other aspect of this collection of information, including suggestions for reducing this burden, to the Office of U.S. Employment Service, Department of Labor, Room N-4470 and/or the Office of IRM Policy, DOL, Room N-1301, 200 Constitution Avenue, N.W., Washington, DC 20210. (1205-0310).

U.S. Department of Justice
Immigration and Naturalization Service

FORM G-325A
BIOGRAPHIC INFORMATION

OMB No. 1115-0066
Approval expires 4-30-85

(Family name)	(First name)	(Middle name)	☐ MALE ☐ FEMALE	BIRTHDATE (Mo.-Day-Yr.)	NATIONALITY	FILE NUMBER A-

ALL OTHER NAMES USED (Including names by previous marriages)	CITY AND COUNTRY OF BIRTH	SOCIAL SECURITY NO. (If any)

	FAMILY NAME	FIRST NAME	DATE, CITY AND COUNTRY OF BIRTH (If known)	CITY AND COUNTRY OF RESIDENCE
FATHER				
MOTHER (Maiden name)				

HUSBAND (If none, so state) OR WIFE	FAMILY NAME (For wife, give maiden name)	FIRST NAME	BIRTHDATE	CITY & COUNTRY OF BIRTH	DATE OF MARRIAGE	PLACE OF MARRIAGE

FORMER HUSBANDS OR WIVES (If none, so state)

FAMILY NAME (For wife, give maiden name)	FIRST NAME	BIRTHDATE	DATE & PLACE OF MARRIAGE	DATE AND PLACE OF TERMINATION OF MARRIAGE

APPLICANT'S RESIDENCE LAST FIVE YEARS, LIST PRESENT ADDRESS FIRST

STREET AND NUMBER	CITY	PROVINCE OR STATE	COUNTRY	FROM		TO	
				MONTH	YEAR	MONTH	YEAR
						PRESENT TIME	

APPLICANT'S LAST ADDRESS OUTSIDE THE UNITED STATES OF MORE THAN ONE YEAR

STREET AND NUMBER	CITY	PROVINCE OR STATE	COUNTRY	FROM		TO	
				MONTH	YEAR	MONTH	YEAR

APPLICANT'S EMPLOYMENT LAST FIVE YEARS. (IF NONE, SO STATE.) LIST PRESENT EMPLOYMENT FIRST

FULL NAME AND ADDRESS OF EMPLOYER	OCCUPATION (SPECIFY)	FROM		TO	
		MONTH	YEAR	MONTH	YEAR
				PRESENT TIME	

Show below last occupation abroad if not shown above. (Include all information requested above.)

THIS FORM IS SUBMITTED IN CONNECTION WITH APPLICATION FOR: ☐ NATURALIZATION ☐ STATUS AS PERMANENT RESIDENT ☐ OTHER (SPECIFY):	SIGNATURE OF APPLICANT	DATE

Are all copies legible? [X] Yes	If your native alphabet is other than roman letters, write your name in your native alphabet here:

PENALTIES: SEVERE PENALTIES ARE PROVIDED BY LAW FOR KNOWINGLY AND WILLFULLY FALSIFYING OR CONCEALING A MATERIAL FACT.

APPLICANT:

BE SURE TO PUT YOUR NAME AND ALIEN REGISTRATION NUMBER IN THE BOX OUTLINED BY HEAVY BORDER BELOW.

COMPLETE THIS BOX (Family Name)	(Given name)	(Middle name)	(Alien registration number)

18. COMPLETE ITEMS ONLY IF JOB IS TEMPORARY		19. IF JOB IS UNIONIZED *(Complete)*	
a. No. of Openings To Be Filled By Aliens Under Job Offer	b. Exact Dates You Expect To Employ Alien	a. Number of Local	b. Name of Local
	From To		
			c. City and State

20. STATEMENT FOR LIVE-AT-WORK JOB OFFERS *(Complete for Private Household Job ONLY)*

a. Description of Residence		b. No. Persons Residing at Place of Employment				c. Will free board and private room not shared with anyone be provided?	*("X" one)*
("X" one)	Number of Rooms	Adults		Children	Ages		☐ YES ☐ NO
☐ House			BOYS				
☐ Apartment			GIRLS				

21. DESCRIBE EFFORTS TO RECRUIT U.S. WORKERS AND THE RESULTS. *(Specify Sources of Recruitment by Name)*

22. Applications require various types of documentation. Please read PART II of the instructions to assure that appropriate supporting documentation is included with your application.

23. EMPLOYER CERTIFICATIONS

By virtue of my signature below, I HEREBY CERTIFY the following conditions of employment.

a. I have enough funds available to pay the wage or salary offered the alien.

b. The wage offered equals or exceeds the prevailing wage and I guarantee that, if a labor certification is granted, the wage paid to the alien when the alien begins work will equal or exceed the prevailing wage which is applicable at the time the alien begins work.

c. The wage offered is not based on commissions, bonuses, or other incentives, unless I guarantee a wage paid on a weekly, bi-weekly or monthly basis.

d. I will be able to place the alien on the payroll on or before the date of the alien's proposed entrance into the United States.

e. The job opportunity does not involve unlawful discrimination by race, creed, color, national origin, age, sex, religion, handicap, or citizenship.

f. The job opportunity is not:

   (1) Vacant because the former occupant is on strike or is being locked out in the course of a labor dispute involving a work stoppage.

   (2) At issue in a labor dispute involving a work stoppage.

g. The job opportunity's terms, conditions and occupational environment are not contrary to Federal, State or local law.

h. The job opportunity has been and is clearly open to any qualified U.S. worker.

24. DECLARATIONS

DECLARATION OF EMPLOYER ➤ *Pursuant to 28 U.S.C. 1746, I declare under penalty of perjury the foregoing is true and correct.*

SIGNATURE	DATE

NAME *(Type or Print)*	TITLE

AUTHORIZATION OF AGENT OF EMPLOYER ➤ *I HEREBY DESIGNATE the agent below to represent me for the purposes of labor certification and I TAKE FULL RESPONSIBILITY for accuracy of any representations made by my agent.*

SIGNATURE OF EMPLOYER	DATE

NAME OF AGENT *(Type or Print)*	ADDRESS OF AGENT *(Number, Street, City, State, ZIP Code)*

U.S. Department of Justice
Immigration and Naturalization Service

For sale by the Superintendent of Documents
U.S. Government Printing Office
Washington, DC 20402

OMB #1115-0168

Petition for a Nonimmigrant Worker

START HERE - Please Type or Print

Part 1. Information about the employer filing this petition.

If the employer is an individual, use the top name line. Organizations should use the second line.

Family Name	Given Name	Middle Initial

Company or Organization Name

Address - Attn:

Street Number and Name		Apt. #
City	State or Province	
Country	ZIP/Postal Code	

IRS Tax #

Part 2. Information about this Petition.

(See instructions to determine the fee).

1. **Requested Nonimmigrant Classification:**
   (write classification symbol at right) _____

2. **Basis for Classification** (check one)
   a. ☐ New employment
   b. ☐ Continuation of previously approved employment without change
   c. ☐ Change in previously approved employment
   d. ☐ New concurrent employment

3. **Prior petition.** If you checked other than "New Employment" in item 2. (above) give the most recent prior petition number for the worker(s):

4. **Requested Action:** (check one)
   a. ☐ Notify the office in Part 4 so the person(s) can obtain a visa or be admitted (NOTE: a petition is not required for an E-1, E-2, or R visa).
   b. ☐ Change the person(s) status and extend their stay since they are all now in the U.S. in another status (see instructions for limitations). This is available only where you check "New Employment" in item 2, above.
   c. ☐ Extend or amend the stay of the person(s) since they now hold this status.

5. **Total number of workers in petition:** _____

   (See instructions for where more than one worker can be included.)

Part 3. Information about the person(s) you are filing for.

Complete the blocks below. Use the continuation sheet to name each person included in this petition.

If an entertainment group, give their group name.

Family Name	Given Name	Middle Initial
Date of Birth (Month/Day/Year)	Country of Birth	
Social Security #	A #	

If in the United States, complete the following:

Date of Arrival (Month/Day/Year)	I-94 #	
Current Nonimmigrant Status	Expires (Month/Day/Year)	

FOR INS USE ONLY

Returned	Receipt
_____	
_____	
Resubmitted	
_____	
_____	
Reloc Sent	
_____	
_____	
Reloc Rec'd	
_____	
_____	

Interviewed
☐ Petitioner
☐ Beneficiary

Class: _____
# of Workers: _____
Priority Number: _____
Validity Dates: From _____
To _____

☐ **Classification Approved**
☐ Consulate/POE/PFI Notified

At: _____
☐ Extension Granted
☐ COS/Extension Granted

Partial Approval (explain)

Action Block

To Be Completed by Attorney or Representative, if any
☐ Fill in box if G-28 is attached to represent the applicant

VOLAG#

ATTY State License #

Form I-129 (Rev. 12/11/91) N   *Continued on back.*

Part 4. Processing Information.

a. If the person named in Part 3 is outside the U.S. or a requested extension of stay or change of status cannot be granted, give the U.S. consulate or inspection facility you want notified if this petition is approved.

Type of Office (check one):	☐ Consulate	☐ Pre-flight inspection	☐ Port of Entry

Office Address (City)	U.S. State or Foreign Country

Person's Foreign Address

b. Does each person in this petition have a valid passport?
    ☐ Not required to have passport   ☐ No - explain on separate paper ☐ Yes

c. Are you filing any other petitions with this one?   ☐ No   ☐ Yes - How many? _____

d. Are applications for replacement/Initial I-94's being filed with this petition?   ☐ No   ☐ Yes - How many? _____

e. Are applications by dependents being filed with this petition?   ☐ No   ☐ Yes - How many? _____

f. Is any person in this petition in exclusion or deportation proceedings?   ☐ No   ☐ Yes - explain on separate paper

g. Have you ever filed an immigrant petition for any person in this petition?   ☐ No   ☐ Yes - explain on separate paper

h. If you indicated you were filing a new petition in Part 2, within the past 7 years has any person in this petition:

    1) ever been given the classification you are now requesting?   ☐ No   ☐ Yes - explain on separate paper

    2) ever been denied the classification you are now requesting?   ☐ No   ☐ Yes - explain on separate paper

i. If you are filing for an entertainment group, has any person in this petition not been with the group for at least 1 year?
    ☐ No   ☐ Yes - explain on separate paper

Part 5. Basic Information about the proposed employment and employer.
Attach the supplement relating to the classification you are requesting.

Job Title	Nontechnical Description of Job

Address where the person(s) will work if different from the address in Part 1.

Is this a full-time position?		Wages per week or per year
☐ No - Hours per week	☐ Yes	

Other Compensation (Explain)	Value per week or per year	Dates of Intended employment From: To:

Type of Petitioner - check one: ☐ U.S. citizen or permanent resident	☐ Organization	☐ Other - explain on separate paper

Type of business:		Year established:

Current Number of Employees	Gross Annual Income	Net Annual Income

Part 6. Signature.
Read the information on penalties in the instructions before completing this section.

I certify, under penalty of perjury under the laws of the United States of America, that this petition, and the evidence submitted with it, is all true and correct. If filing this on behalf of an organization, I certify that I am empowered to do so by that organization. If this petition is to extend a prior petition, I certify that the proposed employment is under the same terms and conditions as in the prior approved petition. I authorize the release of any information from my records, or from the petitioning organization's records, which the Immigration and Naturalization Service needs to determine eligibility for the benefit being sought.

Signature and title	Print Name	Date

Please Note: If you do not completely fill out this form and the required supplement, or fail to submit required documents listed in the instructions, then the person(s) filed for may not be found eligible for the requested benefit, and this petition may be denied.

Part 7. Signature of person preparing form if other than above.

I declare that I prepared this petition at the request of the above person and it is based on all information of which I have any knowledge.

Signature	Print Name	Date

Firm Name and Address

Supplement-1

Attach to Form I-129 when more than one person is included in the petition. *(List each person separately. Do not include the person you named on the form).*

Family Name		Given Name	Middle Initial	Date of Birth (month/day/year)
Country of Birth		Social Security No.		A#

IF IN THE U.S.	Date of Arrival *(month/day/year)*		I-94#	
	Current Nonimmigrant Status:		Expires on *(month/day/year)*	

Country where passport issued	Expiration Date (month/day/year)	Date Started with group

Family Name		Given Name	Middle Initial	Date of Birth (month/day/year)
Country of Birth		Social Security No.		A#

IF IN THE U.S.	Date of Arrival *(month/day/year)*		I-94#	
	Current Nonimmigrant Status:		Expires on *(month/day/year)*	

Country where passport issued	Expiration Date (month/day/year)	Date Started with group

Family Name		Given Name	Middle Initial	Date of Birth (month/day/year)
Country of Birth		Social Security No.		A#

IF IN THE U.S.	Date of Arrival *(month/day/year)*		I-94#	
	Current Nonimmigrant Status:		Expires on *(month/day/year)*	

Country where passport issued	Expiration Date (month/day/year)	Date Started with group

Family Name		Given Name	Middle Initial	Date of Birth (month/day/year)
Country of Birth		Social Security No.		A#

IF IN THE U.S.	Date of Arrival *(month/day/year)*		I-94#	
	Current Nonimmigrant Status:		Expires on *(month/day/year)*	

Country where passport issued	Expiration Date (month/day/year)	Date Started with group

Family Name		Given Name	Middle Initial	Date of Birth (month/day/year)
Country of Birth		Social Security No.		A#

IF IN THE U.S.	Date of Arrival *(month/day/year)*		I-94#	
	Current Nonimmigrant Status:		Expires on *(month/day/year)*	

Country where passport issued	Expiration Date (month/day/year)	Date Started with group

Supplement-1

Attach to Form I-129 when more than one person is included in the petition. *(List each person separately. Do not include the person you named on the form).*

Family Name	Given Name	Middle Initial	Date of Birth (month/day/year)
Country of Birth	Social Security No.		A#

IF IN THE U.S.	Date of Arrival (month/day/year)		I-94#
	Current Nonimmigrant Status:		Expires on (month/day/year)

Country where passport issued	Expiration Date (month/day/year)	Date Started with group

Family Name	Given Name	Middle Initial	Date of Birth (month/day/year)
Country of Birth	Social Security No.		A#

IF IN THE U.S.	Date of Arrival (month/day/year)		I-94#
	Current Nonimmigrant Status:		Expires on (month/day/year)

Country where passport issued	Expiration Date (month/day/year)	Date Started with group

Family Name	Given Name	Middle Initial	Date of Birth (month/day/year)
Country of Birth	Social Security No.		A#

IF IN THE U.S.	Date of Arrival (month/day/year)		I-94#
	Current Nonimmigrant Status:		Expires on (month/day/year)

Country where passport issued	Expiration Date (month/day/year)	Date Started with group

Family Name	Given Name	Middle Initial	Date of Birth (month/day/year)
Country of Birth	Social Security No.		A#

IF IN THE U.S.	Date of Arrival (month/day/year)		I-94#
	Current Nonimmigrant Status:		Expires on (month/day/year)

Country where passport issued	Expiration Date (month/day/year)	Date Started with group

Family Name	Given Name	Middle initial	Date of Birth (month/day/year)
Country of Birth	Social Security No.		A#

IF IN THE U.S.	Date of Arrival (month/day/year)		I-94#
	Current Nonimmigrant Status:		Expires on (month/day/year)

Country where passport issued	Expiration Date (month/day/year)	Date Started with group

Name of person or organization filing petition: | Name of person you are filing for:

Classification sought (check one):
☐ E-1 Treaty trader   ☐ E-2 Treaty investor

Name of country signatory to treaty with U.S.

Section 1.   Information about the Employer Outside the U.S. (if any)

Name | Address

Alien's Position - Title, duties and number of years employed | Principal Product, merchandise or service

Total Number of Employees

Section 2.   Additional Information about the U.S. Employer.

The U.S. company is, to the company outside the U.S. (check one):
☐ Parent   ☐ Branch   ☐ Subsidiary   ☐ Affiliate   ☐ Joint Venture

Date and Place of Incorporation or establishment in the U.S.

Nationality of Ownership (Individual or Corporate)

Name	Nationality	Immigration Status	% Ownership

Assets | Net Worth | Total Annual Income

Staff in the U.S.	Executive/Manager	Specialized Qualifications or Knowledge
Nationals of Treaty Country in E or L Status		
Total number of employees in the U.S.		

Total number of employees the alien would supervise; or describe the nature of the specialized skills essential to the U.S. company.

Section 3.   Complete if filing for an E-1 Treaty Trader

Total Annual Gross Trade/Business of the U.S. company | For Year Ending
$

Percent of total gross trade which is between the U.S. and the country of which the treaty trader organization is a national.

Section 4.   Complete if filing for an E-2 Treaty Investor

Total Investment:	Cash	Equipment	Other
	$	$	$
	Inventory	Premises	Total
	$	$	$

Form I-129 Supplement E/L (12/11/91) N

U.S. Department of Justice
Immigration and Naturalization Service

L Classification
Supplement to Form I-129

Name of person or organization filing petition: _____

Name of person you are filing for: _____

This petition is (check one): ☐ An individual petition   ☐ A blanket petition

Section 1.   Complete this section if filing an individual petition.

Classification sought (check one): ☐ L-1A manager or executive   ☐ L-1B specialized knowledge

List the alien's, and any dependent family members' prior periods of stay in an L classification in the U.S. for the last seven years. Be sure to list only those periods in which the alien and/or family members were actually in the U.S. in an L classification.

_____

_____

Name and address of employer abroad
_____

Dates of alien's employment with this employer. Explain any interruptions in employment.
_____

Description of the alien's duties for the past 3 years.
_____

Description of alien's proposed duties in the U.S.
_____

Summarize the alien's education and work experience.
_____

The U.S. company is, to the company abroad: (check one)
☐ Parent   ☐ Branch   ☐ Subsidiary   ☐ Affiliate   ☐ Joint Venture

Describe the stock ownership and managerial control of each company.
_____

Do the companies currently have the same qualifying relationship as they did during the one-year period of the alien's employment with the company abroad?   ☐ Yes   ☐ No (attach explanation)

Is the alien coming to the U.S. to open a new office?
☐ Yes (explain in detail on separate paper)   ☐ No

Section 2.   Complete this section if filing a Blanket Petition.

List all U.S. and foreign parent, branches, subsidiaries and affiliates included in this petition. (Attach a separate paper if additional space is needed.)

Name and Address	Relationship

Explain in detail on separate paper.

Form I-129 Supplement E/L (12/11/91) N

Name of person or organization filing petition:

Name of person or total number of workers or trainees you are filing for:

List the alien's and any dependent family members; prior periods of stay in H classification in the U.S. for the last six years. Be sure to list only those periods in which the alien and/or family members were actually in the U.S. in an H classification. If more space is needed, attach an additional sheet.

Classification sought (check one):

☐ H-1A   Registered Professional nurse
☐ H-1B1   Specialty occupation
☐ H-1B2   Exceptional services relating to a cooperative research and development project administered by the U.S. Department of Defense
☐ H-1B3   Artist, entertainer or fashion model of national or international acclaim

☐ H-1B4   Artist or entertainer in unique or traditional art form
☐ H-1B5   Athlete
☐ H-1BS   Essential Support Personnel for H-1B entertainer or athlete
☐ H-2A   Agricultural worker
☐ H-2B   Nonagricultural worker
☐ H-3   Trainee
☐ H-3   Special education exchange visitor program

Section 1. Complete this section if filing for H-1A or H-1B classification.

Describe the proposed duties

Alien's present occupation and summary of prior work experience

Statement for H-1B speciality occupations only:

    By filing this petition, I agree to the terms of the labor condition application for the duration of the alien's authorized period of stay for H-1B employment.

Petitioner's Signature   Date

Statement for H-1B specialty occupations and DOD projects:

    As an authorized official of the employer, I certify that the employer will be liable for the reasonable costs of return transportation of the alien abroad if the alien is dismissed from employment by the employer before the end of the period of authorized stay.

Signature of authorized official of employer   Date

Statement for H-1B DOD projects only:

    I certify that the alien will be working on a cooperative research and development project or a coproduction project under a reciprocal Government-to-Government agreement administered by the Department of Defense.

DOD project manager's signature   Date

Section 2. Complete this section if filing for H-2A or H-2B classification.

Employment is: (check one)
☐ Seasonal
☐ Peakload
☐ Intermittent
☐ One-time occurrence

Temporary need is: (check one)
☐ Unpredictable
☐ Periodic
☐ Recurrent annually

Explain your temporary need for the alien's services (attach a separate paper if additional space is needed).

Section 3. Complete this section if filing for H-2A classification.

The petitioner and each employer consent to allow government access to the site where the labor is being performed for the purpose of determining compliance with H-2A requirements. The petitioner further agrees to notify the Service in the manner and within the time frame specified if an H-2A worker absconds or if the authorized employment ends more than five days before the relating certification document expires, and pay liquidated damages of ten dollars for each instance where it cannot demonstrate compliance with this notification requirement. The petitioner also agrees to pay liquidated damages of two hundred dollars for each instance where it cannot be demonstrated that the H-2A worker either departed the United States or obtained authorized status during the period of admission or within five days of early termination, whichever comes first.

The petitioner must execute Part A. If the petitioner is the employer's agent, the employer must execute Part B. If there are joint employers, they must each execute Part C.

Part A. Petitioner:

By filing this petition, I agree to the conditions of H-2A employment, and agree to the notice requirements and limited liabilities defined in 8 CFR 214.2 (h) (3) (vi).

Petitioner's signature   Date

Part B. Employer who is not petitioner:

I certify that I have authorized the party filing this petition to act as my agent in this regard. I assume full responsibility for all representations made by this agent on my behalf, and agree to the conditions of H-2A eligibility.

Employer's signature   Date

Part C. Joint Employers:

I agree to the conditions of H-2A eligibility.

Joint employer's signature(s)   Date

Joint employer's signature(s)   Date

Joint employer's signature(s)   Date

Joint employer's signature(s)   Date

Joint employer's signature(s)   Date

Section 4. Complete this section if filing for H-3 classification.

If you answer "yes" to any of the following questions, attach a full explanation.

		No	Yes
a.	Is the training you intend to provide, or similar training, available in the alien's country?	☐	☐
b.	Will the training benefit the alien in pursuing a career abroad?	☐	☐
c.	Does the training involve productive employment incidental to training?	☐	☐
d.	Does the alien already have skills related to the training?	☐	☐
e.	Is this training an effort to overcome a labor shortage?	☐	☐
f.	Do you intend to employ the alien abroad at the end of this training?	☐	☐

If you do not intend to employ this person abroad at the end of this training, explain why you wish to incur the cost of providing this training, and your expected return from this training.

U.S. Department of Justice
Immigration and Naturalization Service

O and P Classifications
Supplement to Form I-129

Name of person or organization filing petition:

Name of person or group or total number of workers you are filing for:

Classification sought (check one):

☐ O-1 Alien of extraordinary ability in sciences, art, education, or business.

☐ P-2 Artist or entertainer for reciprocal exchange program

☐ P-2S Essential Support Personnel for P-2

Explain the nature of the event

Describe the duties to be performed

If filing for O-2 or P support alien, dates of the alien's prior experience with the O-1 or P alien.

Have you obtained the required written consultations(s)?   ☐ Yes - attached   ☐ No - Copy of request attached
If not, give the following information about the organizations(s) to which you have sent a duplicate of this petition.

O-1 Extraordinary ability

Name of recognized peer group	Phone #
Address	Date sent

O-1 Extraordinary achievement in motion pictures or television

Name of labor organization	Phone #
Address	Date sent
Name of management organization	Phone #
Address	Date sent

O-2 or P alien

Name of labor organization	Phone #
Address	Date sent

Form I-129 Supplement O/P/Q/R (12/11/91) N

OMB #1115-0168

U.S. Department of Justice
Immigration and Naturalization Service

Q & R Classifications
Supplement to Form I-129

Name of person or organization filing petition: Name of person you are filing for:

Section 1.   Complete this section if you are filing for a Q international cultural exchange alien.

I hereby certify that the participant(s) in this international cultural exchange program:
- is at least 18 years of age,
- has the ability to communicate effectively about the cultural attributes of his or her country of nationality to the American public, and
- has not previously been in the United States as a Q nonimmigrant unless he/she has resided and been physically present outside the U.S. for the immediate prior year.

I also certify that the same wages and working conditions are accorded the participants as are provided to similarly employed U.S. workers.

Petitioner's signature   Date

Section 2.   Complete this section if you are filing for an R religious worker.

List the alien's, and any dependent family members, prior periods of stay in R classification in the U.S. for the last six years. Be sure to list only those periods in which the alien and/or family members were actually in the U.S. in an R classification.

Describe the alien's proposed duties in the U.S.

Describe the alien's qualifications for the vocation or occupation

Description of the relationship between the U.S. religious organization and the organization abroad of which the alien was a member.

Form I-129 Supplement O/P/Q/R (12/11/91) N

U.S. Department of Justice
Immigration and Naturalization Service (INS)

OMB #1115-0054

Petition for Alien Fiancé(e)

DO NOT WRITE IN THIS BLOCK

Case ID#	Action Stamp	Fee Stamp
A#		
G-28 or Volag #		
The petition is approved for status under Section 101(a)(15)(k). It is valid for four months from date of action.		AMCON: _____ ☐ Personal Interview ☐ Previously Forwarded ☐ Document Check ☐ Field Investigations

Remarks:

A. Information about you

1. **Name** (Family name in CAPS)   (First)   (Middle)

2. **Address** (Number and Street)   (Apartment Number)

   (Town or City)   (State/Country)   (ZIP/Postal Code)

3. **Place of Birth** (Town or City)   (State/Country)

4. **Date of Birth** (Mo/Day/Yr)
5. **Sex** ☐ Male ☐ Female
6. **Marital Status** ☐ Married ☐ Single ☐ Widowed ☐ Divorced

7. **Other Names Used** (including maiden name)

8. **Social Security Number**
9. **Alien Registration Number** (if any)

10. **Names of Prior Husbands/Wives**
11. **Date(s) Marriages(s) Ended**

12. If you are a U.S. citizen, complete the following:

    My citizenship was acquired through (check one)
    ☐ Birth in the U.S.
    ☐ Naturalization
       Give number of certificate, date and place it was issued

    ☐ Parents
       Have you obtained a certificate of citizenship in your own name?
       ☐ Yes ☐ No
    If "Yes", give number of certificate, date and place it was issued

13. Have you ever filed for this or any other alien fiancé(e) or husband/wife before? ☐ Yes ☐ No
    If you checked "yes," give name of alien, place and date of filing, and result

B. Information about your alien fiancé(e)

1. **Name** (Family name in CAPS)   (First)   (Middle)

2. **Address** (Number and Street)   (Apartment Number)

   (Town or City)   (State/Country)   (ZIP/Postal Code)

3. **Place of Birth** (Town or City)   (State/Country)

4. **Date of Birth** (Mo/Day/Yr)
5. **Sex** ☐ Male ☐ Female
6. **Marital Status** ☐ Married ☐ Single ☐ Widowed ☐ Divorced

7. **Other Names Used** (including maiden name)

8. **Social Security Number**
9. **Alien Registration Number** (if any)

10. **Names of Prior Husbands/Wives**
11. **Date(s) Marriages(s) Ended**

12. Has your fiancé(e) ever been in the U.S.?
    ☐ Yes ☐ No

13. If your fiancé(e) is currently in the U.S., complete the following:
    He or she last arrived as a (visitor, student, exchange alien, crewman, stowaway, temporary worker, witout inspection, etc.)

    Arrival/Departure Record (I-94) Number   Date arrived (Month/Day/Year)

    Date authorized stay expired, or will expire, as shown on Form I-94 or I-95

INITIAL RECEIPT	RESUBMITTED	RELOCATED		COMPLETED		
		Rec'd	Sent	Approved	Denied	Returned

Form I-129F (Rev. 4/11/91) Y

B. (continued) Information about your alien fiancé (e)

14. List all children of your alien fiancé(e) (if any)

(Name)	(Date of Birth)	(Country of Birth)	(Preesent Address)

15. Address in the United States where your fiancé(e) intends to live

(Number and Street)   (Town or City)   (State)

16. Your fiancé (e)'s address abroad

(Number and Street)   (Town or City)   (Province)   (Country)   (Phone Number)

17. If your fiancé (e)'s native alphabet is other than Roman letters, write hs or her name and address abroad in the native alphabet:

(Name)   (Number and Street)   (Town or City)   (Province)   (Country)

18. Your fiancé (e) is related to you.   ☐ Yes   ☐ No

If you are related, state the nature and degree of relationship, e.g., third cousin or maternal uncle, etc.

19. Your fiancé (e) has met and seen you.   ☐ Yes   ☐ No

Describe the circumstances under which you met. If you have not personally met each other, explain how the relationship was established, and explain in detail any reasons you may have for requesting that the requirement that you and your fiancé (e) must have met should not apply to you.

20. Your fiancé (e) will apply for a visa abroad at the American Consulate in _____

(City)   (Country)

(Designation of a consulate outside the country of your fiancé(e)'s last residence does not guarantee acceptance for processing by that consulate. Acceptance is at the discretion of the designated consulate.)

C. Other Information

If you are serving overseas in the armed forces of the United States, please answer the following:

I presently reside or am stationed overseas and my current mailing address is _____

I plan to return to the United States on or about _____

Penalties: You may, by law be imprisoned for not more than five years, or fined $250,000, or both, for entering into a marriage contract for the purpose of evading any provision of the immigration laws and you may be fined up to $10,000 or imprisoned up to five years or both, for knowingly and willfully falsifying or concealing a material fact or using any false document in submitting this petition.

Your Certification

I am legally able to and intend to marry my alien fiancé(e) within 90 days of his or her arrival in the United States. I certify, under penalty of perjury under the laws of the United States of America, that the foregoing is true and correct. Furthermore, I authorize the release of any information from my records which the Immigration and Naturalizaton Service needs to determine eligibility for the benefit that I am seeking.

Signature _____ Date _____ Phone Number _____

Signature of Person Preparing Form if Other than Above

I declare that I prepared this document at the request of the person above and that it is based on all information of which I have any knowledge.

Print Name _____ (Address) _____ (Signature) _____ (Date) _____

G-28 ID Number _____

Volag Number _____

For sale by the Superintendent of Documents, U.S. Government Printing Office
Washington, D.C. 20402

U.S. Department of Justice
Immigration and Naturalization Service (INS)

Petition for Alien Relative

OMB #1115-0054

DO NOT WRITE IN THIS BLOCK - FOR EXAMINING OFFICE ONLY

Case ID#

A#

G-28 or Volag #

Action Stamp

Fee Stamp

Section of Law:
- ☐ 201 (b) spouse
- ☐ 201 (b) child
- ☐ 201 (b) parent
- ☐ 203 (a)(1)
- ☐ 203 (a)(2)
- ☐ 203 (a)(4)
- ☐ 203 (a)(5)

AM CON: _____

Petition was filed on: _____ (priority date)
- ☐ Personal Interview
- ☐ Pet. ☐ Ben. "A" File Reviewed
- ☐ Field Investigations
- ☐ 204 (a)(2)(A) Resolved
- ☐ Previously Forwarded
- ☐ Stateside Criteria
- ☐ I-485 Simultaneously
- ☐ 204 (h) Resolved

Remarks:

A. Relationship

1. The alien relative is my
   - ☐ Husband/Wife
   - ☐ Parent
   - ☐ Brother/Sister
   - ☐ Child

2. Are you related by adoption?
   - ☐ Yes
   - ☐ No

3. Did you gain permanent residence through adoption?
   - ☐ Yes
   - ☐ No

B. Information about you

1. Name (Family name in CAPS) (First) (Middle)

2. Address (Number and Street) (Apartment Number)

   (Town or City) (State/Country) (ZIP/Postal Code)

3. Place of Birth (Town or City) (State/Country)

4. Date of Birth (Mo/Day/Yr)

5. Sex
   - ☐ Male
   - ☐ Female

6. Marital Status
   - ☐ Married
   - ☐ Widowed
   - ☐ Single
   - ☐ Divorced

7. Other Names Used (including maiden name)

8. Date and Place of Present Marriage (if married)

9. Social Security Number

10. Alien Registration Number (if any)

11. Names of Prior Husbands/Wives   12. Date(s) Marriages(s) Ended

13. If you are a U.S. citizen, complete the following:
    My citizenship was acquired through (check one)
    - ☐ Birth in the U.S.
    - ☐ Naturalization (Give number of certificate, date and place it was issued)
    - ☐ Parents
      Have you obtained a certificate of citizenship in your own name?
      - ☐ Yes
      - ☐ No
      If "Yes", give number of certificate, date and place it was issued

14a. If you are a lawful permanent resident alien, complete the following:
    Date and place of admission for, or adjustment to, lawful permanent residence, and class of admission:

14b. Did you gain permanent resident status through marriage to a United States citizen or lawful permanent resident? ☐ Yes ☐ No

C. Information about your alien relative

1. Name (Family name in CAPS) (First) (Middle)

2. Address (Number and Street) (Apartment Number)

   (Town or City) (State/Country) (ZIP/Postal Code)

3. Place of Birth (Town or City) (State/Country)

4. Date of Birth (Mo/Day/Yr)

5. Sex
   - ☐ Male
   - ☐ Female

6. Marital Status
   - ☐ Married
   - ☐ Widowed
   - ☐ Single
   - ☐ Divorced

7. Other Names Used (including maiden name)

8. Date and Place of Present Marriage (if married)

9. Social Security Number

10. Alien Registration Number (if any)

11. Names of Prior Husbands/Wives   12. Date(s) Marriages(s) Ended

13. Has your relative ever been in the U.S.? ☐ Yes ☐ No

14. If your relative is currently in the U.S., complete the following: He or she last arrived as a (visitor, student, stowaway, without inspection, etc.)

    Arrival/Departure Record (I-94) Number   Date arrived (Month/Day/Year)

    Date authorized stay expired, or will expire, as shown on Form I-94 or I-95

15. Name and address of present employer (if any)

    Date this employment began (Month/Day/Year)

16. Has your relative ever been under immigration proceedings?
    - ☐ Yes
    - ☐ No   Where _____ When _____
    - ☐ Exclusion ☐ Deportation ☐ Recission ☐ Judicial Proceedings

---

	INITIAL RECEIPT	RESUBMITTED	RELOCATED		COMPLETED		
			Rec'd	Sent	Approved	Denied	Returned

Form I-130 (Rev. 10/13/98)N

C. (continued) Information about your alien relative

16. List husband/wife and all children of your relative (if your relative is your husband/wife, list only his or her children).
    (Name)   (Relationship)   (Date of Birth)   (Country of Birth)

17. Address in the United States where your relative intends to live
    (Number and Street)   (Town or City)   (State)

18. Your relative's address abroad
    (Number and Street)   (Town or City)   (Province)   (Country)   (Phone Number)

19. If your relative's native alphabet is other than Roman letters, write his or her name and address abroad in the native alphabet:
    (Name)   (Number and Street)   Town or City   (Province)   (Country)

20. If filing for your husband/wife, give last address at which you both lived together: From   To
    (Name)   (Number and Street)   (Town or City)   (Province)   (Country)   (Month)   (Year)   (Month)   (Year)

21. Check the appropriate box below and give the information required for the box you checked:
    ☐ Your relative will apply for a visa abroad at the American Consulate in _____
                                                          (City)   (Country)

    ☐ Your relative is in the United States and will apply for adjustment of status to that of a lawful permanent resident in the office of the Immigration and
    Naturalization Service at _____ . If your relative is not eligible for adjustment of status, he or she will
                              (City)   (State)
    apply for a visa abroad at the American Consulate in _____ ,
                                                          (City)   (Country)

    (Designation of a consulate outside the country of your relative's last residence does not guarantee acceptance for processing by that consulate.
    Acceptance is at the discretion of the designated consulate.)

D. Other Information

1. If separate petitions are also being submitted for other relatives, give names of each and relationship.

2. Have you ever filed a petition for this or any other alien before?   ☐ Yes   ☐ No
   If "Yes," give name, place and date of filing, and result.

Warning: The INS investigates claimed relationships and verifies the validity of documents. The INS seeks criminal prosecutions when family relationships are falsified to obtain visas.

Penalties: You may, by law be imprisoned for not more than five years, or fined $250,000, or both, for entering into a marriage contract for the purpose of evading any provision of the immigration laws and you may be fined up to $10,000 or imprisoned up to five years or both, for knowingly and willfully falsifying or concealing a material fact or using any false document in submitting this petition.

Your Certification: I certify, under penalty of perjury under the laws of the United States of America, that the foregoing is true and correct. Furthermore, I authorize the release of any information from my records which the Immigration and Naturalization Service needs to determine eligibility for the benefit that I am seeking.

Signature _____ Date _____ Phone Number _____

Signature of Person Preparing Form if Other than Above

I declare that I prepared this document at the request of the person above and that it is based on all information of which I have any knowledge.

Print Name _____ (Address) _____ (Signature) _____ (Date) _____

G-28 ID Number _____

Volag Number _____

Form I-130 (Rev. 10/13/98)N

NOTICE TO PERSONS FILING FOR SPOUSES IF MARRIED LESS THAN TWO YEARS

Pursuant to section 216 of the Immigration and Nationality Act, your alien spouse may be granted conditional permanent resident status in the United States as of the date he or she is admitted or adjusted to conditional status by an officer of the Immigration and Naturalization Service. Both you and your conditional permanent resident spouse are required to file a petition, Form I-751, Joint Petition to Remove Conditional Basis of Alien's Permanent Resident Status, during the ninety day period immediately before the second anniversary of the date your alien spouse was granted conditional permanent residence.

Otherwise, the rights, privileges, responsibilities and duties which apply to all other permanent residents apply equally to a conditional permanent resident. A conditional permanent resident is not limited to the right to apply for naturalization, to file petitions in behalf of qualifying relatives, or to reside permanently in the United States as an immigrant in accordance with the immigration laws.

> **Failure to file Form I-751, Joint Petition to Remove the Conditional Basis of Alien's Permanent Resident Status, will result in termination of permanent residence status and initiation of deportation proceedings.**

NOTE: You must complete Items 1 through 6 to assure that petition approval is recorded. Do not write in the section below item 6.

---

1. **Name of relative** (Family name in CAPS)   (First)   (Middle)

2. **Other names used by relative** (Including maiden name)

3. **Country of relative's birth**   4. **Date of relative's birth** (Month/Day/Year)

5. **Your name** (Last name in CAPS) (First)   (Middle)   6. **Your phone number**

Action Stamp

SECTION
- [ ] 201 (b)(spouse)
- [ ] 201 (b)(child)
- [ ] 201 (b)(parent)
- [ ] 203 (a)(1)
- [ ] 203 (a)(2)
- [ ] 203 (a)(4)
- [ ] 203 (a)(5)

DATE PETITION FILED

- [ ] **STATESIDE**
CRITERIA GRANTED

SENT TO CONSUL AT;

CHECKLIST

Have you answered each question?

Have you signed the petition?

Have you enclosed:
- [ ] The filing fee for each petition?
- [ ] Proof of your citizenship or lawful permanent residence?
- [ ] All required supporting documents for each petition?

If you are filing for your husband or wife have you included:
- [ ] Your picture?
- [ ] His or her picture?
- [ ] Your G-325A?
- [ ] His or her G-325A?

Relative Petition Card
Form I-130 (Rev. 10/13/98)N

U.S. Department of Justice
Immigration and Naturalization Service

OMB No.1115-0005

Application for Travel Document

START HERE - Please Type or Print

Part 1.   Information about you.

Family Name	Given Name	Middle Initial

Address - C/O

Street Number and Name		Apt. #
City	State or Province	
Country		ZIP/Postal Code

Date of Birth (Month/Day/Year)	Country of Birth
Social Security #	A #

Part 2.   Application Type (check one).

a. ☐ I am a permanent resident or conditional resident of the United States and I am applying for a Reentry Permit.

b. ☐ I now hold U.S. refugee or asylee status and I am applying for a Refugee Travel Document.

c. ☐ I am a permanent resident as a direct result of refugee or asylee status, and am applying for a Refugee Travel Document.

d. ☐ I am applying for an Advance Parole to allow me to return to the U.S. after temporary foreign travel.

e. ☐ I am outside the U.S. and am applying for an Advance Parole.

f. ☐ I am applying for an Advance Parole for another person who is outside the U.S. *Give the following information about that person:*

Family Name	Given Name	Middle Initial
Date of Birth (Month/Day/Year)	Country of Birth	

Foreign Address - C/O

Street Number and Name		Apt. #
City	State or Province	
Country		ZIP/Postal Code

Part 3.   Processing Information.

Date of Intended departure (Month/Day/Year)	Expected length of trip.

Are you, or any person included in this application, now in exclusion or deportation proceedings?

☐ No   ☐ Yes, at (give office name) _____

If applying for an Advance Parole Document, skip to Part 7.

Have you ever before been issued a Reentry Permit or Refugee Travel Document?

☐ No   ☐ Yes (give the following for the last document issued to you)

Date Issued	Disposition (attached, lost, etc.)

Continued on back.

FOR INS USE ONLY

Returned	Receipt
_____	
_____	
Resubmitted	
_____	
_____	
Reloc Sent	
_____	
_____	
Reloc Rec'd	
_____	
_____	

☐ Applicant Interviewed on

Document Issued
☐ Reentry Permit
☐ Refugee Travel Document
☐ Single Advance Parole
☐ Multiple Advance Parole
Validity to _____

If Reentry Permit or Refugee Travel Document
☐ Mail to Address in Part 2
☐ Mail to American Consulate
☐ Mail to INS overseas office
AT

Remarks:
☐ Document Hand Delivered
On _____ By _____

Action Block

To Be Completed by Attorney or Representative, if any
☐ Fill in box if G-28 is attached to represent the applicant

VOLAG#

ATTY State License #

Form I-131 (Rev. 10/13/98)N

Part 3. Processing Information. (continued)

Where do you want this travel document sent? (check one)

a. ☐ Address in Part 2, above

b. ☐ American Consulate at (give City and Country, below)

c. ☐ INS overseas office at (give City and Country, below)

   City   Country

If you checked b. or c., above, give your overseas address:

Part 4. Information about the Proposed Travel.

Purpose of trip. *If you need more room, continue on a separate sheet of paper.*	List the countries you intend to visit.

Part 5. Complete only if applying for a Reentry Permit.

Since becoming a Permanent Resident (or during the past five years, whichever is less) how much total time have you spent outside the United States?	☐ less than 6 months ☐ 6 months to 1 year ☐ 1 to 2 years	☐ 2 to 3 years ☐ 3 to 4 years ☐ more than 4 years
Since you became a Permanent Resident, have you ever filed a federal income tax return as a nonresident, or failed to file a federal return because you considered yourself to be a nonresident? (if yes, give details on a separate sheet of paper).	☐ Yes	☐ No

Part 6. Complete only if applying for a Refugee Travel Document.

Country from which you are a refugee or asylee:

If you answer yes to any of the following questions, explain on a separate sheet of paper.

Do you plan to travel to the above-named country?	☐ Yes	☐ No
Since you were accorded Refugee/Asylee status, have you ever: returned to the above-named country; applied for an/or obtained a national passport, passport renewal, or entry permit into this country; or applied for an/or received any benefit from such country (for example, health insurance benefits)?	☐ Yes	☐ No
Since being accorded Refugee/Asylee status, have you, by any legal procedure or voluntary act, re-acquired the nationality of the above-named country, acquired a new nationality, or been granted refugee or asylee status in any other country?	☐ Yes	☐ No

Part 7. Complete only if applying for an Advance Parole.

On a separate sheet of paper, please explain how you qualify for an Advance Parole and what circumstances warrant issuance of Advance Parole. Include copies of any documents you wish considered. (See instructions.)

For how may trips do you intend to use this document?   ☐ 1 trip   ☐ More than 1 trip
If outside the U.S., at right give the U.S. Consulate or INS office you wish notified if this application is approved.

Part 8. Signature.   *Read the information on penalties in the instructions before completing this section. You must file this application while in the United States if filing for a reentry permit or refugee travel document.*

I certify under penalty of perjury under the laws of the United States of America that this petition, and the evidence submitted with it, is all true and correct. I authorize the release of any information from my records which the Immigration and Naturalization Service needs to determine eligibility for the benefit I am seeking.

Signature	Date	Daytime Telephone # ( )

Please Note: *If you do not completely fill out this form, or fail to submit required documents listed in the instructions, you may not be found eligible for the requested document and this application will have to be denied.*

Part 9. Signature of person preparing form if other than above. (sign below)

I declare that I prepared this application at the request of the above person and it is based on all information of which I have knowledge.

Signature	Print Your Name	Date

Firm Name and Address		Daytime Telephone # ( )

U. S. Department of Justice
Immigration and Naturalization Service

Affidavit of Support

(ANSWER ALL ITEMS: FILL IN WITH TYPEWRITER OR PRINT IN BLOCK LETTERS IN INK.)

I, _____, *residing at* _____
   (Name)   (Street and Number)

_____
(City)   (State)   (ZIP Code if in U.S.)   (Country)

BEING DULY SWORN DEPOSE AND SAY:

1. I was born on_____at_____
                              (Date)   (City)   (Country)

   If you are *not* a native born United States citizen, answer the following as appropriate:

   a. If a United States citizen through naturalization, give certificate of naturalization number _____

   b. If a United States citizen through parent(s) or marriage, give citizenship certificate number _____

   c. If United States citizenship was derived by some other method, attach a statement of explanation.

   d. If a lawfully admitted permanent resident of the United States, give "A" number _____

2. That I am_____years of age and have resided in the United States since (date) _____

3. That this affidavit is executed in behalf of the following person:

Name		Sex	Age
Citizen of--(Country)	Marital Status	Relationship to Deponent	
Presently resides at--(Street and Number)	(City)	(State)	(Country)

Name of spouse and children accompanying or following to join person:

Spouse	Sex	Age	Child		Sex	Age
Child	Sex	Age	Child		Sex	Age
Child	Sex	Age	Child		Sex	Age

4. That this affidavit is made by me for the purpose of assuring the United States Government that the person(s) named in item 3 will not become a public charge in the United States.

5. That I am willing and able to receive, maintain and support the person(s) named in item 3. That I am ready and willing to deposit a bond, if necessary, to guarantee that such person(s) will not become a public charge during his or her stay in the United States, or to guarantee that the above named will maintain his or her nonimmigrant status if admitted temporarily and will depart prior to the expiration of his or her authorized stay in the United States.

6. That I understand this affidavit will be binding upon me for a period of three (3) years after entry of the person(s) named in item 3 and that the information and documentation provided by me may be made available to the Secretary of Health and Human Services and the Secretary of Agriculture, who may make it available to a public assistance agency.

7. That I am employed as, or engaged in the business of _____with _____
                                                                                   (Type of Business)   (Name of concern)

   at _____
        (Street and Number)   (City)   (State)   (Zip Code)

   I derive an annual income of *(if self-employed, I have attached a copy of my last income tax
   return or report of commercial rating concern which I certify to be true and correct to the best
   of my knowledge and belief. See instruction for nature of evidence of net worth to be
   submitted.)* $_____

   I have on deposit in savings banks in the United States $_____

   I have other personal property, the reasonable value of which is $_____

Form I-134 (Rev. 12-1-84) Y   OVER

I have stocks and bonds with the following market value, as indicated on the attached list which I certify to be true and correct to the best of my knowledge and belief. $ _____

I have life insurance in the sum of $ _____

With a cash surrender value of $ _____

I own real estate valued at $ _____

With mortgages or other encumbrances thereon amounting to $ _____

Which is located at_____
(Street and Number   (City)   (State)   (Zip Code)

8. That the following persons are dependent upon me for support: *(Place an "X" in the appropriate column to indicate whether the person named is **wholly or partially** dependent upon you for support.)*

Name of Person	Wholly Dependent	Partially Dependent	Age	Relationship to Me

9. That I have previously submitted affidavit(s) of support for the following person(s). If none, state *"None"*

Name   Date submitted

_____

_____

10. That I have submitted visa petition(s) to the Immigration and Naturalization Service on behalf of the following person(s). If none, state none.

Name   Relationship   Date submitted

_____

_____

_____

11. *(Complete this block only if the person named in item 3 will be in the United States temporarily.)*
   That I ☐ do intend   ☐ do not intend, to make specific contributions to the support of the person named in item 3. *(If you check "do intend", indicate the exact nature and duration of the contributions. For example, if you intend to furnish room and board, state for how long and, if money, state the amount in United States dollars and state whether it is to be given in a lump sum, weekly, or monthly, or for how long.)*

_____

_____

_____

OATH OR AFFIRMATION OF DEPONENT

I acknowledge at that I have read Part III of the Instructions, Sponsor and Alien Liability, and am aware of my responsibilities as an immigrant sponsor under the Social Security Act, as amended, and the Food Stamp Act, as amended.

I swear (affirm) that I know the contents of this affidavit signed by me and the statements are true and correct.

Signature of deponent _____

Subscribed and sworn to (affirmed) before me this _____*day of* _____ ,19_____

at _____ .*My commission expires on* _____

Signature of Officer Administering Oath _____ *Title* _____

If affidavit prepared by other than deponent, please complete the following: I declare that this document was prepared by me at the request of the deponent and is based on all information of which I have knowledge.

_____

(Signature)   *(Address)*   *(Date)*

START HERE - Please Type or Print

Part 1. Information about the person or organization filing this petition. If you are filing for yourself and do not want to use an alternate mailing address, skip this part and go to part 2.

If an individual is filing, use the top name line. Organizations should use the second line.

Family Name	Given Name	Middle Initial

Company or Organization

Address - Attn:

Street Number and Name		Room #
City	State or Province	
Country	ZIP/Postal Code	

IRS Tax #	Social Security #

FOR INS USE ONLY

Returned	Receipt
Resubmitted	
Reloc Sent	
Reloc Rec'd	

☐ Petitioner Interviewed
☐ Beneficiary Interviewed

Classification
☐ 203(b)(1)(A) Alien Of Extraordinary Ability
☐ 203(b)(1)(B) Outstanding Professor or Researcher
☐ 203(b)(1)(C) Multi-national executive or manager
☐ 203(b)(2) Member of professions w/adv. degree or of exceptional ability
☐ 203(b)(3) (A) (i) Skilled worker
☐ 203(b)(3) (A) (ii) Professional
☐ 203(b)(3) (A) (iii) Other worker
☐ Sec. 124 IMMACT-Employee of U.S. business in Hong Kong

Certification:
Blanket Labor Certification
Schedule A, Group I
Schedule A, Group II

Priority Date	Consulate

Remarks

Action Block

Part 2. Petition Type.

1. This petition is being filed for: *(check one)*

a. ☐ An alien of extraordinary ability
b. ☐ An outstanding professor or researcher
c. ☐ A multinational executive or manager
d. ☐ A member of the professions holding an advanced degree or an alien of exceptional ability
e. ☐ A skilled worker (requiring at least two years of specialized training or experience) or professional
f. ☐ Any other worker (requiring less than two years training or experience)
g. ☐ An employee of a U.S. business operating in Hong Kong
h. ☐ Soviet Scientist

Part 3. Information about the person you are filing for.

Family Name	Given Name	Middle Initial

Address - C/O

Street # and Name		Apt. #
City	State or Province	
Country	Zip or Postal Code	

Date of Birth (Month/Day/Year)	Country of Birth

Social Security # (if any)	A # (if any)

If in the U.S.

Date of Arrival (Month/Day/Year)	I-94#
Current Nonimmigrant Status	Expires on (Month/Day/Year)

To Be Completed by
Attorney or *Representative*, if any
☐ Fill in box if G-28 is attached to represent the petitioner

VOLAG#

ATTY State License #

Continued on back.

Part 4. Processing Information.

A. Check one:
   ☐ The person named in Part 3 is now in the U.S. and an application to adjust status to permanent resident is attached or will be filed in this petition is approved.
   ☐ If the Petition is approved, but the adjustment of status cannot be approved, send the petition to an American Consulate abroad, which the Department of State will identify based on the following information:

   Country of Nationality of person named in Part 3: _____
   Country of current residence or, if no in the U.S., last permanent residence abroad, of person named in part 3: _____
   If you gave a U.S. address in Part 3, print the person's print the person's foreign address below.
   Name: _____ Address: _____

   If your employee's native alphabet is other than Roman Letter, write the foreign address in the native alphabet:

Are you filing any other petitions or applications with this one?	☐ No	☐ Yes -attach an explanation	
Is the person you are filing for in exclusion or deportation proceedings?	☐ No	☐ Yes -attach an explanation	
Has an immigrant visa petition ever been filed by or on behalf of this person?	☐ No	☐ Yes -attach an explanation	

Part 5. Additional Information about the employer.

Type of petitioner (check one)
☐ Self   ☐ Individual U.S. Citizen   ☐ Company or organization
☐ Permanent Resident   ☐ Other - explain _____

If a company, give the following:
   Type of business

Date Established	Current # of employees	Gross Annual Income	Net Annual Income

If an individual, give the following:
Occupation | | Annual Income |

Part 6. Basic Information about the proposed employment.

Job Title	Nontechnical description of job

Address where the person will work if different from address in Part 1.

Is this a full-time position?	☐ Yes No (hours per week _____)	Wages per week

Is this a permanent position?: ☐ Yes ☐ No   Is this a new position? ☐ Yes ☐ No

Part 7. Information on spouse and all children of the person you are filing for.

Provide an attachment listing the family members of the person you are filing for. Be sure to include their full name, relationship, date and country of birth, and present address.

Part 8. Signature. *Read the information on penalties in the instructions before completing this section. If someone helped you prepare this petition, he or she must complete Part 9.*

I certify under penalty of perjury under the laws of the United States of America that this petition and the evidence submitted with it are all true and correct. I authorize the release of any information from my records which the Immigration and Naturalization Service needs to determine eligibility for the benefit I am seeking.

Petitioner's Signature	Print Name	Date	Daytime Telephone No. ( )

Please Note: If you do not completely fill out this form or fail to submit required documents listed in the instructions, you cannot be found eligible for the requested document and this application may be denied.

Part 9. Signature of person preparing form if other than above. *(Sign below)*

I declare that I prepared this application at the request of the above person and it is based on all information of which I have knowledge.

Signature	Print Name	Date	Daytime Telephone No. ( )

Firm Name and Address

Form I-140 (Rev. 10/13/98)N

U.S. Department of Justice

Immigration and Naturalization Service

OMB No. 1115-0032

Application for Advance Permission to Return to Unrelinquished Domicile

(See instructions on reverse. Please typewrite or print plainly in ink)

FEE STAMP

Alien Registration No.

Date

(1) I hereby apply for permission to return to the United States under the authority contained in Section 212(c) of the Immigration and Nationality Act.

MY NAME IS: *(First)*   *(Middle)*   *(Last)*

DATE OF BIRTH: *(Month, day, year)*   PLACE OF BIRTH: *(City, province, country)*   I AM A CITIZEN OF: *(Country)*

PRESENT ADDRESS: *(Street and number, apt. no., city, state, country)*

(2) I was lawfully admitted to the United States for permanent residence at:

PORT: DATE: *(Month, day, year)*   NAME OF VESSEL OR OTHER MEANS OF CONVEYANCE:

(3) Since that admission I have departed from and reentered the United States as follows:

DEPARTED FROM THE UNITED STATES			RETURNED TO THE UNITED STATES			PURPOSE OF TRIP
Port	Date (Month, day, year)	Vessel or Other Means of Conveyance	Port	Date (Month, day, year)	Vessel or Other Means of Conveyance	

(4) During the past 7 years I have resided at the following places: *(List present address first)*

(Complete Address - Include Apt. No.)	From -	To-
		Present time

(5) During the past 7 years I have been employed as follows: *(List present employment first)*

From -	To -	Employer's Name	Address	Occupation or Type of Business

(6) My immediate family consists of the following persons:

Name	Relation	Date and Country of Birth	Citizen of	Present Address

(7) I _____ depart(ed) temporarily from the United States on or about _____ and will remain
(Intend to or have)   *(Date)*

in _____ approximately _____ , for the purpose of
(Country)   *(Length of Time)*

_____ ; and expect to apply for admission at _____
                                                             (Port)

RECEIVED	TRANS. IN	RET'D-TRANS. OUT	COMPLETED

Form I-191 (Rev. 10/13/98)N

(8) I believe I may be inadmissible to the United States for the following reasons:

_____

_____

_____

I understand that the information herein contained may be used in any criminal or civil proceedings, including deportation or exclusion, hereafter instituted against me.

I certify that the statements above are true and correct to the best of my knowledge and belief.

_____

SIGNATURE OF PERSON PREPARING FORM, IF OTHER THAN APPLICANT
I declare that the document was prepared by me at the request of the applicant and is based on all information of which I have any knowledge.

(Signature)	_(Address)_	_(Date)_

Decision: ☐ Application granted upon the following terms and conditions:	DATE OF ACTION DD
	DISTRICT

INSTRUCTIONS TO THE APPLICANT

READ INSTRUCTIONS CAREFULLY - FEE WILL NOT BE REFUNDED

(A) This form when completely executed, should be submitted to the District Director of the Immigration office having jurisdiction over your place of permanent residence.

(B) A fee of one hundred seventy dollars ($170.00) must be paid for filing this application. It cannot be refunded regardless of the action taken on the application.

MAIL CASH. ALL FEES MUST BE SUBMITTED IN THE EXACT AMOUNT. Payment by check or money order must be drawn on a bank or other institution located in the United States and be payable in United States currency. If applicant resides in Guam, check or money order must be payable to the "Treasurer Guam." If Applicant resides in the Virgin Islands, check or money order must be payable to the "Commissioner of Finance of the Virgin Islands". All other applicants must make the check or money order payable to the "Immigration and Naturalization Service." When check is drawn on account of a person other than the applicant, the name of the applicant must be entered on the face of the check. If application is submitted from outside the United States, remittance may be made by bank international money order or foreign draft drawn on a financial institution in the United States and payable to the Immigration and Naturalization Service in United States currency. Personal checks are accepted subject to collectibility. An uncollectible check will render the application and any document issued pursuant thereto invalid. A charge of $30.00 will be imposed if a check in payment of a fee is not honored by the bank on which it is drawn.

(C) If the space provided in the form is insufficient to answer a question fully, you should attach a sheet of paper containing your answer which should be numbered to correspond with the question.

(D) In Part (3) where absences have been numerous as a resident alien border crosser or as a seaman it will be sufficient to give the approximate number of such absences and the years covered thereby.

(E) List specifically and in detail your reasons for possible inadmissibility. For example, if application is made because the applicant may be inadmissible due to conviction of crime, the designation of the crime, the date and place of its commission and of conviction therefor, and the sentence or other judgement of the court shall be stated in the application. In the case of disease, mental or physical defect or other disability, give exact description, duration thereof and date and place last treated.

(F) If applicant is mentally incompetent or is under 14 years of age, the application shall be executed by his parent or guardian.
The authority for collection of the information requested on this form is contained in 8 U.S.C. 1103(a). Submission of the information is voluntary. The principal purpose for which the information is solicited is for use by a District Director of the Immigration and Naturalization Service to determine whether the applicant is eligible for advance permission to return to an unrelinquished domicile pursuant to the provisions of section 212(c) of the Immigration and Nationality Act, 8 U.S.C. 1182(c). The information solicited may also, as a matter of routine use, be disclosed to other federal, state, local, and foreign law enforcement and regulatory agencies, the Department of Defense including any component thereof (if the applicant has served, or is serving in the Armed Forces of the United States), the Department of State, Central Intelligence Agency, Interpol, and individuals and organizations, during the course of investigation to elicit further information required by the Service to carry out its functions. Failure to provide any or all of the solicited information may result in the denial of the application.

Public Reporting Burden. A person is not required to respond to a collection of information unless it displays a currently valid OMB control Number. Reporting burden for this collection of information is estimated to average as follows: 1) _learning about the form,_ 5 minutes; 2) _completing and assembling and mailing the form,_ 10 minutes, for a total of 15 minutes per response. If you have comments regarding the accuracy of this estimate, or suggestions for making this form simpler, you can write to the U.S. Department of Justice, Immigration and Naturalization Service Room 5307, Washington, D.C. 20536; OMB No. 1115-0032, **DO NOT MAIL YOUR COMPLETED APPLICATION TO THIS ADDRESS.**

START HERE - Please Type or Print

FOR INS USE ONLY

Part 1. Information about person or organization filing this petition. (Individuals should use top name line; organizations should use the second line.) *If you are filing for yourself, skip to Part 2. A widow(er) must file for him/her self.*

Family Name	Given Name	Middle Initial

Company or Organization Name

Address - C/O

Street Number and Name		Apt. #
City	State or Province	
Country		ZIP/Postal Code

U.S. Social Security #	A #	IRS Tax # (if any)

Part 2. Classification Requested (check one):

a. ☐ Amerasian

b. ☐ Widow(er) of a U.S. citizen who died within the past 2 years

c. ☐ Special Immigrant Juvenile

d. ☐ Special Immigrant Religious Worker

e. ☐ Special Immigrant based on employment with the Panama Canal Company, Canal Zone Government or U.S. Government in the Canal Zone

f. ☐ Special Immigrant Physician

g. ☐ Special Immigrant International Organization Employee or family member

Part 3. Information about the person this petition is for.

Family Name	Given Name	Middle Initial

Address - C/O

Street Number and Name		Apt. #
City	State or Province	
Country		ZIP/Postal Code

Date of Birth (Month/Day/Year)	Country of Birth
U.S. Social Security # (if any)	A # (if any)

Complete the items below if this person is in the United States:

Date of Arrival (Month/Day/Year)	I-94 #
Current Nonimmigrant Status	Expires on (Month/Day/Year)

FOR INS USE ONLY

Returned

Receipt

Resubmitted

Reloc Sent

Reloc Rec'd

☐ Petitioner/ Applicant Interviewed

☐ Beneficiary Interviewed

☐ I-485 Filed Concurrently
☐ Bene "A" File Reviewed

Classification

Consulate

Priority Date

Remarks:

Action Block

To Be Completed by *Attorney* or *Representative*, if any

☐ Fill in box if G-28 is attached to represent the applicant

VOLAG#

ATTY State License #

Form I-360 (Rev. 09/19/91) N   ***Continued on back.***

Part 4. Processing Information.

Below give the United States Consulate you want notified if this petition is approved and if any requested adjustment of status cannot be granted.

American Consulate: City	Country

If you gave a United States address in Part 3, print the person's foreign address below. If his/her native alphabet does not use Roman letters, print his/her name and foreign address in the native alphabet.

Name	Address

Sex of the person this petition is for.	☐ Male	☐ Female
Are you filing any other petitions or applications with this one?	☐ No	☐ Yes (How many? _____)
Is the person this petition is for in exclusion or deportation proceedings?	☐ No	☐ Yes (Explain on a separate sheet of paper)
Has the person this petition is for ever worked in the U.S. without permission?	☐ No	☐ Yes (Explain on a separate sheet of paper)
Is an application for adjustment of status attached to this petition?	☐ No	☐ Yes

Part 5. Complete only if filing for an Amerasian.

Section A. Information about the mother of the Amerasian

Family Name	Given Name	Middle Initial

Living? ☐ No (Give date of death _____) ☐ Yes (complete address line below) ☐ Unknown (attach a full explanation)

Address

Section B. Information about the father of the Amerasian: If possible, attach a notarized statement from the father regarding parentage. Explain on separate paper any question you cannot fully answer in the space provided on this form.

Family Name	Given Name	Middle Initial

Date of Birth (Month/Day/Year)	Country of Birth

Living? ☐ No (give date of death _____) ☐ Yes (complete address line below) ☐ Unknown (attach a full explanation)

Home Address

Home Phone #	Work Phone #

At the time the Amerasian was conceived:

☐ The father was in the military (indicate branch of service below - and give service number here): _____

    ☐ Army   ☐ Air Force   ☐ Navy   ☐ Marine Corps   ☐ Coast Guard

☐ The father was a civilian employed abroad. Attach a list of names and addresses of organizations which employed him at that time.

☐ If the father was not in the military, and was not a civilian employed abroad. *(Attach a full explanation of the circumstances.)*

Part 6. Complete only if filing for a Juvenile.

Section A. Information about the Juvenile

List any other names used.

Marital Status:	☐ Single	☐ Married	☐ Divorced	☐ Widowed

Answer the following questions regarding the person this petition is for. If you answer "no" explain on a separate sheet of paper.

Is he/she still a juvenile under the laws of the state in which the juvenile

court upon which the alien has been declared dependent is located? ☐ No ☐ Yes

Does he/she continue to be dependent upon the juvenile court? ☐ No ☐ Yes

Does he/she continue to be eligible for long term foster care? ☐ No ☐ Yes

Continued on next page.

Part 7. Complete only if filing for a Widow or Widower.

Section A. Information about the U.S. citizen husband or wife who died.

Family Name	Given Name	Middle Initial

Date of Birth (Month/Day/Year)	Country of Birth	Date of Death (Month/Day/Year)

His/her U.S. citizenship was based on (check one)

☐ Birth in the U.S.   ☐ Birth abroad to U.S. citizen parent(s)   ☐ Naturalization

Section B. Additional Information about you.

How many times have you been married?	How many times was the person in Section A married?

Give the date and place you and the person in Section A were married.

Did you live with this U.S. citizen spouse from the date you were married until he/she died?
☐ Yes   ☐ No (attach explanation)

Were you legally separated at the time of the United States citizen's death?
☐ Yes (attach explanation)   ☐ No

Give your address at the time of the United States citizen's death.

Part 8. Information about the children and spouse of the person this petition is for.
For a widow or widower, include any children of your deceased spouse.

A.	Family Name	Given Name	Middle Initial	Date of Birth (Month/Day/Year)
	Country of Birth	Relationship ☐ Spouse ☐ Child		A #

B.	Family Name	Given Name	Middle Initial	Date of Birth (Month/Day/Year)
	Country of Birth	Relationship ☐ Spouse ☐ Child		A #

C.	Family Name	Given Name	Middle Initial	Date of Birth (Month/Day/Year)
	Country of Birth	Relationship ☐ Spouse ☐ Child		A #

D.	Family Name	Given Name	Middle Initial	Date of Birth (Month/Day/Year)
	Country of Birth	Relationship ☐ Spouse ☐ Child		A #

E.	Family Name	Given Name	Middle Initial	Date of Birth (Month/Day/Year)
	Country of Birth	Relationship ☐ Spouse ☐ Child		A #

F.	Family Name	Given Name	Middle Initial	Date of Birth (Month/Day/Year)
	Country of Birth	Relationship ☐ Spouse ☐ Child		A #

G.	Family Name	Given Name	Middle Initial	Date of Birth (Month/Day/Year)
	Country of Birth	Relationship ☐ Spouse ☐ Child		A #

H.	Family Name	Given Name	Middle Initial	Date of Birth (Month/Day/Year)
	Country of Birth	Relationship ☐ Spouse ☐ Child		A #

Continued on back.

Part 9. Signature. *Read the information on penalties in the instructions before completing this part. If you are going to file this petition at an INS office in the United States, sign below. If you are going to file it at a U.S. consulate or INS office overseas, sign in front of a U.S. INS or consular official.*

I certify, or, if outside the United States, I swear or affirm, under penalty of perjury under the laws of the United States of America, that this petition, and the evidence submitted with it, is all true and correct. If filing this on behalf of an organization, I certify that I am empowered to do so by that organization. I authorize the release of any information from my records, or from the petitioning organization's records, which the Immigration and Naturalization Service needs to determine eligibility for the benefit being sought.

Signature	Date

Signature of INS or Consular Official	Print Name	Date

Please Note: *If you do not completely fill out this form, or fail to submit required documents listed in the instructions, then the person(s) filed for may not be found eligible for a requested benefit, and it may have to be denied.*

Part 10. Signature of person preparing form if other than above. (sign below)

I declare that I prepared this application at the request of the above person and it is based on all information of which I have knowledge.

Signature	Print Your Name	Date

Firm Name
and Address

U.S. Department of Justice
Immigration and Naturalization Service

OMB No. 1115-0053

Application to Register Permanent Residence or Adjust Status

START HERE - Please Type or Print

Part 1.   Information about you.

Family Name	Given Name	Middle Initial

Address - C/O

Street Number and Name		Apt. #

City

State	Zip Code

Date of Birth (month/day/year)	Country of Birth

Social Security #	A # (if any)

Date of Last Arrival (month/day/year)	I-94 #

Current INS Status	Expires on (month/day/year)

Part 2.   Application Type. *(check one)*

I am applying for adjustment to permanent resident status because:

a. ☐ an immigrant petition giving me an immediately available immigrant visa number has been approved (attach a copy of the approval notice), or a relative, special immigrant juvenile, or special immigrant military visa petition filed with this application will give me an immediately available visa number if approved.

b. ☐ My spouse or parent applied for adjustment of status or was granted lawful permanent residence in an immigrant visa category which allows derivative status for spouses and children.

c. ☐ I entered as a K-1 fiance(e) of a U.S. citizen whom I married within 90 days of entry, or I am the K-2 child of such a fiance(e) (attach a copy of the fiance(e) petition approval notice and the marriage certificate).

d. ☐ I was granted asylum or derivative asylum status as the spouse or child of a person granted asylum and am eligible for adjustment.

e. ☐ I am a native or citizen of Cuba admitted or paroled into the U.S. after January 1, 1959, and thereafter have been physically present in the U.S. for at least 1 year.

f. ☐ I am the husband, wife, or minor unmarried child of a Cuban described in (e) and am residing with that person, and was admitted or paroled into the U.S. after January 1, 1959, and thereafter have been physically present in the U.S. for at least 1 year.

g. ☐ I have continuously resided in the U.S. since before January 1, 1972.

h. ☐ Other-explain_____

I am already a permanent resident and am applying to have the date I was granted permanent residence adjusted to the date I originally arrived in the U.S. as a nonimmigrant or parolee, or as of May 2, 1964, whichever is later, and: *(Check one)*

i. ☐ I am a native or citizen of Cuba and meet the description in (e), above.

j. ☐ I am the husband, wife or minor unmarried child of a Cuban, and meet the description in (f), above.

Continued on back.

Form I-485 (Rev. 10/13/98)N

Part 3. Processing Information.

A. City/Town/Village of birth

Current occupation

Your mother's first name

Your father's first name

Give your name exactly how it appears on your Arrival /Departure Record (Form I-94)

Place of last entry into the U.S. (City/State)

In what status did you last enter? *(Visitor, Student, exchange alien, crewman, temporary worker, without inspection, etc.)*

Were you inspected by a U.S. Immigration Officer? □ Yes □ No

Nonimmigrant Visa Number

Consulate where Visa was issued

Date Visa was Issued (month/day/year)

Sex: □ Male □ Female

Marital Status: □ Married □ Single □ Divorced □ Widowed

Have you ever before applied for permanent resident status in the U.S? □ No □ Yes (give date and place of filing and final disposition):

B. List your present husband/wife, all of your sons and daughters (if you have none, write "none". If additional space is needed, use separate paper).

Family Name	Given Name	Middle Initial	Date of Birth (month/day/year)
Country of birth	Relationship	A #	Applying with you? □ Yes □ No
Family Name	Given Name	Middle Initial	Date of Birth (month/day/year)
Country of birth	Relationship	A #	Applying with you? □ Yes □ No
Family Name	Given Name	Middle Initial	Date of Birth (month/day/year)
Country of birth	Relationship	A #	Applying with you? □ Yes □ No
Family Name	Given Name	Middle Initial	Date of Birth (month/day/year)
Country of birth	Relationship	A #	Applying with you? □ Yes □ No
Family Name	Given Name	Middle Initial	Date of Birth (month/day/year)
Country of birth	Relationship	A #	Applying with you? □ Yes □ No

C. List your present and past membership in or affiliation with every political organization, association, fund, foundation, party, club, society, or similar group in the United States or in any other place since your 16th birthday. Include any foreign military service in this part. If none, write "none". Include the name of organization, location, dates of membership from and to, and the nature of the organization. If additional space is needed, use separate paper.

_____

_____

_____

_____

_____

_____

Part 3. Processing Information. *(Continued)*

Please answer the following questions. (If your answer is **"Yes"** on any one of these questions, explain on a separate piece of paper. Answering **"Yes"** does not necessarily mean that you are not entitled to register for permanent residence or adjust status).

1. Have you ever, in or outside the U. S.:
    a. knowingly committed any crime of moral turpitude or a drug-related offense for which you have not been arrested?
    b. been arrested, cited, charged, indicted, fined, or imprisoned for breaking or violating any law or ordinance, excluding traffic violations?
    c. been the beneficiary of a pardon, amnesty, rehabilitation decree, other act of clemency or similar action?
    d. exercised diplomatic immunity to avoid prosecution for a criminal offense in the U. S.?   □ Yes   □ No

2. Have you received public assistance in the U.S. from any source, including the U.S. government or any state, county, city, or municipality (other than emergency medical treatment) , or are you likely to receive public assistance in the future?   □ Yes   □ No

3. Have you ever:
    a. within the past 10 years been a prostitute or procured anyone for prostitution, or intend to engage in such activities in the future?
    b. engaged in any unlawful commercialized vice, including, but not limited to, illegal gambling?
    c. knowingly encouraged, induced, assisted, abetted or aided any alien to try to enter the U.S. illegally?
    d. illicitly trafficked in any controlled substance, or knowingly assisted, abetted or colluded in the illicit trafficking of any controlled substance?   □ Yes   □ No

4. Have you ever engaged in, conspired to engage in, or do you intend to engage in, or have you ever solicited membership or funds for, or have you through any means ever assisted or provided any type of material support to, any person or organization that has ever engaged or conspired to engage, in sabotage, kidnapping, political assassination, hijacking, or any other form of terrorist activity?   □ Yes   □ No

5. Do you intend to engage in the U.S. in:
    a. espionage?
    b. any activity a purpose of which is opposition to, or the control or overthrow of, the Government of the United States, by force, violence or other unlawful means?
    c. any activity to violate or evade any law prohibiting the export from the United States of goods, technology or sensitive information?   □ Yes   □ No

6. Have you ever been a member of, or in any way affiliated with, the Communist Party or any other totalitarian party?   □ Yes   □ No

7. Did you, during the period March 23, 1933 to May 8, 1945, in association with either the Nazi Government of Germany or any organization or government associated or allied with the Nazi Government of Germany, ever order, incite, assist or otherwise participate in the persecution of any person because of race, religion, national origin or political opinion?   □ Yes   □ No

8. Have you ever engaged in genocide, or otherwise ordered, incited, assisted or otherwise participated in the killing of any person because of race, religion, nationality, ethnic origin, or political opinion?   □ Yes   □ No

9. Have you ever been deported from the U.S., or removed from the U.S. at government expense, excluded within the past year, or are you now in exclusion or deportation proceedings?   □ Yes   □ No

10. Are you under a final order of civil penalty for violating section 274C of the Immigration Act for use of fraudulent documents, or have you, by fraud or willful misrepresentation of a material fact, ever sought to procure, or procured, a visa, other documentation, entry into the U.S., or any other immigration benefit?   □ Yes   □ No

11. Have you ever left the U.S. to avoid being drafted into the U.S. Armed Forces?   □ Yes   □ No

12. Have you ever been a J nonimmigrant exchange visitor who was subject to the 2 year foreign residence requirement and not yet complied with that requirement or obtained a waiver?   □ Yes   □ No

13. Are you now withholding custody of a U.S. Citizen child outside the U.S. from a person granted custody of the child?   □ Yes   □ No

14. Do you plan to practice polygamy in the U.S.?   □ Yes   □ No

---

    Continued on back   Form I-485 (Rev. 10/13/98)N

Part 4.   Signature. *(Read the information on penalties in the instructions before completing this section. You must file this application while in the United States.)*

I certify under penalty of perjury under the laws of the United States of America that this application, and the evidence submitted with it, is all true and correct. I authorize the release of any information from my records which the Immigration and Naturalization Service needs to determine eligibility for the benefit I am seeking. I understand that completion of this form by persons required by law to register with the Selective Service System (males 18 through 25 years of age) constitutes such registration in accordance with the Military Selective Service Act.

Signature	Print Your Name	Date	Daytime Phone Number

Please Note: *If you do not completely fill out this form, or fail to submit required documents listed in the instructions, you may not be found eligible for the requested document and this application may be denied.*

Part 5.   Signature of person preparing form if other than above. *(Sign Below)*

I declare that I prepared this application at the request of the above person and it is based on all information of which I have knowledge.

Signature	Print Your Name	Date	Day time Phone Number

Firm Name
and Address

Form I-485 (Rev. 10/13/98)N

START HERE - Please Type or Print

Part 1. Information about Applicant

Family Name	First Name	Middle Name

Address - C/O

Street Number and Name		Apt. Suite
City	State or Province	
Country		ZIP/Postal Code

INS A #	Date of Birth (month/day/year)	Country of Birth

Part 2. Basis for Eligibility (check one)

1. On Form I-485, Part 2, I checked application type (check one):

a. ☐ An immigrant petition . . .   Go to #2.
b. ☐ My spouse or parent applied ...   Go to #2.
c. ☐ I entered as a K-1 fiance ...   Stop Here. Do Not File This Form.
d. ☐ I was granted asylum ...   Stop Here. Do Not File This Form.
e. ☐ I am a native or citizen of Cuba ..   Stop Here. Do Not File This Form.
f. ☐ I am the spouse or child of a Cuban   Stop Here. Do Not File This Form.
g. ☐ I have continuously resided in the U.S. ..   Stop Here. Do Not File This Form.
h. ☐ Other ...   Go to #2.
i. ☐ I am already a permanent resident ...   Stop Here. Do Not File This Form.
j. ☐ I am already a permanent resident and am the spouse or child of a Cuban   Stop Here. Do Not File This Form.

2. I have filed Form I-360; and I am applying for adjustment of status as a special immigrant juvenile court dependent (check one):

   ☐ Yes   Stop Here. Do Not File This Form.   ☐ No   Go to #3.

3. I have filed Form I-360; and I am applying for adjustment of status as a special immigrant who has served in the United States Armed Forces (check one):
   ☐ Yes   Stop Here. Do Not File This Form.   ☐ No   Go to #4.

4. I last entered the United States (check one):

   ☐ Legally as a crewman (D-1/D-2 visa).   Go to #11.   ☐ Legally without a visa   Go to #5.
   ☐ Without inspection.   Go to #11.   ☐ Legally as a parolee.   Go to #5.
   ☐ Legally in transit without visa status.   Go to #11.   ☐ Legally with another type of visa (show type _____) Go to #5.

5. I last entered the United States legally without a visa as a visitor for tourism or business; and I am applying for adjustment of status as the spouse, unmarried child less than 21 years old, parent, widow or widower of a United States citizen (check one):

   ☐ Yes   Stop Here. Do Not File This Form.   ☐ No   Go to #6.

6. I last entered the United States legally as a parolee, or with a visa (except as a crewman), or as a Canadian citizen without a visa; and I am applying for adjustment of status (check one):

   ☐ As the spouse, unmarried child less than 21 years old, parent, widow or widower of a United States citizen.
   Stop Here. Do Not File This Form.

   ☐ As a special immigrant retired international organization employee or family member of an international organization employee or as a special immigrant physician; and I have filed Form I-360.   Stop Here. Do Not File This Form.

   ☐ Under some other category.   Go to #7.

FOR INS USE ONLY

Returned	Receipt

Resubmitted

Reloc Sent

Reloc Rec'd

Interviewed
☐
☐

File Reviewed ☐ ☐	Class of Adjustment Code: _____ _____ _____

To Be Completed by Attorney or Representative, if any

☐ Check if G-28 is attached showing you represent the petitioner

VOLAG#

ATTY State License #

Part 2. continue.

7. I am a national of the (former) Soviet Union, Vietnam, Laos or Cambodia who last entered the United States legally as a public interest parolee after having been denied refugee status; and I am applying for adjustment of status under Public Law 101-167 *(check one)*:

    ☐ Yes   **Stop Here. Do Not File This Form.**   ☐ No **Go to #8.**

8. I have been employed in the United States after 01/01/77 without INS authorization *(check one)*:

    ☐ Yes **Go to #9.**   ☐ No **Go to #10.**

9. I am applying for adjustment of status under the Immigration Nursing Relief Act (INRA); I was employed without INS authorization only on or before 11/29/90; and I have always maintained a lawful immigration status while in the United States after 11/05/86 *(check one)*:

    ☐ Yes   **Stop Here. Do Not File This Form.**   ☐ No **Go to #10.**

10.   I am now in lawful immigration status; and I have always maintained a lawful immigration status while in the United States after 11/05/86 *(check one)*:

    ☐ Yes   **Stop Here. Do Not File This Form .**
    ☐ No, but I believe that INS will determine that my failure to be in or maintain a lawful immigration status was through no fault of my own or for technical reasons. **Stop Here. Do Not File This Form**, and attach an explanation to your Form I-485 application.
    ☐ No   **Go to #11.**

11. I am unmarried and less than 17 years old *(check one)*:

    ☐ Yes   **Stop Here. File This Form and Form I-485.**   **Pay only the fee required with Form I-485.**
    ☐ No   **Go to #12.**

12. I am the unmarried child of a legalized alien and am less than 21 years old, or I am the spouse of a legalized alien; and I have attached a copy of my receipt or approval notice showing that I have properly filed Form I-817, Application for Voluntary Departure under the Family Unity Program *(check one)*:

    ☐ Yes   **Stop Here. File This Form and Form I-485.**   **Pay only the fee required with Form I-485.**
    ☐ No   **Go to #13.**

13.   **File This Form and Form I-485. You must pay the additional sum:**

                $130.00 - Fee required with Form I-485* <u>and</u>
                $650.00 - Additional sum under section 245(i) of the Act

                $780.00 - Total amount you must pay.

*If you filed Form I-485 separately, attach a copy of your filing receipt and pay only the additional sum of $650.00. In #11 and /or #12, show the answer you would have given on the date you filed Form I-485.

Part 3.   Signature. Read the information on penalties in the instructions before completing this section. If someone helped you prepare this petition he or she must complete Part 4.

I certify, under penalty of perjury under the laws of the United States of America, that this application, and the evidence submitted with it, is all true and correct. I authorize the release of any information from my records which the Immigration and Naturalization Service needs to determine eligibility for the benefit I am seeking.

Signature	Print Your Name	Date	Daytime Telephone No.

Please Note: If you do not completely fill out this form or fail to submit required documents listed in the instructions, you may not be found eligible for the requested document and this application may be denied.

Part 4.   Signature of person preparing form if other than above. *(Sign Below)*

I declare that I prepared this application at the request of the above person and it is based on all information of which I have knowledge.

Signature	Print Your Name	Date	Daytime Telephone No.

Firm Name
and Address

U.S. Department of Justice
Immigration and Naturalization Service

OMB No. 1115-0081

Immigrant Petition by Alien Entrepreneur

START HERE - Please Type or Print

Part 1. Information about you.

Family Name	Given Name	Middle Initial

Address - In Care of:

Street # and Name		Apt. #

City or town	State or Province

Country	Zip or Postal Code

Date of Birth (Month/Day/Year)	Country of Birth

Social Security #	A#

If in the U.S.	Date of Arrival (Month/Day/Year)	I-94#
	Current Nonimmigrant Status	Expires on (Month/Day/Year)

Part 2. Application type (Check one).

a. ☐ This petition is based on an investment in a commercial enterprise in a targeted employment area for which the required amount of capital invested has been adjusted downward.

b. ☐ This petition is based on an investment in a commercial enterprise in an area for which the required amount of capital invested has been adjusted upward.

c. ☐ This petition is based on an investment in a commercial enterprise which is not in either a targeted area or in an upward adjustment area.

Part 3. Information about your investment.

Name of Commercial Enterprise Invested In

Street Address

Phone #	Business Organized as (Corporation, partnership, etc...)

Kind of Business
(Example: Furniture Manufacturer)

Date established (Month/Day/Year)	IRS Tax #

Date of your initial investment (Month/Day/Year)	Amount of your initial investment $

Your total capital investment in enterprise to date $	% of enterprise you own

If you are not the sole investor in the new commercial enterprise, list on separate paper the names of all other parties (natural and non-natural) who hold a percentage share of ownership of the new enterprise and indicate whether any of these parties is seeking classifications as an alien entrepreneur. Include the name, percentage of ownership and whether or not the person is seeking classification under section 203(b)(5).

If you indicated in Part 2 that the enterprise was in a targeted employment area or in an upward adjustment area, give the location at right.   County   State

Continued on back.

Form I-526 (Rev. 10/13/98)N

Part 4. Additional Information about the enterprise.

Type of enterprise *(check one):*

□ new commercial enterprise resulting from the creation of a new business.
□ new commercial enterprise resulting from the purchase of an existing business.
□ new commercial enterprise resulting from a capital investment in an existing business.

Assets:

Total amount in U.S. bank account	$ _____
Total value of all assets purchased for use in the enterprise	$ _____
Total value of all property transferred from abroad to the new enterprise	$ _____
Total of all debt financing	$ _____
Total stock purchases	$ _____
Other (explain on separate paper)	$ _____
Total	$ _____

Income: When you made investment   Gross $ _____   Net $ _____
       Now   Gross $ _____   Net $ _____

Net worth When you made investment $ _____   Now $ _____

Part 5. Employment creation Information.

# of full-time employees in Enterprise in U.S. (excluding you, spouse, sons & daughters)

When you made your initial investment _____   Now _____   Difference _____

How many of these new jobs were created by your investment? _____

How many additional new jobs will be created by your additional investment? _____

What is your position, office or title with the new commercial enterprise?

_____

Briefly describe your duties, activities and responsibilities.

_____

_____

Your Salary _____   Cost of Benefits _____

Part 6. Processing information.

Check One:

I am in the United States and an application to adjust status to permanent resident is attached or will be filed if this petition is approved.

After approval, send this petition to an American Consulate abroad, which the Department of State will identify based on the following information:

Your country of Nationality : _____ .

If now in the U.S., the country of your last permanent residence abroad: _____ .

Is an application for adjustment of status attached to this petition?	□ Yes	□ No
Are you in exclusion or deportation proceedings?	□ Yes (If yes, explain on separate paper)	□ No
Have you ever worked in the U.S. without permission?	□ Yes (Explain on separate paper)	□ No

Part 7. Signature. *Read the information on penalties in the instructions before completing this section.*

I certify under penalty of perjury under the laws of the United States of America that this petition, and the evidence submitted with it, is all true and correct. I authorize the release of any information from my records which the Immigration and Naturalization Service needs to determine eligibility for the benefit I am seeking.

Signature _____   Date _____

Please Note: If you do not completely fill out this form, or fail to submit required documents listed in the instructions, you may not be found eligible for the requested document and this application may be denied.

Part 8. Signature of person preparing form if other than above. *(Sign below)*

I declare that I prepared this application at the request of the above person and it is based on all information of which I have knowledge.

Signature _____   Print Your Name _____   Date _____

Firm Name and Address

U.S. Department of Justice
Immigration and Naturalization Service

Application to Extend/ChangeNonimmigrant Status

OMB No.1115-0093

START HERE - Please Type or Print

Part 1. Information about you.

Family Name	Given Name	Middle Initial

Address - In Care of:

Street # and Name	Apt. #

City	State

Zip Code

Date of Birth (month/day/year)	Country of Birth

Social Security # (if any)	A# (if any)

Date of Last Arrival Into the U.S.	I-94#

Current Nonimmigrant Status	Expires on (month/day/year)

Part 2. Application Type.   (See Instructions for fee.)

1. **I am applying for:** (check one)
   a. ☐ an extension of stay in my current status
   b. ☐ a change of status. The new status I am requesting is: _____
2. **Number of people included in this application:** (check one)
   a. ☐ I am the only applicant
   b. ☐ Members of my family are filing this application with me.
      The Total number of people included in this application is _____
      (complete the supplement for each co-applicant)

Part 3.   Processing Information.

1. I/We request that my/our current or requested status be extended until (month/day/year) _____

2. Is this application based on an extension or change of status already granted to your spouse, child or parent?
   ☐ No   ☐ Yes (receipt # _____)

3. Is this application being filed based on a separate petition or application to give your spouse, child or parent an extension or change of status?
   ☐ No   ☐ Yes, filed with this application   ☐ Yes, filed previously and pending with INS

4. If you answered yes to question 3, give the petitioner or applicant name:

   If the application is pending with INS, also give the following information.

   Office filed at_____   Filed on_____ (date)

Part 4.   Additional Information.

1. For applicant #1, provide passport information:

Country of issuance	Valid to: (month/day/year)

2. Foreign address:

Street # and Name	Apt#

City or Town	State or Province

Country	Zip or Postal Code

Continued on back.

Form I-539 (Rev. 10/13/98)N

Part 4.   Additional Information. *(continued)*

3. Answer the following questions. If you answer yes to any question, explain on separate paper.	Yes	No
a. Are you, or any other person included in this application, an applicant for an immigrant visa or adjustment of status to permanent residence?		
b. Has an immigrant petition ever been filed for you, or for any other person included in this application?		
c. Have you, or any other person included in this application ever been arrested or convicted of any criminal offense since last entering the U.S.?		
d. Have you, or any other person included in this application done anything which violated the terms of the nonimmigrant status you now hold?		
e. Are you, or any other person included in this application, now in exclusion or deportation proceedings?		
f. Have you, or any other person included in this application, been employed in the U.S. since last admitted or granted an extension or change of status?		

If you answered YES to question 3f, give the following information on a separate paper: Name of person, name of employer, address of employer, weekly income, and whether specifically authorized by INS.

If you answered NO to question 3f, fully describe how you are supporting yourself on a separate paper. Include the source and the amount and basis for any income.

Part 5.   Signature. *Read the information on penalties in the instructions before completing this section. You must file this application while in the United States.*

I certify under penalty of perjury under the laws of the United States of America that this application, and the evidence submitted with it, is all true and correct. I authorize the release of any information from my records which the Immigration and Naturalization Service needs to determine eligibility for the benefit I am seeking.

Signature	Print your name	Date

Please Note: If you do not completely fill out this form, or fail to submit required documents listed in the instructions, you cannot be found eligible for the requested document and this application will have to be denied.

Part 6.   Signature of person preparing form If other than above. *(Sign below)*

I declare that I prepared this application at the request of the above person and it is based on all information of which I have knowledge.

Signature	Print Your Name	Date

Firm Name
and Address

(Please remember to enclose the mailing label with your application)

Form I-539 (Rev. 10/13/98)N

Supplement-1

Attach to Form I-539 when more than one person is included in the petition or application. *(List each person separately. Do not include the person you named on the form).*

Family Name	Given Name	Middle Initial	Date of Birth (month/day/year)
Country of Birth	Social Security No.		A#

IF IN THE U.S.	Date of Arrival (month/day/year)	I-94#
	Current Nonimmigrant Status:	Expires on (month/day/year)

Country where passport issued	Expiration Date (month/day/year)

Family Name	Given Name	Middle Initial	Date of Birth (month/day/year)
Country of Birth	Social Security No.		A#

IF IN THE U.S.	Date of Arrival (month/day/year)	I-94#
	Current Nonimmigrant Status:	Expires on (month/day/year)

Country where passport issued	Expiration Date (month/day/year)

Family Name	Given Name	Middle Initial	Date of Birth (month/day/year)
Country of Birth	Social Security No.		A#

IF IN THE U.S.	Date of Arrival (month/day/year)	I-94#
	Current Nonimmigrant Status:	Expires on (month/day/year)

Country where passport issued	Expiration Date (month/day/year)

Family Name	Given Name	Middle Initial	Date of Birth (month/day/year)
Country of Birth	Social Security No.		A#

IF IN THE U.S.	Date of Arrival (month/day/year)	I-94#
	Current Nonimmigrant Status:	Expires on (month/day/year)

Country where passport issued	Expiration Date (month/day/year)

Family Name	Given Name	Middle Initial	Date of Birth (month/day/year)
Country of Birth	Social Security No.		A#

IF IN THE U.S.	Date of Arrival (month/day/year)	I-94#
	Current Nonimmigrant Status:	Expires on (month/day/year)

Country where passport issued	Expiration Date (month/day/year)

U.S. Department of Justice
Immigration and Naturalization Service

Application for Asylum and for Withholding of Removal

OMB No. 1115-0086

Start Here - Please Type or Print. USE BLACK INK. SEE THE SEPARATE INSTRUCTION PAMPHLET FOR INFORMATION ABOUT ELIGIBILITY AND HOW TO COMPLETE AND FILE THIS APPLICATION.

PART A. INFORMATION ABOUT YOU.

1. Alien Registration Number(s), if any (A#'s)

2. Social Security Number

3. Complete Last Name

4. First Name

5. Middle Name

6. What Other Names Have You Used? *(Include maiden name and aliases.)*

7. Residence in the U.S.
C/O

Telephone Number

Street Number and Name

Apt. No.

City

State

ZIP Code

8. Mailing Address in the U.S. if Other than Above
C/O

Telephone Number

Street Number and Name

Apt. No.

City

State

ZIP Code

9. Sex
☐ Male   ☐ Female

10. Marital Status:
☐ Single   ☐ Married   ☐ Divorced   ☐ Widowed

11. Date of Birth *(Mo/Day/Yr)*

12. City and Country of Birth

13. Present Nationality *(Citizenship)*

14. Nationality at Birth

15. Race, Ethnic or Tribal Group

16. Religion

17. *Check each box that applies.*
   ☐ I am **not** now in removal, deportation or exclusion proceedings.
   ☐ I was previously in removal, deportation or exclusion proceedings.
   ☐ I am now in removal, deportation or exclusion proceedings.
   ☐ I have never been in removal, deportation or exclusion proceedings.

18. *Complete 18a through 18g.*
   a. When did you last leave your country? *(Mo/Day/Yr)*

   b. When did you last enter the U.S.? *(Mo/Day/Yr)*

   c. Where did you last enter the U.S.?

   d. What was your status when you last entered the U.S.? *(What type of visa did you have, if any)?*

   e. What is your I-94 Number?

   f. What is the expiration date of your authorized stay, if any?

   g. Have you previsously entered the U.S.? ☐ No ☐ Yes. If YES, list place, date, and your status for each entry. *(Attach additional sheets as needed.)*

   Date _____   Place _____   Status _____

   Date _____   Place _____   Status _____

   Date _____   Place _____   Status _____

FOR INS USE ONLY

Returned

Receipt

Resubmitted

Reloc Sent

Reloc Rec'd

Action:
Interview Date:

Asylum:
   Granted
   Denied
   Referred
   Recommended Approval Date _____

Date A.O. final decision or referral issued _____

Total number of persons granted asylum _____

For EOIR Use Only

To Be Completed by Attorney or Representative, if any

Check if G-28/EOIR-28 is attached showing you represent the applicant.

INS VOLAG or PIN #

ATTY State License # _____

Form I-589 (Rev. 05-01-98) N

Information About You - Continued.

19. What is your native language?	20. Are you fluent in English? ☐ Yes ☐ No	21. What other languages do you speak fluently?

22. Have you ever applied to the United States Government or to any other Government(s) for refugee status, asylum, withholding of deportation, or withholding of removal?

☐ No.

☐ I was included in a pending application of my parent(s). However, I am now 21 years old or married so I am filing my own application.

☐ I was included in my spouse's application, but now I wish to file my own application.

☐ Yes. (In what country and what was the decision? Also specify the date of the decision.) Country _____ Date _____

Decision _____

23. What country issued your last passport or travel document?	24. Passport # Travel Document #	25. Expiration Date

26. Prior address in last country of residence or country in which you fear persecution. *(List Address, City/Town, Province, State, Department, and Country)*

27. Provide the following information about your education, beginning with the most recent.

Name of School	Type of School	Location	Attended From (Mo/Yr)	To (Mo/Yr)

28. Provide the following information about your residences during the last five years. List your present address first. *(Use additional sheets of paper if necessary.)*

Number and Street	City	Province or State	Country	Dates From (Mo/Yr)	To (Mo/Yr)

29. Provide the following information about your employment during the last five years. List your present employment first. *(Use additional sheets of paper if necessary.)*

Name and Address of Employer	Your Occupation	Dates From (Mo/Yr)	To (Mo/Yr)

30. Provide the following information about your parents.

Name	Country and City of Birth	Location

PART B. INFORMATION ABOUT YOUR SPOUSE AND CHILDREN.

Your Spouse. ☐ I am not married. *(Skip to Part B, Your Children.)*

1. Alien Registration Number (A#)		2. Passport/ID Card, etc.#	
3. Complete Last Name	4. First Name	5. Middle Name	6. Date of Birth *(Mo/Day/Yr)*
7. Date of Marriage *(Mo/Day/Yr)*	8. Place of Marriage	9. City and Country of Birth	
10. Nationality *(Citizenship)*	11. Race, Ethnic or Tribal Group	12. Sex ☐ Male ☐ Female	

13. Is this person in the U.S.? ☐ Yes. *(Complete blocks 13 to 24.)* ☐ No. *(Specify Location)*

14. Social Security #

15. Place of Last Entry in the U.S.?	16. Date of Last Entry in the U.S.? *(Mo/Day/Yr)*	17. I-94#	18. Status when Last Admitted *(Visa type, if any)*
19. Expiration of Status *(Mo/Day/Yr)*	20. Is your spouse in removal, deportation or exclusion proceedings? ☐ Yes ☐ No		21. If previously in the U.S., Date of Previous Arrival *(Mo/Day/Yr)*
22. Place of Previous Arrival			23. Status at Time of Previous Arrival

24. If in the U.S., is this person to be included in this application? *(Check the appropriate box.)*

 ☐ Yes. *(Attach one (1) photograph of your spouse in the upper right hand corner of Page 3 on the extra copy of the application submitted for this person.)*
 ☐ No, because my spouse is/has:
  ☐ Filing separately.
  ☐ Separate application pending.
  ☐ Other reasons.

All of Your Children, Regardless of Age or Marital Status.

(Use Supplement A Form or attach additional pages and documentation if you have more than two (2) children.)

1. Alien Registration Number (A#)		2. Passport/ID Card, etc.#	
3. Complete Last Name	4. First Name	5. Middle Name	6. Date of Birth *(Mo/Day/Yr)*
7. City and Country of Birth	8. Nationality *(Citizenship)*	9. Race, Ethnic or Tribal Group	10. Sex ☐ Male ☐ Female

11. Is this child in the U.S.? ☐ Yes. *(Complete blocks 12 to 22.)* ☐ No. *(Specify Location)*

12. Social Security #

13. Place of Last Entry in the U.S.?	14. Date of Last Entry in the U.S.? *(Mo/Day/Yr)*	15. I-94#	16. Status when Last Admitted *(Visa type, if any)*
17. Expiration of Status *(Mo/Day/Yr)*	18. Is this child in removal, deportation or exclusion proceedings? ☐ Yes ☐ No		19. If previously in the U.S., Date of Previous Arrival *(Mo/Day/Yr)*
20. Place of Previous Arrival			21. Status at Time of Previous Arrival

22. If in the U.S., is this person to be included in this application? *(Check the appropriate box.)*

 ☐ Yes. *(Attach one (1) photograph of your child in the upper right hand corner of Page 3 on the extra copy of the application submitted for this person.)*
 ☐ No, because child is/has:
  ☐ Filing separately.
  ☐ Separate application pending.
  ☐ Over 21 years of age.
  ☐ Married.
  ☐ Other reasons.

Information About Your Spouse and Children - Continued *(Use Supplement A Form or attach additional sheets of paper to list additional children.)*

All of Your Children, Regardless of Age or Marital Status.

1. Alien Registration Number (A#):	2. Passport/ID Card, etc. #

3. Complete Last Name	4. First Name	5. Middle Name	6. Date of Birth *(Mo/Day/Yr)*

7. City and Country of Birth	8. Nationality *(Citizenship)*	9. Race, Ethnic or Tribal Group	10. Sex ☐ Male ☐ Female

11. Is this person in the U.S.? ☐ Yes. *(Complete blocks 11 to 22.)* ☐ No. *(Specify Location)*	12. Social Security #

13. Place of Last Entry in the U.S.?	14. Date of Last Entry in the U.S.? *(Mo/Day/Yr)*	15. I-94#	16. Status when Last Admitted *(Visa type, if any)*

17. Expiration of Status *(Mo/Day/Yr)*	18. Is this child in removal, deportation or exclusion proceedings? ☐ Yes ☐ No	19. If previously in the U.S., Date of Previous Arrival *(Mo/Day/Yr)*

20. Place of Previous Arrival	21. Status at Time of Previous Arrival

22. If in the U.S., is this person to be included in this application? *(Check the appropriate box.)*

    ☐ Yes. *(Attach one (1) photograph of your child in the upper right hand corner of Page 3 on the extra copy of the application submitted for this person.)*
    ☐ No, because child is/has:
        ☐ Filing separately.
        ☐ Separate application pending.
        ☐ Over 21 years of age.
        ☐ Married.
        ☐ Other reasons.

PART C. INFORMATION ABOUT YOUR CLAIM TO ASYLUM.
(Use Supplement B Form or attach additional sheets of paper as needed to complete your responses to the questions contained in Part C.)

1. Why are you seeking asylum? Explain in detail what the basis is for your claim. *(Attach additional sheets of paper as needed.)*

Information About Your Claim to Asylum - Continued.

2. Have you or any member of your family ever belonged to or been associated with any organizations or groups in your home country, such as, but not limited to, a political party, student group, labor union, religious organization, military or paramilitary group, civil patrol, guerrilla organization, ethnic group, human rights group, or the press or media?

☐ No.   ☐ Yes.   If yes, provide a detailed explanation of your or your relatives' involvement with each group and include the name of each organization or group; the dates of membership or affiliation; the purpose of the organization; your duties or your relatives' duties or responsibilities in the group or organization; and whether you or your relatives are still active in the group(s).   *(Attach additional sheets of paper as needed.)*

3. Have you or any member of your family ever been mistreated or threatened by the authorities of your home country or any other country or by a group or groups that are controlled by the government, or that the government of the country is unable or unwilling to control?

☐ No.   ☐ Yes.   If YES, was it because of any of the following reasons? *(Check each of the following boxes that apply.)*

☐ Race   ☐ Religion   ☐ Nationality   ☐ Membership in a particular social group   ☐ Political Opinion

On a separate sheet of paper, specify for each instance, what occurred and the circumstances; the relationship to you of the person involved; the date; the exact location; who it was who took such action against you or your family member(s); his/her position in the government or group; the reason why the incident occurred.   Attach documents referring to these incidents, if they are available.   *(Attach additional sheets of paper as needed.)*

4. Have you or any member of your family ever been accused, charged, arrested, detained, interrogated, convicted and sentenced, or imprisoned in your country or any other country, including the United States?

☐ No.   ☐ Yes.   If YES, for each instance, specify what occurred and the circumstances; dates; location; the duration of the detention or imprisonment; the reason(s) for the detention or conviction; the treatment received during the detention or imprisonment; any formal charges that were lodged against you or your relatives; the reason for release; treatment after release.   Attach documents referring to these incidents if they are available. *(Attach additional sheets of paper as needed.)*

Information About Your Claim to Asylum - Continued.

5. Do you fear being subjected to torture (severe physical or mental pain or suffering, including rape or other sexual abuse) in your home country or any other country if you return?

☐ No.   ☐ Yes. If YES, explain why. *(Attach additional sheets of paper as needed.)*

6. What do you think would happen to you if you returned to the country from which you claim you would be subjected to persecution? Explain in detail and provide information or documentation to support your statement, if available. *(Attach additional sheets of paper as needed.)*

7. Describe in detail your trip to the United States from your home country. After leaving the country from which you are claiming asylum, did you or your spouse or child(ren), who are now in the United States, travel through or reside in any other country before entering the United States?

☐ No.   ☐ Yes.   If YES, for each person, identify each country and indicate the length of stay; the person's status while there; the reasons for leaving; whether the person is entitled to return for residence purposes; and if the person applied for refugee status or for asylum while there; or why he or she did not do so. *(Attach additional sheets of paper as needed.)*

PART D. ADDITIONAL INFORMATION ABOUT YOUR APPLICATION FOR ASYLUM.

(Use Supplement B Form or attach additional sheets of paper as needed to complete your responses to the questions contained in Part D.)

1. Do you, your spouse, or your child(ren) now hold, or have you ever held, permanent residence, other permanent status, or citizenship, in any country other than the one from which you are now claiming asylum?

    ☐ No. ☐ Yes. If YES, explain. *(Attach additional sheets of paper as needed).*

2. Have you, your spouse, your child(ren), your parents ever filed for, been processed for, or been granted or denied refugee status or asylum by the United States Government?

    ☐ No. ☐ Yes. If YES, explain the decision and what happened to any status you received as a result of that decision. If you have been denied asylum by an Immigration Judge or the Board of Immigration Appeals, please describe any change in country conditions or your own circumstances since the date of the denial that may affect your eligibility for asylum. *(Attach additional sheets of paper as needed.)*

3. Have you, your spouse, your child(ren), or your parents ever filed for, been processed for, or been granted or denied refugee status or asylum by any other country?

    ☐ No. ☐ Yes. If YES, explain the decision and what happened to any status you received as a result of that decision. *(Attach additional sheets of paper as needed.)*

4. Have you, your spouse, or child(ren) ever caused harm or suffering to any person because of his or her race, religion, nationality, membership in a particular social group or belief in a particular political opinion, or ever ordered, assisted, or otherwise participated in such acts?

    ☐ No. ☐ Yes. If YES, describe, in detail, each such incident and your own or your spouse's or child(ren)'s involvement. *(Attach additional sheets of paper as needed.)*

5. After you left your country of claimed persecution for the reasons you have described, did you return to that country?

    ☐ No. ☐ Yes. If YES, describe, in detail, the circumstances of your visit, for example, the date(s) of the trip(s), the purpose(s) of the trip(s), and the length of time you remained in that country for the visit(s). *(Attach additional sheets of paper as needed.)*

6. Are you filing the application more than one year after your last arrival in the United States?

    ☐ No. ☐ Yes. If YES, explain why you did not file within the first year after you arrived. You should be prepared to explain at your interview or hearing why you did not file your asylum application within the first year after you arrived. For guidance in answering this question see Part 1: Filing Instructions, Section V. "Completing the Form," Part D. *(Attach additional sheets of paper as needed.)*

PART E. SIGNATURE.

After reading the information on penalties in the instructions, complete and sign below. If someone helped you prepare this application, he or she must complete Part F.

I certify, under penalty of perjury under the laws of the United States of America, that this application and the evidence submitted with it is all true and correct. Title 18, United States Code, Section 1546, provides in part: "Whoever knowingly makes under oath, or as permitted under penalty of perjury under Section 1746 of Title 28, United States Code, knowingly subscribes as true, any false statement with respect to a material fact in any application, affidavit, or other document required by the immigration laws or regulations prescribed thereunder, or knowingly presents any such application, affidavit, or other document containing any such false statement or which fails to contain any reasonable basis in law or fact -- shall be fined in accordance with this title or imprisoned not more than five years, or both". I authorize the release of any information from my record which the Immigration and Naturalization Service needs to determine eligibility for the benefit I am seeking.

Staple your photograph here.

WARNING: **Applicants who are in the United States illegally are subject to removal if their asylum or withholding claims are not granted by an asylum officer or an Immigration Judge. Any information provided in completing this application may be used as a basis for the institution of, or as evidence in, removal proceedings even if the application is later withdrawn. Applicants determined to have knowingly made a frivolous application for asylum will be permanently ineligible for any benefits under the Immigration and Nationality Act. See INA 208(d)(6) and 8 CFR 208.18.**

Signature of Applicant *(The person named in Part A)*

[_____]   Date *(Mo/Day/Yr)*
              Sign your name so it all appears within the brackets.

Print Name   Write your name in your native alphabet

Did your spouse, parent or child(ren) assist you in completing this application? ☐ No ☐ Yes *(If YES, list their name(s) and relationship.)*

(Name) _____ *(Relationship)* _____ *(Name)* _____ *(Relationship)* _____

Did someone other than you or your spouse, parent or child(ren) prepare this application? ☐ No ☐ Yes *(Complete Part F)*

Asylum applicants may be represented by counsel. Have you been provided with a list of persons who may be available to assist you, at little or no cost, with your asylum claim?   ☐ No   ☐ Yes

PART F. SIGNATURE OF PERSON PREPARING FORM IF OTHER THAN ABOVE.   *Sign below.*

I declare that I have prepared this application at the request of the person named in Part E, that the responses provided are based on all information of which I have knowledge, or which was provided to me by the applicant and that the completed application was read to the applicant in his or her native language for verification before he or she signed the application in my presence. I am aware that the knowing placement of false information on the Form I-589 may also subject me to civil penalties under 8 U.S.C. Section 1324(c).

Signature of Preparer	Print Name	Date *(Mo/Day/Yr)*
Daytime Telephone Number ( )	Address of Preparer: Street Number and Name	

Apt. No.	City	State	ZIP Code

PART G. TO BE COMPLETED AT INTERVIEW.

You will be asked to complete this Part when you appear before an asylum officer of the Immigration and Naturalization Service (INS), or an Immigration Judge of the Executive Office for Immigration Review (EOIR) for examination.

I swear (affirm) that I know the contents of this application that I am signing, including the attached documents and supplements, that they are all true or   not all true to the best of my knowledge and that corrections numbered _____ to _____ were made by me or at my request.

Signed and sworn to before me by the above-name applicant on:

_____   _____
          Signature of Applicant   Date *(Mo/Day/Yr)*

_____   _____
     Write your Name in your Native Alphabet   Signature of Asylum Officer or Immigration Judge

Page 8 (Rev. 05-01-98) N

A# *(If available)*	Date
Applicant's Name	Applicant's Signature

ALL OF YOUR CHILDREN, REGARDLESS OF AGE OR MARITAL STATUS.

(Attach additional pages and documentation if you have more than two (2) children.)

1. Alien Registration Number (A#):	2. Passport/ID Card, etc.#

3. Complete Last Name	4. First Name	5. Middle Name	6. Date of Birth *(Mo/Day/Yr)*

7. City and Country of Birth	8. Nationality *(Citizenship)*	9. Race, Ethnic or Tribal Group	10. Sex ☐ Male ☐ Female

11. Is this child in the U.S.? ☐ Yes. *(Complete blocks 12 to 22.)* ☐ No. *(Specify Location)*	12. Social Security #

13. Place of Last Entry in the U.S.?	14. Date of Last Entry in the U.S.? *(Mo/Day/Yr)*	15. I-94#	16. Status when Last Admitted *(Visa type, if any)*

17. Expiration of Status *(Mo/Day/Yr)*	18. Is this child in removal, deportation or exclusion proceedings? ☐ Yes ☐ No	19. If previously in the U.S., Date of Previous Arrival *(Mo/Day/Yr)*

20. Place of Previous Arrival	21. Status at Time of Previous Arrival

22. If in the U.S., is this person to be included in this application? *(Check the appropriate box.)*

    ☐ Yes. *(Attach one (1) photograph of your child in the upper right hand corner of Page 3 on the extra copy of the application submitted for this person.)*
    ☐ No, because child is/has:
        ☐ Filing separately.
        ☐ Separate application pending.
        ☐ Over 21 years of age.
        ☐ Married.
        ☐ Other reasons.

1. Alien Registration Number (A#):	2. Passport/ID Card, etc.#

3. Complete Last Name	4. First Name	5. Middle Name	6. Date of Birth *(Mo/Day/Yr)*

7. City and Country of Birth	8. Nationality *(Citizenship)*	9. Race, Ethnic or Tribal Group	10. Sex ☐ Male ☐ Female

11. Is this child in the U.S.? ☐ Yes. *(Complete blocks 12 to 22.)* ☐ No. *(Specify Location)*	12. Social Security #

13. Place of Last Entry in the U.S.?	14. Date of Last Entry in the U.S.? *(Mo/Day/Yr)*	15. I-94#	16. Status when Last Admitted *(Visa type, if any)*

17. Expiration of Status *(Mo/Day/Yr)*	18. Is this child in removal, deportation or exclusion proceedings? ☐ Yes ☐ No	19. If previously in the U.S., Date of Previous Arrival *(Mo/Day/Yr)*

20. Place of Previous Arrival	21. Status at Time of Previous Arrival

22. If in the U.S., is this person to be included in this application? *(Check the appropriate box.)*

    ☐ Yes. *(Attach one (1) photograph of your child in the upper right hand corner of Page 3 on the extra copy of the application submitted for this person.)*
    ☐ No, because child is/has:
        ☐ Filing separately.
        ☐ Separate application pending.
        ☐ Over 21 years of age.
        ☐ Married.
        ☐ Other reasons.

ADDITIONAL INFORMATION ABOUT YOUR CLAIM TO ASYLUM.

A# (If available)	Date
Applicant's Name	Applicant's Signature

Use attached blank response sheet to supplement any information requested. Please copy and complete as needed.

PART _____

QUESTION _____

ADDITIONAL INFORMATION ABOUT YOUR CLAIM TO ASYLUM.

A# (*If available*)	Date
Applicant's Name	Applicant's Signature

Use attached blank response sheet to supplement any information requested. Please copy and complete as needed.

PART ____

QUESTION ____

OMB No. 1115-0049

Petition to Classify Orphan as an Immediate Relative

[Section 101 (b)(1)(F) of the Immigration and Nationality Act, as amended.]

Please do not write in this block.

TO THE SECRETARY OF STATE;

The petition was filed by:

☐ Married petitioner ☐ Unmarried petitioner

The petition is approved for orphan:

☐ Adopted abroad ☐ Coming to U.S. for adoption. Preadoption requirements have been met.

Remarks:

Fee Stamp

File number

DATE OF ACTION

DD

DISTRICT

Please type or print legibly in ink. Use a separate petition for each child.

Petition is being made to classify the named orphan as an immediate relative.

BLOCK I - Information About Prospective Petitioner

1. My name is: (Last)   (First)   (Middle)

2. Other names used (including maiden name if appropriate):

3. I reside in the U.S. at: (C/O if appropriate)   (Apt. No.)

   (Number and street)   (Town or city)   (State)   (ZIP Code)

4. Address abroad (if any): (Number and street)   (Apt. No.)

   (Town or city)   (Province)   (Country)

5. I was born on: (Month)   (Day)   (Year)

   In: (Town or City)   (State or Province)   (Country)

6. My phone number is: (Include Area Code)

7. My marital status is:
   ☐ Married
   ☐ Widowed
   ☐ Divorced
   ☐ Single
      ☐ I have never been married.
      ☐ I have been previously married _____ time(s).

8. If you are now married, give the following information:

   Date and place of present marriage

   Name of present spouse (include maiden name of wife)

   Date of birth of spouse   Place of birth of spouse

   Number of prior marriages of spouse

   My spouse resides ☐ With me   ☐ Apart from me
      (provide address below)

   (Apt. No.)   (No. and street)   (City)   (State)   (Country)

9. I am a citizen of the United States through:
   ☐ Birth   ☐ Parents   ☐ Naturalization   ☐ Marriage

   If acquired through naturalization, give name under which naturalized, number of naturalization certificate, and date and place of naturalization:

   If not, submit evidence of citizenship. See Instruction 2.a(2).

   If acquired through parentage or marriage, have you obtained a certificate in your own name based on that acquisition?
   ☐ No   ☐ Yes

   Have you or any person through whom you claimed citizenship ever lost United States citizenship?
   ☐ No   ☐ Yes (If yes, attach detailed explanation.)

Continue on reverse.

Received	Trans. In	Ret'd Trans. Out	Completed

Form I-600 (Rev. 10/13/98)N

BLOCK II - Information About Orphan Beneficiary

10. Name at birth   (First)   (Middle)   (Last)

11. Name at present   (First)   (Middle)   (Last)

12. Any other names by which orphan is or was known.

13. Sex   ☐ Male   **14.** Date of birth (Month/Day/Year)
      ☐ Female

15. Place of birth   (City)   (State or Province)   (Country)

16. The beneficiary is an orphan because (check one):
    ☐ He/she has no parents
    ☐ He/she has only one parent who is the sole or surviving parent.

17. If the orphan has only one parent, answer the following:
   a.   State what has become of the other parent:

   b.   Is the remaining parent capable of providing for the orphan's support?   ☐ Yes   ☐ No

   c.   Has the remaining parent, in writing, irrevocably released the orphan for emigration and adoption?   ☐ Yes   ☐ No

18. Has the orphan been adopted abroad by the petitioner and spouse jointly or the unmarried petitioner?   ☐ Yes   ☐ No

If yes, did the petitioner and spouse or unmarried petitioner personally see and observe the child prior to or during the adoption proceedings?   ☐ Yes   ☐ No

Date of adoption

Place of adoption

19. If either answer in question 18 is "No", answer the following:
   a.   Do petitioner and spouse jointly or does the unmarried petitioner intend to adopt the orphan in the United States?   ☐ Yes   ☐ No

   b.   Have the preadoption requirements, if any, of the orphan's proposed state of residence been met?   ☐ Yes   ☐ No

   c.   If b. is answered "No", will they be met later?   ☐ Yes   ☐ No

20. To petitioner's knowledge, does the orphan have any physical or mental affliction?   ☐ Yes   ☐ No
If "Yes", name the affliction.

21. Who has legal custody of the child?

22. Name of child welfare agency, if any, assisting in this case:

23. Name of attorney abroad, if any, representing petitioner in this case.

Address of above.

24. Address in the United States where orphan will reside.

25. Present address of orphan.

25. If orphan is residing in an institution, give full name of institution.

26. If orphan is not residing in an institution, give full name of person with whom orphan is residing.

27. Give any additional information necessary to locate orphan such as name of district, section, zone or locality in which orphan resides.

28. Location of American Consulate where application for visa will be made.
(City in Foreign Country)   (Foreign Country)

Certification of Prospective Petitioner

I certify under penalty of perjury under the laws of the United States of America that the foregoing is true and correct and that I will care for an orphan/orphans properly if admitted to the United States.

(Signature of Prospective Petitioner)

Executed on (Date)

Certification of Married Prospective Petitioner's Spouse

I certify under penalty of perjury under the laws of the United States of America that the foregoing is true and correct and that my spouse and I will care for an orphan/orphans properly if admitted to the United States.

(Signature of Prospective Petitioner)

Executed on (Date)

Signature of Person Preparing Form if Other Than Petitioner

I declare that this document was prepared by me at the request of the prospective petitioner and is based on all information of which I have any knowledge.

(Signature)

Address

Executed on (Date)

U.S. Department of Justice
Immigration and Naturalization Service

Application for Advance Processing
of Orphan Petition [8CFR 204.1(b)(3)]

Please do not write in this block.

It has been determined that the

☐ Married   ☐ Unmarried

prospective petitioner will furnish proper care to a beneficiary orphan if admitted to the United Sates.

There

☐ are   ☐ are not

preadoptive requirements in the state of the child's proposed residence.

The following is a description of the preadoption requirements, if any, of the state of the child's proposed residence:

The preadoption requirements, if any,

☐ have been met.   ☐ have not been met.

Fee Stamp

DATE OF FAVORABLE DETERMINATION

DD

DISTRICT

File number of petitioner, if applicable

Please type or print legibly in ink.

Application is made by the named prospective petitioner for advance processing of an orphan petition.

BLOCK I - Information About Prospective Petitioner

1. My name is: (Last)   (First)   (Middle)

2. Other names used (including maiden name if appropriate):

3. I reside in the U.S. at: (C/O if appropriate)   (Apt. No.)

   (Number and street)   (Town or city)   (State)   (ZIP Code)

4. Address abroad (if any): (Number and street)   (Apt. No.)

   (Town or city)   (Province)   (Country)

5. I was born on: (Month)   (Day)   (Year)

   In: (Town or City)   (State or Province)   (Country)

6. My phone number is: (Include Area Code)

7. My marital status is:
   ☐ Married
   ☐ Widowed
   ☐ Divorced
   ☐ Single
       ☐ I have never been married.
       ☐ I have been previously married _____ time(s).

8. If you are now married, give the following information:

   Date and place of present marriage

   Name of present spouse (include maiden name of wife)

   Date of birth of spouse   Place of birth of spouse

   Number of prior marriages of spouse

   My spouse resides ☐ With me   ☐ Apart from me
                                   (provide address below)

   (Apt. No.)   (No. and street)   (City)   (State)   (Country)

9. I am a citizen of the United States through:
   ☐ Birth   ☐ Parents   ☐ Naturalization   ☐ Marriage

   If acquired through naturalization, give name under which naturalized, number of naturalization certificate, and date and place of naturalization:

   If not, submit evidence of citizenship. See Instruction 2.a(2).

   If acquired through parentage or marriage, have you obtained a certificate in your own name based on that acquisition?
   ☐ No   ☐ Yes

   Have you or any person through whom you claimed citizenship ever lost United States citizenship?
   ☐ No   ☐ Yes (If yes, attach detailed explanation.)

Continue on reverse.

Received	Trans. In	Ret'd Trans. Out	Completed

Form I-600A (Rev. 10/13/98)N

BLOCK II - General Information

10. Name and address of organization or individual assisting you in locating or identifying an orphan

(Name)

_____

(Address)

11. Do you plan to travel abroad to locate or adopt a child?

☐ Yes ☐ No

12. Does your spouse, if any, plan to travel abroad to locate or adopt a child?

☐ Yes ☐ No

13. If the answer to question 11 or 12 is "yes", give the following information:

a. Your date of intended departure _____

b. Your spouse's date of intended departure _____

c. City, province _____

14.. Will the child come to the United States for adoption after compliance with the preadoption requirements, if any, of the state of proposed residence?

☐ Yes ☐ No

15. If the answer to question 14 is "no", will the child be adopted abroad after having been personally seen and observed by you and your spouse, if married?

☐ Yes ☐ No

16. Where do you wish to file your orphan petition?

The service office located at

_____

The American Consulate or Embassy at

17. Do you plan to adopt more than one child?

☐ Yes ☐ No

If "Yes", how many children do you plan to adopt?

Certification of Prospective Petitioner

I certify under penalty of perjury under the laws of the United States of America that the foregoing is true and correct and that I will care for an orphan/orphans properly if admitted to the United States.

(Signature of Prospective Petitioner)

_____

Executed on (Date)

Certification of Married Prospective Petitioner's Spouse

I certify under penalty of perjury under the laws of the United States of America that the foregoing is true and correct and that my spouse and I will care for an orphan/orphans properly if admitted to the United States.

(Signature of Prospective Petitioner)

_____

Executed on (Date)

Signature of Person Preparing Form if Other Than Petitioner

I declare that this document was prepared by me at the request of the prospective petitioner and is based on all information of which I have any knowledge.

(Signature)

_____

Address

_____

Executed on (Date)

U. S. Department of Justice
Immigration and Naturalization Service

Application for Waiver of Ground of Excludability

DO NOT WRITE IN THIS BLOCK

☐ 212 (a) (1)   ☐ 212 (a) (10)   Fee Stamp
☐ 212 (a) (3)   ☐ 212 (a) (12)
☐ 212 (a) (6)   ☐ 212 (a) (19)
☐ 212 (a) (9)   ☐ 212 (a) (23)

A. Information about applicant -

1. Family Name (Surname In CAPS)   (First)   (Middle)

2. Address (Number and Street)   (Apartment Number)

3. (Town or City) (State/Country)   (Zip/Postal Code)

4. Date of Birth *(Month/ Day/ Year)*   5. I&N File Number
A-

6. City of Birth   7. Country of Birth

8. Date of visa application   9. Visa applied for at:

10. Applicant was declared inadmissible to the United States for the following reasons: (List acts, convictions, or physical or mental conditions. If applicant has active or suspected tuberculosis, the reverse of this page must be fully completed.)

11. Applicant was previously in the United States, as follows:
City & State   From (Date)   To (Date)   I&NS Status

12. Social Security Number

B. Information about relative, through whom applicant claims eligibility for a waiver -

1. Family Name (Surname in CAPS)   (First)   (Middle)

2. Address (Number and Street)   (Apartment Number)

3. (Town or City)   (State/Country)   (Zip/Postal Code)

4. Relationship to applicant   5.I&NS Status

C. Information about applicant's other relatives in the U.S.
(List only U.S. citizens and permanent residents)

1. Family Name (Surname in CAPS)   (First)   (Middle)

2. Address (Number and Street)   (Apartment Number)

3. (Town or City)   (State/Country)   (Zip/Postal Code)

4. Relationship to applicant   5.I&NS Status

1. Family Name (Surname in CAPS)   (First)   (Middle)

2. Address (Number and Street)   (Apartment Number)

3. (Town or City)   (State/Country)   (Zip/Postal Code)

4. Relationship to applicant   5.I&NS Status

1. Family Name (Surname in CAPS)   (First)   (Middle)

2. Address (Number and Street)   (Apartment Number)

3. (Town or City)   (State/Country)   (Zip/Postal Code)

4. Relationship to applicant   5.I&NS Status

Signature (of applicant or petitioning relative)

Relationship to applicant   Date

Signature (of person preparing application, if not the applicant or petitioning relative) I declare that this document was prepared by me at the request of the applicant, or petitioning relative, and is based on all information of which I have any knowledge.
Signature

Address   Date

Initial receipt	Resubmitted	Relocated		Completed		
		Received	Sent	Approved	Denied	Retuned

Form I-601 (Rev. 10/13/98)N

To be completed for applicants with
active tuberculosis or suspected tuberculosis

A. Statement by Applicant

Upon admission to the United States I will:

    1.Go directly to the physician or health facility named in Section B;

    2. Present all X-rays used in the visa medical examination to substantiate diagnosis;

    3. Submit to such examinations, treatment, isolation, and medical regimen as may be required; and

    4. Remain under the prescribed treatment or observation whether on inpatient or outpatient basis, until discharged.

Signature of *Applicant*

Date

B. Statement by Physician or Health Facility

(May be executed by a private physician, health de- partment, other public or private health facility, or military hospital.)

I agree to supply any treatment or observation necessary for the proper management of the alien's tuberculous condition.

I agree to submit Form CDC 75.18 "Report on Alien with Tuberculosis Waiver" to the health officer named in Section D:

    1. Within 30 days of the alien's reporting for care, indicating presumptive diagnosis, test results, and plans for future care of the alien; or

    2. 30 days after receiving Form CDC 75.18 if the alien has not reported.

Satisfactory financial arrangements have been made. (This statement does not relieve the alien from submitting evidence, as required by consul, to establish that the alien is not likely to become a public charge.)

I represent (enter an "X" in the appropriate box and give the complete name and address of the facility below.)

☐ 1. Local Health Department
☐ 2. Other Public or Private Facility
☐ 3. Private Practice
☐ 4. Military Hospital

Name of Facility (please type or print)

Address (Number & Street) (Apartment Number)

City, State & Zip Code

Signature of Physician   Date

C. Applicant's Sponsor in the U.S.

Arrange for medical care of the applicant and have the physician complete Section B.

If medical care will be provided by a physician who checked box 2 or 3, in Section B., have Section D. completed by the local or State Health Officer who has jurisdiction in the area where the applicant plans to reside in the U.S.

If medical care will be provided by a physician who checked box 4., in Section B., forward this form directly to the military facility at the address provided in Section B.

Address where the alien plans to reside in the U.S.

Address (Number & Street)   (Apartment Number)

City, State & ZIP Code

D. Endorsement of Local or State Health Officer

Endorsement signifies recognition of the physician or facility for the purpose of providing care for tuberculosis. If the facility or physician who signed in Section B is not in your health jurisdiction and is not familiar to you, you may wish to contact the health officer responsible for the jurisdiction of the facility or physician prior to endorsing.

Endorsed by: Signature of Health Officer

Date

Enter below the name and address of the Local Health Department to which the "Notice of Arrival of Alien with Tuberculosis Waiver" should be sent when the alien arrives in the U. S.

Official Name of Department

Address (Number & Street)   (Apartment Number)

City, State & ZIP Code

Please read instructions with care.

If further assistance needed, contact the office of the Immigration and Naturalization Service with jurisdiction over the intended place of U.S. residence of the applicant.

U. S. Department of Justice
Immigration and Naturalization Service

OMB No. 1115-0048

Application for Waiver of Ground of Excludability

DO NOT WRITE IN THIS BLOCK

☐ 212 (a) (1) ☐ 212 (a) (10)   Fee Stamp
☐ 212 (a) (3) ☐ 212 (a) (12)
☐ 212 (a) (6) ☐ 212 (a) (19)
☐ 212 (a) (9) ☐ 212 (a) (23)

A. Information about applicant -

1. Family Name (Surname In CAPS)   (First)   (Middle)

2. Address (Number and Street)   (Apartment Number)

3. (Town or City) (State/Country)   (Zip/Postal Code)

4. Date of Birth *(Month/ Day/ Year)*   5. I&N File Number A-

6. City of Birth   7. Country of Birth

8. Date of visa application   9. Visa applied for at:

10. Applicant was declared inadmissible to the United States for the following reasons: (List acts, convictions, or physical or mental conditions. If applicant has active or suspected tuberculosis, the reverse of this page must be fully completed.)

11. Applicant was previously in the United States, as follows:
City & State   From (Date)   To (Date)   I&NS Status

12. Social Security Number

B. Information about relative, through whom applicant claims eligibility for a waiver -

1. Family Name (Surname in CAPS)   (First)   (Middle)

2. Address (Number and Street)   (Apartment Number)

3. (Town or City)   (State/Country)   (Zip/Postal Code)

4. Relationship to applicant   5. I&NS Status

C. Information about applicant's other relatives in the U.S.
(List only U.S. citizens and permanent residents)

1. Family Name (Surname in CAPS)   (First)   (Middle)

2. Address (Number and Street)   (Apartment Number)

3. (Town or City)   (State/Country)   (Zip/Postal Code)

4. Relationship to applicant   5. I&NS Status

1. Family Name (Surname in CAPS)   (First)   (Middle)

2. Address (Number and Street)   (Apartment Number)

3. (Town or City)   (State/Country)   (Zip/Postal Code)

4. Relationship to applicant   5. I&NS Status

1. Family Name (surname in CAPS)   (First)   (Middle)

2. Address (Number and Street)   (Apartment Number)

3. (Town or City)   (State/Country)   (Zip/Postal Code)

4. Relationship to applicant   5. I&NS Status

Additional Information and Instructions

Signature and Title of Requesting Officer

Address   Date

This office will maintain only a folder relating to the applicant pursuant the A.M.

U. S. Department of Justice

Immigration and Naturalization Service

OMB No 1115-0059

Application for Waiver of The Foreign Residence Requirement of Section 212(e) of the Immigration and Nationality Act, as amended

This application must be typewritten or printed legibly in ink with block letters.

Fee Stamp

1. Name (Last in CAPS)	First	Middle	If a married woman, give maiden name

2. Mailing Address (Apt. No.)	(Number and Street)	(Town or City)	(State or Province)	(Country)	(Zip Code, if in U.S.)

Present or last U.S. Residence	(Number and Street)	(City)	(State)	(ZIP Code)

3. Date of Birth	Country of Birth	Country of Nationality	Country of Last Foreign Residence

Alien Registration Number, If Known

4. I believe I am subject to the foreign residence requirements because: (Check appropriate box(es))

A. ☐ I participated in an exchange program which was financed by an agency of the U.S. Government or the government of the country of my nationality or last foreign residence for the purpose of promoting international educational and cultural exchange.

B. ☐ An agency of the Government of the U.S. or the government of the country of my nationality or last foreign residence gave me a grant (such as a Fullbright grant), stipend or allowance for the purpose of participation in an exchange program. Name of U.S. Government agency

or foreign country _____.

C. ☐ I became an exchange visitor after the Secretary of State designated the country of my nationality or last foreign residence as clearly requiring the services of persons with my specialized knowledge or skill.

D. ☐ I entered the United States as, or my status was changed to that of, an exchange visitor on or after January 10, 1977 to participate in graduate medical education or training.

5. I am applying for waiver of the foreign residence requirement on the ground that: (Check appropriate box(es))

A. ☐ My departure from the United States would impose exceptional hardship upon my United States citizen or lawful permanent resident spouse or child.

B. ☐ I cannot return to the country of my nationality or last foreign residence because I would be subject to persecution on account of race, religion, or political opinion.

IMPORTANT: If you have checked Box "A" you must attach to this application a statement dated and signed by you giving a *detailed explanation* of the basis for your belief that compliance by you with the two-year foreign residence requirement of Section 212(e) of the Immigration and Nationality Act, as amended, would impose exceptional hardship upon your spouse or child who is a citizen of the United States or a lawful permanent resident thereof. Without such statement your application is incomplete. You must include in the statement all pertinent information concerning the income and savings of yourself and your spouse. There should also be attached such documentary evidence as may be available to support the allegations of hardship.

If you have checked Box "B" you must attach a statement dated and signed by you setting forth in detail the reason(s) you believe that you cannot return to the country of your nationality or last foreign residence because you would be subject to persecution on account of race, religion, or political opinion. There should also be attached such documentary evidence as may be available to support the allegations of persecution.

6. If married, check appropriate box(es):   (See Instruction No. 4)

A. ☐ My spouse is included in this application.   B. ☐ My spouse is filing a separate application for waiver.

RECEIVED	TRANS. IN	RET'D TRANS. OUT	COMPLETED

Form I-612 (Rev 10/13/98)N

7. List all program numbers and names of *all* program sponsors.

8. Major field of activity (*Check one*)

    ◯ (1) Agriculture   ◯ (4) Engineering   ◯ (7) Natural And Physical Sciences
    ◯ (2) Business Administration   ◯ (5) Humanities   ◯ (8) Social Sciences
    ◯ (3) Education   ◯ (6) Medicine   ◯ (9) Other

9. Occupation

10. Date and port of last arrival in the United States as participant in a designated exchange program.

11. If you are now abroad, give date of departure from U.S.

12. Number of prior marriages of applicant ——————

    If married, number of prior marriages of applicant's spouse ——————

13. Name of spouse	Date and Country of birth	Nationality	Country of last foreign residence
14. Names of children	Date and Country of birth	Nationality	Country of last foreign residence

15. If you checked Box "A" in block 5 above, furnish the following information concerning your spouse or one of your children who is a citizen of the United States and who you believe would suffer exceptional hardship if you resided outside the United States for two years following your departure from this country.

Name of United States citizen spouse or child:

United States citizenship of spouse or child was acquired through (*check one*)

◯ Birth in the United States   ◯ Naturalization   ◯ Parent(s)

If United States citizenship of spouse or child was acquired through naturalization, give the following:

Number of naturalization certificate	Date of naturalization	Place of naturalization

If United States citizenship of spouse or child was acquired through parent(s), has spouse or child obtained a certificate of citizenship? ——————

If so, give number of certificate —————————— If not, submit evidence in accordance with instruction 6(a) (2).

16. If you checked Box "A" in block 5 above and you do not have a spouse or child who is a citizen of the United States, furnish the following information concerning your spouse or one of your children who is a lawful permanent resident of the United States and who you believe would suffer exceptional hardship if you resided outside the United States for two years following your departure from this country.

Name of lawful resident alien spouse or child:

Alien Registration Number

Date, place, and means of admission for lawful permanent residence:

I certify under penalty of perjury under the laws of the United States of America that the foregoing is true and correct.

Executed on ——————————— ——————————— ———————————
              (Date)   *(Place)*   *(Signature of applicant)*

Signature of person preparing form, if other than applicant: I declare that this document was prepared by me at the request of the applicant and is based on all information of which I have any knowledge:

——————————————
                                 (Signature)

—————————————————————— ——————————— ———————————
(Address of person preparing form, if other than applicant)   *(Date)*   *(Occupation)*

Petition to Remove the Conditions on Residence

OMB No. 1115-0145

START HERE - Please Type or Print

Part 1. Information about you.

Family Name	Given Name	Middle Initial

Address - C/O:

Street Number and Name		Apt. #
City	State or Province	
Country	ZIP/Postal Code	

Date of Birth (month/day/year)	Country of Birth
Social Security #	A #

Conditional residence expires on (month/day/year)	▓▓▓▓▓▓▓

Mailing address if different from residence in C/O:

Street Number and Name		Apt #
City	State or Province	
Country	ZIP/Postal Code	

FOR INS USE ONLY

Returned	Receipt
Resubmitted	
Reloc Sent	
Reloc Rec'd	
☐ Applicant Interviewed	

Remarks

Action

Part 2. Basis for petition (check one).

a. ☐ My conditional residence is based on my marriage to a U.S. citizen or permanent resident, and we are filing this petition together.

b. ☐ I am a child who entered as a conditional permanent resident and I am unable to be included in a Joint Petition to Remove the Conditional Basis of Alien's Permanent Residence (Form I-751) filed by my parent(s).

My conditional residence is based on my marriage to a U.S. citizen or permanent resident, but I am unable to file a joint petition and I request a waiver because: (check one)

c. ☐ My spouse is deceased.

d. ☐ I entered into the marriage in good faith, but the marriage was terminated though divorce/annulment.

e. ☐ I am a conditional resident spouse who entered in to the marriage in good faith, or I am a conditional resident child, who has been battered or subjected to extreme mental cruelty by my citizen or permanent resident spouse or parent.

f. ☐ The termination of my status and deportation from the United States would result in an extreme hardship.

Part 3. Additional Information about you.

Other names used (including maiden name):	Telephone #
Date of Marriage	Place of Marriage

If your spouse is deceased, give the date of death (month/day/year)

Are you in deportation or exclusion proceedings?	☐ Yes ☐ No
Was a fee paid to anyone other than an attorney in connection with this petition?	☐ Yes ☐ No

To Be Completed by Attorney or Representative, if any

☐ Fill in box if G-28 is attached to represent the applicant

VOLAG#

ATTY State License #

Continued on back.

Form I-751 (Rev. 10/13/98)N

Part 3. Additional Information about you. (con't)

Since becoming a conditional resident, have you ever been arrested, cited, charged, indicted, convicted, fined or imprisoned for breaking or violating any law or ordinace (excluding traffic regulations), or committed any crime for which you were not arrested?

☐ Yes ☐ No

If you are married, is this a different marriage than the one through which conditional residence status was obtained?

☐ Yes ☐ No

Have you resided at any other address since you became a permanent resident?

☐ Yes ☐ No *(If yes, attach a list of all addresses and dates.)*

Is your spouse currently serving employed by the U. S. government and serving outside the U.S.?

☐ Yes ☐ No

Part 4. Information about the spouse or parent through whom you gained your conditional residence .

Family Name	Given Name	Middle Initial	Phone Number ( )

Address

Date of Birth *(month/day/year)*	Social Security #	A#

Part 5. Information about your children. *List all your children. Attach another sheet if necessary*

	Name	Date of Birth *(month/day/year)*	If in U.S., give A#, current immigration status and U.S. Address	Living with you?
1				☐ Yes ☐ No
2				☐ Yes ☐ No
3				☐ Yes ☐ No
4				☐ Yes ☐ No

Part 6. Complete if you are requesting a waiver of the joint filing petition requirement based on extreme mental cruelty.

Evaluator's ID Number: State: ☐☐ Number: ☐☐☐☐☐☐☐ Expires on *(month/day/year)* Occupation

Last Name	First Name	Address

Part 7. Signature. *Read the information on penalties in the instructions before completing this section. If you checked block "a" in Part 2 your spouse must also sign below.*

I certify, under penalty of perjury under the laws of the United States of America, that this petition, and the evidence submitted with it, is all true and correct. If conditional residence was based on a marriage, I further certify that the marriage was entered into in accordance with the laws of the place where the marriage took place, and was not for the purpose of procuring an immigration benefit. I also authorize the release of any information from my records which the Immigration and Naturalization Service needs to determine eligibility for the benefit being sought.

Signature	Print Name	Date
Signature of Spouse	Print Name	Date

Please note: If you do not completely fill out this form, or fail to submit any required documents listed in the instructions, then you cannot be found eligible for the requested benefit, and this petition may be denied.

Part 8. Signature of person preparing form if other than above.

I declare that I prepared this petition at the request of the above person and it is based on all information of which I have knowledge.

Signature	Print Name	Date

Firm Name and Address

Form I-751 (Rev. 10/13/98)N

U. S. Department of Justice
Immigration and Naturalization Service

OMB # 1115-0163

Application for Employment Authorization

Do Not Write in This Block

Remarks	Action Stamp	Fee Stamp
A#		
Applicant is filing under 274a.12 _____		

☐ Application Approved. Employment Authorized / Extended (Circle One) _____ (Date).
until _____ (Date).
Subject to the following conditions: _____

☐ Application Denied.
   ☐ Failed to establish eligibility under 8 CFR 274a.12 (a) or (c).
   ☐ Failed to establish economic necessity as required in 8 CFR 274a.12(c) (14), (18) and 8 CFR 214.2(f)

I am applying for: ☐ Permission to accept employment
                ☐ Replacement (of lost employment authorization document).
                ☐ Renewal of my permission to accept employment (attach previous employment authorization document).

1. Name (Family Name in CAPS)   (First)   (Middle)

2. Other Names Used (Include Maiden Name)

3. Address in the United States (Number and Street)   (Apt. Number)

   (Town or City)   (State/Country)   (ZIP Code)

4. Country of Citizenship/Nationality

5. Place of Birth (Town or City) (State/Province)   (Country)

6. Date of Birth (Month/Day/Year)   7. Sex   ☐ Male ☐ Female

8. Marital Status   ☐ Married   ☐ Single
                ☐ Widowed   ☐ Divorced

9. Social Security Number (Include all Numbers you have ever used)

10. Alien Registration Number (A-Number) or I-94 Number (if any)

11. Have you ever before applied for employment authorization from INS?
   ☐ Yes (If yes, complete below)   ☐ No
   Which INS Office?   Date(s)

Results (Granted or Denied - attach all documentation)

12. Date of Last Entry into the U.S. (Month/Day/Year)

13. Place of Last Entry into the U.S.

14. Manner of Last Entry (Visitor, Student, etc.)

15. Current Immigration Status (Visitor, Student, etc.)

16. Go to Part 2 of the instructions, Eligibility Categories. In the space below, place the letter and number of the category you selected from the instructions (For example, (a)(8), (c)(17)(iii), etc.).

Eligibility under 8 CFR 274a.12

(   ) (   ) (   )

Certification

Your Certification: I certify, under penalty of perjury under the laws of the United States of America, that the foregoing is true and correct. Furthermore, I authorize the release of any information which the Immigration and Naturalization Service needs to determine eligibility for the benefit I am seeking. I have read the Instructions in Part 2 and have identified the appropriate eligibility category in Block 16.

Signature   Telephone Number   Date

Signature of Person Preparing Form If Other Than Above: I declare that this document was prepared by me at the request of the applicant and is based on all information of which I have any knowledge.

Print Name   Address   Signature   Date

Initial Receipt	Resubmitted	Relocated		Completed		
		Rec'd	Sent	Approved	Denied	Returned

Form I-765 (Rev. 10/13/98)N Page

U.S. Department of Justice
Immigration and Naturalization Service

OMB # 1115-0170

Application for Temporary Protected Status

START HERE - Please Type or Print

Part 1. Type of Application *(check one)*

1. _____ This is my first application to register for Temporary Protected Status.
2. _____ This is my application for annual registration/re-registration. I have previously been granted Temporary Protected Status. I have maintained and continue to maintain the conditions of eligibility for Temporary Protected Status.

Part 2. Information about You

Family Name	First	Middle Initial

U.S. Mailing Address - Care of

Street Number and Name		Apt. #
Town/City	County	
State	ZIP Code	

Place of Birth (Town or City) _____ (State/Country) _____

Country of Residence	Country of Citizenship
Date of Birth *(month/day/year)*	Sex ☐ Male ☐ Female

Marital Status ☐ Single ☐ Married ☐ Divorced ☐ Widowed	Other Names Used *(including maiden name)*
Date of entry into the U.S.	Place of entry into the U.S.

Manner of Arrival *(Visitor, student, stowaway, without inspection, etc.)*

Arrival/Departure Record (I-94) Number	Date authorized stay expired/or will expire, as shown on form I-94 or I-95

Your current immigration Status

In Status *(state nonimmigrant classification e.g. F-1, etc.)*

Out of Status *(state nonimmigrant violation e.g. overstay student etc.; EWI)*

Alien Registration Number *(If any)*	Social Security Number

Are you now or have you ever been under immigration proceedings?
☐ Yes   ☐ No   Where_____ When_____
☐ Exclusion   ☐ Deportation   ☐ Rescission   ☐ Judicial Proceedings

Part 3. Information about Your spouse and children *(if any)*

Name of Spouse Last	First	Middle Initial
Address (number and street)		Apt #
Town/City	State	
Country	Zip/Postal Code	

Form I-821 (Rev. 5/22/91)N   *Continued on back.*

FOR INS USE ONLY

Remarks

Action Stamp

Fee Stamp

Case ID#:

A#:

To Be Completed by
Attorney or Representative, if any
☐ Fill in box if G-28 is attached to represent the applicant

VOLAG#

ATTY State License #

Part 3. Information about your spouse and children (con't)

Date of Birth (month/day/year)	Date and Place of Present Marriage
Name of prior husbands/wives	Date(s) Marriage(s) Ended

List the names, ages, and current residence of any children

Name - (Last)	(First)	(Middle Initial)	Date of Birth	Residence

Part 4. Eligibility Standards

1. Fill in the necessary information:

   I am a national of the foreign state of _____, and I entered the United States on _____, and I have resided in the United States since that time.

2. To be eligible for Temporary Protected Status, you must be admissible as an immigrant to the United States, with certain exceptions. Do any of the following apply to you?

   a. have you been convicted of any felony or 2 or more misdemeanors committed in the United States;

   b. (i) have you ordered, incited, assisted, or otherwise participated in the persecution of any person on account of race, religion, nationality, membership in a particular social group or political opinion;

   (ii) have you been convicted by a final judgment of a particularly serious crime, constituting a danger to the community of the United States (an alien convicted of an aggravated felony is considered to have committed a particularly serious crime);

   (iii) have you committed a serious nonpolitical crime outside of the United States prior to your arrival in the United States; or

   (iv) have you engaged in or are you still engaged in activities that could be reasonable grounds for concluding that you are a danger to the security of the United States;

   c. (i) have you been convicted of, or have you committed acts which constitute the essential elements of a crime (other than a purely political offense) or a violation of or a conspiracy to violate any law relating to a controlled substance as defined in Section 102 of the Controlled Substance Act;

   (ii) have you been convicted of 2 or more offenses (other than purely political offenses) for which the aggregate sentences to confinement actually imposed were 5 years or more;

   (iii) have you trafficked in or do you continue to traffic in any controlled substance or are or have been a knowing assister, abettor, conspirator, or colluder with others in the illicit trafficking of any controlled substance;

   (iv) have you engaged or do you continue to engage solely, principally, or incidentally in any activity related to espionage or sabotage or violate any law involving the export of goods, technology, or sensitive information, any other unlawful activity, or any activity the purpose of which is in opposition, or the control, or overthrow of the government of the United States;

Form I-821 (Rev. 05/22/91)

Continued on next page

(v) have you engaged in or do you continue to engage in terrorist activities;

(vi) have you engaged in or do you continue to engage or plan to engage in activities in the United States that would have potentially serious adverse foreign policy consequences for the United States;

(vii) have you been or do you continue to be a member of the Communist or other totalitarian party, except when membership was involuntary; and

(viii) have you participated in Nazi persecution or genocide.

d.   have you been arrested, cited, charged, indicted, fined, or imprisoned for breaking or violating any law or ordinance, excluding traffic violations, or been the beneficiary of a pardon, amnesty, rehabilitation decree, other act of clemency or similar action;

e.   have you committed a serious criminal offense in the United States and asserted immunity from prosecution;

f.   have you within the past 10 years engaged in prostitution or procurement of prostitution or do you continue to engage in prostitution or procurement of prostitution;

g.   have you been or do you intend to be involved in any other commercial vice;

h.   have you been excluded and deported from the United States within the past year, or have you been deported or removed from the United States at government expense within the last 5 years (20 years if you have been convicted of an aggravated felony);

i   have you ever assisted any other person to enter the United States in violation of the law;

j   (i) do you have a communicable disease of public health significance,

(ii) do you have or have you had a physical or mental disorder and behavior (or a history of behavior that is likely to recur) associated with the disorder which has posed or may pose a threat to the property, safety or welfare of yourself or others;

(iii) are you now or have you been a drug abuser or drug addict;

k.   have you entered the United States as a stowaway;

l.   are you subject to a final order for violation of section 274C (producing and/or using false documentation to unlawfully satisfy a requirement of the Immigration and Nationality Act);

m.   do you practice polygamy;

n.   were you the guardian of, and did you accompany another alien who was ordered excluded and deported from the United States;

o.   have you detained, retained, or withheld the custody of a child, having a lawful claim to United States citizenship, outside the United States from a United States citizen granted custody.

If any of the above statements apply to you, indicate which one(s) by number reference on the line below (for example "2 k") and include a full explanation on a separate piece of paper. If you were ever arrested you should provide the disposition (outcome) of the arrest (for example, "case dismissed") from the appropriate authority.

PLEASE NOTE: If you placed any of the following numbered references on the line above you may be eligible for a waiver of the grounds described in the statements: 2e; 2f; 2g; 2h; 2i; 2j; 2k; 2l; 2m; 2n; 2o. Form I-601 or I-724 are the Service forms used to request a waiver. These forms are available at INS offices.

Part 5. Your Certification

Your Certification: I certify, under penalty of perjury under the laws of the United States of America, that the foregoing is true and correct. Copies of documents submitted are exact photocopies of unaltered original documents and I understand that I may be required to submit original documents to the INS at a later date. Furthermore, I authorize the release of any information from my records which the Immigration and Naturalization Service needs to determine eligibility for the benefit that I am seeking.

Signature:_____ Date:_____ Telephone No.: _____

Signature of Person Preparing Form if other than above:

I declare that I prepared this document at the request of the person above and that it is based on all information of which I have any knowledge.

Print Name: _____ Signature: _____ Date:_____

Address:_____

Part 6. Checklist

____ Have you answered each question?
____ Have you signed the application?

Have you enclosed:

____The filing fee for this application or a written request for a waiver of the filing fee (see instructions, item 12)?

____Supporting evidence to prove identity, nationality, date of entry and residence?

____Other required supporting documents (fingerprint charts, pictures etc.) for each application?

IT IS NOT POSSIBLE TO COVER ALL THE CONDITIONS FOR ELIGIBILITY OR TO GIVE INSTRUCTIONS FOR EVERY SITUATION. IF YOU HAVE CAREFULLY READ ALL THE INSTRUCTIONS AND STILL HAVE QUESTIONS, PLEASE CONTACT YOUR NEAREST INS OFFICE. IT IS RECOMMENDED THAT YOU KEEP A COMPLETE COPY OF THIS APPLICATION FOR YOUR RECORDS.

Petition by Entrepreneur to Remove the Conditions

START HERE - Please Type or Print

FOR INS USE ONLY

Part 1.   Information about you.

Family Name	Given Name	Middle Initial

Address - C/O:

Street Number and Name		Apt. #

City	State or Province

Country	ZIP/Postal Code

Date of Birth (Mo/Day/Yr)	Country of Birth

Social Security #	A #

Form I-526 Receipt Number	

Since becoming a conditional permanent resident, have you ever been arrested, cited, charged, indicted, convicted, fined or imprisoned for breaking or violating any law or ordinance (excluding traffic regulations), or committed any crime for which you were not arrested?   ☐ **Yes**   ☐ **No**

FOR INS USE ONLY

Returned	Receipt
Resubmitted	
Reloc Sent	
Reloc Rec'd	
☐ Applicant Interviewed	

Remarks/Action

Part 2.   Basis for petition. *(Check one)*

a. ☐ My conditional permanent residence is based on an investment in a commercial enterprise.

b. ☐ I am a conditional permanent resident spouse or child of an entrepreneur, and I am unable to be included in a Petition by Entrepreneur to Remove Conditions (Form I-829) filed by my conditional resident spouse or parent.

c. ☐ I am a conditional permanent resident spouse or child of an entrepreneur who is deceased.

To Be Completed by **Attorney or Representative, if any.**
☐ Fill in box if G-28 is attached to represent the applicant
VOLAG#
ATTY State License #

Part 3.   Information about your husband or wife.

Family Name	Given Name	Middle Initial	Sex ☐ Male ☐ Female

List all other names used (i.e. maiden name, aliases)	Date of Birth (Mo/Day/Yr)	Date of Marriage (Mo/Day/Yr)

A #	Current Immigration Status	Is your current immigration status based on the petitioner's current status? ☐ Yes ☐ No

Part 4.   Children. *(List all your children. Attach another sheet if necessary.)*

Name	Date of Birth (Mo/Day/Yr)

A #	Current Immigration Status	Living with you? ☐ Yes ☐ No

Part 4. Children. *(Continued)*

Name		Date of Birth (Mo/Day/Yr)
A #	Current Immigration Status	Living with you? ☐ Yes ☐ No

Part 5. Information about your commercial enterprise.

Type of Enterprise *(Check one):*

☐ New commercial enterprise resulting from the creation of a new business.
☐ New commercial enterprise resulting from the reorganization of an existing business.
☐ New commercial enterprise resulting from a capital investment in an existing business.

Kind of Business *(Be as specific as possible.)*

Date Business Established (Mo/Day/Yr)	Amount of Initial Investment	Date of Initial Investment (Mo/Day/Yr)	% of Enterprise you Own

List number of full-time employees in enterprise in U.S. (excluding you, spouse, sons and daughters):

At the time of your initial investment _____ Presently _____ Difference _____

How many of these new jobs were created by your investment? _____

Subsequent Investment in the Enterprise

Date of Investment	Amount of Investment	Type of Investment

Please provide the gross and net income generated annually by the commercial enterprise since your initial investment. Include all income generated up to date during the present year.

Year	Gross Income	Net Income

Has your commercial enterprise filed for bankruptcy, ceased business operations, or have any changes in its business organization or ownership occurred since the date of your initial investment?   ☐ Yes (Explain on separate sheet)   ☐ No

Has your commercial enterprise sold any corporate assets, shares, property, or had any capital withdrawn since the date of your initial investment?   ☐ Yes (Explain on separate sheet)   ☐ No

Part 6. Signature. *(Read the information on penalties in the instructions before completing this section.)*

I certify, under penalty of perjury under the laws of the United States of America, that this petition and the evidence submitted with it, is all true and correct. I further certify that the investment was made in accordance with the laws of the United States and was not for the purpose of evading United States immigration laws. I also authorize the release of any information from my records which the Immigration and Naturalization Service needs to determine eligibility for the benefit being sought.

Signature of Applicant	Print Name	Date

Please note: If you do not completely fill out this form, or fail to submit any required documents listed in the instructions, you cannot be found eligible for the requested benefit, and this petition may be denied.

Part 6. Signature of person preparing form if other than above.

I declare that I prepared this petition at the request of the above person and it is based on all information of which I have knowledge.

Signature	Print Name	Date

Firm Name
and Address

Form I-829 (Rev. 10/13/98)N

OMB #1115-0214

Affidavit of Support Under Section 213A of the Act

START HERE - Please Type or Print

Part 1.   Information on Sponsor (You)

Last Name	First Name	Middle Name

Mailing Address (Street Number and Name)	Apt/Suite Number

City	State or Province

Country	ZIP/Postal Code	Telephone Number ( )

Place of Residence if different from above (Street Number and Name)	Apt/Suite Number

City	State or Province

Country	ZIP/Postal Code	Telephone Number ( )

Date of Birth (Month, Day, Year)	Place of Birth (City, State, Country)	Are you a U.S. Citizen? ☐ Yes ☐ No

Social Security Number	A-Number (If any)

FOR AGENCY USE ONLY

This Affidavit	Receipt
[ ] Meets	
[ ] Does not meet	

Requirements of Section 213A

Officer's Signature

Location

Date

Part 2.   Basis for Filing Affidavit of Support

I am filing this affidavit of support because (check one):

a. ☐   I filed/am filing the alien relative petition.

b. ☐   I filed/am filing an alien worker petition on behalf of the intending immigrant, who is related to me as my _____.
(relationship)

c. ☐   I have ownership interest of at least 5% of _____.
(name of entity which filed visa petition)
which filed an alien worker petition on behalf of the intending immigrant, who is related to me as my _____.
(relationship)

d. ☐   I am a joint sponsor willing to accept the legal obligations with any other sponsor(s).

Part 3.   Information on the Immigrant(s) You Are Sponsoring

Last Name	First Name	Middle Name

Date of Birth (Month,Day,Year)	Sex: ☐ Male ☐ Female	Social Security Number (If any)

Country of Citizenship	A-Number (If any)

Current Address (Street Number and Name)	Apt/Suite Number	City

State/Province	Country	ZIP/Postal Code	Telephone Number ( )

List any spouse and/or children immigrating with the immigrant named above in this Part: (Use additional sheet of paper if necessary.)

Name	Relationship to Sponsored Immigrant			Date of Birth			A-Number (If any)	Social Security Number (If any)
	Spouse	Son	Daughter	Mo.	Day	Yr.		

Form I-864 (1/21/98)Y

To be a sponsor you must be a U.S. citizen or national or a lawful permanent resident. If you are not the petitioning relative, you must provide proof of status. To prove status, U.S. citizens or nationals must attach a copy of a document proving status, such as a U.S. passport, birth certificate, or certificate of naturalization, and lawful permanent residents must attach a copy of both sides of their Alien Registration Card (Form I-551).

The determination of your eligibility to sponsor an immigrant will be based on an evaluation of your demonstrated ability to maintain an annual income at or above 125 percent of the Federal poverty line (100 percent if you are a petitioner sponsoring your spouse or child and you are on active duty in the U.S. Armed Forces). The assessment of your ability to maintain an adequate income will include your current employment, household size, and household income as shown on the Federal income tax returns for the 3 most recent tax years. Assets that are readily converted to cash and that can be made available for the support of sponsored immigrants if necessary, including any such assets of the immigrant(s) you are sponsoring, may also be considered.

The greatest weight in determining eligibility will be placed on current employment and household income. If a petitioner is unable to demonstrate ability to meet the stated income and asset requirements, a joint sponsor who *can* meet the income and asset requirements is needed. Failure to provide adequate evidence of income and/or assets or an affidavit of support completed by a joint sponsor will result in denial of the immigrant's application for an immigrant visa or adjustment to permanent resident status.

A. Sponsor's Employment

I am: 1.   ☐   Employed by _____ *(Provide evidence of employment)*
Annual salary $ _____ *or* hourly wage $ _____ *(for_____ hours per week)*

2.   ☐   Self employed _____ *(Name of business)*
Nature of employment or business _____

3.   ☐   Unemployed or retired since _____

B. Use of Benefits

Have you or anyone related to you by birth, marriage, or adoption living in your household or listed as a dependent on your most recent income tax return received any type of means-tested public benefit in the past 3 years?

☐Yes   ☐   No *(If yes, provide details, including programs and dates, on a separate sheet of paper)*

C. Sponsor's Household Size   **Number**

1.   Number of persons (related to you by birth, marriage, or adoption) living in your residence, including yourself. *(Do NOT include persons being sponsored in this affidavit.)*   _____
2.   Number of immigrants being sponsored in this affidavit *(Include all persons in Part 3.)*   _____
3.   Number of immigrants **NOT** living in your household whom you are still obligated to support under a previously signed affidavit of support using Form I-864.   _____
4.   Number of persons who are otherwise dependent on you, as claimed in your tax return for the most recent tax year.   _____
5.   Total household size.   *(Add lines 1 through 4.)*   **Total**   _____

List persons below who are included in lines 1 or 3 for whom you previously have submitted INS Form I-864, *if your support obligation has not terminated.*
(If additional space is needed, use additional paper)

Name	A-Number	Date Affidavit of Support Signed	Relationship

D. Sponsor's Annual Household Income

Enter total unadjusted income from your Federal income tax return for the most recent tax year below. If you last filed a joint income tax return but are using only your *own* income to qualify, list total earnings from your W-2 Forms, or, *if* necessary to reach the required income for your household size, include income from other sources listed on your tax return. If your *individual* income does not meet the income requirement for your household size, you may also list total income for anyone related to you by birth, marriage, or adoption currently living with you in your residence if they have lived in your residence for the previous 6 months, or any person shown as a dependent on your Federal income tax return for the most recent tax year, even if not living in the household. For their income to be considered, household members or dependents must be willing to make their income available for support of the sponsored immigrant(s) and to complete and sign Form I-864A, Contract Between Sponsor and Household Member. A sponsored immigrant/household member only need complete Form I-864A if his or her income will be used to determine your ability to support a spouse and/or children immigrating with him or her.

You must attach evidence of current employment and copies of income tax returns as filed with the IRS for the most recent 3 tax years for yourself and all persons whose income is listed below. See "Required Evidence" in Instructions. Income from all 3 years will be considered in determining your ability to support the immigrant(s) you are sponsoring.

☐ I filed a single/separate tax return for the most recent tax year.
☐ I filed a joint return for the most recent tax year which includes only my own income.
☐ I filed a joint return for the most recent tax year which includes income for my spouse and myself.
    ☐ I am submitting documentation of my individual income (Forms W-2 and 1099).
    ☐ I am qualifying using my spouse's income; my spouse is submitting a Form I-864A.

Indicate most recent tax year _____
(tax year)

Sponsor's individual income $_____

or

Sponsor and spouse's combined income $_____
(If joint tax return filed; spouse must submit Form I-864A.)

Income of other qualifying persons.
(List names; include spouse if applicable. Each person must complete Form I-864A.)

_____ $_____

_____ $_____

_____ $_____

Total Household Income $_____

Explain on separate sheet of paper if you or any of the above listed individuals are submitting Federal income tax returns for fewer than 3 years, or if other explanation of income, employment, or evidence is necessary.

E. Determination of Eligibility Based on Income

1.   ☐ I am subject to the 125 percent of poverty line requirement for sponsors.
    ☐ I am subject to the 100 percent of poverty line requirement for sponsors on active duty in the U.S. Armed Forces sponsoring their spouse or child.
2.   Sponsor's total household size, from Part 4.C., line 5 _____.
3.   Minimum income requirement from the Poverty Guidelines chart for the year of _____ is $ _____
    for this household size.   *(year)*

If you are currently employed and your household income for your household size is equal to or greater than the applicable poverty line requirement (from line E.3.), you do not need to list assets (Parts 4.F. and 5) or have a joint sponsor (Part 6) unless you are requested to do so by a Consular or Immigration Officer. You may skip to Part 7, Use of the Affidavit of Support to Overcome Public Charge Ground of Admissibility. Otherwise, you should continue with Part 4.F.

F. Sponsor's Assets and Liabilities

Your assets and those of your qualifying household members and dependents may be used to demonstrate ability to maintain an income at or above 125 percent (or 100 percent, if applicable) of the poverty line *if* they are available for the support of the sponsored immigrant(s) and can readily be converted into cash within 1 year.   The household member, other than the immigrant(s) you are sponsoring, must complete and sign Form I-864A, Contract Between Sponsor and Household Member.   List the cash value of each asset *after* any debts or liens are subtracted.   Supporting evidence must be attached to establish location, ownership, date of acquisition, and value of each asset listed, including any liens and liabilities related to each asset listed.   See "Evidence of Assets" in Instructions.

Type of Asset	Cash Value of Assets *(Subtract any debts)*
Savings deposits	$
Stocks, bonds, certificates of deposit	$
Life insurance cash value	$
Real estate	$
Other *(specify)*	$
Total Cash Value of Assets	$_____

Part 5.   Immigrant's Assets and Offsetting Liabilities

The sponsored immigrant's assets may also be used in support of your ability to maintain income at or above 125 percent of the poverty line *if* the assets are or will be available in the United States for the support of the sponsored immigrant(s) and can readily be converted into cash within 1 year.

The sponsored immigrant should provide information on his or her assets in a format similar to part 4.F. above. Supporting evidence must be attached to establish location, ownership, and value of each asset listed, including any liens and liabilities for each asset listed.   See "Evidence of Assets" in Instructions.

Part 6.   Joint Sponsors

If household income and assets do not meet the appropriate poverty line for your household size, a joint sponsor is required.   There may be more than one joint sponsor, but each joint sponsor must individually meet the 125 percent of poverty line requirement based on his or her household income and/or assets, including any assets of the sponsored immigrant. By submitting a separate Affidavit of Support under Section 213A of the Act (Form I-864), a joint sponsor accepts joint responsibility with the petitioner for the sponsored immigrant(s) until they become U.S. citizens, can be credited with 40 quarters of work, leave the United States permanently, or die.

Part 7.   Use of the Affidavit of Support to Overcome Public Charge Ground of Inadmissibility

Section 212(a)(4)(C) of the Immigration and Nationality Act provides that an alien seeking permanent residence as an immediate relative (including an orphan), as a family-sponsored immigrant, or as an alien who will accompany or follow to join another alien is considered to be likely to become a public charge and is inadmissible to the United States unless a sponsor submits a legally enforceable affidavit of support on behalf of the alien.   Section 212(a)(4)(D) imposes the same requirement on an employment-based immigrant, and those aliens who accompany or follow to join the employment-based immigrant, if the employment-based immigrant will be employed by a relative, or by a firm in which a relative owns a significant interest.   Separate affidavits of support are required for family members at the time they immigrate if they are not included on this affidavit of support or do not apply for an immigrant visa or adjustment of status within 6 months of the date this affidavit of support is originally signed.   The sponsor must provide the sponsored immigrant(s) whatever support is necessary to maintain them at an income that is at least 125 percent of the Federal poverty guidelines.

I submit this affidavit of support in consideration of the sponsored immigrant(s) not being found inadmissible to the United States under section 212(a)(4)(C) (or 212(a)(4)(D) for an employment-based immigrant) and to enable the sponsored immigrant(s) to overcome this ground of inadmissibility.   I agree to provide the sponsored immigrant(s) whatever support is necessary to maintain the sponsored immigrant(s) at an income that is at least 125 percent of the Federal poverty guidelines.   I understand that my obligation will continue until my death or the sponsored immigrant(s) have become U.S. citizens, can be credited with 40 quarters of work, depart the United States permanently, or die.

Notice of Change of Address.

Sponsors are required to provide written notice of any change of address within 30 days of the change in address until the sponsored immigrant(s) have become U.S. citizens, can be credited with 40 quarters of work, depart the United States permanently, or die.   To comply with this requirement, the sponsor must complete INS Form I-865.   Failure to give this notice may subject the sponsor to the civil penalty established under section 213A(d)(2) which ranges from $250 to $2,000, unless the failure to report occurred with the knowledge that the sponsored immigrant(s) had received means-tested public benefits, in which case the penalty ranges from $2,000 to $5,000.

If my address changes for any reason before my obligations under this affidavit of support terminate, I will complete and file INS Form I-865, Sponsor's Notice of Change of Address, within 30 days of the change of address. I understand that failure to give this notice may subject me to civil penalties.

Means-tested Public Benefit Prohibitions and Exceptions.

Under section 403(a) of Public Law 104-193 (Welfare Reform Act), aliens lawfully admitted for permanent residence in the United States, with certain exceptions, are ineligible for most Federally-funded means-tested public benefits during their first 5 years in the United States. This provision does not apply to public benefits specified in section 403(c) of the Welfare Reform Act or to State public benefits, including emergency Medicaid; short-term, non-cash emergency relief; services provided under the National School Lunch and Child Nutrition Acts; immunizations and testing and treatment for communicable diseases; student assistance under the Higher Education Act and the Public Health Service Act; certain forms of foster-care or adoption assistance under the Social Security Act; Head Start programs; means-tested programs under the Elementary and Secondary Education Act; and Job Training Partnership Act programs.

Consideration of Sponsor's Income in Determining Eligibility for Benefits.

If a permanent resident alien is no longer statutorily barred from a Federally-funded means-tested public benefit program and applies for such a benefit, the income and resources of the sponsor and the sponsor's spouse will be considered (or deemed) to be the income and resources of the sponsored immigrant in determining the immigrant's eligibility for Federal means-tested public benefits.   Any State or local government may also choose to consider (or deem) the income and resources of the sponsor and the sponsor's spouse to be the income and resources of the immigrant for the purposes of determining eligibility for their means-tested public benefits. The attribution of the income and resources of the sponsor and the sponsor's spouse to the immigrant will continue until the immigrant becomes a U.S. citizen or has worked or can be credited with 40 qualifying quarters of work, provided that the immigrant or the worker crediting the quarters to the immigrant has not received any Federal means-tested public benefit during any creditable quarter for any period after December 31, 1996.

I understand that, under section 213A of the Immigration and Nationality Act (the Act), as amended, this affidavit of support constitutes a contract between me and the U.S. Government.   This contract is designed to protect the United States Government, and State and local government agencies or private entities that provide means-tested public benefits, from having to pay benefits to or on behalf of the sponsored immigrant(s), for as long as I am obligated to support them under this affidavit of support.   I understand that the sponsored immigrants, or any Federal, State, local, or private entity that pays any means-tested benefit to or on behalf of the sponsored immigrant(s), are entitled to sue me if I fail to meet my obligations under this affidavit of support, as defined by section 213A and INS regulations.

Civil Action to Enforce.

If the immigrant on whose behalf this affidavit of support is executed receives any Federal, State, or local means-tested public benefit before this obligation terminates, the Federal, State, or local agency or private entity may request reimbursement from the sponsor who signed this affidavit.   If the sponsor fails to honor the request for reimbursement, the agency may sue the sponsor in any U.S. District Court or any State court with jurisdiction of civil actions for breach of contract.   INS will provide names, addresses, and Social Security account numbers of sponsors to benefit-providing agencies for this purpose.   Sponsors may also be liable for paying the costs of collection, including legal fees.

I acknowledge that section 213A(a)(1)(B) of the Act grants the sponsored immigrant(s) and any Federal, State, local, or private agency that pays any means-tested public benefit to or on behalf of the sponsored immigrant(s) standing to sue me for failing to meet my obligations under this affidavit of support. I agree to submit to the personal jurisdiction of any court of the United States or of any State, territory, or possession of the United States if the court has subject matter jurisdiction of a civil lawsuit to enforce this affidavit of support. I agree that no lawsuit to enforce this affidavit of support shall be barred by any statute of limitations that might otherwise apply, so long as the plaintiff initiates the civil lawsuit no later than ten (10) years after the date on which a sponsored immigrant last received any means-tested public benefits.

Collection of Judgment.

I acknowledge that a plaintiff may seek specific performance of my support obligation. Furthermore, any money judgment against me based on this affidavit of support may be collected through the use of a judgment lien under 28 U.S.C. 3201, a writ of execution under 28 U.S.C. 3203, a judicial installment payment order under 28 U.S.C. 3204, garnishment under 28 U.S.C. 3205, or through the use of any corresponding remedy under State law. I may also be held liable for costs of collection, including attorney fees.

Concluding Provisions.

I, _____ , *certify under penalty of perjury under the laws of the United States that:*

   (a) I know the contents of this affidavit of support signed by me;
   (b) All the statements in this affidavit of support are true and correct;
   (c) I make this affidavit of support for the consideration stated in Part 7, freely, and without any mental reservation or purpose of evasion;
   (d) Income tax returns submitted in support of this affidavit are true copies of the returns filed with the Internal Revenue Service; and
   (e) Any other evidence submitted is true and correct.

_____   _____
(Sponsor's Signature)   *(Date)*

Subscribed and sworn to *(or affirmed)* before me this

_____ day of _____ , _____
                          (Month)   *(Year)*

at _____ .

My commission expires on _____ .

_____
(Signature of Notary Public or Officer Administering Oath)

_____
(Title)

Part 8.   If someone other than the sponsor prepared this affidavit of support, that person must complete the following:

I certify under penalty of perjury under the laws of the United States that I prepared this affidavit of support at the sponsor's request, and that this affidavit of support is based on all information of which I have knowledge.

Signature	Print Your Name	Date	Daytime Telephone Number
			( )

Firm Name and Address

Sponsor's Name *(Last, First, Middle)*	Social Security Number	A-Number (If any)

General Filing Instructions:

Form I-864A, Contract Between Sponsor and Household Member, is an attachment to Form I-864, Affidavit of Support Under Section 213A of the Immigration and Nationality Act (the Act). The sponsor enters the information above, completes Part 2 of this form, and signs in Part 5. The household member completes Parts 1 and 3 of this form and signs in Part 6. A household member who is also the sponsored immigrant completes Parts 1 and 4 (Instead of Part 3) of this form and signs in Part 6. The Privacy Act Notice and information on penalties for misrepresentation or fraud are included on the instructions to Form I-864.

The signatures on the I-864A must be notarized by a notary public or signed before an Immigration or Consular Officer. A separate form must be used for each household member whose income and/or assets are being used to qualify. This blank form may be photocopied for that purpose. A sponsored immigrant who qualifies as a household member is only required to complete this form if he or she has one or more family members immigrating with him or her and is making his or her *income* available for their support. Sponsored immigrants who are using their *assets* to qualify are not required to complete this form. This completed form is submitted with Form I-864 by the sponsored immigrant with an application for an immigrant visa or adjustment of status.

Purpose:

This contract is intended to benefit the sponsored immigrant(s) and any agency of the Federal Government, any agency of a State or local government, or any private entity to which the sponsor has an obligation under the affidavit of support to reimburse for benefits granted to the sponsored immigrant, and these parties will have the right to enforce this contract in any court with appropriate jurisdiction. This contract must be completed and signed by the sponsor and any household member, including the sponsor's spouse, whose income is included as household income by a person sponsoring one or more immigrants under Section 213A of Act. The contract must also be completed if a sponsor is relying on the assets of a household member who is not the sponsored immigrant to meet the income requirements. If the sponsored immigrant is a household member immigrating with a spouse or children, and is using his or her income to assist the sponsor in meeting the income requirement, he or she must complete and sign this contract as a "sponsored immigrant/household member."

By signing this form, a household member, who is not a sponsored immigrant, agrees to make his or her income and/or assets available to the sponsor to help support the immigrant(s) for whom the sponsor has filed an affidavit of support and to be responsible, along with the sponsor, to pay any debt incurred by the sponsor under the affidavit of support. A sponsored immigrant/household member who signs this contract agrees to make his or her income available to the sponsor to help support any spouse or children immigrating with him or her and to be responsible, along with the sponsor, to pay any debt incurred by the sponsor under the affidavit of support. The obligations of the household member and the sponsored immigrant/household member under this contract terminate when the obligations of the sponsor under the affidavit of support terminate. For additional information see section 213A of the Act, part 213a of title 8 of the Code of Federal Regulations, and Form I-864, Affidavit of Support Under Section 213A of the Act.

Definitions:

1) An "affidavit of support" refers to INS Form I-864, Affidavit of Support Under Section 213A of the Act, which is completed and filed by the sponsor;
2) A "sponsor" is a person, either the petitioning relative, the relative with a significant ownership interest in the petitioning entity, or another person accepting joint and several liability with the sponsor, who completes and files the Affidavit of Support under Section 213A of the Act on behalf of a sponsored immigrant;
3) A "household member" is any person (a) sharing a residence with the sponsor for at least the last 6 months who is related to the sponsor by birth, marriage, or adoption, *or* (b) whom the sponsor has lawfully claimed as a dependent on the sponsor's most recent Federal income tax return even if that person does not live at the same residence as the sponsor, *and* whose income and/or assets will be used to demonstrate the sponsor's ability to maintain the sponsored immigrant(s) at an annual income at the level specified in section 213A(f)(1)(E) or 213A(f)(3) of the Act;
4) A "sponsored immigrant" is a person listed on this form on whose behalf an affidavit of support will be completed and filed; and
5) A "sponsored immigrant/household member" is a sponsored immigrant who is also a household member.

Part 1. Information on Sponsor's Household Member or Sponsored Immigrant/Household Member

Last Name	First Name	Middle Name

Date of Birth *(Month, Day, Year)*	Social Security Number *(Mandatory for non-citizens; voluntary for U.S. citizens)*	A-Number *(If any)*

Address *(Street Number and Name)* Apt Number	City	State/Province	ZIP/Postal Code

Telephone Number ( )	Relationship to Sponsor:_____ I am: ☐ The sponsor's household member. *(Complete Part 3.)* ☐ The sponsored immigrant/household member. *(Complete Part 4.)*	Length of residence with sponsor (_____ years, _____months)

Part 2. Sponsor's Promise

I, THE SPONSOR, _____, in consideration of the household member's promise to support the

(Print name of sponsor)

sponsored immigrant(s) and to be jointly and severally liable for any obligations I incur under the affidavit of support, promise to complete and file an affidavit of support on behalf of the following_____ sponsored immigrant(s):

(Indicate number)

Name of Sponsored Immigrant *(First, Middle, Last)*	Date of Birth *(Month, Day, Year)*	Social Security Number *(If any)*	A-Number *(If any)*

Part 3. Household Member's Promise

I, THE HOUSEHOLD MEMBER, _____, in consideration of the sponsor's

(Print name of household member)

promise to complete and file the affidavit of support on behalf of the sponsored immigrant(s):

1) Promise to provide any and all financial support necessary to assist the sponsor in maintaining the sponsored immigrant(s) at or above the minimum income provided for in section 213A(a)(1)(A) of the Act (not less than 125 percent of the Federal poverty line) during the period in which the affidavit of support is enforceable;

2) Agree to be jointly and severally liable for payment of any and all obligations owed by the sponsor under the affidavit of support to the sponsored immigrant(s), to any agency of the Federal Government, to any agency of a State or local government, or to any private entity;

3) Agree to submit to the personal jurisdiction of any court of the United States or of any State, territory, or possession of the United States if the court has subject matter jurisdiction of a civil lawsuit to enforce this contract or the affidavit of support; and

4) Certify under penalty of perjury under the laws of the United States that all the information provided on this form is true and correct to the best of my knowledge and belief and that the income tax returns I submitted in support of the sponsor's affidavit are true copies of the returns filed with the Internal Revenue Service.

Part 4. Sponsored Immigrant/Household Member's Promise

I, THE SPONSORED IMMIGRANT/HOUSEHOLD MEMBER, _____
(Print name of sponsored immigrant)
in consideration of the sponsor's promise to complete and file the affidavit of support on behalf of the sponsored immigrant(s) accompanying me:

1) Promise to provide any and all financial support necessary to assist the sponsor in maintaining any sponsored immigrant(s) immigrating with me at or above the minimum income provided for in section 213A(a)(1)(A) of the Act (not less than 125 percent of the Federal poverty line) during the period in which the affidavit of support is enforceable;

2) Agree to be jointly and severally liable for payment of any and all obligations owed by the sponsor under the affidavit of support to any sponsored immigrant(s) immigrating with me, to any agency of the Federal Government, to any agency of a State or local government, or to any private entity;

3) Agree to submit to the personal jurisdiction of any court of the United States or of any State, territory, or possession of the United States if the court has subject matter jurisdiction of a civil lawsuit to enforce this contract or the affidavit of support; and

4) Certify under penalty of perjury under the laws of the United States that all the information provided on this form is true and correct to the best of my knowledge and belief and that the income tax returns I submitted in support of the sponsor's affidavit of support are true copies of the returns filed with the Internal Revenue Service.

Part 5. Sponsor's Signature

_____   Date: _____
Sponsor's Signature

Subscribed and sworn to *(or affirmed)* before me this _____ day of _____, _____
(Month)   *(Year)*

at _____. My commission expires on _____.

_____   _____
Signature of Notary Public or Officer Administering Oath   *Title*

Part 6. Household Member's or Sponsored Immigrant/Household Member's Signature

_____   Date: _____
Household Member's or Sponsored Immigrant/Household Member's Signature

Subscribed and sworn to *(or affirmed)* before me this _____ day of _____, _____
(Month)   *(Year)*

at _____. My commission expires on _____.

_____   _____
Signature of Notary Public or Officer Administering Oath   *Title*

1999 Poverty Guidelines*
Minimum Income Requirement For Use in Completing Form I-864

For the 48 Contiguous States, the District of Columbia, Puerto Rico, the U.S. Virgin Islands, and Guam:

Sponsor's Household Size	100% of Poverty Line For sponsors on active duty in the U.S. Armed Forces who are petitioning for their spouse or child	125% of Poverty Line **For all other sponsors**
2	$11,060	**$13,825**
3	13,880	**17,350**
4	16,700	**20,875**
5	19,520	**24,400**
6	22,340	**27,925**
7	25,160	**31,450**
8	27,980	**34,975**
	Add $2,820 for each additional person.	**Add $3,525 for each additional person.**

For Alaska / For Hawaii

Sponsor's Household Size	For Alaska 100% of Poverty Line For sponsors on active duty in the U.S. Armed Forces who are petitioning for their spouse or child	For Alaska 125% of Poverty Line For all other sponsors	For Hawaii 100% of Poverty Line For sponsors on active duty in the U.S. Armed Forces who are petitioning for their spouse or child	For Hawaii 125% of Poverty Line For all other sponsors
2	$13,840	$17,300	$12,730	$15,912
3	17,360	21,700	15,970	19,962
4	20,880	26,100	19,210	24,012
5	24,400	30,500	22,450	28,062
6	27,920	34,900	25,690	32,112
7	31,440	39,300	28,930	36,162
8	34,960	43,700	32,170	40,212
	Add $3,520 for each additional person.	Add $4,400 for each additional person.	Add $3,240 for each additional person.	Add $4,050 for each additional person.

Means-tested Public Benefits

Federal Means-tested Public Benefits.   To date, Federal agencies administering benefit programs have determined that Federal means-tested public benefits include, but are not limited to, Food Stamps, Medicaid, Supplemental Security Income (SSI), Temporary Assistance for Needy Families (TANF), and the State Child Health Insurance Program (CHIP).

State Means-tested Public Benefits.   Each State will determine which, if any, of its public benefits are means-tested.   If a State determines that it has programs which meet this definition, it is encouraged to provide notice to the public on which programs are included.   Check with the State public assistance office to determine which, if any, State assistance programs have been determined to be State means-tested public benefits.

Programs Not Included: The following Federal and State programs are *not* included as means-tested benefits: emergency Medicaid; short-term, non-cash emergency relief;   services provided under the National School Lunch and Child Nutrition Acts; immunizations and testing and treatment for communicable diseases;   student assistance under the Higher Education Act and the Public Health Service Act;   certain forms of foster-care or adoption assistance under the Social Security Act;   Head Start programs; means-tested programs under the Elementary and Secondary Education Act; and Job Training Partnership Act programs.

*Published March 18, 1999; Effective for use with I-864 as of May 1, 1999.

Sponsor's Notice of Change of Address

START HERE - Please Type or Print **Answer all Questions**

Part 1.   Information about Sponsor

Last Name	First Name	Middle Name

Date of Birth *(Month, Day, Year)*	Place of Birth *(City, State, Country)*

A-Number *(If any)*	Social Security Number

My New Mailing Address *(Street Number and Name)*	Apt/Suite Number

FOR AGENCY USE ONLY

Receipt

City	State or Province

Country	ZIP/Postal Code	Telephone Number ( )

My New Place of Residence if different from above *(Street Number and Name)*   Apt/Suite Number

City	State or Province

Country	ZIP/Postal Code	Telephone Number ( )

Effective Date of Change of Address

Part 2.   Sponsor's Signature

I certify under penalty of perjury under the laws of the United States of America that all information on this notice is true and correct.

Signature	Date	Daytime Telephone Number ( )

Part 3.   Signature of person preparing notice if other than sponsor

I declare I prepared this application at the request of the above person and it is based on information of which I have knowledge.

Signature	Date	Daytime Telephone Number ( )

Last Name *(Print)*	First name	Middle Initial

Firm Name and Address   *(Print)*

Form I-865 (10/6/97)

INSTRUCTIONS

Purpose of This Form
Please use this form to report your new address and/or residence, as required by 8 U.S.C. 1183a(d) and 8 CFR 213a.3. You may photocopy the blank form for use in reporting future changes of address.

Who Completes This Form?
A sponsor of an immigrant, under section 213A of the Immigration and Nationality Act, is required to report his or her change of address within 30 days of the change if the sponsorship agreement is still in force. The sponsorship agreement remains in force until the sponsored immigrant becomes a U.S. citizen, can be credited with 40 quarters of work, departs the United States permanently, or dies.

General Filing Instructions
Please answer all questions by typing or clearly printing in black ink. Indicate that an item is not applicable with N/A. If an answer is "none", please so state. If the sponsor is a permanent resident, the sponsor must also comply with the change of address reporting requirement in 8 CFR 265.1.

Where to File This Form
If your new address is in Alabama, Arkansas, Florida, Georgia, Kentucky, Louisiana, Mississippi, New Mexico, North Carolina, Oklahoma, South Carolina, Tennessee, or Texas, mail this form to:

> Texas Service Center
> P.O. Box 152122
> Irving, TX 75015-2122

If your new address is in Connecticut, Delaware, District of Columbia, Maine, Maryland, Massachusetts, New Hampshire, New Jersey, New York, Pennsylvania, Puerto Rico, Rhode Island, Vermont, Virginia, or West Virginia, mail this form to:

> Vermont Service Center
> P.O. Box 9485
> St. Albans, VT 05479-9485

If your new address is in Arizona, California, Hawaii, or Nevada, mail this form to:

> California Service Center
> P.O. Box 10485
> Laguna Niguel, CA 92607-0485

If your new address is elsewhere in the United States, or you have moved abroad, mail this form to:

> Nebraska Service Center
> P.O. Box 87485
> Lincoln, NE 68501-7485

Penalties
If the sponsor fails to give notice of a **change in his or her address**, as required by 8 U.S.C. 1183a(d) and 8 CFR 213a.3, the **sponsor may be liable for the civil penalty** established by 8 U.S.C. 1183a(d). The amount of the civil penalty will depend on whether the sponsor failed to give this notice knowing that the sponsored immigrant(s) have received means-tested public benefits.

Privacy Act Notice.
Authority for the collection of the information requested on this form is contained in 8 U.S.C. 1183a(d). The information will be used principally by the Service to verify a sponsor's compliance with the change of address requirement, and to notify agencies that furnish means-tested public benefits of the sponsor's change of address, if requested. The sponsor is required by statute to provide this change of address.

The information may also, as a matter of routine use, be disclosed to other Federal, State, and local agencies providing means-tested public benefits for use in civil action against the sponsor for breach of contract. It may also be disclosed as a matter of routine use to other Federal, State, local, and foreign law enforcement and regulatory agencies to enable these entities to carry out their law enforcement responsibilities. Failure to provide the information may result in the imposition of the penalty established in 8 U.S.C. 1183a(d).

U.S. Department of Justice
Immigration and Naturalization Service

Application for Suspension of Deportation or Special Rule Cancellation of Removal (pursuant to section 203 of Public Law 105-100 (NACARA))

START HERE - Please Type or Print. If any question does not apply to you, write "None" or "N/A" in the appropriate space.

Part 1. Background Information about YOU

Alien Registration Number(s), if any (List every "A-number" you have been given)

Family Name/Names	Given Name	Middle Initial

What other names have you used? (Include maiden name and aliases)

Address - Street Number and Name (or PO Box)	Apt #

City	State	Zip Code

Date of Birth (month/day/year)	Place of Birth (City or Town and Country)

Social Security #	Gender □ Male □ Female

Present Nationality (Citizenship)	Home Phone # ( ) -

Part 2. Application Type (check all that are applicable to you)

I am eligible to apply for suspension of deportation or special rule cancellation of removal under the Nicaraguan Adjustment and Central American Relief Act (NACARA) because I have not been convicted of an aggravated felony and:

☐ a) I am a national of El Salvador who first entered the United States on or before September 19, 1990, or a national of Guatemala who first entered the United States on or before October 1, 1990. I also registered for benefits under the settlement agreement in *American Baptist Churches v. Thornburgh (ABC)*, 760 F.Supp.796 (N.D.Cal. 1991), either directly or, if Salvadoran, by applying for Temporary Protected Status (TPS), and I have not been apprehended at time of entry after December 19, 1990.

☐ b) I am a national of Guatemala or El Salvador who filed an application for asylum on or before April 1, 1990.

☐ c) I entered the United States on or before December 31, 1990; filed an application for asylum on or before December 31, 1991; and at the time of filing was a national of the Soviet Union (USSR), Russia, any republic of the former Soviet Union, Latvia, Estonia, Lithuania, Poland, Czechoslovakia, Romania, Hungary, Bulgaria, Albania, East Germany, Yugoslavia, or any state of the former Yugoslavia.

☐ d) I am the spouse, child (unmarried and under 21 years of age), unmarried son or unmarried daughter of someone who has already applied for, or is presently filing with me for suspension of deportation or special rule cancellation of removal under NACARA. If I am an unmarried son or unmarried daughter, I entered the United States on or before October 1, 1990, or my parent was granted suspension of deportation or special rule cancellation of removal when I was less than 21 years of age. Attach proof of relationship and provide the following information about that spouse or parent:

Name:
A-number(s):
The person who has applied for special rule cancellation of removal or suspension of deportation is your: ☐ Spouse ☐ Parent
Your spouse or parent applied with: ☐ INS ☐ EOIR (Executive Office for Immigration Review)

FOR INS USE ONLY

Returned	Receipt

Resubmitted

Reloc. Sent

Reloc. Received

Decision

☐ Suspension of Deportation or Special Rule Cancellation of Removal and adjustment of status granted

☐ Referred to Immigration Judge in accordance with 8 CFR Section 240.70.

(Adjudicating Officer's Signature)

(Date of Action)   (Office Location)

EOIR Actions

Attorney or Representative, if any

☐ Check box if G-28 is attached.

VOLAG #

Atty. State License #

Part 3. Information about Your Presence in the United States

1. Provide information about the places where you have resided in the United States during the last 10 years: *(List PRESENT ADDRESS FIRST and work back in time. List only places where you resided 60 days or more. Attach additional sheets of paper as needed.)*

Street and Number - Apt. Or Room # - City or Town - State - ZIP Code	Resided From: (Month / Year)	Resided To: (Month / Year)
		Present

2. Provide information about your first entry into the United States

Name used when first entered the United States: *(Family Name, First, Middle)*	Place of first entry into the United States: *(City and State)*

Your status when you first entered the United States:	Date of first entry into the United States: *(Month/Day/Year)*	Period for which admitted: *(Month/Day/Year)* From: To:

If you changed nonimmigrant status after entry, list status you changed to:	Date you changed status: *(Month/Day/Year)*	Last Extension of Stay expired on: *(Month/Day/Year)*

3. Provide information about any departure from and return to the United States you have made since your first entry: *(Please list all departures, including brief ones. Attach additional sheets of paper as needed.)*

If you have **not** departed the United States since your first date of entry, please mark an X in this box: ☐

Port of Departure: *(Place or Port, City, State)*	Departure Date: *(Month/Day/Year)*	Purpose of Travel:	Destination:
Port of Return: *(Place or Port, City, State)*	Return Date: *(Month/Day/Year)*	Status at Entry:	Inspected and Admitted? ☐ Yes ☐ No
Port of Departure: *(Place or Port, City, State)*	Departure Date: *(Month/Day/Year)*	Purpose of Travel:	Destination:
Port of Return: *(Place or Port, City, State)*	Return Date: *(Month/Day/Year)*	Status at Entry:	Inspected and Admitted? ☐ Yes ☐ No

4. Have you ever :

   a) been ordered deported or removed?   ☐ Yes ☐ No

   b) departed the United States under an order of deportation or removal?   ☐ Yes ☐ No

   c) overstayed a grant of voluntary departure from an Immigration Judge or the INS? ☐ Yes ☐ No

   d) departed the United States pursuant to a grant of voluntary departure?   ☐ Yes ☐ No

   e) failed to appear for deportation or removal?   ☐ Yes ☐ No

If you responded "Yes" to any of the above, please indicate the name and Alien Registration # you were using at that time, along with the date you left the United States, if applicable:_____

If you are unsure about any of your answers to questions 4(a)-(e) above, please indicate which question(s) and explain why you are unsure about the response(s) you have given: *(Attach additional sheets of paper as needed.)*

Part 4. Information about Your Financial Status and Employment

1. Provide information about the places where you have been employed for the last 10 years: *(List PRESENT EMPLOYMENT FIRST and work back in time. Include all employment, even if less than full-time. If you did the same type of work for 3 or more employers during any 6-month period and you do not know the names and addresses of those employers, you may state "multiple employers," indicate the city or region where you did the work, list the type of work you did, and estimate your earnings during that period. Any periods of unemployment, unpaid work (as a homemaker or intern, for example), or school attendance should be specified. Attach additional sheets of paper as needed.)*

Full Name and Address of Employer or School: *(if self employed, give name and address of business.)*	Earnings per Week: *(approximate)*	Type of Work Performed:	Employed From: *(Month/Year)*	Employed To: *(Month / Year)*
				Present

2. Provide information about your assets in the United States and other countries, including those held jointly with your spouse, if you are married, or with others. Do not include the value of clothing and household necessities. If married, provide information about your spouse's assets that he or she does not hold jointly with you:

Self *(including assets jointly owned with Spouse or others)*		Spouse	
Cash, Checking or Savings Accounts:	$	Cash, Checking or Savings Accounts:	$
Motor Vehicle(s): *(Minus any amount owed)*	$	Motor Vehicle(s): *(Minus any amount owed)*	$
Real Estate: *(Minus any amount owed)*	$	Real Estate: *(Minus any amount owed)*	$
Other: *(Describe below, e.g., stocks, bonds)*	$	Other: *(Describe below, e.g., stocks, bonds)*	$
Total:	$	Total:	$

3. Have you filed a federal income tax return while in the United States? ☐Yes ☐ No If "Yes," indicate the years you filed and attach evidence that you filed the returns. If you did not file a tax return during any particular year(s), please explain why you did not file. *(Attach additional sheets of paper as needed.)*:

Part 5. Information about your Marital Status and Spouse

Marital status: □ Married □ Single *(If single, skip this Part and go to Part 6)* □ Divorced □ Separated □ Widower

1. Information About Spouse:

Name: *(Family Name(s), First, Middle)*	Date of Marriage:*(Month/Day/Year)*	Place of Marriage: *(City and Country)*
Place of Birth: *(City and Country)*	Date of Birth:*(Month/Day/Year)*	Citizenship:

Your spouse currently resides at:
(Indicate "with me" if spouse resides with you.) _____

| | Number and Street | Apt. # | City or Town | State/Country | Zip Code |

If presently residing in the United States, your spouse's present status is: □ US Citizen □ Legal Permanent Resident □ Asylee □ Asylum Applicant □ Other *(Please describe)*:_____

His/her alien registration number(s) is *(List all A#s your spouse has been given)*: A #

Your spouse □ is □ is not employed. If employed, please give salary and the name and address of the place(s) of employment:

Full Name and Address of Employer:	Earnings Per Week:*(Approx)*	Type of Work:	Employed from: *(Month/Day/Year)*	Employed to: *(Month/Day/Year)*

2. Information about Previous Spouse(s):

I □ have □ have not been previously married: *(If previously married, list the names of each prior spouse, the dates on which each marriage began and ended, the place where the marriage terminated, and describe how each marriage ended. Attach additional sheets of paper as needed.)*

Name of Prior Spouse: *(Family Name(s), First, Middle Initial)*	Date married: *(Month/ Day/ Year)*	Date marriage ended: *(Month/ Day/Year)*	Place marriage ended: *(City and Country)*	Manner in which marriage was terminated or ended *(i.e. death of spouse, divorce)*:

3. Have you been ordered by any court, or are you otherwise under any legal obligation, to provide child support and/or spousal maintenance? □ Yes □ No If "Yes," on a separate piece of paper please explain what type of obligation you have, to whom it is owed, and whether you are fulfilling that obligation.

Part 6. Information about your CHILD/CHILDREN

1. Do you have children? □ Yes □ No *(If "No," then skip this Part and go to Part 7)*
2. Please list all your children below, regardless of their age, giving the requested information about each of them. *(In the Address box, indicate "with me" if child currently resides with you, or list Number and Street, City, and State or Country of residence. Attach additional sheets of paper as needed.)*

Name of Child: *(Family Name(s), First, Middle)*	A-Number:	Place of Birth:	Date of Birth:	Immigration Status
1)				
Current Address:			Citizenship:	
2)				
Current Address:			Citizenship:	
3)				
Current Address:			Citizenship:	
4)				
Current Address:			Citizenship:	

Part 7. Information about your PARENT/PARENTS

You do not need to provide information about your parents' assets and earnings unless you believe that your removal would result in extreme hardship to your parent or parents.

Name of Parent: *(Family Name(s), First, Middle)*	A-Number	Place of Birth: *(City and Country)*	Date of Birth: *(Month/Day/Year)*	Immigration Status:
Father:				
Current Address: *(Number and Street, City, State or Country)*			Citizenship:	
Estimated total assets: $ Weekly earnings: $				
Mother:				
Current Address:			Citizenship:	
Estimated total assets: $ Weekly earnings: $				

Part 8. Miscellaneous Information

Please respond to the following questions. If you answer "Yes" to any of these questions, please provide an explanation of your answer on an attached sheet of paper.

1. Have you ever (either in the United States or in a foreign country) been arrested, summoned into court as a defendant, convicted, fined, imprisoned, placed on probation, or forfeited collateral for an act involving a felony, misdemeanor, or breach of any public law or ordinance (including, but not limited to, driving violations involving alcohol)?   ☐ Yes ☐ No
    (If you answered "Yes," your explanation should include a brief description of each offense, including the name and location of the offense, date of conviction, any penalty imposed, any sentence imposed, and the time actually served.)

2. Have you ever been:
☐ Yes ☐ No A habitual drunkard?
☐ Yes ☐ No One who has derived income principally from illegal gambling?
☐ Yes ☐ No One who has given false testimony for the purpose of obtaining immigration benefits?
☐ Yes ☐ No One who has engaged in prostitution or unlawful commercialized vice?
☐ Yes ☐ No Involved in a serious criminal offense and asserted immunity from prosecution?
☐ Yes ☐ No One who has aided and/or abetted another to enter the United States illegally?
☐ Yes ☐ No A trafficker of a controlled substance, or one who knowingly assisted, abetted, conspired, or colluded with others in any such trafficking (not including a single offense of simple possession of 30 grams or less of marijuana)?
☐ Yes ☐ No A practicing polygamist?
☐ Yes ☐ No Admitted into the United States as a crewman after June 30, 1964?
☐ Yes ☐ No Admitted into the United States as, or after arrival acquired the status of, an exchange visitor?
☐ Yes ☐ No Inadmissible or deportable on security related grounds under sections 212(a)(3) or 237(a)(4) (for cancellation applicants), or under pre-IIRIRA section 241(a)(4) (for suspension applicants) of the Immigration and Nationality Act (INA)?
☐ Yes ☐ No One who has ordered, incited, assisted, or otherwise participated in the persecution of an individual on account of his or her race, religion, nationality, membership in a particular social group, or political opinion?
☐ Yes ☐ No A person previously granted relief under section 212(c) or 244(a) (suspension of deportation) of the INA or whose removal has previously been canceled under section 240A (cancellation of removal) of the INA?

Part 9. Information about Hardship You and/or Your Family Will Face if You are Deported or Removed from the United States

Please answer the following questions by checking "Yes," "No" or "Not Applicable" in the boxes provided. Where required, please provide an explanation of your answer on an attached sheet of paper. You should reference the number of each question for which you are providing an explanation. Your responses in this Part should be about you and/or your qualifying family member(s), except for your response to question 11. A qualifying family member is a parent, spouse, or child who is a United States citizen or lawful permanent resident of the United States. When providing responses about a family member, please provide the family member's name and his or her relationship to you. **Please attach any documents you have to support the responses you give below.** *(See the Instructions for types of documents that may be submitted.)*

*IMPORTANT: If you meet the eligibility requirements for NACARA suspension of deportation or special rule cancellation of removal listed in (a) or (b) under **Part 2 Application Type** on page 1 of this form and you complete this form, you will be presumed meet the extreme hardship requirement unless evidence in the record establishes that neither you nor your qualified relative are likely to experience extreme hardship if you are deported or removed from the United States. If you qualify for a presumption of extreme hardship, you do not need to submit documents that support your answers below regarding your claim to extreme hardship but you do need to provide explanations to your answers below.*

1. ☐ Yes ☐ No ☐ Not applicable - If you have children, do your children speak, read, and write English?

2. ☐ Yes ☐ No ☐ Not applicable - If you have children, do your children speak, read and write the native language of the country you would be returned to if deported or removed?

3. ☐ Yes ☐ No - Do you or any of your family members suffer or have suffered any illness, health problem, or disability that required medical attention? If yes, indicate on an attached sheet of paper the health problem, the family member who suffers from it and any care the person receives in the United States that would not be available in the country to which you would be deported or removed.

4. ☐ Yes ☐ No - Would you be able to obtain employment in the country to which you would be deported or removed? If yes, explain on an attached sheet of paper the type of employment you would be able to obtain. If no, explain why you would be unable to find employment.

5. ☐ Yes ☐ No ☐ Not applicable - If you or a family member are currently pursuing educational opportunities in the United States, would you or the family member continue to pursue the educational opportunities if deported or removed from the United States? If no, explain why not.

6. ☐ Yes ☐ No ☐ Not applicable - If you are deported or removed from the United States would all members of your family accompany you? If no, list which family member(s) would not accompany you. Also, explain why the family member(s) would not accompany you and how that affects you and your family member(s).

7. ☐ Yes ☐ No - Would you or your family experience any emotional or psychological impact if you were deported or removed from the United States? If yes, please explain.

8. ☐ Yes ☐ No - Would the current conditions in the country to which you would be deported or removed cause you or your family extreme hardship if returned? If yes, please explain.

9. ☐ Yes ☐ No - Do you presently have any other way, besides this application for suspension of deportation or special rule cancellation of removal, to adjust status to that of a permanent resident in the United States? If yes, please explain.

10. ☐ Yes ☐ No ☐ Not applicable - If you belong to any civic, political, religious, community, or social organization, association, foundation, club, or similar group or participate in volunteer activities, would your separation from these community ties and activities affect you if you are deported or removed from the United States? If yes, please explain.

11. ☐ Yes ☐ No - Is there any other type of hardship that you or your family would face if you are deported or removed from the United States? Include any hardship to brothers, sisters, grandparents or other extended family members. If yes, please explain.

Part 10. Signature

After reading the information on penalties in the instructions, complete and sign below.
If someone helped you prepare this application, he or she must complete **Part 11.**

I certify under penalty of perjury under the laws of the United States of America, that this application and the evidence submitted with it is all true and correct. Title 18, United States Code, Section 1546, provides in part: "Whoever knowingly makes under oath, or as permitted under penalty of perjury under Section 1746 of Title 28, United States Code, knowingly subscribes as true, any false statement with respect to a material fact in any application, affidavit, or other document required by the immigration laws or regulations prescribed thereunder, or knowingly presents any such application, affidavit, or other document containing any such false information or which fails to contain any reasonable basis in law or fact-- shall be fined in accordance with this title or imprisoned not more than five years, or both."

I authorize the release of any information from my record which the Immigration and Naturalization Service needs to determine eligibility for the benefit I am seeking.

Staple your

photographs

here

WARNING: Applicants who are in the United States illegally are subject to deportation or removal if their applications are not granted by an asylum officer or an Immigration Judge. Any information provided in completing this application may be used as a basis for the institution of, or as evidence in, deportation or removal proceedings even if the application is later withdrawn.

Signature of Applicant: _____   Date _____

(Month/Day/Year)

Print Name: _____   Write your name in your native alphabet: _____

Part 11. Signature of Person Preparing Form if Other than Above _(Read the following information and sign below.)_

I declare that I have prepared this application at the request of the person named in Part 11, that the responses provided are based on all information of which I have knowledge, or which was provided to me by the applicant, and that the completed application was read to the applicant in a language the applicant speaks fluently for verification before he or she signed the application in my presence. I am aware that the knowing placement of false information on the Form I-881 may subject me to civil penalties under 8 U.S.C. 1324 (c).

Signature of Preparer:	Print Name:	Date: _(Month/Day/Year)_
Daytime Telephone #: ( ) -	Address of Preparer: _(Street # and Name, City or Town, State, Zip Code)_	

Part 12. To be Completed at Interview or Hearing

You will be asked to complete this Part when you appear before an Asylum Officer of the Immigration and Naturalization Service (INS), or an Immigration Judge of the Executive Office for Immigration Review (EOIR) for examination.

I swear (affirm) that I know the contents of this application that I am signing, including the attached documents and supplements, that they are ☐ all true or ☐ not all true to the best of my knowledge and that the corrections numbered _____ to _____ were made by me or at my request.

Signed and sworn to before me by the above-named applicant on:

_____
Signature of Applicant

_____
Date _(Month/Day/Year)_

_____
Write your Name in your Native Alphabet

_____
Signature of Asylum Officer or Immigration Judge

OMB No. 1115-0227

Use this blank sheet to supplement any information requested. Please copy and submit as needed.

A # _____   Print Name _____

Signature of Applicant: _____ Date: _____

Part _____
Question ___

U. S. IMMIGRATION & NATURALIZATION SERVICE

COLOR PHOTOGRAPH SPECIFICATIONS

IDEAL PHOTOGRAPH
◄

IMAGE MUST FIT INSIDE THIS BOX ►

THE PICTURE AT LEFT IS IDEAL SIZE, COLOR, BACKGROUND, AND POSE. THE IMAGE SHOULD BE 30MM (1 3/16IN) FROM THE HAIR TO JUST BELOW THE CHIN, AND 26MM (1 IN) FROM LEFT CHEEK TO RIGHT EAR. THE IMAGE MUST FIT IN THE BOX AT RIGHT.

THE PHOTOGRAPH

* THE OVERALL SIZE OF THE PICTURE, INCLUDING THE BACKGROUND, MUST BE AT LEAST 40MM (1 9/16 INCHES) IN HEIGHT BY 35MM (1 3/8IN) IN WIDTH.

* PHOTOS MUST BE FREE OF SHADOWS AND CONTAIN NO MARKS, SPLOTCHES, OR DISCOLORATIONS.

* PHOTOS SHOULD BE HIGH QUALITY, WITH GOOD BACK LIGHTING OR WRAP AROUND LIGHTING, AND MUST HAVE A WHITE OR OFF-WHITE BACKGROUND.

* PHOTOS MUST BE A GLOSSY OR MATTE FINISH AND UN-RETOUCHED.

* POLAROID FILM HYBRID #5 IS ACCEPTABLE; HOWEVER SX-70 TYPE FILM OR ANY OTHER INSTANT PROCESSING TYPE FILM IS UNACCEPTABLE. NON-PEEL APART FILMS ARE EASILY RECOGNIZED BECAUSE THE BACK OF THE FILM IS BLACK. ACCEPTABLE INSTANT COLOR FILM HAS A GRAY-TONED BACKING.

THE IMAGE OF THE PERSON

* THE DIMENSIONS OF THE IMAGE SHOULD BE 30MM (1 3/16 INCHES) FROM THE HAIR TO THE NECK JUST BELOW THE CHIN, AND 26MM (1 INCH) FROM THE RIGHT EAR TO THE LEFT CHEEK. IMAGE CANNOT EXCEED 32MM BY 28MM (1 1/4IN X 1 1/16IN).

* IF THE IMAGE AREA ON THE PHOTOGRAPH IS TOO LARGE OR TOO SMALL, THE PHOTO CANNOT BE USED.

* PHOTOGRAPHS MUST SHOW THE ENTIRE FACE OF THE PERSON IN A 3/4 VIEW SHOWING THE RIGHT EAR AND LEFT EYE.

* FACIAL FEATURES **MUST BE IDENTIFIABLE.**

* CONTRAST BETWEEN THE IMAGE AND BACKGROUND IS ESSENTIAL. PHOTOS FOR VERY LIGHT SKINNED PEOPLE SHOULD BE SLIGHTLY UNDER-EXPOSED. PHOTOS FOR VERY DARK SKINNED PEOPLE SHOULD BE SLIGHTLY OVER-EXPOSED.

SAMPLES OF UNACCEPTABLE PHOTOGRAPHS

INCORRECT POSE

IMAGE TOO LARGE

IMAGE TOO SMALL

IMAGE TOO DARK UNDER-EXPOSED

IMAGE TOO LIGHT

DARK BACKGROUND

OVER-EXPOSED

SHADOWS ON PIC

Immigration & Naturalization Service
Form M-378 (6-92)

U.S. Department of Justice
Immigration and Naturalization Service

OMB #1115-0009
Application for Naturalization

START HERE - Please Type or Print

FOR INS USE ONLY

Part 1.   Information about you.

Family Name	Given Name	Middle Initial

U.S. Mailing Address - Care of

Street Number and Name	Apt. #

City	County

State	ZIP Code

Date of Birth (month/day/year)	Country of Birth

Social Security #	A #

Part 2.   Basis for Eligibility (check one).

a.   I have been a permanent resident for at least five (5) years .

b.   I have been a permanent resident for at least three (3) years and have been married to a United States Citizen for those three years.

c.   I am a permanent resident child of United States citizen parent(s) .

d.   I am applying on the basis of qualifying military service in the Armed Forces of the U.S. and have attached completed Forms N-426 and G-325B

e.   Other. (Please specify section of law)_____.

Part 3.   Additional information about you.

Date you became a permanent resident (month/day/year)	Port admitted with an immmigrant visa or INS Office where granted adjustment of status.

Citizenship

Name on alien registration card (if different than in Part 1)

Other names used since you became a permanent resident (including maiden name)

Sex Male Female	Height	Marital Status: Single Married	Divorced Widowed

Can you speak, read and write English ?   No Yes.

Absences from the U.S.:

Have you been absent from the U.S. since becoming a permanent resident?   No Yes.

If you answered **"Yes"** , complete the following, Begin with your most recent absence. If you need more room to explain the reason for an absence or to list more trips, continue on separate paper.

Date left U.S.	Date returned	Did absence last 6 months or more?	Destination	Reason for trip
		Yes No		
		Yes No		
		Yes No		
		Yes No		
		Yes No		
		Yes No		

FOR INS USE ONLY

Returned	Receipt
Resubmitted	
Reloc Sent	
Reloc Rec'd	
Applicant Interviewed	

At Interview
request naturalization ceremony at court

Remarks

Action

To Be Completed by
Attorney or *Representative*, if any
Fill in box if G-28 is attached to represent the applicant

VOLAG#

ATTY State License #

Continued on back.

Form N-400 (Rev. 01/15/99)N

Part 4. Information about your residences and employment.

A. List your addresses during the last five (5) years or since you became a permanent resident, whichever is less. Begin with your current address. If you need more space, continue on separate paper:

Street Number and Name, City, State, Country, and Zip Code	Dates (month/day/year)	
	From	To

B. List your employers during the last five (5) years. List your present or most recent employer first. If none, write "None". If you need more space, continue on separate paper.

Employer's Name	Employer's Address Street Name and Number - City, State and ZIP Code	Dates Employed (month/day/year)		Occupation/position
		From	To	

Part 5. Information about your marital history.

A. Total number of times you have been married _____ . If you are now married, complete the following regarding your husband or wife.

Family name	Given name	Middle initial

Address

Date of birth (month/day/year)	Country of birth	Citizenship
Social Security#	A# (if applicable)	Immigration status (If not a U.S. citizen)

Naturalization (If applicable)
(month/day/year)   Place   (City, State)

If you have ever previously been married or if your current spouse has been previously married, please provide the following on separate paper: Name of prior spouse, date of marriage, date marriage ended, how marriage ended and immigration status of prior spouse.

Part 6. Information about your children.

B. Total Number of Children _____ . Complete the following information for each of your children. If the child lives with you, state "with me" in the address column; otherwise give city/state/country of child's current residence. If deceased, write "deceased" in the address column. If you need more space, continue on separate paper.

Full name of child	Date of birth	Country of birth	Citizenship	A - Number	Address

Form N-400 (Rev. 07/17/91)N Internet   **Continued on next page**

Part 7. Additional eligibility factors.

Please answer each of the following questions. If your answer is **"Yes"**, explain on a separate paper.

1. Are you now, or have you ever been a member of, or in any way connected or associated with the Communist Party, or ever knowingly aided or supported the Communist Party directly, or indirectly through another organization, group or person, or ever advocated, taught, believed in, or knowingly supported or furthered the interests of communism?   Yes   No

2. During the period March 23, 1933 to May 8, 1945, did you serve in, or were you in any way affiliated with, either directly or indirectly, any military unit, paramilitary unit, police unit, self-defense unit, vigilante unit, citizen unit of the Nazi party or SS, government agency or office, extermination camp, concentration camp, prisoner of war camp, prison, labor camp, detention camp or transit camp, under the control or affiliated with:

    a.   The Nazi Government of Germany?   Yes   No

    b.   Any government in any area occupied by, allied with, or established with the assistance or cooperation of, the Nazi Government of Germany?   Yes   No

3. Have you at any time, anywhere, ever ordered, incited, assisted, or otherwise participated in the persecution of any person because of race, religion, national origin, or political opinion?   Yes   No

4. Have you ever left the United States to avoid being drafted into the U.S. Armed Forces?   Yes   No

5. Have you ever failed to comply with Selective Service laws?   Yes   No

    If you have registered under the Selective Service laws, complete the following information:

        Selective Service Number:_____   Date Registered:_____

    If you registered before 1978, also provide the following:

        Local Board Number:_____   Classification:_____

6. Did you ever apply for exemption from military service because of alienage, conscientious objections or other reasons?   Yes   No

7. Have you ever deserted from the military, air or naval forces of the United States?   Yes   No

8. Since becoming a permanent resident , have you ever failed to file a federal income tax return ?   Yes   No

9. Since becoming a permanent resident , have you filed a federal income tax return as a nonresident or failed to file a federal return because you considered yourself to be a nonresident?   Yes   No

10 Are deportation proceedings pending against you, or have you ever been deported, or ordered deported, or have you ever applied for suspension of deportation?   Yes   No

11. Have you ever claimed in writing, or in any way, to be a United States citizen?   Yes   No

12. Have you ever:

    a.   been a habitual drunkard?   Yes   No

    b.   advocated or practiced polygamy?   Yes   No

    c.   been a prostitute or procured anyone for prostitution?   Yes   No

    d.   knowingly and for gain helped any alien to enter the U.S. illegally?   Yes   No

    e.   been an illicit trafficker in narcotic drugs or marijuana?   Yes   No

    f.   received income from illegal gambling?   Yes   No

    g.   given false testimony for the purpose of obtaining any immigration benefit?   Yes   No

13. Have you ever been declared legally incompetent or have you ever been confined as a patient in a mental institution?   Yes   No

14. Were you born with, or have you acquired in same way, any title or order of nobility in any foreign State?   Yes   No

15. Have you ever:

    a.   knowingly committed any crime for which you have not been arrested?   Yes   No

    b.   been arrested, cited, charged, indicted, convicted, fined or imprisoned for breaking or violating any law or ordinance excluding traffic regulations?   Yes   No

(If you answer yes to 15 , in your explanation give the following information for each incident or occurrence the **city**, **state**, and **country**, where the offense took place, the **date** and **nature** of the offense, and the **outcome** or **disposition** of the case).

Part 8.   Allegiance to the U.S.

If your answer to any of the following questions is **"NO"**, attach a full explanation:

1.   Do you believe in the Constitution and form of government of the U.S.?   Yes   No

2.   Are you willing to take the full Oath of Allegiance to the U.S.? (see instructions)   Yes   No

3.   If the law requires it, are you willing to bear arms on behalf of the U.S.?   Yes   No

4.   If the law requires it, are you willing to perform noncombatant services in the Armed Forces of the U.S.?   Yes   No

5.   If the law requires it, are you willing to perform work of national importance under civilian direction?   Yes   No

Form N-400 (Rev. 01/15/99)N

Part 9. Memberships and organizations.

A. List your present and past membership in or affiliation with every organization, association, fund, foundation, party, club, society, or similar group in the United States or in any other place. Include any military service in this part. If none, write "none". Include the name of organization, location, dates of membership and the nature of the organization. If additional space is needed, use separate paper.

_____

_____

_____

_____

Part 10. Complete only if you checked block " C " in Part 2.

How many of your parents are U.S. citizens?   One   Both   (Give the following about one U.S. citizen parent:)

Family Name	Given Name	Middle Name

Address

Basis for citizenship:
Birth
Naturalization Cert. No.

Relationship to you (check one):   natural parent   adoptive parent

parent of child legitimated after birth

If adopted or legitimated after birth, give date of adoption or, legitimation: *(month/day/year)*_____ .

Does this parent have legal custody of you?   Yes   No

(Attach a copy of relating evidence to establish that you are the child of this U.S. citizen and evidence of this parent's citizenship.)

Part 11. Signature.   *(Read the information on penalties in the instructions before completing this section).*

I certify or, if outside the United States, I swear or affirm, under penalty of perjury under the laws of the United States of America that this application, and the evidence submitted with it, is all true and correct. I authorize the release of any information from my records which the Immigration and Naturalization Service needs to determine eligibility for the benefit I am seeking.

Signature   **Date**

Please Note: *If you do not completely fill out this form, or fail to submit required documents listed in the instructions, you may not be found eligible for naturalization and this application may be denied.*

Part 12. Signature of person preparing form if other than above. *(Sign below)*

I declare that I prepared this application at the request of the above person and it is based on all information of which I have knowledge.

Signature   **Print Your Name**   **Date**

Firm Name
and Address

DO NOT COMPLETE THE FOLLOWING UNTIL INSTRUCTED TO DO SO AT THE INTERVIEW

I swear that I know the contents of this application, and supplemental pages   1 through____, that the corrections , numbered 1 through____, were made at my request, and that this amended application, is true to the best of my knowledge and belief.

Subscribed and sworn to before me by the applicant.

_____
(Examiner's Signature)   Date

_____
(Complete and true signature of applicant)

OMB No. 1115-0015

Application for Replacement Naturalization/Citizenship Document

START HERE - Please Type or Print

Part 1. Information about you.

Family Name	Given Name	Middle Name

Address - In care of:

Street # and Name		Apt #

City or town	State or Province

Country	Zip or Postal Code

Date of Birth (Month/Day/Year)	Country of Birth

Certificate #	A #

Part 2. Type of application.

1. I hereby apply for: (check one)

a. ☐ a new Certificate of Citizenship

b. ☐ a new Certificate of Naturalization

c. ☐ a new Certificate of Repatriation

d. ☐ a new Declaration of Intention

e. ☐ a special Certificate of Naturalization to obtain recognition of my U.S. citizenship by a foreign country

2. Basis for application: (If you checked other than "e" in Part 1, check one)

a. ☐ my certificate is/was lost, stolen or destroyed (attach a copy of the certificate if you have one). Explain when, where and how _____
_____

b. ☐ my certificate is mutilated (attach the certificate)

c. ☐ my name has been changed (attach the certificate)

d. ☐ my certificate or declaration is incorrect (attach the documents)

Part 3. Processing Information.

SEX ☐ Male ☐ Female	Height	Marital Status	☐ Single ☐ Married	☐ Widowed ☐ Divorced

My last certificate or declaration of intention was issued to me by:

INS Office or Name of court	Date (Month/Day/Year)

Name in which the document was issued:

Other names I have used (if none, so indicate):

Since becoming a citizen, have you lost your citizenship in any manner?

☐ No   ☐ Yes (attach an explanation)

Part 4. Complete if applying for a new document because of name change.

Name changed to present name by: (check one)

☐ Marriage or Divorce on (month/day/year)_____(attach a copy of marriage or divorce certificate)

☐ Court Decree (month/day/year)_____(attach a copy of the court decree)

Continued on back.

FOR INS USE ONLY

Returned	Receipt
Resubmitted	
Reloc Sent	
Reloc Rec'd	
☐ Applicant Interviewed	

☐ Declaration of Intention verified by _____

☐ Citizenship verified by _____

Remarks

Action Block

To Be Completed by Attorney or Representative, If any

☐ Fill in box if G-28 is attached to represent the applicant

VOLAG#

ATTY State License #

Part 5.   Complete if applying to correct your document.

If you are applying for a new certificate or declaration of intention because your current one is incorrect, explain why it is incorrect and attach copies of the documents supporting your request.

_____

_____

_____

_____

Part 6.   Complete if applying for a special certificate of recognition as a citizen of the U.S. by the Government of the foreign country.

Name of Foreign Country _____

Information about official of the country who has requested this certificate (if known)

Name   Official title

_____

Government Agency

Address: Street # and Name		Room #
City	State or Province	
Country		Zip or Postal Code

Part 7.   Signature. *Read the information on penalties in the instructions before completing this part. If you are going to file this application at an INS office in the U.S., sign below.   If you are going to file it at a U.S. INS office overseas, sign in front of a U.S. INS or consular official.*

I certify, or, if outside the United States, I swear or affirm, under penalty of perjury under the laws of the United States of America that this application, and the evidence submitted with it, is all true and correct. I authorize the release of any information from my records which the Immigration and Naturalization Service needs to determine eligibility for the benefit I am seeking.

Signature   **Date**

Signature of INS   Print Name   Date
or Consular Official

Please Note: *If you do not completely fill out this form, or fail to submit required documents listed in the instructions, you may not be found eligible for a certificate and this application may be denied.*

Part 8.   Signature of person preparing form if other than above.   (sign below)

I declare that I prepared this application at the request of the above person and it is based on all information of which I have knowledge.

Signature   **Print Your Name**   **Date**

Firm Name
and Address

Form N-565 (Rev. 10/13/98)N

U.S. Department of Justice
Immigration and Naturalization

APPLICATION FOR CERTIFICATE OF CITIZENSHIP

FEE STAMP

Take or mail this application to:
IMMIGRATION AND NATURALIZATION SERVICE

Date _____

(Print or type) _____ nee _____
(Full, True Name, without Abbreviations)   (Maiden name, if any)

_____
(Apartment number, Street address, and if appropriate, "in care of")

ALIEN REGISTRATION
NO. _____

_____
(City)   (Country)   (State)   (ZIP Code)

_____
(Telephone Number)

(SEE INSTRUCTIONS. BE SURE YOU UNDERSTAND EACH QUESTION BEFORE YOU ANSWER IT.)

I hereby apply to the Commissioner of Immigration and Naturalization for a certificate showing that I am a citizen of the United States of America.

(1) I was born in _____ on _____
                 (City) (State or Country)   (Month) (Day) (Year)

(2) My personal description is: Sex _____; complexion _____; color of eyes _____; color of hair _____; height ____ feet ____ inches;

weight _____ pounds; visible distinctive marks _____

Marital status: ◯ Single; ◯ Married; ◯ Divorced; ◯ Widow(er).

(3) I arrived in the United States at _____ on _____
                       (City and State)   (Month) (Day) (Year)

under the name _____ by means of _____
                                            (Name of ship or other means of arrival)

◯ on U. S. Passport No. _____ issued to me at _____ on _____
                                                   (Month) (Day) (Year)

◯ on an Immigrant Visa. ◯ Other (specify) _____

---

(4) FILL IN THIS BLOCK ONLY IF YOU ARRIVED IN THE UNITED STATES BEFORE JULY 1, 1924.

(a) My last permanent foreign residence was _____
                                          (City)   (Country)

(b) I took the ship or other conveyance to the United States at _____
                                            (City)   (Country)

(c) I was coming to _____ at _____
               (Name of person in the United States)   (City and State where this person was living)

(d) I traveled to the United States with _____
                         (Names of passengers or relatives with whom you traveled, and their relationship to you, if any)

---

(5) Have you been out of the United States since you first arrived? ◯ Yes ◯ No; If "Yes" fill in the following information for every absence.

DATE DEPARTED	DATE RETURNED	Name Of Airlines Or Other Means Used To Return To The United States	Port Of Return To The United States

(6) I _____ filed a petition for naturalization. (*If "have" attach full explanation.*)
    (have) (have not)

TO THE APPLICANT. - Do not write between the double lines below. Continue on next page.

ARRIVAL RECORDS EXAMINED	ARRIVAL RECORD FOUND
Card index _____	Place _____ Date _____
Index books _____	Name _____
Manifests _____	Manner _____
_____	Marital status _____ Age _____
	(Signature of person making search)

(CONTINUE HERE)

(7) I claim United States citizenship through my *(check whichever applicable)* ◯ father; ◯ mother; ◯ both parents;

◯ adoptive parent(s) ◯ husband

(8) My father's name is _____ ; he was born on _____

(Month)   (Day)   (Year)

at _____ ; and resides at _____

(City)   (State or Country)   (Street address, city and State or country. If dead, write

He became a citizen of the United States by ◯ birth; ◯ naturalization on _____

"dead" and date of death.)

(Month)   (Day)   (Year)

in the _____ Certificate of Naturalization No. _____

(Name of court, city and State)

☐ through his parent(s), and _____ **issued Certificate of Citizenship No. A or AA** _____

(was)   (was not)

(If known) His former Alien Registration No. was _____

He _____ lost United States citizenship. *(If citizenship lost, attach full explanation)*

(has)   (has not)

He resided in the United States from _____ to _____ ; from _____ to _____ ; from _____ to _____ ;

(Year)   (Year)   (Year)   (Year)   (Year)   (Year)

from _____ to _____ ; from _____ to _____ ; I am the child of his _____ marriage.

(Year)   (Year)   (Year)   (Year)   (1st, 2d, 3d, etc.)

(9) My mother's present name is _____ ; her maiden name was _____ ;

she was born on _____ ; at _____ ; she resides

(Month) (Day) (Year)   (City) (State or country)

at _____ She became a citizen of the

(Street address, city, and State or country. If dead write "dead" and date of death.)

United States by ◯ birth; ◯ naturalization under the name of _____

on _____ in the _____

(Month) (Day) (Year)   (Name of court, city, and State)

Certificate of Naturalization No. _____ ; ☐ through her parent(s), and _____ issued Certificate of

(was) (was not)

Citizenship No. A or AA _____ (If known) Her former Alien Registration No. was _____

She _____ lost United States citizenship. *(If citizenship lost, attach full explanation .)*

(has) (has not)

She resided in the United States from _____ to _____ ; from _____ to _____ ; from _____ to _____ ;

(Year)   (Year)   (Year)   (Year)   (Year)   (Year)

from _____ to _____ ; from _____ to _____ ; I am the child of her _____ marriage.

(Year)   (Year)   (Year)   (Year)   (1st, 2d, 3d, etc.)

(10) My mother and my father were married to each other on _____ at _____

(Month) (Day) (Year)   (City)   (State or country)

(11) If claim is through adoptive parent(s):

I was adopted on _____ in the _____

(Month) (Day) (Year)   (Name of Court)

at _____ by my _____ who were not United States citizens at that time.

(City or town) (State) (Country)   (mother, father, parents)

(12) My _____ served in the Armed Forces of the United States from _____ to _____ and _____

(father) (mother)   (Date)   (Date)   (was) (was not)

honorably discharged.

(13) I _____ lost my United States citizenship. *(If citizenship lost, attach full explanation.)*

(have) (have not)

(14) I submit the following documents with this application:

Nature of Document   *Names of Persons Concerned*

_____   _____

_____   _____

_____   _____

_____   _____

_____   _____

(2)

(15) Fill in this block if your brother, sister, mother or father ever applied to the Immigration Service for a certificate of citizenship.

NAME OF RELATIVE	RELATIONSHIP	DATE OF BIRTH	WHEN APPLICATION SUBMITTED	CERTIFICATE NO. AND FILE NO., IF KNOWN, AND LOCATION OF OFFICE

(16) Fill in this block only if you are now or ever have been a married woman. I have been married _____ (1, 2, 3 etc.) time(s), as follows:

DATE MARRIED	NAME OF HUSBAND	CITIZENSHIP OF HUSBAND	IF MARRIAGE HAS BEEN TERMINATED: Date Marriage Ended	How Marriage Ended (Death or Divorce)

(17) Fill in this block only if you claim citizenship through a husband. *(Marriage must have occurred prior to September 22, 1922.)*

Name of citizen husband _____ ; he was born on _____
(Give full and complete name)   (Month) (Day) (Year)

at _____ ; and resides at _____ He became a citizen of the
(City) (State or country)   (Street address, city, and State or country. If dead, write ``dead'' and date of death.)

United States by ◯birth; ◯naturalization on _____ in the _____ Certificate of
(Month) (Day) (Year)   (Name of court, city, and state)

Naturalization No. _____ ; ☐through his parent(s), and _____ issued Certificate of
(was) (was not)

Citizenship No. A or AA _____ He _____ since lost United States citizenship. *(If citizenship lost, attach full explanation.)*
(has) (has not)

I am of the _____ race. Before my marriage to him, he was married _____ time(s), as follows:
(1, 2, 3, etc.)

DATE MARRIED	NAME OF WIFE	IF MARRIAGE HAS BEEN TERMINATED: Date Marriage Ended	How Marriage Ended (Death or Divorce)

(18) Fill in this block only if you claim citizenship through your stepfather. *(Applicable only if mother married U. S. Citizen prior to September 22, 1922.)*

The full name of my stepfather is _____ ; he was born on _____ at _____ ;
(Month) (Day) (Year)   (City) (State or country)

and resides at _____ He became a citizen of the United States by ◯ birth;
(Street address, city, and State or country. If dead, write "dead" and date of death.)

◯ naturalization on _____ in the _____ Certificate of Naturalization No. _____ ;
(Month) (Day) (Year)   (Name of court, City and State)

☐ through his parent(s), and _____ issued Certificate of Citizenship No. A or AA _____ He _____ since lost United
(was) (was not)   (has) (has not)

States citizenship. *(If citizenship lost, attach full explanation.)* He and my mother were married to each other on _____ at _____
(Month) (Day) (Year)   (City and State or

_____ My mother is of the _____ race. She _____ issued Certificate of Citizenship No. A _____
country)   (was) (was not)

Before marrying my mother, my stepfather was married _____ time(s), as follows:
(1, 2, 3 etc.)

DATE MARRIED	NAME OF WIFE	IF MARRIAGE HAS BEEN TERMINATED: Date Marriage Ended	How Marriage Ended (Death or Divorce)

(19) I _____ previously applied for a certificate of citizenship on _____ , at _____
(have) (have not)   (Date)   (Office)

(20) Signature of person preparing form. If other than applicant. I declare that this document was prepared by me at the request of the applicant and is based on all information of which I have any knowledge.

SIGNATURE: _____

(SIGN HERE) _____

ADDRESS: _____   DATE: _____

(Signature of applicant or parent or guardian)

(3)

AFFIDAVIT

1, the _____ , do swear
(Applicant, parent, guardian)
that I know and understand the contents of this application, signed by me,
and of attached supplementary pages numbered ( ) to ( ), inclusive; that
the same are true to the best of my knowledge and belief; and that
corrections numbered ( ) to ( ) were made by me or at my request.

Subscribed and sworn to before me upon examination of the applicant
(parent, guardian) at _____
this _____ day of _____, _____
and continued solely for:

_____
(Signature of applicant, parent, guardian)

_____
(Officers Signature and Title)

REPORT AND RECOMMENDATION ON APPLICATION

On the basis of the documents, records, and persons examined, and the identification upon personal appearance of the underage beneficiary, I find that
all the facts and conclusions set forth under oath in this application are _____ true and correct; that the applicant did _____ derive or acquire United
States citizenship on _____, through
(Month) (Day) (Year)

and that (s)he _____ been expatriated since that time. I recommend that this application be _____ and that
(has) (has not)   (granted)   (denied)
_____ Certificate of citizenship be _____ issued in the name of _____
(A) (AA)
In addition to the documents listed in Item 14, the following documents and records have been examined:

Person Examined	Address	Relationship to Applicant	Date Testimony Heard
_____	_____	_____	_____
_____	_____	_____	_____
_____	_____	_____	_____

Supplementary Report(s) No.(s) _____ Attached.
Date _____, _____

_____
(Officer's Signature and Title)

I do _____ concur in the recommendation

Date _____, _____

_____
(Signature of District Director or Officer in Charge)

(4)

U. S. Department of Justice
Immigration and Naturalization Service

OMB No. 1115-0203

Application for Transmission of Citizenship Through a Grandparent

Part A.   INSTRUCTIONS

This is a supplement for Forms N-600 and N-643.   Attach the completed supplement *(Printed or typed in black or blue ink)* to your Form N-600 or Form 643 and take or mail the application to the appropriate INS office in the United States. *(See reverse for more instructions)*

Part B.   INFORMATION ABOUT CHILD *(PRINT OR TYPE)*

Last Name	First Name	Middle Name	Date of Birth *(Month/Day/Year)*

As a United States citizen parent, I am applying for a certificate of citizenship for my child through his or her *(check appropriate box)*
Grandfather   Grandmother

Part C.   INFORMATION ABOUT GRANDFATHER *(PRINT OR TYPE)*

Grandfather's Last Name	First Name	Middle Name	Date of Birth *(Month/Day/Year)*

Place of Birth *(City/State/Country)*	He currently resides at *(Street Address/City/State/Country)* *(If Deceased, So State)*

He became a citizen of the United States by: Birth   Naturalization   Derivation   On *(Month/Day/Year)*: _____

In the *(Name of Court, City, State)* _____,   Certificate of Naturalization Number: _____

Or through his parent(s), and   was   was not   issued a Certificate of Citizenship. If issued provide Number A or AA

_____ . His former Alien Registration Number was _____ . He   has   has not

lost United States citizenship. *(If citizenship lost, attach full explanation)*   He resided in the United States from *(Year)* _____

to *(Year)* _____; from *(Year)* _____ to *(Year)* _____; from *(Year)* _____ to *(Year)* _____

Part D.   INFORMATION ABOUT GRANDMOTHER *(PRINT OR TYPE)*

Grandmother's Last Name	First Name	Middle Name	Date of Birth *(Month/Day/Year)*

Place of Birth *(City/State/Country)*	She currently resides at *(Street Address/City/State/Country)* *(If Deceased, So State)*

She became a citizen of the United States by: Birth   Naturalization   Derivation   On *(Month/Day/Year)*: _____

In the *(Name of Court, City, State)* _____,   Certificate of Naturalization Number: _____

Or through her parent(s), and   was   was not   issued a Certificate of Citizenship.   If issued provide Number A or AA

_____ . Her former Alien Registration Number was _____ . She   has   has not

lost United States citizenship. *(If citizenship lost, attach full explanation)*   She resided in the United States from *(Year)* _____

to *(Year)* _____; from *(Year)* _____ to *(Year)* _____; from *(Year)* _____ to *(Year)* _____ .

My child's grandparents were married to each other on _____ at _____
                                                                                                          (Month/Day/Year)   *(City/State/County/Country)*

I certify, under penalty of perjury under the laws of the United States of America, that this application, and the evidence submitted with it, are all true and correct. I authorize the release of any information from my records which the Immigration and Naturalization Service needs to determine eligibility for the benefit I am seeking.

Signature	Print Your Name	Date

Form N-600/N-643 Supplement A (Rev. 9/4/97)

U.S. Department of Justice
Immigration and Naturalization Service

OMB No. 1115-0152

Certificate of Citizenship on Behalf of Adopted Child

START HERE - Please Type or Print

FOR INS USE ONLY

Part A. Information about adopted child.

Last Name	First	Middle

Address:

Street Number and Name		Apt. #
City	State or Province	
Country	ZIP/Postal Code	

Date of Birth (Mo/Day/Yr)	Place of Birth (City, Country)
Social Security #	A#

Personal Description:

Sex ☐ M ☐ F	Height Ft. _____ In. _____
Marital Status	Visible Marks or Scars

Information about Entry:

Name of Entry (If different from Item A)

Date of Entry	Place of Entry
Date of Adoption (Mo/Day/Yr)	Place of Adoption (City, Country)

Part B. Information about the Adoptive Parents (If there is only one parent write "None" in place of the name of the parent which does not apply.)

Last Name of Adoptive Father	First	Middle

U.S. Citizen by:
☐ Birth in the U.S.
☐ Birth abroad to USC parents (List certificate of citizenship number or passport number)
☐ Naturalized or derived after birth (List naturalization certificate number)

Last Name of Adoptive Mother	First	Middle and Maiden

U.S. Citizen by:
☐ Birth in the U.S.
☐ Birth abroad to USC parents (List certificate of citizenship number or passport number)
☐ Naturalized or derived after birth (List naturalization certificate number)

FOR INS USE ONLY

Returned	Receipt
Resubmitted	
Reloc Sent	
Reloc Rec'd	
☐ Applicant Interviewed	

Action Block

Recommendation of Officer:

Approval ☐   Denial ☐

Concurrence of District Director or Officer in Charge:

I do ☐   do not ☐ concur

Signature

_____

Certificate # _____

To Be Completed by Attorney or Representative, If any

☐ Fill in box if G-28 is attached to represent the applicant

VOLAG#

ATTY State License #

Continued on back.

Form N-643 (Rev. 10/13/98)N

Part B. *Continued.*

Date and Place of Marriage of the Adoptive Parents

Number of Prior Marriages of Adoptive Father	Number of Prior Marriages of Adoptive Mother

Is residence of parents' the same as the child's? ☐ YES ☐ NO (If no, explain on a separate sheet of paper.)

If the residence address is different from Item A, list actual residence address.   Daytime Telephone #
( ) -

Part C. Signature. (Read the information on penalties in the instructions before completing this section.)

I certify that this application, and the evidence submitted with it, is true and correct. I authorize the release of any information from my records, or that of my child, which the Immigration and Naturalization Service needs to determine eligibility for the benefit I am seeking.

Signature	Print Name	Date

Part D. Signature of person preparing form if other than above. *(Sign below)*

I declare that I prepared this application at the request of the above person and it is based on all information of which I have knowledge.

Signature	Print Name	Date

**Firm Name
and Address**

DO NOT COMPLETE THE FOLLOWING UNTIL INSTRUCTED TO DO SO AT THE INTERVIEW

AFFIDAVIT. I, the (parent, guardian) _____ do swear or affirm, under penalty of the perjury laws of the United States, that I know and understand the contents of this application signed by me, and the attached supplementary pages number ( ) to ( ) inclusive; that the same are true and correct to the best of my knowledge, and that corrections numbered ( ) to ( ) were made by me or at my request.

Signature of parent or guardian _____   Date _____

_____   _____   _____
Person Examined   Address   Relationship to Applicant

Sworn or affirmed before me on _____ at _____

Signature of interviewing officer _____ Title _____

Form N-643 (Rev. 10/13/98)N

U.S. Department of Justice
Immigration and Naturalization Service

OMB #1115-0173

Application for Posthumous Citizenship

Space to the right for the use of the **Immigration and Naturalization Service** **ONLY.**	Fee Stamp

PART I - To be Completed by the Applicant

A. Information about you, the Applicant

1. Name (Last/First/Middle)

2. Address (Street Name and Number)

   (Town/City, State/Country, ZIP/Postal Code)

3. If abroad, city/country of nearest American Embassy or Consulate

4. Telephone Number (Include Area Code)

5. Total number of authorization affidavits attached (see instructions)

6. Your Relationship to Decedent at time of his/her death (check one box)

   Next of Kin
   a. Spouse
   b. Parent
   c. Son/Daughter
   d. Brother/Sister

   Representative
   e. Executor or Administrator of Decedent's Estate
   f. Guardian, Conservator, or Committee of Decedent's Next-of-Kin
   g. VA Recognized Service Organization (Name below)

   (Name of Service Organization)

B. Information about the Decedent

1. Name Used During Active Service (Last/First/Middle)

2. Other Names Used

3. Date of Birth (Month/Day/Year)   4. Place of Birth (City/State/Country)

5. Date of Death (Month/Day/Year)   6. Place of Death (City/State/Country)

7. Immigration Status at Time of Death (Permanent Resident, Student, Visitor, etc.)

8. Alien Registration Number or other INS File Number

9. Social Security Number

10. Father's Full Name   a. Living   b. Deceased

11. Mother's Maiden Name   a. Living   b. Deceased

12. Marital Status at time of death   a. Married   b. Widowed   c. Divorced   d. Single

13. Military Service Serial Number (If different from Social Security #)

14. Date Entered Active Duty Service (Month/Day/Year)

15. Place Entered Active Duty Service (City/State/Country)

16. Date Released from Active Duty Service (Month/Day/Year)

17. Branch of Service   18. Type of Discharge

19. Military Rank at Time of Discharge   20. Retired from military?   Yes   No

21. VA Claim Number (if any)

22. Total number of children (if none, write none)

23. Complete the following for each child.

Name (Last, First)	Date of Birth (Month/Day/Year)	
		Living Deceased
		Living Deceased
		Living Deceased

24. Total number of brothers and sisters (if none, write none)

25. Complete the following for each brother and sister.

Name (Last, First)	Date of Birth (Month/Day/Year)	
		Living Deceased
		Living Deceased
		Living Deceased

Certification of Applicant

I certify, under penalty of perjury under the laws of the United States of America, that the information in Part I is true and correct.

Signature   Date

Declaration of Person Preparing Form, if other than above.

I declare that I prepared this document at the request of the person above and that it is based on all information of which I have any knowledge.

Signature   Date

Name (print or type)

Address

Form N-644 (05/30/91) Internet

PART II -
To be Completed by the Applicable Executive Department

1. No Active Duty Records Found For This Individual
2. No Casualty Records Found For This Individual
3. Name of Decedent Correctly Shown
4. Name of Decedent Different in Records
   (List name shown in records)

5. Active Duty Service Records Found
   (complete a through f)
   a. Branch of Service

   b. Date Entered Active Duty Service

   c. Place Entered Active Duty Service (City/State/Country)

   d. Service Number

   e. Date Released from Service

   f. Honorable Service During a Period of Hostilities Specified
      by Law?   Yes   No
6. Individual Entered Service under the Lodge Act?
                 Yes   No   Unable to Determine

7. Record of Death Found
   (Complete a and b)
   a. Date of death

   b. Death resulted from injury or disease incurred in or
      aggravated by active duty service during a period of military
      hostilities specified by law?
               Yes   No   Unable to Determine

8. Certification
   I certify the information given here concerning the
   (check one or both, as appropriate)
        Service   Death
   of the individual named on this form is correct according to the
   records of the (Name below)
        (Specify Executive Department)

   Signature   Date

   Title

PART III - To be Completed by the Department of Defense, Washington Headquarters Services, Directorate for Information Operations and Reports

A. Certification

Based on the information received from the Department of Veterans Affairs concerning the death of the individual named on this form, I certify that the individual died on

Date (Month/Day/Year)

as a result of injury or disease incurred in or aggravated by service during a period of hostilities specified by law.

Signature   Date

Title

B. Unable to Certify

Based on the information received from the Department of Veterans Affairs concerning the death of the individual named on this form, I am unable to certify that the individual died as a result of injury or disease incurred in or aggravated by service during a period of hostilities specified by law.

Signature   Date

Title

Space below (Part IV) for use of the Immigration and Naturalization Service ONLY.

Part IV -
To be Completed by the Immigration and Naturalization Service

Applicant Authorized Next-of-Kin or Representative
Positive Certification Military Service
Positive Certification Service Connected Death
Place of Enlistment Qualifies under INA Section 329(a)(1)
Decedent Admitted for Lawful Permanent Residence

Action Stamp

Cert. #	Date Mailed
A #	Reg. Mail #

Initial Receipt	Resubmitted	Relocated		Completed		
		Rec'd	Sent	App'd	Denied	Ret'd

Part I. THIS SECTION TO BE COMPLETED BY THE APPLICANT *(Please print or type information)*

Last Name	First Name	Middle Name	Social Security Number

Address		Alien Number

City	State	Zip Code

Telephone Number	Date of Birth	Sex

I, _____ authorize _____

              (Applicant's Name)   *(Licensed medical doctor or licensed clinical psychologist)*

to release all relevant physical and mental health information related to my medical status to the INS for the purpose of applying for an exception from the English language and U.S. civics testing requirements for naturalization. I certify under penalty of perjury pursuant to Title 28 U.S.C. Section 1746, that the information on the form and any evidence submitted with it is all true and correct. I am aware that the knowing placement of false information on the Form N-648 and related documents may also subject me to civil penalties under 8 U.S.C. Section 1324c.

Signature _____ Date_____

Part II. THIS SECTION TO BE COMPLETED BY A LICENSED MEDICAL DOCTOR OR LICENSED CLINICAL PSYCHOLOGIST *(see instructions)*

The individual named above is applying for an exception from the English language and U. S. history and civics tests required of applicants for naturalization. The Immigration and Naturalization Service's regulations require that applicants for an exception based on disability submit this certification form, completed by a licensed medical doctor or licensed clinical psychologist, along with a completed application for naturalization (Form N-400).

Please answer the following questions as clearly and completely as possible, using common terminology and complete words and phrases.

1. Date of your most recent examination of the applicant. _____ 19 ___

2. Is this your first examination of the individual? Yes____ No ____

    If yes, who is the regular attending physician? _____

3. Based on your examination, describe any findings of a physical or mental disability or impairment which, in your professional medical opinion, would prevent this applicant from demonstrating knowledge of basic English language and/or U.S. history and civics. Describe in detail. If applicant has a mental disability or impairment, please provide DSM diagnosis.

4. Did the applicant's disability or impairment result from the illegal use of drugs? If the applicant is developmentally disabled, did this condition first manifest itself before age 22? Please explain.

5. What is the duration of the applicant's disability or impairment? Is it temporary (less than 12 months) or permanent? Explain.

6. Please provide your medical speciality. If you are not specialized, provide your medical experience and other qualifications that permit you to make this assessment.

I certify under penalty of perjury under the laws of the United States of America, that the information on the form and any evidence submitted with it is all true and correct. I agree to release this applicant's relevant medical records upon request from the U.S. Immigration and Naturalization Service. I am aware that the knowing placement of false information on the Form N-648 and related documents may also subject me to civil penalties under 8 U.S.C. Section 1324c.

Signature _____ Date _____

Please Type or Print

Last Name	First Name	Middle Name
Business Address	City, State, ZIP Code	Telephone
License Number	Licensing State	

Form **9003** (January 1992)	Department of the Treasury—Internal Revenue Service **Additional Questions to be Completed by All Applicants for Permanent Residence in the United States**	**OMB Clearance No. 1545-1065** **Expires 8-31-94**

This form must accompany your application for permanent residence in the United States

Privacy Act Notice: Your responses to the following questions will be provided to the Internal Revenue Service pursuant to Section 6039E of the Internal Revenue Code of 1986. Use of this information is limited to that needed for tax administration purposes. Failure to provide this information may result in a $500 penalty unless failure is due to reasonable cause.

On the date of issuance of the Alien Registration Receipt Card, the Immigration and Naturalization Service will send the following information to the Internal Revenue Service: your name, social security number, address, date of birth, alien identification number, occupation, class of admission, and answers to IRS Form 9003.

Name *(Last—Surname—Family)*   *(First—Given)*   *(Middle Initial)*

Taxpayer Identification Number . . . .

Enter your Social Security Number (SSN) if you have one. If you do not have an SSN but have used a Taxpayer Identification Number issued to you by the Internal Revenue Service, enter that number. Otherwise, write "NONE" in the space provided; i.e., " ⌞ ⌞ ⌞ ⌞ ⌞ N,O,N,E, ".

	Mark appropriate column	
	Yes	**No**
1. Are you self-employed? Mark "yes" if you own and actively operate a business in which you share in the profits other than as an investor.		
2. Have you been in the United States for 183 days or more during any one of the three calendar years immediately preceding the current calendar year? Mark "yes" if you spent 183 days or more (not necessarily consecutive) in the United States during any **one of the three prior** calendar years **whether or not you worked** in the United States.		
3. During the last three years did you receive income from sources in the United States? Mark "yes" if you received income paid by individuals or institutions located in the United States. Income includes, but is not limited to, compensation for services provided by you, interest, dividends, rents, and royalties.		
4. Did you file a United States Individual Income Tax Return (Forms 1040, 1040A, 1040EZ or 1040NR) in any of the last three years?		

If you answered yes to question 4, for which tax year was the last return filed? . . . . 19 __ __

Paperwork Reduction Act Notice—We ask for the information on this form to carry out the Internal Revenue laws of the United States. You are required to give us the information. We need it to ensure that you are complying with these laws and to allow us to figure and collect the right amount of tax.

The time needed to complete and file this form will vary depending on individual circumstances. The estimated average time is 5 minutes.

If you have comments concerning the accuracy of this time estimate or suggestions for making this form more simple, we would be happy to hear from you. You can write to both the **Internal Revenue Service**, Washington, DC 20224. Attention: IRS Reports Clearance Officer, T:FP, and **Office of Management and Budget.** Paperwork Reduction Project (1545-1065) Washington, DC 20503. **DO NOT send this form to either of these offices. Instead, return it to the appropriate office of the Department of State or the Immigration and Naturalization Service.**

Remarks

Cat. No. 10126D   Form **9003** (Rev. 1-92)

Index

tear-out, Appendix III
Fraud waivers, 25/8

G

Grandfather clause for adjustment of status, 5/6, 25/7
Green cards, 1/3, 2/1, 4/1-4
abandonment of U.S. residence, 4/3-4
B-1 and B-2 visas and, 15/2
categories of applicants for, 1/5-7, 4/1-3
commuter status, 4/4
conditional, 5/3-4, 5/21-22, 7/2, 10/2, 10/13
E-1 visas and, 20/4
E-2 visas and, 21/5
expiration dates, 4/1
F-1 and M-1 visas and, 22/5
H-1B visas and, 16/4
H-2B visas and, 17/4
H-3 visas and, 18/2
J-1 visas and, 23/4
L-1 visas and, 19/4
nonimmigrant visas and, 14/5
O, P and R visas, 24/5
quotas, 1/3, 4/3
time for approval of, 1/3-4
U.S. citizenship and, 4/4
U.S. taxes and, 4/4
See also Visas; specific ways of obtaining green cards
Guatemalans
amnesty for, 4/2
NACARA applications, 13/2-4

H

H-1A visas (nonimmigrant nurses), 16/1
H-1B visas (temporary specialty workers), 16/1-15
academic credential evaluation, 16/3
accompanying relatives, 16/4, 16/13, 16/14
appealing
application denial (consular filing), 16/11-12
application denial (U.S. filing), 16/13-14
petition denial, 16/9
application procedure
consular filing, 16/5, 16/9-12
U.S. filing, 16/5, 16/12-14
for Canadians, 28/2-3
documents
application (consular filing), 16/11
application (U.S. filing), 16/13

petition, 16/8-9
employer requirements, 16/4-5
extensions, 16/14-15
fees, 16/7, 16/9, 16/11, 16/12, 16/14
forms
application (consular filing), 16/11
application (U.S. filing), 16/13
for employer, 16/4-5
petition, 16/7-8
green card application from, 16/4
interviews
application (consular filing), 16/11
application (U.S. filing), 16/13
petition, 16/9
for Mexicans, 28/2-4
for nurses, 16/1
overstays and cancellation of visa, 16/10-11
paperwork, 16/6
petition procedure, 16/5, 16/7-9
privileges and limitations, 16/1
qualifying for, 16/2-4
quotas, 16/2
revalidation, 16/14-15
terminology for participants, 16/6
TN status alternative, 28/2-4
work authorization, 16/14
H-2A visas (temporary agricultural workers), 17/2
H-2B visas (temporary nonagricultural workers), 17/1-21
academic credential evaluation, 17/15
accompanying relatives, 17/4, 17/18, 17/20
appealing
application denial (consular filing), 17/16-17
application denial (U.S. filing), 17/19
petition denial, 17/13-14
Temporary Labor Certification denial, 17/11
application procedure
consular filing, 17/5, 17/14-17
U.S. filing, 17/5, 17/17-19
documents
application (consular filing), 17/16
application (U.S. filing), 17/18-19
petition, 17/13
Temporary Labor Certification, 17/10-11
for entertainment workers, 17/3, 17/13
extensions, 17/19-20
fees, 17/11, 17/14, 17/15, 17/18, 17/19

forms
application (consular filing), 17/16
application (U.S. filing), 17/18
petition, 17/12
Temporary Labor Certification, 17/8-10
green card application from, 17/4
interviews
application (consular filing), 17/16
application (U.S. filing), 17/19
petition, 17/13
paperwork, 17/5-6
petition procedure, 17/5, 17/11-14
privileges and limitations, 17/1
qualifying for, 17/1-4
quotas, 17/1
revalidation, 17/20
Temporary Labor Certification, 17/4-5, 17/6-11, 17/19
terminology for participants, 17/6
work authorization, 17/20
H-3 visas (temporary trainees), 18/1-13
accompanying relatives, 18/2, 18/12
appealing
application denial (consular filing), 18/9
application denial (U.S. filing), 18/11
petition denial, 18/7
application procedure
consular filing, 18/3, 18/7-9
U.S. filing, 18/3, 18/9-11
documents
application (consular filing), 18/8-9
application (U.S. filing), 18/10-11
petition, 18/6
extensions, 18/11-12
fees, 18/4, 18/7, 18/10, 18/11
for foreign medical students, 16/9
forms
application (consular filing), 18/8
application (U.S. filing), 18/10
petition, 18/5-6
green card application from, 18/2
interviews
application (consular filing), 18/9
application (U.S. filing), 18/11
petition, 18/6
paperwork, 18/3-4
petition procedure, 18/3, 18/4-7
privileges and limitations, 18/1
qualifying for, 18/1-2
quotas, 18/1
revalidation, 18/12

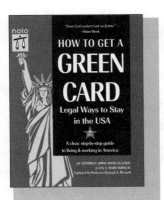

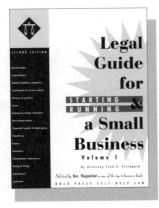

CATALOG

...more from Nolo.com

BUSINESS

	PRICE	CODE
Avoid Employee Lawsuits (Quick & Legal Series)	$24.95	AVEL
⊙ The CA Nonprofit Corp Kit (Binder w/CD-ROM)	$49.95	CNP
▣ Consultant & Independent Contractor Agreements (Book w/Disk—PC)	$24.95	CICA
▣ The Corporate Minutes Book (Book w/Disk—PC)	$69.95	CORMI
The Employer's Legal Handbook	$39.95	EMPL
▣ Form Your Own Limited Liability Company (Book w/Disk—PC)	$44.95	LIAB
▣ Hiring Independent Contractors: The Employer's Legal Guide (Book w/Disk—PC)	$34.95	HICI
▣ How to Create a Buy-Sell Agreement & Control the Destiny of your Small Business (Book w/Disk—PC)	$49.95	BSAG
▣ How to Form a California Professional Corporation (Book w/Disk—PC)	$49.95	PROF
▣ How to Form a Nonprofit Corporation (Book w/Disk —PC)—National Edition	$44.95	NNP
⊙ How to Form a Nonprofit Corporation in California (Book w/CD-ROM)	$44.95	NON
▣ How to Form Your Own California Corporation (Binder w/Disk—PC	$39.95	CACI
▣ How to Form Your Own California Corporation (Book w/Disk—PC)	$39.95	CCOR
▣ How to Form Your Own New York Corporation (Book w/Disk—PC)	$39.95	NYCO
▣ How to Form Your Own Texas Corporation (Book w/Disk—PC)	$39.95	TCOR
How to Write a Business Plan	$29.95	SBS
The Independent Paralegal's Handbook	$29.95	PARA
Legal Guide for Starting & Running a Small Business, Vol. 1	$29.95	RUNS
▣ Legal Guide for Starting & Running a Small Business, Vol. 2: Legal Forms (Book w/Disk—PC)	$29.95	RUNS2
Marketing Without Advertising	$22.00	MWAD
▣ Music Law (Book w/Disk—PC)	$29.95	ML
Nolo's California Quick Corp (Quick & Legal Series)	$19.95	QINC
⊙ Open Your California Business in 24 Hours (Book w/CD-ROM)	$24.95	OPEN
▣ The Partnership Book: How to Write a Partnership Agreement (Book w/Disk—PC)	$39.95	PART
Sexual Harassment on the Job	$24.95	HARS
Starting & Running a Successful Newsletter or Magazine	$29.95	MAG
Take Charge of Your California Workers' Compensation Claim	$34.95	WORK
Tax Savvy for Small Business	$34.95	SAVVY
Wage Slave No More: Law & Taxes for the Self-Employed	$24.95	WAGE
▣ Your Limited Liability Company: An Operating Manual (Book w/Disk—PC)	$49.95	LOP
Your Rights in the Workplace	$24.95	YRW

▣ Book with disk

⊙ Book with CD-ROM

	PRICE	CODE

CONSUMER

Fed Up with the Legal System: What's Wrong & How to Fix It	$9.95	LEG
How to Win Your Personal Injury Claim	$29.95	PICL
Nolo's Everyday Law Book	$24.95	EVL
Nolo's Pocket Guide to California Law	$15.95	CLAW
Trouble-Free Travel...And What to Do When Things Go Wrong	$14.95	TRAV

ESTATE PLANNING & PROBATE

8 Ways to Avoid Probate (Quick & Legal Series)	$16.95	PRO8
9 Ways to Avoid Estate Taxes (Quick & Legal Series)	$24.95	ESTX
Estate Planning Basics (Quick & Legal Series)	$18.95	ESPN
How to Probate an Estate in California	$39.95	PAE
▣ Make Your Own Living Trust (Book w/Disk—PC)	$34.95	LITR
Nolo's Law Form Kit: Wills	$19.95	KWL
▣ Nolo's Will Book (Book w/Disk—PC)	$34.95	SWIL
Plan Your Estate	$34.95	NEST
Quick & Legal Will Book (Quick & Legal Series)	$21.95	QUIC

FAMILY MATTERS

Child Custody: Building Parenting Agreements That Work	$29.95	CUST
Child Support in California: Go to Court to Get More or Pay Less (Quick & Legal Series)	$24.95	CHLD
The Complete IEP Guide	$24.95	IEP
Divorce & Money: How to Make the Best Financial Decisions During Divorce	$34.95	DIMO
Do Your Own Divorce in Oregon	$19.95	ODIV
Get a Life: You Don't Need a Million to Retire Well	$19.95	LIFE
The Guardianship Book for California	$34.95	GB
⊙ How to Adopt Your Stepchild in California (Book w/CD-ROM)	$34.95	ADOP
A Legal Guide for Lesbian and Gay Couples	$25.95	LG
▣ The Living Together Kit (Book w/Disk—PC)	$34.95	LTK
Nolo's Pocket Guide to Family Law	$14.95	FLD
Using Divorce Mediation: Save Your Money & Your Sanity	$21.95	UDMD

GOING TO COURT

Beat Your Ticket: Go To Court and Win! (National Edition)	$19.95	BEYT
The Criminal Law Handbook: Know Your Rights, Survive the System	$29.95	KYR
Everybody's Guide to Small Claims Court (National Edition)	$18.95	NSCC
Everybody's Guide to Small Claims Court in California	$24.95	CSCC
Fight Your Ticket ... and Win! (California Edition)	$24.95	FYT
How to Change Your Name in California	$34.95	NAME
How to Collect When You Win a Lawsuit (California Edition)	$29.95	JUDG
How to Mediate Your Dispute	$18.95	MEDI
How to Seal Your Juvenile & Criminal Records (California Edition)	$29.95	CRIM
How to Sue for Up to $25,000...and Win! (California Edition)	$29.95	MUNI
Mad at Your Lawyer	$21.95	MAD
Nolo's Deposition Handbook	$29.95	DEP
Represent Yourself in Court: How to Prepare & Try a Winning Case	$29.95	RYC

HOMEOWNERS, LANDLORDS & TENANTS

California Tenants' Rights	$24.95	CTEN
▣ Contractors' and Homeowners' Guide to Mechanics' Liens (Book w/Disk—PC)	$39.95	MIEN

▣ Book with disk
⊙ Book with CD-ROM

	PRICE	CODE
The Deeds Book (California Edition)	$24.95	DEED
Dog Law	$14.95	DOG
⊙ Every Landlord's Legal Guide (National Edition, Book w/CD-ROM)	$44.95	ELLI
Every Tenant's Legal Guide	$26.95	EVTEN
For Sale by Owner in California	$24.95	FSBO
How to Buy a House in California	$24.95	BHCA
The Landlord's Law Book, Vol. 1: Rights & Responsibilities (California Edition)	$44.95	LBRT
⊙ The California Landlord's Law Book, Vol. 2: Evictions (Book w/CD-ROM)	$44.95	LBEV
Leases & Rental Agreements (Quick & Legal Series)	$24.95	LEAR
Neighbor Law: Fences, Trees, Boundaries & Noise	$24.95	NEI
⊙ The New York Landlord's Law Book (Book w/CD-ROM)	$39.95	NYLL
Renters' Rights (National Edition—Quick & Legal Series)	$19.95	RENT
Stop Foreclosure Now in California	$34.95	CLOS

HUMOR

	PRICE	CODE
29 Reasons Not to Go to Law School	$12.95	29R
Poetic Justice	$9.95	PJ

IMMIGRATION

	PRICE	CODE
How to Get a Green Card: Legal Ways to Stay in the U.S.A.	$29.95	GRN
U.S. Immigration Made Easy	$44.95	IMEZ

MONEY MATTERS

	PRICE	CODE
⌷ 101 Law Forms for Personal Use (Quick & Legal Series, Book w/disk—PC)	$29.95	SPOT
Bankruptcy: Is It the Right Solution to Your Debt Problems? (Quick & Legal Series)	$19.95	BRS
Chapter 13 Bankruptcy: Repay Your Debts	$29.95	CH13
⌷ Credit Repair (Quick & Legal Series, Book w/disk—PC)	$18.95	CREP
⌷ The Financial Power of Attorney Workbook (Book w/disk—PC)	$29.95	FINPOA
How to File for Chapter 7 Bankruptcy	$29.95	HFB
IRAs, 401(k)s & Other Retirement Plans: Taking Your Money Out	$24.95	RET
Money Troubles: Legal Strategies to Cope With Your Debts	$24.95	MT
Nolo's Law Form Kit: Personal Bankruptcy	$16.95	KBNK
Stand Up to the IRS	$29.95	SIRS
Surviving an IRS Tax Audit (Quick & Legal Series)	$24.95	SAUD
Take Control of Your Student Loan Debt	$24.95	SLOAN

PATENTS AND COPYRIGHTS

	PRICE	CODE
⊙ The Copyright Handbook: How to Protect and Use Written Works (Book w/CD-ROM)	$34.95	COHA
Copyright Your Software	$24.95	CYS
⌷ Getting Permission: How to License and Clear Copyrighted Materials Online and Off (Book w/disk—PC)	$34.95	RIPER
How to Make Patent Drawings Yourself	$29.95	DRAW
The Inventor's Notebook	$19.95	INOT
⌷ License Your Invention (Book w/Disk—PC)	$39.95	LICE
Patent, Copyright & Trademark	$29.95	PCTM
Patent It Yourself	$46.95	PAT
Patent Searching Made Easy	$29.95	PATSE
⊙ Software Development: A Legal Guide (Book with CD-ROM)	$44.95	SFT
Trademark: Legal Care for Your Business and Product Name	$39.95	TRD
The Trademark Registration Kit (Quick & Legal Series)	$19.95	TREG

⌷ Book with disk
⊙ Book with CD-ROM